Contract Law in China

AF741072

Contract Law in China

Lei Chen
Liang Zhao

This book was originally published as a monograph in the International Encyclopaedia of Laws/Contracts.

Founding Editor: Roger Blanpain
General Editor: Frank Hendrickx
Volume Editor: Jacques Herbots

Wolters Kluwer

Published by:
Kluwer Law International B.V.
PO Box 316
2400 AH Alphen aan den Rijn
The Netherlands
E-mail: lrs-sales@wolterskluwer.com
Website: www.wolterskluwer.com/en/solutions/kluwerlawinternational

Sold and distributed by:
Wolters Kluwer Legal & Regulatory U.S.
920 Links Avenue
Landisville, PA 17538
United States of America
E-mail: customer.service@wolterskluwer.com

DISCLAIMER: The material in this volume is in the nature of general comment only. It is not offered as advice on any particular matter and should not be taken as such. The editor and the contributing authors expressly disclaim all liability to any person with regard to anything done or omitted to be done, and with respect to the consequences of anything done or omitted to be done wholly or partly in reliance upon the whole or any part of the contents of this volume. No reader should act or refrain from acting on the basis of any matter contained in this volume without first obtaining professional advice regarding the particular facts and circumstances at issue. Any and all opinions expressed herein are those of the particular author and are not necessarily those of the editor or publisher of this volume.

ISBN 978-94-035-3629-3

e-Book: ISBN 978-94-035-3639-2
web-PDF: ISBN 978-94-035-3649-1

© 2025 Kluwer Law International BV, The Netherlands, and/or subsidiaries, its licensors, and contributors. All rights are reserved, including those for text and data mining, AI training, and similar technologies.

No part of this publication may be reproduced, stored in a retrieval system, or transmitted in any form or by any means, electronic, mechanical, photocopying, recording, or otherwise, without written permission from the publisher.

Permission to use this content must be obtained from the copyright owner. More information can be found at: https://www.wolterskluwer.com/en/solutions/kluwerlawinternational/rights-and-permissions

The Authors

Professor Lei Chen is a Chair in International Arbitration and Chinese Law and the Director of the Durham International Dispute Resolution Institute at Durham University. He is a Member of the European Academy of Sciences and Arts, a Titular Member of the International Academy of Comparative Law, and a Fellow of the European Law Institute. Professor Chen is a member of the International Commercial Expert Committee of the PRC Supreme People's Court. He is a Fellow of the Chartered Institute of Arbitrators, serving on the panel of arbitrators for numerous arbitration institutions worldwide. His publications include monographs on *Property Law in China: Transition and Trend* (Cambridge University Press, 2025), *Chinese Condominium Law* (Intersentia, 2010); edited volumes on *Chinese Contract Law: Civil and Common Law Perspectives* (Cambridge University Press, 2017), Comparative Consumer Sales (Routledge, 2017), The Legal Protection of Personality Rights in Europe and China (Brill 2018); and numerous articles in leading law and interdisciplinary journals. Professor Chen has written the General Introduction and Part I of this monograph.

Dr Liang Zhao is an Associate Professor in Law at Southampton Law School, University of Southampton, UK. He teaches and researches contract law, international trade law, maritime law, insurance law and conflict of laws. He received his LLB at Dalian Maritime University, LLM at the University of Southampton and PhD at The University of Hong Kong. He is the author of *Maritime Law and Practice in China* (Informa Law from Routledge, 2017). He is also a contributor to *Chinese Legal Reform and the Global Legal Order: Adoption and Adaption* (Cambridge University Press, 2017). He is a Fellow of the Chartered Institute of Arbitrators and a supporting member of the London Maritime Arbitrators Association. He is also an arbitrator of Chinese arbitration commissions including the China Maritime Arbitration Commission and local arbitration commissions in China. Dr Zhao has written Part II and Part III of this monograph.

The Authors

Table of Contents

The Authors 3

List of Abbreviations 15

General Introduction 17

§1. The General Background of the Country 17
I. Geography 17
II. Culture 18
III. Political System 19
A. State Structure 19
B. Powers of the State Organs 21

§2. Legal Family: Civil Law Tradition with the Socialist Value 22

§3. The Primacy of Legislation 24

§4. The Position of the Judiciary 24

§5. Introduction to the Law of Contracts 28
I. Definition of Contract 28
II. Historical Background of the Law of Contracts 28
III. Classification of Contracts 30
A. Civil Contracts and Administrative Contracts 31
B. Civil Contracts and Commercial Contracts 34
IV. Contract and Torts 36
V. Contract and Quasi-contract 40
VI. Contract and the Law of Property 41

§6. The Principle of Good Faith 43
I. Concept 43
II. The Overarching Principle of Good Faith 44
III. The Historical, Cultural and Political Dimensions of the Good Faith Principle 46
IV. The Challenges of the Good Faith Principle 48

§7. Sources of the Law of Contracts 50
I. Legal Sources as the Basis for Rulings 50
A. National Legislation: The Civil Code and Other Laws 51

B. Administrative Regulations 52
C. Local Regulations and Autonomy Regulations 52
D. The SPC Judicial Interpretations 52
E. Civil Customs 53
F. International Treaties 54
II. Legal Sources as the Basis for Reasoning 54
A. Departmental Rules 54
B. Local Departmental Documents 55
C. The SPC Judicial Opinions 56
D. The SPC Guiding Cases 56
E. International Customary Practices 58

Part I. General Principles 59

Chapter 1. Contract Formation 59

§1. AGREEMENT AND QUID PRO QUO (RECIPROCITY) 59
I. Offer and Acceptance 59
II. Intention to Create Legal Relations 66
III. Consideration 69
IV. Modifications of the Contract 72

§2. FORMAL AND EVIDENTIAL REQUIREMENTS 74
I. Formal Requirements 74
II. Evidential Requirement-Proof 76
III. Obligation of Means and Obligation of Result 80

§3. LIABILITY AND NEGOTIATIONS 81
I. Pre-contractual Liability 81
II. Preliminary Contracts 84
III. Compensation for Pre-contractual Liability 88

Chapter 2. Validity 91

§1. LEGISLATIVE DEVELOPMENT OF CONTRACT VALIDITY 91

§2. CAPACITY OF THE PARTIES 95

§3. DEFECTS OF CONSENT 96
I. A Sham Manifestation of Intent 96
II. Gross Misunderstanding 100
III. Fraud by Counterparty and a Third Party 105
A. Fraud by Counterparty 105
B. Fraud by a Third Party 107
C. Comparison with English Law of Misrepresentation 109
IV. Coercion 110

V. Improper Pressure and Manifest Unfairness 112
VI. Malicious Collusion 116

§4. Other Conditions of Validity 120
I. Illegality 120
II. Public Order and Good Morals 126
III. Effectiveness of a Contract Subject to Approval 133

§5. The Consequences of Contract Invalidity 137

Chapter 3. The Contents of a Contract 141

§1. Introduction 141

§2. Ascertaining of Express Terms 142
I. Interpretation of Express Terms 142

§3. Implied Terms 149

§4. Standard Terms and Exemption Clauses 152

§5. Arbitration Clauses 155

Chapter 4. Privity of Contract 162

§1. The rule of privity of contract 162
I. Third Parties and the Contract 163
II. Contract for the Benefit of a Third Party 165
III. Contracts Performed by a Third Party 168

§2. Assignment of Contractual Rights 171
I. Subrogation 171
II. Assignment of Contractual Rights by Agreement 179
III. Assignment of Contractual Liabilities 187

§3. The Special Case of a 'Sub-contract' in Commercial Law 190

§4. Actio Pauliana 192

Chapter 5. The Termination of the Contract 200

§1. Concept and Features 200

§2. Performance and Breach 203
I. Anticipatory Breach 203
II. Delayed Performance of the Main Obligation 206

III. Unrealisation of Contract's Purpose 209

§3. Court-Ordered Termination: Breaching Party's Relief and Doctrine of Change of Circumstances 212
I. Breaching Party's Relief 212
II. Change of Circumstances 217

§4. Discharge by Agreement 220

§5. Waiver of Termination Rights 223

§6. Legal Consequences of Termination 225
I. Restitution 225
II. Damages 226
III. Set-Off 227
IV. Ancillary Responsibilities 228
V. Summary 229

Chapter 6. Remedies 230

§1. General Provisions 230

§2. Breach or Non-performance 232
I. Concept 232
II. Strict Liability or Faculty-Based Liability? 233
III. Limitations on the Recoverable Loss 235
A. Force Majeure 235
IV. Mitigation 235
V. Contributory Negligence 237
VI. Reduction of Loss by Gains of the Non-breaching Party 238

§3. Specific Performance and Remedial Measures 239
I. Specific Performance as a Routine Remedy 239
II. Restrictions on Availability of Specific Performance 240
III. Comparative Analysis 241

§4. Damages 243
I. General Rule 243
II. Expected Benefits 244
III. Calculating Expected Benefits 245
IV. Reliance Damages and Restitution Damages 251

§5. Security Deposits 252

§6. Creditor's Unjustified Refusal or Delay to Accept Performance 256

§7. Exceptio Non Adimpleti Contractus (The Defence of Non-performance by the Other Party) 257

§8. Liquidated Damages and Penalty Clauses 260
I. Concept 260
II. Penalty Clause 262
III. Adjusting Liquidated Damages 264
IV. Factors Affecting the Adjustment of Liquidated Damages 266

§9. Limitation of Actions 269
I. Nature and Function 269
II. Suspension of Limitation Period 271
III. Interruption of Limitation Period 272

Part II. Specific Contracts 277

General Introduction 277

Chapter 1. Sales Contracts 279

§1. Concept of Sale Contract 279

§2. Consumer Sale Contract 282

§3. CISG 283
I. Application 283
II. Formation of Contract 284
III. Seller's Obligations and Buyer's Remedies 285
IV. Buyer's Obligations and Seller's Remedies 286
V. Breach and Remedies 288

§4. Ownership under Sale 289

§5. Delivery of the Subject Matter 291

§6. Risks and Transfer 293

§7. Quality Requirements 295

§8. Inspection 298

§9. Payment Obligation 301

§10. Termination of Contract 303

§11. Sale by Sample and Sale by Trial 304

§12. OTHERS 305

§13. SALE OF COMMERCIAL REAL ESTATE 306
I. Commercial Real Estate Sale 306
II. Offer and Validity of Contract 307
III. Risk and Quality Concerns 307
IV. Breach and Remedies 308

Chapter 2. Contracts for the Supply and Use of Electricity, Water, Gas or Heat 311

§1. CONCEPT AND RESPONSIBILITY 311

§2. PERFORMANCE OF CONTRACT 312

Chapter 3. Gift Contracts 314

§1. GENERAL PROVISIONS 314

§2. PERFORMANCE OF CONTRACT 315

Chapter 4. Loan Contracts 317

§1. CONCEPT 317

§2. PERFORMANCE OF LOAN CONTRACTS 319

§3. PRIVATE LOAN CONTRACTS 320

Chapter 5. Guaranty Contracts 325

§1. GENERAL PROVISIONS 325

§2. THE FORMS OF GUARANTY 328

§3. GUARANTY LIABILITY 331
I. Duration of Guaranty 331
II. Scope of Guaranty 333
III. Change of guaranty 334
IV. More Than One Guarantor 336

Chapter 6. Lease Contracts 337

§1. GENERAL PROVISIONS 337

§2. RIGHTS AND OBLIGATIONS OF THE LESSOR 338

§3. Rights and Obligations of the Lessee 342

§4. Lease Contracts on Urban Buildings 344

Chapter 7. Financial Lease Contracts 348

§1. General Provisions 348

§2. Performance of the Financial Lease Contract 350

§3. Termination of Contract 353

Chapter 8. Factoring Contracts 355

Chapter 9. Contracts for Work 360

Chapter 10. Construction Contracts 365

§1. The Construction Contracts 365

§2. Construction Contract and Tendering 367

§3. Subcontracting 368

§4. Void Construction Contracts 370

§5. Contractors' Rights and Obligations 372

§6. The Employer's Rights and Obligations 374

Chapter 11. Transport Contracts 378

§1. General Provisions 378

§2. Carriage of Passengers Contracts 379

§3. Carriage of Goods Contracts 382

§4. Multimodal Transport Contracts 387

Chapter 12. Technology Contracts 389

§1. General Provisions 389

§2. Contracts for Technology Development 392

§3. Contracts for Technology Transfer and Technology Licence 396

§4. Contracts for Technology Consultancy and Technology Services 399

Chapter 13. Safekeeping Contracts 401

Chapter 14. Warehousing Contracts 404

Chapter 15. Mandate Contracts 408

§1. General Provisions 408

§2. Damages 408

§3. Mandate Contracts with Third Parties 410

§4. Termination of Contract 414

Chapter 16. Property Service Contracts 417

§1. General Provisions 417

§2. Performance of Contract 419

§3. Termination of Contract 421

Chapter 17. Contracts of Commission Agency 423

Chapter 18. Intermediary Contracts 425

§1. General Provisions 425

§2. Intermediary's Report Obligation 426

§3. Remuneration and Expenses 428

§4. Application of the Mandate Contract Rules 431

Chapter 19. Partnership Contracts 433

§1. Definition 433

§2. Performance of Contract 434

§3. External Transfer of Share 435

§4. End and Termination of Partnership Contracts 436

Part III. Quasi-contracts 437

§1. Negotiorum Gestio (Unauthorised Management) 437

§2. Unjustified Enrichment 440

Bibliography 445

Table of Cases 455

Table of Legislation 481

Index 485

List of Abbreviations

BEE	Beijing Equity Exchange
BGB	German Civil Code
CC	Civil Code
CCL	Contract Law
CCP	Chinese Communist Party
CIETAC	China International Economic and Trade Arbitration Commission
CISG	Convention for International Goods Sales
CPPCC	Chinese People's Political Consultative Conference
DCC	Doctrine of Change of Circumstances
ECL	Economic Contract Law
FOB	Free on Board
GPCL	General Principles of Civil Law
IOU	I Owe You
IPO	Initial Public Offering
LOI	Letter of Intent
LPR	Loan Prime Rate
NPC	National People's Congress
NPCSC	National People's Congress Standing Committee
NSPA	Nominee Share Purchase Agreements
PRC	People's Republic of China
RLCL	Rural Land Contract Law
SCIA	Shenzhen Court of International Arbitration
SP	Specific Performance
SPC	Supreme People's Court
SPP	Supreme People's Procuracy
UCC	Uniform Commercial Code
UCP	Uniform Customs and Practice
VAT	Value Added Tax
WTO	World Trade Organization

List of Abbreviations

General Introduction

§1. The General Background of the Country

I. Geography

1. The People's Republic of China (PRC) is situated in East Asia, covering an expansive land area of 9.6 million square kilometres, making it one of the largest countries in the world by size.[1] Its territory includes 5,400 offshore islands scattered along a coastline that stretches approximately 22,800 kilometres.[2]

2. China shares land borders with fourteen countries: North Korea to the east; Mongolia to the north; Russia to the northeast and northwest; Kazakhstan, Kyrgyzstan, and Tajikistan to the west; Afghanistan, Pakistan, India, Bhutan and Nepal to the southwest; and Myanmar, Laos, and Vietnam to the south. Additionally, China has maritime boundaries with South Korea, Japan, the Philippines, Brunei, Malaysia, and Indonesia across the Yellow Sea, East China Sea, and South China Sea.[3] Its coastline also includes the Bohai Sea, underscoring its strategic maritime geography.

3. China's terrain is often described as a four-step 'staircase' descending from west to east. The highest step, known as the 'roof of the world', is the Qinghai-Tibet Plateau, averaging over 4,000 metres above sea level. The second step includes the Inner Mongolia, Loess, and Yunnan-Guizhou plateaus, as well as the Tarim, Junggar, and Sichuan basins, with elevations between 1,000 and 2,000 metres. The third step, ranging from 500 to 1,000 metres, is delineated by the Greater Hinggan, Taihang, Wushan, and Xuefeng mountain ranges. The final step comprises the eastern plains. Approximately 25.9% of China's land lies above 3,000 metres, 7% between 2,000 and 3,000 metres, 25% between 500 and 1,000 metres, and the remaining 25.2% below 500 metres.[4]

4. With many rivers streaming down from the Qinghai-Tibet Plateau, China claims to have the most hydropower potential with reserves of 680 million kW. China is also known to be rich in mineral resources and is considered third in the

1. This is the official measurement, which includes Taiwan and Diaoyu island.
2. Information from the Official Web Portal: http://english.gov.cn.
3. *Ibid.*
4. *Ibid.*

world for total reserves of minerals. Petroleum, natural gas, oil shale, phosphorus and sulfur can also be abundant. China has around 400 million ha of grasslands, with natural pasturelands in the north and south of the Tianshan Mountains in Xinjiang that are ideal for stockbreeding. China also hosts more than 5,000 plant species.[5]

5. Concerning cultivation, over 130.04 million ha of land are cultivated. The cultivated part of Northeast Plain grows wheat, corn, sorghum, soybeans, flax and sugarbeet. The North China Plain supplies wheat, corn, millet and cotton. Paddy rice and freshwater fish can be found in the Middle-Lower Yangtze Plain, also called the 'land of fish and rice'. It is also an area that grows tea and silkworms. The Sichuan Basin, known as the 'land of plenty', nurtures plentiful paddy rice, rapeseed and sugarcane, while the Pearl River Delta farms paddy rice.[6]

II. Culture

6. The Chinese population was 1,411.78 million persons as of 2021, increased by 72.06 million persons compared with the population of 1,339.72 million persons in 2010, up by 5.38 per cent. It is also one of the most overcrowded countries in the world, with the majority of the residents occupying less than half of the country's land. According to 2021 statistics, there were 901.99 million people residing in urban areas, comprising 63.89% of the population, and 509.79 million people living in rural areas, making up 36.11%.[7]

7. Although 91.11% of the population is of the Han ethnic, China is also home to dozens of ethnic groups.[8] The Zhuang, Manchu, Hui, Miao, Uygur, Yi, Tujia, Mongolian, Tibetan, Bouyei, Dong, Yao, Korean, Bai, Hani, Li, Kazak and Dai each have a population of over 1 million. Yunnan Province, with residents from over 20 ethnic groups, is most diverse in terms of ethnicity. Some ethnic groups enjoy autonomous rights under the regional ethnic autonomy system developed by the Chinese government. Under this system, Inner Mongolia, Xinjiang Uygur, Guangxi Zhuang, Ningxia Hui and Tibet are autonomous regions with extensive rights governing internal affairs, including economic development, education, and protection of cultural heritage.[9] The Chinese government also recognises 30 autonomous prefectures, 120 autonomous counties and 1,100 ethnic townships.[10]

8. The official language of China is Putonghua Chinese, also known as Mandarin. The government, media, and schools widely use the language. In its generic

5. *Ibid.*
6. *Ibid.*
7. The Seventh National Population Census (the National Bureau of Statistics of China), May 2021, at https://www.stats.gov.cn/english/PressRelease/202105/t20210510_1817185.html.
8. *Ibid.*
9. The Regional Ethnic Autonomy Law (1984) (second session of the 6th NPC)
10. Information from the Official Web Portal: http://english.gov.cn.

sense of the word, it can be said that Chinese is the language used in China. However, various regional dialects and sub-dialects are used in China. A majority (53 of the 55) of the ethnic minority groups speak a different language and use a different system of written script. It is commonly recognised that the spoken and written language used by the Han people is the language appropriately referred to as 'Chinese'.

9. A wide variety of religions are practised in China. There are over 3,000 religious associations established. One of the earliest practised religions is Buddhism, believed to have been introduced to China around the first century AD. This religion is acknowledged as the most influential religion in China after the fourth century. Different forms of Buddhism have been practised in China, for example, Tibetan Buddhism and Hinayana Buddhism. Other main religions in China include Islam, Roman Catholic and Protestant Christianity. Another popular religion among the Han people is Taoism.

III. Political System

A. *State Structure*

10. As enunciated in the Constitution of the PRC (Constitution), China is a socialist state[11] led by a single party, the Chinese Communist Party (CCP).[12]

11. The National People's Congress (NPC) is the formal governmental organ through which state power is exercised, designated by the Constitution as 'the highest organ of state power'.[13] Together with its Standing Committee (NPCSC), the NPC is the primary legislative body, holding legislative authority.[14] The NPCSC also oversees the Supreme People's Court (SPC) and the Supreme People's Procuracy (SPP), which are the highest judicial and prosecutorial bodies, respectively.[15] Apart from legislating and overseeing the SPC and SPP, the key roles and functions of the NPC and the NPCSC also include: supervising the work of the State Council (executive branch),[16] monitoring the implementation of the Constitution,[17] electing or appointing key state officials, such as the President, Premier, and members of the State Council,[18] removing officials from office when necessary,[19] reviewing and approving the state budget and financial reports,[20] approving international treaties

11. Paragraph 1 of Art. 1 of the PRC Constitution.
12. Paragraph 2 of Art. 1 of the PRC Constitution.
13. Article 57 of the PRC Constitution.
14. Article 58 of the PRC Constitution.
15. Article 67 (6) of the PRC Constitution.
16. *Ibid.*
17. Article 67 (1) of the PRC Constitution.
18. Article 62 (5) of the PRC Constitution.
19. Article 63 of the PRC Constitution.
20. Article 62 (11) of the PRC Constitution.

and agreements.[21] Through the NPCSC, the NPC exercises continuous legislative and supervisory authority when not in session, ensuring the effective functioning of the state.[22]

12. The State Council, also known as the Central People's Government, serves as the executive branch,[23] responsible for formulating administrative measures, enacting administrative regulations, issuing decisions and orders and submitting proposals to the NPC or the NPCSC.[24] The State Council operates an audit office to conduct auditing oversight over the revenue and expenditure of all State Council departments and local governments at all levels and over the revenue and expenditure of all state financial institutions, enterprises and public institutions.[25] The State Council is accountable to the NPC and must report its work to the NPC. When the NPC is not in session, the State Council is accountable to the NPCSC and must report its work to the NPCSC.[26]

13. The Executive Leadership of the national government, the President of the PRC, acts as the country's ceremonial leader, with responsibilities that include entering into international treaties and representing China on the global stage. This structure reflects a centralised system where legislative, executive, and judicial functions align under the NPC's ultimate authority.

14. China's eight minor political parties, officially termed 'democratic parties',[27] are integral components of the country's political framework. They operate under the leadership of the CCP within the patriotic united front, a coalition designed to foster cooperation among various social and political groups. These parties participate in the Chinese People's Political Consultative Conference (CPPCC),[28] contributing to state and government affairs through roles such as political consultation and democratic supervision.[29]

15. While these democratic parties engage in the political system, they do not hold independent power at the national level. Their existence and activities are contingent upon accepting the CCP's leading role, and their leadership is vetted by the

---

21. Article 67 (15) of the PRC Constitution.
22. Article 67 (3) of the PRC Constitution.
23. Article 85 of the PRC Constitution.
24. Article 89 of the PRC Constitution.
25. Article 91 of the PRC Constitution.
26. Article 92. of the PRC Constitution.
27. https://www.gov.cn/guoqing/2023-03/10/content_5745769.htm.
28. This system was explained in a statement issued by the CCP on 30 December 1989, the 'Opinion of the CPC Central regarding Insisting on and Perfecting the System of Multiparty Co-operation and Political Consultation under the Leadership of the CCP,' in State council Gazette No. 2, p. 38 (1990). This was subsequently endorsed in 1993 Amendments to the Constitution, in the 10th paragraph of the Preamble.
29. What makes CPC-led multi-party cooperation a success (People's Daily Online), June 2011, at http://english.people.com.cn/90001/90780/91342/7421713.html.

CCP's United Front Work Department. This arrangement ensures that the democratic parties function in an advisory capacity, supporting the CCP's policies and maintaining the appearance of political inclusiveness.

16. The eight democratic parties in China are not opposition parties in the sense of Western political systems. Instead, their role includes providing advisory opinions on state affairs to the CCP Congress and participating in the CPPCC. These parties, while part of the political framework, do not hold actual political power. However, individual members from these parties may be appointed to senior positions in state organs, reflecting their consultative and cooperative roles rather than independent political authority. This arrangement underscores China's unique model of multi-party cooperation under the leadership of the CCP.

17. The NPC is the formal governmental organ through which state power can be exercised. The Constitution calls the NPC 'the highest organ of state power'.[30] Together with the NPCSC, the NPC holds legislative power.[31] The executive branch of the state is the State Council,[32] also referred to as the Central People's Government.[33] The NPC also heads the SPC and the Supreme People's Procuracy (SPP), respectively, the state's highest judiciary and procuratorial body. The Executive Leadership of the National Government serves as the country's figurehead and is responsible, among other things, for entering international treaties.

18. The political structure described above is replicated at lower levels: at the provincial, municipal and county levels.[34] The hierarchy of local government goes in this order descending: counties, cities, municipal districts, townships, nationality townships, and towns.[35] Under the leadership of the NPC, a local people's congress and local people's government are formed. Each local people's congress establishes its standing committee above the county level.[36] As in the case at the national level, the local people's court and people's procuratorates answer to their local people's congress. The local people's congresses can enact local regulations so far as they do not contravene the Constitution and national laws.[37]

B. Powers of the State Organs

19. The main powers of the NPC include amending the Constitution, enacting and amending basic laws and examining and approving important plans on state financial affairs. The NPC also has the power to elect and appoint key state officials

30. *Ibid.*
31. Articles 57–59 of the PRC Constitution.
32. Article 85 of the PRC Constitution.
33. Article 85 of the PRC Constitution.
34. Article 95 of the PRC Constitution.
35. Article 95 of the PRC Constitution.
36. Article 96 of the PRC Constitution.
37. Article 100 of the PRC Constitution.

such as the President and the Vice-president of the PRC,[38] the Premier of the State Council,[39] the Chairman of the Central Military Commission,[40] the President of the SPC[41] and the Procurator-General of the SPP.[42]

20. The NPCSC is the permanent body of the NPC. It carries a supervisory role in enforcing the Constitution[43] and the performance of the State Council, Central Military Commission, the SPC and the SPP.[44] It also holds residual powers to enact, amend and interpret laws and regulations and appoint officials in various state organs.[45] The NPCSC makes decisions over state matters when the NPC is not in session.

21. As mentioned above, the State Council is China's ultimate executive government body. It has wide powers in administering state affairs, such as education, public health, population planning, public security and foreign affairs.[46] In addition to its executive role, the State Council can propose state matters to the NPC. It is responsible for devising and drafting state economic plans and budgets,[47] as well as deciding on dividing powers between the Central Government and other administrative organs.[48]

22. The people's courts and the people's procuratorates are responsible for the enforcement of laws, with the SPC being the highest body in administering justice[49] and the SPP as the highest body supervising law enforcement.[50] The two bodies form the judiciary structure in China. Even though the Constitution stresses the independence of the SPC and the SPP, both bodies are to function under the supervision of the NPC and the NPCSC.[51]

§2. Legal Family: Civil Law Tradition with the Socialist Value

23. Chinese law is considered a *sui generis* system, which does not fit any traditional legal family category in the comparative law scholarship. While David, Zweiget and Kotz regarded Chinese law as distinctive on its own, i.e., Chinese legal

38. Article 62(4) of the PRC Constitution.
39. Article 62(5) of the PRC Constitution.
40. Article 62(6) of the PRC Constitution.
41. Article 62(7) of the PRC Constitution.
42. Article 62(8) of the PRC Constitution.
43. Article 67(1) of the PRC Constitution.
44. Article 67(6) of the PRC Constitution.
45. Article 67(1)–(4), (7)–(8) of the PRC Constitution.
46. Article 89(6)–(9) of the PRC Constitution.
47. Article 89(5) of the PRC Constitution.
48. Article 89(4) of the PRC Constitution.
49. Article 127 of the PRC Constitution.
50. Article 129 of the PRC Constitution.
51. Articles 128 and 133 of the PRC Constitution.

family, Mattei labels it as a Far Eastern Law. While La Porta et al. position Chinese law as of German legal origin, Glenn categorised it as a Confucian legal family.[52]

24. It is widely recognised that Chinese law aligns closely with the civil law tradition, which has its roots in the late Qing Dynasty (1902–1911). During this period, China faced the urgent need to reform its legal system to adapt to the demands of modernity. Although a draft of the Qing Civil Code was prepared, it was never implemented and was not adopted by the subsequent interim Republic government. Nonetheless, it was the first attempt in Chinese legal history to establish a separate civil code from an all-encompassing feudal criminal code. The country moved away from its customary Chinese traditions and Confucian values for the first time. More significantly, this civil code draft laid the foundation for the European civil codes to be used to develop a set of Chinese civil laws.

25. From 1911 to 1928, despite political instability and frequent changes in government, the Republic of China[53] continued its efforts to develop a modern Chinese civil code, showing a commitment to legal modernisation. The Republican Civil Code (1929–1931) had apparent traces of civil law, notably in its statutory framework. It was organised into five books: General Principles, Law of Obligations, Property Law, Family and Succession. This structure was the same as the Qing Civil Code Draft and passed down from the German model. It is fair to say that the German Pandectist influence was ubiquitous in this code.[54]

26. When the PRC was founded in 1949, The Republican legal system, including the Republican Civil Code was repealed without being replaced. Despite the several failures of attempting to introduce a civil code, on 12 April 1986, the NPC enacted the General Principles of Civil Law (GPCL).[55] This law was a milestone since it was a hallmark in China's civil law reconstruction after the Cultural Revolution.

27. Essentially, the civil law tradition underpins Chinese private law. From a historical and comparative perspective, civil law is an important part of the Chinese legal system.[56] Many Chinese jurists value civil law doctrines and hold statute law in high esteem. They pay special attention to studying civil law, which is useful and necessary to modernise the Chinese legal system.[57]

52. Mattias Siems, Comparative Law 87 (Cambridge University Press 2022).
53. The Republic of China was established after the fall of the Qing Dynasty, marking the end of imperial rule in China. It was the first republican government in East Asia. It governed China from 1912 to 1949. Following the victory of the CCP in the civil war, the ROC government retreated to Taiwan, while the PRC was established on the mainland.
54. Lei Chen, The historical development of the Civil Law tradition in China: a private law perspective, 78 (1-2) Tijdschrift voor Rechtsgeschiedenis/Revue d'histoire du droit/The Legal History Review 159-181 (2010).
55. The General Principles of the Civil Law (1987).
56. Shiyuan Han, A Snapshot of Chinese Contract Law from an Historical and Comparative Perspective, in Towards a Chinese Civil Code (Brill Nijhoff 2012).
57. Jingen Wang & Larry A. DiMatteo, Chinese Reception and Transplantation of Western Contract Law, 34 Berkeley J. Int'l L. 44 (2016).

28. In summary, an appropriate characterisation of the Chinese legal system is a civil law tradition coupled with socialist values. When China needed to import foreign legislative ideas in the late Qing period, it was no surprise but a natural choice, for there were conceptual and doctrinal similarities between feudal Chinese law and modern continental civil law.[58] Additionally, the Chinese legal language, legal culture, political structure and colonial history are of a kind that allowed Japan to provide a convenient reference. Moreover, China's reception of the civil law tradition was neither a function of colonisation nor driven by the admirable prestige of civilian codes. There was no time to fancy the prestige, and only after the civil law system had been introduced did the Chinese government and jurists start to value its prestige.

§3. The Primacy of Legislation

29. Legislation is central in governing various aspects of society and is considered the primary source of law. Laws are enacted by the NPC and NPCSC at the national level, as well as by local people's congresses and their standing committees at the regional level. These laws cover various legal subjects, including civil, criminal, and administrative. Additionally, regulations and rules issued by government agencies and administrative bodies are also important components of the legal system, although they derive their authority from higher-level legislation. Overall, legislation is the foundation of the Chinese legal system, guiding the behaviour of individuals, organisations, and government entities.

30. The legislation enacted by the national legislature is the highest source of contract law in China, for example, the Contract Law (CCL) or the Civil Code (CC). According to Article 58 of the Constitution, the NPC or NPCSC exercises the legislative power of the state. Furthermore, the NPC and its Standing Committee are empowered. They may annul any administrative regulations promulgated by the State Council or local regulations promulgated by the state organs of provinces, autonomous regions and municipalities that contravene the legislation.

31. It is common practice under Chinese law for the state to introduce national legislation, followed by implementation rules issued by the State Council or local governments. This is also often followed by a judicial interpretation released by SPC on the new legislation. These subsequent regulations, rules, implementation measures, and judicial interpretations fine-tune the details of the main legislation.

§4. The Position of the Judiciary

32. The judiciary in the Chinese legal system is a key component of the state structure. The people's courts are the judicial organs of the state.[59] The SPC is the

58. Lei Chen, Contextualizing Legal Transplant: China and Hong Kong, in Methods of Comparative Law (Edward Elgar Publishing 2012).
59. Article 128 of the PRC Constitution.

highest judicial authority in the PRC. It oversees the adjudicative work of local courts at all levels and specialised courts. Additionally, higher-level courts supervise the judicial activities of lower-level courts.[60] The SPC is accountable to the NPC and the NPCSC.[61] Local people's courts at various levels are accountable to the state power organs that established them.[62]

33. While the Constitution and laws provide for judicial independence,[63] the judiciary operates under the leadership of the CCP, which may influence court decisions to ensure alignment with state policies and political priorities.[64] It plays a significant role in adjudicating disputes, enforcing laws, and maintaining social order, but its position and function are viewed against the unique structure of China's political-legal framework.

34. The judiciary is organised hierarchically, with the SPC at the apex, followed by high people's courts, intermediate people's courts, and basic people's courts.[65] Specialised courts, such as military, maritime, and intellectual property courts, address specific types of cases.[66]

35. In recent years, judicial reforms have aimed to enhance professionalism, transparency, and public trust in the legal system. These include measures to reduce local government influence over courts, improve judges' qualifications, and promote consistency in legal interpretations through SPC-issued judicial interpretations and case guidance. Recent reforms reflect efforts to modernise and professionalise the judiciary while maintaining its alignment with state policy.

36. The SPC issues judicial interpretations to clarify and unify the application of laws, which effectively serve as binding guidance for lower courts. These interpretations are a critical tool for addressing gaps or ambiguities in legislation. The SPC has also established a system for using 'guiding cases' to promote consistency and predictability in judicial decisions. Although not legally binding as precedent, these cases are influential in shaping the application of law.

60. Article 132 of the PRC Constitution.
61. Article 133 of the PRC Constitution.
62. *Ibid.*
63. Article 131 of the PRC Constitution states that People's courts exercise judicial power independently in accordance with the law, free from interference by administrative organs, social organisations, or individuals.
64. Article 1 of the PRC Constitution states that the leadership of the CCP is the core essence of the socialist rule of law with Chinese characteristics. 'The judicial power exercised by the courts is an integral part of the Party's leadership and governance authority. It represents a key mechanism through which the Party exercises its leadership and governance, serving as a powerful tool for maintaining and advancing the Party's long-term governance and ensuring the nation's lasting stability and security'; Maintain Social Fairness with Strict and Impartial Justice (People's Court Daily), Jan. 2023, at https://www.chinacourt.org/article/detail/2023/01/id/7112342.shtml.
65. Articles 12 and 13 of the Organic Law of the People's Courts.
66. Article 15 of the Organic Law of the People's Courts.

37. Given the size of China and regional variation in social and economic conditions, legislation cannot cover every situation, especially as society and the economy evolve. Judges often face legislation short in detail and must make judgments based on changing circumstances. As a result, courts, particularly SPC, play a significant role in shaping how contracts are enforced.[67] Judges also need to address unclear laws in new situations. Therefore, judicial interpretations issued by the SPC are considered the most important source of clarification for contract law. Judges at all levels of Chinese courts can refer to the provisions of the SPC judicial interpretations as a legal basis supporting the ruling in the judgments.

38. Only the SPC, as the highest judicial body in the country, has the authority to provide judicial interpretations. The SPC issued three major judicial interpretations concerning the application of CCL prior to the enactment of the CC in 2020.[68] For example, the SPC Interpretation on Issues Concerning the Application of the Contract Law (I) and (II) (the SPC Interpretation on the Contract Law (I) (1999); the SPC Interpretation on the Contract Law (II) (2009)) are guidelines for all levels of courts when dealing with specific contract law issues. These interpretations clarify how the CCL should be applied in various situations.

39. For instance, SPC Interpretation on Contract Law (II) (2009), issued after the 2008 financial crisis, focuses on contract validity, performance, and breach. It emphasises the principle of party autonomy, allowing parties to choose the court for disputes and reinforcing the validity of oral contracts. The CCL does not explicitly mention the doctrine of 'change of circumstances' as a reason to excuse the performance of a contract. However, the SPC Interpretation on Contract Law (II) (2009) formalises this principle.[69] This means courts can now officially use it to relieve parties from their contractual obligations if unexpected circumstances arise. The concept first appeared in a 1992 court case.[70] This SPC interpretation confirms that the CCL implicitly allows such exemptions in hardship cases.

40. While the SPC offers detailed guidance through interpretations that fill in gaps left by statutes, the exact power of these interpretations is debated. While some argue they hold the same weight as legislation, others point out that statutes precede internal court rules. These rules lack a strong legal foundation, and legal scholars

67. Lei Chen & Larry A. DiMatteo, History of Chinese Contract Law 1-2, in Chinese Contract Law: Civil and Common Law Perspectives (Larry A. DiMatteo & Lei Chen ed., Cambridge University Press 2017).
68. The SPC Interpretation on Issues Concerning the Application of the Contract Law (I) (1999); The SPC Interpretation on Issues Concerning the Application of the Contract Law (II) (2009); and the SPC Interpretation on Issues Concerning the Application of Law in the Trial of Disputes Over Sales Contracts (2012, 2020 revision).
69. This rule has now been incorporated into the Art. 533 CC.
70. *Wuhan Gas Company v. Chongqing Detection Instrument Factory*, Gazette Case of the SPC, Issue 2, 1996; 武汉市煤气公司诉重庆检测仪表厂，《最高人民法院公报》案例，1996年02期.

disagree on the true force of SPC interpretations and precedent-setting cases. Regular SPC decisions do not hold the same weight as legislation.[71] However, published decisions in the SPC Gazette are seen as significant 'soft law' that indirectly influences contract law.[72]

41. After the CC was introduced, the SPC issued a judicial interpretation in 2023 on Several Issues Concerning the Application of the General Provisions of the Contract Book of the Civil Code (the SPC Interpretation on the Contract Book (2023)) to provide detailed guidance on the application and implementation of the CC's contract-related provisions.[73]

42. The SPC interpretation resolves ambiguities in the CC by offering specific explanations of general principles and rules, ensuring consistent application across courts. It promotes uniform application of the law, reducing discrepancies in how courts interpret and enforce contractual provisions. It serves as an authoritative reference for lower courts when handling contract disputes, improving the efficiency and quality of judicial decisions. This judicial interpretation demonstrates the SPC's proactive role in ensuring that the CC is effectively implemented and adapted to meet the needs of China's legal and economic environment. It bridges gaps between the law's broad principles and the complexities of real-world applications.

43. Beyond issuing interpretations, the SPC has also issued the Judicial Meeting Minutes to unify judicial thinking, regulate judges' discretion, and enhance the transparency and predictability of civil and commercial adjudication. The purpose is to ensure the uniform application of laws to foster judicial credibility. The Judicial Meeting Minutes are not judicial interpretations and cannot be cited as a ruling basis for judgment. However, as one of the court documents, minutes guide judicial activities. It is crucial to distinguish between different forms of minutes carefully. Minutes issued under the SPC name can influence judicial activities comparable to judicial interpretations. For example, the SPC Minutes of the National Conference on Civil and Commercial Trial Work of Courts Nationwide were issued by the SPC on 8 November 2019 (The SPC Trial Minutes (2019)). A Trial Minute is an official document issued by Chinese courts after an internal formal conference containing a set of judge-made rules articulated in a detailed way to interpret relevant legislation. A Trial Minute issued by the SPC somewhat resembles a judicial interpretation, though the right of issuance of the former is not limited to the SPC, but applies to lower courts as well. A SPC Minute is generally regarded as less binding in judicial practice compared to a judicial interpretation.

44. However, minutes and judicial interpretations are not substitutes but rather complementary. Although minutes belong to normative documents, they do not

71. It is worth noting that the SPC judicial interpretations are not mentioned in the Legislation Law (2018 revision) which sets out the principles, processes, and hierarchy for enacting, amending, and interpreting laws.
72. Lei Chen & Larry A. DiMatteo, History of Chinese Contract Law (2017).
73. The SPC Interpretation on Several Issues Concerning the Application of the General Provisions of the Contract Book of the Civil Code (2023).

carry the same legally binding force or status as judicial interpretations. Their authority stems from the majority consensus among judges, and their binding force is lower.

§5. Introduction to the Law of Contracts

I. Definition of Contract

45. A contract is an agreement between civil subjects to create, alter, and terminate a civil legal relationship.[74] First, it is an agreement between parties with equal standing. The contract can involve natural persons, legal persons (companies), or other organisations, but all parties involved have equal footing in the agreement. Second, the agreement establishes, alters, or terminates a relationship involving their civil rights and obligations.

46. Agreements related to civil status, such as marriage, adoption, and guardianship, shall be governed by the relevant provisions of other applicable laws. If none, the rules in the Contract Book of the CC shall be applicable, given the nature of the civil status involved.[75]

II. Historical Background of the Law of Contracts

47. With major social, political, and economic changes following the founding of the PRC in 1949, the CCP swiftly discarded the legal system of the previous government (Kuomintang). They replaced it with new 'Judicial Principles' designed for the 'liberated areas'.[76] This shift reflected a core socialist belief: laws under the previous regime, seen as tools for the ruling class, needed to be replaced with new laws reflecting the interests of the working class.[77] China's first contract law regulations came in 1950,[78] but freedom of contract was stifled during the Cultural Revolution (1966-1970s) due to the centrally planned economy. This period prioritised government decisions over fair trade principles, leaving China without a comprehensive contract law for over thirty years. Until 1981, China relied on regulations for specific types of contracts rather than a general contract law.

---

74. Paragraph 1 of Art. 464 CC.
75. Paragraph 2 of Art. 464 CC.
76. Liberated Areas are ones that had been controlled by the CCP before the Kuomintang was completely defeated in Chinese Civil Law.
77. Lei Chen, The Historical Development of the Civil Law Tradition in China: a Private Law Perspective, 159-181 (2010).
78. The Provisional Measure Concerning Contract Making by the Government Offices, State-run Enterprises and Co-operatives, issued by the Government Administration Council of the Central People's Government on 27 September 1950.

48. When the Cultural Revolution ended, China's economic reforms took a major step forward in 1981 by enacting the Economic Contract Law (ECL).[79] This law, the first codified contract law in PRC's history, aimed to provide a reliable legal framework for all economic activities. It initially focused on ten specific contract types, like sales and transportation. Recognising the growing market economy and international trade, China expanded its legal framework in 1985 with Economic Contracts Law Involving Foreign Interests.[80]

49. China's embrace of international trade was evident in joining the Convention for International Goods Sales (CISG) in 1981. This period (late 1970s to 1990s) saw significant progress in Chinese contract law. First, the 1987 Technology Contract Law recognised technical knowledge as valuable, a shift from the past focus on manual labour.[81] Second, the GPCL marked a turning point by using the broader term 'contract' instead of 'economic contract'. This milestone legislation and specific laws for different contract types served as a bridge between the planned economy and the emerging market system.

50. China's economic reforms and growing role in international trade highlighted the limitations of their existing contract law. The patchwork of specific contract laws was seen as unclear, outdated, and impractical. Joining the World Trade Organization (WTO) added pressure to modernise China's legal system to attract foreign investment. Chinese leaders recognised the need for a consistent, user-friendly, and business-oriented contract law to support international trade. This meant replacing the fragmented system with a modern and unified law.[82]

51. Therefore, the CCL draft was officially adopted in 1999.[83] The CCL represents the culmination of efforts to consolidate and reconcile various preceding contract law frameworks.[84] Concurrently with promulgating the CCL, previous laws pertaining to specific types of contracts were repealed.[85] After introducing the CCL, the SPC issued three judicial interpretations to clarify certain provisions within the

79. The Economic Contract Law was enacted on 13 December 1981 and came into effect on 1 July 1982. There are a total of seven chapters and forty-seven articles.
80. The Economic Contract Law Involving Foreign Interests was promulgated on 21 March 1985, and came into effect on 1 July 1985. The entire law consists of seven chapters, comprising a total of forty-three articles.
81. The Technology Contract Law was enacted on 23 June 1987 and came into effect on 1 December 1987. There are a total of seven chapters and fifty-five articles, mainly covering the following: the scope of application of the Technology Contract Law, principles for the conclusion of technology contracts, and ownership of technical achievements; the conclusion, performance, modification, and termination of technology contracts; technology development contracts; technology transfer contracts; technology consulting contracts and technology service contracts; arbitration and litigation of disputes arising from technology contracts.
82. Lei Chen & Larry A. DiMatteo, History of Chinese Contract Law (2017).
83. The Contract Law was enacted on 15 March 1999 and came into effect on 1 October 1999.
84. Lei Chen & Larry A. DiMatteo, History of Chinese Contract Law 10-14 (2017).
85. Jing Leng & Wei Shen, The Evolution of Contract Law in China: Convergence in Law but Divergence in Enforcement, in Private Law in China and Taiwan – Legal and Economic Analyses Ch. 3 (Chung, Shen & Wang ed., Cambridge University Press 2016).

law.[86] These interpretations aim to clarify legal ambiguities and ensure consistent application of the CCL in judicial practice. These interpretations also contribute to the codification of contract law.

52. The CC was effective on 1 January 2021. The CCL was simultaneously repealed. In the Contract Book of the CC, the pre-existing contract law provisions have been largely retained without significant changes.[87] The CC incorporates certain rules that were originally established in judicial interpretations, including the doctrine of changed circumstances.[88]

53. The CC differs from the German Civil Code (BGB) and the Dutch Civil Code, lacking a general section governing the law of obligations. Interestingly, the Qing Civil Code Draft and the Kuomintang Civil Code, still applicable in Taiwan with numerous revisions, contain a separate section outlining general rules governing the law of obligations. However, the CC does not include such provisions. This decision likely stems from the belief that the CCL has significantly developed over approximately twenty years of judicial practice. Therefore, extensive modifications are considered unnecessary and costly for lawmakers.

54. Consequently, the Contract Book in the CC is a quasi-contract, referencing concepts such as unjust enrichment and *negotiorum gestio*.[89] The Contract Book comprises 526 articles, from Article 463 to Article 988, making up 41.7% of the total 1260 articles in the CC. This makes it the largest section of the CC regarding article count.

III. Classification of Contracts

55. Contracts can vary significantly regarding their financial magnitude, duration, and content. They may involve substantial or trivial amounts of money, have long or short durations and encompass many subjects such as sale agreements, hire-purchase agreements, employment contracts, and marriage contracts. However, this monograph does not cover all types of contracts. Contracts related to employment and marriage are largely outside the scope of this monograph.

---

86. First, the SPC Interpretation on Several Issues Concerning the Application of Law in the Trial of Cases Involving Disputes over Contracts (I): This interpretation was issued on 1 December, 1999. Second, the SPC Interpretation on Several Issues Concerning the Application of Law in the Trial of Cases Involving Disputes over Contracts (II) was issued on 24 April 2009. Third, the SPC Interpretation on Several Issues Concerning the Application of Law in the Trial of Cases Involving Sale Contracts was released on 31 March 2012.
87. Jacques Henri Herbots, The Chinese new Civil Code and the law of contract, 7 China-EU Law Journal 39-49 (2021).
88. Lei Chen, Continuity and change: some reflections on the Chinese Civil Code, 29(2) Asia Pacific Law Review 287–305 (2021).
89. Unjust enrichment is a legal doctrine that prevents one party from being unjustly enriched at the expense of another. It is governed by Arts 985–988 CC. *Negotiorum gestio* is a legal doctrine found in Arts 979–984 CC. It refers to the voluntary management of another person's affairs without their authorisation or request, typically in their absence or when they are unable to act.

56. The CC specifically regulates nominate contracts (also known as typical contracts) with detailed provisions for their formation, performance, and termination. Examples are sales contracts, lease contracts, loan contracts, construction contracts, service contracts and agency contracts.

57. Based on the way of formation, it is divided into formal contracts and informal ones. Formal contracts require specific forms for validity, such as writing, registration, or approval. Informal contracts do not require any particular form and can be oral or written as long as the essential elements of the contract are fulfilled. For example, verbal agreements for small transactions.

58. From the perspective of the time of performance, there are instantaneous contracts and continuous contracts. The former refers to the contract's obligations being performed immediately upon agreement. The latter's obligations are performed over a period.

59. The distinction between long-term contracts and short-term contracts lies primarily in their duration of performance. Long-term Contracts refer to agreements intended to establish a sustained legal relationship over an extended period, typically involving continuous or repeated performance. An example is lease agreements for commercial properties, supply chain contracts, and construction contracts. They typically allocate risks related to market fluctuations, inflation, or regulatory changes over time. Price adjustment or renegotiation clauses are common. Courts may modify or terminate the contract if unforeseen events fundamentally alter its basis.[90] For example, a long-term construction contract may include provisions for adjusting prices due to material cost increases.

60. Short-term contracts refer to agreements where obligations are fulfilled within a relatively short timeframe, often involving instantaneous or one-time performance. Examples are spot sales or one-time transport contracts. Risks are limited to the immediate transaction and are typically borne by the obligated party without long-term considerations. They are rarely subject to adjustments due to their brief duration, making the principle of changed circumstances less relevant.

61. Contracts under Chinese law are classified into various types to accommodate the diverse legal and practical needs of parties.

A. Civil Contracts and Administrative Contracts

62. The distinction between administrative contracts and civil contracts is a significant issue in Chinese legal theory. The core of the distinction lies in the nature of the parties involved, the purpose of the contract, and the characteristics of the rights and obligations in the performance of the contract.

90. Article 533 CC.

63. Civil contracts are agreements between equal parties in civil legal relationships. These contracts involve individuals, legal persons, or other organisations, and they typically pertain to private interests. Administrative contracts, on the other hand, involve administrative organs or public institutions as one of the contracting parties. These contracts are between administrative agencies and individuals, legal persons, or other organisations, often concerning administrative matters or public services.

64. Civil contracts primarily address private legal relationships, such as sales, lease, and loan contracts, to fulfil the parties' private interests. The purpose is to satisfy the personal or commercial interests of the parties involved, such as sales, leases, or loans, which are purely transactional in nature.

65. Administrative contracts are related to administrative activities or public services. They may include contracts for the provision of public utilities, land use contracts, or contracts related to administrative permits and licences. A certain level of inequality characterises the relationship.

66. The administrative agency has administrative authority and may unilaterally influence the performance of the contract, such as by terminating the contract or supervising the other party's actions. The primary aim is to achieve public interests or fulfil administrative management functions.[91] For instance, a public infrastructure project contract signed by the government aims to realise specific public policy goals.

67. The regulatory framework differs, too. The CC primarily governs civil contracts, other relevant laws and regulations and SPC Judicial Interpretations. Administrative contracts are regulated by administrative laws and regulations which specifically govern administrative contracts' formation, performance, modification, and termination.

68. Disputes arising from civil contracts are generally resolved through civil litigation procedures in the people's courts. Disputes related to administrative contracts may be adjudicated through administrative proceedings or, in some cases, through civil litigation. Administrative litigation procedures are used when contesting administrative actions, decisions, or contracts involving administrative agencies.

69. Addressing administrative contracts into administrative litigation serves two main purposes: first, it enables the supervision of administrative organs to ensure they fulfil their duties under the law, thereby preventing them from circumventing legal obligations through contract agreements. Second, it strengthens oversight of the exercise of administrative power, preventing administrative organs from abusing their authority or using it unfairly to infringe upon the legitimate rights and interests of the other party involved.

91. Wang Liming, Studies on Contract Law, vol. 1, 57 (Renmin University of China Press, 2002).

70. Despite the conceptual differences between the two, at the practical level, an overlapping jurisdiction issue may arise. Due to the lack of specific legislation concerning administrative contracts in China, theoretical standards are overly abstract. Consequently, some contracts brought to the court fail to be adequately differentiated, highlighting the need for further legal refinement.

71. Additionally, inconsistencies exist among current laws, as illustrated by the example of rural land contracting management contracts. While the Administrative Reconsideration Law designates them as administrative contracts, the Rural Land Contract Law (RLCL) implies they are civil contracts, creating ambiguity. For example, the land use rights created over the rural land for the village households under RLCL is a private property right.[92] The distinction between administrative and civil contracts forms the foundation of administrative adjudication, but the lack of clear criteria presents significant challenges. Legislative action is required to establish unified standards and clarify differentiation rules.

72. The main distinction between administrative agreements and civil contracts lies in whether they involve rights and obligations under administrative law.[93] This can be assessed from three key aspects to examine:

1. whether the agreement contains provisions related to the exercise of administrative powers or the performance of administrative duties;
2. whether the agreement is aimed at achieving public interest objectives or fulfilling administrative management goals.
3. Whether the administrative agency, based on the agreement or legal provisions, possesses unilateral rights such as termination or modification of the agreement.[94]

73. A vexing issue illustrating the overlapping between the two realms is seeking approval from an administrative agency after a civil or commercial contract is concluded. For instance, Article 8 of the SPC Interpretation on Contract Law (II) (2009) mandates that parties to contracts must register their contracts with relevant government administrative bodies if required by administrative regulations. This illustrates the intertwining of contract law with administrative law and procedures.

---

92. Article 333 CC stipulates that the right to contract and manage land is established upon the effectiveness of the land contracting and management agreement. The registration authority shall issue certificates such as the land contracting and management rights certificate or forestry rights certificate to the holders of such rights, register them in official records, and confirm the land contracting and management rights.
93. Paragraph 1 of Art. 11 of the SPC Interpretation on Several Issues Concerning the Application of the Administrative Litigation Law (2018) provides 'an agreement containing rights and obligations under administrative law, concluded by an administrative agency in consultation with a citizen, legal person, or other organization to achieve public interest or administrative management objectives within the scope of its statutory duties, constitutes an administrative agreement as stipulated in Art. 12, para. 1, Item 11 of the Administrative Litigation Law.'
94. *Jinsha County Lengshuihe Tourism Development Co., Ltd. v. Jinsha County People's Government*, the Supreme People's Court, (2020) SPC Min Shen No. 6933; 金沙县冷水河旅游开发有限责任公司诉金沙县人民政府，最高人民法院（2020）最高法民申6933号.

74. Although Chinese scholars often classify contract law as part of private law, it is important to note that administrative regulations issued by the State Council also serve as sources of contract law. Therefore, administrative regulations are considered primary sources in shaping contract law. The relationship between contract law and administrative law has garnered significant academic attention. Failure to complete such approval procedures does not affect the validity of obligations related to approval or related clauses in the contract. If a party obligated to apply for approval or other procedures fails to fulfil this obligation, the other party may request them to bear responsibility for violating it.[95]

75. The SPC Interpretation on the Contract Book (2023) provides that if a party fails to fulfil or improperly fulfils an obligation to seek approval, the court should support the other party's request to continue the obligation or to terminate the contract and claim damages.[96] If a party disregards a court order to fulfil the approval obligation, and the other party seeks termination and damages, the court should uphold the request.[97]

76. Before approval is obtained, if one party sues to enforce the contract's main obligations without amending their claims after clarification, the court should dismiss the case, though this does not preclude filing a separate lawsuit.[98] Where approval is denied despite the obligated party fulfilling their obligations, the court should not award damages unless the denial is due to delays caused by that party, in which case compensation for resulting losses is governed by Article 157 of the CC.[99]

77. In summary, while both civil contracts and administrative contracts involve agreements between parties, they differ in terms of the nature of the parties involved, the purpose and subject matter of the contracts, the regulatory framework governing them, and the methods for resolving disputes.

B. Civil Contracts and Commercial Contracts

78. Chinese law traditionally follows a unified legislative model for civil and commercial law, as reflected in the Contract Book of the CC. This approach maintains the principle of 'unity of civil and commercial law' while incorporating numerous commercial legal norms, including financing leases, factoring, warehousing, construction projects, and agency – typical examples of commercial contracts.

79. Despite this legislative model, civil contracts and commercial contracts differ primarily in terms of their purpose, applicable rules, and the nature of the parties

95. Article 502 CC.
96. Article 12 of the SPC Interpretation on the Contract Book (2023).
97. *Ibid.*
98. *Ibid.*
99. *Ibid.*; Art. 157 CC.

involved. While both fall under the general framework of the CC, specific differences arise due to the unique characteristics of commercial transactions.[100]

80. Conceptually, civil contracts and commercial contracts differ in their focus and purpose. Civil contracts typically address personal interests, such as purchasing goods for personal use, leasing residential properties, or providing services to individuals. These contracts typically involve individuals or entities acting in a non-commercial capacity. A common example is a consumer sale.

81. In contrast, commercial contracts involve business entities – such as companies, corporations, or partnerships – conducting transactions aimed at commercial or profit-driven objectives. These contracts are primarily oriented toward profit and commercial enterprise. For example, A supply agreement between a manufacturer and a retailer for the wholesale purchase of goods for resale. Understanding the contract's purpose helps the court tailor its interpretation and enforcement to the nature of the obligations and expectations of the parties.

82. Commercial contracts often involve more sophisticated arrangements, such as international trade, financing leases, or large-scale supply agreements, which may require special rules for risk allocation, performance, and dispute resolution. Courts recognise that commercial contracts are usually negotiated between parties with equal bargaining power, unlike civil contracts that may involve individual consumers requiring greater legal protection.

83. The principle of privity of contract is more strictly observed in the realm of civil contracts, where parties define their mutual rights and obligations and, in principle, cannot dispose of the rights of third parties or impose obligations on them. In contrast, commercial contracts often allow for more flexibility, with certain exceptions to this principle being more common.[101] For instance, in factoring contracts, where the factor knowingly accepts fictitious accounts receivable created by the creditor and debtor as the subject of the assignment, the debtor of the accounts receivable is entitled to challenge the factor's claim for payment by asserting the non-existence of the accounts receivable.[102] From the perspective of the underlying contract that generates the accounts receivable, it can be said that this contract conditionally binds the factor, a third party, thereby breaking the traditional principle of contractual privity.[103]

100. Gu Zhang, Commercial Law, the Hermit Crab: On the Independence and Characteristics of Commercial Law, 2 Tsinghua Rule of Law 1-51 (2005).
101. This will be extensively discussed in the chapter Privity of Contract of this monograph.
102. Article 763 CC.
103. Jianyuan Cui, The Distinction between Civil Contracts and Commercial Contracts, 1 Political and Legal Forum 56 (2022).

84. A breach of a civil contract generally leads to remedies to cover personal losses, such as compensation for damages, specific performance, or contract termination, as provided under the CC and the Consumer Protection Law.[104] In contrast, a breach of a commercial contract may involve similar remedies but often includes additional provisions tailored to business needs, such as arbitration clauses, liquidated damages or penalty clauses tailored to the business context. As a result, in a consumer dispute, the court may apply stricter standards to protect the buyer. In a business-to-business dispute, the court may enforce penalty clauses or industry practices more readily.

85. Civil contracts, especially consumer contracts, are subject to public policy concerns, including protecting weaker parties and ensuring fairness. Courts aim to balance the interests of individual consumers and promote equity, while commercial contracts operate in a competitive market environment with less intervention.

86. The judiciary in China distinguishes between civil contracts and commercial contracts during trials, especially when applying relevant laws and determining the nature of the dispute.[105] This distinction is not formally codified as separate legal regimes but arises from the practical need to adapt judicial reasoning to the specific characteristics and purposes of the contract in question.

87. In summary, while civil contracts focus on personal and non-commercial relationships, commercial contracts are oriented toward profit-driven, business-related activities. The governing principles, applicable laws, and the nature of the parties significantly influence how these contracts are formed, performed, and enforced under Chinese law.

88. Examining the differences between civil and commercial contracts highlights the need to account for the unique characteristics and requirements of commercial contracts when applying the law. It also helps differentiate various commercial transactions, addressing their complexities and nuances effectively. Therefore, the design of the legal framework or judicial reasoning should clearly differentiate between the rules governing civil and commercial contracts to ensure precision and adaptability in regulating these distinct areas.

IV. Contract and Torts

89. A challenge arises in delineating the contract law within the broader scope of civil obligations. The commitments made through binding promises should be honoured, forming the basis of contract law. Compensation should be provided for

104. The Consumer Protection Law was originally enacted in 1993 with the most significant revision occurring in 2013. It aims to protect the rights of consumers to safety, fair transactions, truthful information, free choice, and compensation for damages.
105. For example, the SPC Second Civil Division (commercial tribunal) has published a biannual periodical specifically on commercial dispute resolution since 2010: The Guidance on Commercial Adjudication (The SPC Second Civil Division ed., Beijing: the People's Court Press 2010).

wrongful harm inflicted, as evident in the tort law. Tort law pertains to civil wrongs, such as negligence or defamation. For instance, if A negligently drives her car and injures B, A has committed the tort of negligence. In such cases, compensation aims not to fulfil B's expectations but to restore B to her pre-accident state, safeguarding B's 'reliance interest' or reinstating the 'status quo'.

90. With the deepening development of modern society, the scope of application of tort liability law continues to expand, increasingly encroaching into the traditional domain of contract law. The traditional boundaries between contract law and tort liability law face significant challenges. This is evident in the introduction of third-party inducement liability, broader protection for economic losses, the development of economic torts, impact on breach of product liability, and extension to areas such as medical malpractice and traffic accidents. These trends highlight the growing influence of tort liability law.

91. While it protects private rights and remedies damages in society, traditional contract law may encounter limitations in safeguarding rights due to its inherent relational nature, which often excludes third-party involvement. Modern contract transactions, however, often involve interconnected relationships, potentially impacting third-party rights or subjecting parties to harm caused by third-party actions.

92. In such cases, tort liability law offers a legal framework and protection for injured parties seeking redress. In the intersection of contract and tort liability law, it is crucial to recognise that tort law offers more robust protection, enabling individuals to secure better compensation and remedies through tort claims. Unlike contract law, tort liability law can effectively integrate with liability insurance and social assistance programs.

93. One example illustrating the expanding scope of tort liability protection is that non-pecuniary loss can be readily recovered in a tort action[106] while it is rarely awarded in very exceptional circumstances under the contract realm.[107] Article 1183 of the CC provides that where a person's right to life or health is infringed upon, causing serious mental harm to others, the injured party may claim compensation for mental damages.[108] Therefore, compensation for mental damages only applies in cases where tortious acts cause serious mental harm. Thus, it generally applies within the scope of tort liability, not contract liability. Only when the victim sues for compensation for mental damages on the grounds of tort can the court accept it.[109]

106. Article 21 of the Provisions of the Supreme People's Court on Several Issues Concerning the Application of Law in the Trial of Cases about travel service contracts disputes.
107. Lei Chen, Damages and Specific Performance in Chinese Contract Law, in Chinese Contract Law: Civil law and Common Law Perspectives 377-403 (Lei Chen & Larry A. DiMatteo ed., Cambridge University Press 2017).
108. Article 1183 CC.
109. Article 1 of the SPC Interpretation on Several Issues Concerning the Ascertainment of Compensation Liability for Emotional Damages in Civil Torts (2001, 2020 revision).

94. The boundary between contractual liability and tort liability under Chinese law is often blurred, particularly in cases involving overlapping obligations or concurrent claims. The distinction depends on the legal basis for the claim: contractual liability arises from the breach of agreed obligations, while tort liability addresses the harm caused by violating general duties of care.

95. Contractual and tort claims offer different remedies. Contract claims emphasise expectation damages (placing the claimant in the position they would have been had the contract been performed), while tort claims focus on compensatory damages (restoring the status quo). This disparity creates confusion in concurrent liability cases. A buyer harmed by defective goods may seek tort damages for personal injury or contractual damages for breach of the sales agreement.

96. The CC stipulates that if one party's breach of contract infringes upon the personal or property rights of the other party, the injured party has the right to choose to claim either contractual liability or tort liability.[110] According to this provision, when tort liability and contractual liability overlap, the party has the right to choose one to pursue. However, if one party opts for tort compensation, can the other party invoke contractual terms as a defence?

97. In cases of concurrent liability, the connection between tort and contractual liability cannot be entirely severed. A Chinese court held that it is essential to protect one party's right to choose the type of claim while safeguarding the other party's legal right to raise defences.[111] Allowing one party to select tort compensation while prohibiting the other party from invoking contractual terms as a defence would render the contractual relationship meaningless, violate the principle of good faith, and prevent market participants from reasonably managing and mitigating normal commercial risks through the contract system.[112]

98. Further, some property rights disputes are often resolved using tort liability norms. For instance, trespass or damage to property may be treated as tort cases, even when arising from contractual breaches, blurring the boundaries further. Chinese courts often treat property rights claims as tort claims, effectively substituting tort liability for property rights disputes.

99. When contractual and tort liabilities overlap, the plaintiff may choose the cause of action and jurisdiction most favourable to their case.[113] The court's jurisdiction should be determined based on the plaintiff's claims and the selected cause of action. In one case, a Service Agreement specified that 'disputes arising from the

110. Article 186 CC.

111. *Tokio Marine Nichido Fire Insurance (China) Co., Ltd. Shanghai Branch v. Xinjie Logistics Group Co., Ltd.*, Gazette Case of the SPC, Issue 12, 2019; 东京海上日动火灾保险(中国)有限公司上海分公司诉新杰物流集团股份有限公司，最高人民法院公报》案例，2019年12期.

112. *Ibid.*

113. *Liangxi District Manze Road Trading Company v. Zhejiang S.F. Express Co., Ltd.*, the Supreme People's Court, (2023) SPC Min Xia No. 142; 梁溪区漫泽道商贸商行诉浙江顺丰速运有限公司，最高人民法院民（2023）最高法民辖142号

conclusion, performance, termination, or rescission of this agreement shall fall under the jurisdiction of the court at the place of the agreement's conclusion'. However, the SPC ruled that this clause applies exclusively to contractual disputes and does not cover tort claims. Therefore, statutory jurisdiction was deemed applicable in this case.[114]

100. Hence, when tort liability and contractual liability overlap, the injured party may choose one basis to file a claim for damages. However, if the chosen claim is unsuccessful, may the injured party pursue the alternative claim to seek compensation? In judicial practice, there is no consistent understanding. This raises the question of whether the alternative claim is extinguished following the failure of the first claim or, in other words, whether the injured party's right to choose is a one-time opportunity.

101. The key issue in determining whether a claim constitutes repeated litigation lies in the identity of the cause of action. Specifically, it depends on whether the rights, obligations or legal relationships under substantive law are the same.[115] Tort and contract claims, based on distinct legal relationships, do not constitute repeated litigation.[116] Therefore, in this ruling, the party can still pursue the alternative claim after the chosen claim is unsuccessful. This should be a recommended approach. Moreover, lawsuits based on these two types of claims differ significantly in terms of the burden of proof and the scope of damages. The injured party bears the burden of proof and claim damages based on the specific legal relationship underlying each claim.[117]

102. The CC grants injured parties the right to choose between contractual and tort liability in cases of overlap, aiming to respect their autonomy and maximise protection. If the initial claim is unsuccessful, the injured party should be allowed to pursue an alternative claim to safeguard their rights better. Claims based on distinct legal relationships, such as tort and contract, generating different causes of action, do not constitute repeated litigation.

---

114. *Ibid.*

115. The standard for determining repeated litigation is outlined in Art. 247 of the SPC Interpretation of on the Application of the Civil Procedure Law (2015, 2021 revision). According to this provision, a repeated lawsuit is established if a party initiates a second lawsuit concerning the same matter either during the litigation process or after a judgment has become legally effective, and all of the following conditions are met: 1) the parties in the subsequent lawsuit are the same as in the previous lawsuit; 2) the cause of action in the subsequent lawsuit is the same as in the previous lawsuit; 3) the claims in the subsequent lawsuit are the same as those in the previous lawsuit, or the claims in the subsequent lawsuit essentially negate the outcome of the previous judgment. This provision embodies the principle of *res judicata* in civil litigation and establishes the criteria for determining whether a case constitutes repeated litigation.

116. *Du Yang & Feng Xuan v. Yuan Hairong & Zhao Qiang*, Beijing No. 3 Intermediate People's Court (2019) Jing 03 Min Zhong No. 6313; 杜洋、冯轩诉袁海荣、赵强，北京市第三中级人民法院（2019）京03民终6313号.

117. *Ibid.*

V. Contract and Quasi-contract

103. The relationship between contract and quasi-contract is one of distinct legal concepts with different bases and applications. A contract is a legally binding agreement between parties where rights and obligations are established and enforceable. It requires mutual consent, legality of object, and lawful form to be valid.

104. On the other hand, a quasi-contract, also known as an implied contract or contract implied in law, refers to situations where no formal contract exists between parties. However, the law imposes obligations akin to those arising from a contract to prevent unjust enrichment or detriment to one party. The unjust enrichment doctrine aims to prevent one party from benefiting at the expense of another without a valid legal reason.

105. A person may be required to return what they have unjustly gained where she has received a benefit from another party; the receiving party has no legal basis for retaining the benefit, and the benefit has been acquired at the expense of another party under the CC.[118]

106. Negotiorum gestio refers to the legal concept of 'management of affairs without mandate' or 'unauthorised management'. It occurs when an individual, known as the gestor, voluntarily manages the affairs or property of another person, the dominus, without authorisation or mandate.[119]

107. Under the CC, a gestor who manages the affairs of another person without authorisation shall be responsible for any resulting losses caused by negligence or violation of instructions. The gestor may also be entitled to reimbursement of necessary expenses and reasonable remuneration for their services unless otherwise agreed or implied by law.

108. In essence, *negotiorum gestio* regulates situations where a person intervenes in the affairs of another without express authority, outlining the rights and obligations of the gestor in such circumstances. Quasi-contractual obligations are not based on the parties' express agreement but on equitable principles.

109. While parties voluntarily enter into contracts, quasi-contracts are imposed by law to ensure fairness and justice. Therefore, the relationship between contract and quasi-contract lies in their distinct nature and the circumstances under which they arise: contracts arise from the explicit agreement of parties, while quasi-contracts arise from legal principles aimed at preventing unjust enrichment or unjust detriment.

---

118. Article 987 CC.
119. Article 979 CC.

VI. Contract and the Law of Property

110. Contracts and property relationships are closely intertwined but distinct legal concepts. As part of the law of obligations, contracts refer to legally binding agreements between parties where rights and obligations are established. Property relationships encompass individuals' legal rights and interests concerning property, including ownership, possession, use, and disposal. Property relationships can arise from various sources, such as contracts, inheritance, gifts, or statutory rights.

111. While contracts often involve the transfer or use of property, they are distinct from property relationships. Contracts create legal obligations between parties based on mutual agreement, whereas property relationships concern individuals' legal rights and interests concerning specific assets or properties.[120]

112. However, it is important to note that contracts can affect property relationships and vice versa. For example, a contract for property sale establishes rights and obligations between the buyer and seller, which may impact their respective property interests. Similarly, property rights may be subject to contractual arrangements, such as leases, mortgages, or easements.

113. Chinese law treats an actual agreement between the present and the would-be owner as both a necessary and a sufficient condition for property transfer. It should be emphasised that ownership does not pass on account of mere agreements between the parties but only on delivery or registration, as required by the formality rules.[121]

114. The agreement giving rise to transfer is strictly separated from the delivery or registration itself.[122] Immovable property is transferred by registration and movables by delivery. The conventional wisdom by Chinese legal academics rejects the German-style separation. At the same time, it contends that Chinese law does have a 'separation' principle (区分原则) in property transfers: the cause of a conveyance is separate from the result of that conveyance.[123]

115. What these Chinese academics mean by the separation principle is, in reality, 'intent plus' in that transferring ownership to movables and immovables requires

120. Lei Chen, Private Property with Chinese Characteristics: A Critical Analysis of the Chinese Law on Property of 2007, 18(5) European Review of Private Law 983-1004 (2010).
121. Article 215 CC. While this is the case under the Chinese law, in the German legal system, registration and delivery are not merely formalities but are juridical acts with the transferor's intent to convey embodied in the real contract.
122. Article 208 CC.
123. Huixing Liang, Is Juridical Act of Real Rights Recognised in Chinese Civil Law?, 6 Chinese Journal of Law 56 (1989); Liming Wang, On Several Issues Concerning Juridical Act of Real Right, 3 Chinese Legal Science 58 (1997); Xianzhong Sun, The Principle of Separation Between the Reason and the Result of the Alteration of Property Rights 5 Chinese Journal of Law 28 (1999).

the contract and delivery or registration, respectively.[124] Therefore, Chinese law exemplifies how a jurisdiction operates the 'intent plus' system while rejecting the separatist approach.[125]

116. Chinese law adopts a causal system rather than an abstract system.[126] There has been a long-standing debate among Chinese scholars over whether Chinese law should adopt abstraction[127] or causality[128] since the 1980s. Although valuing its doctrinal refinement as von Savigny and his disciples advocated, most Chinese legal scholars took a dim view of this theory. Among those, the strongest anti-abstractionist argument is that the 'causal system plus bona fide acquisition' model strikes a perfect balance between the security of the property and the security of the transaction.

117. Such a model protects good faith purchasers, so they are prioritised over the transferor as long as all constituent elements of bona fide acquisition are met.[129] Bad faith purchasers do not enjoy this protection. It is worth noting that Chinese law doctrinally views a bona fide acquisition as an independent acquisition by operation of law.[130]

118. Paragraph 1 of Article 597 of the CC provides that if the seller lacks the authority to dispose of the subject matter, preventing the transfer of ownership, the buyer has the right to terminate the contract and insist that the seller be held responsible for the breach of contract.[131]

119. Meanwhile, Article 15 of the Property Law was reproduced word by word in Article 215 of the CC. It states that 'A contract entered into by the parties concerning the creation, alteration, transfer or extinction of immovable property rights

124. Articles 209 and 224 CC. For an English translation of the CC; The Civil Code of the People's Republic of China: English Translation (Lei Chen et al. ed., Nijhoff: Brill, 2021).
125. Zhicheng Wu & Lei Chen, Revisiting property transfer theory: English law and Chinese law compared, 43 (2) Legal Studies 259-277 (2023).
126. *Ibid.*
127. Xianzhong Sun, General Principles of Real Rights Law of China 412–56 (2nd edn, Beijing: Law Press, 2009); Yunsong Ge, Study on the Theory of Real Juridical Act, 6 Peking University Law Journal 702 (2004); Diyu. Xu, A Teleological Explanation of the Abstraction Principle, 2 Chinese Legal Science 84 (2005).
128. Yi Wang, On the Transfer of Real Rights 311–32 (Beijing: Renmin University Press, 2001); Tian Yin, Comments and Thoughts on Property Law Theories 190–215 (Beijing: Renmin University Press, 2004); Jianyuan Cui, A Positivist Analysis of the Concept of Juridical Act of Real Rights and Chinese Civil Law, 2 Journal of Comparative Law 60 (2004).
129. Huixing Liang & Huabin Chen, Property Law 97 (Law Press China, 2016); Liming Wang, Property Law 56 (Renmin University of China Press, 2015).
130. Articles 311 and 313 CC; Jianyuan Cui, Commentaries of the Chinese Civil Code: Book on Property Rights vol. I, 528 (Beijing: Renmin University Press, 2020); Commentaries of the Civil Code: Book on Property Rights vol. I, 476 (Xianzhong Sun & Guangxin Zhu ed., Beijing: China Legal Publishing House, 2020). In contrast, English law doctrinally considers the good faith purchase as a mere exception to the nemo dat starting point. *See* William Swadling, Restitution and Bona Fide Purchase in The Limits of Restitutionary Claims: A Comparative Analysis (W. Swadling ed., London: UKNCCL, 1997).
131. Paragraph 1 of Art. 597 CC.

shall become effective upon the formation of the contract unless otherwise provided by law or agreed by the parties, and the failure to register the property right shall not affect the validity of the contract.'

120. Thus, the above provisions clarify that the transferor's power of disposition is a determining factor of the validity of the conveyance but not necessarily of the underlying contract.[132] While the scholarly debates are ongoing and unsettled as to whether the Chinese law should remain unitary or go towards a separatist approach, the SPC interpreted such a change in the CC in a pro-separatist way.[133]

121. Overall, contracts and property relationships are fundamental aspects of the legal framework governing transactions and property rights in the CC, each with its own rules and principles but often interconnected in practice.

§6. The Principle of Good Faith

I. Concept

122. The principle of good faith, also known as the doctrine of honesty and trustworthiness, is a fundamental principle of civil law and is often referred to as the omnipotent principle of civil law.[134] It requires civil subjects to act with honesty, goodwill, and trustworthiness in all civil activities, including exercising civil rights, performing civil obligations, and assuming civil liabilities.

123. The principle of good faith is highly abstract and generalised. Terms such as 'integrity' and 'acting with honesty and honouring commitments' can be understood as requiring parties in civil activities not to prioritise their own interests exclusively but also to consider the interests of relevant stakeholders. This highly abstract connotation has been criticised as 'a highly utopian portrait of what scholars believe is to be desired'.[135] A sensible view suggests that good faith is a standard of conduct imposed on parties, either as a customary norm within the community where the transaction occurs or as dictated by fairness and reasonableness in the specific circumstances of a case.[136] However, this may risk pegging the good faith with the principle of fairness.

124. Whatever the understanding of good faith should be, Chinese law imposes this moral duty on the parties. This stands in contrast to the laissez-faire approach of common law, which refrains from applying overarching principles to regulate the

132. Liming Wang, Property Law 69–70 (Renmin University of China Press, 2015).
133. Understanding and Applying the Book on Contracts of the Chinese Civil Code 861 (Enforcement of Civil Code Group of the SPC ed., Beijing: People's Court Press, 2020).
134. Article 7 CC.
135. Ewan McKendrick & Qiao Liu, Good Faith in Contract Performance in the Chinese and Common Laws, in Chinese Contract Law: Civil and Common Law Perspectives 44-71 (Lei Chen & Larry A. DiMatteo ed., Cambridge: Cambridge University Press 2017.
136. Bing Ling, Contract Law in China 54 (Sweet & Maxwell, 2002).

behaviour of contracting parties. The common law approach highlights the adversarial nature of contractual relationships, permitting parties to prioritise their own interests without being legally required to act cooperatively.[137] Notably, Common law legal systems have taken varying approaches at different times.[138]

125. The CISG appears to provide a middle ground. Article 7(1) of CISG addresses courts and arbitral tribunals, instructing them to uphold good faith in international trade when interpreting the Convention. It does not impose a direct duty of good faith on the parties themselves.[139] The UNIDROIT Principles of International Commercial Contracts, the Principles of European Contract Law, and the European Draft Common Frame of Reference mandate a duty of good faith for all parties and explicitly forbid any attempts to exclude this obligation through contractual agreements.[140]

II. The Overarching Principle of Good Faith

126. The provisions related to good faith serve as specific general clauses reflecting this principle. For instance, the prohibition of the abuse of rights is a fundamental provision regulating the exercise of rights in Chinese civil law.[141] This clause embodies the principle of exercising rights in good faith from a restrictive perspective – imposing internal limits on rights and legal statuses to prevent abuse. Article 132 constitutes an essential specific type or general clause of the principle of good faith. Other similar general clauses include:

Article 142: Interpretation of declarations of intent based on good faith.
Article 466: Contract interpretation guided by good faith.
Article 500: Pre-contractual liability arising from conduct violating good faith.
Article 509(2): Ancillary obligations derived from good faith.
Article 558: Post-contractual obligations arising from good faith.

137. Christian Twigg-Flesner, General Principles of Chinese Contract Law: An English Common Law Perspective, in Chinese Contract Law: Civil and Common Law Perspectives 29-43 ((Lei Chen & Larry A. DiMatteo ed., Cambridge: Cambridge University Press 2017).
138. A few common law jurisdictions have moved to a direction of recognising a principle of good faith. For US law, *see* Section 1-304 of the Uniform Commercial Code, which states that 'every contract or duty within [the UCC] imposes an obligation of good faith in its performance and enforcement'. Also, *see* Section 205 of the American Restatement (Second) of Contracts; for Canadian law, *see Bhasin v. Hrynew, 2014 SCC 71, (2014) 379 DLR (4th) 385*; for Australian law, *see Renard Constructions (ME) Pty v. Minister for Public Works (1992) 44 NSWLR 349.*
139. This is despite that a different view exists to suggest the principle of good faith also applies to the contracting parties. Michael J. Bonell, Interpretation of Convention, in Commentary on the International Sales Law (Cesare M. Bianca & Michael J. Bonell ed., Guiffre: Milan, 1987) 84–85.
140. Article 1.7 of the UNIDROIT Principles of International Commercial Contracts; Art. 1:201 of Section 2 of the Principles of European Contract Law; Definitions and Model Rules of European Private Law: Draft Common Frame of Reference III.-1:103 (Christian von Bar et al. ed., OUP Oxford 2010).
141. Article 132 CC.

127. These provisions reflect the broad application of the principle of good faith throughout the CC. For example, good faith governs pre-contractual negotiations, ensuring that parties act transparently and fairly.[142] If one party negotiates in bad faith by withdrawing without justification after creating legitimate expectations, they may be held liable for damages. The principle imposes a duty on parties to cooperate and fulfil their obligations honestly and reasonably. Courts may use good faith to prevent opportunistic behaviour, such as exploiting technicalities to avoid performance.

128. When contract terms are ambiguous, courts interpret them in line with good faith to reflect the true intentions of the parties and the principle of fairness. Good faith also influences the extent of liability and the determination of remedies.[143] A party acting in bad faith may face harsher consequences. In addition, good faith may limit the right to terminate a contract if the terminating party's conduct is deemed unreasonable or opportunistic. The doctrine plays a role in interpreting provisions related to unforeseen circumstances, encouraging renegotiation and equitable adjustments rather than outright termination.[144]

129. However, the outer limits of the good faith principle are under-articulated in the Chinese legal community.[145] The issue arises when courts cite the principle of good faith as a ruling basis without proper reasoning. As a fundamental principle, it has been argued that the principle of good faith should not serve as the direct basis for adjudication alone.[146] Instead, it must be concretised into specific rules tailored to the particular case to be applicable. When specific rules are present, these should be applied instead; otherwise, it constitutes an evasion into general clauses.[147]

130. In judicial practice, however, there are often instances of applying the good faith principle in ways that are either substantively meaningless or constitute an escape into general clauses.[148] The substantively meaningless application is characterised by declarative usage, where courts state phrases like 'civil activities shall adhere to the principle of good faith' without any further articulation. The escape

---

142. *Tan v. Chang & Chang*, Liaocheng Intermediate People's Court of Shandong Province, (2023) Lu 15 Min Zhong No. 3926; 谭某祥诉常某龙、常某峰，山东省聊城市中级人民法院（2023）鲁15民终3926号.
143. *Jianfuxin Software Development Co., Ltd. v. Zhuhai Jinshan Office Software Co., Ltd.*, the Supreme People's Court, (2020) SPC Zhi Min Zhong No. 1319; 福建福昕软件开发股份有限公司诉珠海金山办公软件有限公司，最高人民法院（2020）最高法知民终1319号.
144. *Zhangjiakou Xin Million Catering Co., Ltd. v. Xuanhua Hotel Co., Ltd.*, Zhangjiakou Intermediate People's Court (2007) Zhang Shang Zhong Zi No. 74; 张家口市鑫百万餐饮有限公司诉宣化饭店有限责任公司，张家口市中级人民法院（2007）张商终字第74号.
145. Ewan McKendrick & Qiao Liu, Good Faith in Contract Performance in the Chinese and Common Law 44-71 (2017).
146. Shiyuan Han,General Principles under the CCL, in Chinese Contract Law: Civil and Common Law Perspectives 27-28 (Lei Chen & Larry A. DiMatteo ed., Cambridge: Cambridge University Press 2017).
147. Huixing Liang, General Introduction of Civil Law 374-375 (5th edition, Law Press China, 2017).
148. Ziyi Pan, The Typological Application of the Principle of Good Faith in China's Civil Law[J]. Jurisprudence, 2023(9): 125-141

into general clauses refers to situations where courts, despite the existence of specific provisions, still directly invoke the principle of good faith, thereby avoiding the duty to provide proper reasoning. This issue reflects a tension between the proper function of fundamental principles as guiding norms and the need for legal certainty and accountability in judicial decision making.

III. The Historical, Cultural and Political Dimensions of the Good Faith Principle

131. The prominence of good faith in Chinese law can be attributed to both legal and cultural factors, alongside its roots in civil law traditions. Below, I outline its importance and role in different aspects of contract disputes, as well as its cultural underpinnings.

132. The first one is a cultural factor, which is attributed to a deep-rooted tradition of paternalistic governance and collectivism.[149] Confucianism emphasises trustworthiness (信用) and social harmony, which align closely with the concept of good faith. Contracts in traditional Chinese culture are seen not merely as legal tools but as moral commitments reflecting mutual respect and cooperation. The principle of good faith echoes these ideals by promoting integrity and reciprocity in civil and commercial relationships.[150] Historically, Chinese society relied on customs and norms like li (propriety) and yi (righteousness) to guide behaviour. Good faith embodies these values by ensuring fairness and ethical behaviour in legal relationships.[151]

133. Chinese dispute resolution historically prioritises reconciliation over strict legal adjudication. Good faith complements this approach by emphasising equitable solutions. These cultural influences have, at times, fostered a tendency among Chinese lawyers to blur the lines between law and morality.[152] This has led to an overreliance on ethical principles, even when they conflict with fixed legal rules or clear contractual terms. Nonetheless, it provided a moral and ethical foundation in a system where formal rules were still maturing.

134. Second, there is a political legitimacy explanation driven by the socialist value system.[153] In a socialist framework, relationships are not solely based on individual self-interest but also on cooperation and the broader public good. The

149. Patricia Pattison & Daniel Herron, The Mountains are High and the Emperor Is Far Away: Sanctity of Contract in China, 40 American Business Law Journal 459 (2003).
150. Larry A. DiMatteo, Rule of Law in China: The Confrontation of Formal Law with Cultural Norms 391, Cornell Int'l LJ 51 (2018).
151. Simona Novaretti, General Clauses and Practice: The Use of the Principle of Good Faith in the Decisions of Chinese Courts, , 5 (18) European Review of Private Law 953-981 (2010).
152. Ewan McKendrick & Qiao Liu, . Good Faith in Contract Performance in the Chinese and Common Laws, 81 (2017).
153. Chunlin Leonhard, A Legal Chameleon: An Examination of the Doctrine of Good Faith in Chinese and American Contract Law, 25 Connecticut Journal of International Law 305 (2010).

Chinese government places a high value on social stability, which is central to its political legitimacy. The Chinese legal system often prioritises maintaining social harmony and stability, key tenets of socialism.[154] Good faith is seen as a way to integrate moral obligations into legal rules, emphasising ethical behaviour over strict individualism. This reflects the party's broader agenda of embedding socialist values into all aspects of governance, including the legal system.[155] Good faith serves as a normative principle to promote cooperation and prevent conflict in contractual relationships, thereby contributing to the overarching goal of maintaining social harmony. By encouraging equitable and reasonable behaviour, good faith reduces the risk of disputes escalating into broader societal instability.

135. The Chinese government views the law as an instrument of governance, with the legal system expected to reflect state policies and ideological goals. Good faith aligns with the state's efforts to project an image of a fair and just legal system, which is essential for both domestic governance and international legitimacy. Good faith provides a mechanism for the state to intervene in private contracts when necessary to ensure that they align with public policy and social goals. For example, contracts that violate public interests or state policies can be deemed unenforceable under the guise of violating good faith. It reflects the 'law-based governance' (依法治国) policy, where the law is used to guide moral and ethical behaviour in society.

136. Third, with the civil law family, which hinges on general clauses in civil codes.[156] China's civil law tradition significantly contributes to the emphasis on the principle of good faith. Civil law systems rely heavily on codification, where principles like good faith are explicitly stated in the legal code. The Chinese legal system draws heavily from continental European civil law traditions, particularly German law, which places significant emphasis on good faith (Treu und Glauben). In the BGB, Article 242 explicitly establishes good faith as a guiding principle. This influence has shaped the incorporation of good faith as a foundational principle in Chinese civil law.

137. As a result, expectations that parties will cooperate and assist one another beyond the contract's terms are considered reasonable. Maintaining equilibrium in the reciprocal exchange between parties is regarded as a fundamental aspect of contract justice. It serves as a bridge between traditional civil law principles and the unique political and social context of China. While this principle brings significant flexibility, it also poses challenges in balancing legal predictability with broader social and political objectives.

---

154. Notice of the Supreme People's Court on Issuing Some Opinions of the Supreme People's Court about Providing Judicial Protection for the Construction of Socialist Harmonious Society (2007).
155. Article 1 CC; Several Opinions of the Supreme People's Court on Cultivating and Practicing the Socialism Core Values (2015).
156. Liming Wang & Chuanxi Xu, Fundamental Principles of China's Contract Law, 13 Colum. J. Asian L. 1 (1999).

138. Good faith serves as a 'safety valve' that allows judges to address gaps in legislation, resolve ambiguities, and achieve equitable outcomes in specific cases. It serves as a gap-filling principle, offering solutions when explicit legal rules or contractual terms are absent. It also ensures fairness and balances the rights and obligations of parties, particularly in unequal bargaining situations. Beyond contract law, good faith influences various areas of civil law, such as obligations of honesty and fairness in property transactions, tortious liability, fiduciary relationships, and even family law disputes.

IV. The Challenges of the Good Faith Principle

139. Good faith serves as a powerful tool for courts to adapt legal principles to rapidly changing socio-economic conditions. In a maturing legal system like China's, good faith bridges gaps where specific statutory rules are absent or inadequate, allowing courts to address novel or unforeseen issues. While its widespread application is a strength in promoting fairness and adaptability, it also brings certain risks and limitations that can undermine legal certainty and consistency.

140. The broad nature of good faith can lead to inconsistent judicial decisions, as it depends on the discretion of judges. The broad and subjective nature of the principle makes it difficult to predict how courts will apply it in specific cases. This undermines legal certainty, which is crucial for contractual stability. Parties may face difficulties in assessing their legal risks, leading to inefficiency in commercial transactions.

141. Courts may rely on good faith excessively, bypassing more specific legal provisions. This phenomenon, often referred to as a 'general clause escape', avoids detailed reasoning and diminishes the rule-of-law principle.[157] In some cases, the invocation of good faith is merely declarative, adding no substantive reasoning or analytical value to the judgment. This weakens its credibility as a guiding principle.

142. When courts frequently resolve disputes by invoking good faith, it reduces the urgency to develop specific statutory provisions for recurring issues. Instead of fostering a mature legal system, it may perpetuate reliance on vague principles. For example, instead of clarifying rules on pre-contractual liability, courts may broadly cite good faith to impose remedies, leaving the exact scope and nature of such liability undefined. In complex or rapidly evolving fields (e.g., digital contracts, financial contracts), reliance on good faith can delay the development of specialised legal doctrines tailored to the unique challenges of these areas.

157. Some Chinese courts have taken some measures to address this issue. For example, Art. 4 of the Beijing High People's Court's Reference Opinions on the Implementation of the Civil Procedure Law in Civil Trial Work (2012) specifies that the principle of good faith should generally be implemented through specific provisions, with the legal consequences of violating the principle determined in accordance with relevant regulations. It is not appropriate to directly rely on the principle of good faith as the sole basis for handling related litigation actions.

143. Some courts might invoke good faith to override clear contractual rules, which can lead to accusations of judicial activism or arbitrariness.[158] When the application of specific rules conflicts with the principle of good faith and results in an intolerable injustice in a particular case, the good faith principle serves a corrective legal function.[159] It has been argued that when the good faith principle was invoked to override the specific rules, 'the benefits of realizing a general principle outweigh the combined benefits of applying a rule and maintaining legal certainty'.[160] In such cases, any loss to legal certainty is justified and necessary. However, the essence of this corrective function is not to establish an entirely new rule outside the existing law by modifying the law itself but rather to create an exception within specific rules for certain special cases.[161]

144. Parties may invoke good faith opportunistically to avoid obligations or renegotiate unfavourable contracts, leading to strategic litigation and increased transaction costs. Parties may claim that the other party's actions violated the principle of good faith, even when the alleged breach is tenuous or unrelated to actual performance. For example, a debtor may argue that a creditor's insistence on strict compliance with payment deadlines constitutes a lack of good faith, even when the debtor's financial difficulties are self-inflicted. Good faith is often invoked to justify renegotiations, especially when market conditions or unforeseen events make a contract economically burdensome for one party. For example, a supplier facing rising production costs might use good faith to demand higher prices from a buyer, even when the contract explicitly fixes the price.

145. The principle of good faith essentially functions as a 'blank check' given to judges, as its application heavily depends on courts and individual judges presiding over cases. Judges might bypass more rigorous analyses of statutory law or contractual terms by citing good faith, leading to decisions that lack depth and undermine the rule of law. Consequently, the establishment of the good faith principle may increase the risk of arbitrariness in judicial decisions and become a justification for some judges to rationalise subjective or inconsistent rulings.

146. In summary, the principle of good faith is a cornerstone of Chinese law, serving as a fundamental guiding principle across various legal domains. Its primary function is to ensure fairness, equity, and mutual respect in civil and commercial activities, reflecting the moral and ethical underpinnings of Chinese legal

158. A typical example is seen in Art. 29 of the SPC Interpretation of the Contract Law II, which stipulates that the adjustment of the amount of liquidated damages should adhere to the principle of good faith, reflecting its function of balancing interests.
159. Huixing Liang, The Principle of Good Faith and Supplementing Loopholes, 2 Legal Studies 27 (1994).
160. Fei Yu, The Case-based Application of the Corrective Legal Function of the Principle of Good Faith —— the Supreme People's Court's judgment in the Huacheng Case as the object of analysis 22 (2) Chinese Journal of Law 63-70, 69 (2022).
161. Xiaxu Li, The Application and Limits of the Legal Corrective Function of the Principle of Good Faith, 2 Law Science 241 (2021).

tradition. As China's legal system continues to mature, the principle plays a dual role: promoting flexibility and adaptability while introducing challenges that necessitate careful management.

147. Good faith is indispensable for addressing gaps in statutory law, providing courts with discretion to achieve equitable outcomes in complex or unforeseen circumstances. It facilitates fairness in contractual relationships and balances the power dynamics between parties, particularly in a rapidly evolving economic and social context. However, its broad and flexible nature can lead to judicial inconsistency and potential arbitrariness, as decisions heavily depend on individual judges' interpretations. This ambiguity risks undermining legal certainty and predictability, essential for a stable legal system.

§7. Sources of the Law of Contracts

148. Under Chinese law, the sources of contract law are categorised into two types: the legal sources directly referenced in judicial rulings as legal basis and those that courts rely upon to articulate and justify their reasoning in judicial rulings. Simply put, the former serves as the basis for rulings, while the latter is used as the basis for reasoning.[162]

I. Legal Sources as the Basis for Rulings

149. Legal sources as the basis for rulings include national legislation, administrative regulations, local regulations (including Autonomy Regulations and Separate Regulations), the SPC judicial Interpretations, the international treaties which China ratified and civil customs.[163]

150. Under China's Legislation Law, the hierarchy of legal sources is as follows: The Constitution stands as the supreme law. Below it are laws (national legislation) enacted by the NPC and the NPCSC. Next are administrative regulations issued by the State Council, followed by local regulations formulated by provincial or municipal people's congresses. Autonomy regulations and separate regulations are specific to autonomous regions. The SPC judicial interpretations can be cited as the legal basis for rulings guide but are not legislative acts. It is worth noting that

162. Article 2 of the SPC Provisions on Citing Laws, Regulations, and Other Normative Legal Documents in Judicial Decisions (2009) stipulates that when multiple normative legal documents are cited concurrently, the order of citation is as follows: laws and legal interpretations, administrative regulations, local regulations, autonomy regulations or separate regulations, and judicial interpretations. When citing two or more laws, basic laws should be cited first, followed by other laws. If both substantive law and procedural law are cited, substantive law should be cited first, followed by procedural law.

163. Article 4 of the SPC Provisions on Citing Laws (2009) provides civil judicial documents shall cite laws, legal interpretations, or judicial interpretations. Administrative regulations, local regulations, or autonomy regulations and separate regulations that are applicable may be directly cited.

although international treaties are not mentioned in the SPC's Provisions on Citing Laws, it is an established practice for Chinese courts to directly cite certain international treaties that China has ratified, such as the CISG, as a basis for their rulings.[164]

A. *National Legislation: The Civil Code and Other Laws*

151. The primary legislative source is the Contract Book of the CC, the most sizeable one in the CC.[165] The Contract Book represents the culmination of decades of legal development, replacing the GPCL and the 1999 Contract Law with a modern, unified, and comprehensive framework. This evolution reflects China's commitment to aligning its contract law with both domestic needs and international practices, ensuring consistency and adaptability in an ever-changing legal and commercial landscape.

152. The Contract Book of the CC consists of three parts. General Provisions outline principles for all contracts, covering formation, validity, performance, modification, termination, and liability for breach. Specific Provisions detail rules for particular contract types, such as sales, services, leases, loans, and construction. This ensures clarity in addressing unique contractual relationships. Finally, the Quasi-Contracts section governs obligations without formal agreements, including unjust enrichment and *negotiorum gestio* (management of another's affairs without consent). There is no general part governing the law of obligations in the CC, as contained in the German BGB and Dutch Civil Code.[166]

153. Many national legislations are relevant to the application of contract law. Examples include E-Commerce Law,[167] Consumer Protection Law,[168] Company Law,[169] Insurance Law,[170] Maritime Law,[171] Construction Law,[172] and Foreign Investment Law.[173]

---

164. Qiao Liu & Xiang Ren, CISG in Chinese Courts: The Issue of Applicability, 65 (4) The American Journal of Comparative Law 873–918 (2017); Shiyuan Han, Application of CISG in International Commercial Arbitration in China, 5 China Law Science 218-238 (2016).
165. The Contract Book contains 526 articles (Article 463–Article 988), which occupies 41.7% of the total 1260 articles, thus forming the most sizable Book of the CC.
166. Lei Chen, Continuity and change: some reflections on the Chinese Civil Code 287–305 (2021).
167. E-Commerce Law, promulgated on 31 August 2018.
168. Consumer Protection Law, promulgated on 31 October 1993, revised on 27 August 2009 and 25 October 2013 subsequently.
169. Company Law, adopted at the Fifth Meeting of the Standing Committee of the Eighth National People's Congress on 29 December 1993, subsequently revised on 25 December 1999; 28 August 2004; 27 October 2005;
28 December 2013; 26 October 2018; and 29 December 2023.
170. Insurance Law. Adopted on 30 June, 1995, revised on 28 October 2002, 28 February, 2009, 31 August, 2014 and 24 April, 2015.
171. Maritime Law, promulgated on 7 November 1992.
172. Construction Law, promulgated on 1 November 1997, revised on 22 April 2011 and 23 April 2019.
173. Foreign Investment Law, promulgated on 15 March 2019.

B. Administrative Regulations

154. While the CC primarily governs CCL, administrative regulations play a significant role in addressing specific issues. These regulations supplement the national framework, providing detailed guidance in specialised areas or addressing local needs. The State Council issues administrative regulations which have a nationwide application.

155. They address issues that require detailed provisions not covered by national laws. An example is the *Regulations on Online Transactions (2021)* issued by the State Council to clarify rights and obligations in e-commerce contracts. They set rules on the liability of platforms for contractual breaches by merchants, complementing the E-Commerce Law and the CC. Another example is *the Regulations on Contracts for Government Procurement of Services*. These regulations detail the requirements for contracts involving the purchase of services by government entities, ensuring transparency and fairness.

C. Local Regulations and Autonomy Regulations

156. Local regulations are enacted by the people's congresses or their standing committees at the provincial level, autonomous regions, and municipalities directly under the central government. They cater to the unique legal and economic circumstances of specific regions. *The Guangdong Province Regulations on Business Environment Optimization (2021)* provides provisions for simplifying contract-related procedures, such as registration and notarisation, to improve business efficiency. It also offers region-specific guidance on handling contractual disputes, particularly in international trade hubs like Shenzhen and Guangzhou.

157. An example of autonomy regulations is the *Inner Mongolia Autonomy Regulation on Resource Contracts*, which governs resource extraction contracts, balancing commercial interests with environmental and cultural preservation. Contracts involving mining or energy development require additional clauses to respect local traditions and ecological concerns.

D. The SPC Judicial Interpretations

158. Since the CC is principle-based and short in details, it is supplemented by governmental regulations and judicial interpretations of the SPC. The courts, especially the SPC, are influential in spelling concrete rules concerning contractual disputes. Judicial interpretations serve as the 'most important and active interpretation authority' in China.[174]

174. Peng Zhongli, An Inquiry into the Legal Status of Judicial Interpretation Documents Issued by the Supreme People's Court, 26(3) Science of Law 14-29 (2018).

159. Judicial interpretations issued by the SPC, though not enacted by the legislature, are often referred to as 'quasi-legislation'. These interpretations are binding on courts at all levels and can be cited as authoritative legal bases for rulings in Chinese court judgments.

160. After promulgating the CC, the SPC has issued several judicial interpretations to facilitate the effective implementation of the CC, which came into effect on 1 January 2021. These interpretations serve as authoritative guidelines for courts across the country, ensuring consistent application of the law. They include the SPC Interpretation on Several Issues Concerning the Application of the General Provisions of the Civil Code (2022) (2022),[175] the SPC Interpretation on the Contract Book (2023),[176] the SPC Interpretation on Several Issues Concerning the Application of the Security System in the Civil Code (2021),[177] the SPC Interpretation on Several Issues Concerning the Application of the Property Rights Book of the Civil Code (2021),[178] the SPC Interpretation on Several Issues Concerning the Application of International Treaties and International Customary Practices in Foreign-Related Civil and Commercial Cases (2023).[179]

E. Civil Customs

161. Civil customs (民事习惯) play an important role as a supplementary legal source in the Chinese legal system. They refer to commonly accepted practices and norms observed in civil activities, which are recognised and applied by courts when statutory law or contractual agreements are silent as long as they do not conflict with public order and good morals.[180]

162. Civil customs provide practical solutions in areas not fully addressed by statutory law. Courts may rely on civil customs to interpret vague or undefined terms in contracts. If a lease agreement mentions 'reasonable rent', local customary rent rates may be used to determine the amount.

163. By incorporating social norms, civil customs ensure that the legal system remains flexible and responsive to societal changes. In commercial disputes, long-standing trade practices within a local market might influence how a court interprets a contract breach. In a country as diverse as China, civil customs allow courts

175. The SPC Interpretation on Several Issues Concerning the Application of the General Provisions of the Civil Code (2022).
176. The SPC Interpretation on the Contract Book (2023).
177. the SPC Interpretation on Several Issues Concerning the Application of the Security System in the Civil Code (2020).
178. The SPC Interpretation on Several Issues Concerning the Application of the Property Rights Book of the Civil Code (2021)
179. The SPC Interpretation on Several Issues Concerning the Application of International Treaties and International Customary Practices in Foreign-Related Civil and Commercial Cases (2023).
180. Article 10 CC.

to account for regional variations in norms and practices, particularly in areas like property use, family relationships, and community interactions.

164. Parties invoking civil customs must demonstrate their prevalence and acceptance within a specific community or industry. This can be challenging, particularly for unwritten customs. Civil customs cannot override statutory provisions or mandatory rules. If a custom conflicts with higher-level laws, courts must prioritise formal legal norms.

F. International Treaties

165. In China, international treaties serve as a legal basis for rulings under specific conditions. If an international treaty ratified by China contains provisions differing from domestic law, the treaty prevails unless China has declared reservations.[181]

166. Treaties are commonly applied in foreign-related civil and commercial cases, such as trade and investment disputes. Courts also use treaties like the CISG to interpret contractual obligations. When parties have referred to an international treaty or Convention that China has not ratified, Chinese courts may still determine the rights and obligations between the contracting parties based on the provisions of that treaty, provided it reflects the parties' mutual agreement and does not conflict with mandatory Chinese laws or public policy.[182]

II. Legal Sources as the Basis for Reasoning

A. Departmental Rules

167. In the Chinese legal system, departmental rules (部门规章) refer to normative documents issued by ministries, commissions, or agencies under the State Council. While they are not considered laws enacted by the NPC or the NPCSC, nor administrative regulations issued by the State Council, departmental rules play an important role in governance and legal reasoning.

168. Departmental rules are subordinate to laws and administrative regulations in China's legal hierarchy. They cannot contravene laws, administrative regulations, or the Constitution. If a conflict arises, courts must prioritise higher-level norms. They are issued to provide detailed and technical implementation guidelines for

---

181. Article 1 of the SPC Interpretation on the Application of International Treaties and International Customary Practices (2023).
182. Article 4 of the SPC Interpretation on the Application of International Treaties and International Customary Practices (2023).

higher-level laws or regulations. Examples include rules from the Ministry of Commerce, Ministry of Justice, or China Banking and Insurance Regulatory Commission.

169. Departmental rules are binding on relevant administrative entities and individuals within their regulatory scope. In practice, judges may reference departmental rules when laws or administrative regulations lack specificity or fail to address detailed procedural or substantive issues. For example, a departmental rule from the Ministry of Housing and Urban-Rural Development may provide detailed standards for construction safety, supplementing the broader provisions of the CC.[183]

170. Nonetheless, over-reliance on departmental rules may lead to perceptions of judicial overreach, where courts appear to enforce administrative policy rather than applying statutory law. Some departmental rules are not widely publicised or easily accessible, creating challenges for parties seeking to understand their legal obligations. The use of departmental rules in reasoning may raise concerns about the judiciary's independence if it appears to align too closely with administrative agencies.

B. Local Departmental Documents

171. Local government documents play a unique role in the Chinese legal system. While not strictly part of the formal legislative hierarchy, they can influence judicial reasoning and administrative practices in specific contexts. Their use as a legal basis for reasoning reflects the decentralised nature of governance and the interplay between local regulations and national laws.

172. Local government rules are issued by local governments (e.g., provincial or municipal governments) to provide implementation details for laws or administrative regulations. Examples include zoning regulations, environmental protection measures, and housing policies. Administrative Decisions or Notices (政府通知或决议) are issued by local governments to address specific issues or provide administrative guidance. They are usually not legally binding but carry significant practical weight within the jurisdiction.

173. Local government documents play a vital role in supplementing national laws and adapting them to regional needs, but their use in judicial reasoning must be carefully managed to avoid conflicts with higher-level laws and ensure fairness. By balancing local flexibility with legal consistency, these documents can effectively contribute to the development of China's legal system while maintaining adherence to the rule of law.

183. The Administrative Measures for the Quality Inspection of Construction Projects was issued on 29 December 2022.

C. The SPC Judicial Opinions

174. The SPC issued a number of trial minutes, judicial opinions and other normative judicial documents. However, technically, they are not as formally binding as judicial interpretations. For instance, trial minutes are internal summaries or records produced after judicial discussions during meetings of SPC judges or panels. They consolidate viewpoints on how courts should handle specific types of cases. Trial minutes are not formally binding but have significant influence in guiding judicial practice. They are generally regarded as internal references for judges rather than formal legal documents. They address practical issues encountered by judges in handling cases and often reflect emerging or unresolved legal challenges. They are mainly used as a consensus document rather than enforceable rules. A notable example is the SPC Trial Minutes (2019).

175. Judicial opinions are policy-oriented documents issued by the SPC to provide general guidance on judicial priorities, principles, or methodologies. Judicial opinions are not binding legal documents and cannot serve as the basis for court judgments. They are more forward-looking and often address broader legal or policy trends. They serve as guidelines for reforming judicial practices or improving the quality of case handling. Therefore, they exert impacts on how laws and judicial interpretations should be understood in a broader context. For example, the SPC Opinion on Strengthening the Judicial Protection of Intellectual Property Rights (2020).[184]

176. Normative judicial documents are administrative or procedural rules issued by the SPC to regulate court operations or processes. They lack the formal authority of judicial interpretations but are widely followed as administrative guidance. An example is the SPC Notice on Improving Online Filing Procedures (2020).[185]

177. While judicial interpretations carry quasi-legislative authority and are binding across the judiciary, other documents like trial minutes, judicial opinions, and normative judicial documents serve complementary but distinct roles. They guide judges in practice, influence policy, or regulate court administration without having the binding force or formal status of judicial interpretations.

D. The SPC Guiding Cases

178. The SPC guiding cases are a set of judicial decisions selected and published by the SPC to serve as models for judicial reasoning and decision making in China. Although not formally binding as in common law systems, they hold significant persuasive authority in ensuring consistency and quality in judicial practice.

184. The SPC Opinion on Strengthening the Judicial Protection of Intellectual Property Rights (2020).
185. The SPC Notice on Improving Online Filing Procedures (2020).

179. Guiding cases provide consistent interpretations of laws and principles across different regions and courts, reducing disparities in judicial outcomes. While China's civil law system does not traditionally rely on legal precedent like common law systems, the SPC introduced a 'guiding cases' system in 2010.[186] The guiding cases system, uniquely tailored to China's legal landscape, was instituted by the SPC to tackle disparities in social and economic development across regions, resolve intricate and varied litigation disputes, and address the issue of inconsistent rulings by local courts in similar cases. It aims to consolidate trial experiences promptly, provide guidance for the judicial work of all levels of people's courts, standardise judicial practices, and unify trial standards.

180. In areas where statutory laws or judicial interpretations are silent, guiding cases provide concrete legal reasoning to address specific scenarios. The publication of guiding cases increases public understanding of how courts interpret and apply laws, fostering trust in the judiciary. Guiding cases serve as benchmarks for judicial reasoning, ensuring that judges at all levels follow consistent methodologies in similar cases.

181. In 2011, the SPC's Case Guidance Office released the first set of 'guiding cases' for courts, including two specifically related to contracts.[187] As of 1 December 2024, the SPC has issued 41 batches of 236 guiding cases.[188]

182. In 2020, the SPC issued the Guiding Opinions on Unifying the Application of Laws to Strengthen the Retrieval of Similar Cases (for Trial Implementation), which introduced the concept of similar cases.[189] Similar cases are defined as previous cases with comparable basic facts, focal points of dispute, or legal application issues to the current case. Suppose a judge identifies a guiding case that may resemble a pending case during the trial proceedings or encounters a situation where a party, attorney, or prosecutor suggests referring to and applying a guiding case. In that case, the judge should compile a report on the search for similar cases.[190]

183. While not binding precedents, guiding cases carry significant persuasive weight and are frequently cited in judicial decisions as a basis for reasonings. Courts are encouraged, though not strictly required, to refer to guiding cases when adjudicating similar disputes. This 'soft precedent' system enhances consistency without rigidly binding judges.

---

186. The SPC Provisions Concerning Work on Case Guidance (2010); the Detailed Implementing Rules on the SPC Provisions Concerning Work on Case Guidance (2015).
187. Notice of the Supreme People's Court on Issuing the First Set of Guiding Cases (2011).
188. Notice by the Supreme People's Court of Issuing the Forty-First Group of Guiding Cases (2024).
189. The SPC Guiding Opinions on Unifying the Application of Laws to Strengthen the Retrieval of Similar Cases (for Trial Implementation) (2020).
190. *Ibid.*

184. The challenges of guiding cases are as significant as their benefits. The lack of a binding precedent system means that lower courts may not always follow guiding cases consistently. Some judges may refer to guiding cases selectively or disregard them entirely. The number of guiding cases issued is relatively small compared to the volume of cases adjudicated in China, limiting their practical influence. It is recommended to expand the number of guiding cases to cover a broader range of legal issues.

185. SPC guiding cases are an innovative mechanism in China's legal system, bridging the gap between civil law traditions and the need for consistent judicial reasoning. Their continued development and refinement will be crucial in advancing the maturity and predictability of Chinese judicial practices.

E. *International Customary Practices*

186. International customary practices or international usages in the Chinese legal system refer to widely recognised practices and norms in international trade, commerce, or specific professional fields. While not formal law, international customary practices often serve as a supplementary source of legal reasoning, particularly in disputes involving cross-border transactions or foreign-related civil and commercial matters.

187. When Chinese laws or regulations do not provide clear guidance, courts can turn to international customary practices to fill gaps. In a dispute over international shipping, the INCOTERMS (International Commercial Terms) may clarify responsibilities and risk allocation between buyers and sellers.

188. Parties in cross-border transactions often rely on international customary practices to regulate their agreements. Courts respect this autonomy by enforcing such practices where no conflicts with Chinese law exist. For example, payment methods like letters of credit governed by the UCP 600 (Uniform Customs and Practice for Documentary Credits) are treated as international customary practices and commonly enforced in payment disputes.

Part I. General Principles

Chapter 1. Contract Formation

§1. Agreement and Quid Pro Quo (Reciprocity)

189. Almost all legal systems impose two requirements in determining whether there has been a binding contract. First, the parties must have manifested their intention to be bound (contractual liability is consensual). Second, the agreement to which they manifested their intention must be definite enough to be enforceable (protection of expectation interest).

I. Offer and Acceptance

190. Most contracts are concluded by way of offer and acceptance.[191] However, at the conceptual level, in common law jurisdictions, contracts are defined objectively as they require an exchange of promises. In civil law countries, more emphasis is put on the subjective element of the meeting of minds. This also leads to a different approach to contract interpretation.

191. Despite the conceptual differences, the eventual results are often similar. Contract law characteristically envisions the process of agreement in terms of a discrete offer by one party and an acceptance by the other.

192. An offer is a proposal made by one party (the offeror) to another party (the offeree) indicating a willingness to enter into a contract on specified terms, which is intended to become binding as soon as the offeree accepts it.[192] There are two elements to constitute a valid offer. First, the offer must be clear and definite and express the intention to create legal obligations. Second, it must be sufficiently detailed regarding the rights and obligations it intends to create.

193. To satisfy the first condition as stated above, the contents of an offer must be clear and definite, and express the intent to create legal obligations. The contents of a contract generally contain the following items: (1) names or business names

191. Article 471 CC provides that the parties may conclude a contract by means of offer and acceptance, or by other means.
192. Article 472 CC.

and domiciles of the parties; (2) subject matter; (3) quantity; (4) quality; (5) price or remuneration; (6) time, place and manner of performance Ambiguities in terms of the offer or a lack of serious intent to be bound can invalidate the offer; (7) liability for breach of contract; and (8) means of dispute resolution.[193] The parties may conclude a contract by referencing a model text of each type of contract.[194]

194. The essential elements of a contract vary depending on its nature and type. The requirements of completeness and definiteness typically apply to the main obligations of the contract, which are often outlined in the initial paragraphs. For example, an offer for a lease must specify the start and end dates, the rent amount, and the specific property being leased, as these are the fundamental obligations of the parties involved under Article 704 of the Civil Code.[195]

195. Nonetheless, under Chinese law, a contract does not become void simply because the price or another essential term is not specified at the time of agreement. According to the Civil Code, if the parties do not determine the price, the court or arbitrator can fill in the missing terms based on several factors:

1) Statutory or government-set prices: If there are applicable government or statutory tariffs, those will be used.[196]
2) Customary or market prices: In the absence of statutory tariffs, the court may determine the price based on customary practices or the market price at the time and place of performance.[197]
3) Parties' agreement: If the parties later agree on the price or leave it to be determined by a third party, that decision will be upheld.[198]

196. Thus, Chinese law allows flexibility in dealing with incomplete terms and ensures the contract remains valid where performance is expected in exchange for compensation.[199]

197. Under Chinese law, as in many legal systems, there is a critical distinction between an invitation to offer (sometimes called an invitation to treat) and an offer. This distinction is important because it influences the point at which a legally binding agreement is initiated. An invitation to offer is generally a preliminary communication that indicates a willingness to negotiate or invites others to make an offer.[200] This could include advertising a product or service, sending a catalogue, or

193. Article 470 CC.
194. *Ibid.*
195. Article 704 CC stipulates that the content of a lease contract generally includes terms as to the name, quantity and use of the leased item, term of lease, rent, time and means of payment of rent, and the maintenance and repair of the leased item, etc.
196. Article 511(2) CC.
197. Articles 510 and Art 511 (2) CC.
198. Article 510 CC.
199. Article 3 of the SPC Interpretation on Several Issues Concerning the Application of the General Provisions of the Contract Book of the Civil Code (2023)
200. Article 473 of the CC.

displaying goods for sale. The key characteristic of an invitation to offer is that it does not legally bind the person making it; it is merely an invitation for others to submit proposals or offers.

198. However, commercial advertisements and promotions can be a valid offer if they meet the criteria of an offer.[201] The difference between offers and invitations to treat reflects a straightforward and practical idea. During negotiations, parties will engage in various communications, not all of which are meant to create binding legal obligations. Invitations to treat essentially serve to kickstart negotiation discussions and do not commit the initiator legally to any agreement. On the other hand, offers are communicated with the intention to commit legally and establish binding agreements once they are accepted.

199. An offer has no binding force and can be revoked at any time before acceptance, provided the revocation reaches the offeree before or at the same time as the offer.[202] Where an expression of intent to revoke an offer is made in dialogue, the content of such expression should be known to the offeree before the acceptance is made; where an expression of intent to revoke an offer is made in forms other than dialogue, such expression shall reach the offeree before the acceptance is made.[203] However, an offer cannot be revoked if the offeror indicates a fixed time for acceptance or otherwise explicitly states that the offer is irrevocable or the offeree has reason to believe that the offer is irrevocable and has made reasonable preparation to perform the contract.[204]

200. An offer becomes effective when it reaches the offeree. This means the offer must be communicated to the offeree in such a way that the offeree is aware of the offer and can make a decision regarding acceptance.[205] An offer ceases to be effective under any of the following circumstances: (1) the offer is declined; (2) the offer is revoked following the law; (3) the offeree fails to dispatch an acceptance before the expiry of the time for acceptance; and (4) the offeree makes substantial changes to the contents of the offer.[206] Certainly, the offer also ceases to be effective upon the death of the offeror as a natural person.[207]

201. Once the offer is accepted, the parties are bound by the contract. An acceptance is the expression of an intent by the offeree to assent to the offer.[208] The acceptance is made in the form of a notice, except where acceptance may be made by an act based on trade practice or as expressed in the offer.[209] Acceptance must occur within the time specified by the offeror. If no time is specified, acceptance must

201. *Ibid.*
202. Articles 475 and 141 CC.
203. Article 477 CC.
204. Article 476 CC.
205. Articles 137 and 474 CC.
206. Article 478 CC.
207. Article 13 CC.
208. Article 479 CC.
209. Article 480 CC.

occur within a reasonable time.[210] The reasonableness of the time can sometimes be more flexibly interpreted based on the circumstances of communication and the nature of the transaction. However, the Civil Code provides a clear rule on when to start running for the time limit:

> Article 482: Where an offer is made by letter or telegram, the time limit for acceptance shall run from the date shown in the letter or from the date on which the telegram is handed in for dispatch. If no such date is shown in the letter, it shall be accrued from the postmark date on the envelope. Where an offer is made by means of instantaneous communication, such as telephone, facsimile, email, and so forth, the time limit for acceptance shall run from the moment that the offer reaches the offeree.

202. Acceptance is effective when it reaches the offeror.[211] To be effective, an acceptance must be communicated to the offeror. A person who decides to accept an offer but does not inform the offeror this has not, in law, accepted the offer.

203. The contract is formed when the acceptance is communicated to the offeror, provided it is within the stipulated or reasonable time.[212] In other words, acceptance takes effect when it comes to the offeror's attention. This receipt rule is consistent with the general rule in contract law that acceptance must be communicated to the offeror to be effective. This aligns with the receipt rule used in many civil law countries, where acceptance is only effective upon receipt by the offeror. In contrast, common law generally follows the postal acceptance rule;[213] acceptance is effective when sent, not when received, except in instances where stipulations require receipt.

204. In terms of manner and form of acceptance, it must conform to the requirements specified in the offer. If the offer specifies a particular method or condition for how acceptance should be conveyed, the acceptance must comply with those terms. For example, if the offer dictates that acceptance must be sent to a particular address or must be in written and signed form, the acceptance is only valid if it conforms to these stipulations unless the offeror explicitly or implicitly waives these stipulations.

205. The rationale for this rule is to allow parties to tailor the contract formation process to suit their specific requirements. For instance, if a party desires a documented, signed record of the agreement process, a requirement that acceptance be signed serves this purpose.

---

210. Article 481 CC: An acceptance shall reach the offeror within the time limit prescribed in the offer. Where no time limit is prescribed in the offer, the acceptance shall reach the offeror in accordance with the following provisions: (1) if the offer is made in dialogue, the acceptance shall be made instantly;(2) if the offer is made in forms other than a dialogue, the acceptance shall reach the offeror within a reasonable period of time.
211. Articles 137 and 484 CC.
212. Article 483 CC.
213. *See Adams v. Lindsell* (1818) 1 B & Ald 681.

206. Similarly, suppose a party seeks to avoid the risks associated with postal delivery, such as a letter getting lost. In that case, they can enhance reliability by stipulating that the acceptance must be sent via courier or delivered by hand. This flexibility in specifying acceptance terms helps ensure that both parties have a clear and secure understanding of how the contract is to be formally agreed upon.

207. If no method is specified, acceptance can take any form that reasonably conveys the acceptance to the offeror. This requirement ensures that acceptance is unequivocal and clearly communicated. Acceptance can be expressed (clearly stated verbally or in writing) or implied (conducted in a way that clearly indicates acceptance, such as taking action that is consistent with accepting the terms of the offer).[214]

208. A late acceptance is treated as a new offer unless the offeror informs the offeree that it still considers the acceptance effective despite the delay.[215] Nonetheless, if the offeree posted the acceptance within the time limit for acceptance, and under normal circumstances, the acceptance would have reached the offeror in due time, but due to other reasons, the acceptance reaches the offeror after the time limit for acceptance has expired, such acceptance is effective unless the offeror notifies the offeree in a timely manner that it does not accept the acceptance due to the acceptance's late arrival.[216]

209. The essential features required for an act or statement to qualify as an acceptance include responding directly to the offer, being unconditional, and matching the offer's terms exactly. This requirement that acceptance must strictly adhere to the terms set out in the offer is commonly referred to as the mirror-image rule. This rule ensures that an acceptance is unequivocal, aligning precisely with the original offer without modifications. However, Chinese law adopts a relaxed approach to this mirror-image rule as in real life, the absolute adherence to the exact contents of the offer is rigid and not conducive to free bargaining.

210. Therefore, an acceptance that makes substantial modifications to the terms of the offer is considered a rejection of the original offer and, simultaneously, a new offer.[217] Where an acceptance does not substantially modify the contents of the offer, it shall be effective, and the contents of the contract shall be subject to those of the acceptance unless the offeror promptly indicates its objection or the offer has stated that no acceptance may make any change to the contents of the offer.[218]

---

214. Shiyuan Han, General Principles of Contract Law 152-153 (4th edn, Law Press China 2018).
215. Article 486 CC.
216. Article 487 CC.
217. Article 488: The contents of an acceptance shall accord with those of the offer. If the offeree substantially modifies the contents of the offer, that constitutes a new offer. The modification relating to the subject matter, quality, quantity, price or remuneration, time or place or manner of performance, liabilities for breach of contract and means of dispute resolution so forth, constitutes the substantial modification of an offer.
218. Article 489 of the CC.

211. For example, in *Zhang Jie v. Shanghai Haitong Securities Asset Management Co., Ltd.,* although the defendant required the Claimant to provide a written response by no later than 2:00 PM on 23 January 2015, the Claimant's actual response with his signature was at 2:14 PM.[219] The SPC held that the late response did not modify the content of the offer substantially 'since the exact time of the response was not a substantive requirement for the effectiveness of the confirmation letter, and the Defendant Company did not express any objections upon receiving it, both parties have already performed according to the content of the confirmation letter'.[220]

212. The offeree risks revocation only during the time between the arrival of the offer and the dispatch of acceptance. An acceptance can be revoked, but the revocation must reach the offeror before or simultaneously with the acceptance.[221] The ability to revoke acceptance before it reaches the offeror is a feature that provides flexibility and reflects the dynamics of negotiation in real life. This feature is somewhat unique as, in many common law jurisdictions, once acceptance is sent following the postal rule, it generally cannot be revoked.

213. These rules ensure that all parties' intentions are aligned when a contract is formed, thus reducing potential disputes and enhancing the predictability of business transactions. The specificity and structured nature of Chinese acceptance rules provide a strong legal framework for domestic and international traders and investors operating in or with China.

214. The principles of offer and acceptance are effective for straightforward transactions but can become less practical in complex negotiations. In these more intricate scenarios, courts may opt to determine whether an agreement has been reached by using criteria that extend beyond the traditional framework of offer and acceptance. Negotiation often involves scenarios where contract formation is not straightforward but requires a detailed, prolonged process of discussion covering a wide array of terms and issues. This is particularly true in cases involving complex negotiations where parties engage in extended discussions to hash out the nuances of their agreement.

215. It also applies to scenarios known as 'battle of the forms', where each party uses its standard contract forms, leading to a situation where the acceptance of terms becomes a negotiation in itself.[222] These situations demand flexibility in understanding how and when a contract is formed, as traditional notions of offer and

---

219. *Zhang Jie v. Shanghai Haitong Securities Asset Management Co., Ltd.* The SPC (2018) SPC Civil Min Shen No. 1423. 张杰、上海海通证券资产管理有限公司委托理财合同纠纷案，中华人民共和国最高人民法院（2018）最高法民申1423号.

220. *Ibid.*

221. Article 485 CC.

222. Nicole Kornet, Contracting in China: Comparative Observations on Freedom of Contract, Contract Formation, Battle of Forms and Standard Form Contracts, Maastricht European Private Law Institute Working Paper No. 2011/06 (2011) https://ssrn.com/abstract=1756750 or http://dx.doi.org/10.2139/ssrn.1756750 accessed on 3 November 2024.

acceptance may not adequately address the complexities of the iterative process of reaching a mutual agreement. The flexible approach allows for a more nuanced assessment of the interactions and intentions of the parties involved, recognising that the formalities of offer and acceptance may not fully capture the dynamics of complicated contractual agreements.

216. While the legal test for determining whether the parties have reached a binding agreement appears clear, in practice, it often requires judicial interpretation and the exercise of judicial discretion. For instance, Article 472(2) of the Civil Code stipulates that an offer's content must be 'specific and clear', but how should a judge determine whether the parties' intentions meet this standard?

217. One viewpoint holds that because acceptance cannot alter the substance of an offer, the offer must include all substantive terms. In other words, the intention of the parties must encompass all the terms listed in Article 488 of the Civil Code (such as subject matter, quantity, quality, price or remuneration, performance period, place and method of performance, breach liability, and dispute resolution) for the offer to be valid. However, this interpretation does not align with the reality of commercial transactions or the provisions of the Civil Code.

218. In actual transactions, many contracts do not contain all the substantive terms specified in Article 488. Moreover, Article 510 of the Civil Code provides that if, after a contract becomes effective, the parties have not agreed upon or clearly defined terms such as quality, price, or place of performance, they can supplement these terms by agreement. If they fail to agree, the terms can be determined based on the contract's relevant clauses or trade practices. Article 511 further allows for the determination of contract terms even if no agreement is reached, thus reinforcing that the content specified in Article 488 is not mandatory for an offer to be valid.

219. While Article 488 specifies that a substantive change by the offeree amounts to a counteroffer and that filling in missing substantive terms creates a new offer, these provisions are not exhaustive in determining whether an intention constitutes an offer. The broader context of contract formation requires a nuanced approach, as the presence of an offer is inherently tied to the clarity of intent, the specificity of terms, and the parties' conduct.

220. For instance, determining whether an intention amounts to an offer must consider whether the proposal demonstrates a clear intention to be bound upon acceptance. This principle is grounded in the need to distinguish between mere negotiations and a binding proposal. Merely adding or clarifying terms may reflect a willingness to explore contractual terms rather than a definitive intention to enter into a contract.

221. Furthermore, the overall context of the communication between the parties plays a crucial role. Courts may examine the language used, the parties' relationship, and industry practices to assess whether an invitation qualifies as an offer or remains part of the negotiation process. For example, preliminary agreements or letters of intent, such as in commercial transactions, might include substantive terms, yet these documents/terms may lack the intention required for the constitution of a binding offer.

222. Additionally, the offeree's conduct and subsequent actions after making amendments or additions to terms may further illuminate their intent. If the offeree's changes are accompanied by actions that align with further negotiation rather than acceptance, this supports the view that such changes do not immediately create a binding offer.

223. In summary, while substantive changes and the inclusion of missing terms are critical factors in identifying counteroffers and new offers under Article 488, they should not be the sole criteria. A holistic evaluation of intent, context, and conduct is essential to ensure a balanced and accurate determination of whether a valid offer exists. This approach aligns with the principles of good faith and reasonableness in contract law, ensuring that legal interpretations reflect the realities of commercial and personal dealings.

II. Intention to Create Legal Relations

224. In Chinese contract law, the intention to create legal relations is an essential element for the formation of a contract. This concept is similar to other legal systems where the parties must have a mutual understanding that their agreement will result in legal obligations enforceable by law. There is no standalone provision specifically addressing the intention to create legal relations as a constituting element of contract formation. However, such an element was highlighted in the statutory definitions of offer and acceptance.

225. The Civil Code defines an offer as an expression of intent to enter into a contract with another party. Such intent must meet the following criteria: (1) it is specific and definite, and (2) it indicates that the offeror will be bound upon acceptance by the offeree.[223] An acceptance is the offeree's expression of intent to agree to the offer.[224]

226. The intention to create legal relations is assessed primarily by the outward expressions or conduct of the parties, not their internal, subjective intentions.[225] This means the focus is on how the parties' intentions appear through their actions and statements rather than their internal, subjective state of mind. This objective

223. Article 472 CC.
224. Article 479 CC.
225. Shiyuan Han, General Principles of Contract Law 102 (2018).

approach focuses on whether a reasonable person, based on the parties' actions and statements, would conclude that they intended to form a legally binding agreement.[226]

227. Parties entering into a contract must have the legal capacity to do so. This includes age, mental capacity, and not being restricted by other legal constraints.[227] The parties must demonstrate a sufficiently serious intention to be bound by the contract. This is evaluated based on the context of the agreement, the conduct of the parties, and possibly the type of contract.

228. The purpose of this element is to define where legal enforceability ends. In daily life, people often make casual arrangements – such as agreeing to meet at a specific time, offering rides, or participating in activities like hiking. Typically, these are not considered legally enforceable. For instance, if someone plans to meet a friend at a café, they would not expect to be legally liable if they fail to show up. These are seen as social commitments, not contractual obligations. Even if a decent person would honour such an agreement, it remains unenforceable without an intention to create legal relations.

229. In legal terms, social agreements are not legally binding and are recognised through the principle that parties must intend to create legal relations for a contract to be formed. Without this intention, no legally enforceable contract exists, regardless of whether the parties have agreed on terms. This principle helps distinguish between social arrangements and agreements meant to be legally binding. A typical example of situations where parties do not intend to create legal relations is found in social or familial arrangements. These types of agreements are generally understood not to carry legal obligations, reflecting the understanding that such interactions are meant to be informal and based on personal relationships rather than legal commitments.

230. Determining whether parties intend to enter into legal relations typically relies heavily on the specific circumstances surrounding the agreement rather than strict legal rules or principles. Courts often examine the context in which the agreement was made, including the relationship between the parties, the nature of the agreement, and the language used. These factors help judges infer whether the parties envisioned their agreement as legally binding. In this way, the decision is largely based on the factual nuances of each case, allowing for a tailored evaluation of each party's intentions.

231. In legal evaluations, courts typically presume that familial or social agreements are not intended to create legal relations. However, this presumption can be

226. The exception is that where to determine whether the contract is made under duress or fraud, the actual intention of the parties is the key test.
227. Articles 143–145 CC.

overturned with evidence showing that the parties intended the agreement to be legally binding.

232. However, in a business context, the situation differs significantly, as commercial agreements are generally presumed to involve the intention to create legal obligations. This presumption reflects the nature of business dealings, where parties enter into negotiations with the understanding that their commitments will be enforceable. Unlike casual or social arrangements, commercial agreements often involve financial stakes, mutual obligations, and an expectation of performance that is crucial to maintaining business relationships and market stability.

233. For example, when companies negotiate contracts for the supply of goods or services, they rely on the enforceability of these contracts to plan operations, manage resources, and mitigate risks. The certainty that comes from legally binding commitments is vital in the business world, as it ensures predictability and accountability between the parties involved. While the intention to create legal relations can be rebutted in exceptional circumstances – such as if evidence shows that the parties expressly intended not to be legally bound – this is uncommon in commercial settings, where legal enforceability is a fundamental expectation.

234. Therefore, in commercial transactions, the default presumption is that the parties intended to create legal relations, reflecting the expectation of legal accountability in such dealings. The burden falls on the party asserting otherwise to prove there was no intent to form a binding agreement. These presumptions and their rebuttals enable courts to tailor their evaluations to the specific context and intentions of the parties in each case.

235. The requirement of intention to create legal relations primarily impacts non-commercial areas, especially in the context of relationships among friends and family. Here, the doctrine ensures that many informal arrangements are not subject to legal enforcement. This is based on the rationale that such agreements, typically made in a personal or social setting, are unlikely to have been formed with the intention of creating legally binding obligations.[228] The requirement serves to maintain the informal nature of personal interactions, preventing the legal system from imposing formalities and potential liabilities on relationships meant to be governed by mutual understanding and trust rather than legal commitments.

236. The distinction between social arrangements (non-binding) and contractual relations (binding) is often blurred and challenging to delineate in practice clearly. How can a judge conclusively determine that parties in a familial or social context lacked the intention to create legal relations? In situations involving friends or family, the inherent informality and the assumption that parties do not intend to be

228. Lei Wang, On the distinction between the informal/social arrangements and Civil Legal Conduct, 6 Tsinghua Law Journal 157 (2013).

legally bound complicate this assessment. Chinese law, like many legal systems, offers no explicit criteria or detailed guidance to help a judge navigate such distinctions, leaving significant discretion to judicial interpretation.

237. In practice, courts tend to infer the parties' intentions based on contextual factors, such as the language used in the arrangement, the formality of their communication, and whether any financial considerations were involved. However, these factors are inherently subjective and may be interpreted differently depending on the specific circumstances of the case. Courts often rely on the principle of reasonableness – evaluating whether a reasonable person would regard the agreement as legally binding.[229] This approach can be particularly difficult in close personal relationships, where a mix of personal trust and informal commitments may easily blur the lines of enforceability.

238. One argument is that in such cases, courts tend to prioritise public policy over the strict application of contract formation rules.[230] In other words, public policy considerations, such as avoiding the flood of trivial disputes or maintaining social harmony, may play a pivotal role in judicial decisions.[231] Recognising informal social promises as legally binding could lead to an overwhelming number of cases and undermine the very social bonds these promises are intended to foster. Courts often consider the implications of declaring informal agreements enforceable, as doing so could strain family relations or disrupt social dynamics.

239. However, emphasising public policy implies that the objective test – whether a reasonable person would believe the agreement was intended to be legally binding – is applied inconsistently. The absence of clear statutory guidelines provides judges with considerable discretion, which can result in variations in how similar cases are decided. While this flexibility allows judges to account for the unique circumstances of each case, it also creates uncertainty for parties involved in social or familial disputes.

240. Thus, the distinction between social arrangements and enforceable contracts remains context-sensitive and subject to judicial discretion. It is often guided as much by public policy as by a strict evaluation of intent.

III. Consideration

241. In distinguishing legally binding and non-binding arrangements, courts usually assess whether the parties intended to create legal relations. In common law

229. Yufei Liang, Judicial identification and handling of informal/social arrangements, 2 Law Application Journal (Fa Lv Shi Yong) 30 (2014).
230. Lei Wang, On the distinction between the informal/social arrangements and Civil Legal Conduct 157 (2013).
231. Hongfei Xie, On the Intention to Establish Legal Relationships: The Limits of Legal Intervention in Social Life, 3 Global Law Review 5 (2012).

jurisdictions, a further requirement is that a promise must be supported by valid consideration – something of value exchanged between the parties.[232] However, this contrasts with Chinese law, which, following the civil law tradition,[233] does not require consideration for a contract to be valid.[234] Instead, Chinese law emphasises mutual consent and the lawful purpose of the agreement as the primary elements for contract formation.

242. Consent must be genuine, free from coercion, fraud, or mistake, as it forms the foundation of the contractual obligation in Chinese law rather than an exchange of value. Additionally, the contract's purpose must be lawful, meaning it cannot involve illegal activities, breach public order or good morals, or violate legal prohibitions. The requirement of a lawful purpose is crucial for a contract's validity, serving a role in Chinese law comparable to consideration's function in ensuring an agreement's legality in common law systems.

243. Some types of contracts may have specific formal requirements that must be fulfilled for the contract to be valid. For example, contracts related to real estate transactions must be in writing and properly registered.[235] These formalities serve a similar purpose to consideration in that they provide evidence of the parties' intent and the seriousness of the transaction. Under Chinese law, contracts must be negotiated, executed, and enforced according to the principle of good faith.[236] This principle demands that parties act honestly and not engage in behaviour that undermines the spirit of the agreement.[237] This requirement is intended to ensure fair dealing between parties, akin to how consideration aims to balance the equities of a transaction.

244. Although Chinese contract law does not recognise consideration, it emphasises the concept of reciprocal obligations. This principle requires each party to perform their contractual duties, and failure to do so can result in legal consequences. These may include the other party's right to seek enforcement, claim compensation, or terminate the contract.

245. In summary, Chinese contract law emphasises lawful purpose, mutual consent, and adherence to formal and procedural norms over the common law concept

232. Lon L. Fuller, Consideration and Form, 41 Columbia Law Review 799 (1941); John Adams and Roger Brownsword, Contract, Consideration and the Critical Path, 53 The Modern Law Review 536 (1990).
233. Lei Chen, Contextualizing Legal Transplant: China and Hong Kong, in Methods of Comparative Law 192-212 (P.G. Monateri ed., Elgar Edward 2012).
234. Chunyan Ding, Contract Formation Under Chinese Law, in Studies in the Contract Laws of Asia II: Formation and Third Party Beneficiaries (Mindy Chen-Wishart, Alexander Loke, and Stefan Vogenauer eds., Oxford University Press 2018) https://ssrn.com/abstract=3237320 accessed October 4 2024.
235. Article 15 of the Urban Real Estate Administration Law.
236. Article 7 CC.
237. Liming, Wang, and Chuanxi Xu, Fundamental Principles of China's Contract Law, 13 Colum. J. Asian L. 1 (1999).

of consideration. These elements ensure that contracts are formed based on mutual agreement and legally permissible objectives, aligning with the broader principles of contract law in civil law jurisdictions.

246. As discussed, consideration is not required to make a valid contract under Chinese law. The core principles of the doctrine of consideration focus on the concepts of value and reciprocal exchange. Then what about the law of gifts? Under Chinese law, the concept of a gift is treated distinctly from nominate contracts (typical contracts).[238] This statutory structure provides detailed rules governing gratuitous gifts. More to the point, it has specific requirements that differentiate it from contracts that involve an exchange of considerations.

247. A gift contract in Chinese law is defined as a unilateral promise where one party (the donor) transfers property to another party (the donee) without expecting anything in return, and the donee accepts the gift.[239] Unlike other contracts that might require consideration or reciprocal obligations, a gift is characterised by its gratuitous nature. However, certain gifts must be made in a written form. For example, for a gift involving real estate or other significant assets, a written form may be required to validate the gift contract.[240] This requirement ensures clarity and legal certainty about the donor's intention and the details of the property being gifted. Similar to real estate transactions, gifts involving real estate must be registered to effectuate the transfer of property rights legally.[241]

248. The donor must have the legal capacity to make the gift, and the consent must be freely given without coercion, fraud, or misunderstanding. The donee must also accept the gift, either explicitly or implicitly, for the gift contract to be complete. Generally, gift contracts are revocable until the gift is actually delivered to the donee.[242] Additionally, the donor may cease to perform the gift contract where its financial position deteriorates so markedly that its business or family life has been severely affected.[243] Once the gift is delivered, the donor usually cannot revoke the gift unless specific conditions justify such revocation (e.g., if the donee commits a serious offence against the donor or the donor's close relatives).

249. A special exception rule introduced in the Civil Code states that gift contracts that have been notarised or legally irrevocable gift contracts of a public interest or moral obligation nature involving disaster relief, poverty alleviation, disability aids, etc., cannot be revoked.[244] Where the donor fails to deliver the property through notarisation or concerning public interests, the donee may seek to

238. Chapter 12 Gift Contract in the Contract Law Book of the Civil Code: Arts 657-666.
239. Article 657 CC.
240. Articles 37 and 41 of the Urban Real Estate Administration Law.
241. Article 659 CC.
242. Paragraph 1 of Art. 658 CC.
243. Article 666 CC.
244. Paragraph 2 of Art. 658 CC.

enforce delivery.[245] Where such property to be delivered has been damaged, destroyed or lost due to deliberate acts or gross negligence on the part of the donor, the donor shall be liable for damages.[246]

250. Gifts made for illegal purposes or that contravene public morals are not valid. There are restrictions regarding gifts made in anticipation of death or those that affect the mandatory share of inheritance that heirs are entitled to under succession laws.[247]

251. In conclusion, while the general formation of contracts does not emphasise the exchange of considerations as in common law systems, the law of gifts is clearly defined with its unique requirements focusing on the gratuitous transfer of assets and the intentions of the parties involved. This makes the gift a distinct legal category governed by specific rules that ensure the proper execution and legal recognition of such transfers.

252. Nonetheless, this by no means suggests that Chinese law would consider introducing a doctrine of consideration. The complexities surrounding the doctrine of consideration and the modifications it has undergone in both England and other common law jurisdictions have led some scholars to question its validity or call for its abolition.[248] Furthermore, the doctrine has garnered little support in efforts to harmonise contract laws internationally.[249]

IV. Modifications of the Contract

253. Under Chinese law, modifications to a contract are treated with care and specificity, as the stability of contractual relations is highly valued. As with contract formation, the primary requirement for modifying a contract is the mutual consent of all parties involved.[250] One party cannot unilaterally modify the terms of the contract without the other party's consent. A public announcement of intent to modify a contract, followed by the other party's silence by the end of the announcement period, does not constitute implicit consent to the modification.[251]

245. Paragraph 1 of Art. 660 CC.
246. Paragraph 2 of Art. 660 CC.
247. Article 664 CC.
248. Lord Wright, Ought the Doctrine of Consideration to be Abolished from the Common Law? 49 Harvard LR 1225, 1226 (1936). Also *see* the contrasting view, Gamage, David, and Allon Kedem. 'Commodification and Contract Formation: Placing the Consideration Doctrine on Stronger Foundations.' (2006) 73 U. Chi. L. Rev. 1299.
249. Hein Kötz, Comparative Contract Law, in The Oxford Handbook of Comparative Law (Mathias Reimann and Reinhard Zimmermann eds., Oxford University Press 2019) https://doi.org/10.1093/oxfordhb/9780198810230.013.29 accessed 12 April 2024.
250. Article 543 CC.
251. Paragraph 2 of Art. 140 CC.

254. If the parties' agreement on the terms of a modification is unclear or cannot be determined, it is presumed that the contract has not been modified.[252] This is intended to protect the interests and expectations of all parties involved. Any changes to the contract must be agreed upon by the parties, reflecting the principle that contracts are based on the meeting of the minds.

255. Depending on the initial form of the contract, amendments may need to be made in writing to be effective, especially if the original contract was required to be in writing or registered (e.g., real estate transactions). In the absence of explicit legal provisions, the form of a contract modification should generally be consistent with the form of the original contract.

256. If the original contract required approval or registration (such as in the case of property transfers), modifications to the contract also need to be approved or registered to be enforceable.[253]

257. Chinese law tends to emphasise the formality of contract modifications more than some common law jurisdictions. While common law also requires mutual consent for modifications, the formality of these modifications can sometimes be less stringent, depending on the nature of the contract and the jurisdictions involved. In China, regulatory oversight on contract modifications can be more pronounced, especially in sectors involving real estate or other significant economic interests.[254] This is partly due to the socio-economic implications of contractual dealings in these sectors.

258. In cases of statutory contract modification, a party may request the court to modify the contract without requiring mutual agreement between the parties. Apart from modifications made through mutual agreement, a contract may also be modified when circumstances arise as provided by law. In such cases, the modification can be done at the court's order without the need for both parties to agree. For example, during the performance of a contract, if a change of circumstances occurs, a party may request the court to modify the contract.[255]

259. It is worth noting that under Chinese Law, there is a distinction between contract modification (合同变更) and contract replacement（合同更新）. Contract modification refers to the partial amendment or supplementation of its terms rather than a complete alteration of its content. If the parties make it explicit that the new contract supersedes or replaces all the pre-existing contracts, agreements or arrangements, that clause will prevail. Such a scenario is not considered a contract modification but rather a contract replacement.

252. Article 544 CC.
253. Paragraph 3 of Art. 502 CC.
254. *Ibid.*
255. Article 533 CC.

260. Contract replacement was not explicitly provided in the Civil Code but was widely employed and reasoned by courts.[256] This is because the Civil Code provides a principle of freedom to contract, meaning contract parties are free to conclude, modify, and terminate contracts.[257] The difference between the two concepts is that in the case of contract modification, the prior arrangements or contractual relationships continue to exist subject to the modified terms. Nevertheless, in case of contract replacement, the new contract will supersede, extinguish or replace the prior arrangements or contracts.

§2. Formal and Evidential Requirements

I. Formal Requirements

261. Contracts can be established in various forms, including written, oral (via phone or face-to-face), and other methods.[258] All legal systems have statutory rules mandating that certain contracts are only valid and enforceable if they follow a specific legal form. Chinese law is no exception. Certain types of contracts, however, must be in writing due to specific legal requirements. For instance, the Civil Code mandates that contracts dealing with the construction land use right transfer, the habitation right, the servitude right, the mortgage right, and the pledge must be in writing and signed by all involved parties.

262. Similarly, the Arbitration Law specifies that agreements to resolve disputes through arbitration need to be documented in writing or through another written method.[259] 'Written form' refers to a form that conveys the contents in a tangible manner, such as formal contracts, letters, telegrams, telexes, and facsimiles.[260] The contents which can be tangibly expressed by electronic data texts, emails, and so forth, and which can be accessible at any time upon request, are regarded as 'written form'.[261]

263. Recognising modern commerce dynamics, the Civil Code acknowledges electronic contracts if the information contained therein is accessible for future reference. This accommodates contracts formed via emails, text messages, or electronic contract platforms, provided they meet the requirements of authenticity, integrity, and reliability.[262]

---

256. For example, *Su Yueniu & Zhu Zhiping v. Wang Zhengpeng & Wang Zhenyou* Intermediate People's Court of Xuancheng Anhui (2020) Wan 18 Min Zhong No. 1328. 苏月牛、朱治平股权转让纠纷案，安徽省宣城市中级人民法院（2020）皖18民终1328号.
257. Article 5 CC.
258. Paragraph 1 of Art. 469 CC.
259. Article 16 of the Arbitration Law.
260. Paragraph 2 of Art. 469 CC.
261. Paragraph 3 of Art. 469 CC.
262. Article 491 CC.

264. Apart from specific instances where written form must be employed to form a special contract under the relevant statutory stipulations,[263] contracts can be formed in any manner the parties agree upon. Most contracts do not involve formal documents; they are often formed through informal means like text messages, phone calls, emails, or casual conversations.

265. This flexibility necessitates clear legal rules that specify how and when contracts are established because disputes frequently arise about the formation of contracts. One common defence in contract disputes is to argue that no valid contract was formed, so there are no binding obligations.

266. Nonetheless, formalities are crucial as they dictate the validity of a contract and protect the interests of the parties involved. They ensure that all legal provisions are followed and that the contract can be enforced under Chinese law. The key question concerns the legal consequence of non-conformity with the statutorily stipulated written formality requirement.

267. Will a contract that does not adhere to the formal requirements stipulated by law or the Civil Code be deemed invalid or unenforceable? The response is primarily determined by the nature of the requirement and the stipulations of the legislation that establishes it. For example, the Civil Code only provides that 'to create a right of habitation, the parties shall conclude the underlying contract of right of habitation in writing'.[264] It does not address where the underlying contract of habitation right was not made in writing. The same loophole occurs in other special types of contracts, which require to be made in writing.

268. First and foremost, the Civil Code provides a chance to cure the non-conformity of the written formality rule, which provides that:

> Where a contract is to be concluded in written form as required by relevant laws and administrative regulations or as agreed by the parties, and the parties have failed to conclude the contract in written form if one party has performed the principal obligation and the other party has accepted it, the contract is established.[265]

269. When the written form is stipulated as a requirement for the formation of a contract, the rationale is to convey that the decisive factor in determining whether a contract is established is not the parties' mutual consent but the written form as the contractual formality. Under this legislative intent, even if the parties have factually reached an agreement, but this agreement is not clothed in the legally mandated or agreed written form, the contract cannot be established. Therefore, at this

263. It should be highlighted that there are many other instances where certain contracts must be formed in writing under the Chinese law other than the examples mentioned. Examples are leasing of immovable property for a period exceeding six months (Art. 707 CC), and technology development contracts (Art. 851 CC).
264. Article 367 CC.
265. Paragraph 2 of Art. 490 CC.

juncture, the effectiveness of a contract is attributed not so much to the mutual assent of the parties but to the written form. This appears to be against the parties' intention and over-rigid.

270. Therefore, to mitigate such rigidity, the Civil Code does not confirm that failure to comply with the written formalities will always lead to invalidity. If one party has fulfilled their main contractual obligation and the other party has accepted this performance, the contract is considered established.

271. This means that even if a contract was not initially formalised in writing or explicitly agreed upon, the performance and acceptance of obligations can confirm its existence and validity. This principle emphasises that actions demonstrating a commitment to the terms can establish a contract, with substantial performance effectively curing the lack of written formalities. Without such performance, the contract cannot be recognised due to the unresolved formality defect.

272. However, this rule's drawback is that the parties can effectively bypass the written formality requirement through their conduct. If a party's actions in performing the contract are taken as evidence of agreement, this undermines the necessity for written formalities. This raises an important question: Why impose a rule requiring written formalities if non-compliance can be remedied by subsequent performance?

273. While the rule that performance can remedy the absence of written formalities offers flexibility, it also weakens the rationale behind mandating written agreements. It raises a broader issue about balancing the need for formal safeguards with the practicalities of enforcing agreements based on parties' conduct. This tension highlights the importance of legal frameworks that carefully delineate when and how performance can substitute for formalities without undermining the integrity of contractual law.

II. Evidential Requirement-Proof

274. Formal requirements provide evidence of an agreement, reducing disputes over the existence and timing of oral agreements. While the parol evidence rule in common law jurisdictions restricts the use of extrinsic evidence to alter, explain, or contradict the terms of a written contract, no direct equivalent exists in Chinese law. However, Chinese contract law does regulate the use of external evidence in interpreting contracts, focusing on clarifying the parties' intentions rather than imposing strict evidentiary limitations.

275. The rules for interpreting contracts do allow consideration of relevant external factors. Specifically, the interpretation of a contract shall ascertain the true intentions of the parties according to the terms and nature of the contract, the relevant practices, and the principle of good faith.[266] This suggests a more flexible approach than the strict parol evidence rule of common law systems, allowing for a broader range of evidence to determine the parties' intentions. Courts still consider external evidence to interpret unclear contract terms, to determine the real intent of the contracting parties, or where there may be a typo or clerical error. Chinese law also allows for the supplementation of contract terms through reference to relevant laws, customary practices, or through mutual agreement if the contract is silent on specific issues.[267]

276. The use of customary practices and previous dealings between the parties to interpret the contract indicates an openness to external evidence beyond the written document. Therefore, while the written contract holds significant authority, the courts are not as restrictive as common law jurisdictions concerning external evidence. This approach aims to ascertain the true intentions of the parties and promote fairness and equity in contractual dealings.

277. In practice, Chinese courts can and often do look beyond the written contract to ascertain the parties' real intentions, especially in cases where the terms are ambiguous or incomplete. This flexibility enables a broader interpretation of contractual obligations and rights but may also create uncertainty regarding the predictability of contract enforcement.

278. For businesses and legal practitioners, it is crucial to draft clear and comprehensive contracts while being prepared for courts to consider a wide range of evidence to interpret the terms and intent of those contracts in case of disputes.

279. The evidential requirements for contract formation are established to ensure that the existence and terms of a contract can be appropriately verified. These requirements are crucial for resolving disputes and enforcing contracts. The Civil Code allows contracts to be formed in various forms, including written, oral and other forms such as by conduct. Chinese law emphasises the necessity of written or electronic forms for certain types of contracts but allows for oral contracts in many situations. This hybrid approach aims to balance the traditional civil law preference for formalism with the need for flexibility in modern commerce.

280. First, written contracts are generally the most straightforward in terms of evidential proof. The contract document serves as the primary evidence of the agreement and its terms. It provides clear, tangible evidence that can be easily referenced and verified, reducing ambiguity in disputes. As discussed in the previous

266. Article 142 CC.
267. Article 510 CC: Where, after the contract becomes effective, there is no agreement in the contract between the parties on such contents as quality, price or remuneration, or place of performance etc., or such agreement is ambiguous, the parties may agree upon supplementary terms; if a supplementary agreement cannot be reached, such terms shall be determined in accordance with the relevant terms, nature and purpose of the contract, or the trade practices.

section, certain types of contracts, such as real estate transactions or long-term leases for more than six months, are required by law to be in writing.

281. Second, electronic contracts are recognised similarly to written contracts if they can be stored and reproduced. Evidence can include emails, text messages, digital signatures, or any data stored electronically. Convenient and adaptable to modern business practices, electronic contracts are especially popular for e-commerce and international transactions. Many jurisdictions, including China, have laws specifically addressing the validity and recognition of electronic contracts and signatures, such as the Electronic Signature Law.[268] For contracts that legally require a written form, documents signed by the parties, electronic texts, emails, or other forms of written communication that can be stored and reproduced are acceptable.

282. Third, establishing the existence and terms of an oral contract is often more difficult than with written agreements. Evidence can include witness testimonies, records of verbal agreements (like recorded phone calls, where legally permissible), and the actions or conduct of the parties that imply an agreement. However, there is a greater potential for disputes over the terms or even the existence of the contract due to the lack of physical documentation. The contact was made by 'other forms', including contracts implied by conduct or those established through customary practices among parties.

283. Article 2 of the SPC Interpretation on the Contract Law II 2009 provided that:

> if a contract has not been formed in writing or oral form by the relevant parties, but their civil conduct can ascertain the intention of entering into a legal relationship from both parties, then the Courts may find that the contract has been formed in 'other forms' according to the first paragraph of Article 10 of the Contract Law, except where it is otherwise provided under other law.

284. While this SPC judicial interpretation was repealed when the Civil Code was introduced, it shows that courts have taken a flexible approach to questions of evidence of the existence of a contract. The oral contracts allow flexibility and immediacy in making agreements without the formalities of written contracts. Evidence is often derived from the conduct of the parties that consistently suggests an agreement. For example, in *Wang Weibin v. Chen Jing*,[269] there was a dispute on whether an entrusted financial investment contract was formed between the parties. The contract was found to be formed by the court based on the following facts: (a) QQ chat records, (b) email exchanges, and (c) before the parties signed the formal

268. The Electronic Signature Law was passed on 28 August 2004. It came into effect on 1 April 2005. The current version of the law was on 23 April 2019.
269. *Wang Weibin v. Chen Jing* No.2 Intermediate People's Court of Shanghai (2016) Hu 02 Min Zhong No. 5427; 王伟斌与陈婧委托理财合同纠纷案，上海市第二中级人民法院（2016）沪02民终5427号.

written joint investment agreement, one party had already been recommended by the other party to start investing. The court found that the three factors at (a) to (c) confirmed the contractual relationship of entrusted investment arrangement between the parties.

285. Like oral contracts, contracts implied by conduct can lead to disputes due to their less formal nature and the difficulty in proving specific terms. When there is a dispute over whether a contract has been established, and if the court can confirm the parties' names or titles, the subject matter, and the quantity involved, it should generally rule that the contract has been formed.[270] This implies that the basic elements necessary to recognise a contract's existence are the identification of parties involved and agreement on the key terms of the contract (such as the subject matter and quantity). The contract may not be formed if there are specific legal provisions or agreements between the parties that dictate otherwise. This highlights the importance of the specific terms agreed upon by the parties and any relevant laws that might impact contract formation.

286. If a contract is deemed to have been formed, but some content is missing, the court should determine what the contract lacks based on relevant provisions of the Civil Code, specifically Articles 510 and 511.[271] These articles help the court to fill gaps in the contract by interpreting the likely intentions of the parties and applying general principles of contract law, ensuring that the contract is complete and enforceable. This rule illustrates the need for clear evidence of key contract terms and party intentions while also providing mechanisms to address any gaps or ambiguities in contract documentation. It underscores the importance of judicial discretion in ensuring justice is served in contract disputes.

287. Where the parties conclude a contract with a formal written contract, the contract is concluded at the time when it is signed and sealed or fingerprinted by both parties. The contract is established if one party has fulfilled the principal obligation and another party has accepted it before a contract is signed and sealed or fingerprinted.[272] If the parties conclude a contract through letters or electronic data texts and require a letter of confirmation, the contract is deemed established when the confirmation letter is signed.[273]

288. If the goods or services information released by one party through the internet or other information networks meet the criteria for an offer, the contract is established upon selection and successful submission of the order for goods or services of another party, except as otherwise agreed upon by the parties.[274] With the increasing use of digital communications and transactions, electronic evidence of contract

270. Article 3 of the SPC Interpretation on the Contract Book (2023).
271. *Ibid.*
272. Paragraph 1 Art. 490 CC.
273. Paragraph 1 Art. 491 CC.
274. Paragraph 1 Art 491 CC.

formation, such as text messages, emails, or blockchain entries, is recognised, provided it meets standards of integrity, reliability, and appropriateness for the nature of the contract.

289. In cases where the contract form is not prescribed or where disputes arise about oral agreements, testimony from witnesses, recordings, or other relevant evidence may be used to prove the formation and terms of the contract. Parties are encouraged to maintain good records of communications and agreements to support any future need to prove the contract's existence or content, especially in business contexts where disputes may arise. In any legal dispute regarding a contract, the burden of proof typically lies with the party seeking to enforce the contract. This party must provide sufficient evidence to demonstrate the existence of the contract and its terms.

III. Obligation of Means and Obligation of Result

290. In Chinese law, the concepts of 'obligation of means' (also known as an obligation to use best efforts) and 'obligation of result' (where the focus is on achieving a specific outcome) are not as formally codified or distinctly categorised as they are in some civil law systems like French law. However, the principles underlying these obligations exist and are applied in contract performance under the Civil Code.

291. Obligation of result implies that a party is contractually bound to achieve a specific result. Failure to deliver the promised result constitutes a breach of contract, regardless of the efforts made. In Chinese law, this is often seen in contracts where the performance is clearly defined by objective criteria or standards, like delivery contracts where goods must meet specific requirements or construction contracts where a building must be completed by a certain date to the agreed specifications.

292. Obligation of Means entails that a party is required to make all reasonable efforts to achieve a certain result, but the actual achievement of that result is not guaranteed. The focus is on the behaviour and actions of the obligated party rather than the outcome. In Chinese law, this typically applies to service contracts, such as management services or consultancy agreements, where the service provider promises to work towards a goal without guaranteeing the result.

293. For example, the Civil Code specifies that an obligor should fulfil its obligations according to the terms and nature of the contract and the principle of good faith.[275] This can encompass both obligations of result and obligations of means, depending on the nature of the contract and the intentions of the parties.

275. Article 509 CC.

294. Articles 580 and 581 deal with liability for breach of contract. They state that if a party fails to perform its obligations or its performance does not conform to the agreement, it shall bear the breach of contract liabilities.[276] This applies to both results and means, though the application might differ based on contract types and contents.

295. In practice, whether a contractual obligation is treated as an obligation of results or an obligation of means depends on the contractual terms and the nature of the obligations involved. Courts will look at the agreement itself, the attending circumstances, and the parties' intents to determine the nature of the obligation.

296. Chinese law emphasises the parties' intention and the principle of fairness, often allowing for some flexibility in determining how obligations are categorised and enforced. Thus, while the terminology may not be explicitly used, the essence of these obligations is recognised and applied depending on the contractual context. For parties engaging in contracts governed by Chinese law, it is crucial to clearly define the nature of the obligations in the contract terms to ensure there is no ambiguity regarding the expectations and legal standards applicable to the performance of the contract.

§3. Liability and Negotiations

I. Pre-contractual Liability

297. Pre-contractual liability is a crucial aspect of Chinese contract law, designed to ensure fairness and integrity during the negotiation phase of contract formation. By examining case law and comparing it to other legal systems, particularly common law traditions, we can better understand its role in shaping contractual relationships.

298. Article 500 of the Civil Code specifies the circumstances under which a party may be held liable for damages incurred during negotiations. It states:

> A party which, during contract negotiations, engages in any of the following conduct that causes damage to the other party shall be liable for damages: (i) negotiating in bad faith under the pretence of entering into a contract; (ii) intentionally concealing material facts or providing false information related to contract formation; (iii) engaging in other conduct contrary to the principle of good faith.[277]

276. Articles 580 and 581 CC.
277. Article 500 CC.

299. This provision emphasises the importance of good faith (bona fides) in contract negotiations, a principle central to civil law traditions.[278] The first two circumstances cover situations where one party acts in bad faith, potentially preventing the other party from pursuing business opportunities, such as withholding negotiations with third parties. The third circumstance is a broad, catch-all provision that grants courts significant discretion in resolving disputes. Notably, German law has a similar concept known as '*culpa in contrahendo*' (fault in contracting).[279] It is a unique concept that shifts between contract and tort, at times taking on characteristics of either obligation category.[280]

300. In essence, Article 500 establishes the legal framework for holding parties liable for damages incurred during the pre-contractual phase. This includes bad-faith negotiations, the concealment of material facts, providing false information, or violating the principle of good faith.

301. This principle establishes that a relationship of trust can emerge during the early stages of a contract or similar business interactions, obligating parties to exercise due care toward each other. Even though no contractual rights or obligations exist before a contract is finalised, the frequency of interactions often leads to increased mutual trust. Pre-contractual liability thus operates as a form of liability that lies between a contractual breach and a tort liability.[281] Its purpose is to protect transactional security by outlining the duty of care parties must uphold during the negotiation phase. Under Chinese law, they include: (1) a duty to negotiate in good faith,[282] (2) a duty to inform,[283] and (3) a duty of confidentiality.[284]

302. These obligations differ from the contractual obligations that arise once a contract takes effect and also from the general duty of care established in tort law. Pre-contractual liability stems from the 'granting of relied trust', meaning that if one party breaches their duty of care during the negotiation phase, they may be held liable for damages.[285] This liability covers losses incurred by the other party who reasonably relied on the breaching party's conduct. Essentially, it ensures compensation for harm caused when trust reasonably placed in the other party's actions is violated.

---

278. Kessler and Fine, Culpa in Contrahendo, Bargaining in Good Faith, and Freedom of Contract: A Comparative Study 77 Harvard LR 401 (1964).
279. Rudolf von Jhering, Culpa in contrahendo, 4 JherJb (1861).
280. Markesinis, Basil S., Hannes Unberath, and Angus C. Johnston, The German Law of Contract: a comparative treatise 93 (Bloomsbury Publishing 2006).
281. Stefan Lorenz, Die culpa in contrahendo im französischen Recht, ZEuP 218 (1994).
282. Article 500 (1) CC.
283. Article 500 (2) CC.
284. Article 501 CC stipulates that a trade secret or other confidential information the parties come to know in concluding a contract shall not be disclosed or improperly exploited, no matter whether the contract is established or not. The party shall be liable for damages if it discloses or improperly exploits such trade secret or confidential information and thus causes losses to the other party.
285. While we aim to provide an overview in this chapter, it would be misleading to cover all aspects of the topic solely within the context of contract formation. It characteristically involves tort law discussions.

303. In light of Article 500 of the Civil Code, Chinese courts have increasingly recognised and enforced pre-contractual liability, demonstrating a commitment to fairness and integrity in commercial transactions. Notable cases highlight how courts interpret and apply Article 500. In one landmark case, a company was found liable for negotiating a contract without genuine intent, causing the other party to incur significant costs with the expectation of reaching an agreement. The court ruled that this behaviour constituted bad faith under Article 500(i), obligating the defendant to compensate for the damages.[286]

304. In another case, a party was held liable for concealing critical information that would have influenced the negotiation process. Based on Article 500(ii), this decision highlighted that intentionally withholding material facts breaches the obligation of good faith in negotiations. Collectively, such cases emphasise the judiciary's role in enforcing ethical standards during the pre-contractual phase.

305. A comparative analysis reveals notable contrasts and similarities between Chinese law and common law systems regarding pre-contractual liability. In common law jurisdictions, such as English law, the concept of 'culpa in contrahendo' is not explicitly codified but is addressed through various doctrines that aim to prevent unfair conduct during negotiations. These doctrines, such as misrepresentation, promissory estoppel, or unjust enrichment, provide remedies when one party suffers harm due to the bad faith or misleading actions of the other during pre-contractual discussions.

306. How do common law systems address issues of pre-contractual liability without explicit good faith requirements? It has been argued that while common law jurisdictions do not mandate good faith in negotiations, they still protect reasonable expectations and sanction misconduct through various legal doctrines.[287] For example, the common law principle of misrepresentation provides a remedy for parties who have been induced to conclude a contract based on false statements. Similarly, the doctrine of promissory estoppel can be invoked to enforce promises made during negotiations, provided that the promisee has relied on such promises to their detriment.[288]

307. Legal recognition of pre-contractual liability requires parties to negotiate with transparency and integrity to avoid legal repercussions, particularly in international transactions where differing legal practices may lead to misunderstandings. Pre-contractual liability in China mandates good faith negotiations and penalises bad faith conduct, intentional concealment, and other dishonest behaviour. While

---

286. *Wen Bin v. Yunnan Radio and Television Real Estate Development Co., Ltd.*, The SPC (2020) SPC Civil Zai No. 194; 文斌、云南广电房地产开发有限公司缔约过失责任纠纷案，最高人民法院（2020）最高法民再194号
287. Alexander Loke. Pre-contractual Liability through the Looking Glass of the Common Law, in Chinese Contract Law: Civil and Common Law Perspectives 190-212 (DiMatteo LA and Lei C eds., Cambridge University Press 2017).
288. Crabb V. Arun DC (1976) 1 Ch 179.

the Civil Code does not explicitly regulate third-party liability, it does address third-party actions involving fraud or coercion that lead to the nullification of a contract. Under Article 157, after a contract is rescinded, the injured party may assert pre-contractual negligence liability against the third party responsible for fraud or coercion. This indirect acknowledgement of third-party liability marks a significant development, though such liability is often classified as tortious.

308. Through judicial decisions and academic contributions, the interpretation of pre-contractual liability in China continues to evolve, reflecting the commitment to ethical standards in commercial transactions. Comparatively, China's approach differs from common law systems, highlighting its distinct methods of protecting negotiating parties.

II. Preliminary Contracts

309. In contract negotiations, two common scenarios arise. The first involves extensive negotiations leading to the creation of a final contract. The second occurs when parties reach an interim agreement on certain terms and formalise these points in a preliminary agreement, signalling their intention to continue negotiations toward a final contract.

310. In the first scenario, Article 500 of the Civil Code applies directly, focusing on bad faith behaviour. In the second scenario, the key question is whether the preliminary agreement is legally binding.

311. Article 495 of the Civil Code clarifies that, under Chinese law, a preliminary contract is an agreement where the parties commit to entering into a contract within a specified period.[289] Documents such as subscription agreements, purchase orders, and reservation agreements to enter into a contract within a specified future period or provide earnest money/security deposit to secure the future conclusion of a contract, and the key elements of the future contract, such as the parties and the subject matter, can be clearly determined, constitute a binding preliminary contract.[290]

312. Does it mean that subscription agreements, purchase orders, or reservation agreements automatically constitute preliminary contracts (预约合同) simply because they are labelled as pre-agreements? It may well be the case that these documents merely express an intention to contract rather than agree to enter into a contract within a specified future period. In such circumstances, they may not have legal binding force as contracts.[291]

289. Article 495 CC.
290. Paragraph 1 of Art. 6 of the SPC Interpretation on the Contract Book (2023).
291. Paragraph 2 of Art. 6 of the SPC Interpretation on the Contract Book (2023).

313. Therefore, documents like Letters of Intent (LoI) and Memoranda of Understanding (MoU), are often taken as non-binding. Where the parties, through signing a Letter of Intent (LOI) or MoU, only express their intention to enter into a transaction without agreeing to enter into a contract within a specified period in the future, it is not taken as a preliminary contract.[292] In other words, the courts will look into the substance of the LOI instead of the title the parties choose to label.

314. A preliminary contract is binding, so it must naturally meet the requirements for contract formation. In other words, for a preliminary contract to be established, its terms must be clear and specific. If the parties fail to agree on essential terms such as the subject matter, quantity, price, or remuneration, it cannot be deemed a valid preliminary contract.[293] This raises a critical question: if a preliminary contract includes agreements on these essential elements, what distinguishes it from the main contract?

315. The distinction lies in the level of detail in the contractual terms. While a preliminary contract may specify the subject matter, price, or remuneration, it often lacks detailed terms such as payment methods, guarantees, the creation and arrangement of related contracts, dispute resolution clauses, or other substantive provisions. Therefore, it is less comprehensive than the main contract.

316. It is essential to underline why parties might choose to sign a preliminary contract rather than directly entering into the main contract. First, the conditions for concluding the main contract may not yet be fully matured. Second, the parties may wish to avoid prematurely committing to the main contract, which could leave them in a disadvantaged position. By signing a preliminary contract, they retain the right to decide whether to finalise the main contract. Thus, a preliminary contract arises in situations where the parties have agreed on the essential terms required for contract formation but have not yet reached a consensus on all substantive matters of mutual concern.

317. The core characteristic of a preliminary contract is that it grants legally binding force to the results of phased negotiations while requiring the parties to agree on all substantive matters of mutual concern to complete the transaction. Considering that a preliminary contract already satisfies the requirements for contract formation, if the parties do not explicitly state within the agreement that they will enter a future main contract, or if such an agreement exists but one party has already performed, and the other party has accepted the performance, the document should not be regarded as a preliminary contract but instead as the main contract itself.[294]

318. The formation of a contract is a process with distinct stages. As transactions become increasingly complex, this staged nature of contract formation becomes more pronounced, placing higher demands on the density of legal rules.

292. Article 6 of the SPC Interpretation on the Contract Book (2023).
293. *Ibid.*
294. Paragraph 3 of Art. 6 of the SPC Interpretation on the Contract Book (2023).

This is because parties in different stages of a transaction require varying levels of protection to ensure the security of their dealings.

319. After a preliminary contract comes into effect, its binding nature obligates the parties to act in good faith and cooperate in concluding the main contract as agreed. When one party refuses to conclude the main contract or violates the principle of good faith during negotiations, such as by delaying negotiations, introducing unreasonable terms, or acting in a manner contrary to the agreed purpose of the preliminary contract, such party has breached their obligations under the preliminary contract.[295]

320. This breach can have significant legal implications. The non-defaulting party may seek remedies such as compensation for damages caused by the breach of the preliminary contract. These damages could include expenses incurred during the negotiation process or lost opportunities that arise from the failure to conclude the main contract. The remedy is not merely punitive but also ensures that the non-defaulting party's legitimate expectations are safeguarded.

321. The principle of good faith, enshrined in Chinese civil law, serves as a fundamental guideline in this context. It requires that parties not only comply with the express terms of the preliminary contract but also conduct themselves in a manner that aligns with the trust and cooperation inherent in contractual obligations. For example, the relevant factors in determining whether this party violates the principle of good faith are whether the conditions proposed by that party during the negotiations significantly deviate from the terms agreed upon in the preliminary contract or whether the party has made reasonable efforts to engage in good-faith discussions.[296] For instance, if a party introduces terms during the negotiations that are materially inconsistent with the preliminary agreement – such as altering the agreed-upon price, scope of performance, or timelines without justification – this could be deemed as acting in bad faith. Similarly, a lack of active participation in the negotiation process, such as deliberate delays or unresponsiveness, may also constitute a breach of the principle. As a result, the more comprehensive the preliminary contract, the stronger the obligation to proceed in good faith toward concluding the main contract.

322. For the damages due to the breach of a preliminary contract, if the parties have an agreement on the scope or method of compensation, the court shall respect that agreement.[297] In the absence of such an agreement, the court should determine the compensation amount by comprehensively considering factors such as the completeness of the preliminary contract's content and the extent to which the conditions for concluding the main contract have been fulfilled.[298]

295. Paragraph 1 of Art. 7 of the SPC Interpretation on the Contract Book (2023).
296. Paragraph 2 of Art. 7 of the SPC Interpretation on the Contract Book (2023).
297. Article 8 of the SPC Interpretation on the Contract Book (2023).
298. *Ibid.*

323. The completeness of the preliminary contract refers to the extent to which the contract has specified essential terms such as the subject matter, quantity, price, and other key provisions. A more detailed preliminary contract increases the predictability of the main contract's terms, which in turn strengthens the basis for assessing losses caused by non-performance.

324. The extent to which conditions for the main contract are fulfilled refers to the degree of readiness for the main contract's conclusion. For example, where external approvals, technical verifications, or procedural conditions have been met, the non-fulfilment of the main contract by one party may cause greater losses for the other party, justifying higher compensation.

325. Nonetheless, whether the damages arising from a breach of a preliminary contract are to cover the expectation loss or reliance loss is not addressed directly by the SPC. Differing views arise. In some cases, it was held that 'when determining the scope of compensation for such liability, it should be limited to the reliance interest losses incurred by the counterparty. This does not include loss of opportunity or anticipated profits'.[299] However, in another case, the courts held that 'if one party fails to fulfil their obligations of a preliminary contractual nature, they shall compensate the counterparty for expectation interest, meaning the losses corresponding to the benefits the counterparty would have gained if the contract had been performed.[300]

326. In a judgment handed down by the SPC, it was held that the damages for breach of a preliminary contract shall follow the general rules for liability for breach of contract. The scope of damages includes all losses caused by the breach.[301] Where the amount of loss is difficult to calculate, it should be determined based on the foreseeability of the loss at the time the preliminary contract was signed, adhering to the principle of compensation for actual loss. It further reasoned that the court should consider various factors, including the degree of fault of the breaching party, the performance efforts of the non-breaching party, reasonable costs incurred, opportunity costs of the main contract, the content of the preliminary contract, the

---

299. *Cao Canru v. Shanghai Lines Real Estate Co., Ltd.*, No. 2 Intermediate People's Court of Shanghai (2010) Hu Er Zhong Min Er (Civil) Zhong Zi No.609; 曹灿如与上海莱因思置业有限公司, 上海二中院（2010）沪二中民二（民）终字第609; *Zhang Jun and Xi'an Daniel Real Estate Development Co., Ltd*, Shaanxi Province Xi'an Intermediate People's Court (2009) Xi Min Er Zhong Zi No.1376; 张军与西安丹尼尔房地产开发有限公司买卖合同纠纷案，陕西省西安市中级人民法院（2009）西民二终字第1376号; *Cheng Meiju v. Jiangxi Huirong Real Estate Investment and Development Co., Ltd.* Jiangxi High People's Court (2016) Gan Civil Zai No.46; 程美菊与江西惠荣房地产投资开发有限公司商品房预约合同纠纷案， 江西省高级人民法院 （2016）赣民再46号.

300. *Beijing Yougaoya Decoration Engineering Co., Ltd. v. Beijing Henry Dai Art Furniture Co., Ltd. Beijing No.* 2 Intermediate People's Court Er Zhong Min Zhong Zi No.01756; 北京优高雅装饰工程有限公司诉北京亨利戴艺术家具有限公司， 北京二中院（2007）二中民终字第01756号.

301. *Huang Wengui v. Beijing Ningke Real Estate Co., Ltd.* The SPC (2019) SPC Min Shen No.2868; 黄文贵、北京宁科置业有限责任公司房屋买卖合同纠纷案， 最高人民法院（2019）最高法民申2826号.

parties' intention to conclude the main contract, objective obstacles, market risks, policy factors, and other reasons that led to the failure to conclude the main contract. Based on these considerations, the court should determine the amount of loss at its discretion.[302]

327. To summarise, for preliminary contracts, the calculation of losses is often complex due to the uncertainty surrounding the main contract. Courts typically adopt a discretionary approach, relying on evidence such as the nature and detail of the preliminary contract's terms and the parties' demonstrated intent to proceed with the main contract.[303] In cases where the amount of loss is particularly difficult to calculate, courts may limit damages to reliance interest, avoiding speculative awards for expectation interest. This approach ensures fairness while recognising the unique transitional role of preliminary contracts. Compensation for breach of a preliminary contract reflects the complexity of balancing reliance and expectation interests. Courts must exercise discretion by considering the foreseeability of losses, the degree of fault, and the unique context of each case.

328. In conclusion, a party's refusal to fulfil the obligations of a preliminary contract or their bad faith actions during negotiations not only constitutes a breach of the preliminary agreement but also undermines the broader principle of good faith, which is fundamental to maintaining fairness and trust in contractual relationships. The courts, therefore, play a crucial role in ensuring that such breaches are addressed appropriately, protecting the integrity of contractual commitments and the interests of the non-defaulting party.

III. Compensation for Pre-contractual Liability

329. While there may be disputes among the parties about whether they should bear pre-contractual liability, the most challenging aspect, in practice, is defining the scope of compensation for pre-contractual liability. The compensation in such cases typically covers the reliance losses suffered by the party that reasonably relied on the conduct of the breaching party during the negotiation phase. This can include actual expenses incurred, such as travel costs, preparation costs, legal fees, and lost opportunities, but it generally does not cover the expected interest losses that would have been realised had the contract been concluded.

330. Compensation for pre-contractual liability is different from damages due to a breach of a preliminary contract. A preliminary contract is taken as a binding contract. Unlike damages for a breach of contract, pre-contractual liability usually does not cover expectation losses – the profit or benefit the non-breaching party expected to gain from the contract. Courts often assess whether the aggrieved party had reasonable grounds to believe that the contract would be finalised and whether the

302. *Ibid.*
303. Guixiang Liu, Issues Regarding the Formation of Contracts, 4 Law Application (Fa Lv Shi Yong) 3 (2022).

expenses incurred were directly tied to that belief. The court's focus is on protecting the integrity of negotiations and ensuring that parties act in good faith, even if the contract is not ultimately concluded.

331. When determining the scope of property restitution or compensation following the non-formation, invalidation, or rescission of a contract, the distribution must be done reasonably between the parties in accordance with the principle of good faith. The non-performing party should not be allowed to benefit from the non-formation, invalidation, or rescission of the contract.[304] The pre-contractual liability borne by the parties in such circumstances should not exceed the performance interest of the contract.[305] For example, according to if a construction contract is deemed invalid, but the construction project has been completed and passed inspection, payment for the project may be made with reference to the contract.[306] However, unless new projects beyond the contract's original scope have been added, the payment generally should not exceed the amount stipulated in the contract.[307]

332. Both reliance interest and expectation interest encompass loss of opportunity interest, but the key distinction lies in the timing. Loss of opportunity interest in reliance interest pertains to opportunities lost at the time of contracting, while in expectation interest, it refers to opportunities lost during performance.

333. For example, Mr Li was negotiating to purchase a house from Ms Wang when Mr Zhang falsely claimed to offer his house to Mr Li at a low price, engaging in malicious negotiations. As a result, Mr Li missed the chance to finalise a contract with Ms Wang. This illustrates how loss of opportunity interest can arise at different stages of the contractual process.

334. Suppose Mr Li and Ms Wang initially agreed on a price of RMB 2 million, but due to Mr Zhang's interference, Mr Li signed a contract with Ms Wang for RMB 2.2 million. Ms Wang then sold the house to Ms Chen for RMB 2.5 million, breaching her contract with Mr Li. As a result, Mr Li had to buy a similar house from Mr Sun for RMB 2.5 million.

335. In this case, Mr Li is entitled to claim breach liability from Ms Wang and seek compensation for the loss of performance interest, which includes the loss of opportunity interest. This opportunity loss would amount to RMB 300,000 (RMB 2.5 million deducts RMB 2.2 million), representing the difference between the price Mr Li paid and the contract price with Ms Wang. Additionally, Mr Li could have originally negotiated a deal with Ms Wang for RMB 2 million but signed at RMB

304. Article 32 (2) of the SPC Trial Minutes (2019).
305. *Ibid.*
306. Article 2 of the SPC Interpretation on the Application of Law in the Trial of Construction Contract Disputes.
307. *Ibid.*

2.2 million due to Mr Zhang's interference. Mr Zhang should, therefore, compensate Mr Li for the loss of opportunity interest caused by his interference, amounting to RMB 200,000 (RMB 2.2 million deducts RMB 2 million).

336. It is important to note that whether the loss pertains to expectation interest or reliance interest if the loss of opportunity is recoverable, the costs incurred by the parties to obtain this opportunity should not be included in the compensation. For instance, if Mr Li seeks RMB 200,000 in reliance interest from Mr Zhang, any costs incurred to secure that opportunity should not be part of the claim.

337. To summarise, compensation typically covers reliance losses, including actual expenses like travel, legal fees, and preparation costs incurred during negotiations. However, expectation losses – the profit a party expected if the contract had been concluded – are generally not included. Compensation is limited to foreseeable losses at the time of the breach. Courts assess whether the breaching party could reasonably foresee the damages and whether the aggrieved party had reasonable grounds to believe the contract would be finalised. The focus is on good faith and preventing any party from unfairly benefiting from the non-formation or invalidation of a contract.

338. Both reliance interest and expectation interest include loss of opportunity interest, but the timing differs: reliance interest focuses on the opportunity lost at the time of contracting, while expectation interest looks at the opportunity lost during performance. It can be concluded from the above scenario that the costs incurred to secure the opportunity should not be included in compensation for opportunity interest.

Chapter 2. Validity

§1. Legislative Development of Contract Validity

339. The Economic CCL, effective on 1 July 1982, and the Foreign Economic CCL, effective on 1 July 1985, adopted a dichotomy of valid and invalid contracts and made specific provisions on the circumstances under which contracts are considered invalid.[308] The GPCL, effective 1 January 1987, defined civil legal acts as 'legal acts by citizens or legal persons to establish, change, or terminate civil rights and obligations'.[309] The GPCL adopted a model with four different types: valid contracts, invalid contracts, voidable contracts, and contracts' effectiveness to be determined.[310]

340. The CCL, which was introduced in 1999, provided regulations on the effectiveness of contracts in a special chapter (Chapter Three), adopting a model with five different types: valid contracts, invalid contracts,[311] voidable contracts,[312] contracts' effectiveness to be determined,[313] and contracts not yet effective.[314] Specifically, there are three situations where the validity of a contract is to be determined or pending: contracts signed by persons with limited civil capacity, contracts signed without proper authorisation, and contracts signed by individuals lacking a right of disposal. In addition, the contract not yet effective refers to a situation where laws or administrative regulations prescribe that procedures such as approval or registration shall be completed for effectiveness, and such provisions shall apply.[315]

341. Compared with the GPCL, the CCL narrowed the scope of invalid contracts. For example, contracts entered into by persons with limited civil capacity were regarded as invalid under the GPCL[316] and have become voidable under the CCL.[317] Additionally, under the GPCL, a contract is invalid when it violates a statutory provision in laws or social public interest.[318] Under the CCL, a caveat is cautioned that only contracts that violate mandatory provisions of laws or administrative regulations are invalid.[319]

308. Article 7 of the Economic CCL; Arts 9 and 10 of the Foreign Economic CCL.
309. Article 54 of the GPCL.
310. Articles 55, 58, 59, 66 of the GPCL.
311. Article 52 of the CCL.
312. Articles 54 and 55 of the CCL.
313. Articles 47, 48 and 51 of the CCL.
314. Article 44 of the CCL.
315. Paragraph 2 of Art. 44 of the CCL.
316. Article 58 (2) of the GPCL.
317. Article 47 of the CCL.
318. Article 55 of the GPCL.
319. Article 52 of the CCL.

342. The Civil Code further narrowed the scope of invalid contracts by providing an exception to the invalidity of legal acts resulting from violations of mandatory provisions of laws and administrative regulations.[320] As a matter of principle, a civil juridical act violating any mandatory provision of law or administrative regulation is void. However, a caveat states, 'unless the mandatory provision in question does not lead to the voidness of the civil juridical act'.[321] This is significant as it implies that even when a contract violates a mandatory provision of law, it may not be invalid. It is still necessary to examine whether such a violation of mandatory legal provisions renders the contract invalid. This essentially introduces a proportionality test to look into the individual circumstances of each case. Therefore, this gives the SPC a space to introduce a judicial interpretation in this regard.[322]

343. Second, the Civil Code changed from 'infringing upon social public interests' as grounds for invalidating a contract under the CCL[323] to 'contravening public order and social morals'.[324] This begs the question of to what extent the ambit of public order and social morals is narrower than one of social public interest. This remains to be seen when the Chinese courts handed down more rulings.

344. Third, while deleting the provision that contracts are invalid if they conceal illegal purposes under a legal form under the CCL,[325] The Civil Code introduced a provision that legal acts with fraudulent misrepresentations are invalid. However, the effectiveness of hidden legal acts should be handled according to relevant laws.[326] As a result, it seems that where there is a hidden contract, it is not considered invalid anymore. A nuanced approach is taken to investigate whether the concealed contract is invalid per Article 153 of the Civil Code.

345. After the Civil Code was enacted, the SPC conducted a comprehensive review of its previous judicial interpretations in line with the Civil Code. It has gone through a tidying-up process in line with the Civil Code. Specifically, the SPC modified the *Interpretation on Issues Concerning the Application of Law in the Trial of Disputes over Sales Contracts* by deleting Article 3, which pertains to the invalidity of contracts due to lack of disposal rights.[327]

346. In addition, the SPC revised its Interpretation on the Application of Laws in the Adjudication of Disputes over Contracts concerning State-owned Land Use Rights (2005, 2020 revision) (the 'SPC Interpretation on State-owned Land Use

---

320. Paragraph 1 of Art. 153 CC.
321. *Ibid.*
322. Articles 16,17 and 18 of the *SPC Interpretation on the Contract Book (2023).*
323. Article 52 (4) of the CCL.
324. Paragraph 2 of Art. 153 CC.
325. Article 52 (3) of the CCL.
326. Article 146 CC.
327. Article 3 of the SPC Interpretation on Issues Concerning the Application of Law in the Trial of Disputes over Sales Contracts (2012, 2020 revision).

Rights Contracts (2020)') by removing Article 11, which declares contracts for the transfer of land use rights without approval as invalid.[328]

347. Furthermore, the SPC amended the Reply on Issues concerning Whether State-owned Transferred Land Use Rights of Bankrupt Enterprises Should be Included in Bankruptcy Property (2002), changing the provision regarding the invalidity of mortgages on transferred land use rights without approval to state that lack of approval does not affect the validity of contracts.[329] Furthermore, it clarified that 'State-owned enterprises mortgaging key equipment, complete sets of equipment, or buildings should not be deemed invalid solely due to lack of approval by the competent government department unless there are other statutory grounds for invalidity.'[330]

348. It is worth mentioning that the *SPC Interpretation on Certain Issues of Security System Concerning the Application of the Civil Code (2020)* (the 'SPC Interpretation on Security System (2020)'). It provides numerous provisions concerning the determination of the effectiveness of guarantee contracts:

1. A legal representative's provision of guarantees without the company's resolution, in violation of Article 16 of the Company Law,[331] constitutes unauthorised representation. Except in cases of apparent representation, such acts do not bind the company.[332] It also specifies situations where no company resolution is required and the effectiveness of guarantees provided by listed companies.[333]
2. The use of property with unclear or disputed ownership or property lawfully seized, detained, or supervised as collateral does not affect the validity of the mortgage contract.[334]
3. Mortgages on illegally constructed buildings are void unless legal procedures are completed before the conclusion of the first-instance court debate. Where

---

328. Article 11 of the SPC Interpretation on the Application of Laws in the Adjudication of Disputes over Contracts concerning State-owned Land Use Rights (2005, 2020 revision).
329. The Reply on Issues concerning Whether State-owned Transferred Land Use Rights of Bankrupt Enterprises Should be Included in Bankruptcy Property. This judicial interpretation addresses the treatment of state owned transferred land use rights in bankruptcy proceedings, providing clarity on their inclusion as bankruptcy assets.
330. *Ibid.*
331. Article 16 of the Company Law provides when a company intends to provide a guarantee for another party, the following rules apply: For a limited liability company, the provision of a guarantee must be approved by a resolution of its board of directors, shareholders' meeting, or shareholders' assembly, depending on the specific corporate governance structure. For a joint stock company, any guarantee provided must be approved by a resolution of its board of directors or shareholders' general meeting in accordance with its articles of association. If the company provides a guarantee for a shareholder or an actual controller, the matter must be resolved by the shareholders' meeting or the general shareholders' assembly. The shareholder or the actual controller involved in the matter cannot participate in the voting process.
332. Article 7 of the SPC Interpretation on Certain Issues of Security System Concerning the Application of the Civil Code (2020).
333. Articles 8 and 9 of the SPC Interpretation on Security System (2020).
334. Article 37 of the SPC Interpretation on Security System (2020).

a party claims invalidity of a mortgage contract due to illegally constructed buildings on land mortgaged for land use rights, the contract will remain valid if the necessary legal procedures are finalised in time.[335]

4. If a mortgagor mortgages buildings on allocated construction land or mortgages allocated land use rights, the mortgage contract will remain valid even if issues such as the inability to mortgage the land use rights or lack of approval procedures are raised.[336]

349. The validity of a contract is governed by Article 143 of the Civil Code, which sets out the general requirements for the validity of civil legal acts. A civil legal act is considered valid if it meets three conditions: (1) the actor possesses civil capacity; (2) the expression of intent is genuine; and (3) the act complies with mandatory provisions of laws or administrative regulations and does not contravene public order or good morals.[337] When these criteria are met, the law recognises and protects the outcomes of such actions.

350. On the contrary, the legal grounds for contract invalidity are found in Articles 144, 146, 153, and 154 of the Civil Code. The four articles, as mentioned earlier, specify five reasons for contract invalidity:

1. Civil legal acts performed by individuals lacking the capacity for civil conduct are invalid.[338]
2. Acts of deception in collusion are invalid.[339]
3. Civil legal acts that violate mandatory provisions of laws or administrative regulations are invalid.[340]
4. Civil legal acts that contravene public order and good morals are invalid.[341]
5. Civil legal acts conducted by collusion between the actor and the counterparty, causing harm to the legitimate rights and interests of others, are invalid.[342]

351. From the GPCL in 1986 to the Civil Code in 2020, rules on invalid civil juridical acts have remained consistent. The overarching trend reflects an increasing respect for party autonomy in civil matters, coupled with a cautious approach to invalidating civil legal acts.

335. Article 49 of the SPC Interpretation on Security System (2020).
336. Article 50 of the SPC Interpretation on Security System (2020).
337. Article 143 CC
338. Article 144 CC.
339. Article 146 CC.
340. Article 153 (1) CC.
341. Article 153 (2) CC.
342. Article 154 CC.

§2. CAPACITY OF THE PARTIES

352. The law imposes limits on the capacity of certain persons to bind themselves by contract to protect individuals who may lack the ability to understand the nature and consequences of their actions or to safeguard broader societal interests. These limitations are typically applied to categories such as minors, persons with mental incapacities, and those under legal guardianship.

353. Hence, acts undertaken by individuals lacking the capacity for civil conduct are deemed invalid, and their consequences are neither recognised nor protected, even if the act appears solely beneficial to the individual.[343] For instance, a contract signed on behalf of an infant would be considered void.

354. There are two categories of persons with limited capacity. First, minors over eight who lack full capacity for civil conduct are individuals with restricted capacity. They often lack full contractual capacity, with contracts entered into by minors being voidable or requiring ratification by their statutory agents, such as a parent or guardian.[344] However, they may independently conduct civil legal acts solely for their benefit or appropriate to their age and intelligence.[345] This rule protects minors from exploitation while allowing them to engage in necessary or beneficial transactions, such as purchasing everyday essentials.

355. Second, adults who cannot fully understand their actions are individuals with restricted capacity for civil conduct.[346] Their civil legal acts are represented by their statutory agents or require the consent or ratification of their statutory agents.[347] Persons with mental incapacities may be restricted from forming legally binding agreements if they are unable to understand the contract's implications due to conditions such as mental illness. Contracts made under such circumstances may be deemed void or voidable to prevent unfair advantage. However, they may independently conduct civil legal acts solely for their benefit or appropriate to their intelligence and mental health status.[348]

356. Chinese law allows persons with limited civil capacity (8 years old) to receive rewards, donations or payments, reflecting its acceptance of non-reciprocal contracts.[349] If such individuals exceed their capacity, their actions need approval or affirmation from their legal representative.[350] Whether to affirm or negate the act's effectiveness is solely at the discretion of the statutory agent. Before the consent or ratification of the statutory agent, the effectiveness of such acts remains

343. Article 144 CC provides that 'civil legal actions carried out by individuals lacking capacity for civil conduct are invalid.'
344. Article 23 CC.
345. Article 19 CC.
346. Article 22 CC.
347. *Ibid.*
348. Paragraph 1 of Art. 145 CC.
349. Article 19 CC.
350. *Ibid.*

uncertain, and this state of uncertainty should not persist indefinitely. The Civil Code grants the relative party the right of notification to avoid prolonged uncertainty and safeguard transaction security. By sending a notice to the statutory agent, the counterparty may urge the statutory agent to ratify it within thirty days from the date the statutory agent receives such notice.[351]

357. The statutory agent's silence is seen as his or her refusal of ratification.[352] This is because when the statutory agent does not express an opinion on ratification, it implies a passive and neglectful attitude towards the effectiveness of ratification. In such cases, it should be considered a refusal to ratify; thus, the act does not take legal effect. The bona fide counterparty can rescind the juridical act if the rescission is done before the ratification.[353]

358. Under Chinese law, civil conduct, including a contract, can be rescinded because of a 'lack of judgment'.[354] What amounts to a lack of judgment is articulated by the SPC, which states that if one party is a natural person, based on the age, intelligence, knowledge, and experience of that party, and considering the complexity of the transaction, if it can be determined that the individual lacks the necessary cognitive ability regarding the nature of the contract, the legal consequences of entering into the contract, or specific risks in the transaction, it causes the 'lack of judgment'.[355]

359. To summarise, except for civil legal acts purely for obtaining benefits or civil legal acts suitable for their age, intelligence, and mental condition, the implementation of civil legal acts by persons with limited capacity shall require the consent or ratification of their statutory agents.[356] Consent is a prior and explicit acknowledgement, while ratification is a subsequent acknowledgement.

§3. Defects of Consent

I. A Sham Manifestation of Intent

360. Recently, cases of collusive false representations in commercial litigation have risen significantly. These include sham contracts in construction, real estate

351. Paragraph 2 of Art. 145 CC.
352. *Ibid.*
353. *Ibid.*
354. Article 151 CC provides that the aggrieved party has the power to rescind the civil juridical act which is obviously unfair at the moment of its formation via the People's Court or arbitral tribunal, as long as the counterparty takes advantage of the aggrieved party's distress, lack of judgement, or other similar circumstances.
355. Article 11 of the SPC Interpretation on the Contract Book (2023).
356. Article 5 of the SPC Interpretation on the General Provisions of Civil Code states that civil legal acts performed by persons with limited capacity for civil conduct must align with their age, intelligence, and mental health. Courts may assess this alignment by considering the extent to which the act relates to their daily life, their ability to understand their actions and foresee consequences, and factors such as the subject matter, quantity, price, or remuneration.

transactions, and financial agreements such as letters of credit, factoring, financial leasing, and trusts. Courts handling such cases face challenges in three key areas: identifying the parties' true intentions, nullifying the sham contract, and characterising and evaluating concealed actions.

361. To address this issue, Article 146 of the Civil Code establishes a legal framework for collusive sham representations, drawing inspiration from Article 117 of the German Civil Code (BGB) on Scheingeschäft (sham transactions).[357] This provision replaces the earlier rule under the GPCL and CCL regarding 'legally valid forms concealing illegal purposes'. It distinguishes between acts based on false representations of intent and the concealed actions they aim to obscure.

362. A juridical act carried out by an actor and the counterparty based on a sham manifestation of intent is void.[358] Civil legal acts implemented with false expressions of intent are collusive sham representations. They refer to false civil legal acts that the actor and counterparty jointly implement with a false expression of intent for a specific purpose. For example, falsely donating property to evade debts, falsely fabricating a divorce to evade real estate fees, and falsely divorcing to circumvent the housing purchase restriction policy. These acts do not have a true expression of intent, so the law intervenes in the legal effects of such acts to ensure normal civil order. Specifically, the purpose of the collusion is to deceive a third party, such as a creditor or a government agency. The collusion must be between two or more parties. The false expression of intent must be material to the civil legal act.

363. The elements constituting collusive sham representations include (1) the presence of intentional expressions of intent, (2) a discrepancy between the intended purpose and the expressed behaviour, (3) intentional collusion between the party expressing intent and the counterparty, and (4) the mutual knowledge of collusion between the expressing party and the counterparty.

364. In practice, collusive sham representations can be successfully invoked in three situations. First, contracting parties may admit that their contract is a sham driven by their litigation interests and the desire to mitigate or evade legal liabilities. This phenomenon is prevalent in factoring disputes, particularly when creditors and debtors confess to the fictitious nature of debts to evade payment obligations to the factor.[359] Courts typically give careful consideration, and sometimes even adopt, the self-acknowledgement made by the parties involved. However, the court holds ultimate decision-making authority on this matter. If the court's

357. Article 117 of BGB on Sham transaction: (1) If a declaration of intent that is to be made to another person is, with his consent, only made for the sake of appearance, it is void. (2) If a sham transaction hides another legal transaction, the provisions applicable to the hidden transaction apply.

358. Paragraph 1 of Art. 146 CC.

359. *China Xiamen Construction Group Co., Ltd. v. China Construction Bank Corporation Shanghai Second Branch*, the Supreme People's Court, (2019) SPC Min Shen 1518; 中国建设银行股份有限公司上海第二支行诉中厦建设集团有限公司， 最高人民法院（2019）最高法民申1518号.

findings differ from the admissions made by the parties, the court's determination prevails. This aligns with standard rules regarding litigation evidence.

365. Second, it is found in transactions that defy commercial logic. This often occurs in circular trading arrangements. In such scenarios, the involved parties form a complete closed-loop transaction chain, where one party both sells and buys, accepting losses willingly, which is inconsistent with the role of profit-making entities. Additionally, these transactions typically involve only the circulation of funds without actual delivery of goods. Therefore, such circular trading activities are not buying and selling but financing or lending transactions.[360]

366. Third, it can be found where there is non-conformity between actual performance and contractual terms. *In Shenyang Huajin Real Estate Co., Ltd. v. Shenyang Sujiatun District People's Government & Shenyang Municipal Bureau of Natural Resources Sujiatun Branch*,[361] on 13 September 2011, the Defendant and the Claimant, the District government agency of Shenyang, signed the 'Contract for the Assignment of the Right to Use State-owned Construction Land' and agreed:

> Article 6: The transferor agrees to deliver the assigned parcel to the transferee before September 1, 2011, and the parcel should meet the land conditions specified in item (1) of this article when the land is delivered:
>
> > Article 37: The transferor must deliver the transferred land on time under the Contract. If not, for each day of extension, the transferor shall pay the transferee liquidated damages at 1‰ of the transfer price of the state-owned construction land use right paid by the transferee, and the land use period shall be calculated from the date of actual delivery of the land. If the land delivery exceeds 60 days, the transferee shall have the right to terminate the Contract, and the transferor shall return double the deposit and return the rest of the transfer price paid to compensate for the loss.

367. On 21 September 2011, the Defendant obtained the State-owned Land Use Certificate. However, some buildings on the land had not been expropriated or demolished at the time, delaying delivery of that portion of the land to Defendant. The first-instance court ruled that the government agency must pay Huajin Company RMB 50 million in liquidated damages for the delay. On appeal, the second-instance court reduced the amount to RMB 36.89 million. Upon retrial, the SPC found that the contract, signed on 13 September 2011, stipulated a land delivery deadline of 1 September 2011. Since the land did not meet delivery standards at the

360. *Coal Sales Department of Rizhao Port Group Co., Ltd. v. Shanxi Coking Coal Group International Development Co., Ltd.*, the Supreme People's Court, (2015) SPC Min Ti No. 74; 日照港集团有限公司煤炭运销部诉山西焦煤集团国际发展股份有限公司，最高人民法院（2015）民提字第74号.

361. *Shenyang Huajin Real Estate Co., Ltd. v. Shenyang Sujiatun District People's Government & Shenyang Municipal Bureau of Natural Resources Sujiatun Branch*, the Supreme People's Court, (2021) SPC Min Zai No. 351; 沈阳华锦置业有限公司诉沈阳市苏家屯区人民政府、沈阳市自然资源局苏家屯分局，最高人民法院（2021）最高法民再351号.

time of signing, the breach had already occurred. The SPC held that the clauses concerning the delivery deadline and liability for the delay did not reflect the parties' true intentions.

368. The SPC concluded that the clauses regarding the land delivery deadline and liquidated damages were collusive false representations by both parties. It overruled the first and second-instance judgments, holding the government agency liable for damages capped at RMB 11 million.

369. Two related questions arise: how should the validity of a hidden contract be determined? Should it automatically be deemed invalid due to the collusive sham representation? Article 146(2) of the Civil Code states that the validity of a juridical act concealed behind a sham representation must be assessed according to relevant legal provisions.[362] Thus, hidden civil legal acts may be legal or illegal, depending on the applicable laws.

370. For example, in cases of tax evasion, parties may create a sham contract alongside a hidden contract that reflects their true agreement. The sham contract, often intended to deceive third parties like tax authorities or regulators, misrepresents the actual terms of the transaction. Courts will carefully evaluate factors such as the contract's background, purpose, structure, and parties involved to determine whether the contract's appearance aligns with the actual circumstances. The legal effect of a hidden contract based on the parties' true intentions can be categorised further based on its compliance with legal provisions.

371. Where the parties use false expressions of intent to conceal their true intentions in an attempt to circumvent mandatory provisions of laws or administrative regulations, the hidden contract shall be deemed invalid if it violates such provisions. However, if the mandatory provisions do not expressly render the civil legal act invalid, the hidden contract may still be considered valid.[363]

372. Where the parties use false expressions of intent to conceal their true intentions to circumvent laws and administrative regulations requiring contract approval, the contract must still undergo the necessary approval procedures. If the lack of approval affects the contract's effectiveness, it will be deemed not to have come into effect. However, this does not affect the validity of clauses requiring the completion of approval procedures or other related provisions within the contract.[364]

373. The invalidity of hidden contracts that breach public order and good morals under Article 153(2) underscores the Civil Code's emphasis on aligning private agreements with broader societal interests.[365] This principle ensures that contracts not only serve the parties' intentions but also adhere to ethical and legal standards

362. Paragraph 2 of Art. 146 CC.
363. Article 14 of the SPC Interpretation on the Contract Book.
364. *Ibid.*
365. Paragraph 2 of Art. 153 CC.

essential for a well-functioning society. Courts play a critical role in identifying and invalidating such contracts to preserve public trust in the legal system.

374. When multiple contracts for the same transaction reflect the true intentions of the parties and no factors affect their validity, the court shall determine whether the contract terms have changed by examining the order of their establishment and actual performance. However, if laws or administrative regulations prohibit such changes, the court shall declare the changes invalid.[366]

375. Finally, it is notable that the invalid partial provisions due to collusive sham representations do not affect the contract's validity. For example, in the retrial case of *Shenzhen Hengchang Disheng Technology Co., Ltd. v. Xiamen Yongtongchang Investment Co., Ltd.*,[367] the SPC held that although the price clause of the 'Equity Transfer Agreement' signed by the parties in 2015 was not their true intent and thus invalid, the agreement served the purpose of implementing the 'Equity Transfer Agreement' signed by both parties in 2014. The clauses concerning equity transfer ratio, equity transfer registration, and other provisions in the 2015 agreement represented the genuine intentions of both parties. Therefore, while the price clause in the 2015 agreement was invalidated, the price stipulated in the 2014 agreement should apply, and it does not affect the overall legality and validity of the 2015 agreement. This ruling aligns with the relevant provisions of Article 156 of the Civil Code: Where the partial voidness of a civil juridical act does not affect the validity of the other part, the other part remains valid.[368]

II. Gross Misunderstanding

376. A civil legal act based on a gross misunderstanding refers to a legal act carried out by one party due to a gross misunderstanding of the content or nature of the legal act, resulting from their own fault. Such legal acts are considered voidable rather than void. Voidable civil legal acts possess three characteristics: first, they primarily involve legal acts with misrepresented intentions; second, the right to revoke such acts must be actively exercised by the party with the right of revocation; third, revocable civil legal acts remain valid until revoked.

377. The Civil Code does not adopt the concept of mistake as found in many other civil law and common law systems. Instead, it builds upon Article 59(1) of the GPCL 1986 by introducing the notion of gross misunderstanding in Article 147. The misunderstanding must be gross for the party expressing it. If the misunderstanding is not gross/material, the law does not permit the party to exercise the right

366. *Ibid.*
367. *Shenzhen Hengchang Disheng Technology Co., Ltd. v. Xiamen Yongtongchang Investment Co., Ltd.*, the Supreme People's Court (2018) SPC Min Shen No. 5290; 深圳市恒昌廸生科技有限公司诉厦门永同昌投资有限公司，最高人民法院（2018）最高法民申5290号.
368. Article 156 CC.

of rescission based on such misunderstanding. In such cases, where the misunderstanding has minimal impact on the party, the law favours protecting the counterparty's interests and ensuring transactional security. Otherwise, if parties were allowed to rescind contracts at will based on minor misunderstandings regarding the nature of the transaction, normal transactional order would be compromised.

378. The Civil Code provides that the mistaken actor has the power to rescind the civil juridical act done by gross misunderstanding via courts or arbitral tribunals.[369] The misunderstandings may pertain to the nature of the transaction, the identity of the counterparty, or the characteristics of the subject matter, including its variety, quality, specifications, price, quantity so on. For instance, mistaking a lease agreement for a loan agreement constitutes a misunderstanding of the transaction's nature; entering into a processing contract with Company A under the mistaken belief that it is Company B constitutes a misunderstanding of the counterparty; mistaking an artificial crystal for a natural diamond constitutes a misunderstanding of the subject matter.

379. However, due to the lack of a clear definition in the Civil Code, gross misunderstanding remains ambiguous, particularly regarding what constitutes 'gross', leading to uncertainty. Therefore, courts are left discretion to clarify under the specific circumstances of individual cases. To ensure consistency in judicial practice, the SPC provides guidelines for determining gross misunderstanding in Article 19 of the 'SPC Interpretation on the General Provisions of the Civil Code (2022)'.[370]

380. The SPC Interpretation on the General Provisions of the Civil Code (2022) clarifies that:

> If a party's actions stem from a misapprehension about the nature of the action, the identity of the other party, or the characteristics, quality, specifications, price, quantity so on., of the subject matter, and according to a common understanding, absent this misunderstanding, the party would not have made the same statement, the court may deem this as a gross misunderstanding under Article 147 of the Civil Code.[371]

381. The SPC Interpretation provision regarding gross misunderstanding is derived from the legal test outlined in Article 71 of the SPC Opinions on Several Issues Concerning the Implementation of the General Principles of Civil Law (For Trial Implementation, 1988) (the 'SPC Opinions on the Implementation of the GPCL (1988)'),[372] which states that:

369. Article 147 CC.
370. Article 19 of the SPC Interpretation on Several Issues Concerning the Application of the General Provisions of the Civil Code (2022).
371. Article 19(1) of the SPC Interpretation on the General Provisions of the Civil Code (2022).
372. The SPC Opinions on Several Issues Concerning the Implementation of the GPCL (1988).

> Where a party's mistaken understanding about the nature of the act, the counterparty, the type, quality, specifications, and quantity of the subject matter leads to outcomes contradictory to their intention and causes significant losses, it may be classified as a material misunderstanding.[373]

382. With scrutiny of the two versions, the remarkable changes in the SPC Inter pretation on the General Provisions of the Civil Code (2022) include the following:

1. First, the criteria for determining the significance of gross misunderstanding have been revised. Previously, it relied on causing significant losses.[374] However, it now hinges on whether, based on common understanding, the party would have made the same statement if the misunderstanding had not occurred.[375] This change departs from the previous emphasis on causing significant losses. The reason is twofold. First, it addresses the challenges in defining such losses. Second, gross misunderstanding should not depend on causing significant losses as a constitutive element. For instance, if a seller confuses the colour of an item desired by the buyer or selects the wrong bouquet for a holiday, even if no significant losses occur, the contract's purpose may still be frustrated, constituting gross misunderstanding.
2. Second, the new rule enhances the restrictions on rescission claims by explicitly delineating the burden of proof. The new rule mandates that a party asserting rescission of a civil legal act on the ground of gross misunderstanding must substantiate the existence of such misunderstanding at the time of taking action.[376] The party must proactively exercise this right and present it to the court or arbitration institution. In such a circumstance, the expressing party bears the burden of proof.[377]
3. Third, it should be noted that not all civil legal acts executed based on a gross misunderstanding will be revoked. For example, in transactions involving antiques, calligraphy, and artwork, where it is customary for buyers to rely on their own judgment, even if the material or age of the artwork does not meet their expectations, the buyer cannot claim to have experienced a gross misunderstanding. In such cases, the buyer has no right to request the revocation of the contract based on a significant misunderstanding. Acknowledging the distinctive nature of transactions like antique trading, it includes a provision exempting parties from seeking rescission based on gross misunderstanding in adherence to trade customs. Considering the particularity of trading customs

373. Article 71 of the SPC Opinions on the Implementation of the GPCL (1988).
374. However, some scholars still hold that under the Civil Code, the criterion of 'gross' is essentially consequentialist, i.e., defined by its outcomes by reference to Article 151. *See* Wei Shen, The Doctrine of Mistake and the Rule on Gross Misunderstanding in Chinese Contract Law, in Invalidity 29-48 (Mindy Chen-Wishart, Hiroo Sono, and Stefan Vogenauer eds., Oxford 2022).
375. Article 19(1) of the SPC Interpretation on the General Provisions of the Civil Code (2022).
376. Article 19(2) of the SPC Interpretation on the General Provisions of the Civil Code (2022).
377. *Ibid.*

for specific commodities, such an exception respects the principle of appearance in certain commercial activities and protects innocent counterparties' interests.[378]

383. Before the SPC guidance introduced the exception of trading customs, courts were cautious in applying the doctrine of gross misunderstanding due to the lack of specific actionable standards. It is anticipated that courts would rely on 'trade customs' as a criterion when applying this doctrine: misunderstanding falling outside the realm of trade custom interpretations may be considered gross misunderstandings, whereas misunderstanding consistent with trade custom interpretations may not meet the threshold and therefore might not be deemed gross misunderstandings. Benchmarking 'trade customs' for judicial discretion is an innovative and systematic approach to make judicial rulings predictable and consistent.

384. It is worth highlighting that the presence or absence of fault on the part of the expressing party, whether in good faith or otherwise, does not impact the right of a mistaken party to seek rescission based on a gross misunderstanding. However, deliberate actions by the expressing party to induce misunderstanding may most likely constitute fraud.

385. In cases of gross misunderstanding, the interests of the mistaken party acting in good faith are safeguarded in the consequences of rescinding civil legal acts, and the expressing party at fault is liable to compensate the other party for any resulting losses. However, suppose the mistaken party exhibits gross negligence in taking an action. In that case, it is inappropriate to allow it to seek rescission. However, the SPC Interpretation on the General Provisions of Civil Code (2022) does not provide a definite answer and leaves room for interpretation.

386. As elucidated above, there may be a potential overlap between gross misunderstanding and fraud. If a party can directly prove that the counterparty acted intentionally, they can claim rescission on grounds of fraud. However, if difficult or too costly to prove, they may alternatively claim gross misunderstanding. Chinese law allows parties to select their claims based on the cost-benefit analysis, whether fraud or gross misunderstanding.

387. There are instances in practice where gross misunderstanding appears to be user-friendly to the claimant. For example, one party, with a duty to inform or explain, intentionally conceals the true situation during the conclusion of a contract, leading the other party to misunderstand. This is particularly common in selling used cars and real estate transactions.

388. In such cases, concurrence between fraud and gross misunderstanding is possible. In a used car transaction, the buyer often discovers post-purchase issues such as false mileage, vehicle age, and previous accidents. When the buyer initiates litigation on the grounds of fraud, and the seller denies fraud or claims ignorance,

378. *Ibid.*

the buyer typically faces difficulties proving the seller's fraudulent intent. At this point, the gross misunderstanding doctrine becomes advantageous with its comparatively favourable burden of proof on the seller. When existing evidence fails to establish the seller's fraud, courts would be content with the gross misunderstanding doctrine to protect the buyer's interests.

389. In *Nie Jiawei v. Xinjiang Balingjiuling Automobile Service Co., Ltd.*, the court opined that although the seller, as a professional used car trading company, could not be conclusively proven to have engaged in fraudulent behaviour, it failed to fulfil its duty to carefully examine the involved vehicle for significant accidents during the transaction.[379] Instead, the seller sold the vehicle to the buyer as accident-free, leading the buyer to make a purchasing decision due to gross misunderstanding. Therefore, the court supported the buyer's claim to rescind the vehicle purchase contract and return the purchase price.[380]

390. Finally, if a party seeks to revoke a civil juridical act due to an error in the transmission of a third party's expression of intent, Article 19 in the SPC Interpretation on the General Provisions of Civil Code (2022) will govern the situation.[381] This provision incorporates the incorrect convey of an expression of intent by a third party into the rule governing gross misunderstanding. This was so decided primarily because the communicator is legally deemed as or equivalent to the spokesperson of the expressing party.

391. The concept of gross misunderstanding in Chinese law is functionally equivalent to mistake in English contract law, particularly unilateral mistake or mutual mistake. Both concepts address situations where one or both parties operate under a significant misunderstanding about the facts or terms of the contract, leading to disputes about its validity.

392. Both gross misunderstanding and mistake require the misunderstanding to be about a fundamental fact or term of the contract. In both systems, the misunderstanding must significantly impact the party's decision to enter the contract. Both allow for rescission of the contract, aiming to restore parties to their pre-contractual positions.

393. English law categorises mistakes in contracts into three types: unilateral mistake, where one party is mistaken, and the other party knows or ought to know about the mistake; mutual mistake, where both parties are mistaken about the same fundamental fact but misunderstand each other's intentions; and common mistake, where both parties share the same incorrect belief about a fundamental aspect of the

---

379. *Nie Jiawei v. Xinjiang Balingjiuling Automobile Service Co., Ltd.*, the People's Court of Shuimogou District, Urumqi City, Xinjiang Uygur Autonomous Region (2022) Xin 0105 Min Chu No. 5620; 聂嘉伟诉新疆捌零玖零汽车服务有限公司， 新疆维吾尔自治区乌鲁木齐市水磨沟区人民法院（2022）新0105民初5620号.

380. *Ibid.*

381. Article 20 of the SPC Interpretation on the General Provisions of Civil Code (2022).

contract.[382] Chinese law under gross misunderstanding focuses on a single party's significant misunderstanding without categorising it as unilateral or mutual.

394. In English law, for unilateral mistakes to void a contract, the non-mistaken party must know or should reasonably know of the mistake.[383] In Chinese law, the emphasis is on the existence and impact of the misunderstanding rather than the other party's knowledge. Chinese courts focus on fairness and the party's ability to demonstrate the misunderstanding's impact. English courts balance mistakes with the principle of caveat emptor (buyer beware) and uphold contracts unless the mistake is egregious.

395. While gross misunderstanding in Chinese law and mistakes in English law share the goal of addressing significant errors in contracting, they differ in scope and application. Chinese law adopts a broad, fairness-oriented approach focused on the effect of the misunderstanding, whereas English law maintains stricter boundaries to protect contractual certainty and stability.

III. Fraud by Counterparty and a Third Party

A. Fraud by Counterparty

396. The GPCL provision stipulated that a party's act in violation of its true intent induced by fraud, coercion, or taking advantage of the other party's predicament shall be void.[384] Further clarification on fraudulent behaviour was provided soon after the enactment of the GPCL by the SPC, which specified that intentional communication of false information or deliberate concealment of true information to induce the other party to make erroneous expressions of intent constitutes fraud.[385]

397. Subsequently, Article 52(1) of the CCL stipulated that 'a contract entered into through fraud or coercion that damages national interests shall be void'.[386] Article 54(2) of the CCL provides that 'a party who, through fraud, coercion, or taking advantage of the other party's predicament, enters into a contract in violation of its true intent, may request the people's court or an arbitration institution to alter or rescind it'.[387] In brief, under the CCL, fraud can be grounds for invalidating or revoking the contract, depending on whether there is damage to state interest.

398. Unlike the rules in the CCL, the Civil Code stipulates fraudulent conduct as revocable primarily because it does not harm the interests of third parties and

382. Ewan McKendrick, Contract Law: Text, Cases, and Materials 515 (7th edn, OUP 2016).
383. *Smith v. Hughes* (1871) LR 6 QB597.
384. Article 58(1) item 3 of the GPCL.
385. Article 68 of the SPC Opinions on the Implementation of the GPCL (1988).
386. Article 52(1) of the CCL.
387. Article 54(2) of the CCL.

does not involve public order. Granting the defrauded party the right of rescission allows them to decide whether to exercise this right independently. This effectively safeguards their civil rights.

399. In cases involving fraud against the state, granting the state the discretion to rescind contracts is also sufficient to protect state interests. If differentiation were to be mandated, rendering contracts fraudulent against the state void *ab initio* could potentially disadvantage the protection of state interests. Therefore, the Civil Code clarifies that the defrauded actor has the power to rescind the civil juridical act fraudulently induced by the counterparty and, hence, against the defrauded actor's genuine intent via the courts or arbitral tribunals.[388]

400. Fraud refers to the intentional act of one party informing the other party of false circumstances or intentionally concealing the true circumstances, thereby inducing the other party to make a mistaken expression of intent. The aggrieved party can request a court or arbitration institution to rescind such acts.[389] The following conditions must be met for a civil legal act made based on fraud to be rescinded:

401. First, the fraudulent party must have the intent to deceive. The purpose of the intent is to deceive the other party and thereby obtain an improper advantage. Fraud can be either active (intentionally informing the other party of false information) or passive (deliberately concealing the truth by a person who has a duty to disclose).[390] In *Liu Xiangqian v. Anbang Property Insurance Co., Ltd.*,[391] the court held that when an insurance event occurs, if the insurance company, as a professional claim-handling institution, knows or should have known that the incident falls within the scope of compensation based on its professional experience and understanding of the insurance contract, intentionally conceals important facts that the insured is entitled to insurance compensation without legal or contractual basis, and induces the insured to reach a settlement agreement on this basis, the insured has made an untruthful expression of intent. The insurance company's behaviour violates the principle of good faith and constitutes fraud. The court supports the claim made by the insured to revoke the settlement agreement.

402. Second, the fraudulent party must have committed a fraudulent act. Fraudulent acts generally fall into two categories: (1) intentionally informing the other party of false information), i.e., the actor actively causes the other party to make a mistake by fabricating false facts and providing misleading information; (2) the person with the duty to inform intentionally conceals the true situation, i.e., the actor, in the presence of a duty to inform, passively fails to provide important transaction

388. Article 148 CC.
389. *Ibid.*
390. Article 21 of the SPC Interpretation on the General Provisions of the Civil Code.
391. *Liu Xiangqian v. Anbang Property Insurance Co., Ltd.*, Gazette Case of the SPC, Issue 8, 2013; 刘向前诉安邦财产保险公司,《最高人民法院公报》案例, 2013年第08期.

information, causing the counterparty to make a mistake.[392] The duty to inform can arise from legal provisions, contractual agreements, the principle of good faith, trading practices so on. The courts have the discretion to determine whether a particular act constitutes fraud. Fraud is a complex issue; no single, bright-line rule can be applied in all cases.

403. Third, these misrepresentations were material to the decision to enter into the contract.[393] The defrauded party's mistake is the result of the fraud of the fraudulent party. In other words, if the fraudulent party had not committed the fraud, the defrauded party would not have made a mistake. The aggrieved party relied on these misrepresentations to enter into the contract. If the fraudulent party intends to deceive, the defrauded party is not mistaken. As a result, it does not constitute fraud. In short, there is a causal relationship between the fraudulent act of the fraudulent party and the civil legal act implemented by the defrauded party.

404. If a contract is revoked due to fraud, the parties must be restored to their original positions as if the contract had never been made. The power of rescission is extinguished if the defrauded party fails to exercise the power of rescission within one year from the date on which the party knows or ought to know the cause of rescission.[394] If this restitution is not possible or sufficient, compensation for losses may be required.

405. In brief, fraud provides that a contract is voidable if one party induces the other party to enter into the contract through fraudulent means. Fraudulent conduct typically involves intentional deception, where one party knowingly provides false information or conceals material facts to induce the other party to make a decision they would not have otherwise made. Fraudulent contracts are voidable to ensure fairness and protect the interests of parties who were misled into entering agreements. The focus is on the fraudulent intent of the deceiving party and the causal link between the fraud and the victim's decision to contract.

B. Fraud by a Third Party

406. It is not uncommon that a contract was entered into due to the fraudulent act of a third party. In such a situation, the defrauded actor has the power to rescind the contract fraudulently induced by a third party and hence against the defrauded actor's genuine intent via the courts or arbitral tribunal, as long as the counterparty knows or ought to know of the fraud.[395]

---

392. Article 21 of the SPC Interpretation the General Provisions of the Civil Code (2022).
393. *Ibid.*
394. Article 152(1) CC.
395. Article 149 CC.

407. For example, a producer engages in false advertising, causing consumers to be deceived. Since the contractual relationship is established between the consumer and the seller, the producer is a third party. If the seller is not aware of the producer's false advertising and should not be aware of it, the consumer cannot claim to rescind the contract; if the seller knows or should know that the producer has engaged in false advertising, the consumer has the right to request to rescind the contract.

408. The defrauded party has the burden of proving that the third party's fraud caused them to make a mistake. The right to rescind must be exercised within a reasonable time after the defrauded party discovers the fraud. Rescission has the effect of restoring the parties to their pre-contractual positions. The right to rescind a civil legal act implemented due to fraud by a third party is designed to protect the interests of the defrauded party. It is important for parties to civil transactions to be aware of this right and to exercise it promptly if they believe they have been the victim of fraud.

409. Under the Civil Code, the following conditions must be met for a civil legal act implemented due to fraud by a third party to be rescinded:

> A third party outside of the parties to the transaction committed the fraud. The third party here generally refers to anyone other than the contracting parties, their agents, or their legal representatives. If a party's agent or legal representative commits fraud, it should be considered fraud committed by one party, not a third party.[396]

410. The defrauded party may enter into a contract as a result of the fraudulent act of a third party. To establish fraud, there must be a clear causal relationship between the fraudulent act and the decision of the defrauded party to form the contract. The defrauded party must demonstrate that they relied on a false statement or a concealed material fact presented by the third party. This reliance must be reasonable, meaning that a typical, prudent person in similar circumstances could also have been misled by the fraudulent representation or omission.

411. Reasonableness of reliance includes factors such as the context of the transaction, the nature of the falsehood, the sophistication of the defrauded party, and whether the party had an opportunity or obligation to verify the facts. For instance, if the false statement involved technical details that a layperson could not reasonably verify, reliance may be deemed more justifiable.

412. If the other party knows or should reasonably know that a civil legal act performed by one party resulted from the fraudulent act of a third party, the defrauded party has the right to rescind the contract. However, if the other party was unaware of the third party's fraudulent behaviour, the defrauded party cannot rescind the contract. This distinction protects parties acting in good faith and

396. *Ibid.*

ensures fairness in legal relationships. To prevent the abuse of the right to rescind, the defrauded party must exercise this right through litigation or arbitration rather than merely notifying the other party. This formal requirement ensures that the validity of the rescission is subjected to judicial or arbitral scrutiny, safeguarding against arbitrary or unfounded rescission claims. It also provides an opportunity for the other party to present evidence of their lack of knowledge of the fraud, ensuring that rescission is granted only in justified cases.

C. Comparison with English Law of Misrepresentation

413. The functional equivalent of the Chinese law of fraud is the English law of misrepresentation, despite notable differences. Both systems protect parties who enter into contracts under false pretences, but their procedural approaches and legal reasoning reflect the foundational differences between common and civil law traditions. It is categorised as misrepresentation (innocent, negligent, section 2(1) Misrepresentation Act 1967 or fraudulent)[397] under English law.

414. Both systems require that the false statement or conduct materially influences the party's decision to contract. In Chinese law, this causal relationship is essential for proving fraud. Both systems allow the aggrieved party to seek rescission of the contract and/or claim damages.

415. English law offers a more nuanced framework with distinct categories and tailored remedies for misrepresentation.[398] In contrast, Chinese law focuses on fraudulent conduct with broader principles and fewer categories, reflecting its civil law tradition. In English law, rescission is available for all types of misrepresentation. Damages may be available in tort (fraudulent or negligent misrepresentation) or under the Misrepresentation Act 1967.[399] In Chinese law, rescission is the primary remedy for fraud and compensation for damages is possible if fraud results in harm, but only under general tort principles.

416. In English law, fraudulent misrepresentation requires proof that the statement was made knowingly, recklessly, or without belief in its truth.[400] In Chinese law, fraud generally requires intentional deception, but there is no equivalent concept for negligent misrepresentation under English law, which addresses liability when a party makes a statement carelessly, causing reliance and loss.[401]

397. Ewan McKendrick, Contract Law, section 13.6 (14th edn, Red Globe Press 2021).
398. The general remedies for misrepresentation are recession of contract or damages; depending on the type of misrepresentation, different remedies may apply. i.e., if innocent misrepresentation under the Misrepresentation Act 1967 arises, the remedy would be recession or damages in lieu of recession under section 2(2) of the 1967 Act.
399. *See* Section 2 of the Misrepresentation Act 1967.
400. *Derry v. Peek* (1889) App Cas 337.
401. *See* section 2(1) of the Misrepresentation Act 1967.

417. Chinese law explicitly addresses fraud by third parties, allowing rescission if the other contracting party knew or should have known of the third party's fraud. In English law, liability for third-party misrepresentation depends on the principles of the agency or whether the party has a duty to disclose the third party's misrepresentation.[402]

IV. Coercion

418. Coercion, also known as duress, in the context of contract validity, is addressed under the Civil Code as a significant factor affecting contract validity. Coercion involves the use of threats, force, or other means to create fear or undue pressure, compelling the coerced party to act against their genuine intent. Coercion can be exerted by either the counterparty to the contract or by a third party. The coerced actor can rescind the civil juridical act under duress via the courts or arbitral tribunals.[403]

419. Coercion refers to the act of using the threat of causing harm to the personal rights, property rights, and other legitimate interests of natural persons or their close relatives or causing harm to the reputation, honour, and property rights of legal persons or unincorporated organisations, to coerce them into making declarations of intent based on fear.[404] The threat can be to cause physical harm, financial harm, or damage to their reputation. Examples are threatening to physically harm someone if they do not sign a contract, threatening to damage someone's reputation if they do not agree to a certain deal, and threatening to withhold financial support from someone if they do not comply with demands, to name a few.

420. Compared with the CCL, the Civil Code made the following changes regarding the rule of coercion. First, the Civil Code addresses coercion by a party to the contract and a third party outside the contractual relationship.

421. Second, the Civil Code does not have a separate provision addressing the situation where a party uses coercion to conclude a contract to the detriment of national interests. In cases where a party uses coercion to conclude a contract that harms national interests, reference could be made to Article 153 (2) of the Civil Code, which deems such contracts as violating public order and good morals and, therefore, invalid.

---

402. For example, in *Bradford Third Equitable Benefit Building Society v. Borders* [1941] 2 All ER 205 (HL), it was discussed that the Party that made the untrue statement could also face liability had he manifestly approved and adopted a representation made by a third party.
403. Article 150 CC.
404. Article 22 of the SPC Interpretation on the General Provisions of the Civil Code (2022).

422. Third, when one party uses coercion to make the other party perform a contract action contrary to their true intentions, the Civil Code only allow the coerced party to request a court or an arbitration institution to rescind the contract without permitting the coerced party to request the modification of the contract.

423. Coercion can be physical or psychological. It can be directed at the coerced person or their loved ones. The threat must be credible and imminent. The coerced party must have no reasonable alternative but to comply with the demand. The right to rescind a civil legal act implemented due to coercion is designed to protect the interests of the coerced party. It is important for parties to civil transactions to be aware of this right and to exercise it promptly if they believe they have been coerced.

424. The following conditions must be met for a civil legal act implemented due to coercion to be rescinded. First, the actor objectively implemented a coercive act. That is, to threaten to implement a certain act of harm, forcing the coerced object to produce a feeling of fear. The coercion here must reach the point where the coerced party feels fear, regardless of whether the harm is serious.

425. Second, the actor subjectively has the intent to coerce. That is, to intentionally threaten to harm the legitimate rights and interests of the coerced object and implement the desired civil legal act.

426. Third, the coercion must be illegal, including the illegality of the means and the purpose. If one party has a legitimate basis to exert pressure on the other, it does not constitute coercion. Coercion should not be confused with self-help behaviour. For example, when a person leaves a restaurant without paying after eating, the owner asks to pay before leaving. Although this behaviour temporarily restricts personal freedom, it does not constitute coercion. Because eating in a restaurant requires paying money, and when the money is still owed, the restaurant owner's behaviour of not letting him leave is a self-help behaviour, which is legal, so it does not constitute an illegal act of coercion.

427. Fourth, a direct and sufficient causal relationship must exist between the coercion and the coerced party's decision to enter the contract. The coercion must be the decisive factor in the coerced party's action. The coerced party produces a feeling of fear due to the coercion and manifests intent due to the fear. If the coerced person did not feel fear due to the coercion, or even if there was fear, it was not caused by the coercive act, or even if there was fear, but did not manifest intent, then it does not constitute coercion under civil law.

428. The coerced party can rescind a civil legal act implemented through coercion. The coerced party must exercise the right to rescind through litigation or arbitration within the prescribed time limit[405] and cannot use the form of notifying the other party.[406]

429. The concept of coercion under Chinese law aligns closely with the English law doctrine of duress. Both focus on protecting the voluntariness of consent in contractual agreements, ensuring that contracts formed under improper pressure can be rescinded. Coercion under Chinese law involves threats or acts that induce a party to enter a contract against their genuine intent, often involving threats to personal safety, property, or other significant interests. In English law, duress encompasses improper pressure, such as threats of harm, that leave the victim with no reasonable alternative but to agree to the contract.[407] Rescission is the primary remedy in both legal systems. Both require a sufficient causal relationship between the coercion/duress and the coerced party's decision to contract.

430. Chinese law explicitly includes threats from third parties and applies to all civil legal acts, whereas English law primarily focuses on duress within contractual relationships and has developed economic duress as a distinct category, as recognised in *The Siboen and The Sibotre* [1976].[408] While economic duress is codified in English law, it is not explicitly defined in Chinese law.[409] Additionally, Chinese law imposes a one-year statutory time limit for seeking rescission, whereas English law relies on equitable doctrines, such as laches, to determine whether rescission remains available, with no fixed statutory time frame. Chinese law codifies coercion with explicit procedural rules, while English law evolves through case law and equitable principles, offering broader recognition of economic duress.

V. Improper Pressure and Manifest Unfairness

431. A contract affected by manifest unfairness refers to a situation where one party takes advantage of the other party's vulnerable or incapacitated state such as distress, lack of judgment, or similar circumstances, leading to a significant imbalance in rights and obligations when the contract is concluded. In this situation, the disadvantaged party has the right to request rescission via court or arbitration proceedings.[410] The elements constituting manifest unfairness include both objective and subjective aspects.

---

405. Article 152(2) CC provides that the power of rescission is extinguished. The coerced party fails to exercise the power of rescission within one year from the date on which the very duress comes to an end.
406. *Du Changhang v. Wang Xuewei*, Liaoning Shenyang Intermediate People's Court (2021) Liao 01 Min Zhong No. 12917; 杜畅航诉王学伟，辽宁沈阳中院（2021）辽01民终12917号.
407. *Barton v. Armstrong* [1976] AC 104
408. *Occidental Worldwide Investment Corp. v. Skibs A/S Avanti, Skibs A/S Glarona, Skibs A/S Navalis (The 'Siboen' and the 'Sibotre')* [1976] 1 Lloyd's Rep 293 (QB).
409. Yi Wang, Duress and Exploitation in Chinese Contract Law, in Invalidity 52 (Mindy Chen-Wishart, Hiroo Sono, and Stefan Vogenauer eds., Oxford 2022) https://doi.org/10.1093/oso/9780192859341.003.0003 accessed 1 Jan. 2025.
410. Article 151 CC.

1. Articles 54 of the CCL and 59 of the GPCL do not explicitly define the concept of 'manifestly unfair'. However, guidance is provided in Article 72 of the SPC Opinions on the Implementation of the GPCL. It suggests that manifest unfairness may be established when one party exploits its advantageous position or the other party's lack of experience, leading to a significant imbalance in the principles of fairness and reciprocal compensation between rights and obligations. This interpretation helps address situations where one party unjustly benefits at the expense of the other.
2. Neither the CCL nor the GPCL explicitly addresses the subjective element, i.e., the subjective reasons causing manifest unfairness. However, invoking the principle of manifest unfairness to revoke a contract requires not only the objective condition of the contract's content being manifestly unfair but also typically necessitates specific subjective elements.
3. This means that besides the contract terms being unfair in terms of rights and obligations, it must also be proven that such unfairness is caused by specific subjective reasons, such as one party exploiting its advantageous position or the lack of experience of the other party. These subjective factors indicate that manifest unfairness is not merely an objective state of unequal terms but also includes the result of unfairness reliant on the subjective actions of one of the parties.

432. Article 72 of the SPC Opinions on the Implementation of the GPCL explicitly mentions these subjective reasons, stating that if one party 'takes advantage of its superiority or the lack of experience of the other party', leading to a significant violation of the principles of fairness and equivalent compensation in the contract, such a situation can be deemed as manifestly unfair. The 'taking advantage of superiority' and 'exploiting the other party's lack of experience' highlight the subjective causes behind the outcome of manifest unfairness. In *Dawa Tianruixiang Chemical Co., Ltd. v. Jin'ao Technology (Hubei) Chemical Co., Ltd.*,[411] the court held that whether the lawsuit filed by Dawa Company can be supported by law depends critically on examining whether the agreement in question possesses the subjective and objective elements necessary to constitute manifest unfairness.[412]

433. Subjective elements pertain to the intentional exploitation of advantages or the reckless nature or lack of experience of the other party in concluding a contract, resulting in the conclusion of a manifestly unfair contract. Such a subjective state indicates a departure from the requirement of good faith. Several typical scenarios of the subjective requirement include:

1. Exploiting the other party's distress typically involves taking advantage of their temporary financial hardship or urgent need for essential resources. For

411. *Dawa Tianruixiang Chemical Co., Ltd. v. Jin'ao Technology (Hubei) Chemical Co., Ltd.*, Hanjiang Intermediate People's Court, Hubei Province (2016) E 96 Min Zhong No. 245; 大洼天瑞祥化工有限公司诉金澳科技（湖北）化工有限公司，湖北省汉江中级人民法院（2016）鄂96民终245号.

412. *Ibid.*

instance, if someone urgently needs to raise funds for a family member's sudden serious illness treatment and another party exploits this urgent need by persuading them to sell their property at a significantly lower price, it may constitute manifest unfairness. Parties may reach a compensation agreement privately or through mediation in personal injury compensation disputes.

2. If the compensation amount in the agreement is significantly lower than the statutory standard, the principle of manifest unfairness may apply. This often occurs between employers, workers, and hospitals and patients. Specifically, after an accident, employers tend to exploit the economic hardship, lack of experience (especially among migrant workers), and even the difficulty of providing evidence (such as not having a written labour contract) of the workers. At the same time, hospitals might also take advantage of their position in determining the consequences of injuries. Here, based on the contract's objective unfairness and the relevant entities' structural advantages, subjective elements can be inferred.[413]
3. Exploiting the other party's lack of judgment refers to taking advantage of their limited experience in life or business transactions. For example, financial institution employees selling high-risk financial products to elderly individuals with lower levels of education in urban areas, who lack judgment capability, may constitute manifest unfairness due to their purchase of high-risk financial products.
4. It should be noted that while it is likely for manifest unfairness to apply in civil or consumer contracts, in commercial transactions, the parties to a contract are usually at arm's length, thus curtailing the likelihood of finding a manifest unfairness. Specifically, if both parties to the contract are commercial entities, the subjective elements, i.e., the 'lack of judgment capacity', usually do not substantiate.[414]

434. Therefore, when evaluating whether a contract is manifestly unfair, it is essential not only to consider whether the contract content itself contravenes the principles of fairness and equivalent exchange (objective conditions) but also to examine whether this unfairness is due to the specific subjective actions of one of the parties (subjective elements). The proof of such subjective behaviour is crucial for requesting the modification or rescission of a contract deemed manifestly unfair.

435. On objective elements, manifest unfairness involves a clear and substantial imbalance in the exchange of rights, obligations, or benefits between the parties. For example, one party may receive significantly less value or bear an excessive burden compared to the other. This imbalance is not merely incidental or minor but is so pronounced that it deviates significantly from accepted standards of fairness.

413. Jian He, Commentary on Article 54 (1), Item 2 of the Contract Law (Unconscionability), 01 The Jurist, 155-174 (2017).
414. *Zhu Junmin, Wang Yazhuang & Zheng Lu v. Shanghai Yuankai (Group) Co., Ltd. & Song Guizhong*, the Supreme People's Court, (2020) SPC Min Shen No. 4426; 祝军民、王亚壮、郑路诉上海源恺（集团）有限公司、宋贵中，最高人民法院（2020）最高法民申4426号.

436. The doctrine of manifest unfairness aims not to eliminate the commercial risks that parties should bear but to prohibit or restrict one party from gaining 'windfall profits' that do not comply with transaction rules. Imbalances in interests often occur in transactions, and such imbalances are typically the normal risks that parties should bear in transactions.[415] Specific circumstances of various transaction relationships should be considered to determine whether there is a significant imbalance, particularly by assessing factors such as supply and demand dynamics and price fluctuations.

437. Only when the imbalance in interests reaches a 'significant' level can the doctrine of manifest unfairness be applied to revoke the transaction. The resulting transaction must go beyond being simply harsh or unwise; it must rise to the level of being exploitative and excessively burdensome.

438. Manifest unfairness must be assessed at the time of the formation of the contract. Suppose circumstances change after the contract is concluded, causing manifest unfairness in both parties' treatment of obligations or payments. In such cases, the rules regarding changes in circumstances should be applied instead of invoking the doctrine of manifest unfairness.

439. The manifest unfairness in Chinese law can be compared to undue influence and unconscionable bargains in English law. These doctrines aim to address situations where the fairness of a contract is compromised by an abuse of power or a significant imbalance in bargaining positions. Undue influence arises when one party uses their influence over another to obtain an unfair advantage.[416] English law divides undue influence into actual undue influence proven by specific evidence of coercion or manipulation and presumed undue influence, which arises from certain relationships (e.g., solicitor-client, parent-child) where one party is in a position of trust.[417]

440. English law also recognises the concept of unconscionable bargains, where one party takes advantage of the other's vulnerability to secure an unreasonably favourable contract.[418] To prove unconscionability, there must be a special disadvantage (e.g., lack of education, financial distress) affecting one party.[419] The stronger party must have exploited this disadvantage.[420]

---

415. *Tibet Zhongtaihengyuan Industrial Co., Ltd. v. Lhasa Liuwu New District Urban Investment, Construction and Development Group Co., Ltd.*, the Supreme People's Court (2019) SPC Min Zhong No. 760; 西藏中太恒源实业有限公司诉拉萨市柳梧新区城市投资建设发展集团有限公司, 最高人民法院（2019）最高法民终760号.

416. *R v. A-G for England and Wales* [2003] UKPC 22, Lord Hoffman at para [21]: 'Undue influence has concentrated in particular upon the unfair exploitation by one party of a relationship which gives him ascendancy or influence over the over.'

417. *Royal Bank of Scotland plc v. Etridge (No. 2)* [2001] UKHL 44, Lord Nicolls at para [18].

418. *Lloyds Bank v. Bundy* [1975] QB 326, Lord Denning at para [339].

419. *Strydom v. Vendside Ltd* [2009] EWHC 2130 (QB); [2009] All ER (D) 135 (Aug) Justice Blair at para [36].

420. *Ibid.*

441. Chinese law focuses on the exploitation of specific circumstances, such as distress, lack of judgment, or inexperience, leading to manifest unfairness in the transaction. English law also addresses vulnerability but distinguishes between undue influence (focused on relationships) and unconscionable bargains (focused on the transaction's terms and circumstances). Hence, Chinese law's manifest unfairness provision is broader, encompassing any significantly imbalanced transaction caused by vulnerability exploitation. By contrast, English law applies undue influence primarily in fiduciary or trust-based relationships and unconscionable bargains in specific, egregious cases of inequality.

442. Both legal systems aim to address situations where one party secures an excessive advantage. Chinese law emphasises the 'significant violation of fairness' standard. English law focuses on whether the weaker party's consent was freely given or if the stronger party's conduct was unconscionable.

443. The concepts of manifest unfairness in Chinese law and undue influence/unconscionable bargains in English law serve similar purposes: protecting weaker parties from exploitative contracts. However, Chinese law adopts a statutory framework focusing on fairness and equity in contractual transactions. English law relies on equitable doctrines rooted in case law, with a greater emphasis on the relationship between the parties and procedural safeguards.

VI. Malicious Collusion

444. Malicious collusion, which refers to the illegal collusion between two parties to carry out certain civil legal acts, causing harm to other's rights and interests, is an act of malicious collusion. Such behaviours manifest in various forms, including the abuse of agency rights,[421] fraudulent acts against creditors, unauthorised disposition, selling the same item to multiple buyers, obtaining guarantees through deceit, evading legal obligations, colluding in auctions, and collusive bidding, among others. Acts of malicious collusion violate the principle of good faith, harming the interests of specific third parties and damaging the normal order of transactions.

445. The Civil Code, following its predecessors such as the GPCL and the CCL, explicitly addresses malicious collusion, particularly in contexts where such actions

421. Incidents where agents, and counterparties collude maliciously to harm the interests of principals occur frequently. Art. 154 CC states that malicious collusion by the actor and the counterparty to harm the lawful rights and interests of others causes the contract to be invalid. However, the agent concludes contracts in the name of the principal, and it is the principal's interests that are harmed, not 'others'' interests, courts cannot declare the contract invalid based on this provision. Furthermore, while Art. 164 CC stipulates that 'agents and counterparties who collude maliciously to harm the lawful rights and interests of the principal shall bear joint liability,' it does not explicitly address the legal effect of contracts formed through such collusion. This deserves a special attention in case law.

harm the state, collective, or third parties' interests.[422] It deems acts of malicious collusion as inherently invalid. This stance has been widely recognised in judicial practice. This principle is firmly rooted in protecting public order and good morals, emphasising the protection of lawful rights and interests against acts conducted in bad faith.

446. However, the boundary between acts of malicious collusion and acts against public order and good morals is blurred. In both the GPCL and the CCL, malicious collusion was framed as 'civil acts that are maliciously colluded to harm the interests of the state, collective, or third parties are invalid'.[423] From a textual interpretation, state and collective interests are usually considered important to public order and good morals and should be interpreted as 'social public interests'. It is often understood that the rule against malicious collusion is, in nature, a sub-set provision of the principle of public order and good morals.

447. In acts of malicious collusion, the parties have malicious intent, and the purpose of performing the legal act is to harm the legal rights and interests of others, which fits the situations targeted by the principle of public order and good morals. Therefore, according to the provisions of the GPCL and the CCL, both the interests of third parties and the public interest are protected. If this legislative logic is followed, then the rule against malicious collusion harming the interests of third parties does not have independent value and can be encompassed within the rules against violating public order and good morals.

448. Therefore, Article 154 of the Civil Code removed the terms 'national interest' and 'collective interest' and directly changed them to 'civil legal acts in which the actor colludes maliciously with the counterparty, harming the lawful rights and interests of others, are invalid'.[424] Notably, not everyone can claim that the contract is invalid. Only the specific third parties who have suffered harm can claim the contract as invalid because of malicious collusion.

449. The Civil Code categorises acts of malicious collusion as a type of invalid civil legal act. It places it alongside acts that violate public order and good morals as grounds for invalidation. Although some typical forms of malicious collusion, such as bid rigging, are specified by certain special laws,[425] the malicious collusion conducts are diverse and require a general rule, as found in Article 154. However, it should be noted that providing malicious collusion as a general rule does risk being overly abstract. In its application, it is necessary to concretise its constitutive requirements to ensure the accurate application of the rule.

---

422. Article 58(4) of the GPCL; Art. 52(2) of the CCL.
423. *Ibid.*
424. Article 154 CC.
425. Articles 50–57 of the Bidding Law (1999, 2017 revision).

450. In *Swiss Cargill International v. Fujian Jinshi Oil Manufacturing Co., Ltd and others*,[426] the SPC provides guidance on the relevant factors taken into account to determine a malicious collusion and the legal consequences of the malicious collusion. In this case, the Claimant, *Swiss Cargill International*, is an arbitral award creditor against the defendant. The Claimant filed a suit at Xiamen Intermediate People's Court to enforce the foreign arbitral award in May 2006 and a year later, the foreign arbitral award was recognised by the Court. However, when the Claimant sought to enforce the award, it was discovered that on 8 May 2006, the defendant signed a State-owned Land Use Right and Asset Sale Contract with Fujian Tianyuan Bio-Protein Technology Co., Ltd. (Tianyuan Company).

451. It was agreed that the defendant would transfer all its fixed assets, including the state-owned land use rights, factory buildings, office buildings, and oil production equipment, to Tianyuan Company for the price of RMB 25.69 million. On 21 February 2008, Tianyuan Company signed a 'Sales Contract' with Zhangzhou Huifengyuan Trading Co., Ltd. (Huifengyuan Company). It was agreed that Huifengyuan Company would purchase the aforementioned land use rights, buildings, and equipment on the land for a total price of RMB 26.69 million.

452. Due to Fujian Jinshi Company having no assets available for execution, making it impossible to carry out enforcement, Cargill Inc. thus filed a lawsuit with the Fujian High People's Court, requesting the following:

1. To declare the 'State-owned Land Use Right and Asset Sale Contract' signed between Fujian Company and China Textiles Company as invalid.
2. To declare the state-owned land use rights and asset 'Sales Contract' signed between China Textiles Company and HSBC Yuan Company as invalid.
3. To order HSBC Yuan Company and China Textiles Company to return the properties obtained under the contracts to the property owners.

453. The SPC held that the issue is whether the contracts established among these parties constitute 'malicious collusion to harm the interests of a third party'.

454. First, during the signing and execution of the 'State-owned Land Use Right and Asset Sale Contract', it was found that the actual controllers of the defendant and Tianyuan Company were a married couple acting as the legal representatives for both companies and signing the contracts. Therefore, it can be determined that during the signing and execution of the contract, Tianyuan Company was aware of the arbitral award debts incurred by the defendant. This familial relationship between the two legal representatives of two sale contracts raises inquiries about potential conflicts of interest and the genuine nature of the transaction, suggesting

426. *Swiss Cargill International v. Fujian Jinshi Oil Manufacturing Co., Ltd and others*, SPC Guiding Case No. 33; 瑞士嘉吉国际公司诉福建金石制油有限公司等, 最高人民法院第33号指导性案例.

that the dealings may have been structured to strategically manipulate assets and liabilities, particularly in ways that could undermine the interests of external creditors like Cargill Inc.

455. Second, the contract price of the Sale Contract established on 8 May 2006 was not based on any formal appraisal from an accredited valuer. Upon review, the trial court examined the defendant's balance sheet dated 31 May 2006, which detailed the original price of fixed assets at RMB 44,042,705.75, with a net value post-depreciation of RMB 32,354,833.70.[427] Given this data, the court noted that the RMB 21.05 million valuation for buildings and equipment set in the contract was significantly lower than the net value indicated in the balance sheet. This disparity in valuation led the court to determine that the asset pricing was unreasonably low, and given that Tianyuan Company was aware of Fujian Jinshi's considerable debts to Cargill Inc., the transaction was deemed to exhibit malice. Tianyuan's decision to purchase the assets at such a low price, despite knowing about Fujian Jinshi's financial obligations, suggested a deliberate attempt to undervalue the assets. This action was interpreted as malicious collusion aimed at shielding assets from legitimate creditor claims and thereby harming the interests of Cargill Inc., the creditor.

456. Third, when HFY Company entered into the Sales Contract with Tianyuan Company, it was fully aware of the origin of the assets being transferred as well as the significant debts owed by the defendant to Cargill Inc. The contract stipulated a purchase price of RMB 26.69 million, which was only slightly higher than the price at which Tianyuan Company had acquired the assets from Fujian Jinshi Company. It was found that HFY Company had paid RMB 5.69 million to Tianyuan Company but had not settled the remaining amount. Based on these facts, the trial court determined that HFY Company and Tianyuan Company had colluded maliciously when signing the Sales Contract. This collusion was judged sufficient to harm the interests of the creditor, Cargill Inc.

457. Therefore, the SPC ruled that the State-owned Land Use Right and Asset Sale Contract signed between the Defedant and Tianyuan Company, as well as the 'Sales Contract' between Tianyuan Company and Huifengyuan Company, were identified as contracts involving malicious collusion intended to harm the interests of Cargill Inc and such contracts should be invalid.

---

427. *Ibid.* On 23 October 2011, the Fujian Provincial High People's Court issued Civil Judgment No. 2007 Min Min Chu Zi No. 37, confirming that the 'State-owned Land Use Right and Asset Sale Contract' and the 'Sales Contract' were invalid. The court ordered HFY Company to return the state-owned land use rights acquired under the aforementioned contract to the defendant within thirty days of the judgment taking effect. Similarly, Tianyuan Company was ordered to return the buildings and equipment acquired under the contract to the Defendant within thirty days of the judgment taking effect. Following the judgment, the Defendant appealed the decision. On 22 August 2012, the SPC issued Civil Judgment No. (2012) Min Si Zhong Zi No. 1, dismissing the appeal and upholding the original judgment.

458. This ruling highlights the importance of fair asset valuation in transactions, especially under circumstances where a party is known to be financially compromised. The court's judgment aimed to protect creditors' rights and ensure that asset transfers in the context of debt are conducted transparently and fairly, preventing any deliberate undervaluation that could undermine creditor recoveries.

459. More to the point, this ruling underscores the importance of intent and awareness in transactions involving potentially distressed assets. The court recognised that the subsequent transaction between Tianyuan and Huifengyuan not only followed an initial underpriced transfer but was also carried out with full knowledge of the existing financial liabilities of Fujian Jinshi to Cargill. The slight increase in the resale price in the contract with Huifengyuan, coupled with incomplete payment, suggested a continuation of efforts to circumvent the rightful claims of creditors, particularly Cargill Inc.

460. The case reflects judicial scrutiny of asset transfers that might be structured to shield assets from creditors, emphasising the legal requirement for fair dealing and transparency in transactions, especially when the parties involved are aware of underlying financial distress and existing creditor claims.

461. The malicious collusion rule under the Civil Code has three features. First, there is an explicit recognition of malicious collusion as inherently invalid. Second, it focuses on protecting third parties from harm. Third, it is rooted in the broader principle of public order and good morals.

§4. Other Conditions of Validity

462. Regardless of how strongly a legal system upholds the principle of freedom of contract, it cannot enforce contracts that violate the law, good morals, or public policy. Legislative provisions addressing such contracts are often broad and imprecise, typically distinguishing between illegal contracts and those that contravene ethical or moral standards. The discussion below examines the illegality of public order and good morals separately, followed by an analysis of the validity of contracts requiring approval.

I. Illegality

463. Article 153(1) of the Civil Code provides that 'civil legal acts violating mandatory provisions of laws or administrative regulations are invalid'.[428] This provision limits the scope of contract invalidity to violations of mandatory provisions in laws and administrative regulations. However, it does not provide a statutory definition of what constitutes mandatory provisions in such laws or regulations.

428. Article 153(1) CC.

464. The phrase 'except where such mandatory provisions do not render the civil legal act invalid' in Article 153(2) is generally interpreted to encompass both mandatory provisions concerning validity (效力性强制性规定) and mandatory provisions concerning regulation (管理性强制性规定).[429] However, neither category has been clearly defined by statute.

465. The key practical distinction lies in the consequences of a violation: a contract is deemed invalid if the violated rule is determined to be a mandatory provision on validity. Conversely, if classified as a mandatory provision on regulation, the contract typically remains valid. This creates a logical circularity in distinguishing between the two categories, leaving courts with significant discretion to interpret the nature of a legal provision in each case. Without further clarification, this discretion could lead to inconsistent applications of the law.

466. For example, China has a foreign exchange control. Article 17 of the *Foreign Exchange Control Regulations* provides that:

> A domestic institution or individual that makes direct investment or issues or trades negotiable securities or derivative products overseas shall handle the registration formalities at the foreign exchange administrative department of the State Council. If the relevant state provisions require the approval of the competent department or archive the issue with the competent department, it/he shall do so before handling the registration formalities.[430]

467. Whether the above provision constitutes a mandatory provision concerning validity or regulation remains unsettled under Chinese law. Different courts have taken varying approaches to determine whether a transaction is tainted by illegality due to violations of foreign exchange control regulations.

468. For instance, in *Chen Jing v. Wang Weibin*, the courts held that the contract was invalid because it violated foreign exchange control regulations.[431] However, in other cases, such as *Ni Xiuping v. Yang Xigen and Li Ruifen*, the courts reached a different conclusion.[432] In *Ni Huiping*, the court reasoned that the relevant regulation aimed to facilitate personal foreign exchange income and expenditures, simplify procedures, and regulate foreign exchange management.[433] It found that the entrustment agreement between Yang Xigen and Ni Huiping, wherein Ni Huiping

---

429. Article 153(2) CC.
430. Article 17 of the Foreign Exchange Control Regulations (1996, 2008 revision).
431. *Chen Jing v. Wang Weibin*, Shanghai No. 2 Intermediate People's Court, (2016) Hu 02 Min Zhong No. 5427; 陈婧诉王伟斌，上海市第二中级人民法院（2016）沪02民终5427号. Shanghai No. 2 Intermediate People's Court ruled that the contract was invalid as there was a violation of a mandatory legal provision.
432. *Ni Xiuping v. Yang Xigen & Li Ruifen*, Wuxi Intermediate People's Court, (2017) Su 02 Min Zhong No. 1560; 倪惠平诉杨锡根、李瑞芬，江苏省无锡市中级人民法院（2017）苏02民终1560号. Wuxi Intermediate People's Court found there was a valid contract (despite violations of the Foreign Exchange Control Regulations).
433. *Ibid.*

invested RMB 3.15 million to entrust Yang Xigen to purchase PGCG stock, did not involve foreign exchange receipts, expenditures, or business activities. Therefore, the court determined that the regulation invoked by Ni Huiping was not a mandatory provision concerning validity and rejected the claim that the agreement was invalid.[434] This divergence in judicial reasoning underscores the ongoing uncertainty in Chinese law regarding the classification and consequences of violating such provisions.

469. To tackle this inconsistency, the SPC issued a judicial guiding opinion in 2009, which provides that when determining whether the validity of the contract has been tainted by illegality:

> The people's court should holistically consider the legislative intent of laws and regulations and balance/weigh conflicting rights and interests, such as the types of rights and interests at hand, transaction security, and the objects they regulate, and comprehensively determine the mandatory provisions. Suppose the mandatory provisions concern the contract behaviour, that is, as long as the contract behaviour occurs. In that case, if it harms the national or social public interest, the People's Court should affirm the contract as invalid. If mandatory provisions regulate the parties' 'market access' qualifications rather than certain types of contract behaviours or regulate the performance of a certain contract rather than a certain type of contract behaviour, the people's court shall determine this type of contract as valid. It should be handled carefully, and when necessary, the opinions of relevant legislative departments should be sought, or the people's court at a higher level should be consulted.[435]

470. However, in some cases, the statute specifies that a party violating the rule will face penalties, such as fines, licence revocation, or other sanctions, but it does not address whether a contract formed in violation of the rule is void. In such instances, the judge's determination regarding the breach of the statutory rule depends on public policy considerations, taking into account the harm the statute aims to prevent, its language, scope, purpose, the impact on the innocent party, and any other relevant factors.

471. In 2019, the SPC issued The SPC Minutes of the National Conference on Civil and Commercial Trial Work of Courts Nationwide (2019) to clarify this. When adjudicating contract disputes, the Courts must carefully assess the nature of 'mandatory provisions' under Article 153(1) of the Civil Code and Article 14 of the SPC Interpretation on the CCL (II) (2009).[436] The list of relevant factors includes the

434. *Ibid.*
435. The Guiding Opinions on Several Issues Concerning the Trial of Civil and Commercial Contract Disputes under Current Situations (2009).
436. Article 30 of the SPC Minutes of the National Conference on Civil and Commercial Trial Work of Courts Nationwide (2019) provides some guidance: 'some people's courts frequently deem contracts invalid on the grounds of violating the mandatory provisions of laws and administrative regulations, and improperly expand the scope of invalid contracts, … Some people's courts believe

types of legal interests protected by mandatory provisions, the legal consequences of illegal acts, and transaction security protection.

472. Mandatory provisions concerning validity include those related to financial security, market order, national macroeconomic policies, and public order and good morals. Examples include prohibitions on trading certain goods or services, such as human organs, drugs, or firearms; violations of franchising regulations, such as over-the-counter margin trading contracts; contracts formed through illegal transaction methods, such as violations of tendering rules; and illegal trading venues, such as unauthorised futures trading. In contrast, mandatory provisions concerning regulation typically govern aspects like business scope, trading time, and trading quantity and do not generally affect the validity of contracts.[437]

473. Mandatory provisions concerning regulations are intended to regulate market behaviour and administrative processes without necessarily invalidating contracts that fail to comply with them. In the case of *Hebi Broadhouse Real Estate Co., Ltd. v. Qixian Rural Credit Cooperatives*,[438] the SPC declined to invalidate a contract for violating mandatory provisions concerning regulations. The SPC reasoned that the Regulations on Loans, issued as departmental rules by the People's Bank of China, primarily serve as administrative guidelines for managing deposits and loans. These rules are distinct from mandatory provisions concerning validity, as mentioned in Articles 143 and 153 of the Civil Code, which address legal requirements for the enforceability of contracts.[439] This case highlights the distinction between provisions aimed at ensuring administrative compliance and those that directly affect the legitimacy and enforceability of contracts.

474. Judicial practice generally holds that only contracts violating mandatory provisions of law concerning validity are rendered invalid. This distinction is crucial for protecting party autonomy, ensuring transactional security, promoting good faith, encouraging transactions, and preventing misuse of mandatory provisions as a pretext for malicious breach of contract.

475. However, courts often vary in their interpretations and standards for distinguishing between mandatory provisions concerning validity and those concerning regulations. Chinese law contains numerous mandatory provisions, legal terms, and administrative regulations with differing legislative purposes. Despite guidance from the SPC, no clear standard has emerged to determine which provisions render contracts invalid. This uncertainty poses risks to judicial credibility, as it undermines consistency and predictability in the application of the law.

---

that all mandatory provisions of an administrative nature are 'mandatory provisions of management' and do not affect the validity of the Contract. This method of identification should be corrected … '.

437. *Ibid.*

438. *Hebi Broadhouse Real Estate Co., Ltd. v. Qixian Rural Credit Cooperatives*, the Supreme People's Cour, (2019) Min Shen No. 4756; 淇县农村信用合作联社诉鹤壁市广厦房产置业有限公司，最高人民法院（2019）最高法民申4756号.

439. Articles 143 and 153 CC.

476. As such, Article 16 of the SPC Interpretation on the Contract Book (2023) adopts a new approach by abandoning the concept of mandatory provisions concerning validity. It now requires judges to determine the validity of civil legal acts according to the actual effect of mandatory provisions.

477. Specifically, suppose a contract violates mandatory provisions of laws or administrative regulations. In that case, the Chinese courts may determine that the contract is not void due to a violation of mandatory provisions in one of the following situations:[440]

1. First, if the actual performance of the contract has a negligible effect on public order, declaring the contract void could lead to unfair or unjust outcomes.
2. Second, when mandatory provisions aim to protect government interests (e.g., tax revenue, land transfer fees, or other legitimate third-party interests), upholding the contract's validity may still achieve the regulatory purpose.
3. Third, if the mandatory provisions are designed to ensure one party's internal risk control or management, and the other party lacks the ability or duty to verify compliance, declaring the contract void could unfairly penalise the non-breaching party.
4. Fourth, a party that violated mandatory provisions during contract formation but later gains the ability to rectify the breach and refuses to do so in violation of the principle of good faith may still be held accountable.
5. Fifth, additional scenarios outlined in laws, judicial interpretations, or administrative regulations may influence the determination of contract validity.

478. In such situations, Chinese courts would refrain from declaring a contract void based on violations of mandatory provisions at the request of a contracting party. This approach shifts the focus from a rigid interpretation of whether a mandatory provision directly invalidates a civil legal act to a broader evaluation of how such norms influence the overall effectiveness of the transaction. By allowing greater judicial discretion, this framework enables judges to assess the specific impact of mandatory provisions on civil legal acts, fostering a more nuanced, context-sensitive, and equitable application of the law.

479. This flexibility enables judges to consider the specific circumstances of each case and make more informed decisions. It allows for a more balanced assessment of all parties' interests rather than simply applying rigid legal rules. Assessing the effectiveness of mandatory norms in light of their practical impact aligns with the principle of achieving the law's intended purpose.

480. What is worth mentioning is that where a contract is deemed valid, but the parties' illegal actions have not been addressed, courts may issue judicial recommendations to the relevant administrative authorities.[441] If the parties' actions are suspected of a crime, the case should be referred to the criminal investigation

440. Article 16 of the SPC Interpretation on the Contract Book (2023).
441. *Ibid.*

authorities.[442] This approach addresses the long-standing issue of lack of coordination between courts and relevant regulatory agencies when mandatory provisions are violated.

481. Nonetheless, the downside of the new approach is that it could still lead to uncertainty in legal outcomes since it introduces subjective elements into the decision-making process. The interpretation of the 'corrective effect' of mandatory norms can differ based on individual judges' perspectives, which may result in inconsistent rulings. Overall, it is a step towards adapting legal principles to real-world complexities, but its success will ultimately depend on its implementation and the guidance provided to judges.

482. In modern society, laws and regulations permeate all aspects of life. This is particularly relevant in China, a nation characterised by top-down, regulation-oriented governance. Whether national or local, legislative or regulatory, industry standards or codes of conduct, they are so extensive that many business activities – including contract formation – risk violating these rules. This highlights the growing need to revisit the issue of contracts that breach legal provisions. The trend toward more flexible remedies suggests that the rigidity of traditional solutions may no longer be the most suitable approach in modern times.[443]

483. While Chinese law does not explicitly use a proportionality test as a formal doctrine as found in the common law system,[444] the courts do apply a form of balancing test. They consider whether the illegal act justifies voiding the entire contract or if the illegal portion can be severed, allowing the valid portions of the contract to remain enforceable. Additionally, where the illegal behaviour has not been addressed, the court may issue recommendations to administrative authorities or refer the matter for criminal investigation. Hence, the approach resembles a proportionality assessment, as the courts weigh the impact of the illegality on the contract's validity while ensuring that public interest and legal standards are upheld.

484. To summarise, under Chinese law, the validity of a contract tainted by illegality is assessed based on whether the illegal element fundamentally affects the contract's core purpose. Contracts that violate mandatory legal provisions are generally deemed invalid. However, the SPC steered a new course by making this rule less rigid and less absolute. The Chinese courts may consider factors such as the nature and severity of the illegality, the connection between the illegal act and the contract's main obligations, and whether the public interest or social order at stake has been significantly affected by the violation. This way allows courts to weigh factors like deterrence, public policy, and proportionality to achieve equitable outcomes based on the context of each case.

---

442. *Ibid.*
443. Rossella Esther Cerchia, A Comparative Viewpoint on Illegal Contracts: In Favor of Flexibility and Proportionality, 21.2 Global Jurist 447-479 (2021).
444. The UK Supreme Court in *Patel v. Mirza [2016] UKSC 42* adopted a more flexible approach which openly addressed the underlying policy considerations involved and invited Courts to reach a balanced judgment in each case, permitting account to be taken of the proportionality of the outcome.

II. Public Order and Good Morals

485. Article 153(2) of the Civil Code states that 'civil juridical acts violating public order and good morals are invalid'. The principle of public order and good morals is a supplement to 'violating mandatory provisions of laws or administrative regulations'. It is generally believed that such a principle encompasses public order and good morals. Public order can be understood as the order that conforms to the interests of the state and social public interests, while good morals can be understood as good moral concepts or norms. Therefore, public order and good morals refer to the collection of fundamental principles and norms considered essential for society's orderly functioning and moral welfare. These include legal and moral standards widely recognised and accepted in society.

486. Although civil juridical acts are primarily based on the principle of party autonomy, Chinese law places a high premium on public order and good morals in the sense that the civil juridical act, including a contract, does not harm the interests of the state or social public interests and should adhere to good moral norms. The rule of public order and good morals is a fundamental principle that governs the legality and validity of civil acts and transactions.

487. This rule is designed to ensure that all civil legal actions and agreements do not contravene society's basic values and legal norms. Laws that violate public order and good morals are considered invalid or unenforceable. This rule applies to a wide range of civil activities, including contracts, property transactions, marriage, and family relations. Civil acts that directly conflict with societal norms and legal standards may be deemed invalid.

488. For example, the parties still signed a lease contract when the involved property has been identified as a dangerous building with serious structural dangers which may cause major safety accidents. It was agreed to lease the building as a business hotel that may endanger the safety of the general public's life and property. The court held that this damages social public interests and violates public order and good morals.[445] Therefore, the lease contract is invalid, and the legal responsibilities to be borne by each party should be determined based on the extent of fault of both parties.

489. Nonetheless, the scope of public order, good morals, and its connotation are uncertain and vague, leaving room for interpretation. It is worth noting that various provisions and regulations may indirectly relate to the concept of public order and good morals throughout the Civil Code. For example, provisions regarding contracts, property rights, tort liability, and family relations may all incorporate considerations of public order and good morals to ensure that civil actions are conducted consistent with societal norms and values.

---

445. *Rao Guoli v. Jiangxi Provincial Prison Administration Material Supply Station*, the Supreme People's Court, (2019) SPC Min Zai No. 97; 饶国礼诉江西省监狱管理局物资供应站，最高人民法院（2019）最高法民再97号.

490. Applying the rule of public order and good morals in Chinese courts involves a judicial assessment of whether a particular civil act or legal transaction contravenes the fundamental legal and moral standards recognised by society. Courts apply the rule based on each case's specifics, considering the act's nature and its impact on societal norms and legal standards. There is no one-size-fits-all approach, as the determination heavily depends on the act's context.

491. The interpretation and application of public order and good morals can be dynamic and context-specific, with courts relying on legal principles, precedents, and societal standards to determine whether a particular action violates public order and good morals. As a consequence, judges have considerable discretion in applying the rule. They evaluate whether an act violates society's collective sense of justice, legality, and morality. This evaluation is grounded in social, cultural, and legal contexts.

492. One major controversy lies in the inherent vagueness and subjectivity of the rule. What constitutes public order and good morals can vary widely and change over time, leading to potential unpredictability in its application. The broad discretion granted to judges in interpreting and applying the rule can lead to inconsistent outcomes. While this allows for flexibility in adjudication, it also raises concerns about legal certainty and fairness. This is particularly the case in adjudicating the new type of cases.

493. In *Shanghai Qinju Co Ltd. v. Beijing Yuner Computing Technology Ltd.*, a Beijing computing tech company agreed to buy Bitcoin mining machines from a Shanghai company, with ownership retained by the Shanghai company until payment was completed.[446] They agreed to host these servers at the Beijing company's cloud centre. After the conclusion of the contract, the Shanghai company arranged with another Shanghai industrial company to handle technical service agreements, including paying for electricity and receiving Bitcoin. Later, the industrial company and the Beijing tech company signed an agreement for the Beijing company to provide technical services for the servers, ensuring power supply and continuous operation. Due to several power outages, the industrial company sued the Beijing tech company for breach of contract, seeking over RMB 5.3 million in compensation for lost Bitcoin income.[447]

494. In its first instance judgment, the Beijing Dongcheng District Court considered Bitcoin 'mining' essentially a risk investment activity aimed at gaining virtual goods profits.[448] On 3 September 2021, China's National Development and Reform Commission and other departments issued a notice on rectifying virtual currency

446. *Shanghai Qinju Co Ltd. v. Beijing Yuner Computing Technology Ltd.*, Beijing Dongcheng District People's Court, (2021) Jing 0101 Min Chu No. 6309; 上海勤鞠实业有限公司诉北京云尔计算科技有限公司，北京市东城区人民法院（2021）京0101民初6309号.

447. *Ibid.*

448. *Ibid.*

'mining' activities, categorising them as industries to be eliminated and banning investments in them according to relevant regulations. Article 19 of the State Council's 'Interim Provisions on Promoting Industrial Structure Adjustment' prohibits investment in projects classified for elimination. Bitcoin mining, characterised by its massive electricity consumption, is not conducive to high-quality development, energy conservation, emission reduction, and achieving carbon peak and neutrality goals.

495. For the Beijing Court, it contradicts the 'green principle' in Article 9 of the Civil Code. It does not comply with relevant policies, regulations, and regulatory requirements for industrial structure adjustment, violating public order and good morals. Therefore, the contract involved in maintaining Bitcoin 'mining machines' and 'mining' should be considered invalid.[449]

496. Notably, all the government documents are departmental rules, which do not qualify as mandatory rules of laws or administrative regulations. Article 153(2) of the Civil Code, as a supplementary provision for invalidity of contracts violating mandatory provisions, functions as a fallback ground for invalidating contracts without explicit statutory provisions. This may reduce predictability for parties regarding judicial outcomes.

497. Another controversial aspect is balancing individual rights and freedoms with societal morals and interests. Excessive emphasis on public order and good morals could unduly restrict individual liberties or commercial freedoms. Rapid societal changes can shift what is considered acceptable or moral, challenging courts to adapt their interpretations of public order and good morals without clear legislative guidance. It is not uncommon for the court to invalidate a financial contract concluded by sophisticated parties.

498. For example, in *Nanjing Gaoke Xinjun Growth Phase I Equity Investment Partnership (Limited Partnership) v. Fang Yongsheng and Liang Xilin*, the parties agreed to subscribe to 100 million yuan of additional capital in Shaoxing RunKang Biomedical Equity Investment Partnership (Limited Partnership).[450] Subsequently, the parties signed an Amended Partnership Agreement, which includes Clause 4.2 about the post-initial public offering (IPO) put option: within six months from the date Jiangsu ShuoShi completes its qualified IPO, the investors have the right to demand any put obligor (the defendants or Shaoxing RunKang) to buy back all or part of their partnership shares at a prescribed price. The post-IPO repurchase price

449. *Ibid.*

450. *Nanjing Gaoke Xinjun Growth Phase I Equity Investment Partnership (Limited Partnership) v. Fang Yongsheng and Liang Xilin*, Shanghai No. 2 Intermediate People's Court, (2020) Hu 02 Min Chu No. 234; 南京高科新浚成长一期股权投资合伙企业（有限合伙）诉房永生、梁锡林，上海市第二中级人民法院（2020）沪02民初234号.

will be calculated based on the average closing price of Jiangsu ShuoShi's shares in the secondary market over the 30 trading days preceding the put notice issuance.

499. In December 2019, Jiangsu ShuoShi was listed on the Shanghai Stock Exchange's STAR Market. According to Article 10 of the Shanghai Stock Exchange Science and Technology Innovation Board Stock Issuance and Listing Review Practice Guide, the Clause mentioned above 4.2 agreement is considered an earn-out agreement that should have been disclosed before applying for the STAR Market IPO. However, during the application process, Jiangsu ShuoShi did not disclose the repurchase clause as required by regulations. The Claimant issued a Repurchase Notice to the defendants, demanding the performance of the post-IPO repurchase obligation.

500. The Shanghai No. 2 Intermediate People's Court held that the validity of earn-out agreements following a company's public listing not only implicates adjustments within the company's internal relationships but also affects securities regulatory requirements, undermining the stability of securities market transactions and financial security.[451] Suppose parties conceal undisclosed earn-out clauses explicitly required by listing review rules to be rectified before listing.

501. In that case, the determination of their validity must carefully consider the public order embodied in these rules, whether the regulatory focus is on the actions of trading or qualifications for market access, and the implications for financial security and social impact. Provisions directly tied to stock market value, such as buy-back clauses, pose a risk of investors deliberately manipulating stock prices in the secondary market during the exercise period for their investment benefits. Therefore, such an agreement should be considered invalid.[452] The Shanghai High People's Court affirmed this reasoning on appeal.[453]

502. In this case, the agreement included a repurchase clause directly linked to the secondary market stock value, violating the securities industry guidelines issued by the Shanghai Stock Exchange. Nevertheless, the court invoked public order and good morals as a fatal ground to invalidate the agreement.[454]

503. In summary, while the rule of public order and good morals serves as a crucial mechanism for aligning legal transactions with societal values, its application is marked by complexities and controversies, especially regarding its subjective nature and the balance between societal interests and individual rights.

451. *Ibid.*
452. *Ibid.*
453. *Nanjing Gaoke Xinjun Growth Phase I Equity Investment Partnership (Limited Partnership) v. Fang Yongsheng and Liang Xilin*, Shanghai High People's Court, (2020) Hu 02 Min Chu No. 234; 南京高科新浚成长一期股权投资合伙企业（有限合伙）诉房永生、梁锡林， 上海市高级人民法院（2021）沪民终745号.
454. *Ibid.*

504. Article 31 of the SPC Trial Minutes 2019 stipulates that:[455]

> violations of regulations generally do not affect the validity of contracts, but if the content of the regulation involves public order and good morals such as financial security, market order, and national macro policies, the contract should be deemed invalid. When determining whether regulations involve public order and good morals, the courts should carefully consider the scope of regulation objects, regulatory intensity, transaction security protection, and social impact, and provide sufficient reasoning in their judgments.

505. In its reasons for determining the invalidity of contracts violating regulations, the SPC has, to some extent, narrowed the scope of public order and good morals through a listing approach, reflecting a tendency in judicial practice to cautiously apply public order and good morals in determining the invalidity of contracts. After implementing the Civil Code, courts may continue invoking public order and good morals as grounds for the invalidity of contracts. However, the scope of application of public order and good morals will be further tested in practice.

506. It is suggested that extreme caution should still be exercised when invoking the ground of violating public order and good morals. Otherwise, there is a risk of indirectly expanding the scope of invalidity, which could undermine the intended purpose of party autonomy and related judicial interpretations that strictly limit the scope of illegal invalidity. To address this concern, the SPC further articulated how the Chinese courts should apply the rule of public order and good morals in practice as a judicial interpretation. Article 17 of the SPC Interpretation on the Contract Book (2023) provides that:[456]

> When determining whether a contract violates public order and good morals, the People's Court should be guided by socialist core values, taking into account factors such as the parties' subjective motives and transaction purposes, the intensity of government regulation, the frequency of similar transactions by the parties within a certain period, and the social consequences of the actions. The reasoning should be fully articulated in the judgment documents. If the transaction is conducted out of life necessity, does not significantly impact public order, does not affect national security, or does not contravene good morals, the People's Court should not declare the contract invalid.

507. Take the example of purchasing property under another person's name (nominee purchasing). The issue is whether the agreement between the parties, namely, the nominee purchasing agreement, is invalid due to violations of the local government's property purchase restriction regulations.

---

455. Article 31 of the SPC Trial Minute (2019).
456. Article 17 of the SPC Interpretation on the Contract Book (2023).

508. In practice, one viewpoint suggests that although property purchase restriction regulations are stipulated by local government agencies rather than by the State Council, these regulations involve macro-control of the real estate market by the state, thus involving social public interests or public order and good morals. Therefore, parties attempting to evade these regulations using a nominee approach inevitably violate public order and good morals, making the nominee purchasing agreement invalid.

509. A different view holds, however, that it is necessary to clarify the ownership of the property in case of the nominee purchasing. Although most of these agreements stipulate that the purchased property belongs to the actual money provider, with the nominee acting only as a holder on behalf of the money provider, the provisions regarding changes in real property rights in the Property Rights section of the Civil Code are mandatory regulations.

510. In cases where there is a change in real property rights based on legal acts, the parties must agree to the change in property rights, and registration must be completed. Otherwise, the property rights will not pass. Therefore, if there is only an agreement between the parties regarding property ownership, but registration cannot be completed due to violations of purchase restriction regulations, the nominee will not acquire ownership of the purchased property and will face significant legal risks, such as the possibility of the property being disposed of by the nominator.

511. This implies that the regulatory purpose of purchase restrictions has been achieved, and it is not necessary further to deem the nominee purchasing agreement between the parties invalid. If the nominee purchasing agreement is deemed invalid, it may trigger the parties' dishonesty. For example, in the event of a surge in property prices, the nominator may refuse to fulfil the contract or bear another breach of contract liabilities on the grounds of the agreement being invalid, thereby obtaining substantial profits from the increased value of the property. In such a circumstance, public order and good morals may not be invoked as grounds to invalidate the nominee purchasing agreement.

512. The same reasoning also applies to the cases of nominee share purchase agreements (the 'NSPA'), where one party is the nominee holding a company's equity for the actual investor. However, while the NSPA in a non-listed company can be taken as valid, the Chinese courts have developed a consistent position over the NSPA of listed companies in the last decade. Where the subject matter to be purchased is a share in a listed company in an NSPA, such an agreement is invalid.

513. In *Yang Jinguo v. Lin Jinkun, Changzhou Yamadun Co., Ltd.*,[457] the SPC held that the NSPA violated a series of regulatory provisions related to the listing of companies. While some are regulatory provisions of government departments, they

457. *Yang Jinguo v. Lin Jinkun*, the Supreme People's Court, (2017) SPC Min Shen No. 2454; 杨金国诉林金坤，最高人民法院（2017）最高法民申2454号.

provide important safeguards for the interests of the general non-specific investors and necessary protection for social public interests. Therefore, under Article 52 of the CCL, the disputed agreements in this case should be deemed invalid.

514. In *Sugiura Tatsumi v. Gong Yin*, the Claimant, Sugiura Tatsushin, a Japanese national and Gong Yin, the Defendant, signed an NSPA stipulating that the Claimant would purchase 880,000 shares of a company at RMB 4.36 per share and entrust the Defendant with management, with Defendant transferring all profits to Sugiura promptly.[458] In 2017, the company was publicly listed on the Shanghai Stock Exchange. During the IPO process, Defendant, as a shareholder, repeatedly issued declarations confirming she was a genuine shareholder and was not a nominee on behalf of an actual investor. In 2018, the listed company distributed cash dividends of RMB 4 per 10 shares to all shareholders and increased its share capital by four shares for every ten shares through capital reserves.[459] Subsequently, the number of Company A shares under Defendant's name increased to 1,232,000 shares. A dispute arose between the parties as to the profit distribution.

515. The Shanghai Financial Court reasoned that this is a typical NSPA where the Claimant is the actual investor and the Defendant is the nominal holder. Defendant did not disclose during the IPO of Company A that she held the disputed shares in a nominee capacity. Nor did the Claimant disclose the nominee holding situation to the company or regulatory authorities before or after the IPO.[460] Following the IPO, the disputed shares were registered under the Defendant's name. The Court held that the undisclosed nominee holding violates the public order that must be observed in the securities market. Therefore, the hidden nominee holding of the disputed shares is invalid due to violating the public order in the securities market.[461]

516. In Shanghai Honghua Cultural Entrepreneurship Investment Co., Ltd. v. Chen Haokang & Shenzhen Quance Management Consulting Co., Ltd.& Li Ye,[462] the parties entered an NSPA. The Court of First Instance held that the content of the 'Shareholding Proxy Memorandum' at issue constitutes hidden nominee holding of shares in the listed company in substance.[463] Listed companies must truthfully disclose the ownership of shares, and investing in the shares of a listed company through a nominee violates regulatory rules regarding clear ownership of shares, thereby harming social public interests. According to Article 8, Article 143, and

458. *Sugiura Tatsumi v. Gong Yin*, Shanghai Financial Court, (2018) Hu 74 Min Chu No. 585; 杉浦立身诉龚茵，上海金融法院（2018）沪74民初585号.

459. *Ibid.*

460. *Ibid.*

461. *Ibid.*

462. *Shanghai Honghua Cultural Entrepreneurship Investment Co., Ltd. V. Chen Haokang & Shenzhen Quance Management Consulting Co., Ltd. & Li Ye*, Shanghai No. 1 Intermediate People's Court, (2019) Hu 01 Min Chu No. 46; 上海宏华文化创业投资有限责任公司诉陈灏康、深圳市权策管理咨询有限公司、李野，上海市第一中级人民法院（2019）沪01民初46号.

463. *Ibid.*

Article 153 of the Civil Code, the 'Shareholding Proxy Memorandum' is invalid.[464] On appeal, the Shanghai High People's Court upholds the ruling by the Court of First Instance.[465]

517. From the above three cases, it can be seen that Chinese courts decided that the hidden nominee holding shares in the listed company violated regulatory rules, thereby harming social public interests and contravening public order and good morals, rendering it invalid. However, the legal consequences of the invalid NSPA are crucial on whether the actual investor can demand the return of the investment funds, interests and profits if any. This will be discussed in detail in section 5.

518. For the present purpose, it is important to acknowledge the boundaries of public order and good morals to prevent it from becoming a tool for enforcing a purely instinctive sense of 'justice between individuals'[466] rather than a clearly defined legal principle. Otherwise, public order and good morals would become an unriddled horse, intruding unpredictably into areas of private law, undermining legal certainty and the rule of law.

519. Without well-defined limits, public order and immorality risk becoming a mechanism of ad hoc judicial intervention driven by subjective notions of fairness rather than established legal frameworks. This would erode the predictability essential for private transactions and dispute resolution, discouraging both parties from placing trust in contractual obligations. Public order and good morals must, therefore, remain grounded in legal consistency and principle, functioning not as a catch-all doctrine but as a safeguard for fundamental societal values, used sparingly and with clarity.

III. Effectiveness of a Contract Subject to Approval

520. Generally, a valid contract becomes effective upon establishment, except as otherwise stipulated by law or agreed upon by the parties.[467] Some contracts are subject to approval as stipulated by relevant laws or administrative regulations. The CCL does not provide clear guidance on the effectiveness of a contract subject to approval but not being approved.

---

464. *Ibid.*
465. *Shanghai Honghua Cultural Entrepreneurship Investment Co., Ltd. v. Chen Haokang & Shenzhen Quance Management Consulting Co., Ltd. & Li Ye*, Shanghai High People's Court, (2020) Hu Min Zhong No. 512; 上海宏华文化创业投资有限责任公司诉陈灏康、深圳市权策管理咨询有限公司、李野，上海市高级人民法院（2020）沪民终512号.
466. Hector Lewis MacQueen, Illegality and Immorality in Contracts: Towards European Principles, in Towards a European Civil Code 555-570 (4th edn, Arthur S. Hartkamp, Martijn W. Hesselink, Ewoud Hondius, C Mak, Edgar Du Perron eds., Kluwer Law International–Ars Aequi Libri 2011).
467. Paragraph 1 of Art. 502 CC.

521. The evolution of relevant judicial interpretations and policies illustrates that the SPC has itself undergone a process of continually deepening its understanding. Initially, unapproved contracts were classified as contracts not yet in effect, distinguishing them from invalid contracts.[468] The former still has the potential to become effective after completing the approval procedures, whereas the latter is inherently and definitively invalid from the outset.

522. However, the *SPC Interpretation on the Contract Law (I) (1999)* does not provide specific provisions on how to facilitate the transformation of an ineffective contract into an effective one. This omission has led courts, in judicial practice, to often deem contracts as ineffective but ultimately regard them as invalid contracts, failing to achieve the intended effect.[469]

523. In response, *the SPC Interpretation on the Contract Law (II) (2009)* stipulates that for contracts requiring approval to become effective, the court may, based on the specifics of the case and at the request of the counterparty, order that the counterparty may handle the necessary approval procedures themselves, with the party who failed to fulfil the obligation to seek approval bearing the related costs and losses.[470] This provision allows the counterparty to independently apply for approval, meaning that even when the entire contract is not yet effective, the obligation to seek approval becomes independently effective. This is commendable.

524. However, due to the complexity of the approval procedures and the necessity of cooperation from the party obligated to seek approval, the counterparty often struggles to assemble all the required documents for the application. This makes it challenging to ultimately obtain approval, rendering the provision difficult to implement effectively as expected.

525. Recognising the above drawbacks, the SPC has recently pronounced that the clauses concerning the obligation to seek approval become independently effective and that the party obligated to seek approval must bear liability for breach of contract if they fail to fulfil this obligation.[471] Further, the SPC clearly states that if the court orders the obligated party to perform the approval-seeking obligation and the obligated party still refuses, then the counterparty may request that the obligated party bear liability for breaching the entire contract – that is, compensate for

468. Article 9 of SPC Interpretation of Several Issues concerning the Application of the Contract Law of the People's Republic of China on Contract Law (I) (1999).
469. Guixiang Liu & Guangrong Wu, Thinking Methods in the Application of Contract Law Book in the Civil Code: Focusing on the Interpretation of the General Principles of Contract Book, 01 The Jurist 57-73 (2024).
470. Article 8 of the SPC Interpretation of Several Issues concerning the Application of the Contract Law of the People's Republic of China (II) (2009).
471. Article 1 of the SPC Provisions on Certain Issues Concerning the Adjudication of Cases Involving Foreign-Invested Enterprises (I) (2010).

the full performance interest.[472] In addressing the repercussions of not adhering to approval duties, the SPC proposes a sequential approach to assign responsibility to those obligated to obtain approvals.[473]

526. Such a new approach taken in the above recent SPC Interpretations was adopted in the Civil Code. When the approval procedure has not been processed, causing the contract to be ineffective will not affect the effectiveness of clauses requiring the fulfilment of the obligation to apply for approval.[474] If the party required to carry out relevant procedures fails to fulfil such obligation, the other party may request it to bear liability for breach of this obligation.[475]

527. This means that the legal obligations and rights stipulated in the contract come into force only after the approval is granted. A contract not yet in effect essentially means it lacks enforceability, indicating that neither party can enforce the main terms agreed upon in the contract. This, however, does not suggest that the contract is devoid of any legal effects. For instance, a contract awaiting effectuation still maintains legally binding power, distinguishing it from an invalid contract. For example, in the case of a legally valid contract that is not yet effective, its legally binding power can enforce obligations on both parties to neither independently modify nor dissolve the contract,[476] as well as obligations against maliciously hindering or facilitating the realisation of conditions.[477] Moreover, it can impose proactive duties, such as the party's obligation to secure approvals to complete those approval processes.[478]

528. Prior to approval, the parties involved may have limited obligations towards each other, often centred around acting in good faith to obtain the necessary approval. There is often a requirement for the party responsible for obtaining approval to notify the other party of the approval status. Failure to do so promptly can have legal consequences and may give rise to claims for damages. Two related issues need to be examined:

1. First, when the obligated party fails to seek approval, can the counterparty directly request to terminate the contract and claim damages from the approval

---

472. Articles 6 and 7 of the SPC Interpretation on Several Issues Concerning the Application of Law in the Trial of Disputes over Mining Rights (2017); Art. 38 of the SPC Trial Minutes (2019).
473. *Ibid.*
474. Paragraph 2 of Art. 502 CC.
475. *Ibid.*
476. Article 136 CC provides that a juridical act becomes effective at the moment of formation, except as otherwise provided for by law or agreed by parties. The actor shall not alter or terminate such juridical act unilaterally except as otherwise provided for by law or acquiring the counterparty's consent.
477. Article 159 CC provides that in the case of a civil juridical act subject to a condition, if such condition is unjustly prevented from being fulfilled by a party for his or her own interest, it will be seen as fulfilled; if such condition is unjustly fulfilled by a party for his or her own interest, it will be seen as not fulfilled.
478. Article 502 CC.

obligor? When the approval obligor refuses to perform the approval obligation, it constitutes a breach of the independently effective obligation. The counterparty is entitled to request the termination of the contract due to the breach.[479] This is because the failure to seek approval prevents the contract from becoming effective, fundamentally frustrating the purpose of the agreement. The counterparty can claim compensation for losses resulting from the approval obligor's breach of the obligation to seek approval. Damages may include expenses incurred, lost profits, and other direct losses caused by the breach.[480]

2. Second, when the approval obligor has performed the approval obligation, but the contract is not approved, does the approval obligor bear no liability? The approval obligor must diligently perform the approval obligation, which includes preparing necessary documents and submitting applications to the relevant government agency. If the contract is not approved despite the approval obligor's diligent efforts, and the non-approval is due to factors beyond their control (e.g., policy changes, regulatory decisions), the obligor generally does not bear liability.[481] This is because the obligated party has discharged its duty by seeking the approval properly. Certainly, if the non-approval results from the obligor's negligence or fault, such as submitting incomplete or incorrect information, failing to comply with procedural requirements, or engaging in fraudulent activities. In such cases, the approval obligor may be held liable for breach of contract.[482]

529. This is to say, if the required approval is not obtained within a specified period or it becomes apparent that approval will not be granted due to the obligated party's conduct, the contract may be considered void or voidable. The parties may then be returned to their pre-contractual status, and any benefits transferred under the contract may need to be returned.[483] This approach has been formalised in the SPC Interpretation on the Contract Book (2023).[484]

530. The requirement for approval introduces an element of uncertainty into contractual relationships. However, it serves important regulatory and policy purposes by ensuring that certain types of contracts receive scrutiny from relevant authorities before they can produce legal effects. The Civil Code and the SPC Interpretation on the Contract Book (2023) aim to promote the transformation of ineffective contracts into effective ones and protect the legitimate interests of the parties involved by providing clear guidelines on obligations and liabilities in such situations.

---

479. Paragraph 1 of Art. 12 of the SPC Interpretation on the Contract Book (2023).
480. Paragraph 2 of Art. 12 of the SPC Interpretation on the Contract Book (2023); Guixiang Liu & Guangrong Wu, Thinking Methods in the Application of Contract Law Book in the Civil Code: Focusing on the Interpretation of the General Principles of Contract Book, 01 The Jurist 57-73 (2024).
481. Paragraph 4 of Art. 12 of the SPC Interpretation on the Contract Book (2023).
482. *Ibid.*
483. Article 157 CC.
484. Article 12 of SPC Interpretation on the Contract Law (2023).

§5. The Consequences of Contract Invalidity

531. Under the Civil Code, the grounds affecting contract validity can be divided into two categories: (1) void contracts, and (2) voidable contracts, as illustrated in the table below:

Category	*Sub-categories*
Void Contracts	- Collusive sham representation
	- Fraud against state interests
	- Lack of Capacity
	- Violation of Mandatory Laws and Regulations (with exceptions)
	- Violating public order and social morals
	-Malicious collusion
Voidable Contracts	- Gross misunderstanding
	- Fraud by another contracting party or a third party
	- Obviously unfair at the time of establishment
	- Duress (entered under coercion by a contracting party or a third party)

532. Void contracts are automatically invalid from the outset, while voidable contracts can be invalidated at the selection of the affected party. Where the partial voidness of a civil juridical act does not affect the validity of the other part, then the other part remains valid.[485]

533. The legal consequences of a contract being declared invalid are set out in Article 157 of the Civil Code, which is largely modelled after Article 58 of the CCL. It is noteworthy that under the Civil Code, the same legal consequences apply to invalidity, revocation, confirmation of ineffectiveness of the contract and where the civil juridical act is not established.[486]

534. Article 157 provides that 'after a contract has been declared invalid or revoked, all property obtained by reason of the said contract shall be returned; where the property cannot be returned, or there is no need to return it, compensation shall be paid on the basis of the depreciated value of the property. A party at fault can compensate the other party for its resulting losses. Where both parties are at fault, each party shall bear the relevant liability. *If any contrary legal provision is provided elsewhere, such provision prevails*'.

485. Article 156 CC.
486. Article 23 of the SPC Interpretation on the General Provisions of the Civil Code (2022).

535. The last sentence in Article 157 (underlined) is a new addition to Article 58 of the CCL. There are four portions to Article 157.

536. The first portion – 'after a contract has been declared invalid or revoked, all property obtained by reason of the said contract shall be returned' – addresses the return of the property in relation to the now-invalidated or revoked contract. When a contract is invalidated or revoked, it signifies the absence of any contractual relationship between the parties. Therefore, the parties' financial status should be restored to the condition as if the contract had never been entered into. The return of property is aimed at restoring the financial relationship with the state prior to the formation of the contract. Thus, regardless of whether the recipient of the property is at fault, there is an obligation to return the property. However, the return of property primarily applies to situations where performance has already been undertaken. If the parties have not yet begun performance or the property has not been delivered, the principle of returning property should not be applied.

537. Article 460 of the Civil Code provides that the interest, being a civil fruit, should also be returned but subject to payment of the expenses incurred for maintaining the immovable or movable property to a bona fide possessor.[487] Contracts with money as the subject matter, such as loan contracts, pose specific considerations when deemed invalid. In such cases, the party that utilised the funds is generally obligated to return the interest. According to the Civil Code, the general principle refers to the Loan Prime Rate (LPR) for repayment.[488] It is clear from case law that the principal sum and interests should be returned. Many judicial decisions made by both SPC and local courts have followed this approach.[489]

538. The second portion – 'where the property cannot be returned or there is no need to return it, compensation shall be paid based on the depreciated value of the property' In some situations, it may not be possible or necessary to return property. In such cases, in order to achieve the objective of restoring the original state, compensation should be provided to the other party. Non-returnability of property can be categorised into legal non-returnability and factual non-returnability. Legal non-returnability primarily stems from limitations imposed by the bona fide acquisition system.

539. When one party transfers received property to a third party, and the third party acquires the property in good faith without knowing that the contract between the parties is invalid or revoked, the bona fide third party may not return the original property if it is irreplaceable. In this scenario, the party cannot return the property and must compensate the other party based on the property's market value at

487. Article 460 CC.
488. The Second Division of Civil Trial of the Supreme People's Court, Understanding and Application of the Minutes of the National Conference on Civil and Commercial Trial Work of Courts Nationwide 267, People's Court Press, 2019).
489. *Shanghai Minsheng Investment Co., Ltd. V. Jilin Dongli Comprehensive Investment (Group) Co., Ltd.*, Supreme People's Court, (2006) Min Er Zhong Zi No. 145; 上海民生投资有限公司诉吉林省东力综合投资（集团）有限公司，最高人民法院（2006）民二终字第145号.

that time. Factual non-returnability refers to situations where the subject matter is lost, rendering it impossible to return the original property, especially if it is irreplaceable. In such cases, the party acquiring the property should compensate the other party based on the property's market value at the time.

540. What amounts to 'no need for return' is typically decided by the court, but it can also arise from mutual agreement between the parties involved.[490] If the property received by a party consists of services or benefits that cannot be restored to their original state, compensation should be calculated based on the price set by the state at that time. If there is no set price by the state, compensation should be based on the market price or the remuneration standard for similar services, provided in monetary form. Suppose one party benefits from the use of intellectual property rights, and such rights are intangible. In that case, the party may compensate the other party based on the market value of the intellectual property rights.

541. The third portion – 'A party that is at fault is liable to compensate the other party for its resulting losses, and where both parties are at fault, then each party shall bear the relevant liability respectively' – concerns the fault liability compensation rule where a loss has been caused. In addition to property return or compensation, if a party still incurs losses, they can simultaneously demand the other party to bear responsibility based on fault. Parties only bear compensation liability when they are at fault. No liability is incurred if there is no fault, even if the other party suffers losses.

542. When determining the scope of damages compensation, it is essential to reasonably establish liability based on the degree of fault of the parties and consider factors such as property appreciation or depreciation already taken into account when determining the scope of property return. This helps avoid scenarios of double gains or double losses. Moreover, property return and compensation are based on the principle of good faith and fair dealing, which already allocates losses due to property depreciation among the parties. Therefore, in practice, there is minimal room for awarding compensation.

543. The fourth portion: 'If there are other provisions in the law, follow those provisions.' This provision serves as an exception to the first three legal effects. Some notable examples are the construction, lease, and employment contracts. Where a construction contract is void, but the construction is nevertheless inspected and accepted, the contractor may be compensated by reference to the contract provisions for the price of the construction.[491] If a housing lease contract is invalid, the lessee should refer to the agreed rental standard and pay the lessor an occupancy fee.[492] In cases where a labour contract is invalid, the remuneration shall be determined based

490. *Chen Guangyu v. Lin Mingqiang & Wang Ying*, Intermediate People's Court of Haikou City, Hainan Province, (2018) Qiong 01 Min Zhong No. 1393; 陈光玉诉林明强、王颖，海南省海口市中级人民法院（2018）琼01民终1393号.

491. Article 793 CC.

492. Article 4 of the SPC Interpretation on Issues concerning the Application of Law in the Trial of Cases Involving Disputes over Financial Lease Contracts (2020).

on the remuneration of workers in the same or similar positions within the same unit.[493] These special law provisions will take precedence over the general position under the Civil Code.

544. A vexing issue is whether and how a profit or investment return is returned when the contract is invalid. The court needs to consider the market fluctuation, the entrusted business operation, and its link with the investment returns to distribute the investment returns proportionally.[494] The purpose is to avoid a situation where a party could benefit from the contract invalidity. The SPC has instructed all levels of Chinese courts to consider the changes in property value, whether appreciation or depreciation when adjudicating cases. If both parties have gained property through the contract, they should return it to each other. In instances where the property, such as stocks or real estate, has increased or decreased in value compared to the contract price, the court should consider various factors, including market conditions, the actions of the transferee, and the reasons behind the property's change in value. The aim is to ensure a fair and reasonable allocation or sharing of the property between the parties, thereby preventing one party from unjustly benefiting from an invalid or revoked contract.[495]

545. In *Sugiura Tatsumi v. Gong Yin*, the Shanghai Financial Court provided the following rationale for quantifying the sums to be returned due to the contract's invalidity.[496] The court reasoned that the increase in investment returns resulting from dividends and the company's successful listing is not part of the original benefits before the contract was concluded but represents newly added benefits after the contract's performance.[497] The distribution of these returns should be determined through negotiation between the parties. If negotiation fails, the principle of fairness should be applied to ensure a reasonable distribution. This means that the distribution of investment returns should be based on the level of contribution to investment income and the extent of risk borne by each party. In essence, it should adhere to the principles of 'the party who invests reaps the benefits' and 'benefits should align with risks'.[498]

546. Therefore, considering all the relevant factors, the Court granted 70% of the investment returns to the Claimant and 30% to the Defendant.[499] The Shanghai Financial Court's reasoning is in line with the SPC Trial Minutes (2019). The principal is entitled to request the return of the investment returns but is subject to the remunerations of the entrusted, the associated management expenses and other relevant market factors.

---

493. Article 28 of the Labor CCL.
494. Article 32 of the SPC Trial Minutes (2019)
495. Article 33 of the SPC Trial Minutes (2019).
496. *Sugiura Tatsumi v. Gong Yin*, Shanghai Financial Court, (2018) Hu 74 Min Chu No. 585; 杉浦立身诉龚茵，上海金融法院（2018）沪74民初585号.
497. *Ibid.*
498. *Ibid.*
499. *Ibid.*

Chapter 3. The Contents of a Contract

§1. Introduction

547. When parties and their representatives arrange terms for future transactions, they often cannot anticipate every possible circumstance, even if they possess extensive business experience and legal knowledge. Future contingencies may not even be describable. Consequently, some contract provisions may be vague, ambiguous, or even contain gaps. Moreover, the concept of incomplete contract theory suggests that parties may intentionally draft contract terms in a simplified or rough manner to allow flexibility in interpretation.[500] The 'strategic ambiguity hypothesis' posits that parties may intentionally leave formal contracts incomplete. By using deliberate ambiguity, companies can navigate around legal limitations, making it difficult to invalidate such agreements or for the law to effectively hinder their creation and execution.[501]

548. This tendency toward intentionally 'incomplete' contracts reflects a strategic choice, as parties may wish to maintain negotiation leeway, adapt to unforeseen developments, or foster a cooperative relationship by leaving room for interpretation. In complex or long-term contracts, for example, it is often impractical to specify each detail due to the unpredictable nature of future events. By drafting broader terms, the parties create a framework that can evolve with changing circumstances, thereby reducing the need for constant renegotiation or the addition of lengthy amendments.

549. However, this approach also introduces risks. Vague or incomplete clauses may lead to disputes over the interpretation of the parties' obligations, potentially requiring judicial or arbitral intervention to clarify the contract's intent. In such cases, courts may apply principles like purposive interpretation or the use of trade customs to determine the parties' true intent within the broader context of the contract.

550. Thus, while incomplete contracts allow for flexibility, they also underscore the importance of well-defined interpretative principles that can bridge gaps without distorting the contract's purpose. Incomplete contract theory thereby serves as both a practical tool and a reminder of the need for effective mechanisms – such as judicial interpretation and the application of good faith – to manage the inherent uncertainties in contractual relationships.

---

500. Melvin A Eisenberg, Incomplete Contracts, in Foundational Principles of Contract Law ch. 36 (Oxford University Press, 2018); Eric Maskin & Jean Tirole, Unforeseen Contingencies and Incomplete Contracts, 66 (1) The Review of Economic Studies 83–114 (1999).
501. Sarath Sanga, Incomplete Contracts: An Empirical Approach, 34 (4) The Journal of Law, Economics, and Organization 650–679 (2018).

§2. Ascertaining of Express Terms

551. Express terms form the primary foundation for determining the rights and obligations of the contracting parties. When a term is explicitly stated in the contract, it is presumed to reflect the parties' genuine intentions and will generally be enforced unless it conflicts with mandatory legal provisions or public policy. Express terms are the specific provisions agreed upon by the parties, and the interpretation of these terms follows an objective standard, focusing on how a reasonable person would understand them within the contract's context.

I. Interpretation of Express Terms

552. In interpreting express terms, Courts strive to determine the parties' true intentions rather than rigidly interpreting the literal wording of the agreement. This requires reading the express terms within the contract as a whole, ensuring that individual provisions align with the contract's overall purpose and the actual relationship between the parties. Such contextual reading supports a holistic understanding that captures the nuances of contractual obligations and avoids a fragmented or overly rigid interpretation.

553. Where an express term is ambiguous or lacks clarity, courts may look to customary practices within the relevant industry or field to give meaning to the term, as long as these practices do not conflict with mandatory legal rules or public interest. This approach allows for flexibility in interpretation, recognising that some contract terms might rely on implicit, widely understood industry norms. However, the reliance on customary practices can introduce complexity, as these customs must be consistent with the contractual framework and must not override express terms that clearly indicate the parties' contrary intentions.

554. In what follows, we will examine the key principles and steps for determining express terms in a contract, including considerations such as contextual interpretation, the relevance of industry customs, and how courts resolve ambiguities. Additionally, we will explore some challenging issues that can arise, such as reconciling express terms with implied terms, balancing literal and purposive interpretations, and addressing conflicts between express terms and overarching legal principles. These considerations highlight the delicate balance courts must maintain between respecting party autonomy and ensuring that contractual interpretations align with fairness, policy considerations, and legal mandates.

555. The primary rule is to interpret the express terms of a contract based on the ordinary meaning of the words used, as per Article 142 of the Civil Code, which is set out below:

> A manifestation of intent involving a counter-party shall be interpreted in light of the wording, relevant clauses, nature and purpose of the conduct, custom, as well as the principle of good faith, in order to determine the meaning of such manifestation of intent.
>
> A manifestation of intent involving no counter-party shall not be rigidly interpreted in light of its wording but shall instead be interpreted in light of the relevant clauses, nature and purpose of the conduct, custom, as well as the principle of good faith, in order to determine the genuine intent of the actor.[502]

556. Article 466 further provides a guideline on the interpretation of contractual terms:

> If there is a dispute between the parties over the meaning of any clause of the contract, the rules specified in Article 142(1) of this Civil Code apply to ascertain the true meaning of the disputing clauses.
>
> Where a contract is concluded in two or more languages, and it is agreed that all versions are equally authentic, the words and expressions in each version are construed as having the same meaning. In the case of any discrepancy in the literal expressions used in the different language versions, they shall be interpreted in the light of the related term of the contract, the nature and purpose of the contract, and the principle of good faith.[503]

557. The above provisions make it clear that words should be understood in their usual and customary sense unless the context clearly indicates otherwise. In other words, when there is an express term, the primary rule to apply is literal interpretation. Where the counterparty's expression of intent is absent, or in the case of any discrepancies in the literal expressions used across different language versions, contextual interpretation and other interpretative methods will be applied.

558. Despite the rules, ambiguities and vague terms can still create significant interpretation challenges.[504] Different parties might have different understandings of the same term, leading to disputes. It is for this reason that the SPC pronounced a guideline on contract interpretation in its Judicial Interpretation:[505]

> When interpreting contractual terms in accordance with Article 142, Clause 1, and Article 466, Clause 1 of the Civil Code, the People's Court shall base its interpretation on the ordinary meaning of the words used. This interpretation should consider relevant clauses, the nature and purpose of the contract, customs, and the principle of good faith while also referencing factors such as the context of the contract formation, negotiation process, and performance actions to determine the meaning of disputed terms.

502. Article 142 CC.
503. Article 466 CC.
504. Daixiong Yang, The Principle of Interpretation of the Expression of Intent, 7 Law Science 41-56 (2020).
505. Article 1 of the SPC Interpretation on Several Issues Concerning the Application of the General Provisions of the Contract Book of the Civil Code (2023).

If there is evidence showing a mutual understanding between the parties regarding a contractual term that differs from the ordinary meaning of the words, and one party argues for interpreting the term according to its usual meaning, the People's Court shall not uphold this claim.

Where multiple interpretations of a contractual term exist that may impact its validity, the People's Court shall adopt the interpretation that supports the term's validity. In the case of gratuitous contracts, the interpretation that imposes a lighter burden on the debtor shall be preferred.

559. Paragraph 1 specifies that contract interpretation should begin with the ordinary meaning of the words used, in conjunction with relevant clauses, the nature and purpose of the contract, customs, and the principle of good faith. Factors such as the contract's context, negotiation process, and performance should also be considered. This establishes that a literal interpretation is the starting point.[506] If the literal meaning is ambiguous or unclear, terms should be interpreted in the context of other related clauses within the entire contract.[507] Clauses should not be read in isolation; instead, terms should be interpreted in relation to other provisions to maintain coherence and consistency throughout the contract.

560. Express terms must also be interpreted in light of the contract's purpose. Courts will consider the nature of the transaction and the overall intent behind the agreement, including the circumstances under which it was concluded and the practices established between the parties.[508] Systematic interpretation (体系解释), or contextual interpretation, treats all relevant clauses, correspondence, and documents as an integrated whole.[509] This holistic approach seeks coherence within the contractual structure, resolving conflicting clauses by examining the overarching contract purpose and the relationships between clauses. This method aligns with integrative principles found in international practices, such as those stipulated by the UNIDROIT Principles.[510]

561. Unlike purely literal interpretation, which looks only at the exact words used in the document, purposive interpretation encourages courts to go beyond the language to understand the meaning behind the text. Under Chinese law, purposive interpretation seeks to align the textual meaning of contract terms with the underlying goals and shared objectives of the contracting parties in a way that best

506. Paragraph 1 of Article 1 of the SPC Interpretation on the Contract Book (2023).

507. *Hong Kong Rilong Investment Co., Ltd. v. Shenzhen Lexin Enma Electronics Co., Ltd. & Shenzhen Lexin Jingmi Industry Co., Ltd*, the Supreme People's Court, (2017)SPC Min Zai No. 370; 日隆投资有限公司诉深圳乐新恩玛电子有限公司、深圳乐新精密工业有限公司， 最高人民法院（2017）最高法民再370号.

508. The Second Division of Civil Trial of the SPC & SPC Research Office, Understanding and Application of the Judicial Interpretation of the General Principles of Contract Book of the Civil Code 44 (People's Court Press, 2023).

509. The Second Division of Civil Trial of the SPC & SPC Research Office, Understanding and Application of the Judicial Interpretation of the General Principles of Contract Book of the Civil Code 45 (2023).

510. Article 4.3 of the UNIDROIT Principles of International Commercial Contracts (1994, 2004, 2010, and 2016 revisions).

achieves the underlying objectives or purpose for which the document was created. The objective standard in this approach focuses on what a reasonable person would understand the purpose of the contract or legal provision to be, considering the context and circumstances of its formation.[511]

562. Trade customs and good faith serve as valuable supplementary tools for interpretation, especially in instances where textual or systematic interpretations fall short. By incorporating these principles, courts can adopt a broader, socially responsible perspective that ensures contractual obligations align with ethical standards and commercial norms. However, because of the general nature of these principles, their application must be cautious to avoid compromising legal certainty and predictability, which are foundational to contract law.

563. The court will prioritise the actual, mutually understood meaning of the term over its literal interpretation if it can be demonstrated that both parties had a different, specific understanding of it.[512] This approach emphasises the true intent of the parties over rigid adherence to the plain meaning of the language, reflecting the principle that contracts should be enforced in accordance with the shared understanding of the parties involved.[513] In essence, if both parties have a common understanding of a term that differs from its usual interpretation, their shared meaning prevails, respecting their true intent over conventional usage.

564. The SPC explicitly introduces two other interpretative principles: the principle of validity and the principle of systematic coherence.[514] The principle of validity mandates that when multiple interpretations of a contractual term affect its enforceability, the interpretation that upholds the term's validity should be adopted. This approach aligns with the common objective of contracting parties: to create enforceable obligations, not ineffective ones. This principle, prominent in comparative law, mirrors provisions found in the civil codes of countries like Italy and Chile, as well as international frameworks such as the UNIDROIT Principles of International Commercial Contracts and the Principles of European Contract Law. By choosing interpretations that favour enforceability, this rule respects the presumption that parties intend for their agreements to produce legal effects.

565. Furthermore, the principle of systematic coherence suggests that when contradictions exist among contract terms, interpreters should strive to harmonise them rather than disregard or nullify specific clauses. In contracts with vague or incomplete provisions, an approach that treats them as invalid could unjustly negate

511. *Zaozhuang Mining (Group) Co., Ltd. Chaili Coal Mine v. Huaxia Bank Co., Ltd. Qingdao Branch & Qingdao Free Trade Zone International Trade Co., Ltd*, Gazette Case of the SPC, Issue 6, 2010; 枣庄矿业（集团）有限公司柴里煤矿诉华夏银行股份有限公司青岛分行、青岛保税区画的国际贸易有限公司，《最高人民法院公报》案例，2010年06期.

512. Paragraph 2 of Art. 1 of the SPC Interpretation on the Contract Book (2023).

513. The Second Division of Civil Trial of the SPC & SPC Research Office, Understanding and Application of the Judicial Interpretation of the General Principles of Contract Book of the Civil Code 44 (2023).

514. Paragraph 3 of Art. 1 of the SPC Interpretation on the Contract Book (2023).

numerous transactions. Therefore, harmonising contradictory terms aligns with the principle of coherence, ensuring that the contract reflects the genuine intent of both parties, maintains its practical effect, and honours the overall contractual framework.

566. In summary, purposive interpretation, supported by the principles of harmless misrepresentation, validity, and systematic coherence, allows courts to adopt a flexible yet principled approach. By balancing the parties' intent with commercial customs, ethical considerations, and the need for legal effectiveness, this approach promotes a balanced and realistic interpretation of contracts that serves both contractual integrity and fairness.

567. From an economic perspective, interpreting contracts as invalid in such cases is inefficient and contradicts the market economy's goal of promoting transactions. When a contract can be interpreted as either valid or invalid, a validity-oriented approach encourages trade, prevents resource loss and waste, and respects the original intent and objectives of the parties. By favouring interpretations that uphold the enforceability of contracts, courts support a stable transactional environment, which benefits the overall economy by reducing uncertainty and facilitating predictable commercial interactions.

568. There is the principle of debtor-favourability in the interpretation of gratuitous contracts. This principle suggests that when multiple interpretations are possible, the interpretation that imposes a lighter burden on the debtor should be preferred. Gratuitous contracts are generally one-sided, with the debtor incurring obligations without receiving a corresponding benefit or consideration. Favouring interpretations that ease the debtor's burden protects their interests and prevents the imposition of an unduly onerous obligation. Since the debtor does not receive compensation in a gratuitous contract, imposing a lighter obligation is considered fair and equitable, acknowledging that it would be unjust to hold a party to stricter obligations without mutual benefit.[515]

569. Together, these principles – favouring contract validity and protecting debtor interests in gratuitous agreements – align with both economic efficiency and fairness. They uphold the core values of contract law by ensuring that parties are bound by terms that reflect their true intentions while also respecting economic realities and equity. If there are two or more interpretations of a contract clause that could affect its validity, the courts will choose the interpretation that favours the validity of the clause.[516] In the case of a gratuitous contract, the interpretation that imposes a lighter burden on the debtor should be selected.[517] However, in practice, ambiguities, incomplete terms, contradictions, and changing circumstances can create significant challenges.

515. For example, granting the donor the right to revoke a gift at will (Art. 658 (1) CC) and requiring the gratuitous custodian to bear only a lower duty of care (Art. 897 CC).
516. Paragraph 3 of Article 1 of the SPC Interpretation on the Contract Book.
517. *Ibid.*

570. It is remarkable that despite the above principles and rules under Chinese law, there has been relatively little research on the interpretation of contracts, and it has not received adequate attention. In contrast, common law jurisdictions have conducted detailed studies on this topic, resulting in a significant body of research.[518] Therefore, it is necessary to make a comparison between Chinese law and common law in this regard.

571. The common law approach to contract interpretation, as outlined by Lord Hoffmann's five principles, emphasises a contextual interpretation based on what a reasonable person with all relevant background knowledge would understand the contract to mean.[519]

572. Lord Hoffmann's approach considers anything within the 'matrix of fact' that could affect the meaning of the language used, emphasising that interpretation should not be strictly literal but should include the relevant context in which the contract was made.[520] Similarly, Chinese law also supports a contextual interpretation of contracts. Article 142 of the Civil Code explicitly states that the expression of intent shall be interpreted according to the ordinary meaning of words, taking into account the relevant clauses, nature, purpose, and background of the contract, along with customary practices and the principle of good faith.

573. Both legal systems adopt an objective standard for interpretation. In common law, in defending the minority dissent of *Investors Compensation Scheme Ltd.*, it was forcefully argued that interpretation should be an entirely objective process.[521] Altering the terms of an agreement without clear evidence that the revised language reflects the parties' actual intentions is ambitious and potentially speculative. The written contract is the best evidence of the parties' objective intent, and if it is unambiguous, there is no need for further investigation into its meaning.[522] Chinese law also focuses on objective intent by considering how an ordinary person would interpret the parties' intentions based on their external expressions (i.e., the written terms of the contract and their behaviour). The emphasis is on how the contract terms would be understood by someone with reasonable knowledge of the relevant context rather than the private, uncommunicated thoughts of the contracting parties.

574. In common law, contract interpretation should consider the overall purpose of the contract, implying that courts should attempt to determine what the parties

518. Richard Calnan, Principles of Contractual Interpretation (2nd edn, Oxford University Press 2017).
519. *Investors Compensation Scheme Ltd. v. West Bromwich Building Society* [1997] UKHL 28.
520. Adam Kramer, Common Sense Principles of Contract Interpretation (and how we've been using them all along), 23(2) Oxford Journal of Legal Studies 173–196 (2003).
521. Paul S. Davies, Construing Commercial Contracts: No Need for Violence in, Law and Language: Current Legal Issues Volume 15, Current Legal Issues ch. 26, 434-456 (Michael Freeman, and Fiona Smith eds., Oxford University Press, 2013).
522. *Ibid.*

reasonably intended the contract to achieve.[523] Similarly, in Chinese law, Article 466 of the Civil Code and its judicial interpretations encourage judges to consider the nature and purpose of the transaction in interpreting the contract.

575. The key differences, however, are noteworthy. One of the major distinctions is the treatment of prior negotiations. In common law, prior negotiations are explicitly excluded from the contextual background used in contract interpretation, primarily to reduce litigation costs and prevent the courts from being bogged down with extrinsic evidence regarding what parties said before the final contract was signed.[524] In contrast, Chinese law does not categorically exclude prior negotiations. The SPC Judicial interpretations indicate that prior negotiations and established practices between the parties may be used to help interpret ambiguous terms. This more inclusive approach allows Chinese courts to consider the parties' behaviour before and during the formation of the contract to understand their real intent, which contrasts with the more restrictive common law approach.[525]

576. In addition, while common law interpretation relies on principles of reasonableness and assumes that people do not generally make linguistic mistakes,[526] Chinese law explicitly incorporates the principle of good faith as a guiding principle for interpreting contracts. This principle is fundamental in Chinese law, which requires that parties conduct themselves with honesty and integrity in both interpreting and performing their contractual obligations. Chinese judges are encouraged to use good faith as a lens through which they assess the behaviour of contracting parties. This principle introduces a more moral and ethical dimension to contract interpretation in China compared to the common law approach, which tends to be more commercially pragmatic and focused on reasonableness.

577. Furthermore, common law (as seen through Lord Hoffmann's approach) asserts that the meaning of contract terms should not be deduced literally but should be determined in light of their context. This means that the court will look beyond the literal meaning to understand what the parties intended the language to mean in the given context.[527] In Chinese law, while contextual interpretation is also valued, there is a somewhat stronger emphasis on starting with the ordinary and literal meaning of the terms used, as outlined in Article 142 of the Civil Code. Chinese judges are first expected to interpret words based on their ordinary, common meaning, and only if ambiguities arise will they consider the broader context, including commercial practices, the purpose of the contract, and the negotiations between the parties.

---

523. Lord Nicholls, My Kingdom for a Horse: the Meaning of Words, 121 Law Quarterly Review 577 (2005).
524. Christopher Staughton, How do the courts interpret commercial contracts?, 58 Cambridge Law Journal 303 (1999).
525. James Spigelman, From text to context: Contemporary contractual interpretation, 81 Australian Law Journal 322 (2007).
526. Alan Berg, Thrashing through the undergrowth, 122 Law Quarterly Review 354 (2006).
527. Gerard McMeel, The Construction of Contracts: Interpretation, Implication and Rectification (3rd edn. Oxford University Press 2017).

578. The common law's emphasis on excluding prior negotiations and focusing on the objective reasonable person test helps limit judicial discretion to a degree, providing a more predictable and uniform interpretation methodology.[528] In contrast, Chinese law grants judges significant discretion to interpret contract terms based on public policy considerations, the principle of good faith, and the need to promote social harmony. This discretion means that courts may go beyond strict contractual language to achieve an outcome that they view as fair and aligned with broader social or economic policies.

579. Both legal systems consider customary practices in interpreting contracts, but Chinese law places particular emphasis on the local customs and established practices between the parties. In common law, customary practices are considered part of the factual matrix, but they tend to be secondary to the objective interpretation of the contractual language, and the focus is more on commercially reasonable expectations rather than on local customs per se.

580. In summary, in both common law and Chinese law, the interpretation of contracts emphasises the context and the reasonable understanding of the parties, but there are significant differences in how this principle is applied. While common law focuses on excluding prior negotiations to ensure consistency and avoid excessive litigation, Chinese law adopts a more inclusive approach, giving weight to prior negotiations, good faith, and local customs. These differences reflect the underlying philosophies of the two legal systems, with common law favouring objective certainty and predictability and Chinese law emphasising fairness, flexibility, and good faith to adapt to the unique social and economic context of transactions.

§3. Implied Terms

581. A manifestation of intent may be made expressly or impliedly.[529] A contract reflects the common intention of the parties. Both parties have agreed on the essential terms and share the same intent regarding the obligations and rights under the contract. In this context, the court would interpret the contract by considering the true intentions of the parties rather than just the literal meaning of the words, ensuring that the terms reflect the agreed-upon purpose. Along with this logic, implied terms are introduced to complete contracts where certain essential aspects are missing to give effectiveness to the contract and ensure that the agreement functions as intended. Implied terms help bridge gaps where explicit provisions are absent but necessary for the proper performance of the contract.

582. Implied terms are those not explicitly stated but are understood to be part of the contract based on the nature of the agreement, the relationship between the parties, and customary practices.[530] Implied terms should be consistent with the

528. Paul S. Davies, Construing Commercial Contracts: No Need for Violence 434–456 (2013).
529. Article 140 CC.
530. Articles 510 and 511 CC.

nature and purpose of the contract. They are inferred based on what the parties reasonably intended at the time the contract was formed. Certain terms may be implied by statutory provisions, such as Articles 510 and 511 of the Civil Code.

583. Implied terms can be derived from customary practices in the relevant industry or trade. When individuals engage in a specific market, a custom related to that market may be implicitly included in their contract unless the custom contradicts the express terms of the contract or other terms that are implied independently of the custom. English law determines whether a custom is deemed reasonable to be binding upon parties. The assessment of reasonableness is a legal question, and if a custom is deemed reasonable, it is binding on both parties, regardless of whether they were aware of it.[531]

584. Nonetheless, under Chinese law, only the following two specific types of practices can be recognised as trade customs, provided they do not contradict the mandatory provisions of national legislation or administrative regulations and social morality and public order.[532] First, a practice that has become customary between the parties during their course of dealing.[533] This means that if two parties have consistently adopted a particular way of doing things in their past transactions, this way of doing things can be considered a trade custom between them. Such a practice reflects their common understanding of how certain aspects of their transactions should be conducted, even if these are not explicitly stated in the contract.

585. Second, a practice that is generally followed in the location where the transaction takes place or within a particular field or industry and is known (or ought to be known) to the parties at the time of contracting.[534] This recognises that certain practices are so prevalent in a specific industry or area that they can be assumed to form part of the contractual context unless explicitly excluded.

586. The party invoking the existence of a trade custom bears the burden of proof.[535] This means that it is up to the party asserting the existence of a relevant trade custom to provide sufficient evidence demonstrating its existence and applicability to the situation at hand.

587. First, it does not contradict the mandatory provisions of national legislation or administrative regulations. Second, it does not violate social morality and public order. Third, it is the habitual practices or norms that parties typically follow when engaging in transactions within a specific industry or market. Fourth, practices that are commonly adopted in local trading activities or within a specific field or industry, which the parties involved should know or are expected to know when entering into a contract.

531. *Robinson v. Mollett* (1875) LR 7 HL 802.
532. Article 2 of the SPC Interpretation on the Contract Book (2023).
533. *Ibid.*
534. *Ibid.*
535. *Ibid.*

588. Contracts that lack detail or omit important terms can cause confusion. Determining the intentions of the parties in such cases often requires supplementary interpretation, which can be contentious. When terms are missing or incomplete, supplementary interpretations may be used to fill in gaps based on the nature of the contract and the principle of fairness.[536]

589. Where express terms do not cover certain aspects of the contract (such as price, quality, or time of performance), the court may supplement these missing terms based on (1) statutory rules (2) customary practices in the relevant industry, and (3) market prices at the time and place of performance, to ensure that a contract remains enforceable even if it lacks certain specific express terms.

590. Contracts sometimes contain contradictory terms or provisions that are difficult to reconcile. Resolving these contradictions requires careful analysis and often the consideration of which term reflects the primary intention of the parties. Determining the subjective intentions of the parties can be problematic, especially when the negotiation history or communications are unclear or incomplete. This can lead to different interpretations and potential litigation.

591. Over time, circumstances may change in ways that affect the interpretation of contract terms. Adapting the terms to reflect the current reality while respecting the original agreement can be difficult. In contracts involving foreign parties, cultural and language differences can lead to misunderstandings and disputes over the meaning of express terms. The interpretation must bridge these gaps effectively.

592. Hence, the Chinese courts are willing to imply a term to 'fill in the gaps' as long as it is (1) able to be expressed clearly based on the common understanding and in line with prior dealings and (2) necessary to make the contract work. The court will incorporate terms into the contract that the parties are presumed to have understood based on their prior dealings or established business relationships.[537] This approach assumes that certain expectations and customary practices have developed between the parties over time, even if these are not explicitly stated in the current contract. By implying such terms, the court aims to give effect to what it deems as the parties' shared understanding, ensuring that the contract reflects the practical realities and intentions underlying their past transactions.

593. However, courts are not required to adhere strictly to the natural and ordinary meaning of the words used. In exceptional cases, such as when a contract is poorly drafted, they may deviate from that meaning to fulfil the objective intentions of the parties substantiated by admissible evidence.[538] When interpreting legal

536. Article 6 CC.
537. Article 1(2) of the SPC Interpretation on the Contract Book (2023).
538. Paragraph 2 of Art. 1 of the SPC Interpretation on the Contract Book (2023).

documents or contracts, courts should favour interpretations that give effect to the intentions of the parties and the validity of the agreement rather than rendering it void or ineffective.[539]

594. The SPC upholds contractual obligations and ensures that agreements are enforced whenever possible, rather than allowing them to fail due to technicalities or ambiguities. What the SPC does not make explicit but should be recommended is that when evaluating the various possible interpretations of a disputed term, the court should consider which interpretation is more commercially sensible and generally tends to favour the interpretation that aligns with commercial logic rather than one that does not.

595. In common law, courts apply specific tests to imply terms in contracts, such as the business efficacy test, where courts imply terms when they are necessary for the contract to make sense and function properly. The officious bystander test is also often employed by common law courts, meaning if an officious bystander were present and suggested a term during contract formation, and both parties would clearly agree it was meant to be part of the contract, the term is implied.

596. In Chinese law, there are no direct equivalents of these specific tests. Instead, implied terms are inferred based on the principle of good faith, contract purpose, and reasonable expectations of the parties. Chinese law takes a more general approach, focusing on what is necessary to uphold the fairness and purpose of the contract in accordance with established legal principles and social norms.

597. Therefore, Chinese law is different from the English approach by not focusing on reasonableness but rather on the awareness of the parties when entering into the contract. These practices are considered to reflect the standard expectations and obligations of parties in similar contractual relationships. For example, in construction contracts, if the parties have agreed that, upon receiving the completion settlement documents, the employer (the project owner) does not respond within the agreed time, it shall be deemed as acceptance of the completion settlement documents, and the matter shall be handled according to the agreement. The court should support the claim made by the contractor on the settlement of the project payment based on the completion settlement documents.[540]

§4. Standard Terms and Exemption Clauses

598. Standard terms (also known as 'boilerplate clauses') are pre-drafted terms prepared by one party and presented to the other party on a 'take it or leave it' basis.

539. Paragraph 3 of Art. 1 of the SPC Interpretation on the Contract Book (2023).
540. Article 21 of the SPC Interpretation on Issues concerning the Application of Law in the Trial of Cases Regarding Disputes over Construction Contracts for Construction Projects (I) (2020).

The Civil Code recognises standard terms as clauses that are prepared in advance by one party for repeated use and are not negotiated with the other party when the contract is concluded.[541]

599. Notably, repeated use is a constituting element in the standard term. Therefore, Chinese law presupposes the repeated use as a default position unless clear evidence rebuts the presumption. *The SPC Interpretation on the Contract Book (2023)*provides:

> If a party engaged in commercial activities claims that a contract clause, which was pre-drafted without negotiation with the other party, is not a standard term solely because it has not been repeatedly used, the People's Court will not support this argument. However, an exception is made if there is evidence proving that the clause was not pre-drafted for repeated use.[542]

600. In addition, standard terms are often non-negotiable and imposed on the weaker party, such as in consumer contracts. Legal rules governing these terms seek to ensure a balance between fairness and enforceability, protecting the interests of both parties in contractual agreements.

601. A key requirement for the validity of standard terms is transparency and clarity, also referred to as the duty of disclosure. This means the party offering standard terms must explicitly inform the other party and provide a clear explanation, particularly for any terms that restrict the other party's rights or increase its obligations. If these terms are not adequately disclosed and explained, they risk being declared invalid and unenforceable. This duty promotes fairness by ensuring that parties fully understand the terms they are agreeing to, thus preventing the stronger party from imposing potentially unfair or hidden obligations on the weaker party.[543]

602. Contracts, including their exception clauses, must be based on the principles of good faith and fairness. Any clause that significantly tilts the balance of rights and obligations in favour of one party, particularly if that party has a stronger bargaining position, could be challenged and invalidated if deemed unfair.[544]

603. According to the Civil Code, standard terms that exclude or limit liability for personal injury or property damage caused intentionally or through gross negligence are generally not enforceable.[545] This ensures that parties cannot escape responsibility for serious breaches or intentionally harmful actions.

604. In the case of standard form contracts (contracts where one party provides the terms with little or no negotiation), if an exception clause results in an unfair

541. Paragraph 1 of Art. 496 CC.
542. Article 9 of the SPC Interpretation on the Contract Book (2023).
543. Paragraph 2 of Art. 496 CC.
544. Article 7 CC.
545. Article 506 CC.

disadvantage to the other party, often known as unfair terms, the court may deem it invalid. For example, the party providing the standard terms exempts itself from or mitigates its liabilities unreasonably or increases the liabilities or limits the material rights of the other party.[546] The law seeks to protect parties who might otherwise be subjected to unfair terms due to an imbalance in bargaining power. Standard terms must be fair and reasonable. Terms that unfairly favour one party over the other or are excessively harsh, such as where the party providing the standard terms deprives the other party of the material rights, may be deemed invalid.[547]

605. If there is ambiguity in the wording of an exception clause, Article 498 of the Civil Code mandates that the clause be interpreted against the party that drafted it.[548] This principle of *contra proferentem* ensures that ambiguities do not disadvantage the adhering party and unfairly benefit the party who created the terms.

606. In addition to the Civil Code, the Consumer Protection Law provides additional protections for consumers. Exception clauses that attempt to waive or limit a consumer's statutory rights, particularly in relation to safety or product defects, are often deemed invalid.[549] From a socio-legal perspective, the rules governing standard terms and exemption clauses are crucial for consumer protection. They ensure that consumers are not unfairly disadvantaged by terms they had no opportunity to negotiate. These rules help maintain fairness in contractual relationships, especially in situations where there is a significant power imbalance between the contracting parties, such as between large corporations and individual consumers. The requirement for clear disclosure and explanation of standard terms promotes transparency and helps ensure that consumers are fully aware of their rights and obligations, thus enhancing informed consent.

607. In summary, the rules concerning standard terms and exemption clauses in the Civil Code emphasise fairness, reasonableness, and transparency. These rules aim to protect weaker parties in contractual relationships, ensuring that terms are clear, fair, and not overly burdensome. From a socio-legal perspective, these provisions are crucial for consumer protection and maintaining equitable contractual practices. Comparatively, the principles in Chinese law align closely with those in other major legal systems, reflecting a global consensus on the need to regulate standard terms and exemption clauses to protect against unfair practices.[550]

546. Article 497 CC.
547. *Ibid.*
548. Article 498 CC.
549. Article 24 of the Consumer Protection Law (1993, 2013 revisions).
550. The EU has extensive regulations on standard terms and exemption clauses aimed at protecting consumers, similar to Chinese law. The Unfair Terms in Consumer Contracts Directive (93/13/EEC) prohibits unfair terms in contracts between consumers and sellers or suppliers. In the U.S., the Uniform Commercial Code (UCC) and common law principles govern standard terms and exemption clauses. Courts typically scrutinise these clauses for fairness and may apply the doctrine of unconscionability to invalidate overly harsh or one-sided terms. The German Civil Code (BGB) has detailed provisions on standard terms (AGB - Allgemeine Geschäftsbedingungen). It includes strict requirements for transparency, fairness, and the invalidation of clauses that unreasonably disadvantage the adhering party. The UK's Unfair Contract Terms Act 1977 and the Consumer Rights

§5. ARBITRATION CLAUSES

608. Under Chinese law, arbitration clauses must be in written form to be valid.[551] This can be included in the main contract or as a separate arbitration agreement. The arbitration clause must clearly express the parties' intent to resolve disputes through arbitration rather than litigation. The clause must specify a particular arbitration commission to administer the arbitration.[552] Vague or general references to arbitration without naming a specific commission can render the clause invalid.[553]

609. Failure to name a specific arbitration commission can lead to the invalidity of the arbitration agreement. This contrasts with some jurisdictions where a general agreement to arbitrate may be sufficient. Unlike some jurisdictions that permit ad hoc arbitration, Chinese law emphasises institutional arbitration. This means parties must choose an established arbitration institution to administer the arbitration, providing more structured and standardised procedures. For example, in a contract dispute, the arbitration clause stated that any disputes would be resolved by 'an arbitration commission in Beijing' without specifying which commission.[554] In the past, the Chinese court ruled the arbitration clause invalid due to the lack of specificity, as multiple arbitration commissions operate in Beijing, such as China International Economic and Trade Arbitration Commission (CIETAC) and Beijing Arbitration Commission.

610. Consequently, the court assumed jurisdiction over the dispute. However, the recent trend has suggested that Chinese courts generally support arbitration as an alternative dispute resolution method.[555] While Chinese courts strictly scrutinise the arbitration clauses to ensure compliance with statutory requirements, they should interpret them in a manner that favours the validity of the arbitration agreement when reviewing whether an arbitration agreement specifies a clearly designated arbitration institution.[556] For example, where the parties do not specify a particular arbitration institution in the arbitration agreement but agree to apply the

---

Act 2015 provide comprehensive regulations on exemption clauses and standard terms, focusing on ensuring fairness and preventing the exclusion of liability for personal injury or death caused by negligence.

551. Paragraph 1 of Art. 16 of the Arbitration Law.

552. Paragraph 2 of Art. 16 of the Arbitration Law.

553. Article 18 of the Arbitration Law provides that if an arbitration agreement does not specify the matters to be arbitrated or the arbitral commission, or if the terms are unclear, the parties may enter a supplementary agreement. If they are unable to reach such an agreement, the arbitration agreement shall be deemed invalid.

554. *Beijing Shiying Hezhong Digital Technology Co., Ltd. v. Union Software (Beijing) Co., Ltd.*, the Supreme People's Court, (2019) SPC Zhi Min Xia No. 477; 北京世盈合众数字技术有限公司诉系联软件（北京）有限公司，最高人民法院（2019）最高法知民辖终477号.

555. The Civil Division No. 4 of the SPC on 31 December 2021 published a judicial document as a guideline for all Chinese courts to adjudicate the international commercial and maritime cases, including the judicial review of the arbitration, namely, *the Minutes of the National Courts Symposium on Foreign-Related Commercial and Maritime Adjudication Work* (the 'Minutes on Foreign-Related Commercial and Maritime Adjudication Work').

556. Article 93 of the Minutes on Foreign-Related Commercial and Maritime Adjudication Work.

arbitration rules of a certain institution, it is considered that they have chosen that institution for arbitration unless the arbitration rules state otherwise.[557]

611. A valid arbitration agreement should include an expression of intent to submit to arbitration.[558] A 'choice of arbitration or litigation' clause – where the parties agree that disputes may either be arbitrated or litigated – was at issue in the case of *Datang Huxian No. 2 Thermal Power Plant v. Shandong Sanrong Environmental Protection Engineering Co., Ltd.*[559] In the arbitration clause under dispute, the parties agreed that 'either party may submit the dispute to the arbitration committee specified in this contract or bring the matter before the People's Court'. What is the Chinese judicial position on the validity of such a clause? The prevailing view holds that such 'choice of arbitration or litigation' clauses do not create a valid arbitration agreement.[560]

612. In *BY.O v. Yushang Group Co., Ltd*,[561] the arbitration clause provided that 'disputes shall first be resolved through arbitration at the Singapore International Arbitration Centre. If either party disagrees with the arbitration result of the Singapore International Arbitration Centre, either party shall have the right to submit the dispute to the competent commercial court in the location of Party A for litigation'. The court ruled that the part of the clause requiring submission to arbitration was valid.

613. However, the provision allowing either party to litigate following arbitration was deemed invalid. This reflects judicial respect for party autonomy and the agreed-upon forum for resolving disputes. However, the second part of the clause, which permitted the parties to seek litigation if they disagreed with the arbitration outcome, was invalidated on the grounds that it contradicted the finality principle embedded in China's arbitration framework.

614. This ruling underscores the commitment of Chinese courts to enforcing the finality of arbitration and serves as a cautionary example for contract drafters. Multi-tiered dispute resolution clauses, which seek to combine arbitration with subsequent litigation, may be viewed as contrary to the legal principles of binding arbitration in China. Courts in China generally do not permit 'arbitration followed by

---

557. Article 95 of the Minutes on Foreign-Related Commercial and Maritime Adjudication Work.
558. Paragraph 2 of Art. 16 of the Arbitration Law.
559. *Datang Huxian No. 2 Thermal Power Plant v. Shandong Sanrong Environmental Protection Engineering Co., Ltd.*, the Supreme People's Court, (2017) SPC Min Xia Zhong No. 83; 山东三融环保工程有限公司诉大唐户县第二热电厂，最高人民法院（2017）最高法民辖终83号.
560. Reply of the Supreme People's Court to the Request for Instructions on the Case of Dispute over outstanding debts in sales contract between Xiamen Sakura Garment Co., Ltd. and Japan Xijiasi Co., Ltd., (2002) Min Si Ta Zi No. 33; *Jiuyi Global (Jiamusi) Mining Equipment Co., Ltd. v. Datong Longmei Coal Mining Machinery Sales Co., Ltd*, the Supreme People's Court, (2016) SPC Min Xia Zhong No. 39; 久益环球（佳木斯）采矿设备有限公司诉大同市龙煤煤矿机械销售有限公司，最高人民法院，（2016）最高法民辖终39号.
561. *BY.O v. Yushang Group Co., Ltd*, Gazette Case of the SPC, Issue 11, 2021; BY.0诉豫商集团有限公司，《最高人民法院公报》案例，2021年11期.

litigation' structures because they create uncertainty, disrupt the arbitral process, and increase costs by potentially allowing parties to relitigate disputes. Parties need to be mindful that while certain dispute resolution frameworks may be acceptable in one legal system, they may be unenforceable or problematic in another. Here, even though the clause allowed for a second option (litigation) in the event of dissatisfaction with the arbitration result, Chinese law's strict adherence to the finality principle invalidated this provision.

615. In summary, the court's decision reinforces the primacy of arbitration as a single, conclusive method for dispute resolution in the Chinese legal system. It serves as a reminder to contracting parties to ensure that arbitration agreements comply with jurisdictional standards and to avoid provisions that conflict with fundamental principles such as finality, which is designed to uphold the efficiency and integrity of arbitration as an alternative to litigation.

616. Chinese courts have the authority to review arbitration agreements to determine their validity.[562] In addition to the specificity of arbitration institution requirement, an arbitration agreement is deemed invalid if (1) the agreed arbitration matters exceed the legally permitted scope of arbitration; (2) the arbitration agreement was concluded by a person with no or limited civil capacity; or (3) one party was coerced into concluding the arbitration agreement.[563]

617. Arbitration is restricted to certain types of disputes, typically commercial and contractual, which the law allows to be resolved through arbitration. If the arbitration agreement covers issues outside this permitted scope – such as criminal matters or other non-arbitrable disputes – the agreement will be considered invalid. This limitation safeguards the judicial system's jurisdiction over areas that require judicial authority and oversight. Chinese law allows for arbitration of civil and commercial disputes. However, disputes related to administrative, family law, or criminal matters are not arbitrable.

618. For an arbitration agreement to be valid, both parties must have the legal capacity to enter into contracts. If one of the parties lacks this capacity – such as minors or individuals with cognitive impairments – the agreement will not be recognised. This rule protects vulnerable individuals from being bound by agreements they are not legally competent to understand or consent to.

619. If one party used threats or coercion to compel the other into agreeing to arbitration, the agreement would be rendered invalid. The general rule of contract validity applies here. Arbitration is fundamentally based on mutual consent; thus, agreements secured through duress violate the principle of free consent and fairness in contractual relationships.

---

562. Article 20 of the Arbitration Law.
563. Article 17 of the Arbitration Law.

620. Under Chinese law, the doctrine of separability is a well-established legal principle that treats an arbitration clause within a contract as an independent, self-contained agreement distinct from the other terms of the contract. In China, this doctrine is statutorily embedded in both the Arbitration Law[564] and the Civil Code.[565] According to this principle, an arbitration clause, or agreement, is considered a separate agreement from the main contract (or 'matrix contract') to which it is attached.

621. The principle of the separability of arbitration agreements has long been a topic of considerable debate, with ongoing attention given to the independent nature of an arbitration agreement within a contract. Simply put, the separability principle asserts that an arbitration clause within a contract remains unaffected by the invalidity or termination of the main contract, as it functions as a distinct agreement. However, whether the principle of the separability of an arbitration agreement automatically applies in cases where the main contract itself is not formed – meaning whether the arbitration clause, as part of the unformed contract, is therefore also considered invalid – remains a contentious issue with ongoing debate in both academic and judicial circles.

622. In *DHL Project & Chartering Ltd v. Gemini Ocean Shipping Co Ltd*,[566] the UK Court of Appeal distinguished cases where it is claimed that the main (or 'matrix') contract was never actually concluded and cases where an established matrix contract is alleged to be void or otherwise ineffective. In the latter situation, the arbitration agreement may remain valid and enforceable despite the underlying contract being void or ineffective under the doctrine of separability. The Court determined that the present case fell into the former category, as the charter party (the main contract) had not been concluded. It held that it was necessary to assess whether the parties had indeed entered into an arbitration agreement, relying on the ordinary principles of contract formation. In this context, the doctrine of separability was deemed to have no substantial role, as the primary issue was whether an agreement to arbitrate had been established at all.

623. In addressing contract formation, the Court of Appeal determined that the 'subject to approval' provision acted as a pre-condition for the entire contract, including the arbitration clause. The commercial purpose of this clause was to allow either party to withdraw from the contract if the specified conditions were not met. Although the parties agreed that the contract would contain an arbitration clause, this agreement alone did not constitute an enforceable arbitration agreement. The ruling also clarifies that merely agreeing to include an arbitration clause in a contract does not automatically create a standalone arbitration agreement.

624. For an arbitration agreement to be binding, it must be based on the parties' clear intent to arbitrate disputes unconditionally. Conditional language, like 'subject

---

564. Article 19 of the Arbitration Law.
565. Article 507 CC.
566. *DHL Project & Chartering Ltd v. Gemini Ocean Shipping Co Ltd* [2022] EWCA 1555.

to approval', indicates that the parties do not yet consider themselves bound, thus precluding the immediate enforceability of the arbitration clause. This careful analysis of conditional terms ensures that arbitration is only enforced where there is unequivocal agreement to arbitrate, respecting both contractual autonomy and the intention underlying conditional agreements. The Singapore judiciary adopts a similar approach.[567]

625. Chinese law seems to chart a different path. *The SPC Interpretation Concerning Some Issues on Application of the Arbitration Law of the People's Republic of China* (2006, 2008 revision) ('The SPC Interpretation on Arbitration Law (2008 revision)') makes it explicit that if the parties reach an arbitration agreement when concluding a contract, the validity of the arbitration agreement is not affected by the contract's failure to be established.[568] In a leading case handed down by the SPC,[569] Yunyu Company (the 'Yunyu') listed for transfer its 100% equity in Newpower Enterprises Inc. (hereinafter 'Newpower') through the Beijing Equity Exchange ('BEE'). Zhongyuancheng Company (the 'ZYC') was identified as the sole qualified prospective transferee. Subsequently, both parties engaged in extensive negotiations via email regarding the Equity Transaction Contract and Debt Settlement Agreement. It was agreed that preliminary versions of both documents would require final confirmation from BEE, Yunyu Company, and the higher-level China Tourism Group Corporation ('China Tourism') before formal signing.[570]

626. Yunyu required ZYC to complete overseas investment procedures in compliance with national regulations and to make payments for transactions in foreign currency from outside China. On 27 October 2017, Yunyu issued a Notification Letter to ZYC, stating that, despite repeated reminders to complete the necessary legal formalities, ZYC had failed to comply. Consequently, Yunyu formally notified ZYC of the cancellation of the transaction.[571] On November 12, ZYC responded by requesting that Yunyu proceed with arranging the signing and provide the necessary documents to apply for relevant approvals with regulatory authorities. On November 27, Yunyu replied, reiterating that it had issued a transaction cancellation notice on October 27. Yunyu also proposed that both parties initiate procedures with the BEE for the return of the deposit.

627. On 4 April 2018, ZYC filed an arbitration request with the Shenzhen Court of International Arbitration (SCIA), citing Article 16.2 of the preliminary Equity Transaction Contract and Article 12 of the preliminary Debt Settlement Agreement. Yunyu and other relevant parties were named as co-respondents in the arbitration

---

567. *BCY v. BCZ* [2017] 3 SLR 357.
568. Paragraph 2 of Art. 10 of the SPC Interpretation Concerning Some Issues on Application of the Arbitration Law of the People's Republic of China (2006, 2008 revision).
569. *Yunyu Co., Ltd. v. Shenzhen Zhongyuancheng Commercial Investment Holding Co., Ltd.*, the Supreme People's Court, (2019) SPC Min Te No. 1; 运裕有限公司与深圳市中苑城商业投资控股有限公司，最高人民法院（2019）最高法民特1号.
570. *Ibid.*
571. *Ibid.*

application. The central issue in this case is whether the arbitration clause in question is valid and enforceable. The SPC reasoned as follows:[572]

> In judicial practice, questions about whether a contract has been established and whether the arbitration clause within it is valid often become entangled. However, Article 19, Paragraph 1 of the Arbitration Law, which begins with 'an arbitration agreement exists independently', provides a broad, overarching statement that should cover the question of whether the arbitration agreement itself exists or has been established. The following provisions further emphasize that certain listed situations do not affect the validity of the arbitration agreement. Additionally, Article 10, Paragraph 2 of the Interpretation of the Arbitration Law clarifies: 'If the parties reach an arbitration agreement concerning disputes at the time of entering into the contract, the fact that the contract has not been established does not affect the validity of the arbitration agreement.' Therefore, when determining the validity of an arbitration clause – including whether it has been established – it is appropriate first to assess the validity of the arbitration clause itself. Only if necessary should the validity of the entire contract, including whether it has been established, be examined. This case follows this rule by first assessing, based on the specific circumstances, whether the arbitration clause has been validly established.[573]

628. For SPC, the fact has been ascertained that the arbitration clauses in the Equity Transaction Contract and Debt Settlement Agreement were established. Subsequently, the parties negotiated certain other aspects of the contracts, but the arbitration clauses themselves were never disputed. Although Yunyu did not stamp the final contract document, nor did their legal representatives sign it, which is a requirement for the contract to take effect after being signed and stamped by the legal representatives or authorised representatives of both parties, the validity of the arbitration clause remains unaffected.[574] Since the parties have reached an arbitration agreement, there is no need to determine the validity of the main contract in this case; this issue should instead be addressed in arbitration.[575]

629. Chinese courts favour a presumption that arbitration clauses are valid whenever possible, guided by the Arbitration Law and judicial interpretations aimed at preserving arbitration agreements to the extent possible. The court in Yunyu interpreted the arbitration agreement's intent broadly to facilitate dispute resolution, following a rule favouring arbitration in cases of ambiguity.

630. Chinese law explicitly states that an arbitration clause is valid even if the main contract is deemed not to have been formed. This position ensures that the parties' intention to arbitrate survives regardless of issues with the primary contract's formal execution. In the Yunyu case, the court held that the arbitration agreement

572. *Ibid.*
573. *Ibid.*
574. *Ibid.*
575. *Ibid.*

remains valid even though the main contract lacked signatures or official seals, as the intent to arbitrate had been confirmed by both parties.

631. However, in *DHL Project & Chartering Ltd v. Gemini Ocean Shipping Co Ltd*,[576] the English court considered whether the parties' agreement to arbitrate could be upheld independently, especially where the broader contract formation was in dispute. In English law, while an arbitration clause can survive defects in the main contract, courts may examine formal elements to determine if the parties intended to establish a binding arbitration agreement. If formalities are lacking and no binding contract is found, English courts may be less likely to enforce the arbitration clause, particularly where mutual assent is unclear.

632. In summary, Chinese law tends to provide broader protection for arbitration clauses, emphasising enforceability and a pro-arbitration stance, even if formal requirements in the main contract are unmet. English law, while also recognising separability, is more inclined to focus on contract formalities and mutual intent. The difference reveals a pragmatic approach in China aimed at maximising dispute resolution options and a more cautious, formalistic approach in England that seeks clear mutual intent before enforcing arbitration agreements.

633. To conclude, arbitration clauses under Chinese law are characterised by strict formal requirements, particularly the need to name a specific arbitration institution under the current Arbitration Law. This requirement is designed to ensure clarity and enforceability but can lead to challenges if not properly addressed. In recent years, this rigid approach has been relaxed by the SPC in order to cultivate an arbitration-friendly legal environment. From a comparative perspective, the emphasis on institutional arbitration and the detailed scrutiny of arbitration agreements by Chinese courts are notable features. To avoid potential pitfalls, parties entering into contracts governed by Chinese law should ensure their arbitration clauses are precise, clearly express the intent to arbitrate, and specify a recognised arbitration institution.

576. *DHL Project & Chartering Ltd v. Gemini Ocean Shipping Co Ltd* [2022] EWCA 1555.

Chapter 4. Privity of Contract

§1. The Rule of Privity of Contract

634. The principle of privity of contract traditionally holds that only the parties to a contract are entitled to its rights and bound by its obligations. Under the Civil Code, the rights and obligations created by a contract are typically binding only on the parties involved and cannot extend to or affect third parties.[577] However, the Civil Code has specific provisions that elaborate on exceptions to this general rule, reflecting its unique legal and social environment.[578]

635. The principle of privity dictates that a contract generally has no legal effect beyond the parties to the contract.[579] To be specific, the principle of privity consists of two general rules. First, a third party cannot be subject to a burden by a contract to which he is not a party. There is no controversy about this. It would be irrational and unreasonable for a law to allow two contracting parties to impose a burden on a third party. The second rule is that a third party, an outsider to a contract, cannot enforce the promised performance, even when the contract is concluded with a clear intention of benefiting him. This rule is controversial as it has been criticised for causing hardship and is therefore not conducive to commercial life.

636. Below is a table listing the sixteen categories of statutory exceptions to the principle of privity of contract under the Chinese legal framework.

Category	Legal Basis
1. Non-cancellation of leases upon sale of property	Civil Code, Article 725
2. True interest third-party contracts	Civil Code, Article 522(2)
3. Rights of beneficiaries under life insurance contracts	Insurance Law, Article 18(3)
4. Rights of third parties under liability insurance contracts	Insurance Law, Article 65(2)
5. Rights of beneficiaries under trust contracts	Trust Law, Article 2
6. Rights of other victims under consumer contracts	Consumer Rights Protection Law, Article 49

577. Paragraph 2 of Art. 465 CC.
578. *Ibid.*
579. Prior to the Civil Code, Article 8(1) of the CCL 1999 provides that 'a lawfully established contract shall be legally binding on the parties thereto, each of whom shall perform its own obligations in accordance with the terms of the contract ...'. This is a clear expression of the Roman legal maxim stipulatio alteri non potest (a contract purporting to benefit a third party would be invalid).

Category	Legal Basis
7. Rights of victims under product sales contracts	The Product Quality Law, Article 43
8. Rights of individual tourists under group travel contracts	The SPC Provisions on Issues Concerning the Trial of Tourism Dispute Cases, Article 2
9. Creditor's subrogation rights	The Civil Code, Article 535(1)
10. Creditor's rights to preserve subrogation	The Civil Code, Article 536
11. Creditor's right to revoke debtor's gratuitous disposition	The Civil Code, Article 538
12. Creditor's right to revoke debtor's onerous disposition	The Civil Code, Article 539
13. Joint liability of carriers under multimodal transport contracts	The Civil Code, Article 834
14. Joint liability of subcontractors under construction contracts	Civil Code, Article 791(2)
15. Joint liability of the contractor and illegal subcontractor or transferor	The SPC Interpretation on Issues Concerning the Trial of Construction Contract Dispute Cases (I), Article 43(2)
16. The right of the client to intervene and the third party's right to choose	Civil Code, Article 926

I. Third Parties and the Contract

637. As a civil law jurisdiction inspired by continental European systems, the Chinese legal system explicitly established the concept of relativity (privity) of contracts. Paragraph 2 of Article 465 of the Civil Code provides that 'a lawfully formed contract will be legally binding only on the parties, except otherwise provided by law'.

638. The main rationale for keeping the privity principle is twofold. First, contractual rights and obligations are relative or personal to those who voluntarily create them. Defining them in this way entails three elements, namely: (1) the contract creates the legal relation between the specific contracting parties only; (2) only the contracting parties are bound by the contract; and (3) the liability for breach of contract is owed only to the contracting parties. Consequently, as a matter of principle, the right of enforcement by a third party should be disallowed. This has long been accepted as a distinguishing feature of the law of obligations, in contrast to property rights, which are absolute in that they generally bind the whole world. The distinction between rights in rem (rights against the world) and rights in personam (rights against a specific person or persons) is foundational in property and obligation law.[580] A right in rem (Latin for 'against the thing') is a right that is enforceable against the whole world (erga omnes). It pertains to the ownership or possession of a thing (e.g., land, a car, or intellectual property).[581] A right in personam (Latin for 'against the person') is a right that is enforceable only against a specific person or group of persons. It arises typically out of contracts or obligations.[582]

639. Second, there was a fear among the drafters of the Contract Law that without the privity principle, anyone could potentially enforce a contract, thus opening the floodgate for unnecessary litigation. In a similar vein, without the principle, the drafters cautioned that Chinese courts could potentially order any third party to join the litigation and pay damages for which the contracting parties were not liable. This would essentially impose an unfettered burden on a third party. It is necessary to comply with the privity of contract principle to fend off potential abuses of third-party rights and obligations in court proceedings.

640. Nonetheless, while the privity of the contract remains a foundational principle, the law is adaptable to accommodate scenarios where third-party rights or interests are justifiably involved. This flexibility is particularly relevant in a commercial environment where complex transactions may affect parties not directly involved in the initial contract. Thus, the Chinese legal approach to the privity of contract balances adherence to traditional contract principles with necessary exceptions to accommodate social and economic realities. For example, The Civil Code provides that a creditor may exercise the rights of the debtor against a third party when the debtor fails to act and such failure harms the creditor's interests.[583] In the realm of insurance law, an insurer may step into the shoes of the insured to recover funds owed by a third party to the insured, ensuring economic efficiency in debt recovery.[584]

641. The fundamental argument supporting the latter rule is that a contract is a *vinculum iuris* (a bond of law) binding contracting parties. This is true even if the contracting parties agree that each of them may discharge their liability by rendering performance to someone else. When the buyer, at the seller's request, pays the price to the seller's creditor instead of the seller himself, in rendering performance to the seller's third-party creditor, the buyer is performing an obligation he owes to the seller, a party to the contract, and not to the third party creditor. Nonetheless,

580. Peter Birks, An Introduction to the Law of Restitution 33-43 (Clarendon Press 1985).
581. Kevin Gray and Susan Francis Gray, Elements of Land Law 99-114 (5th edn, Oxford University Press 2009).
582. Wesley Newcomb Hohfeld, Fundamental Legal Conceptions as Applied in Judicial Reasoning 12-22 (Yale University Press 1919).
583. Article 535 CC.
584. Article 44 of the Insurance Law.

what if the seller's creditor wants to demand payment in his own name from the buyer? Here, we need to address the Chinese position on contracts for the benefit of third parties.

II. Contract for the Benefit of a Third Party

642. Before the implementation of the Civil Code, special legislation such as the Insurance Law and the Trust Law already contained relevant rules on genuine third-party beneficiary contracts, but these rules were scattered and lacked systematic coherence. There are distinct provisions in the Civil Code that cater to scenarios involving third parties in contract law. These provisions address two specific concepts: contracts for the benefit of a third party and contracts performed by a third party. Each of these has particular stipulations under the law, providing a structured approach to contractual relationships that affect or involve persons other than the contracting parties.

643. First, the Civil Code formally recognises contracts that benefit third parties, even if they are not direct parties to the contract. It also grants legal standing to third-party beneficiaries, allowing them to enforce contractual obligations directly. This is outlined in Article 522, which states that:

> Where the parties agree that the obligor shall perform the obligations to a third party, and the obligor fails to perform its obligations to such third party or its performance of the obligations is not in conformity with the agreement, the obligor shall be liable to the obligee for breach of contract.
>
> If a third party may directly request the obligor to perform its obligations in accordance with the provisions of law or agreement between the parties and the third party does not explicitly express refusal within a reasonable period of time, it may request the obligor to accept liability for breach of contract where the obligor fails to perform its obligations to such third party or its performance of the obligations is not in conformity with the agreement. The defence that the obligor claims against the obligee may be claimed against such third party.[585]

644. This provision explicitly allows for contracts where the benefit is intended for a third party, constituting a breakthrough in the principle of contract privity. Before the enactment of the Civil Code, Articles 64 and 65 of the CCL appear to suggest that a third party does not have a direct right of action.[586] However, these two articles do not explicitly rule out the possibility of a third-party right when the contracting parties agree to confer it on the third party.[587]

585. Article 525 CC.
586. Yi Tian, On Third-Party Contracts, 1 Legal Studies 33 (2001).
587. Shiyuan Han, On Contracts for Performance to a Third Party: An Interpretation of Article 64 of the Chinese Contract Law, 22 Science of Law (Journal of Northwest University of Political Science and Law) 100 (2004).

645. The third party's rights are derived from the parties' intention, as found in the contract. This type of contract recognises that a party to a contract (the promisee) can negotiate terms that confer rights on a third party (the beneficiary), who is not a party to the contract. The third party can demand that the promisor (the party obligated to perform under the contract) fulfil its obligations as per the contract terms. This right is enforceable unless the contract explicitly states otherwise or the nature of the contract precludes such enforcement.[588] This provision enables third parties to be direct beneficiaries of contract terms without the necessity of becoming contracting parties themselves.

646. To be specific, the first paragraph of Article 522 addresses the situation of non-genuine third-party contracts, which is actually a special form of contract performance.[589] In this scenario, a third party, in their own name and for the benefit of the creditor, passively accepts the performance from the debtor. The third party only receives a purely factual economic benefit from the performance. Therefore, the third party does not have the right to demand performance from the debtor directly. If the debtor fails to perform or performs non-compliantly, they are still liable to the creditor for breach of contract.

647. The second paragraph addresses genuine third-party contracts,[590] which differ from non-genuine ones stipulated in the first paragraph because the contract's effectiveness extends to a third party, who acquires the right to demand performance.[591] The third party enjoys independent legal interests; therefore, if the debtor fails to perform or performs non-compliantly, the third party can demand that the debtor assume liability for breach of contract.

648. Whether a contract is a genuine third-party contract is determined based on the true intent of the parties and the creditor-debtor relationship and ownership of rights established by the contract. This determination should not be confined to the wording of the contract alone. While such expressions granting a right of action to a third party are indicative of the formation of a genuine third-party contract, the absence of such wording does not necessarily mean that a genuine third-party contract is not established.[592]

649. Where a contract stipulates that the contract debtor needs to perform the contract to a third party and there is an arbitration agreement between the contracting parties, the contract debtor failed its obligation. An arbitral award was in favour

588. Jianyuan Cui, On Contracts for the Benefit of a Third Party, 62 Jilin University Journal Social Science Edition 152 (2022).
589. Paragraph 1 of Art. 522 CC.
590. Paragraph 2 of Art. 522 CC.
591. Yan Zhu, A Study on Contracts Benefiting Third Parties, 23 Science of Law (Journal of Northwest University of Political Science and Law) 55 (2005).
592. *Lu Suyan v. Wujiang Taihu Industrial Waste Disposal Co., Ltd. & Others* People's Court of New District Shanghai (2022) Hu 0115 Min Chu No. 95925 陆肃燕与吴江市太湖工业废弃物处理有限公司等其他与公司有关的纠纷一审民事判决书 上海市浦东新区人民法院（2022）沪0115民初95925号.

of a third party addressed in the contract. In this situation, can the contract debtor successfully challenge the arbitral award, arguing that the third party is a non-privy of the arbitration agreement?

650. In a case handed down by a Beijing Court,[593] the Evening News Agency claimed that the arbitration decision requiring it to pay compensation to a third party, Ms Yang, falls outside the scope of the arbitration clause. The agreement in question includes an arbitration clause. Although Yang was not a signatory to the agreement, the Evening News Agency and the Air Media Company agreed in the agreement to fulfil certain obligations towards the third party, Ms Yang. The claim by Air Media Company and the arbitration decision requiring the Evening News Agency to pay compensation to Yang were based on contractual terms and did not exceed the scope of the arbitration clause in the agreement.

651. The Evening News Agency raised this issue during the arbitration proceedings, and the arbitration tribunal made its decision based on the contractual terms and legal provisions in accordance with the arbitration agreement. Therefore, the court did not support the Evening News Agency's claim.[594] A third party's interest will not be affected by an arbitration agreement between the contracting parties under Chinese law.

652. It should be noted that while the third party has the right to request the debtor to fulfil the debt towards them independently, they do not have associated contractual rights such as the right of revocation or the right of termination.[595] Although the third party benefits from the contract, they are not original parties to the contract. The rights of revocation and termination are typically reserved for the parties who have negotiated and entered into the contract, as they are the ones who have contractual privity and mutual obligations.[596]

653. Extending additional rights, such as revocation or termination, could lead to conflicts and undermine the original parties' intentions.[597] It is essential to maintain the integrity and predictability of contracts by restricting such significant rights to the original contracting parties. If third-party beneficiaries were granted extensive rights like revocation or termination, it could lead to potential abuse. For instance, a third party might terminate a contract for personal gain or out of spite, which could be detrimental to the contracting parties' interests.

---

593. *Legal Evening News Agency v. Beiqing Hangmei Technology and Media Communication Co., Ltd.,* No. 4 Intermediate People's Court of Beijing (2021) Jing 04 Min Te No.164 法制晚报社与北青航媒科技传播有限公司申请撤销仲裁裁决民事裁定书 北京市第四中级人民法院（2021）京04民特164号.
594. *Ibid.*
595. Article 29 of the SPC Interpretation on the Contract Book (2023).
596. Liming Wan, Contract Law Studies (Volume 1) 162-163 (China Renmin University Press 2015).
597. *Cen Mingguang v. Tengxian Tianping Agricultural Development Co., Ltd,* Intermediate People's Court of Wuzhou City, Guangxi Zhuang Autonomous Region (2015) Wu Min Er Zhong Zi No.94; 岑明广与梁志宏、藤县天平农业发展有限公司与公司有关的纠纷二审民事判决书， 广西壮族自治区梧州市中级人民法院（2015）梧民二终字第94号.

654. The primary purpose of including a third-party beneficiary in a contract is to confer a specific benefit. By limiting the third-party rights to claim this benefit, the law ensures that the contract's primary objective is achieved without introducing additional legal complexities.

655. Where the debtor performs the obligation to the third party as agreed, and the third party refuses to accept it, the creditor can request the debtor to perform the obligation to themselves, except when the debtor has extinguished the debt through measures such as escrow.[598] If the third party refuses to accept or delays acceptance, the debtor is entitled to request the creditor to compensate for the resulting losses.[599] The provision clarifies the legal remedies available to the parties involved in the contract.

656. The primary goal is to ensure that the obligations under the contract are fulfilled. If the third party refuses to accept the performance, the rule provides a mechanism for the creditor to request the debtor to perform the obligation to themselves. The rule protects the debtor from being unfairly penalised when they have performed their obligation as agreed.

657. If the third party refuses to accept the performance, the debtor is not left in an indefinite state of obligation. By allowing the debtor to seek compensation from the creditor for any resulting losses due to the third party's refusal or delay, the debtor's interests are safeguarded. Hence, the contracting parties can be assured that there are legal mechanisms to enforce the performance of obligations and to seek redress in case of refusal or delay by the third party.

III. Contracts Performed by a Third Party

658. Another type of contract is a contract performed by a third party, which addresses situations where the performance of a contract is delegated to a third party who is not originally a party to the contract.[600] Such a contract explicitly provides performance by the third party rendered to the creditor. If the third party either fails to perform or performs in a manner that does not comply with the agreement, the debtor shall bear liability for breach of contract to the creditor.[601]

659. The rule that a debtor remains liable to the creditor if a third party fails to fulfil the agreed obligation underscores the principle that delegation of performance does not absolve the original debtor from their contractual responsibilities. When a debtor arranges for a third party to fulfil the obligation, this arrangement is viewed as a convenience for the debtor rather than a transfer of liability. The creditor, who

598. Paragraph 3 of Art. 29 of the SPC Interpretation on the Contract Book (2023).
599. *Ibid.*
600. Article 523 CC.
601. *Ibid.*

did not directly engage with the third party, retains their right to expect the performance they bargained for from the original contracting party.[602]

660. By holding the original debtor liable, it is made clear that any risk associated with the third party's involvement falls on the debtor, who chose to delegate rather than personally perform the obligation.[603] This encourages parties to carefully select and manage any third parties involved, as their failures could lead to significant financial or reputational repercussions for the debtor.

661. Moreover, in the absence of an explicit novation agreement, where all parties, including the creditor, agree to substitute a new party in place of the original debtor, the original debtor cannot transfer the ultimate liability.

662. Another scenario may arise when the debtor fails to perform their obligation. In such a situation, a third party with a legitimate interest in the performance of that obligation has the right to fulfil it on behalf of the debtor.[604]

663. This rule introduces the concept of third-party performance, which serves as an important mechanism to ensure that creditors receive the performance they are entitled to, even if the debtor defaults.[605] The third party's right to fulfil the obligation is particularly significant when that third party has a legitimate interest in the fulfilment – such as a guarantor, co-investor, or any party that might suffer economic or reputational harm if the debtor defaults.[606]

664. By allowing a range of parties to intervene, the law acknowledges that third parties often have a vested interest in preventing negative consequences, such as asset loss or financial harm, that may arise from the debtor's failure to fulfil their obligations.[607]

602. Lei Chen, Relaxations of Contractual Privity and the Need for Third Party Rights in Chinese Contract Law, in Formation and Third Party Beneficiaries 45-63 (Mindy Chen-Wishart, Alexander Loke, and Stefan Vogenauer eds., Oxford University Press 2018).
603. Shiyuan Han, The General Principles of Contract Law 375-378 (4th edn, Law Press China 2018).
604. Paragraph 1 of Art. 524 CC.
605. Liming Wang, On Performance by a Third Party: Focusing on Article 524 of the Civil Code, 8 LAW 5 (2021).
606. Paragraph 1 of Art. 30 of the SPC Interpretation on the Contract Book (2023) specifies that the court can recognise the following entities as having a legitimate interest in the performance of the debtor's obligation: 1. guarantor or a third party providing collateral; 2. assignee, usufructuary, or lawful possessor of property used as collateral; 3. subsequent priority secured creditors on the collateral; 4. third parties with legal interests in the debtor's property, where such interests may be lost if the property is subject to compulsory enforcement; 5. shareholders or founders of a debtor that is a corporation or an unincorporated organisation; 6. close relatives of a debtor who is a natural person; 7. other third parties with a legitimate interest in the performance of the obligation.
607. Shengping Gao & Xinming Tao, On the Legal Application of Third-Party Debt Repayment: An Analysis Based on Article 30 of Interpretations of the General Provisions of the Contract Section of the Civil Code, 1 Social Science Research 42 (2024).

665. However, this right is subject to limitations based on the nature of the obligation. If the obligation is *intuitu personae* (i.e., one requiring personal performance because of specific skills, expertise, or trust placed in the debtor), then the third party cannot step in.[608] For example, a contract requiring a specific artist to paint a portrait cannot be fulfilled by someone else. Likewise, if the parties explicitly agree that only the debtor can perform the obligation, this right of third-party substitution is excluded. Apart from this exception, the original parties are not allowed to refuse the performance of the third party with a legitimate interest in the contract performance.[609]

666. If the creditor accepts performance from the third party, the creditor's claim against the debtor transfers to the third party unless there is an alternative agreement between the debtor and the third party.[610] This rule relates to the transfer of rights after performance by the third party. Essentially, the third party, having performed the debtor's obligation, takes over the creditor's rights against the debtor. This transfer ensures that the third party, who has fulfilled the debt, can seek reimbursement or compensation from the debtor. It is a form of subrogation, allowing the third party to stand in the shoes of the creditor with regard to the original debtor.

667. However, this transfer of rights can be modified by an agreement between the debtor and the third party.[611] Such an agreement might specify that the third party cannot pursue the debtor for reimbursement after performing the obligation, which may happen if the third party, such as a close family member or a strategic business partner, wishes to absorb the loss themselves without pursuing recovery.

668. It is also crucial to note that the third party's acquisition of the creditor's rights cannot harm the creditor's interests.[612] This ensures that the creditor retains the upper hand and prevents potential manipulations that could disadvantage them, particularly if multiple third parties are involved.

669. Regarding guarantors, if they perform the obligation, they may seek compensation or enforce rights against other guarantors involved in the obligation. This follows specific provisions under the SPC Interpretation on the Security System, which provide guidance on how such intra-guarantor claims should be managed.[613] These rules prevent disputes about contribution and compensation among those who share the guarantee burden.

670. The above rule allows third parties with legitimate interests to mitigate potential losses, and it holds the debtor accountable through the potential liability to

608. Paragraph 1 of Art. 524 CC.
609. Keping Ran, The System of Third-Party Payment from the Perspective of the Codification of the Civil Code, 2 FASHANG YANJIU (Journal of South Central Institute of Political Science and Law) 36 (2015).
610. Paragraph 2 of Art. 524 CC.
611. *Ibid.*
612. Paragraph 2 of Art. 30 of the SPC Interpretation on the Contract Book (2023)
613. Paragraph 3 of Art. 30 of the SPC Interpretation on the Contract Book (2023).

the third party who performed the obligation. Moreover, this mechanism encourages greater contractual stability and flexibility, as parties involved can more effectively manage risks and obligations, knowing that third-party performance is a viable option under certain circumstances.

§2. Assignment of Contractual Rights

671. Chinese law allows a third party to enforce a contract for his benefit if the right has been assigned to him. Assignment involves transferring a contractual right from the original promisee to the third party without the original debtor's consent, serving as an exception to the privity principle. Assignment can occur either by operation of law (such as through succession and subrogation) or by agreement between the assignor and assignee.

I. Subrogation

672. Subrogation claims allow a creditor to step into the shoes of a debtor to enforce rights against a third party (the 'counterparty') when the debtor fails to do so, protecting the creditor's ability to recover what is owed. It ensures the protection of creditors' rights by preventing debtors from harming the creditor's ability to recover debts through inaction or negligence. Subrogation is particularly relevant in complex financial or commercial transactions, such as when a debtor refuses or neglects to pursue its claim against a counterparty or in bankruptcy proceedings where timely registration of claims is critical.

673. Specifically, under Chinese law, if a debtor neglects to exercise their own claims or associated ancillary rights, thereby endangering the creditor's ability to recover a due debt, the creditor is entitled to act in their own name to assert the debtor's rights against a third party (the 'counterparty').[614] A debtor is deemed negligent in exercising its rights (or related ancillary rights) if it fails to pursue claims against its counterparties through litigation or arbitration, causing the creditor's due claims to remain unrealised.[615] This provision clarifies 'negligence' and emphasises that the debtor's inaction must materially harm the creditor's ability to recover their debt.

674. Nonetheless, if a debtor is unable to exercise their rights due to objective reasons, such as being imprisoned or losing their capacity to act without a designated guardian, they do not have the capability to initiate arbitration or litigation. This is important because subrogation targets debtors who have the ability but lack the willingness to exercise their rights. For instance, if a debtor has been imprisoned, the proof of release shows the debtor was unable to pursue their claims until

614. Paragraph 1 of Art. 535 CC.
615. Article 33 of the SPC Interpretation on the Contract Book (2023).

his sentence was complete. Once released, if the debtor promptly goes to his debtor's location to collect the debt, it demonstrates that the debtor was not neglecting their rights. Thus, a subrogation claim filed by the creditor would not meet the necessary conditions for subrogation, as the debtor did not intentionally fail to exercise their rights.[616]

675. The distinction between inability and unwillingness to enforce rights becomes critical in understanding the legitimacy of a subrogation claim. The example given demonstrates a situation where the debtor's inability was beyond their control. Such circumstances, like imprisonment or the loss of legal capacity without a designated guardian, mean that the debtor physically or legally could not pursue their rights rather than refusing to do so.

676. This distinction is vital because subrogation claims are exceptional remedies intended to prevent the undue harm to creditors that results when a debtor unjustifiably fails to collect or enforce a debt. In the case of an objectively incapacitated debtor, they are clearly hindered by circumstances beyond their control, thus not meeting the condition of being a 'neglectful' debtor. Subrogation is designed to address scenarios where debtors fail to act despite having the opportunity and means to do so and not to penalise those unable to act for legitimate reasons.

677. There is an important policy consideration here. By ensuring that subrogation claims cannot be initiated against debtors facing genuine incapacities, the law seeks to maintain a balance in the debtor-creditor relationship. This balance ensures that the creditor's rights are not advanced at the unfair expense of a debtor who, due to unavoidable reasons, could not enforce their rights.

678. A tricky question arises when the debtor has already taken a legal action by initiating and winning litigation or arbitration but subsequently failed to take action to execute the favourable judgment.[617] Under such a circumstance, can the creditor exercise the right of subrogation? One view is that the Civil Code and the SPC Interpretation on the Contract Book (2023) only mentioned that the subrogation right can be invoked when the debtor initiates litigation or arbitration. When a binding judgment or award is issued, the creditor has lost the ground to invoke subrogation.[618] A more sensible view perhaps suggests that so long as the debtor fails to prove it

---

616. *Yang Meihua v. Yang Wanyong and Others*, The People's Court of Wusu City, Xinjiang Uyghur Autonomous Region (2021) Xin 4202 Min Chu No. 5407; 杨某花 杨某勇等债权人代位权纠纷案，新疆维吾尔自治区乌苏市人民法院（2021）新4202民初5407号判决书.

617. Bingwan Xiong, The determination of neglect in exercising authority affecting the realisation of due claims, in Interpretation and Commentary on the Judicial Interpretation of the General Provisions of the Contract Book in the Civil Code 393 (Liming Wang & Hu Zhu eds., Renmin University Press 2024).

618. *Zhang & Cao v. Dongfeng County Hengdaohecheng Honest Development and Construction Co., Ltd.* The People's Court of Longshan District, Liaoyuan City, Jilin Province, (2021) Liao 0882 Min Chu No.4534; 张某，曹某廷诉东丰县横道河诚实开发建设有限公司，东丰县东风建设有限责任公司， 吉林省辽源市龙山区人民法院（2021）辽0882 民初4534号.

was hindered by circumstances beyond their control to execute the judgment or award, the creditor can still exercise the right of subrogation.[619]

679. In this scenario, the refusal to proceed with enforcement constitutes a failure to act in good faith to protect the creditor's interests. This refusal is likely to be seen as unjustifiable negligence. The key test is whether such an unjustifiable negligence 'affects the realisation of the creditor's due claim' as specified in Article 535 of the Civil Code. Back to basics, subrogation rights are specifically designed to address situations where a debtor's refusal to act directly impacts the creditor's ability to recover what they are owed.[620] As such, This inaction satisfies the conditions for subrogation, as it constitutes an unjustified failure by the debtor to exercise their rights, directly affecting the creditor's ability to recover their claim. The creditor may, therefore, step in to enforce the judgment or award on behalf of the debtor to ensure that their rights are protected.

680. The subrogation does not apply to rights that are personal to the debtor and cannot be transferred or exercised by others (e.g., rights closely tied to the debtor's personality or discretion).[621] Certain rights are explicitly excluded from subrogation as they are personal to the debtor, such as maintenance, support, or alimony claims; claims for personal injury compensation; labour remuneration claims, except for amounts exceeding the debtor's and dependents' basic living needs; claims for social security benefits (e.g., pensions, unemployment insurance, minimum living allowances).[622] These exclusions ensure that subrogation does not interfere with the debtor's fundamental rights or basic living standards. The creditor's exercise of the subrogation right is limited to the amount necessary to satisfy the creditor's due claim.[623] The scope of subrogation is strictly tied to the creditor's due claim, avoiding overreach. Necessary costs incurred by the creditor while exercising this right are borne by the debtor.[624] The counterparty can assert defences against the creditor that they would otherwise have against the debtor (e.g., claiming set-off or other legal defences).[625] Allowing the counterparty to raise defences ensures fairness, preventing the creditor from gaining greater rights than the debtor could assert.

681. Before the creditor's claim against the debtor is due, if the debtor's rights are at risk of being time-barred (e.g., due to an expiring statute of limitations) or the

619. *Shanghai Zhongxiang (Group) v. Shanghai Zhabei District Economic Commission*, High People's Court of Shanghai, (2009) Hu Gao Min Yi Min Zi Zhong No. 21; 上海中祥（集团）与上海市闸北区经济委员会等代位权纠纷案，上海市高级人民法院，（2009）沪高民一 民终字第21号.
620. Article 535 CC.
621. Paragraph 1 of Art. 535 CC.
622. Article 34 of the SPC Interpretation on the Contract Book (2023).
623. Paragraph 2 of Art. 535 CC.
624. *Ibid.*
625. Paragraph 3 of Art. 535 CC.

debtor fails to register a claim in bankruptcy, the creditor can step in and take necessary actions to protect the claim. Such actions may include compelling the counterparty to perform its obligations to the debtor or filing a claim with a bankruptcy administrator.[626]

682. One critical scenario is when the debtor's rights are in danger of being time-barred due to the impending expiration of the statute of limitations. If the debtor fails to exercise their rights within a certain time frame, the claim may become unenforceable. This, in turn, would reduce the debtor's overall asset pool, directly affecting the creditor's chances of recovery. The creditor, therefore, has a vested interest in ensuring that the debtor takes action to preserve these claims. If the debtor fails to do so, the creditor is entitled to step in and initiate the necessary legal proceedings to prevent the claim from being extinguished by the statute of limitations.

683. In cases involving bankruptcy, the situation is similarly precarious. If the debtor fails to register a claim in bankruptcy proceedings, they may lose the right to receive payment from the bankrupt estate, thus diminishing the debtor's ability to fulfil their obligations to the creditor. In such situations, the creditor may intervene by filing the claim on behalf of the debtor with the bankruptcy administrator. This right to act is particularly crucial in bankruptcy scenarios, where the orderly distribution of assets depends heavily on all claims being filed in a timely manner. The failure to register a claim may lead to a loss of entitlement, thereby reducing the pool of assets available to settle the debtor's obligations.

684. The proactive intervention permitted by law serves as a mechanism for maintaining the integrity of the debtor's asset pool. It prevents a situation where a debtor's failure to act results in the loss of valuable rights or assets, thereby safeguarding the creditor's interest in being repaid.

685. When a court recognises a creditor's subrogation claim, it effectively allows the creditor to enforce a right that originally belonged to the debtor against a third party (the counterparty). Once the subrogation claim is granted, the counterparty must fulfil the obligation directly to the creditor.[627] Once the creditor successfully recovers what is due through subrogation, the creditor-debtor relationship is partially or fully extinguished, depending on the extent of the performance.[628] Hence, the debtor is relieved of that corresponding part of their liability toward the creditor. Essentially, the debtor's obligation to the creditor is satisfied with the amount that the creditor has recovered through the subrogation claim.[629]

---

626. Article 536 CC.
627. Article 537 CC.
628. *Ibid.*
629. The Research Office of the Second Civil Division of the Supreme People's Court, Understanding and Application of the SPC Interpretation of the General Provisions of the Contract Section of the Civil Code 385 (People's Court Press 2023).

686. Once the counterparty fulfils its obligation directly to the creditor, the original debtor-counterparty relationship is also terminated.[630] It is crucial to recognise that the counterparty's performance under subrogation is as if they had fulfilled their original obligation toward the debtor, meaning that they can no longer be pursued by the debtor for the same obligation.

687. In some cases, the debtor's rights against the counterparty may have been preserved by the court – such as through asset freezing or injunctions – to prevent the debtor from jeopardising the creditor's interests by transferring or depleting their rights. When the creditor exercises subrogation, these preservation measures may continue to ensure that the obligation is appropriately fulfilled.[631] Likewise, if the debtor's rights against the counterparty are under court-ordered execution, such as being auctioned or otherwise enforced to satisfy outstanding debts, the creditor's subrogation right may be exercised in coordination with these execution measures.[632]

688. If the debtor is undergoing bankruptcy, the creditor's subrogation right must be exercised in accordance with bankruptcy laws. In bankruptcy proceedings, all claims and rights of the debtor become subject to collective enforcement under the oversight of a bankruptcy administrator.[633]

689. In sum, when the court recognises a creditor's subrogation claim, the subsequent fulfilment by the counterparty results in the termination of related legal relationships – between the creditor and debtor, as well as between the debtor and counterparty. The interplay between subrogation, preservation, execution, and bankruptcy measures further strengthens the creditor's position, allowing them to take necessary steps to protect their rights while respecting broader legal safeguards that apply to the debtor's assets. The legal structure surrounding subrogation thereby balances the rights and obligations of all involved, promoting orderly and just debt enforcement.

690. The SPC further spells out the details of the jurisdiction of subrogation claims. They are governed by the court in the location of the defendant's domicile unless there are exclusive jurisdiction requirements.[634] It is remarkable that a jurisdictional agreement between the debtor and their counterparty does not affect the court's jurisdiction in subrogation claims.[635] This rule has significant implications, as it underscores the protective nature of subrogation. Subrogation claims are meant to allow creditors to act on behalf of a debtor when the debtor fails to enforce their rights. If the debtor and their counterparty had the ability to alter the jurisdiction through private agreements, it could undermine the effectiveness of subrogation by adding procedural hurdles for the creditor.

---

630. Article 537 CC.
631. *Ibid.*
632. *Ibid.*
633. *Ibid.*
634. Article 35 of the SPC Interpretation on the Contract Book (2023).
635. *Ibid.*

691. Another doctrinal significance is that the independence of subrogation claims from the original debtor-counterparty agreement demonstrates the unique nature of subrogation as a remedy. Unlike typical contractual claims, which may be subject to various negotiated clauses including jurisdiction, subrogation is an independent right exercised by the creditor. It arises out of the debtor's failure to protect their rights and directly impacts the creditor's interests. The creditor exercises subrogation not as a party to the original contract but as a beneficiary whose interests are at stake due to the debtor's failure. As such, the original agreement's jurisdictional stipulations cannot limit or affect the creditor's ability to pursue the claim in the appropriate legal venue.

692. It is important to note that the SPC provides a clear rule on the interplay between the court's subrogation claim and the arbitration agreement between the debtor and the counterparty. If the debtor or the counterparty cites an arbitration agreement to challenge the court's jurisdiction, the court will not uphold this objection.[636] However, if arbitration is initiated before the first court hearing, the subrogation lawsuit can be stayed.[637] The primary rationale behind denying an objection based on an arbitration agreement is to protect the creditor's right to enforce the debtor's claim against a third party. Subrogation is designed to allow creditors to act when the debtor is unwilling to do so, and permitting an arbitration agreement to dictate jurisdiction could create significant obstacles for the creditor.

693. Arbitration agreements are essentially contractual arrangements between the debtor and the counterparty, and the creditor is not a direct party to that agreement.[638] Allowing arbitration clauses to limit the court's jurisdiction over subrogation claims could leave creditors unable to effectively exercise their rights, particularly if arbitration is inaccessible, costly, or unfavourable to them.[639] Thus, the rule is designed to prevent an undue burden on the creditor, ensuring they can pursue the claim in a straightforward and effective manner.[640] The court's jurisdiction is thus prioritised over arbitration in the interest of ensuring that subrogation litigation remains an effective remedy for creditors.

---

636. Article 36 of the SPC Interpretation on the Contract Book (2023).
637. *Ibid.*
638. *Fu Jiaqun v. Hubei Rongxingda Trading Co., Ltd.* Intermediate People's Court of Hubei (2017) E 01 Min Zhong No.1576 付家群、湖北荣兴达贸易有限公司, 湖北省武汉市中级人民法院（2017）鄂01民终1576号民事裁定书
639. Liming Wang, The Impact of Arbitration Agreements on the Exercise of Subrogation Rights: A Commentary on Article 36 of the Interpretation of the General Provisions of the Contract Code, 1 Guangdong Social Science (Guangdong She Hui Ke Xue) 221 (2024).
640. *China Railway 15th Bureau Group Second Engineering Co., Ltd. v. China Railway 15th Bureau Group Second Engineering Co., Ltd. Kunming Branch and Lin Jihui*, No. 2 Intermediate People's Court of Shanghai, (2018) Hu 02 Min Xia Zhong No. 617; 中铁十五局集团第二工程有限公司与中铁十五局集团第二工程有限公司昆明分公司、林际晖， 上海市第二中级人民法院（2018）沪02民辖终617号民事裁定书.

694. Nonetheless, the rule does allow for arbitration to be given effect if initiated before the first court hearing.[641] This reflects an attempt to balance the creditor's rights with the parties' original intention to arbitrate disputes. If arbitration proceedings are initiated promptly, the stay on the subrogation lawsuit recognises the parties' initial agreement and respects the arbitration process as a legitimate alternative dispute resolution mechanism. This ensures that arbitration agreements are not entirely disregarded, but rather, they are only given effect if they do not cause undue delay or obstruct the creditor's subrogation rights.

695. The downside of the rule allowing a stay if arbitration is initiated before the first hearing is likely to encourage strategic behaviour by debtors or counterparties. They may wait until the last possible moment before the first court hearing to initiate arbitration in order to delay enforcement actions. This could be used as a tactic to buy time, complicating the process for creditors and increasing costs associated with enforcement. Such behaviour could undermine the creditor's right to a timely remedy, as the debtor or counterparty may exploit the provision to slow down the subrogation process without genuine intent to resolve the dispute through arbitration.

696. Nonetheless, a counterargument is when the creditor exercises subrogation rights, they also enjoy all of the debtor's rights against the secondary debtor. Correspondingly, the secondary debtor can assert any defences against the creditor that they could have raised against the debtor, including requiring the creditor to adhere to an arbitration agreement between the debtor and the secondary debtor, thus exercising subrogation rights through arbitration.[642] In this context, Article 535 of the Civil Code, which stipulates that subrogation can only be exercised through a court, appears inappropriate.[643] The restriction imposed by Article 535 of the Civil Code, which limits the exercise of subrogation rights to court proceedings, raises significant challenges concerning contractual autonomy, parity between parties, and the efficacy of arbitration as a dispute resolution mechanism. While it seeks to provide a streamlined process for subrogation claims, it may inadvertently create inequities and disparities that disadvantage the secondary debtor and undermine the broader utility of arbitration.

697. Allowing arbitration to play a role in subrogation claims within the context of the privity of contract is complex, given that the subrogating creditor is not an original party to the arbitration agreement between the debtor and the secondary debtor. An exception could be made by treating the subrogating creditor as a 'third-party beneficiary' of the arbitration agreement. In this context, the creditor, while not an original party, is directly affected by the contractual relationship between the debtor and the counterparty. Allowing arbitration could be based on the notion that

641. Article 36 of the SPC Interpretation on the Contract Book (2023).

642. Defeng Xu, The Responsible Assets of the Debtor: The Common Basis of the Creditor's Right of Revocation, Subrogation, and the Corporate Creditor Protection System, 1 Tsinghua University Law Journal 25, 38 (2024).

643. *Ibid.*

the creditor derives rights from the debtor and, as such, should also adhere to the dispute resolution methods agreed to by the debtor. This approach would require the arbitration clause to be interpreted broadly, allowing for the inclusion of parties who step into the shoes of one of the original contracting parties through mechanisms such as subrogation.

698. The SPC's current approach, which restricts subrogation claims to court jurisdiction, is a feasible and practical solution given the current stage of development in China's arbitration practice. It ensures predictability, protects creditor rights, and avoids the complexities associated with non-signatory arbitration participation. However, as arbitration institutions continue to evolve, gain experience, and improve their capacity to handle third-party rights effectively, the feasibility of allowing arbitration to play a role in subrogation claims could be reconsidered.

699. If a creditor initiates a subrogation lawsuit without including the debtor as a third party, the court should add the debtor.[644] The mandatory inclusion of the debtor as a third party in subrogation suits is crucial to maintain transparency regarding the rights and responsibilities of all parties involved, thus enhancing procedural fairness.

700. If multiple creditors bring subrogation claims against the same counterparty, the court may consolidate the claims. If the debtor's claim against the counterparty is insufficient to satisfy all creditors, the court will apportion the claim among the creditors based on the amount of their debts.[645] Consolidating multiple claims by different creditors against the same counterparty not only improves judicial efficiency but also establishes a fair allocation mechanism when the debtor's rights are insufficient to meet all obligations. By apportioning claims based on the debt proportions, the court ensures an equitable outcome for all involved creditors.

701. Subrogation claims against the debtor's counterparty may be consolidated with existing claims against the debtor if they fall under the jurisdiction of the same court.[646] If these cases are under different jurisdictions, the court will inform the creditor to initiate a new lawsuit in the appropriate jurisdiction, and subrogation claims should be stayed until the conclusion of the main action.[647] The provisions regarding consolidation and jurisdictional challenges aim to prevent debtors or counterparties from using procedural objections to delay or complicate recovery efforts.

702. If the court finds that the creditor's subrogation claim does not meet the necessary conditions, it will dismiss the claim. This does not preclude the creditor from initiating a new lawsuit based on new facts.[648] The counterparty cannot object

644. Paragraph 1 of Art. 35 of the SPC Interpretation on the Contract Book (2023).
645. Paragraph 2 of Art. 35 of the SPC Interpretation on the Contract Book (2023).
646. Articles 38 and 39 of the SPC Interpretation on the Contract Book (2023).
647. *Ibid.*
648. Paragraph 1 of Art. 40 of the SPC Interpretation on the Contract Book (2023).

to the subrogation solely on the basis that the creditor-debtor relationship has not been confirmed by an effective legal document.[649] This rule prevents the counterparty from disputing the subrogation on purely procedural grounds, like the absence of an enforceable creditor-debtor relationship, thereby upholding substantive justice over procedural obstacles.

703. After a subrogation claim is initiated, a debtor could be incentivised to reduce the debt or extend repayment terms to disadvantage the creditor or limit their ability to recover. Such changes cannot be used by the counterparty to defend against the creditor's claim and serve as a safeguard, reinforcing that subrogation is designed to place the creditor in the debtor's position with the same rights, regardless of the debtor's subsequent behaviour.[650]

704. Chinese civil law uses subrogation as a creditor protection tool, focusing on safeguarding the creditor's ability to recover their debts while ensuring that procedural defences do not unreasonably hinder the enforcement of legitimate claims. By providing clear jurisdictional rules, enabling third-party substitution, and regulating debtor behaviour after claims are filed, these rules facilitate debt recovery under procedural efficiency and fairness.

II. Assignment of Contractual Rights by Agreement

705. The Civil Code provides a detailed framework for the transfer of contractual rights, ensuring clarity and protecting the interests of all parties involved. By requiring notification and allowing defences and set-offs, the law aims to balance the rights of the transferor, transferee, and obligor, promoting fairness and stability in contractual relationships.

706. Specifically, a party to a contract may assign its rights under the contract, either wholly or partially, to a third party, except as otherwise stipulated by law, agreed by the parties, or prohibited by the nature of the contract.[651] The assignment of rights shall be in accordance with legal procedures and meet any conditions specified in the contract. Assignment of claims refers to the process by which a creditor (assignor) transfers a claim to a third party (assignee) without altering the substance of the claim.[652]

707. The system of claim assignment is closely related to a variety of financial transactions, including factoring, collection, discounting, asset securitisation, and secured financing. By allowing the assignment of claims, the law enables a wide range of financial transactions to occur.

649. Paragraph 2 of Art. 40 of the SPC Interpretation on the Contract Book (2023).
650. Article 41 of the SPC Interpretation on the Contract Book (2023).
651. Article 545 CC.
652. Article 547 CC.

708. The ability to assign claims plays a fundamental role in modern finance, providing flexibility and liquidity to creditors and opening new avenues for asset management. In practice, claim assignment allows creditors to manage their risk by transferring the right to collect debts to a third party, which can be advantageous in circumstances where immediate cash flow is needed or where managing multiple claims directly would be inefficient. For instance, in factoring arrangements, businesses sell their accounts receivable to a factoring company at a discount, allowing them to access funds without waiting for customers to pay.[653]

709. Asset securitisation also relies heavily on claim assignment. In securitisation, a pool of assets, such as loan receivables, is bundled and sold to investors in the form of securities. This transfer of claims facilitates the transformation of relatively illiquid assets into tradable securities, thereby improving market liquidity and enabling banks and financial institutions to redistribute risk and free up capital for further lending. In secured financing, claim assignment allows creditors to use future receivables as collateral to secure loans, providing a mechanism for borrowers to access credit based on their anticipated income.[654] This practice not only supports businesses in securing financing but also offers lenders some protection by giving them a direct right to certain future income streams.

710. When a creditor assigns their rights, they must notify the debtor, and the notification becomes effective upon reaching the debtor.[655] The assignment is not effective against the debtor until such notice has been given.[656] Once the debtor receives this notification, they are obligated to recognise the assignee as the new creditor and may no longer discharge the debt to the original creditor or take any other action that would release their obligation toward the debt.

711. Since the debtor cannot be expected to redirect their performance without notification, the law recognises any payments or actions made in favour of the original creditor (assignor) before receiving notice as valid and final.[657] This protects debtors from unexpected claims by assignees when they were not aware of the transfer.[658] Once the debtor receives the notice of assignment, however, they are legally required to recognise the assignee as the new creditor.[659] In this situation, the assignee's request for performance from the debtor is justified, as the debtor is now aware of the assignee's rights and is responsible for fulfilling obligations accordingly.

---

653. Article 761 CC.
654. Jing Zhang, Recent developments in the law of secured transactions of movables under the new Chinese Civil Code, 26 Uniform Law Review 191 (2021).
655. Paragraph 1 of Art. 546 CC.
656. *Ibid.*
657. Paragraph 1 of Art. 48 of the SPC Interpretation on the Contract Book (2023).
658. *Chongqing Port Logistics Group Industrial Co., Ltd. v. Chongqing Metallurgical Rolling Mill,* Supreme People's Court (2016) SPC Min Shen No.3 020; 重庆港务物流集团实业有限公司诉重庆冶金轧钢厂，最高人民法院（2016）最高法民申3020号.
659. Article 48 of the SPC Interpretation of Contract Book (2023).

712. The party for giving notice of assignment is not restricted to the original creditor alone. If the original creditor authorises the assignee to provide notice of assignment, this notice is deemed valid.[660] Therefore, if a debtor receives a notice of assignment by post and argues that it was posted by the assignee instead of the original creditor, this defence is not valid.[661] The fact that the notice was posted by the assignee does not alter the fact that it was issued by the original creditor.

713. The Civil Code does not specify a particular form for giving notice of assignment, meaning the creditor has the discretion to choose the form of notification. This flexibility allows the creditor to decide whether to notify the debtor by means such as mail, electronic communication, or in-person delivery, depending on what is most appropriate under the circumstances. However, despite this flexibility, the creditor must ensure that the notification is delivered in such a way that the debtor can receive the information in a timely and accurate manner.[662] The goal is to make certain that the debtor is fully aware of the assignment of debt and can properly understand their new obligations under the changed creditor relationship.

714. A notice to assign the creditor's rights shall not be revoked unless such revocation is consented to by the assignee.[663] Any withdrawal of this notification requires the assignee's consent. If the assignee agrees to the withdrawal, it signifies that the assignee, now the new creditor, effectively re-assigns the claim back to the original creditor.

715. Upon receipt of the notice of assignment of rights, the debtor may claim against the assignee any defences it has against the assignor.[664] If, after the assignment of a claim, the debtor raises a defence against the assignee based on a defence they had against the assignor, the assignor would be added by the Chinese courts as a third party to the proceedings. When a party transfers both their contractual rights and obligations, and either the opposing party raises a defence against the assignee or the assignee raises a defence against the opposing party based on the contract, the Chinese courts may add the assignor as a third party to the proceedings.[665]

---

660. *Beijing Zuotengfei Refrigeration Equipment Engineering Co., Ltd. v. Guodian Power Jiuquan Power Generation Co., Ltd.,* Supreme People's Court (2016) SPC Min Shen No. 2296; 北京佐腾飞制冷设备工程有限公司与国电电力酒泉发电有限公司债权转让合同纠纷申诉、申请民事裁定书 最高人民法院（2016）最高法民申2296号.
661. *Qinghai Salt Lake Industrial Co., Ltd. v. Qinghai Haolin Machinery Equipment Leasing Co., Ltd., Qinghai Salt Lake Energy Co., Ltd., and Wan Shiliang*, Supreme People's Court (2016) SPC Min Zhong No. 27; 青海盐湖工业股份有限公司与青海皓林机械设备租赁有限公司与青海盐湖能源有限公司与万世良债权转让合同纠纷二审民事判决书 最高人民法院（2016）最高法民终27号.
662. *Fuxin Shengjin Investment Management Co., Ltd. v. Shenyang Ke Laisite International Real Estate First Co., Ltd. and Shenyang Jiazhou Yangguang Garden Housing Development Co., Ltd*. Supreme People's Court (2016) SPC Zhi Fu No. 48; 阜新盛金投资管理有限公司与沈阳克莱斯特国际置业第一有限公司、沈阳加州阳光花园房屋开发有限公司， 最高人民法院（2016）最高法执复48号.
663. Paragraph 2 of Art. 546 CC.
664. Article 548 CC.
665. Article 47 of the SPC Interpretation on the Contract Book (2023).

716. By allowing the Chinese courts to add the original party (assignor or original debtor) as a third party to the proceedings, the court ensures that any defence based on the pre-existing relationship is fully considered, providing an accurate reflection of the original contractual obligations and rights.[666] The rule thereby respects the initial contractual relationship and its nuances, preventing either party from exploiting the transfer as a way to evade or alter their original commitments.

717. The valid existence of a contract is a fundamental prerequisite for the assignment of rights and obligations under that contract. If the contract was never established, is declared invalid, or has been terminated, any assignment conducted in such circumstances is also invalid. In these cases, the assignor is liable for damages to compensate the bona fide assignee for any losses incurred.

718. If, after receiving notification of the assignment, the assignor requests performance from the debtor on the grounds that the assignment contract was not established, is invalid, has been revoked, or has been determined to be ineffective, the Chinese court will reject the assignor's request for performance from the debtor.[667] This rule serves a crucial function in promoting transactional certainty. Once a notice of assignment is properly served, the debtor should have clear guidance on whom to discharge their obligations to, and they should not be placed in a position of uncertainty due to disputes between the assignor and assignee.

719. However, an exception applies if a notice of assignment itself has been legally revoked.[668] If the notice of assignment notification itself is revoked, the assignor regains the right to request performance from the debtor. For example, if it is proven that the notice was given based on fraudulent activity or an error that renders the assignment invalid, the debtor may have grounds to refuse to perform their obligations to the assignee. This exception acknowledges the possibility of legitimate reasons for assignment retraction, such as a mutual agreement to cancel the assignment or legal grounds that invalidate the initial assignment notification.

720. Certain rights under a contract may not be assigned due to the nature of the contract itself. These are generally contracts based on specific personal relationships, where transferring rights to a third party would alter the contract's substance, undermine its purpose, and compromise the original parties' legitimate interests.[669] Common types of such non-transferable rights include:

1. First, rights based on personal trust must be performed by or received by a specific individual due to a relationship of personal trust. Examples include rights arising from contracts based on agency, training, employment, or gifts. In

666. Wang Liming & Zhu Hu, The Commentary of the SPC Interpretation of the Contract Book 492 (Renmin University Press 2024).
667. Article 49 of the SPC Interpretation on the Contract Book(2023).
668. Paragraph 1 of Art. 49 of the SPC Interpretation on the Contract Book (2023).
669. Item (1) para. 1 of Art. 545 CC.

these cases, the assignor's characteristics or skills are essential, and transferring the rights to a third party would defeat the expectations of the contract.

2. Second, rights are dependent on the identity of a particular creditor. For instance, in a performance contract involving a specific actor, the rights created are based on the unique talent and reputation of that performer. Assigning these rights to another individual would alter the contract's fundamental basis and breach the original parties' expectations.
3. Third, negative obligations include rights where the primary obligation is for one party to refrain from specific actions, such as prohibiting someone from re-assigning a right to another after the initial transfer or restricting a person's use of particular land. These obligations are inherently non-transferable, as they are tied to personal restrictions and cannot reasonably be passed on to a third party without altering the contract's purpose.
4. Fourth, accessory rights are subordinate rights that exist in connection with a primary right and transfer only to the primary right. An accessory right is generally not allowed to be separated from the primary right and assigned independently, as it contravenes the nature of the dependent relationship between primary and accessory rights.

721. A creditor may transfer all or part of the contractual rights to a third party, except where the parties have agreed that such rights may not be transferred.[670] Such agreements prohibiting the transfer of creditor rights are recognised as having definite legal effect.[671] However, even before the introduction of the Civil Code, the SPC relaxed the rule of non-transferability by the parties' agreement in certain types of contracts.[672] The Civil Code now imposes certain limitations on these prohibitions:

> If the parties agree that a non-monetary claim may not be transferred, this restriction cannot be asserted against a bona fide third party. If the parties agree that a monetary claim may not be transferred, this restriction cannot be asserted against any third party.[673]

722. Such a key limitation on non-transferability agreements reflects a balance between contractual autonomy and the protection of third-party interests. Under the Civil Code, agreements prohibiting the transfer of non-monetary claims cannot be

---

670. Item (2) para. 1 of Art. 545 CC.
671. *Lu Yuxiang v. China Power Engineering Co., Ltd.* No. 1 Intermediate People's Court of Beijing, (2015), Yi Zhong Min (Comm) Zhong Zi No. 543; 鲁于翔与中国电力工程有限公司买卖合同纠纷二审民事裁定书，北京市第一中级人民法院（2015）一中民（商）终字第543号.
672. In the SPC Opinions on Several Specific Issues in Current Commercial Trials (2015), the SPC stated that, regarding factoring contracts: 'If the factor knowingly accepts the assignment of receivables despite the underlying contract prohibiting the transfer of such receivables, two key points should be noted: such a prohibition does not automatically affect the validity of the factoring contract. However, when the factor asserts claims against the debtor of the underlying contract based on the factoring agreement, the debtor is not bound by the factoring contract and may invoke the non-assignability clause as a defence.'
673. Paragraph 2 of Art. 545 CC.

enforced against a third party acting in good faith. For monetary claims, the restriction is even broader, as it cannot be enforced against any third party, regardless of their knowledge of the restriction.[674]

723. These limitations serve multiple purposes. First, they protect third parties who acquire claims in good faith or through legitimate transactions, preventing them from being disadvantaged by restrictions they may not have known about. This approach promotes market fluidity and credit circulation by supporting the free transfer of claims, particularly monetary claims, which are often integral to financial transactions. The assignee does not need to review the original agreement between the creditor and the debtor to determine whether any restrictions on assignment exist. This facilitates the free transfer of claims, aligning with current economic trends favouring the securitisation of claims and the use of claims as assets in transactions and financing.[675]

724. Second, the law distinguishes between monetary and non-monetary claims, likely due to the distinct economic roles they play. Monetary claims are often treated as assets with high liquidity, so allowing broad restrictions on their transferability could disrupt the market and reduce access to credit. Conversely, non-monetary claims may involve specific performances or obligations tied closely to the original parties, justifying slightly greater protection for restrictions on transfer, though not against bona fide third parties.

725. In light of this rule, debtors will find it more difficult to protect themselves by including non-assignment clauses in contracts. For greater protection of their interests, debtors may instead rely on the rules of notification in claim assignments, ensuring they receive timely and valid notification to avoid the risk of making double payments. Additionally, debtors might consider imposing higher liquidated damages on the creditor for unauthorised assignments, thus increasing the cost to the creditor of transferring the claim without consent.

726. Any additional performance costs arising from the assignment of a claim are to be borne by the assignor.[676] One of the primary goals of this rule is to protect the debtor from unexpected costs due to a claim assignment.[677] When entering into a contract, the debtor has a reasonable expectation of their performance obligations, including the associated costs. Where the assignment of the claim results in additional expenses for the debtor – such as administrative fees, payment processing charges, or logistical adjustments – these costs are borne by the assignor but not unfairly imposed on the debtor, who did not initiate or control the assignment.

674. Hu Zhu, A Study on the Scope and Effectiveness of Prohibition of Assignment of Claims: Focusing on the Rules of the Civil Code, 5 Science of Law (Journal of Northwest University of Political Science and Law) 121 (2020).
675. Liming Wang, A Study on Major Complex Issues in the General Provisions of the Contract Section of the Civil Code, 1 Social Science in Yunan (Yunnan She Hui Ke Xue) 77 (2020).
676. Article 550 CC.
677. Yu Li, A Legislative Analysis of Factoring Contracts, 12 Law Science 45 (2019).

727. By placing the burden on the assignor, the law respects the debtor's original contractual expectations. If additional costs due to an assignment were imposed on the debtor, it could discourage them from cooperating or complying with assigned claims, potentially complicating the enforceability of assignments in practice.

728. Where there is an assignment of a single debt to multiple assignees, what is the rule to determine the priority of enforcement rights? Simply put, it is based on the timing of notification to the debtor under Chinese law. This rule seeks to address potential conflicts that arise when the same claim is assigned to more than one party.

729. If a debtor has received notifications of assignment from multiple assignees, the debtor may fulfil its obligation to the first notified assignee, and such performance will be valid. If the debtor has fulfilled its obligation to the assignee who first provided notice, the debtor is considered to have discharged its debt.[678] If the debtor knowingly fulfils its obligation to a later assignee rather than the first notified assignee, the first notified assignee retains the right to demand either continued performance from the debtor or breach of contract damages from the assignor.[679]

730. The rule limits the first assignee's ability to claim the return of property from a later assignee who has already received performance unless the later assignee was aware of the prior assignment at the time they accepted performance.[680] This limits the legal exposure of subsequent assignees and preserves the finality of transactions made in good faith.

731. To summarise, the conditions under which the first notified assignee may request the debtor to continue performance are as follows:

The debtor has already performed or partially performed the obligation.
The recipient of the debtor's performance is not the first notified assignee.
The debtor knowingly (not merely should have known) performed to the incorrect assignee.

732. These conditions clarify when a first notified assignee can demand further performance from the debtor if the debtor has mistakenly performed to a subsequent assignee. The 'first notified' standard is based on the timing of the notice's arrival to the debtor.[681] In case of disputes over notification timing, courts will consider factors such as the method of notification, not merely the debtor's acknowledgement or the

678. Paragraph 1 of Art. 50 of the SPC Interpretation on the Contract Book (2023).
679. *Ibid.*
680. *Ibid.*
681. Paragraph 2 of Art. 50 of the SPC Interpretation on the Contract Book (2023)

date indicated on the notice itself.[682] For notices sent via mail or electronic communication, the postmark or electronic timestamp will serve as evidence of the notification's timing.[683]

733. This Chinese rule shares similarities with doctrines in other legal systems but also has unique characteristics. Under English law, the rule 'first in time, first in right' generally applies, meaning that the first assignee has priority if the debtor has notice of their assignment.[684] However, English law places the onus on the first assignee to provide notice to the debtor. If a debtor unknowingly fulfils their obligation to a later assignee without knowledge of a prior assignment, English law may still discharge the debtor's obligation, though the first assignee retains the right to pursue remedies against the assignor.[685]

734. In the United States, particularly under Article 9 of the Uniform Commercial Code (UCC) for secured transactions, priority often depends on factors such as filing and notice.[686] However, for unsecured debt assignments, priority can be affected by the timing of the assignment and notice. If the debtor is informed of multiple assignments, the first to give notice generally has priority, aligning with the Chinese rule in practical effect.[687]

735. In German civil law, similar to Chinese law, performance made to the first notified creditor is valid. Under § 407 BGB, if the debtor is unaware of the assignment and fulfils the debt to the original creditor, they are discharged of their obligation.[688] This approach echoes the Chinese approach by focusing on the debtor's knowledge of the assignment and the sequence of notifications.

736. The Chinese rule allows the debtor to discharge obligations upon performance to the first notified assignee and limits the recourse against the debtor when

---

682. *Ibid.*
683. *Ibid.*
684. For a legal assignment to be valid and enforceable against the debtor, it must comply with Section 136 of the Law of Property Act 1925. If multiple legal assignments exist, the 'first in time, first in right' principle applies, prioritising the earliest assignment that satisfies these requirements. Where the assignments are equitable (i.e., they do not meet the formalities of Section 136), the priority is determined by the rule in *Dearle v. Hall* [1828] 38 ER 475, favouring the first assignment for which notice is given to the debtor.
685. *William Brandt's Sons & Co v. Dunlop Rubber Co Ltd* [1905] AC 454.
686. Section 9-322(a)(1) of UCC establishes the first-to-file-or-perfect rule, which means that the security interest with the earliest filing date or perfection date (if perfection occurs without filing) takes priority, provided it continues to be perfected. Section 9-501(a) specifies where and how financing statements must be filed to perfect a security interest, which is crucial for establishing priority under § 9-322.
687. The priority of unsecured debt assignments is grounded in equitable principles and articulated in Section 336(3) of the Restatement (Second) of Contracts, which prioritise the first assignee to notify the debtor.
688. Article 407 (1) BGB.

subsequent performance has been made in good faith. Additionally, it underscores procedural clarity, providing objective criteria (like postmarks or electronic timestamps) to determine notification timing. This procedural clarity is distinctive and reflects the Chinese legal system's increasing emphasis on formality and reliability in contractual disputes.

737. This rule contained in the judicial interpretation is consistent with broader civil and common law principles regarding assignment priority based on notice timing. However, its nuanced provisions around the debtor's knowledge and return of property reflect a balance between protecting the debtor's reliance on the first notice and safeguarding the first assignee's interests. The detailed procedural guidance for establishing notification timing underlines the importance of procedural fairness and clarity, aligning with international best practices while tailoring to the specific needs of China's legal system.

III. Assignment of Contractual Liabilities

738. The assignment of contractual liabilities requires the consent of the creditor.[689] The debtor and the new debtor must notify the creditor, and the transfer is not effective until the creditor consents.[690] The debtor or the third party (the potential new debtor) may urge the creditor to approve within a reasonable period. The failure of the creditor to express consent shall be deemed disapproval.[691] When a debtor transfers their debt, the new debtor is required to assume any accessory obligations related to the principal debt. However, accessory obligations that are specific to the original debtor are excluded from this transfer.[692]

739. This rule ensures that the transfer of debt includes not only the main obligation but also related accessory obligations, such as interest, penalties, or any guarantees that support the principal debt. This inclusion strengthens the creditor's position as the new debtor steps into the financial role of the original debtor, carrying with it the full scope of the debt obligation. By transferring these accessory obligations, the creditor's rights are preserved, allowing them to enforce the debt with the same protections and benefits as they would have against the original debtor.

740. However, the exception for accessory obligations that are uniquely tied to the original debtor's personal characteristics, abilities, or status safeguards against transferring obligations that depend on specific personal qualities of the original debtor. For instance, if an accessory obligation involves a personal guarantee based

689. Paragraph 1 of Art. 551 CC.
690. *Ibid.*
691. Paragraph 2 of Art. 551 CC.
692. Article 554 CC.

on the original debtor's specific financial profile or a requirement that they fulfil certain obligations due to their qualifications, these would not be transferred to the new debtor. This limitation respects the nature of obligations that another party cannot reasonably fulfil.

741. Chinese law allows a third party to join an existing debt by reaching an agreement with the debtor and notifying the creditor. If the third party expresses a willingness to assume part or all of the debt and the creditor does not explicitly reject this within a reasonable period, the creditor may hold the third party jointly and severally liable with the debtor, to the extent that the third party agreed to assume the debt.[693]

742. When a third party assumes a debt, it will bear joint and several liabilities within the scope of the debt the third party agrees to undertake. Therefore, the third party may clearly define the scope of its assumed liability based on its own intentions. The parties may agree on forms of liability that are different from joint and several liability. For instance, the third party and the original debtor can agree to bear the debt proportionally, with each party responsible for a specific share of the obligation. Alternatively, they may distinguish the third party and the original debtor as primary and secondary debtors.[694] In this arrangement, the third party assumes responsibility to repay the debt within their agreed scope first, while the original debtor is responsible for any remaining amount if the third party's payment is insufficient.

743. This flexibility allows the liability structure to adapt to the needs and agreements of the parties involved. However, where the third party does not explicitly specify the scope of their assumed liability, neither the Civil Code nor the SPC Interpretation on the Contract Book provides guidance, causing the legal position to be contentious.[695]

744. Where the debtor assigns its obligations, the new debtor, the assignee, may exercise any defence that the original debtor had against the creditor; the new debtor may not claim an offset against the creditor if the original debtor enjoys the creditor's rights against the creditor.[696]

745. If a third party joins an existing debt with an agreement granting them the right to seek reimbursement (or recourse) from the original debtor, and the third

693. Article 552 CC.

694. *Shanxi Gonghe Chuangzhan Investment Co., Ltd. & Shanxi Puda Coal Industry Group Co., Ltd. & Zhao Ming v. Shanxi Shuozhou Shanyin Youyi Coal Industry Co., Ltd.* Supreme People's Court (2019) SPC Min Zhong No. 1104; 山西共合创展投资有限公司、山西普大煤业集团有限公司合同纠纷二审民事判决书，最高人民法院（2019）最高法民终1104号.

695. Haohan Xia, The Distinction Between Debt Assumption and Guarantee: Analysis and Development Based on Judicial Divergences, 6 Jurist 102 (2019).

696. Article 553 CC.

party fulfils the debt obligation, the court would allow their claim for reimbursement from the debtor.[697] If there is no explicit agreement granting recourse, the third party may still seek reimbursement from the debtor, following the principles of unjust enrichment under the Civil Code, for the amount they paid to the creditor.[698] However, an exception applies if the third party knew or should have known that joining the debt would harm the debtor's interests.[699] Additionally, if the debtor has defences available against the creditor, they may assert these defences against the third party who joined the debt.[700]

746. This rule reflects a balance between encouraging third-party assistance in debt obligations and protecting the legitimate interests of the debtor.[701] By providing clear rights to reimbursement, recognising unjust enrichment claims, and safeguarding the debtor's defences, it promotes fairness and accountability in debt relationships.[702] By recognising a third party's right to reimbursement if they pay the debt on behalf of the debtor, this rule encourages third-party involvement in debt situations, providing additional flexibility in debt management.[703] When the third party and the debtor agree to a right of recourse, this gives the third party a clear legal path to recover their payment.[704]

747. If there is no explicit recourse agreement, the rule provides an alternative path for reimbursement through unjust enrichment principles, which allows third parties to avoid financial loss due to their assumption of debt on behalf of another. By compensating the third party within the amount they paid to the creditor, this provision ensures that individuals acting in good faith are not unfairly disadvantaged.[705] This rule is based on the idea that the debtor should not benefit from the third party's payment without compensating them, which aligns with fairness principles.[706]

---

697. Paragraph 1 of Art. 51 of the SPC Interpretation on the Contract Book (2023).
698. *Ibid.*
699. *Ibid.*
700. Paragraph 2 of Art. 51 of the SPC Interpretation on the Contract Book (2023).
701. Jun Xiao, Types and Structures of Debt Assumption: Starting from Article 552 of the Civil Code, 6 Oriental Law 125 (2020).
702. Lei Chen, The Security Interests in Chinese Law: Some Nuances, in The Making of the Civil Code: Promises and Persistent Problems (Hao Jiang & Pietro Sirena eds., Cambridge University Press 2023).
703. *Jiangsu Jintao Investment Holding Co., Ltd. v. Jiangxi Kete Investment Co., Ltd.* Supreme People's Court (2020) SPC Min Zhong No. 295; 江苏金涛投资控股有限公司、江西省科特投资有限公司借款合同纠纷二审民事判决书，最高人民法院(2020)最高法民终 295 号民事判决书司.
704. Yu Xian, A Study on Practical Legal Issues of Debt Assumption: Summary of the Supreme People's Court's Adjudication Rules, 18 People's Judicature 44 (2015).
705. Weiping Li, The Reference Application of Debt Assumption to Guarantee Contract Rules, 4 Journal of CUPL 110 (2022).
706. *Heilongjiang Kunfeng Agricultural Development Group Co., Ltd. v. Wengfu Group Agricultural Materials Co., Ltd. & Keshan Xinglong Agriculture Co., Ltd.* Supreme People's Court (2019) SPC Min Zhong No. 1451 黑龙江昆丰农业发展集团有限公司、瓮福集团农资有限责任公司企业借贷纠纷二审民事判决书，最高人民法院(2019)最高法民终1451号民事判决书.

748. Notably, certain relationships, such as partnerships, guarantors (personal or property guarantors), or close family members, may have a legally recognised interest in performing the debt on behalf of the debtor. In these situations, the third party may exercise reimbursement rights after fulfilling the obligation. This recognition of legitimate interest ensures that third parties acting for personal or financial interest are not left at a loss for assuming another's debt.[707]

749. The rule includes a key exception: if the third party knew or should have known that assuming the debt would harm the debtor's interests, they are not entitled to seek reimbursement. This exception respects the debtor's interests, preventing third parties from acting in a way that might create additional financial pressure or obligations detrimental to the debtor. By imposing this requirement, the rule encourages third parties to consider the broader impact on the debtor's financial standing, promoting responsible and considerate debt management practices. It also discourages opportunistic behaviour where a third party might assume debt obligations with the intent to seek excessive reimbursement or create financial leverage over the debtor.

§3. The Special Case of a 'Sub-contract' in Commercial Law

750. Under Chinese law, various commercial statutes, such as those related to agency, insurance, carriage of goods by sea, trust, and construction, have circumvented the privity of contract doctrine in specific situations.[708]

751. In construction contract disputes, the primary parties involved include the employer (the project owner) and the main contractor. Subcontractors and actual builders. In judicial practice concerning construction project disputes, the strict principle of privity of contract may sometimes fail to fully meet the initial intentions of the contracting parties and may even contradict the objectives for which the contract was established.

752. For instance, in a dispute over construction quality, the principle of privity of contract limits the employer to hold only the main contractor accountable for quality obligations under the contract. The main contractor may attempt to avoid liability by referencing any subcontracting arrangements. Although the subcontractors or actual workers are the ones carrying out the work, they cannot be held directly responsible for the project's quality, as they lack a contractual relationship with the employer.

---

707. Liming Wang, On the Right of Recourse of the Debt Assumer: Focusing on Article 51 of the SPC Interpretation of the General Provisions of the Contract Sections of the Civil Code, 41 Studies in Law and Business 3 (2024).

708. Lei Chen, Relaxations of Contractual Privity and the Need for Third Party Rights in Chinese Contract Law, in Formation and Third Party Beneficiaries (Mindy Chen-Wishart, Alexander Loke, and Stefan Vogenauer eds., Oxford University Press 2018).

753. Another example is that after finishing their construction tasks, actual workers often encounter the risk of delayed payments. Lacking a direct contractual relationship with the employer, they cannot claim payment directly from the employer, which raises significant concerns about protecting vulnerable groups, such as migrant workers. These discrepancies have prompted the need to break through the principle of privity of contract in certain cases.

754. Therefore, in the event of a dispute arising from construction project quality, the employer (the project owner) may file a lawsuit against the general contractor, subcontractor, and actual constructor as joint defendants.[709] The actual builder may file a lawsuit against the employer as the defendant, even in the absence of a contract between the two parties.[710] In that case, the court will add the subcontractor as a third party to the case. After determining the amount of construction project payments owed by the employer to the subcontractor, the court may rule that the employer is liable to the actual builder within the scope of the unpaid construction project payments.[711]

755. In agency contracts, the principal grants authority to the agent to act on his behalf.[712] The agent can receive performance from the promisor on behalf of the principal or enter into a contract with the promisor on the principal's behalf. In the latter scenario, the contract binds the principal if the agent acts in the principal's name and the promisor knows or has reason to know that the contract will bind the principal.[713]

756. This means the principal acquires rights and incurs liabilities. Strictly speaking, the principal is not a third party, as the promisor is aware of the principal's existence throughout the process when the agent has actual authority. However, under the principle of apparent authority, where the principal is not explicitly disclosed, but the agent acts within apparent authority, the principal may still have the right to sue and be sued.[714]

757. In insurance contracts, the beneficiary can directly enforce the benefit provided by the insurer.[715] Under trust law, a third party may claim directly based on a property right. The third-party beneficiary has the right to enforce performance against the trustee, relying on his proprietary interest in the subject matter rather than on any contract made by others.[716]

---

709. Articles 7 and 15 of the SPC Interpretation on Issues Concerning the Application of Law in the Trial of Cases Regarding Disputes over Construction Contracts for Construction Projects (I) (2020).
710. Article 43 of the SPC Interpretation on Construction Contracts (I) (2020).
711. *Ibid.*
712. Article 919 CC.
713. Article 925 CC.
714. Article 926 CC.
715. Article 23 of the Insurance Law.
716. Article 4 of the Trust Law.

758. In addition, Article 67 of the Maritime Law allows the consignee to assert rights against the carrier in maritime cargo transport directly, even if the consignee is not a party to the original contract.[717]

759. The above framework highlights various exceptions to the principle of privity under Chinese commercial law, allowing third parties to enforce contractual rights under specific conditions.

§4. Actio Pauliana

760. Article 538 of the Civil Code addresses the right of creditors to request the court to annul transactions that are intended to defraud them.[718] Specifically, If a debtor disposes of their assets or rights without compensation – such as by waiving their own claims,[719] waiving collateral security,[720] or transferring assets gratuitously[721] – or if they maliciously extend the repayment term of their due claims,[722] thereby affecting the creditor's ability to recover their debt, the creditor may request that the court revoke the debtor's actions. This is akin to the *actio pauliana* concept in other legal systems.

761. Actio Pauliana is a legal remedy originating from Roman law, which allows creditors to challenge transactions made by a debtor that are deemed fraudulent or detrimental to the creditor's interests. Specifically, it enables creditors to annul transactions where the debtor has transferred assets to third parties to avoid paying debts, especially when such transfers are done with the intent to defraud creditors. In Chinese law, a similar concept exists under the Civil Code, as shown in Article 538, though it might not be referred to explicitly as *actio Pauliana*.[723]

---

717. Article 67 of the Maritime Law.
718. Article 538 CC.
719. *China Water Resources and Electric Power Foreign Company v. Shanghai Fumin Reclamation and Dredging Co., Ltd., Longwan Port Group Shanghai Industrial Co., Ltd., and Hainan Longwan Port Dredging Group Co., Ltd.* Supreme People's Court (2009) Min Er Ti Zi No. 58; 中国水利电力对外公司诉上海福岷围垦疏浚有限公司、龙湾港集团上海实业有限责任公司、海南龙湾港疏浚集团有限公司，最高人民法院（2009）民二提字第58号民事判决书; Mengyong Dai, 'Debtor's Waiver of Matured Claims' and the Creditor's Right of Revocation, 5 Journal of CUPL 48 (2014).
720. The Supreme People's Court Civil Code Implementation Leadership Group, Understanding and Application of the Contract Section of the Civil Code of the People's Republic of China (Volume I) 527 (People's Court Press 2020).
721. *Huang Ruzhen v. Lin Ping*, Fujian High People's Court (2016) Min Zhong No. 927; 黄如震、林萍债权人撤销权纠纷二审民事判决书，福建省高级人民法院(2016)闽民终972号民事判决书.
722. *Wang Xiaoli v. Dong Xunhu & Dong Xunlong,* Anhui High People's Court (2020) Wan Min Zhong No. 229; 王小丽、董训龙债权人撤销权纠纷二审民事判决书，安徽省高级人民法院(2020)皖民终229号民事判决书.
723. Hongliang Wang, Commentary on Article 538 of the Civil Code (Revocation of Gratuitous Acts by the Debtor), 58 Journal of Nanjing University (Philosophy, Humanities and Social Sciences) 133 (2021).

762. This rule provides creditors with a legal remedy when a debtor's actions significantly hinder the creditor's ability to collect on their claim.[724] By allowing the creditor to request the court's intervention, the rule seeks to prevent a debtor from deliberately or recklessly diminishing the value of assets that could otherwise satisfy the creditor's claim. It affords protection against asset stripping.

763. The rule addresses scenarios where a debtor might strip assets or reduce the collateral securing a debt, potentially leaving little to fulfil the creditor's claim. When a creditor, in a lawsuit exercising the right of revocation, simultaneously requests that the counterparty of the debtor bear legal consequences such as returning property to the debtor, compensating for the price difference, or performing due obligations, the court shall support such requests.[725] This provision gives creditors a safeguard against such manoeuvres.[726]

764. It also prevents fraudulent extensions of terms – debtors may attempt to extend the repayment term of their receivables with third parties in bad faith, deliberately delaying their collection to prevent creditors from accessing these funds.[727] By including these delays within the scope of revocable actions, the rule helps ensure that creditors are not unfairly denied timely access to assets that could satisfy their claims.

765. When a debtor gratuitously disposes of their property interests by means such as waiving their claims, relinquishing security interests, or transferring property without compensation, the creditor's right to revoke does not require a subjective element; it only necessitates the objective element of a fraudulent act to exercise the right of revocation.[728]

---

724. *Ibid.*; *China Water Resources and Electric Power Foreign Company v. Shanghai Fumin Reclamation and Dredging Co., Ltd., Longwan Port Group Shanghai Industrial Co., Ltd., and Hainan Longwan Port Dredging Group Co., Ltd.* Supreme People's Court (2009) Min Er Ti Zi No. 58; 中国水利电力对外公司诉上海福岷围垦疏浚有限公司、龙湾港集团上海实业有限责任公司、海南龙湾港疏浚集团有限公司， 最高人民法院（2009）民二提字第58号民事判决书. The Court held that the so-called harm to the creditor's rights refers to the debtor's actions leading to a reduction in their ability to fulfil obligations, thereby rendering them unable to satisfy the creditor's claims and causing damage to the realisation of the creditor's rights.

725. Article 46 of the SPC Interpretation on the Contract Book (2023).

726. Liming Wangd and Chongyang Pan, On the Triple Protection of the Revocation Right Holder under the Interpretation of the Contract Section: Focusing on Article 46 of the Interpretation of the Contract Section, 1 Journal of Shanghai University of Political Science and Law 1 (2024).

727. *China National Petroleum Corporation North China Sales Branch v. Beijing Tianlong Construction Engineering Co., Ltd.*, No. 2 Intermediate People's Court of Beijing (2014) Er Zhong Zhi Zi No. 542; 中国石油天然气股份有限公司华北销售分公司申请执行北京天龙建筑工程有限公司国内非涉外仲裁裁决纠纷强制执行裁定书， 北京市第二中级人民法院(2014)二中执字第542号执行裁定书.

728. *Zhou Lihui v. Huang Huili*, High People's Court of Henan (2020) Yu Min Zai No. 515; 周利辉诉黄惠丽，河南省高级人民法院（2020）豫民再515号.

766. The reason for not requiring a subjective element is not that the debtor lacks subjective malice but rather that the creditor is not obligated to provide evidence of the debtor's subjective malice.[729] The nature of the debtor's gratuitous disposal inherently harms the realisation of the creditor's rights, and such behaviour is intrinsically malicious, logically presuming the debtor's subjective malice.[730] Of course, the debtor has the right to rebut this legal presumption of subjective malice.

767. It is worth noting that 'malice' in a debtor's 'malicious extension of the performance period of their due claim' refers to knowingly extending the period, aware it harms the creditor's ability to realise their rights, yet proceeding intentionally or recklessly.[731]

768. Specifically, whether an action constitutes 'malice' depends on whether extending the disputed debt is a commercially reasonable act and whether the extension brings direct benefits to the debtor that clearly outweigh the loss of the time value due to the extension. For example, where the debtor extends the performance period of a due claim against a third party only after the creditor has filed a lawsuit against them or has initiated a subrogation lawsuit against the third party, this is generally recognised as 'malice'.

769. Conversely, if the debtor holds multiple claims against the third party and extends the performance period for a claim that the third party is temporarily unable to repay, thereby alleviating the third party's liquidity pressure and preventing their business operations from collapsing – ultimately better ensuring the realisation of subsequent claims – then even if the debtor knows that the extension may jeopardise the creditor's rights, the debtor is not acting with 'malice'. In fact, maliciously extending the performance period of a not-yet-due claim can also affect the realisation of the creditor's rights and should be analogously governed by Article 538 of the Civil Code.

770. When determining the malice of a debtor, the following points should be noted: first, it is sufficient that the debtor is aware that their fraudulent action is harmful to creditors; there is no need for an active intention to cause harm. Second, it is enough for the debtor to recognise that the action is detrimental to creditors in

729. *Li Wenyuan v. Hong Meiliang & Wu Jiafu*, High People's Court of Zhejiang (2013) Zhe Min Zai Zi No. 21;
李文渊诉洪美良、吴加富，浙江省高级人民法（2013）浙民再字第21号.

730. *China International Water & Electric Corp v. Shanghai Fumin Reclamation and Dredging Co., Ltd, Longwan Port Group Shanghai Industrial Co., Ltd & Hainan Longwan Port Dredging Group Co., Ltd,* The Supreme People's Court (2009) Min Er Ti Zi No. 58; 中国水利电力对外公司诉上海福岷围垦疏浚有限公司、龙湾港集团上海实业有限责任公司、海南龙湾港疏浚集团有限公司，最高人民法院（2009）民二提字第58号.

731. Jianyuan Cui, On the Elements of the Creditor's Right of Revocation, 3 Tsinghua University Law Journal 133, 147 (2020).

general without needing to identify harm to a specific creditor. Third, it only requires the debtor's malice and does not extend to requiring such malice from the debtor's counterparty.[732]

771. While debtors generally have the freedom to manage their assets, this rule imposes a limit when such actions clearly harm creditors' interests. This balance ensures that debtors cannot abuse their asset disposal rights to evade liabilities, protecting creditors' ability to recover owed amounts. In practice, this rule empowers creditors to act proactively in preserving their financial interests while reinforcing a system where debtors must consider the rights of their creditors in managing assets that impact their financial obligations.

772. Furthermore, the Civil Code empowers creditors to protect their interests when a debtor engages in transactions that unjustly diminish their assets, making it difficult for creditors to collect what is owed. Article 5 39 of the Civil Code provides:

> If a debtor transfers property at an obviously unreasonable low price, acquires property from others at an obviously unreasonable high price, or provides a guarantee for another person's debt, thereby affecting the realisation of the creditor's claim, and the counterparty of the debtor knew or should have known of this situation, the creditor may request the People's Court to revoke the debtor's action.[733]

773. The key elements of this rule are (1) the debtor's detrimental actions; (2) the debtor's actions must adversely affect the creditor's ability to realise their claim; (3) The debtor's counterparty (the other party in the transaction) knew or should have known about the unreasonableness of the transaction and its potential impact on the creditor. If all these three elements are present, the creditor may exercise its right to seek revocation.

774. A typical example of the debtor's detrimental actions is transferring assets at 'obviously unreasonable low prices' below market value, effectively reducing the pool of assets available to satisfy creditors.[734] It also includes acquiring assets at unreasonably high prices. For example, the debtor purchases assets at inflated prices, which can deplete their resources and hinder the creditor's ability to claim debts. The third example is providing guarantees for others' debts. The debtor uses their assets to secure someone else's debt, potentially jeopardising the creditor's claim on those assets.

---

732. *Ibid.*
733. Article 539 CC.
734. *China Development Bank v. Shenyang High-Voltage Switchgear Co., Ltd., New Northeast Electric (Shenyang) High-Voltage Switchgear Co., Ltd., New Northeast Electric (Shenyang) High-Voltage Disconnecting Switch Co., Ltd., and Shenyang Beifu Machinery Manufacturing Co., Ltd.*, Gazette Case of the SPC, Issue 12, 2008; 国家开发银行与沈阳高压开关有限责任公司、新东北电气(沈阳)高压开关有限公司、新东北电气(沈阳)高压隔离开关有限公司、沈阳北富机械制造有限公司等借款合同、撤销权纠纷案，《最高人民法院公报》2008年第12期.

775. The SPC additionally provides other circumstances where the debtor could conduct detrimental actions. If a debtor, using an obviously unreasonable price, engages in property exchange, debt settlement through assets, property rental (as either landlord or tenant), intellectual property licensing, or similar actions that impact the creditor's ability to collect on their claim, and if the counterparty knew or should have known about this impact, the creditor may request the court to revoke the debtor's actions.[735]

776. The detrimental transaction done by the debtors has materially diminished the debtor's net assets, undermining the creditor's prospects of debt recovery.

777. The debtor's counterparty's knowledge about the unreasonableness of the transaction and its potential impact on the creditor.[736] This element protects innocent third parties who engage in good-faith transactions.

778. Under such circumstances, the creditor has the right to request the court to revoke the debtor's action. This legal remedy aims to restore the debtor's asset pool, enhancing the creditor's chances of recovering the debt. This rule encourages creditors to be vigilant in monitoring debtor transactions and offers them a legal remedy to counteract detrimental actions. It also signals to debtors that asset management decisions must reflect reasonable value and protect creditors' interests, especially when entering into significant or irregular transactions.

779. It is notable that criteria for obviously unreasonable low prices adopt an objective standard. This implies a clear disparity between the transaction price and the fair market value, evident to any reasonable person. Minor deviations are insufficient; the price difference must be substantial and unjustifiable. To be specific, the courts should assess the transaction by considering what a reasonable operator in the local market would determine, using as reference the market price or government guideline price at the time and place of the transaction.[737]

780. When the transfer price is less than 70% of the market or guideline price at the time and location of the transaction, it may generally be regarded as an 'obviously unreasonable low price. Similarly, if the purchase price exceeds the market or guideline price by more than 30%, it may generally be regarded as an 'obviously

735. Articles 42 and 43 of the SPC Interpretation on the Contract Book (2023).
736. *Li Li v. Hunan Caixin Trust Co., Ltd.* (2021) Supreme People's Court (2021) SPC Min Shen No.1754; 李莉、湖南省财信信托有限责任公司债权人撤销权纠纷再审审查与审判监督民事裁定书，最高人民法院（2021）最高法民申1754号案例. In this case, the debtor and the counterparty of the gratuitous transfer of equity were spouses. The Supreme People's Court ultimately determined that the counterparty acted in bad faith, and the creditor's right of revocation was upheld.
737. Paragraph 1 of Art. 42 of the SPC Interpretation on the Contract Book (2023).

unreasonable high price'.[738] However, if there is a familial or affiliated relationship between the debtor and the counterparty, the 70% and 30% thresholds do not apply.[739]

781. The rule relies on objective market standards to define reasonable transaction prices, helping to ensure consistency and fairness. The 70% threshold for low prices and 30% threshold for high prices serve as clear indicators, helping creditors, debtors, and courts easily identify transactions that may be problematic. These thresholds allow creditors to challenge transactions that appear to undervalue or overvalue assets in a way that could impede debt recovery.

782. When a debtor transacts with a family member or affiliate, the rule removes the 70% and 30% thresholds, as such relationships may lead to favourable treatment that does not reflect market value. The removal of these thresholds in related-party transactions recognises that these situations may require additional scrutiny. In these cases, courts can examine the relationship and context more closely to ensure that the transaction was conducted fairly and without intent to defraud creditors.

783. With regards to the counterparty's knowledge, it includes actual knowledge and situations where the counterparty, through due diligence, ought to have been aware of the transaction's unfair nature. The burden of proof is borne by the creditor, who must demonstrate the unreasonableness of the transaction, its impact on their claim, and the counterparty's knowledge. Creditors should act promptly upon discovering such transactions to prevent further dissipation of assets. The right of revocation must be exercised within one year from the date on which the creditor knew or should have known the grounds for revocation. If the right is not exercised within five years from the date of the debtor's action, the right of revocation is extinguished.[740]

784. The primary remedy is to annul the transaction, effectively reversing the asset transfer. Assets may be returned to the debtor's estate, or compensation may be ordered if restitution in kind is impossible.[741] The acts affecting the realisation of the creditor's rights of the obligee that are revoked shall have no legally binding force from the very beginning.[742] By declaring such actions void from the beginning, the rule ensures that any impact on the creditor's rights is effectively erased, restoring the creditor to their original position as if the debtor's action had never occurred.

785. The SPC rule strengthens the creditor's ability to challenge questionable transactions by allowing both the debtor and the counterparty to be brought before

738. Paragraph 2 of Art. 42 of the SPC Interpretation on the Contract Book (2023).
739. Paragraph 3 of Art. 42 of the SPC Interpretation on the Contract Book (2023).
740. Article 541 CC.
741. Article 46 of the SPC Interpretation on the Contract Book (2023).
742. Article 542 CC.

the court as co-defendants.[743] Naming both parties as co-defendants enhances accountability and ensures a comprehensive review of the transaction's validity.

786. The exercise of the right of revocation is limited to the extent of the creditor's claim.[744] When the subject matter of the action being revoked is divisible, the court should entertain the request that the revocation be limited to the extent of the affected debt.[745] Limiting the revocation to the portion that affects the creditor's rights supports proportionality. This approach prevents the court from unnecessarily overturning parts of a transaction that do not impact the creditor's claim.

787. However, if the subject matter is indivisible, such as a single transfer of an asset or a one-time contract with an entire value, the court may support the creditor's request for full revocation.[746] This ensures that the creditor's claim is fully protected, as partial revocation would not sufficiently address the impact on their recovery rights. This approach respects the practical limitations of the transaction and prioritises the creditor's ability to recover fully.

788. Any necessary expenses incurred by the creditor in exercising this right are to be borne by the debtor.[747] The reasonable attorney fees, travel expenses, and other costs incurred by a creditor in exercising the right of revocation may be recognised as 'necessary expenses'.[748] The rule places the financial responsibility for the costs of exercising revocation on the debtor, acknowledging that it was the debtor's actions that prompted the creditor to seek legal recourse.

789. In practice, when a creditor seeks to exercise the right of revocation, the court often first reviews the contract's validity, applying the rule that contracts formed through malicious collusion are void.[749] This suggests that the rule on void contracts due to malicious collusion takes precedence over the creditor's right of revocation. It is proposed that when the rules on contract invalidity from malicious collusion and the creditor's right of revocation intersect, the rule on contract invalidity should not automatically take precedence.[750] Instead, the creditor should have the option to either challenge the contract's validity or exercise their right of revocation.

743. Article 44 of the SPC Interpretation on the Contract Book (2023).
744. Article 540 CC.
745. Paragraph 1 of Art. 45 of the SPC Interpretation on the Contract Book (2023).
746. *Ibid.*
747. Article 540 CC.
748. Paragraph 2 of Art. 45 of the SPC Interpretation on the Contract Book (2023).
749. *Cargill International S.A. v. Fujian Jinshi Oil Manufacturing Co., Ltd.* SPC Guiding Case No. 33; 瑞士嘉吉国际公司诉福建金石制油有限公司等确认合同无效纠纷案，最高人民法院指导案例33号.
750. Hongliang Wang, Commentary on Article 538 of the Civil Code (Revocation of Gratuitous Acts by the Debtor), 58 Journal of Nanjing University (Philosophy, Humanities and Social Sciences) 133 (2021).

790. While the term 'Actio Pauliana' may not be explicitly used in Chinese law, the underlying principle is very much present and is codified in the Civil Code. This provision ensures that creditors have the means to protect their interests against fraudulent transfers by debtors.

Chapter 5. The Termination of the Contract

§1. CONCEPT AND FEATURES

791. Contract termination under Chinese law has several distinctive features that reflect the country's unique legal, economic, and cultural context. A clear understanding of these features is essential when managing contractual relationships with Chinese entities.

792. Before examining the specific characteristics of contract termination under Chinese law, it is helpful to outline the general grounds for termination. Contracts may be terminated by mutual agreement, which requires the consent of all parties involved. The first form of termination, therefore, occurs when all parties mutually agree to end an existing contract through a new agreement (consensual termination by mutual consent).[751] Importantly, without such consensus, no valid termination exists. For instance, if both parties accuse each other of breach, this does not qualify as a mutually agreed termination. Similarly, if one party issues a termination notice and the other acknowledges it but both parties demand that the other be liable for breach, it is not considered an agreed termination, and each party retains the right to claim damages.

793. The second form of termination applies when specific conditions in the contract are met, allowing the non-breaching party to terminate the agreement according to previously stipulated terms (consensual termination based on a prior contractual clause).[752]

794. In addition, contracts can be terminated if their performance becomes impossible due to objective circumstances, such as force majeure.[753] Furthermore, where there has been a sufficiently serious breach of contract by one party, the non-breaching party may choose to terminate the contract, also known as termination by breach.[754] Under Chinese law, the ability of the innocent party to terminate a contract largely hinges on the severity of the breach. If the breach significantly undermines the purpose of the contract, rendering the agreed objectives unattainable, the courts are likely to permit the innocent party to terminate the agreement upon their request.[755]

795. Finally, a contract may be terminated on statutory grounds, such as the doctrine of change of circumstances (DCC).[756] Certain special statutes may provide specific grounds for contract termination relevant to particular types of contracts or

751. Article 562 CC.
752. *Ibid.*
753. Article 563 (1) CC.
754. Article 563 (2) - (4) CC.
755. Article 563 (4) CC.
756. Article 533 CC.

industries.[757] However, the Civil Code has generalised certain rules as a general rule.[758] A party wishing to terminate a contract generally must notify the other party.[759] The law often requires that this notification be given in writing and sometimes within a specific timeframe.[760]

796. Termination due to breach often entails compensation.[761] The non-breaching party may claim damages resulting from the breach. In addition to the liquidated damages or agreed sum, Chinese contracts often include penalty clauses that specify amounts payable in the event of a breach leading to termination. The enforceability of these penalties can be subject to limitations set by Chinese courts.

797. First, a key distinguishing feature of Chinese contract law is its emphasis on judicial oversight in contract termination. Contract disputes, including issues of termination, are commonly resolved in court or through arbitration rather than being left solely to contractual stipulations. For example, even if a contract specifies that the buyer has the right to terminate due to the seller's delayed performance, termination is not automatic. Instead, the court retains discretion to decide whether termination should be permitted based on the buyer's request.[762]

798. The main criterion for this determination is whether the seller's delay constitutes a fundamental breach that undermines the contract's primary purpose.[763] In practice, courts often apply two overarching principles to restrict terminations: the principle of good faith and the prohibition of rights abuse.[764] While many Chinese courts popularly received this view, it was not adopted by the subsequently enacted Civil Code and the SPC Interpretation on the Contract Book (2023). Therefore, it remains persuasive and influential but not legally binding.

757. Special rules on contractual termination can also be found in statutes other than the CC. Arts 50 and 51 of the Trust Law states the scenarios where the beneficiary and the settlor may terminate the trust. Art. 18 of the Enterprise Bankruptcy Law empowers the insolvency office-holder to terminate the insolvent company's executory contracts. Arts 15 and 16 of the Insurance Law contains many provisions involving contractual termination in various contexts. Art. 14 of the Labour Law and Art. 63 of the Tourism Law similarly have such provisions. When land is involved, contractual termination of a contract to grant usufructuary rights is expressly mentioned in Art. 25 of the Rural Land Contract Law and Art. 16 of the Urban Real Estate Administration Law.

758. Paragraph 2 of Art. 563 CC: For indefinite-term contracts that involve ongoing obligations, either party may terminate the contract at any time, but they must notify the other party within a reasonable period before doing so.

759. Article 565 CC.

760. Article 564 CC.

761. Article 566 CC.

762. Article 47 of the SPC Minutes of the National Conference on Civil and Commercial Trial Work of Courts Nationwide (2019).

763. *Ibid.*

764. *Dongyang Shangjiang Ham Factory v. Zhejiang Xuefang Industry and Trade Co., Ltd.*, Supreme People's Court (2014) Min Shen Zi No. 1233; 东阳市上蒋火腿厂诉浙江雪舫工贸有限公司, 最高人民法院（2014）民申字第1233号.

799. Second, in line with broader cultural norms that value harmony and face-saving, there is often a collateral obligation that parties should attempt to negotiate a resolution before moving to terminate a contract formally at the court or the arbitration tribunal.[765]

800. Third, parties can exercise termination rights for contracts that have been formed but are not yet effective. For contracts that have been formed but are not yet effective, the rules regarding contract termination can still apply because the parties have obligations related to facilitating the effectiveness and preparing for the performance of the contract.[766]

801. Fourth, in certain circumstances specified in Article 580 of the Civil Code, a breaching party may request to terminate the contract at the court or arbitration institution.[767] The court or arbitration institution has discretion on whether to terminate the contract, given the individual circumstances of each case. Usually, in cases where the breach of one party triggers the contract termination, only the non-breaching party has the right to terminate the contract; the breaching party does not have the right to terminate. However, the Civil Code shifted a new paradigm in shaping the contract equilibrium.

802. These features illustrate how Chinese contract law blends international legal principles with domestic regulatory and cultural characteristics. Many principles within Chinese law, such as good faith, change of circumstances, and prohibition of abuse of rights, will be recognisable to Western jurists. However, it is essential to explore how these imported doctrines are adapted and applied within the context of Chinese cultural values.

803. One approach is to analyse how Chinese courts resolve conflicts between different legal norms. For instance, examining whether courts choose to uphold a contract's agreed termination clause or restrict parties' autonomy by invoking principles of good faith and fairness can provide insights into this adaptation process. For businesses and individuals engaged in contractual agreements under Chinese jurisdiction, a thorough understanding of these features is essential to manage legal risks and maintain healthy contractual relationships.

---

765. Article 533 CC. The CC formalised the negotiation as a procedural element before a party invokes the doctrine of change of circumstances before the court. It provides that: 'the adversely affected party may renegotiate with the other party. If the negotiation fails within a reasonable period, the parties may request the People's Court or arbitration institution to modify or terminate the contract'.

766. *Hangzhou Yishang Investment Management Partnership (General Partnership) v. Zhongzhu Medical Holdings Co., Ltd.*, the Supreme People's Court, (2020) SPC Min Zhong No. 137; 杭州忆上投资管理合伙企业(普通合伙)诉中珠医疗控股股份有限公司,最高人民法院 (2020) 最高法民终137号.

767. Paragraph 2 of Art. 580 CC.

§2. PERFORMANCE AND BREACH

804. The key provision in the Civil Code governing contract termination against breach is Article 563, which outlines several conditions under which parties to a contract may exercise their statutory right to terminate under Chinese law:

> The parties to a contract may terminate the contract under any of the following circumstances:
>
> (1) where it is rendered impossible to achieve the purpose of the contract due to an event of force majeure;
> (2) where prior to the expiry date of performance, the other party expressly states, or indicates through its conduct, that it will not perform its principal obligation;
> (3) where the other party delays the performance of its principal obligation and fails to perform within a reasonable period after the demand;
> (4) where it is rendered impossible to achieve the purpose of a contract due to the delayed performance of the obligations or other breach of contract by the other party;
> (5) other circumstances as provided by law.
>
> A party may terminate a contract requiring the successive performance of the obligations without a term at any time, provided that the other party is notified within a reasonable period.[768]

805. Items (2), (3) and (4) of Paragraph 1 of Article 562 address anticipatory breach, delayed performance and failure due to delay or other breach.

I. Anticipatory Breach

806. First, an anticipatory breach occurs when a principal obligation is breached either explicitly or implicitly before it is due. If, before the due date of performance, one party clearly states or suggests through their actions that they will not fulfil their main obligation, the contract may be terminated. An explicit anticipatory breach happens when a party clearly states its intention not to fulfil the contract before the duty arises. Implied anticipatory breach involves actions suggesting that a party will not perform its obligations when due. Where one party explicitly expresses or indicates by its conduct that it will not perform its obligations under a contract, the other party may request it to bear the liability for the breach of contract before the due date of the performance.[769]

807. Judges can readily identify explicit anticipatory breach when a party directly expresses its intention not to perform or to stop performing to the other

768. For an English translation of the Chinese Civil Code, *see* The Civil Code of the People's Republic of China: English Translation (Lei Chen and others eds, Brill 2021).

769. Article 578 CC.

party. In cases of explicit anticipatory breach, the aggrieved party has the option to either (1) acknowledge the anticipatory breach or (2) reject the anticipatory breach. In the former, if the aggrieved party believes that the breaching party will not retract their intention to breach, or if waiting for the performance to be due would result in greater losses, they may demand that the breaching party assumes liability for a breach before the performance is due.[770]

808. On the other hand, in the latter, if the aggrieved party believes that the breaching party may retract their intention to breach before the performance is due, or if seeking remedies after the performance is due is more advantageous for protecting their legal rights, they may refuse to accept the breaching party's explicit anticipatory breach. Instead, they can unilaterally insist on the continuation of the contract and, upon the arrival of the performance period, demand that the breaching party fulfil their contractual obligations or assume liability corresponding to an actual breach.

809. However, implied anticipatory breach can be more complex to ascertain. While not all cases of implied anticipatory breach are straightforward, the law outlines specific scenarios that constitute implied breach by law or constructive anticipatory breach. Under the Civil Code, both the right of anticipatory breach and the right of insecurity are stipulated. Articles 527 and 528 of the Civil Code address the right of insecurity, specifically granting this right to the party who has an obligation to perform first in the contract. To be specific, Article 527 of the Civil Code allows a party required to perform first to withhold performance if there is decisive evidence indicating that the other party is in a precarious situation, such as serious business deterioration, asset transfers or fund withdrawals to evade debts, loss of business credibility, or other situations that might impede its performance ability.[771]

810. If a party unjustifiably suspends performance without such conclusive evidence, it will be held liable for breach of contract. Article 528 further explains that if a party rightfully suspends performance under Article 527, it must immediately inform the other party.[772] If the other party provides adequate assurances of its performance, the suspending party must resume its obligations.[773] When the other party cannot restore its capability to perform or provide assurances within a reasonable time, this failure constitutes a non-performance of its principal obligation, allowing the suspending party to terminate the contract and seek damages for breach.[774]

770. *Chongqing Boda Mining Co., Ltd. V. Aluminum Corporation of China Chongqing Branch & Aluminum Corporation of China Limited*, the Supreme People's Court, (2019) SPC Min Zhong No. 511; 重庆博达矿业有限公司诉中国铝业股份有限公司重庆分公司、中国铝业股份有限公司，最高人民法院（2019）最高法民终511号.

771. Article 527 CC.

772. Article 528 CC.

773. *Ibid.*

774. *Baiyin Nonferrous Group Co., Ltd. v. Kaifeng Tokyo Air Separation Group Co., Ltd. & Henan Sijian Co., Ltd*, the Supreme People's Court, (2018) SPC Min Zhong No. 377; 白银有色集团股份有限公司诉开封东京空分集团有限公司、河南四建股份有限公司，最高人民法院（2018）最高法民终377号.

811. The elements constituting an implied anticipatory breach differ from those of an explicit one in that the breaching party does not unequivocally express an intention not to fulfil the contract obligations when performance is due. The criteria for an implied anticipatory breach include:

1. First, the party must display one of the situations specified in Article 527 of the Civil Code, which includes severely deteriorating business conditions, transferring assets or withdrawing funds to evade debts, losing business credibility, or other situations indicating a loss or potential loss of the ability to fulfil obligations. While these situations may not explicitly indicate a breach, based on the party's actions or capacity to perform, it can be determined that they will likely fail to meet their contractual duties, thus making it difficult for the other party to realise their expected rights.
2. Second, the foreseeability of the other party's breach at the time of performance is a subjective judgment. Objective standards must support it to determine whether an implied anticipatory breach exists. Otherwise, subjective assumptions could lead to misuse of legal remedies, harming the legitimate rights and interests of the other party. The foreseeing party must provide evidence proving that the other party will definitely not be able to, or will choose not to, perform the obligations. The adequacy of such evidence should be assessed based on the situations listed in Article 527 of the Civil Code. Regarding the exercise of the right of insecurity, the standard adopted under Chinese law is that of concrete evidence. This approach prevents subjective speculation about the contract performance capabilities of the party due to perform later.[775]

   Consequently, the standard of proof required is stringent. In recent years, judicial decisions have indicated that courts tend to restrict the application of insecurity. A determination must consider the actual circumstances of the debtor. For example, in a claim concerning the criterion of loss of business credibility, the SPC reasoned that:

> However, a party's breach of contract does not equate to 'loss of commercial credibility' or the inability to fulfil contractual obligations. The exercise of the right of insecurity should be based on concrete evidence provided by the party obligated to perform first, demonstrating a significant decline in the performance capability of the party obligated to perform subsequently and a real risk that they will not fulfil their counter-performance. Only under these conditions does the party obligated to perform first have the right to propose a suspension of performance.[776]

775. *Tianjin Metal Tools Company v. Peishi Investment Company*, Gazette Case of the SPC, Issue 4, 2003; 天津市金属工具公司诉沛时投资有限公司，《最高人民法院公报》案例，2003年04期.
776. *Wang Jian v. Manzhouli China International Travel Service Industrial Co., Ltd.*, the Supreme People's Court, (2019) SPC Min Shen No. 568; 王健诉满洲里中国国际旅行社实业有限公司，最高人民法院（2019）最高法民申568号.

3. Third, even if there is concrete evidence indicating that one party will not perform the contract, it cannot immediately be concluded that a breach has occurred. To establish a breach, the non-breaching party must first demand that the other party provide a performance guarantee.[777] A breach can only be confirmed if the other party fails to provide such assurance, and then the non-performing party can be held liable for anticipatory breach.[778]

812. This approach underscores the legal framework's emphasis on ensuring that contractual obligations are taken seriously and providing mechanisms for protection when a party's ability to perform is in doubt. These provisions link the right to withhold performance with the right of termination in cases of anticipatory breach, reflecting a principle that is also upheld in judicial practice. However, it appears to be overlapping to a great extent to have both rules of insecurity and anticipatory breach in the Civil Code. It is possible to consolidate the contents of Articles 527 and 528 into the implied anticipatory breach system and eliminate the provisions regarding the right of insecurity. This is because, although the right of insecurity can function similarly to implied anticipatory breach when there is a time order in performance, the implied anticipatory breach is more effective in protecting the legal rights of the parties to a contract and promoting transactional security in the market.

II. Delayed Performance of the Main Obligation

813. Termination is allowed if one party delays fulfilling their main obligation and still fails to perform after being given a reasonable time to do so following a demand. Under Chinese law, if there is a delay in fulfilling a principal obligation that does not make it impossible to achieve the contract's purpose, the concept of Nachfrist is applied.[779] This mechanism allows the aggrieved party – typically the creditor – to issue a demand to the party at fault. This demand stipulates that if the obligation is not satisfactorily met within a specified timeframe, the contract will be terminated.

814. While the demand can be made in any form, it is commonly issued in writing for clarity and record-keeping. For the demand to initiate Nachfrist, it must be made post-delay. Any pre-emptive demand issued before the obligation's due date does not qualify. The demand should clearly specify the obligation in question, the

777. Article 528 CC.

778. *Shenyang Narnia Biomedical Technology Co., Ltd. V. Shanghai Jingfeng Pharmaceutical Co., Ltd.*, the Supreme People's Court, (2022) SPC Zhi Min Zhong No. 781; 沈阳纳尼亚生物医药科技有限公诉上海景峰制药有限公司，最高人民法院（2022）最高法知民终781号.

779. Nachfrist refers to a grace period or additional deadline given to the debtor to fulfil their obligation after the initial non-performance. Article 281 BGB provides that the creditor may claim damages instead of performance if the debtor fails to perform within a reasonable period (Nachfrist) set by the creditor. Article 323 BGB allows the creditor to withdraw from the contract if the debtor fails to perform within the set Nachfrist. Article 286 BGB explains when the debtor is in default and how a Nachfrist can influence the default status.

additional time allowed for its fulfilment, and the implications of failing to meet the deadline (i.e., termination of the contract). The period extended for completion must be reasonable, a determination often left to the courts.

815. The contract is terminated upon the receipt of the notice by the non-breaching party. Where the notice states that the contract will be terminated by the obligor's failure to perform the obligations within a time limit, and the obligor fails to do so, the contract shall be terminated at the stipulated deadline. If the other party objects to such termination, either party may apply to the court or an arbitration institution to confirm the effectiveness of the termination of the contract promptly.

816. To give a breaching party a right to challenge the termination notice is to prevent the abuse of the termination right exercisable by the non-breaching party. However, a practical issue arises when the recipient of the termination notice remains silent but files litigation when the sending party treats it as terminated. In such cases, the court should not conduct a substantive review to determine whether the termination complies with legal conditions.[780]

817. The SPC further clarifies that if one party unilaterally terminates a contract through notification and asserts that the contract has been terminated due to the other party's failure to raise objections within an agreed-upon or otherwise reasonable timeframe, the court should review whether the party had the legal or contractual right to terminate.[781] Upon review, if the party does indeed hold the right of termination, the contract is considered terminated from the moment the notice reaches the other party. If the party lacks the right of termination, the contract is not considered terminated.[782]

818. In a landmark case published by the SPC, a real estate development company and Mr Sun signed a Cooperation Development Agreement in May 2014.[783] Under the Agreement, Mr Sun was to contribute an initial RMB 500 million deposit, followed by an additional RMB 500 million if the sales proceeds were insufficient to cover construction costs. Failure to contribute was to be treated as a breach.[784] In October 2014, the Real Estate Company issued a coordination letter, raising concerns over the second RMB 500 million contribution.

819. By 20 January 2015, the Real Estate Company formally notified Mr Sun to fulfil his obligations within five days or face termination of the contract. Mr Sun

780. *Chaoyang Qinghua Mining Co., Ltd. v. Chaoyang Jinchang Mining Co., Ltd.* , the Supreme People's Court, (2013) SPC Min Shen No. 2018; 朝阳青花矿业有限公司诉朝阳金昌矿业有限公司，最高人民法院（2013）民申字第2018号.

781. Article 53 of the SPC Interpretation on the Contract Book (2023).

782. *Ibid.*

783. *Sun v. Real Estate Company*, Case No. 7 of The Typical Cases Related to the SPC Interpretation on Several Issues Concerning the Application of the General Provisions of the Contract Book of the Civil Code; 孙某诉某房地产公司， 最高人民法院《关于适用＜中华人民共和国民法典＞合同编通则若干问题的解释》相关典型案例，第7号案例.

784. *Ibid.*

did not contest the payment requirement after receiving the notification but responded on 23 January 2015, requesting the launch of the sales plan for certain buildings with his approval and the establishment of a joint project fund management account. On 13 March 2015, the Real Estate Company issued a contract termination notice. Mr Sun did not raise objections to the notice's form or content.

820. On 17 July 2015, Mr Sun sent a letter requesting strict adherence to the agreement and an update on sales progress. In the first instance court proceeding, Mr Sun demanded a profit-sharing of RMB 30 million from the project. The Real Estate Company's Counterclaim: They sought liquidated damages of RMB 3 million from Mr Sun for breach of contract. Both the first-instance and appellate courts held that Mr Sun did not challenge the termination notice's validity within the legal timeframe. The Cooperation Development Agreement was, therefore, terminated.[785] Mr Sun was dissatisfied with the appellate ruling and applied for a retrial at the SPC.

821. The SPC held that for the termination notice to produce legal effect, the company must have had either a statutory or contractual right to terminate.[786] Under the terms of the Agreement, Mr Sun's obligation to make the second RMB 500 million investment was conditional on the Real Estate Company conducting sales for the project. Only if the sales revenue was insufficient to cover construction costs could the Real Estate Company demand the second instalment from Mr Sun.[787]

822. The SPC pointed out that the first-instance and appellate courts failed to examine whether the Real Estate Company fulfilled its obligations and, therefore, had a valid right to terminate the contract.[788] Instead, they based their judgment solely on the fact that Mr Sun did not request judicial or arbitral confirmation of the termination's validity within the statutory period; whether the Real Estate Company had the right to terminate the contract hinges on whether it fulfilled its obligations under the Cooperation Development Agreement.[789]

823. The rule ensures that the court reviews unilateral terminations based on a party's claim of contract breach or other grounds. This oversight prevents abuse, as parties cannot simply rely on the other's silence as grounds for termination without the proper authority. By requiring a valid right of termination, the rule provides objective criteria, ensuring that termination is only legally recognised when supported by the contract or law. If termination is justified, the rule's recognition that the contract ends upon receipt of notice supports effective communication between parties, emphasising that proper notice is critical in triggering termination rights.

785. *Ibid.*
786. *Ibid.*
787. *Ibid.*
788. *Ibid.*
789. *Ibid.*

III. Unrealisation of Contract's Purpose

824. Unrealisation of the contract's purpose is a catchphrase under Chinese contract law. It plays a significant role in determining the severity of a contract breach. If the breach causes the unrealisation of the contract's purpose, contract termination may be awarded by the court or arbitration institution. Contrarily, a claim of contract termination may most likely not be supported by the courts or arbitration institutions. Article 563 of the Civil Code employs the standard of 'unrealisation of contract purpose' in two situations where a contract can be terminated. Both items 1 and 4 use such a notion.

825. For item 1, the essential component is the unrealisation of the contract's purpose. Although this must result from an event of force majeure, the occurrence of force majeure alone does not automatically justify contract termination. Consequently, if a non-performance caused by force majeure does not prevent the fulfilment of the contract's purpose, parties cannot use this event as a basis to terminate the contract.[790]

826. Item 4 of Article 563 clarifies where the factor making it impossible to realise the purpose of the contract is not a force majeure event but a party's act of breach. The right of immediate termination arises, regardless of the type of term or the nature of duty breached.[791] When the purpose of the contract cannot be achieved due to a breach by one party, termination is justified. This is also known as a fundamental non-performance. This approach allows the aggrieved party to terminate the contract immediately if the breach is considered fundamental.

827. In judicial practice, the standard for determining that 'the purpose of the contract cannot be realised' is commonly equated with the one for determining a fundamental breach. Under such circumstances, since the creditor's interest in performance is frustrated, there is no longer a need to continue performing the contract. Therefore, the Courts need to address how to ascertain the purpose of the contract in each contract termination dispute.

828. The purpose of a contract is typically determined by the main obligation of payment as stipulated in the contract rather than by the subjective motives of the parties at the time of contract formation. For example, in transactions where control over a real estate project or a mining development project company is acquired through equity transfer, although the motive may be to gain control of the real estate business or the mining rights, the transaction between the parties is an equity transfer. The seller's purpose is to receive the transfer payment, and the buyer's purpose is to acquire the target company's shares. Whether there are defects in the right to

790. *Li Guohui v. Zhang Li*, Guangdong Province Shaoguan City Intermediate People's Court, (2022) Yue 02 Min Zhong No. 2240; 李国辉诉张力，广东省韶关市中级人民法院（2022）粤02民终2240号.

791. Wenjie Zhao, A Commentary on Article 94 of Contract Law (Termination), 4 The Jurist 175 (2019).

use the land for construction or mining rights is generally considered a business risk that parties should bear in an equity transfer transaction, not the purpose of the contract. In this case, the contract purpose should be determined by the content of the main obligation of payment stipulated in the contract. Certainly, parties are at liberty to include defects in the right to use construction land or mining rights as conditions for contract termination to control transaction risks.

829. When a deceptive representation is used to conceal a legal act, the apparent conduct, being a result of collusive intent between the parties, is invalid. Therefore, the purpose of the contract should not be determined by the contract provisions that reflect the apparent conduct but by the hidden one. For example, in equity transfer transactions used as collateral, the equity transfer might be a false representation, with the hidden purpose of providing collateral for a loan agreement. The contract's purpose is not to transfer equity but to acquire the loan. In such a situation, the contract purpose should be ascertained based on the nature of the legal relationship.

830. In scenarios involving multiple transactions that form a transaction bundle, the main contractual purpose should be determined based on the nature of the overall legal relationship entailed in the transaction. For example, in real estate development transactions, there may be multiple transaction actions such as equity transfer, debt restructuring, cooperative development, and rights distribution. Here, the main contractual purpose should be determined based on the essence of the transaction, the text of the contract, and the contract performance situation.

831. It is important to note that in ascertaining the main contractual purpose of multiple and linked transactions unless a false intention conceals a civil legal act, the determination should strictly adhere to the literal meaning expressed in the contract text. The contract's provisions should be primarily referred to rather than presuming the motive as the purpose of the contract.

832. In the case of *Beijing Junfield Real Estate Development Ltd v. Cinda Investment Limited and others,*[792] the issue is whether the respondent has the right to terminate the 'Framework Agreement' and the 'Supplementary Agreement III to the Framework Agreement' on the grounds of the unrealisation of the contract's purpose. It is first necessary to clearly identify the main contractual purpose of the series of agreements signed by the parties.

833. The SPC held that the dispute involves a significant and complex commercial transaction concerning project transfer, debt restructuring, and cooperative development. The court reasoned that the main purpose of the agreements at issue was project transfer and debt restructuring, based on four aspects: the specific provisions of the contract, the distribution of contract clauses, the performance of the

792. *Beijing Junfield Real Estate Development Ltd v. Cinda Investment Limited and others*, the Supreme People's Court, (2020) SPC Min Zai No. 15; 北京庄胜房地产开发有限公司诉信达投资有限公司等，最高人民法院（2020）最高法民再15号.

contract, and the performance of the cooperative development project by both parties. The court found that cooperative development was only a small part of the entire framework agreement.

834. It was held that the main clauses of the 'Framework Agreement' and 'Supplementary Agreement (III) to the Framework Agreement' had been fully performed, and the main purpose of the contract had been achieved. Since the main purpose of the contract had been realised and the other objectives could also be achieved, the case did not meet the conditions for statutory termination of a contract under Article 94 of the Contract Law (now Article 563 of the Civil Code). Consequently, the respondent does not have the right to terminate the Agreements.[793]

835. It is worth noting that Article 563 of the Civil Code stipulates two scenarios regarding the termination of a contract due to delayed performance: First, the debtor delays the performance of a principal obligation and fails to fulfil it within a reasonable period after being prompted (item 3). Second, the delay in performance makes it impossible to achieve the contract's purpose (item 4).

836. In the first scenario, three elements must be present: (1) the obligation that the party has delayed is a principal obligation of the contract; (2) the creditor must formally demand performance from the debtor. Without this demand, even if the debtor delays, the contract typically cannot be directly terminated; (3) the debtor still fails to perform within a reasonable period after being prompted.

837. The creditor must demand performance from the debtor after the contract's performance period has expired. When the creditor demands performance or security from the debtor before the expiration of the performance period due to a risk of the debtor losing the performance ability, this falls within the ambit of the anticipatory breach and the rule of insecurity. If a reasonable period is explicitly defined by relevant statutory instruments or an agreement between the parties, it should be followed. For example, Article 11 of the SPC Interpretation on the Sale and Purchase Contract of Commercial Housing specifies a reasonable period of three months.[794]

838. If there is no explicit rule or contractual agreement, the parties may negotiate to determine it. If no agreement is reached, the reasonable period can be determined based on the type of contract, customary practices, and the actual circumstances of the case. In practice, if the creditor has made multiple demands on the debtor, it is typically considered that the reasonable period has been met.

839. In the second scenario, when the performance deadline stipulated in a contract is crucial for achieving the contract's purpose, such as goods customised for a

793. *Ibid.*
794. Article 11 of the SPC Interpretation on Certain Issues Concerning the Application of Law in Trying Cases Involving Disputes over Contracts on Sale of Commercial Real Estate (2003, 2020 revision).

specific marketing event, the significance of fulfilling the contract diminishes once that specific time has passed. Therefore, if a delay in performance results in the inability to achieve the contract's purpose, the creditor has the right to terminate the contract directly, without the need to go through a demand process or provide the debtor with a reasonable grace period.

840. Therefore, when there is no evidence to prove that the delayed performance of a principal obligation has made it impossible to achieve the contract's purpose, and the creditor has not carried out the demand procedure, they do not have the right to statutory termination.[795]

§3. Court-Ordered Termination: Breaching Party's Relief and Doctrine of Change of Circumstances

841. The court has the authority to terminate a contract based on a party's request in two particular scenarios. The first, which was a subject of considerable debate during the codification process, involves the court terminating a contract at the behest of the party responsible for the breach. The second scenario is where the court may terminate a contract due to a change of circumstances at the request of the party seeking relief.

I. Breaching Party's Relief

842. Court-ordered termination at the request of the contract-breaker is a two-step process: the first is the application of a contract-breaker, and the second is the court's exercise of judicial discretion on whether to award an order to terminate the contract. The contract-breaker does not have any right of termination but is only in a position to present a petition to the court; satisfying the constituent requirements to present the petition does not guarantee a result in favour of the contract-breaker.

843. The application step is provided in Article 580 of the Civil Code.[796] To be an eligible applicant, the contract-breaker must have committed a breach of a non-pecuniary obligation,[797] which has caused frustration with the contract's purpose, and the contract-breaker positively applies to the court for an order to terminate the contract.[798]

795. *Ningxia Qianzongbao Diabetes Kidney Disease Institute v. Jiangsu Hongrui Pharmaceutical Co., Ltd.*, the Supreme People's Court, (2019) SPC Min Shen No. 1173; 宁夏千宗宝糖尿病肾病研究所诉江苏红瑞制药有限公司，最高人民法院（2019）最高法民申1173号.

796. Article 580 CC.

797. Article 579 CC holds a legal fiction that a pecuniary obligation is seen as always capable of being performed, which is in stark contrast to the mindset of Art. 2 of the Enterprise Bankruptcy Law, as otherwise a company in financial distress would have never be in a position where it is unable to pay its debts.

798. Commentaries of the Book on Contracts of the Chinese Civil Code 273–274 (Wei Huang ed., Law Press 2020).

844. The second step is the court's decision. Interestingly, six months before the entire mechanism was formally set out in the Civil Code, the SPC had already decided on the factors that judges ought to consider when a contract-breaker applies for termination. Specifically, the SPC Trial Minutes (2019) says:

> A contract-breaker does not have the right to terminate the contract unilaterally. However, when parties come to a deadlock regarding the performance of some types of long-term contracts, it is against both parties' interest for the court to disallow the contract-breaker to terminate the contract by bringing such an action. Based on this prerequisite, where all the following conditions are met, the court shall support the contract breaker's claim:
>
> (1) the contract-breaker was not in bad faith when committing the breach;
> (2) it is obviously unfair to order specific performance against the contract-breaker;
> (3) it is against the principle of good faith for the aggrieved party to insist on the contract-breaker's specific performance.
>
> The order of termination does not diminish or extinguish the contract-breaker's liability for breach of contract.[799]

845. The SPC reaffirmed such a test after the promulgation of the Code,[800] which lower courts have followed.[801]

846. The Civil Code and the SPC Trial Minutes (2019) allow the contract-breaker to request contract termination in order to address contract deadlock.[802] When one party requests to terminate the contractual rights and obligations relationship in accordance with Article 580, Paragraph 2 of the Civil Code, the judicial interpretation designates the time when the copy of the complaint is served as the general termination time for a contract.[803] At the same time, it grants the court a degree of discretion. If, based on the circumstances of the case, designating another time as the contract termination time better aligns with the principles of fairness and good faith, the court must fully explain the reasons in the judgment documents.[804]

---

799. Article 48 of the SPC Trial Minutes (2019).
800. Understanding and Applying the Contract Book of the Chinese Civil Code (II) 741 (Enforcement of Civil Code Group of the Supreme People's Court ed., People's Court Press 2020) .
801. *Cui Chengqi v. Shandong Baoan Real Estate Development Ltd.*, Shandong Province Weihai City Intermediate People's Court, (2023) Lu 10 Min Zhong No. 229; 崔承歧诉山东宝安房地产开发有限公司, 山东省威海市中级人民法院（2023）鲁10民终229号; *Zibo Zichuan Ganglian Material Ltd. v. Building & Installing Engineer Co. Ltd. of China Railway 12th Bureau Group* Shandong Province Zibo City Intermediate People's Court, (2023) Lu 03 Min Zhong No. 1307; 淄博市淄川钢联物资有限公司诉中铁十二局集团建筑安装工程有限公司， 山东省淄博市中级人民法院（2023）鲁03民终1307号.
802. Paragraph 2 of Art. 580 CC.
803. Article 59 of the SPC Interpretation on the Contract Book (2023).
804. *Ibid.*

847. A leading *Xinyu Case*, though published in the Gazette Case of the SPC in 2006,[805] explains what contract deadlock entails. The court ruled in favour of the breaching party's request to terminate the contract. This case was widely believed to set a precedent to allow the breaching party to terminate the contract. Subsequent judicial practice frequently cited the reasoning in the *Xinyu Case*, gradually forming a normative standard for similar cases. This also led to the inclusion of Article 48 in the SPC Trial Minutes (2019).

848. The claimant, Xinyu Company, is a developer and operator of a retail mall. It concluded a sale and purchase agreement with the defendant for a shop unit in the mall. Purchasers of shop units were permitted to enter into possession before the title transfer had been registered. Subsequently, the new management team of Xinyu Company decided to change the type of business operated in the mall.

849. Consequently, Xinyu Company offered to buy back the shop unit from the defendant. However, the defendant asked for a price of around RMB 6.6 million, while she had bought the unit from Xinyu for only RMB 368,184. The market value was appraised at RMB 531,700 by an accredited property valuer. As such, Xinyu Company sued to terminate the purchase agreements on the grounds of the change of circumstances. Xinyu Company averted that Xinyu had bought back all the 150 shop units in the retail mall since the business had been reconceptualised by the new management board, except for two units, including the defendant's unit. The original purpose of operating the boutique shop area in the mall under the new layout plan could no longer be fulfilled.

850. The defendant challenged the termination of the contract and refused to vacate the premises. This situation resulted in a contract deadlock, as the innocent party, the defendant, did not want to take legal action to terminate the contract, whereas the defaulting party, Xinyu Company, wished to terminate.

851. The court of first instance supported the termination request made by the defaulting party, Xinyu Company. The reasoning was that it would be a social waste if such a deadlock continued to exist. The shop unit held by the defendant was just one of 150 units in the mall. Most unit purchasers agreed to return the units to Xinyu Company to reconceptualise the business style. The sooner the defendant vacated the premises, the less waste it would generate. Guided by the principles of good faith and fairness, the court of first instance held that when the cost of performance outweighed the benefits to be obtained for the performance of the contract, specific performance was out of the question.

852. In addition, the court reasoned that shop unit purchasers needed to consider and follow the collective decision of the majority. Therefore, the court ordered the contract to be terminated and the defaulting party to pay compensatory damages. The court of the second instance affirmed the order for termination.

---

805. *Xinyu Company v. Feng Yumei*, Gazette Case of the SPC, Issue 6, 2006; 新宇公司诉冯玉梅，《最高人民法院公报》案例，2006年06期.

853. The *Xinyu Case* is a landmark case in that it challenged the age-old doctrine that only the innocent party can request contract termination before the court. First, the age-old doctrine aligns with the principle of *pacta sunt servanda*, which means contracts must be kept. A valid contract is binding on the parties involved, and neither party may unilaterally alter or terminate the contract without statutory or agreed-upon termination rights or a mutual agreement. In cases of breach, granting the non-breaching party the right to terminate the contract and claim compensation encourages the breaching party to consider the consequences of their actions, thereby promoting strict adherence to the contract. If the law grants the breaching party termination rights, it would encourage breaches, undermining contract termination's role in upholding contract integrity.

854. Second, it helps reduce moral hazard. Once a contractual relationship is established, parties should strictly adhere to the contract terms. In the event of a breach, the non-breaching party has the right to demand continued performance by the breaching party to achieve the contractual purpose. Recognising the statutory termination right exercisable by the breaching party would lead to situations where, in cases of difficult or economically unreasonable performance, the breaching party might choose to breach the contract deliberately. This introduces moral hazards, contradicts the principles of fairness and justice, and violates the principle that no one should profit from their wrongful acts. For instance, in the context of rising housing prices, the breaching party might engage in selling the same property multiple times or maliciously terminating contracts, behaviours that are frequently observed in practice. Recognising such acts would severely jeopardise transaction security and order.

855. Third, it aligns with the nature of contract termination. If, after a breach, the non-breaching party believes that continued performance would cause greater harm and prefers to be released from the original contract to seek new partners, they may choose to terminate the contract. In this sense, contract termination serves as a remedy for breach, a right enjoyed by the non-breaching party, typically corresponding with remedies such as damages or specific performance. Therefore, recognising that the breaching party holds the right to terminate the contract would contradict the nature of contract termination as a remedy available to the non-breaching party.

856. Gleaned from the *Xinyu Case*, a contract deadlock occurs when changes in subjective or objective conditions during the contract's performance make it difficult to continue, thus preventing the contract's objectives from being fulfilled. In such cases, one party seeks to terminate the contract while the other refuses, leading to a standoff. When courts support the breaching party's right to terminate the contract, they typically examine three main criteria: 'the breaching party did not act in bad faith', 'continuing the contract would be extremely unfair to the breaching party' and 'the non-breaching party's refusal to terminate the contract breaches the principle of good faith'.

857. If these conditions are met, the court will rule in favour of terminating the contract. Given the growing number of contract deadlock cases that the Chinese courts faced when the Civil Code was being drafted and prompted by the reasoning of the *Xinyu Case*, the final version of the Civil Code allows the contract-breaker in very exceptional circumstances to request the court to terminate the contract.

858. However controversial it may be, such a rule is driven by the high premium placed on societal interests in China. In the event of a contract deadlock, when the party entitled to terminate the contract refuses to exercise this right, it is often to demand a higher price from the other party, which violates the principles of good faith and fairness. Allowing the non-breaching party to refuse termination could result in a severe imbalance of interests between both parties. In addition, breaking the contract deadlock can reduce transaction costs from a societal interest perspective. It allows parties to promptly exit the deadlock and engage in other transactions, which overall lowers transaction costs and expenses.

859. The disadvantage of this rule is that it may disrupt the balance between the creditor and the debtor in contractual relationships. If invoked too liberally, it could open the way for debtors to exit their contractual obligations prematurely. This raises the question of whether the rule adequately considers the interests of contract creditors. Essentially, the rule prioritises broader societal benefits over the specific interests of creditors. Thus, to prevent potential misuse by contract debtors, cautious application of this rule is necessary.

860. It is often argued that it should be left to the discretion of the courts to decide on contract termination, taking into account the specifics of each case. However, judicial discretion can also introduce uncertainty. Therefore, it is recommended that Chinese courts exercise restraint in using this discretion to avoid overly broad applications.

861. The application ranges of the SPC Trial Minutes (2019) and the Civil Code differ in scope and focus. The former allows a party who has breached a contract to request termination, but this applies only to long-term contracts, which do not necessarily have to involve non-monetary obligations. On the other hand, the latter specifically addresses the non-performance of non-monetary obligations without the requirement that the contracts be long term.

862. Although there is some overlap, the two can also be inconsistent. For instance, during the COVID-19 pandemic, many small business owners faced severe financial difficulties. Consider a scenario where a business leasing commercial property under a 3-year contract becomes insolvent six months into the lease and fails to pay rent. In this case, the lessee might seek to terminate the contract. Here, the non-performance involves a monetary obligation – rent payment – meaning that Article 580 (2) of the Civil Code does not apply. The situation may fall under the scope of the SPC Trial Minutes (2019), though it would also raise questions about whether a three-year term qualifies as a long-term contract. Given these inconsistencies, it is anticipated that the legislature may look to harmonise these rules by integrating the approach of the SPC Trial Minutes (2019) into the Civil Code in the future. This integration would help clarify and unify the legal framework for contract terminations.

II. Change of Circumstances

863. The DCC is recognised under the Civil Code. It allows for the modification or termination of a contract when significant changes occur after the contract has been signed, which are unforeseen, not attributable to any party, and render the performance of contractual obligations unreasonably onerous or cause the purpose of the contract to be defeated.[806] Essentially, the DCC operates as a default rule under Chinese law. In business contracts governed by Chinese law that lack a specific clause addressing changes in circumstances, the statutory DCC may apply and be available to the parties. If the parties attempt to exclude the application of Article 533 by contract pre-emptively, such exclusions are deemed invalid by the courts.[807] This provision emphasises the mandatory nature of the DCC as a safeguard for fairness and public interest, preventing parties from undermining its purpose through private agreements.

864. The key legal elements of this doctrine under Chinese law are: first, the significant change in circumstances must be unforeseeable at the time the contract was formed. If the event could have been anticipated and accounted for in the contract, this doctrine cannot be invoked. This means that neither party could have reasonably predicted the occurrence of the events leading to the change when the contract was signed.

865. Second, the circumstances underlying the contract must have undergone a substantial and fundamental change. The change must affect the basic assumptions or foundation upon which the contract was concluded. Examples include policy adjustments or abnormal changes in market supply and demand.[808] The change must make a continued performance manifestly unfair to one party or otherwise undermine the purpose of the contract.[809] The unfairness must be severe enough to justify judicial intervention.

866. Third, the changes must have occurred after the contract was entered into. Any changes that were already occurring or could be anticipated during the contract negotiations are not covered under this doctrine.

867. Fourth, the change must be external to both parties and not due to either party's action or inaction. It must arise from events beyond the control of both parties involved. The change must not fall within the scope of ordinary commercial

806. Article 533CC.
807. Paragraph 4 of Art. 32 of the SPC Interpretation on the Contract Book (2023).
808. Paragraph 1 of Art. 32 of the SPC Interpretation on the Contract Book (2023).
809. *Ibid.*

risks. This element ensures that normal business risks, such as market fluctuations for typical commodities, are borne by the contracting parties. Contracts involving highly volatile markets, such as commodities, stocks, or futures, inherently involve price fluctuations, and parties are presumed to accept these risks when entering such contracts.

868. Fifth, the change must fundamentally alter the equilibrium of the contract, either by making the performance of the contract unreasonably burdensome or by obliterating the underlying purpose of the contract. This alteration must be so significant that it impacts the very basis on which the contract was agreed.

869. In addition to these five elements, Article 533 of the Civil Code introduces a procedural requirement, namely, that the parties must renegotiate before resorting to the court or arbitration institution. The party seeking relief under this doctrine must have attempted to negotiate in good faith to adjust the contract terms in response to the changed circumstances before seeking legal remedies. The court considers the parties' renegotiation efforts when determining an appropriate remedy.

870. If these criteria are met, the affected party may request the court or an arbitral tribunal to invoke the DCC to modify or terminate the contract. If parties request the modification of the contract only, the court shall not terminate the contract on its own inherent jurisdiction.[810] If one party requests contract modification due to the change, and the other party requests termination (or vice versa), the court must assess the specific circumstances and make a fair judgment to either modify or terminate the contract.[811] In such cases, the court has the discretion to either modify or terminate the contract, guided by the principle of fairness and taking into account the specific circumstances of the situation.[812] This effectively grants the court the discretion to revise certain terms of the parties' contract to mitigate the unfairness arising from the changed circumstances.[813]

871. The relevant factors to consider by the court include the timing of the significant change in circumstances, the parties' renegotiation efforts, and the losses incurred due to the modification or termination of the contract.[814] The court must specify the effective date of modification or termination in its ruling, ensuring clarity and enforceability.[815] Courts are tasked with a case-specific analysis that balances the principle of pacta sunt servanda (contracts must be honoured) with the principle of fairness. This requires a nuanced understanding of market dynamics, contract purpose, and the reasonable expectations of the parties.

---

810. Paragraph 2 of Art. 32 of the SPC Interpretation on the Contract Book (2023).
811. *Ibid.*
812. *Ibid.*
813. Lei Chen & Qiyu Wang, Demystifying the Doctrine of Change of Circumstances under Chinese Law—A Comparative Perspective from Singapore and English Common Law, 6 Journal of Business Law 475-496 (2021).
814. Paragraph 3 of Art. 32 of the SPC Interpretation on the Contract Book (2023).
815. *Ibid.*

872. Chinese courts have applied the DCC in various cases where significant price increases rendered performance excessively burdensome for one of the contracting parties. For instance, in the *Shenyang High-Grade Highway Construction Case*[816] and the *Wuhan Gas Company Case,*[817] the SPC applied the DCC to address the unfairness resulting from a doubling of diesel oil prices and a nearly twofold increase in the production costs of gas meters.

873. The SPC Interpretation on the Contract Book (2023) clearly allows the Chinese court to invoke the DCC to terminate or modify the contract in case of a dramatic change in the contract price.[818] However, it is a misconception to assume that Chinese courts will disregard the parties' intentions by rewriting the contract or compelling them to continue performance against their wishes. A clear example is provided in the *Wuhan Gas Company Case*, where the lower court facilitated mediation efforts, ultimately leading the parties to reach a settlement agreement voluntarily. This outcome highlights the courts' preference for enabling the parties to address unforeseen circumstances collaboratively and in a manner aligned with their mutual interests.

874. Rather than imposing solutions unilaterally, courts prioritise maintaining the integrity of the parties' original agreement while providing a framework for renegotiation when necessary. This approach reflects the principles of autonomy of will and good faith in Chinese law, ensuring that judicial intervention remains minimal and supportive rather than coercive. By fostering amicable settlements, the courts help mitigate the disruption caused by unforeseen circumstances while respecting the foundational intent of the contract. This procedural emphasis also underscores the importance of mediation in Chinese dispute resolution, aiming to preserve business relationships and reduce the adversarial nature of litigation.

875. It is important to note that while a court order can terminate a contract if a DCC was pleaded successfully, modification is a practical remedy, providing parties with a commercially reasonable solution in exceptional circumstances. When courts decide to exercise their discretion to modify a contract, the adjustments are still guided by the parties' intentions and the original terms of the agreement. In the

---

816. *Sun Jianfa v. Shenyang High-grade Highway Construction Corporation & Shenyang High-grade Highway Construction Corporation Materials and Equipment Company*, the Supreme People's Court, (2017) SPC Min Shen No. 3108; 孙建发诉沈阳高等级公路建设总公司、沈阳高等级公路建设总公司材料设备公司, 最高人民法院（2017）最高法民申3108号.

817. *Wuhan Gas Company v. Chongqing Detection Instrument Factory*, Gazette Case of the SPC, Issue 2, 1996; 武汉市煤气公司诉重庆检测仪表厂,《最高人民法院公报》案例，1996年02期.

818. Article 32 of the SPC Interpretation on the Contract Book (2023) provides that after a contract is established, if, due to policy adjustments or abnormal changes in market supply and demand relationships, there occurs a rise or fall in prices that was unforeseeable at the time of contract formation and is not considered a business risk, and if continuing to perform the contract is clearly unfair to one party, the People's Court should recognise that a 'major change' has occurred in the foundational conditions of the contract as stipulated in para. 1 of Art. 533 CC. However, this does not apply to contracts involving commodities with active market characteristics, which have long experienced significant price fluctuations, or to risk investment financial products such as stocks and futures.

Chengdu Pengwei Case,[819] the court took into account the parties' shared intention for the plaintiff to mine for 150-160 days before adjusting the contract to establish a fairer price. Thus, it would be incorrect to assume that modification necessarily involves a total disregard for the parties' original contractual intentions.

876. The SPC has directed lower courts to exercise caution in applying the doctrine, requiring them to seek prior review and approval from higher courts and, when necessary, from the SPC itself.[820] The added procedural safeguards ensure that the Chinese doctrine remains appropriately constrained and is applied solely in exceptional circumstances.

877. From a comparative law perspective, this rule shares similarities with the English doctrine of frustration, though it differs in its outcomes. Under English law, frustration typically leads to the termination of the contract rather than modification. In contrast, Chinese law allows courts to modify contracts, reflecting a more interventionist approach aimed at preserving contractual relationships where possible.[821] The rule also resonates with hardship provisions in international frameworks like the UNIDROIT Principles of International Commercial Contracts, which provide for renegotiation or adaptation of contracts in light of significant changes in circumstances.[822]

878. It enhances judicial flexibility while safeguarding fairness, making it a critical tool for contract governance in complex and volatile economic environments. By promoting judicial oversight and equitable resolutions, this rule ensures that contracts remain instruments of cooperation and fairness, even amid unforeseen disruptions.

§4. Discharge by Agreement

879. The parties may terminate a contract if they reach a consensus through consultation.[823] A contract may be deemed terminated by the court even if the strict legal conditions for termination are not fully satisfied. For example, one party asserts the exercise of the statutory or contractually agreed right of termination, but

819. *Chengdu Pengwei Industrial Co., Ltd. v. Jiangsu Province Yongxiu County Government & the Office of the Leading Group for Sand Mining Management of Poyang Lake in Yongxiu County*, Gazette Case of the SPC, Issue 4, 2010; 成都鹏伟实业有限公司诉江西省永修县人民政府、永修县鄱阳湖采砂管理工作领导小组办公室,《最高人民法院公报》案例, 2010年04期.
820. Article 2 of the SPC Interpretation on Issues Concerning the Application of the Contract Law (II) (2009).
821. Lei Chen & Qiyu Wang, Demystifying the Doctrine of Change of Circumstances under Chinese Law—A Comparative Perspective from Singapore and English Common Law, 6 Journal of Business Law 475-496 (2021).
822. André Janssen & Christian Johannes Wahnschaffe, COVID-19 and international sale contracts: unprecedented grounds for exemption or business as usual?, 25 (4) Uniform Law Review 466–495 (2020).
823. Paragraph 1 of Art. 562 CC.

upon examination, it is found that the conditions for exercising the termination right are not met; however, the other party agrees to terminate. In this situation, the court may terminate the contract.[824] Another scenario where the court terminates the contract is where neither party meets the conditions for exercising the termination right, but both parties claim to terminate the contract.[825] This provision reinforces the significance of mutual consent and party autonomy in contractual relationships.

880. Termination by agreement does not necessarily eliminate any liability for breach of contract. This is to say, where parties have reached a consensus to end the contract but do not make clear their intentions about whether any pre-existing breach of contract would be waived, the default position taken by the SPC is that the contract-breaker cannot raise the counterparty's agreement to terminate the contract as a defence in an action of breach of contract.[826]

881. If a contract is terminated for breach, the party with the right of termination may request the party in breach to bear liability for breach of contract unless otherwise agreed upon by the parties.[827] Furthermore, the termination of rights and obligations under a contract does not impact the validity of clauses pertaining to the final settlement of accounts and liquidation.[828]

882. If the parties mutually agree to terminate a contract but leave unresolved issues like liability for breach, settlement, and post-termination clearance, and one party asserts that the contract has indeed been terminated, the People's Court should uphold this claim unless the parties have specifically agreed otherwise.[829]

883. The Chinese courts may also deem a contract terminated in the following situations unless one party indicates otherwise:

1) One party claims the right to terminate the contract based on legal or contractual grounds, and while the conditions for termination are not met, the other party agrees to the termination.
2) Neither party fulfils the conditions required to exercise the right of termination, but both parties nonetheless seek to terminate the contract.[830]

884. The rule reinforces that a contract may be considered terminated if both parties express an intent to end the contractual relationship, even if the formalities for post-termination obligations are not addressed. This approach supports practical business needs, recognising the parties' mutual consent to end the contract rather

824. Article 52 of the SPC Interpretation on the Contract Book (2023).
825. *Ibid.*
826. Understanding and Applying the Contract Book of the Chinese Civil Code (I) 633 (Enforcement of Civil Code Group of the Supreme People's Court ed., People's Court Press 2020)
827. Paragraph 2 of Art. 566 CC.
828. Article 567 CC.
829. Paragraph 1 of Art. 52 of the SPC Interpretation on the Contract Book (2023).
830. Paragraph 2 of Art. 52 of the SPC Interpretation on the Contract Book (2023).

than leaving it unresolved. The provision also respects contractual autonomy, allowing parties to set their own post-termination agreements.

885. However, if no alternative arrangement is made, the rule provides a default solution for judicial recognition, ensuring that the contract's termination is acknowledged and not left in a state of ambiguity. The rule strikes a balance between formal termination conditions and the parties' practical agreement to end the contract. It allows parties the flexibility to mutually terminate contracts without strictly fulfilling every formal condition, provided there is no disagreement.

886. Parties have the option to include clauses in their contracts that define specific grounds for termination.[831] These grounds can range from breaches committed by a party to objective events that are beyond the control of any party. The effect of the occurrence of the stipulated event is to terminate the contract without either party being in breach of contract. The key issue here is how courts view the enforceability of such termination clauses. According to a straightforward reading of the statutory provision, courts should uphold an aggrieved party's right to terminate the contract if the conditions outlined in the termination clause are met. However, the SPC Trial Minute (2019) adopted a different stance.

887. The SPC Trial Minutes (2019) state that courts should not automatically validate a termination claim based on contract-stipulated grounds. Instead, courts are expected to apply the principle of good faith, assessing the gravity of the breach and its impact on the aggrieved party's objectives in entering the contract. Suppose the breach is deemed minor and does not substantially frustrate the contract's purpose. In that case, the court may decide not to support the termination claim, even if the contract specifies that such an event would justify termination.[832]

888. These principles ensure that terminations are reasonable and prevent parties from ending contracts for minor reasons or in bad faith. However, this view is not universally shared by all the Chinese courts[833] as it risks undermining the certainty of the contractual terms designed and agreed upon by the parties, granting the court almost unfettered discretion.[834] It is for this reason that such a view-- a minor breach of stipulated contractual cause cannot invoke contract termination, was not adopted in the Civil Code and the SPC Interpretation on the Contract Book (2023).

889. Another example to illustrate the heavy-handed judicial oversight on contract termination is that if the non-breaching party intends to terminate the contract

---

831. Paragraph 2 of Art. 562 CC .
832. Article 47 of the SPC Trial Minutes (2019) .
833. *Foshan Sanshui Huatongsheng Textile Printing and Dyeing Co., Ltd. v. Wu Shuxin*, Foshan Intermediate People's Court of Guangdong Province, (2018) Yue 06 Min Chu No. 141; 佛山市三水华通盛纺织印染有限公司诉吴树新，广东省佛山市中级人民法院（2018）粤06民初141号.
834. Ning Liu, Challenge to the right to terminate the agreement under the limitation of minor breaches, 4 Law Science 74-89 (2023).

when the breaching party meets the conditions stipulated in the contract, the non-breaching party must notify the breaching party of their intent to terminate the contract.[835] Only through such notification can the legal effect of exercising the agreed termination right be achieved. If the non-breaching party fails to provide the required notice, the termination will not take legal effect, potentially exposing them to claims of continued performance.[836]

890. The notice cannot merely demand the return of payments and the assumption of liability for breach of contract; it must explicitly state the intent to terminate the contract.[837] Otherwise, the notice will not produce the legal effect of terminating the contract. Requiring notification as an essential condition for exercising agreed termination rights reflects the procedural rigour and fairness principles embedded in Chinese contract law. However, disputes may arise regarding the adequacy of the notice.

§5. Waiver of Termination Rights

891. The time limits for exercising termination rights under the Civil Code reflect the principles of legal certainty and diligence. Parties must carefully monitor the timing of termination events and act promptly to avoid losing their rights. If the law or the parties stipulate a period for exercising the right of termination, and the party entitled to terminate does not exercise it within the period, the right is extinguished.[838] Where the law does not stipulate, or the parties do not agree on a period for exercising the right of termination, the right is extinguished if it is not exercised within one year from the date the terminating party knew or should have known the cause for termination, or if it is not exercised within a reasonable period after being urged by the other party.[839]

892. Contracting parties, considering factors such as commercial interests and cooperative relationships, often choose not to immediately exercise their termination rights when the conditions for termination are met. Instead, they may continue to perform contractual obligations, demanding or accepting the other party's performance, and later assert the termination of the contract within the period allowed for exercising the termination right. The Civil Code does not provide any guidance on

835. Article 565 CC.
836. *Xi'an Qinghe Real Estate Co., Ltd. v. Electronic Comprehensive Survey and Research Institute of the Ministry of Information Industry*, the Supreme People's Court, (2022) SPC Min Shen No. 725; 西安清河置业有限公司诉信息产业部电子综合勘察研究，最高人民法院（2022）最高法民申725号.
837. *Beijing Shangshi Culture Communication Co., Ltd. v. Mokexing Pictures (Beijing) Co., Ltd.*, Beijing Chaoyang District People's Court, (2021) Jing 0105 Min Chu No. 85353; 北京上狮文化传播有限公司诉墨客行影业（北京）有限公司，北京市朝阳区人民法院（2021）京0105民初85353号.
838. Paragraph 1 of Art. 564 CC.
839. Paragraph 2 of Art. 564 CC.

whether the non-breaching party waived or lost its termination right. Therefore, the courts are granted wide discretion by attending to the individual circumstances of each case.

893. One view holds that by continuing to perform the contract or accepting the other party's performance, a party may be deemed to have waived their right to terminate,[840] especially if their actions indicate an intention to affirm the contract or, at least, weaken a later claim for termination.[841] Where the non-breaching party's actions lead the breaching party to believe that termination will not be pursued reasonably, the non-breaching party may be estopped from later asserting the termination right. If the breaching party can prove reliance on the continued performance, they may counterclaim for damages or seek to limit the non-breaching party's remedies.[842]

894. On the other hand, it can be argued that parties may delay termination to preserve a valuable business relationship or complete pending transactions, even if the termination conditions are met. Continuing performance may be a strategy to minimise losses or fulfil obligations under other related agreements.

895. The rationale is that the waiver of rights must be explicitly expressed to be effective because the waiver of such civil rights pertains to the vital interests of the parties involved.[843] The non-breaching party may, within the limitation period, weigh the advantages and disadvantages and autonomously choose to exercise the termination right at any time. More to the point, although the reasonable reliance of the breaching party deserves protection, the fact remains that the breaching party was at fault first. The breaching party's initial fault makes their position less favourable. Therefore, the interests of the good-faith non-breaching party are generally more deserving of legal protection. As such, the non-breaching party's right of termination under the law should not be easily denied.

896. Hence, whether the non-breaching party waives the termination right requires a nuanced approach to balance the interests of both parties while preserving contractual fairness. First, a party-oriented approach allows the non-breaching party to reserve their termination rights even while accepting performance explicitly. This way helps preserve the non-breaching party's right to terminate without the risk of implied waiver, thus reducing ambiguity and potential disputes.

---

840. Article 9 of the Answers of the Jilin High People's Court to Several Questions on the Application of the Contract Termination System in Commercial Cases (2014).

841. Article 1 (11) of the Opinions of the Civil Division II of the Guangdong High People's Court on Resolving Difficult Legal Issues in Civil and Commercial Trial Practice (2012).

842. *Hunan Hongji Industrial Development Co., Ltd. v. Hengyang Mulin Real Estate Development Co., Ltd.*, the Supreme People's Court, (2019) SPC Min Zhong No. 1464; 湖南宏基实业开发有限公司诉衡阳市沐林房地产开发有限公司，最高人民法院（2019）最高法民终1464号.

843. *Gu Ming & Wang Youheng & Jiangsu Ruihao Real Estate Co., Ltd. v. Yancheng Dafeng District People's Government & Yancheng Dafeng District Land and Resources Bureau*, the Supreme People's Court, (2016) SPC Min Zhong No. 822; 顾明、汪有恒、江苏瑞豪置业有限公司诉盐城市大丰区人民政府、盐城市大丰区国土资源局，最高人民法院（2016）最高法民终822号.

897. Second, courts should distinguish between mere acceptance of performance and conduct that amounts to affirming the contract. The court acknowledges that accepting partial or delayed performance may be practical rather than an intent to continue the contract. This prevents the breaching party from unfairly benefiting from the non-breaching party's efforts to mitigate losses. Courts should evaluate the context of the acceptance, focusing on whether it reasonably implies a decision to affirm the contract.

898. A combination of explicit reservation of rights, contextual evaluation of conduct, and clear contractual terms can provide the flexibility and fairness needed to resolve disputes.

§6. Legal Consequences of Termination

899. The first consequence of contractual termination is that rights and duties stipulated in the contract no longer bind the parties. Notably, there have been debates about whether contractual termination is retroactive. Recent judgments show that the practical value of such a debate is undermined by the courts' flexible position when dealing with different types of contracts. Where the contract in question is a one-off contract, the courts have said that termination is retroactive and use this to justify why restitution should be a legal response to termination.[844] Where the terminated contract is a long-term, executory or partly executory one, the courts have said that termination is not retroactive. Hence, past performance and future performance should be treated differently because the former, in principle, does not trigger restitution.[845]

I. Restitution

900. Article 566, paragraph 1 states: 'After the termination of a contract … if the contract has been performed, a party may, in accordance with the circumstances of performance or the nature of the contract, request the other party to restore such party to its original state or adopt other remedial measures, and such party shall have the right to demand compensation for losses.'[846]

901. This provision highlights a significant aspect of post-termination remedies in contractual relationships. Specifically, it provides for the restoration of the parties to their original state and other remedial measures following the termination of

844. *Xu Tingde v. Linyi Yishui Hongxin Mall Ltd*, Shandong Province Linyi City Intermediate People's Court, (2021) Lu 13 Min Zhong No. 3740; 徐廷德诉临沂市沂水虹鑫商城有限公司, 山东省临沂市中级人民法院（2021）鲁13民终3740号.

845. *Suiyang Anjie Motor Carriage of Goods Ltd. v. Tu Zhengui*, Guizhou Province Zunyi City Intermediate People's Court, (2021) Qian 03 Min Zhong No. 10651;.绥阳县安捷汽车货运有限责任公司诉涂珍贵, 贵州省遵义市中级人民法院（2021）黔03民终10651号.

846. Paragraph 1 of Art. 566 CC.

a contract while also allowing claims for compensation for losses. This provision reflects principles of restitution and unjust enrichment in Chinese law.

902. When a contract is terminated, the parties may need to return benefits received under the contract, such as payments, goods, or services. If a party has received tangible goods or property, they must return it in its original form where possible. For benefits that cannot be returned (e.g., services rendered), monetary compensation may be required to reflect the value of the benefit received. Courts examine how much of the contract has been performed before termination. For instance, if one party delivered goods but received only partial payment, they may seek restitution for the unpaid portion and the return of the goods.

903. Neither party unjustly benefits at the expense of the other after contract termination. Defences to unjustified enrichment (e.g., change of position,[847] bona fide purchase,[848] and illegality[849]) will apply in the restitution in response to the contract termination.[850]

II. Damages

904. Article 566, paragraph 2 of the Civil Code provides that 'if a contract is terminated due to a breach, the party with the termination right may require the breaching party to assume liability for the breach unless otherwise stipulated by the parties'. The term 'liability for breach of contract' in this context should be understood as referring to damages or monetary compensation. Furthermore, Article 584 implies that the expectation interest, within the bounds of foreseeability, is recoverable.[851]

905. In the case of contract termination, however, compensation should cover only actual losses incurred and should not include anticipated profits, even if they were foreseeable. This approach reflects a conservative stance in post-termination compensation under Chinese contract law, focusing on compensating tangible losses rather than hypothetical gains.

847. Article 986 CC.
848. Articles 987 and 988 CC.
849. Article 157 CC; Arts 32–34 of the SPC Trial Minutes (2019).
850. Zhicheng Wu & William Swadling, Unjustified Enrichment in the Chinese Civil Code: Questions from the Common Law, 29 (2) Asia Pacific Law Review 402, 413–415 (2021).
851. Article 584 CC provides: Where a party fails to perform its obligations under the contract or its performance fails to satisfy the contract, thereby causing losses to the other party, the amount of compensation for losses shall be equal to the losses caused by the breach of contract, including the benefits receivable after the performance of the contract, provided that it does not exceed the probable losses caused by the breach that has been foreseen or ought to be foreseen when the party in breach concludes the contract.

906. This interpretation limits post-termination damages to real, quantifiable losses, effectively narrowing the compensation scope by excluding anticipated profits. By doing so, the law reduces the financial risk and potential burden on the breaching party, aligning with the principle of mitigating excessive liabilities and preserving fairness in contractual relationships. The distinction drawn here between actual losses and anticipated profits underscores the importance of foreseeability as a limiting factor in awarding damages. While expectation damages are generally recoverable, Chinese contract law appears to restrict this principle in termination cases, emphasising that only losses directly tied to the breach should be compensated. This approach to post-termination liability highlights a cautious view in Chinese contract law, reinforcing contract stability and providing certainty by prioritising tangible losses over speculative gains.

907. The termination of a contract's rights and obligations does not affect the validity of settlement and clearance provisions within the contract.[852] This rule clarifies that contract termination is not a blanket release from all obligations. By preserving the enforceability of settlement and clearance terms, Chinese law ensures that both parties address outstanding financial and procedural matters, fostering a fair and complete conclusion to contractual relationships.

III. Set-Off

908. When parties owe each other debts involving obligations of the same type and quality, either party may offset their debt against the other's due debt. However, offset is not permitted if prohibited by the nature of the debt, by agreement between the parties, or by legal provisions.[853]

909. If a party wishes to claim offset, they must notify the other party, and the offset takes effect upon the notification's arrival. Offset cannot be conditional or time-bound.[854] When the court determines that the right to offset is valid, the court should recognise that, upon receipt of the offset notice, mutual debts – including principal obligations, interest, liquidated damages, or compensation – are extinguished to the extent of the equal amounts owed.[855] If the obligations between the parties involve different types or qualities, an offset may still be allowed if both parties reach an agreement.[856]

910. This rule supports efficient debt management, allowing mutual obligations to be resolved through offset when appropriate. It promotes transparency through the notification requirement and respects contractual autonomy by allowing parties to restrict offset through agreement.

852. Article 567 CC.
853. Paragraph 1 of Art. 568 CC.
854. Paragraph 2 of Art. 568 CC.
855. Article 55 of the SPC Interpretation on the Contract Book (2023).
856. Article 569 CC.

911. When parties owe mutual debts, if one party notifies the other of their intention to offset using a claim for which the statute of limitations has already expired, and the other party raises a defence based on the expired statute of limitations, the Chinese courts should uphold this defence.[857] However, if one party's claim has expired due to the statute of limitations and the other party seeks to offset it, the courts would allow the offset.[858] The rule allows a party to use an offset against a claim that has expired. This provides the party with a means to balance their obligations, even if the debt is no longer enforceable through direct action. It recognises that offset, unlike direct claims, functions as a defensive measure rather than an active demand, making it fair to permit its use for expired claims. This rule clarifies that expired claims can still play a role in offset under certain conditions, encouraging efficient resolution of debts.

IV. Ancillary Responsibilities

912. After the termination of rights and obligations, parties should adhere to principles such as good faith and, in line with trade customs, fulfil duties, including providing notice, offering assistance, maintaining confidentiality, and, where applicable, retrieving used materials.[859] This rule emphasises that even after the formal conclusion of a contract, parties are expected to act responsibly and uphold certain obligations that ensure an orderly conclusion of their relationship. The obligation to act in good faith persists beyond the termination of the contract, aiming to prevent harm or inconvenience after the contractual relationship ends.

913. Specified duties like providing notification, cooperating, maintaining confidentiality, and retrieving used items are common in various industries and help ensure a smooth transition post-termination. For example, notifying the other party of termination or cooperating in finalising outstanding matters prevents misunderstandings and supports both parties in completing residual tasks. The inclusion of confidentiality as a post-termination duty protects sensitive information obtained during the contract's duration. This expectation is particularly important in fields where proprietary information, trade secrets, or personal data are shared and should remain protected even after the contract ends. The duty to retrieve used items, where applicable, reflects an environmentally conscious approach by promoting the proper disposal or recycling of materials. In practice, this duty helps avoid unnecessary waste and ensures that neither party bears an undue burden due to leftover materials.

914. This rule supports the orderly dissolution of contractual relationships and ensures that parties continue to cooperate in ways that uphold mutual respect, environmental responsibility, and the ethical management of sensitive information.

857. Article 58 of the SPC Interpretation on the Contract Book (2023).
858. *Ibid.*
859. Article 558 CC.

V. Summary

915. Chinese law tends to favour a remedial approach that encourages parties to preserve their contractual relationship rather than abandoning it when complications arise. This is evidenced by (1) prioritising remedies such as the cure of performance issues and price adjustments that facilitate ongoing relationships and (2) granting courts considerable leeway to determine whether a breach warrants termination. While this approach may lead to uncertainty and lack of predictability, a strictly defined rule could lack the flexibility needed to ensure fair outcomes tailored to the specifics of each case.

916. This flexibility is especially crucial in the context of Chinese law, which emphasises societal collective interests and the principle of good faith, as demonstrated in cases like the *Xinyu Case*. These values are strongly upheld by Chinese courts, reflecting a preference for solutions that maintain business relations and contractual integrity.

Chapter 6. Remedies

§1. General Provisions

917. Contracting parties primarily focus on ensuring the fulfilment of contractual terms, with the expectation of receiving the benefits of proper performance by the other party. Lawyers, however, often deal with challenges arising from breaches of contract and the corresponding remedies. Contractual remedies serve a critical purpose: they aim to place the non-breaching party in the position they would have occupied had the contract been performed as promised. Without effective remedies, a contract would lack its value as a reliable and enforceable agreement between parties. This focus on protecting the performance interest is fundamental to the nature of a contractual relationship.

918. The essence of ensuring performance lies in the enforceability of remedies. Two principal categories of remedies are available to uphold this principle. The first involves the defaulting party providing monetary compensation, either to enable the non-breaching party to secure substitute performance or to compensate for the lost profits that the promised performance would have generated. This type of remedy is commonly known as 'damages'. The second category requires the defaulting party to fulfil the actual obligations as stipulated in the contract, a remedy referred to as 'specific performance'.

919. Damages, as a monetary remedy, aim to compensate for economic loss and are generally awarded where substitute performance or financial restitution can adequately address the harm caused by the breach.[860] Courts often calculate damages based on the expected interest of the non-breaching party, striving to replicate the benefit they would have received if the contract had been fully performed. This approach aligns with the principle of ensuring efficient compensation and minimising unnecessary litigation.

920. Specific performance, on the other hand, is a remedy of equitable origin and is typically reserved for cases where monetary compensation is insufficient to address the harm. It is most commonly awarded in contracts involving unique goods, real estate, or other circumstances where substitute performance cannot replicate the promised outcome.[861] Courts exercise discretion in granting specific performance, balancing factors such as feasibility, the impact on the defaulting party, and broader considerations of fairness.[862]

860. Article 579 CC provides that if one party fails to pay the price, remuneration, rent, interest, or fulfil other monetary obligations, the other party may request payment.
861. *Grant v. Dawkins* [1973] 1 WLR 1406.
862. Lei Chen, Availability of Specific Remedies in Chinese Contract Law, in Remedies for Breach of Contract (Mindy Chen-Wishart, Alexander Loke and Ong Burton eds., Oxford University Press 2016).

921. Both remedies are essential tools in contract law, serving complementary purposes. Damages provide flexibility and practicality, while specific performance underscores the binding nature of contractual commitments in cases of exceptional importance. Together, these remedies uphold the integrity of contractual relationships, reinforcing the principle that promises made are promises kept.

922. Under Chinese law, parties generally have the freedom to request the remedy they consider most appropriate in cases of contractual breach, subject to the discretion of the courts. Article 577 of the Civil Code provides that if one party fails to perform its contractual obligations or performs them in a manner that does not conform to the agreement, it shall bear liability for breach of contract, which may include continued performance (also known as specific performance),[863] taking remedial measures, or compensating for losses.[864]

923. This discretion is exercised with due regard to the specific circumstances of each case, reflecting the balance between party autonomy and judicial oversight inherent in the Chinese legal framework. However, exploring the nuances of contractual remedies under Chinese law raises several intriguing questions rooted in its interplay with broader legal principles and public policy considerations.

924. A central question in Chinese contract law is whether damages for breach of contract are contingent on proving fault. The extent to which Chinese courts award specific performance for breach and the factors that influence their choice of remedy in such cases. Is specific performance a less favoured remedy? Another significant issue is that parties can stipulate liquidated damages in their contracts, but courts retain the power to adjust these amounts if they are deemed excessively punitive or unreasonably low.[865] Finally, an intriguing issue is whether the practical application of contractual remedies in Chinese courts reveals a convergence with common law practices.

925. In order to answer these questions, this chapter focuses its discussion on damages and specific performance. It first explains the meaning of breach and non-fault liability in the contract breach. Specifically, this part attempts to address whether the Chinese Civil Code has adopted the terminology of fundamental breach and how it is determined if the breach has made the 'realisation of the contract purpose impossible'. Subsequently, rules on damages will be extensively discussed.

863. The notion of continued performance is broader in Chinese law than in common law, for instance, (1) SP is basically an equitable relief in common law while continued performance in China is a statutory remedy; (2) SP in common law is available only if legal remedies are not adequate, but the application of performance continuation in Chinese law contains no such restrictions; (3) SP in common law mainly applies to non-monetary obligations (property in most cases), in contrast with the fact that continued performance in China applies to both monetary and non-monetary obligations; 4) continued performance under Chinese law includes execution or performance of the contract by a third party at the expense of the debtor, provided there is a binding judicial order. *See* Lei Chen, Specific Performance as a Contractual Remedy in Chinese Courts: An Empirical Study, 7 The Chinese Journal of Comparative Law 95 (2019).

864. Article 577 CC.

865. This is seen in Chapter 4 Contract Content.

The compensatory nature of damages has been statutorily stressed in Chinese law, and this has impacted the shaping of concrete contract rules.

926. On the issue of whether non-pecuniary loss can be recovered under Chinese law, there appears to be a discrepancy between judicial attitude and scholarly opinions. Looking closer, it appears that there are different understandings even between the SPC and lower courts at the municipal level. The more important issues concern the way damages are calculated and the extent of damages awarded. What are the limiting factors applicable to the recovery of damages? The last section of Part 15.3 covers the ongoing debates on penalty clauses.

927. In Part 15.4, the rule of specific performance is explored, and it is demonstrated that Chinese law does not enshrine a hierarchy of legal remedies for breach of contract. While it is regarded as a routine remedy at the choice of the non-defaulting party, specific performance is not considered by Chinese courts a primary or default remedy, unlike many other civil law jurisdictions. Although specific performance is generally available to claimants as a remedy alongside damages, it is rarely pursued due to practical considerations. It is argued that despite the doctrinal differences between Chinese law and common law, different legal systems have reached similar results on the practical level. Part 15.5 provides a conclusion from a comparative law perspective.

§2. Breach or Non-performance

I. Concept

928. As a civil law jurisdiction, the Chinese Civil Code incorporates the concepts of both 'non-performance' (不履行) and 'breach' (违约). The distinction between 'non-performance' and 'breach' is nuanced. Some scholars argue that the scope of 'non-performance' is broader, encompassing situations beyond contractual breaches, such as those involving tortious liability or unjust enrichment. Nevertheless, in practical application, the terms are often treated synonymously when addressing the failure to fulfil contractual obligations. Articles 577 and 578 consistently use the term 'non-performance of obligations' (不履行合同义务), reflecting its centrality in the regulation of contractual obligations.[866]

929. Article 577 provides a foundational provision for addressing breaches of contract. This provision emphasises that a breach does not automatically terminate the contract. Instead, it grants the aggrieved party a range of remedies, which may include continued performance, rectification, or monetary compensation. However, Article 577 is not exhaustive in detailing the legal consequences of a breach. By preserving the contract and offering remedial measures, Chinese law encourages performance and minimises the economic disruption caused by breaches. At the same time, the aggrieved party retains flexibility in choosing the most suitable remedy,

866. Articles 577 and 578 CC.

whether it is specific performance, rectification, or monetary damages. The nature and extent of remedies available depend on two key considerations:

930. Breaches may be excused under specific circumstances, such as force majeure, mutual agreement, or statutory exceptions. Lawful excuses can shield the breaching party from liability, transforming what might otherwise be a breach into an excusable non-performance.

931. Remedies vary depending on whether the breach is minor or fundamental. A minor breach may only warrant damages, while a fundamental breach – such as one that defeats the entire purpose of the contract – may allow for contract termination or more stringent remedies.

932. The dual concepts of 'non-performance' and 'breach' in the Civil Code underscore the complexity and adaptability of Chinese contract law. By providing a framework that accommodates both strict liability and lawful excuses, the Civil Code ensures a nuanced and fair approach to contractual breaches. This legal flexibility fosters greater consistency and predictability in contract enforcement, aligning China's approach with global practices while retaining its distinct civil law characteristics. Further exploration of how these remedies are applied in practice can offer deeper insights into the evolving landscape of Chinese contract law and its interaction with international norms.

II. Strict Liability or Faculty-Based Liability?

933. In contrast, Chinese law, as codified in the Civil Code, generally adopts a principle of strict liability for contractual breaches.[867] A defaulting party cannot escape liability for damages by arguing the absence of fault. For example, a seller's liability for defective goods is essentially absolute under the provisions governing sales contracts. The seller cannot defeat the buyer's claim by proving the absence of personal fault in causing the defect. This reflects the broader aim of protecting the non-defaulting party and ensuring commercial certainty in contractual relations.

934. Chinese law also recognises limited exceptions where fault-based liability applies, particularly in contracts involving obligations of care and skill. For instance, in agency contracts, an agent is expected to exercise the level of care and diligence required by the principal's instructions and the nature of the task.[868] Similarly, in storage contracts, the custodian is liable for loss or damage to the stored items only if they failed to exercise the reasonable care expected under the agreement.[869] In these contexts, a failure to meet the requisite standard of care constitutes a fault, thereby triggering liability.

867. Article 577 CC.
868. Article 929 CC.
869. Article 897 CC.

935. This nuanced approach under Chinese law reflects a hybrid liability regime, blending strict liability as the default rule with fault-based exceptions tailored to specific contractual contexts. The rationale for such differentiation lies in the nature of the obligations involved. Contracts imposing duties of care and skill inherently demand a subjective assessment of the defaulting party's conduct, as these duties are not absolute but contingent upon contextually reasonable performance. In contrast, strict liability in areas such as sales and product defects promotes predictability and allocates risks efficiently between the parties.

936. By comparison, under common law, particularly in jurisdictions like England and Wales, the general principle is that fault is not a prerequisite for contractual liability.[870] This aligns more closely with the strict liability model observed in China.[871] In common law, the primary obligation in a contract is to perform as agreed.[872] Any deviation from the contract's terms may be considered a breach, regardless of whether the breach was intentional or occurred without fault. If a party fails to perform (non-performance) or performs defectively (imperfect performance), they are typically liable for breach of contract regardless of fault. The common law position favours predictability in commercial contracts by imposing liability based on non-performance rather than subjective fault.[873] This approach encourages contracting parties to allocate risks explicitly through negotiated terms (e.g., force majeure clauses), emphasising autonomy and the freedom of contract.[874] At the same time, the doctrine of frustration and the emphasis on reasonable care in certain types of contracts provide some flexibility to account for fairness and context-specific expectations.[875]

937. The interplay between fault and strict liability raises intriguing questions about fairness, efficiency, and risk allocation in contract law. These comparative insights underscore the adaptability of legal doctrines to the practical needs of commercial and social contexts while maintaining coherence within the overarching legal system.

870. *Parsons (Livestock) Ltd v. Uttley Ingham & Co Ltd* [1978] QB 791.
871. Lei Chen, Damages and Specific Performance in Chinese Contract Law, in Chinese Contract Law: Civil and Common Law Perspectives 375–376 (L.A. DiMatteo and Lei Chen eds., Cambridge University Press 2017) .
872. *Hadley v. Baxendale* (1854) 9 Exch 341.
873. *Arcos Ltd v. Ronaasen & Son* [1933] AC 470.
874. *Photo Production Ltd v. Securicor Transport Ltd* [1980] AC 827.
875. *Taylor v. Caldwell* (1863) 3 B & S 826; also, under the Sale of Goods Act 1979, particularly Sections 13-14, there is an implied obligation that goods must be fit for purpose and of satisfactory quality. Where goods are sold by description, there is an implied term that they must correspond to the description. If the seller is a professional, they are held to a standard of reasonable care and skill.

III. Limitations on the Recoverable Loss

938. To avoid the unreasonable allocation of risks caused by the breaching party bearing absolute liability for breach of contract, some rules for exemption and mitigation of liability for breach are introduced in the Civil Code.

A. *Force Majeure*

939. Force majeure refers to an extraordinary event or circumstance beyond the control of the parties, which prevents one or both of them from fulfilling their contractual obligations. These events are typically unforeseen, unavoidable, and external, and they render performance impracticable, impossible, or illegal.

940. If a party is unable to perform the contract due to force majeure, they may be partially or entirely exempted from liability depending on the impact of the force majeure.[876] The party affected by force majeure must notify the other party in a timely manner and provide proof within a reasonable period.[877] This provision imposes a duty on the affected party to notify the other party promptly and to provide evidence of the force majeure event to claim the exemption.

941. However, if the force majeure occurs after a delay in performance, the liability for breach is not exempted.[878] The Civil Code defines force majeure as 'any objective circumstance that is unforeseeable, unavoidable, and insurmountable'.[879] This definition establishes the conditions under which an event can be classified as force majeure: it must be unforeseeable at the time of contracting, unavoidable in its occurrence, and insurmountable in its effects.

942. Force majeure can be grounds for terminating a contract if the purpose of the contract becomes impossible to achieve due to the force majeure event.[880] This allows either party to terminate the contract, provided that performance has become impracticable or the contract's purpose cannot be fulfilled.

IV. Mitigation

943. The non-breaching party has an obligation to prevent further losses.[881] This mitigation rule ensures that losses are minimised and prevents the breaching party from being unfairly burdened by avoidable damages. If the non-breaching party fails to take appropriate measures, resulting in increased losses, they cannot claim

876. Paragraph 1 of Art. 590 CC.
877. *Ibid.*
878. Paragraph 2 of Art. 590 CC.
879. Article 180 CC.
880. Article 563 CC.
881. Paragraph 1 of Art. 591 CC.

compensation for the expanded portion of the loss.[882] In other words, the breaching party can request to deduct losses caused by the non-breaching party's failure to mitigate.[883] Reasonable expenses incurred to mitigate losses should be borne by the breaching party.[884]

944. The breaching party is liable for the reasonable costs incurred by the non-breaching party in mitigating losses. This includes expenses such as hiring replacement services, temporary storage, or emergency measures to prevent further damage. The costs must be directly related to the mitigation efforts and deemed reasonable under the circumstances. For example, a buyer breaches a contract for the purchase of goods. The seller must take reasonable steps to resell the goods to another buyer to minimise losses. If the seller delays or refuses to resell, they cannot claim compensation for storage costs during the delay.

945. Another example is in a lease agreement where a tenant vacates a leased property prematurely. The landlord must make reasonable efforts to find a new tenant. Failure to do so may limit the landlord's ability to recover unpaid rent.[885]

946. The non-breaching party is required to take reasonable measures to reduce further losses when faced with a breach of contract. However, disputes may arise over what constitutes 'reasonable' mitigation measures and costs. What constitutes 'reasonable measures' depends on the specific circumstances of the case, including the nature of the contract, the type of breach, and the means available to mitigate losses. The actions taken to mitigate losses must be proportionate and appropriate under the circumstances. The non-breaching party is not required to go beyond what is reasonable or to bear an undue burden in the process of mitigating losses.

947. Subjectivity in this assessment can lead to uncertainty. If the injured party undertakes mitigation efforts that turn out to be ineffective or more expensive than alternatives, disputes may arise about whether the costs are proportional and reasonable. The non-breaching party must prove that their mitigation measures were necessary and that the expenses incurred were reasonable. This may involve significant evidentiary challenges. The process could be made fairer by requiring the non-breaching party to provide prima facie evidence that they have taken reasonable steps to mitigate losses. Once this initial showing is made, the burden could then shift to the breaching party to contest it. This two-step process would help ensure

---

882. *Ibid.*
883. Paragraph 3 of Art. 63 of the SPC Interpretation on the Contract Book (2023).
884. Paragraph 2 of Art. 591 CC.
885. *Shizong Hongxin Manganese Industry Co., Ltd. v. Li Yinghui and Wang Duxian* Supreme People's Court (2020) SPC Min Shen No.4691; 师宗宏鑫锰业有限责任公司、王都贤租赁合同纠纷再审审查与审判监督民事裁定书， 最高人民法院（2020）最高法民申4691号; *Zhongcang Palace (Beijing) Culture Media Co., Ltd. Shanghai Branch & Zhongcang Palace (Beijing) Culture Media Co., Ltd. v. Shanghai Huanyu Hui Commercial Management Co., Ltd.* No.2 Intermediate People's Court of Shanghai (2020) Hu 02 Min Zhong 3179; 中藏宫(北京)文化传媒有限公司与上海寰宇汇商业管理有限公司房屋租赁合同纠纷二审民事判决书， 上海市第二中级人民法院（2020）沪02民终3179.

both parties are held accountable while making the litigation process more balanced. It is recommended that the non-breaching party should document their mitigation efforts and associated costs thoroughly to support claims for compensation.

948. Another possible drawback is that there are limited incentives for the non-breaching party to act promptly when mitigating losses. The law primarily focuses on what measures are taken without placing sufficient emphasis on the timing of those measures. Delayed action in mitigating losses can result in larger damages, which may ultimately be harder to recover. The law could be refined to emphasise the importance of timely mitigation by providing that failure to mitigate within a reasonable timeframe can lead to a reduction in the amount of recoverable damages.

V. Contributory Negligence

949. Contributory negligence is invoked to the allocation of liability when a party's actions have contributed to the damage or loss caused by a breach of contract. The rules governing contributory negligence reflect an effort to achieve fairness by considering the relative fault of both parties.

950. If both parties breach the contract, they must each bear their respective liabilities.[886] If one party's breach causes a loss to the other party, and the injured party has contributed to the occurrence of the loss, the compensation amount may be reduced accordingly.[887] Contributory negligence (过失相抵) under Chinese contract law serves as a principle to limit the liability of the breaching party if the non-breaching party's own negligence contributed to the loss. For example, a company hires a contractor to install machinery but negligently interferes with the process, causing damage. The court may attribute partial responsibility to the company and reduce the damages payable by the contractor.

951. The reduction is proportional to the degree of fault. The non-breaching party's negligence must have a causal connection to the resulting loss. If their fault is unrelated to the breach, the principle does not apply. The reduction in compensation is determined based on the proportional fault of the non-breaching party. If the court finds that the non-breaching party's actions or inactions played a role in aggravating the damages, it will adjust the compensation accordingly. Courts have significant discretion in determining the extent of the non-breaching party's fault.

952. In cases involving contributory negligence, the burden of proof typically lies with the breaching party to demonstrate that the non-breaching party's negligence contributed to the damages. The breaching party must provide evidence showing that the losses could have been reduced if the non-breaching party had acted with reasonable care.

---

886. Paragraph 1 of Art. 592 CC.
887. Paragraph 2 of Art. 592 CC.

953. By imposing consequences for negligence, the rule incentivises the non-breaching party to act responsibly and avoid exacerbating losses. However, establishing the non-breaching party's fault and its causal link to the loss can be challenging, particularly in complex commercial disputes. The broad discretion granted to courts may result in inconsistent application of the rule, creating uncertainty for parties.

954. In some cases, distinguishing between intentional actions and negligence in determining contributory fault can be challenging. Greater clarity in defining negligence versus intentional misconduct and how they affect liability could enhance fairness and consistency in judicial practice.

955. Judicial practice in China reinforces these principles by assessing the proportionality of fault, the reasonableness of actions, and the causal link between the non-breaching party's conduct and the damages incurred.

VI. Reduction of Loss by Gains of the Non-breaching Party

956. The principle of loss to be reduced by gains of the non-breaching party (损益相抵) is a widely accepted concept in Chinese contract law.[888] It ensures that damages awarded to the non-breaching party are adjusted to reflect any benefits or savings they received as a result of the breach. This principle aligns with the overarching goal of compensation: to restore the injured party to the position they would have been in had the contract been performed without providing unjust enrichment.[889]

957. The non-breaching party is entitled to compensation for their losses but must deduct any benefits they obtained as a result of the breach.[890] The gains must be directly attributable to the breach. Unrelated benefits are not deducted. The principle prevents the non-breaching party from recovering more than the actual loss, ensuring damages do not lead to a financial windfall.

958. Disputes may arise over what constitutes a gain directly attributable to the breach, especially in complex commercial scenarios. The principle of reducing losses by gains of the non-breaching party serves as a vital mechanism for ensuring fairness and avoiding unjust enrichment. However, clearer guidelines and enhanced evidentiary standards could improve its application and consistency in practice.

888. Article 23 of the SPC Interpretation on Issues Concerning the Application of Law in the Trial of Disputes Over Sales Contract (2012, 2020 revision).
889. Article 10 of the SPC Guiding Opinions on Several Issues Concerning the Trial of Civil and Commercial Contract Dispute Cases under the Current Situation (2009).
890. Paragraph 3 of Art. 63 of the SPC Interpretation on the Contract Book (2023).

§3. Specific Performance and Remedial Measures

I. Specific Performance as a Routine Remedy

959. Comparative legal studies reveal a notable divergence in the treatment of contractual remedies between common law and civil law systems.[891] Common law jurisdictions typically prioritise awarding damages as the primary remedy for breaches of contract, reflecting a preference for monetary compensation over the enforcement of specific performance.[892] In contrast, civil law systems traditionally treat specific performance as a fundamental remedy, emphasising the fulfilment of contractual obligations.[893] Chinese law adopts a distinctive middle-ground approach, viewing specific performance as a standard remedy while not exhibiting a hierarchical preference between specific performance and damages.[894]

960. Under Chinese law, creditors have the freedom to request specific performance or other preferred remedies.[895] This flexibility aligns with the principle of protecting the performance interest, which is central to contractual relationships. The routine availability of specific performance under Chinese law contrasts with the common law approach, where specific performance is typically considered an exceptional remedy, granted only when damages are inadequate. By providing creditors with a choice between specific performance and damages, the Chinese legal framework seeks to uphold party autonomy while maintaining fairness and efficiency through its carefully tailored restrictions.

961. In Chinese legal terminology, specific performance is framed as a 'remedial right' (履行请求权) rather than being grouped under the broader category of 'remedies' (救济). This conceptual distinction underscores the direct relationship between the creditor's right to performance and the debtor's obligation to fulfil the contract. It also reflects the civil law tradition, where the enforcement of obligations is seen as a natural consequence of breach rather than as an exceptional remedy.[896] Specific performance remains a routine remedy under Chinese law. Creditors are generally free to choose between requesting specific performance (SP) or damages,

891. Lei Chen and Larry A. Di Matteo, Inefficiency of Specific Performance as a Contractual Remedy in Chinese Courts: An Empirical and Normative Analysis, 40 Nw. J. Int'l L. & Bus. 275 (2009); Gerard De Vries, Right to Specific Performance: Is There a Divergence between Civil- and Common-Law Systems and, If So, How Has It Been Bridged in the DCFR?, 17 European Review of Private Law 581 (2009).

892. George Klass, To Perform or Pay Damages, 98 Virginia Law Rev 143, 158 (2012); Steven Shavell, Specific Performance versus Damages for Breach of Contract: An Economic Analysis, 84 Texas Law Rev 831 (2005).

893. Vanessa Mak, Performance-Oriented Remedies in European Sale of Goods Law (Hart Publishing 2009)

894. Lei Chen, The Availability of Specific Performance in Chinese Contract Law, in Remedies for Breach in Asia 21-39 (Mindy Chen-Wishart, Alexander Loke and Burton Ong eds., OUP 2016).

895. Lei Chen, Specific Performance as a Contractual Remedy in Chinese Courts: An Empirical Study, 7 The Chinese Journal of Comparative Law 95 (2019).

896. Lei Chen and Larry A. Di Matteo, Inefficiency of Specific Performance as a Contractual Remedy in Chinese Courts: An Empirical and Normative Analysis, 40 Nw. J. Int'l L. & Bus. 275 (2019).

depending on what better protects their interests. For instance, in contracts involving unique or irreplaceable goods, SP is often the preferred remedy. In contrast, where performance can be readily substituted (e.g., monetary payments or mass-produced goods), damages may be more practical.

II. Restrictions on Availability of Specific Performance

962. Although specific performance is generally available under Chinese law, its application is curtailed under certain conditions.[897] To enhance efficiency and balance the protection of the aggrieved party's interests with fairness, specific performance and its sub-remedies, such as repair and replacement, are subject to several important restrictions under Chinese law. These restrictions aim to prevent the over-protection of creditors and ensure proportionality in contractual remedies. The limitations on the general availability of specific performance are as significant as the remedy itself, reflecting a nuanced approach to enforcement.[898]

963. When the performance of the obligation becomes impossible or excessively burdensome, specific performance is not enforced.

964. If the cost of enforcing specific performance is disproportionate to the benefit obtained, damages may be awarded instead. This limitation reflects the practical and equitable considerations inherent in contract law, ensuring that remedies do not impose undue burdens on the legal system or the breaching party while achieving only minimal benefits for the aggrieved party. In such cases, damages are typically awarded as a more efficient and proportionate alternative.

965. Creditors must act promptly to request specific performance. A delay or failure to mitigate losses may contravene the good faith principle, limiting the availability of this remedy. This principle, deeply embedded in Chinese contract law, underscores the importance of equitable conduct in the enforcement of contractual rights. A creditor's delay or inaction can have significant implications, potentially limiting or even precluding the availability of specific performance as a remedy.

966. Debtor's hardship or change of circumstance: specific performance may be denied if it causes undue hardship to the debtor, particularly in cases involving significant changes in circumstances.[899] This limitation reflects the equitable principle of fairness, ensuring that contractual remedies do not become instruments of injustice or economic oppression. The notion of 'change of circumstances' (情势变更)

897. Articles 580 and 533 CC.
898. Paragraph 1 of Art. 580 CC.
899. Article 533 CC.

plays a crucial role in this context, allowing courts to consider unforeseen and substantial changes that disrupt the contractual equilibrium.[900]

967. A significant and unforeseen change in circumstances, such as an economic crisis, a sudden change in market conditions, or a natural disaster, may render performance fundamentally different from what was originally anticipated. This aligns with the doctrine of *rebus sic stantibus* (things thus standing), which is recognised in many civil law jurisdictions as a means of adjusting or terminating obligations when circumstances change drastically.

968. Notably, if one party fails to fulfil their contractual obligations or performs them inadequately, and specific performance is infeasible due to the nature of the obligation, the other party is entitled to recover the costs incurred in engaging a third party to fulfil the obligation.[901] This rule applies both to non-performance (complete failure to perform the obligation) and defective performance (failure to meet agreed standards or terms). It ensures that the aggrieved party has a remedy regardless of the type of breach.

969. The rule recognises that some obligations, by their nature, cannot be specifically enforced. For example, in contracts involving personal skills or expertise (e.g., a painter or performer) or unique or time-sensitive obligations (e.g., delivering a product within a specific timeframe), alternative remedies are necessary. When specific performance is not possible, the aggrieved party is permitted to arrange for a third party to fulfil the obligation. The breaching party is required to cover the expenses incurred by the aggrieved party in obtaining substitute performance.

III. Comparative Analysis

970. In common law jurisdictions, the concept is similar. If a specific performance is unavailable due to the nature of the obligation, the non-breaching party can mitigate their loss by arranging for a substitute performance.[902] They may then claim damages reflecting the cost of such performance. However, English law emphasises mitigation, requiring the non-breaching party to take reasonable steps to minimise their losses.[903]

971. Under German law, substitute performance (Ersatzvornahme) is explicitly recognised. § 637 BGB (German Civil Code) allows for substitute performance at

900. Lei Chen and Qiyu Wang, Demystifying the Doctrine of Change of Circumstances under Chinese Law-A Comparative Perspective from Singapore and English Common Law, 6 Journal of Business Law 475 (2021).
901. Article 581 CC.
902. *Co-operative Insurance Society Ltd v. Argyll Stores (Holdings) Ltd* [1997] 3 All ER 297.
903. *British Westinghouse Electric & Manufacturing Co Ltd v. Underground Electric Railways Co of London Ltd* [1912] AC 673.

the breaching party's expense, particularly in contracts for services or construction.[904] Similar to the Chinese rule, the injured party can recover costs incurred for such replacement performance. Under the Uniform Commercial Code (UCC), particularly in cases of breach of a contract for goods, the buyer may 'cover' by purchasing substitute goods and recover the additional costs from the seller (UCC § 2-712).[905] Similarly, the Restatement (Second) of Contracts allows for damages based on the cost of substitute performance.[906]

972. At first glance, there might appear to be significant differences in the approach to specific performance between common law and Chinese law. However, in practice, the outcomes often converge, leading to a narrower distinction than the theoretical frameworks suggest. While specific performance remains a key remedy, the restrictions placed on its application introduce a degree of flexibility that mirrors certain common law concerns about practicality and efficiency. This hybrid model suggests a pragmatic approach that seeks to balance the creditor's right to performance with broader considerations of fairness, feasibility, and economic efficiency.

973. Empirically, the Chinese judiciary rarely awards specific performance across all levels of Chinese courts.[907] Specific performance appears to be only cautiously and judiciously awarded. Common law's preference for damages aligns with the Chinese principle of efficiency in cases where damages provide an adequate remedy. In both systems, specific performance is generally reserved for cases where damages are insufficient to restore the injured party's position.

974. Under Chinese law, when a debtor's performance does not conform to the contract, the creditor can request remedies such as repair, redoing, or replacement, depending on the nature of the subject matter and the extent of the loss.[908] If these remedies are impossible, unreasonable, or ineffective, or if the debtor refuses or fails to perform within a reasonable time, the creditor may request alternative remedies, such as returning goods, reducing the price or remuneration, or pursuing other forms of redress.[909]

---

904. German Civil Code (BGB), § 637 – 'Self-Help Remedy of Defects'. This provision allows the non-breaching party to carry out substitute performance at the breaching party's expense if the breaching party fails to rectify defects within a reasonable time period after being given notice.
905. Uniform Commercial Code (UCC) § 2-712 – 'Cover; Buyer's Procurement of Substitute Goods.' This section allows the buyer, upon a seller's breach, to purchase substitute goods ('cover') and recover the difference in cost between the cover price and the original contract price, along with any incidental or consequential damages.
906. Restatement (Second) of Contracts, § 347 – 'Measure of Damages in General.' This section provides that the injured party has a right to damages based on their expectation interest, which may include the cost of substitute performance.
907. Lei Chen, Specific Performance as a Contractual Remedy in Chinese Courts: An Empirical Study, 7 The Chinese Journal of Comparative Law 95 (2019).
908. Article 582 CC.
909. *Ibid.*

975. Article 582 elaborates on the broader framework of remedial measures under Article 577. The latter emphasises the debtor's obligation to take necessary actions to address non-performance.[910] Repair, redoing, and replacement are specific examples of such measures. These remedies collectively constitute the legal framework for addressing defective performance. The remedies under Article 582 align closely with civil law traditions but differ from common law systems, where specific performance is often an exceptional remedy. Chinese law's emphasis on repair, redoing, or replacement reflects its roots in civil law, favouring the preservation of the contract over monetary compensation. However, the alternative remedies, including price reduction and return of goods, introduce a practical flexibility that aligns with modern commercial practices.

976. Chinese law's treatment of specific performance reflects a nuanced stance that bridges the gap between common law and civil law traditions. This middle-ground approach highlights the dynamic nature of Chinese contract law, which strives to uphold the integrity of contractual obligations while addressing the complexities of modern commercial relationships.

§4. Damages

I. General Rule

977. The primary aim of an award of damages for a breach of contract under Chinese law is to compensate the non-defaulting party for losses incurred due to the breach.[911] This principle aligns with the broader goal of ensuring the aggrieved party receives the monetary equivalent of the benefit they would have enjoyed if the contract had been performed as promised. It is worth noting that the breaching party's liability extends beyond mere performance or remedial action to include compensation for consequential damages suffered by the non-breaching party.[912]

978. The party claiming damages must prove that the loss was caused by the breach or wrongful act of the other party. The link between the breach and the damage must be direct and not overly remote. Damages must compensate for losses caused by the breach.[913] Causation serves as a threshold test, excluding losses that are incidental or speculative, ensuring damages reflect only the actual harm caused.

910. Sébastien De Rey and Lei Chen, Non-monetary relief for breach of contract : a European perspective on Chinese contract law, 29 Asia Pacific Law Review 325 (2021).
911. Article 584 CC.
912. Article 583 CC provides that if one party fails to perform their contractual obligations or performs them in a manner inconsistent with the agreement, even after fulfiling the obligation or taking remedial measures, they are still liable to compensate the other party for any additional losses incurred.
913. Article 584 CC.

A breaching party is liable only for losses that were foreseeable at the time the contract was made.[914] This rule limits damages to those that could reasonably have been anticipated as a result of the breach.[915]

979. Under Chinese law, the default remedy for breach of contract is expectation damages. These are calculated to place the non-defaulting party in the same financial position they would have been in if the contract had been fully performed. This principle ensures the enforcement of contractual promises and incentivises performance. The Civil Code clearly spells out that damages are calculated to reflect the expected improvement in the non-defaulting party's position rather than merely restoring them to their pre-contractual state.[916]

980. This approach includes not only actual losses but also anticipated profits, emphasising the concept of expectation damages as the central remedy. The use of the term 'including' in Article 584 suggests that expected benefits (可得利益) are part of the broader concept of 'losses' (损失), indicating a relationship of part to whole. This means that, in addition to expected benefits, other losses caused by the breach of contract can also be compensated.

981. What other losses are recoverable? The necessary expenses incurred by the non-defaulting party for normal contract performance should not be ascertained as other losses. This is because these costs are inherently part of the expected benefits and have a corresponding value exchange relationship. Any extra expenses incurred by the non-defaulting party due to the breach should be included in the compensation. These costs arise solely due to the breach and are not part of the expected performance costs.

II. Expected Benefits

982. Traditionally, Chinese courts have been cautious in supporting claims for expected benefits (可得利益) due to the inherent uncertainties in both evidence and calculation. For example, in a ruling handed down by the SPC, it was reasoned that 'hypothetical or potential losses cannot be claimed as compensable damages for breach of contract'.[917] This reflects the rigid requirement for certainty and reasonableness in claims for breach of contract damages.[918] This caution stems from

914. *Ibid.*

915. *Xinjiang Yakun Trading Co., Ltd. v. Xinjiang Jinghe County Kangrui Cotton Processing Co., Ltd.* (Gazette Case of the SPC, Issue 11, 2006); 新疆亚坤商贸有限公司与新疆精河县康瑞棉花加工有限公司买卖合同纠纷案，《最高人民法院公报》案例，2006年11期.

916. Article 584 CC.

917. *Shanxi Shuyuan Huashi Chemical Energy Co., Ltd. v. Shanxi Sanwei Group Co., Ltd. Supreme People's Court* (2012) Min Yi Zhong Zi No.67; 山西数源华石化工能源有限公司、山西三维集团股份有限公司租赁合同纠纷，最高人民法院二审，（2012）民一终字第67号.

918. *Yuhe Building Materials Factory of Moyu County, Xinjiang Uygur Autonomous Region v. Agricultural Bank of China, Moyu County Branch*, Supreme People's Court (2004) Min Er Zhong Zi No.228; 新疆维吾尔自治区墨玉县玉河建材厂与中国农业银行墨玉县支行为借款合同纠纷

the difficulty in reliably proving the non-defaulting party's expected profits or benefits and quantifying them with precision.

983. The SPC has previously held in its judgments that business profits of enterprises are influenced by numerous factors, making both their status and amount inherently uncertain.[919] In another ruling, the SPC held that 'the overall profit or loss status of an enterprise during a certain period does not necessarily prove whether the expected profits of a specific contract were actually lost'.[920] This position underscores the challenges associated with awarding damages for lost profits in commercial disputes.

984. However, expected benefits represent the very essence of why parties enter into contracts – they embody the core purpose of the contract. The expectation of achieving these benefits is often the driving factor behind contractual obligations. Denying compensation for expected benefits risks undermining the fundamental principle of contract law: to ensure that parties can rely on agreements and be restored, as far as possible, to the position they would have been in had the contract been performed.

III. Calculating Expected Benefits

985. In this context, although uncertainties in evidence and calculation are real challenges, the courts should not overshadow the importance of safeguarding the contractual expectations of the non-defaulting party.[921] Judicial discretion, coupled with clear evidentiary requirements and reasonable methodologies for calculating anticipated benefits, can strike a balance between caution and the need to uphold the purpose of contracts. For this reason, the SPC elaborated on the calculation of

---

新疆维吾尔自治区墨玉县玉河建材厂与中国农业银行墨玉县支行为借款合同纠纷，最高人民法院二审，（2004）民二终字第228号; *Ke Guoqing v. Maoming Weiheng Real Estate Co., Ltd., Maoming Bohui Investment Co., Ltd., and Others*, Supreme People's Court (2015) Min Ti Zi No.221; 柯国庆与茂名市伟恒地产有限公司、茂名市博汇投资有限公司、茂名市志同贸易有限公司与黄世就民间借贷纠纷，最高人民法院再审，（2015）民提字第211号.

919. *Shanxi Shuyuan Huashi Chemical Energy Co., Ltd. v. Shanxi Sanwei Group Co., Ltd. Supreme People's Court* (2012) Min Yi Zhong Zi No.67; 山西数源华石化工能源有限公司、山西三维集团股份有限公司租赁合同纠纷，最高人民法院二审，（2012）民一终字第67号.

920. *Shanghai Zhedong Aluminium Co., Ltd. v. Changzhou Shifang International Trade Co., Ltd.*, Supreme People's Court (2013) Min Er Zhong Zi No.76; 上海浙东铝业有限公司与常州世方国际贸易有限公司一般买卖合同纠纷，最高人民法院二审，（2013）民二终字第76号.

921. *Civil Affairs Bureau of Linwei District, Weinan City, Shaanxi Province v. Weinan Xiangshan Cemetery Operations Management Co., Ltd. and Others*, Supreme People's Court (2021) SPC Min Shen No.4557; 陕西省渭南市临渭区民政局、渭南象山公墓运营管理有限公司等合同纠纷案，最高人民法院民事申请再审审查民事裁定书，（2021）最高法民申4557号. In this case, the SPC held that the determination of expected profits is not contingent on whether the continuation of the contract would have resulted in profit or loss. Although this ruling represents a minority position, which upholds the claim for expected profits, sends a positive signal regarding the recognition of anticipated benefits as compensable damages in contract disputes.

expected benefit losses in 2023. Depending on the circumstances, three methods of calculation are provided: the profit method, the substitute transaction method, and the market price method.

986. First, the profit method is the general approach for calculating expected benefits (可得利益).[922] This method centres on calculating the anticipated profits that the non-defaulting party could reasonably have expected to earn from the contract's performance. Courts may now calculate these expectation benefits based on production profits, operational profits, or resale profits that the non-defaulting party could have earned.[923] This calculation should be made after deducting reasonable costs, such as expenses incurred by the non-defaulting party for the conclusion and performance of the contract.[924] For example, in contracts involving the sale of production equipment or raw materials, if the seller breaches the contract, the resulting loss to the buyer's expected benefits typically falls under production profit loss. This occurs because the buyer is unable to use the equipment or materials to generate the expected production-related income.

987. In contracts such as those for contract-based operations, leasing arrangements, or the provision of services or labour, a breach by one party usually leads to a loss of operational profits for the other party. These are the profits that would have been earned through the ongoing operation or use of the leased or contracted resources. Furthermore, when it comes to sequential sales contracts, if the seller breaches the original contracts, the loss of expected benefits for the buyer in the subsequent resale contract is typically classified as resale profit loss. This occurs when the breach in the original contract disrupts the buyer's ability to resell the goods at the expected profit margin.

988. Second, when the non-defaulting party exercises the right to terminate the contract and conducts a substitute transaction, they may claim the benefits they could have obtained when the contract was performed. Such benefits should be calculated based on the difference between the substitute transaction price and the original contract price.[925] However, where the substitute transaction price significantly deviates from the local market price, and the breaching party argues that the benefits should instead be calculated based on the difference between the market price and the original contract price, the court shall support this argument.[926]

989. A substitute transaction occurs when one party breaches a contract, and the non-breaching party undertakes another transaction to replace the original

---

922. Article 60, para. 1 of the SPC Interpretation of Contract Book (2023) references Art. 9 of the SPC Guiding Opinions on Civil and Commercial Contract Dispute Cases (2009) in this current situation.
923. Paragraph 1 of Article 60 of the SPC Interpretation on the Contract Book (2003).
924. *Ibid.*
925. Paragraph 2 of Art. 60 of the SPC Interpretation on Contract Book (2023).
926. *Ibid.*

contract's performance. For example, in a sales contract, if the seller refuses to deliver the goods, the buyer may purchase similar goods elsewhere, and the difference in price between the substitute transaction and the original contract price is used to determine the loss of anticipated benefits. The essence of a substitute transaction is encouraging transactions. This approach allows for significant mitigation of the losses caused by the breaching party's failure to perform and ensures that the economic purpose of the contract is fulfilled to the extent possible. By reducing the impact of the breach, substitute transactions also help to avoid the waste of social resources, fostering efficiency and continuity in market activity. The substitute transaction method for calculating damages applies under the following circumstances:

1. The breach must be so serious that it constitutes a fundamental breach, allowing the non-breaching party to terminate the contract. In such cases, the non-breaching party is permitted to conduct a substitute transaction.
2. The subject matter of the contract must be a fungible good or replaceable item. If the subject matter is a unique or specific item, the substitute transaction method becomes impractical for calculating losses, and other methods must be applied.
3. Relying solely on the execution of a substitute transaction contract as the basis for damages calculation could lead to moral hazards, such as collusion between the non-breaching party and the substitute transaction counterparty. To mitigate this risk, courts must comprehensively evaluate the qualifications and performance capacity of the substitute transaction counterparty. The non-breaching party bears an elevated burden of proof to demonstrate the legitimacy and fairness of the substitute transaction.
4. The substitute transaction must be reasonable, with price being a critical factor. If the substitute transaction price significantly deviates from the local market price at the time of the transaction, the court may instead use the market price to calculate damages. In such cases, the breaching party bears the burden of proving the deviation. However, even if there is a significant price deviation, if the non-breaching party can prove that failing to conduct the substitute transaction would have led to greater losses, the substitute transaction method should still be used to calculate damages.

990. Third, if the non-defaulting party exercises the right to terminate the contract but does not conduct a substitute transaction, the benefits they can claim are based on the difference between the market price at the place of performance within *a reasonable period* after the breach and the original contract price.[927] It is important to carefully interpret the concept of *a reasonable period* when determining the time point for assessing the market price. The question arises: should the market price be determined

927. Paragraph 3 of Art. 60 of the SPC Interpretation on the Contract Book (2023).

at the time of the breach or at the time of contract termination? After a breach occurs, the parties may engage in negotiations or attempt to resolve the issue rather than immediately seeking remedies. Therefore, basing the market price solely on the time of breach might overlook the possibility of mitigating losses through further communication. Conversely, if the market price is universally tied to the time of contract termination, it could incentivise the non-breaching party to delay exercising the right to terminate the contract, potentially inflating losses to seek higher compensation. This approach risks undermining the principles of good faith.

991. Therefore, courts should be granted the discretion to decide the appropriate time point for determining the market price based on the specific circumstances of the case. In cases where the non-breaching party delays termination, courts may scrutinise whether such a delay was justifiable or intended to inflate losses. If the delay appears unreasonable or strategic, courts may choose to base the market price on the time of the breach to prevent unjust enrichment.

992. If the non-breaching party acts in a timely and reasonable manner, the market price at the time of termination could serve as the reference point, reflecting the real economic impact of the breach.[928]

993. Furthermore, the SPC provides detailed rules in terms of fixed-term contracts involving continuous performance obligations, such as the payment of price or rent, such as long-term tenancy agreements or commercial lease contracts. Under such contracts, if one party fails to pay rent and the other party chooses to terminate the contract, the courts should consider factors such as the subject matter of the contract, type of transaction, market price changes, and remaining performance period to determine a reasonable period for the non-breaching party to conduct a substitute transaction.[929] The expected benefits after contract performance may then be determined based on the price, rent, or equivalent amount corresponding to this reasonable period after deducting the corresponding performance costs that the non-breaching party would have incurred.[930]

994. For instance, in lease contracts, where the performance period is long, significant resources are invested, and uncertainties in performance are evident, calculating expected benefits solely based on the rent corresponding to the remaining lease term after contract termination can lead to unfair outcomes. Such an approach

928. *Stone company v. Quarry Company*, Case No. 9 of The SPC Typical Cases Related to the SPC Interpretation on the General Provisions of the Contract Book, 2023; 某石材公司与某采石公司买卖合同纠纷案，《关于适用中华人民共和国民法典合同编通则若干问题的解释》相关典型案例，第9号案例.

929. Paragraph 1 of Art. 61 of the SPC Interpretation on the Contract Book (2023).

930. *Ibid.*

allows the non-breaching party to neglect their duty to mitigate losses, even when a timely substitute transaction could reasonably reduce the losses. This failure to mitigate could result in unnecessary losses and harm the overall efficiency of market transactions.

995. The courts will not support a claim for expected benefits based on the price, rent, or equivalent amount for the whole remaining contract period after termination.[931] However, an exception applies if the remaining performance period is shorter than the reasonable period for a substitute transaction.[932] The expected benefits should be calculated based on the reasonable period required for the non-breaching party to find a substitute transaction rather than automatically extending the calculation to the entire remaining lease term. In disputes arising from a tenant's breach of a lease contract, judicial practice often adjusts compensation based on the length of the remaining lease term. If the remaining lease period is relatively long, courts generally award damages equivalent to three to six months of rent starting from the date of contract termination. This approach assumes that three to six months is a reasonable time frame for the landlord to find a new tenant and minimises the risk of the landlord neglecting to seek a substitute lease agreement.[933]

996. In a published case by the SPC, a concluded tenancy agreement provides that Mr Chai entrusted the management company to manage and operate the residential property from 24 July 2018 to 16 October 2021.[934] On 3 November 2020, the management company unilaterally issued a termination notice. Mr Chai did not accept the company's unilateral termination. Mr Chai filed a lawsuit demanding rent for the period 17 October 2020 to 16 October 2021, totalling RMB 114,577.2; overdue interest and liquidated damage of RMB 19,096.2; and compensation for the unfulfilled remaining period of the lease term, calculated at RMB 7,956.75. On 8 October 2021, the court ruled to terminate the contract.[935]

997. The court held that when one party breaches a contract, the other party has a duty to take appropriate measures to prevent the loss from escalating. If they fail to do so and allow the loss to increase, they cannot claim compensation for the portion of the loss that could have been avoided.[936] In this case, before the contract was

---

931. Paragraph 2 of Art. 61 of the SPC Interpretation on the Contract Book (2023).
932. *Ibid.*
933. *Malai Gen and Others v. Nanjing Jiangning Urban Construction and Development Co., Ltd.* Intermediate People's Court of Nanjing Jiangsu (2017) Su 01 Min Zhong No.9469; 马来根等诉南京江宁城镇建设开发有限责任公司房屋租赁合同纠纷案 江苏省南京市中级人民法院（2017）苏01民终9469号; *Shanghai Oriental Cultural Development Center v. Shanghai Shennan Real Estate Co., Ltd.* Intermediate People's Court of Shanghai (2014), Hu Yi Zhong Min Er (Civil) Zhong Zi No.1; 上海东方文化发展中心诉上海申南置业有限公司等房屋租赁合同纠纷案 上海第一中级人民法院(2014)沪一中民二(民)终字第1号.
934. *Chai v. Management Company*, Case No. 10 of The SPC Typical Cases Related to the SPC Interpretation on the General Provisions of the Contract Book, 2023; 某石材公司与某采石公司买卖合同纠纷案，《关于适用中华人民共和国民法典合同编通则若干问题的解释》相关典型案例，第10号案例.
935. *Ibid.*
936. *Ibid.*

formally terminated, the management company was obligated to pay rent to Mr Chai as agreed. However, the management company had, through multiple means, expressed its intent to terminate the contract and provided Mr Chai with the password to the property's electronic lock. Mr Chai, however, consistently refused to accept the property, resulting in its prolonged vacancy. As a result, Mr Chai bears responsibility for the escalated losses caused by his refusal to take possession of the property.[937] Considering the parties' statements, the actual performance of the contract, and the evidence on record, the court partially supported Mr Chai's claim for rent. The court awarded rent up to 30 January 2021 (one month after the management company provided the electronic lock password), amounting to RMB 33,418.35.[938]

998. By limiting compensation to a reasonable period, the courts encourage landlords to actively seek substitute tenants and reduce the risk of inflated claims for extended rental losses. This aligns with the principles of fairness (preventing undue enrichment of the landlord) and efficiency (promoting resource optimisation and market activity). In summary, in long-term lease disputes, the calculation of expected benefits must account for the duty to mitigate losses by using the rent corresponding to a reasonable substitute transaction period as the basis.

999. Nonetheless, in court and arbitration rulings, proving and assessing damages for breach of contract is a common challenge. In areas such as tort liability and intellectual property disputes, the practice of calculating the injured party's losses based on the profits gained by the infringer[939] has not yet been introduced into the calculation of damages for contract breaches. However, it is undeniable that in many contract disputes, breaching parties gain significant profits through their breach, especially in cases of malicious breaches. These parties often exploit the difficulty for the non-breaching party to provide evidence of their losses, continuing to act in breach without accountability.

1000. The legal maxim 'no one should benefit from unlawful acts' should not remain merely a principle in tort law but should also be enforceable in contract disputes. In cases of malicious breach, where the breaching party reaps substantial profits at the expense of the non-breaching party, returning these gains becomes a matter of fairness and justice. It is against this background that the SPC also sells out another rule in its 2023 judicial interpretation.

1001. Where the expected benefits that the non-breaching party could have obtained after contract performance cannot be determined under the provisions of Articles 60 and 61 of this interpretation, the court may consider the following factors to determine the damages: the benefits gained by the breaching party due to the breach, the degree of fault of the breaching party, and other circumstances of the

937. *Ibid.*
938. *Ibid.*
939. Article 1182 CC.

breach. In determining the damages, the court should adhere to the principles of fairness and good faith, ensuring that the outcome aligns with equitable and ethical standards.[940]

1002. This rule represents a significant step toward addressing the challenges of evidence insufficiency and profit-based breaches in contract disputes. Allowing courts to disgorge profits obtained through breach reinforces the principle that contracts are to be honoured and prevents unjust enrichment by the breaching party.

1003. Articles 60, 61, and 62 of the SPC Interpretation of the General Provisions of the Contract Book of the Civil Code collectively form the rule system for calculating anticipated benefits. These articles establish a hierarchical framework for the application, ensuring clarity and precision in assessing damages for lost anticipated benefits. Specifically, Article 60 outlines the general rules for calculating anticipated benefits and applies to all types of contracts. Article 61 provides a special provision for calculating anticipated benefits in continuous and periodic contracts, such as leases or supply agreements.

1004. As a specific rule, it takes precedence over the general rules in Article 60 and must be applied first when the contract type falls within its scope. Article 62 acts as a residual rule for cases where anticipated benefits cannot be determined under Articles 60 or 61. It introduces the concept of 'gains from breach', allowing the court to consider the profits the breaching party earned through their violation as a basis for compensating the non-breaching party.

1005. The non-breaching party may choose the appropriate method based on the specific circumstances. Prioritising specific provisions, offering flexible general rules, and providing a residual mechanism ensures both legal certainty and fairness in addressing the economic consequences of contractual breaches.

IV. Reliance Damages and Restitution Damages

1006. In addition to expectation damages, Chinese law also recognises reliance damages[941] and restitution damages[942] as alternative bases for recovery in special circumstances. Reliance losses refer to compensation for expenses incurred in reliance on the contract. These aim to restore the non-defaulting party to the position they were in before entering the contract if expectation damages are too speculative or uncertain. Restitution losses mean recovery of any benefits unjustly enriched by the breaching party at the expense of the non-defaulting party. This applies in situations where enforcing performance or expectation damages would be inequitable. The non-defaulting party generally has the right to choose the remedy they deem

940. Article 62 the SPC International on the Contract Book (2023).
941. Article 500 CC.
942. Article 157 CC.

most appropriate if performance does not conform to the agreement – whether expectation, reliance, or restitution damages – subject to the court's approval.

1007. The compensatory purpose of damages under Chinese law emphasises the expectation of losses to uphold the contractual bargain. By including categories such as non-performance loss, incidental loss, consequential loss, and loss of profit, Chinese law ensures comprehensive protection for the non-defaulting party. At the same time, the recognition of reliance and restitution damages, coupled with judicial discretion, demonstrates the system's adaptability to unique cases, promoting fairness and efficiency.

§5. Security Deposits

1008. Chinese law's position on deposits (定金) reflects the principle of ensuring security for contractual obligations. A deposit agreement is valid only when the deposit is actually delivered, distinguishing it from a mere promise to provide security.[943] This requirement ensures clarity and minimises disputes about whether the deposit obligation was fulfilled. Parties are free to agree on the deposit amount, but it cannot exceed 20% of the value of the main contract.[944] This limitation prevents excessive deposits that could impose an unreasonable burden on one party and ensures proportionality relative to the main obligation. Any amount exceeding the 20% threshold has no legal effect,[945] aligning with the principle of proportionality and protecting the debtor from excessive liability. If the actual delivered deposit differs from the agreed amount, it is deemed a modification of the original agreement.[946] This flexibility acknowledges the practical realities of transactions and allows parties to adapt their agreements without requiring a formal renegotiation or invalidating the deposit's legal effect.

1009. When the debtor performs their obligations, the deposit should either be credited towards the payment or returned to the debtor, depending on the terms of the agreement.[947] The deposit serves as a security for performance, incentivising parties to fulfil their obligations. If the party providing the deposit defaults, resulting in the contract's purpose being unfulfilled, the other party may retain the deposit as compensation.[948] Conversely, if the receiving party defaults, causing the contract's purpose to be unfulfilled, they must return the deposit plus an equal amount as compensation.[949] The Civil Code establishes the failure to achieve the contract's purpose as a prerequisite for applying the penalty provisions related to deposits and

943. Paragraph 1 of Art. 586 CC.
944. Paragraph 2 of Art. 586 CC.
945. *Ibid.*
946. *Ibid.*
947. Article 587 CC.
948. *Ibid.*
949. *Ibid.*

does not permit parties to agree otherwise freely. This approach effectively narrows the scope of application for deposit penalty provisions and grants the courts wide discretion.

1010. For instance, consider a commercial lease contract stipulating that the landowner must deliver the leased property to the lessee by 1 August 2024. The contract also includes a clause stating that if the landowner delays delivery by more than one month, they must return double the deposit paid by the lessee. If the prerequisite of failure to achieve the contract's purpose were not required, any delay of more than one month would automatically obligate the landowner to return double the deposit, as stipulated. However, under the rule introduced by the Civil Code, ambiguity arises as to whether a one-month delay constitutes a fundamental breach, thereby frustrating the purpose of the contract. This uncertainty grants courts the discretion to determine whether the penalty clause should be enforced and whether double the deposit must be returned.

1011. If both parties commit breaches that prevent the achievement of the contract's purpose, the court will not uphold the application of the deposit penalty provisions by either party.[950] This ensures that the legal system does not reward or penalise one party disproportionately when both are responsible for the failure of the contract. It aligns with the principle of proportionality, avoiding unfair outcomes when both parties are significantly at fault. However, if one party's breach is minor, while the other party's breach is such that it prevents the realisation of the contract's purpose, the court will support the minor breaching party's claim to apply the deposit penalty provisions.[951] The court will not accept the defence of the party whose breach frustrated the contract's purpose, even if they argue that the minor breaching party also committed a breach.[952] By allowing the minor breaching party to invoke the deposit penalty, the rationale of this rule lies in that liability is allocated fairly in line with the severity of the breaches. This approach also reflects the principle of fairness, where parties should not exploit minor breaches as a defence to avoid liability for their own significant breaches. The rule provides clear standards for courts to assess the severity and impact of breaches, reducing ambiguity in decision making.

1012. It is worth noting that if the failure to conclude the commercial housing sale contract is due to reasons not attributable to either party, the developer is not required to pay double the deposit as a penalty.[953] Instead, the developer is only obligated to return the full deposit to the purchaser. If the failure to conclude the contract results from a breach by one or both parties, the deposit penalty rules apply,[954] i.e., the breaching party forfeits the deposit (if the purchaser breaches) or

950. Paragraph 1 of Art. 68 of the SPC Interpretation on the Contract Book (2023).
951. *Ibid.*
952. *Ibid.*
953. Article 4 of the SPC Interpretation on Certain Issues Concerning the Application of Law in Trying Cases Involving Disputes over Contracts on Sale of Commercial Real Estate (2003, 2020 revision).
954. *Ibid.*

returns double the deposit (if the developer breaches). This rule ensures a proportional response to contractual disputes in commercial housing sale contracts. It avoids penalising parties for non-performance caused by uncontrollable factors. It also enforces deposit penalties where breaches occur, reinforcing the deposit's function as both a security and penalty mechanism.

1013. Where the parties have not explicitly agreed on the deposit's nature (e.g., whether it serves as a penalty deposit under Article 587), and one party seeks to invoke the penalty provisions, the court will not support the claim.[955] This ensures that deposits without an explicitly defined legal nature are treated as ordinary contractual arrangements rather than penalty deposits. The principle of party autonomy and the need for clarity in agreements are upheld, preventing speculative or unilateral claims about the deposit's intended purpose. This provision complements Article 587 by ensuring that the penalty deposit mechanism is applied only when the parties have expressly agreed on its nature. Where the deposit is explicitly agreed to have the nature of a penalty deposit, but the type of deposit (e.g., default deposit, advance payment, or another type) is undefined or ambiguous, the court will interpret it as a default penalty deposit.[956] This approach balances party autonomy with judicial oversight, ensuring that deposits remain a practical and proportional tool in contract enforcement. This interpretation protects the non-breaching party's expectation that the deposit serves as security for performance.

1014. When the parties agree to use a deposit as security for concluding a contract, and one party either refuses to finalise the contract or engages in bad faith during negotiations, leading to the failure to conclude the contract, the court should support the other party's request to enforce the penalty provisions under Article 587 of the Civil Code.[957] The deposit, in this scenario, serves as security for the commitment to finalise a contract. This rule incentivises parties to act responsibly during pre-contractual negotiations and ensures they are held accountable for unjustified failures to fulfil their commitments. It deters opportunistic behaviour, such as stringing along negotiations without genuine intent to conclude the contract. By holding parties accountable for refusing to conclude contracts or acting in bad faith, it upholds the principles of fairness and good faith in contractual relationships.

1015. If the parties agree that the payment of a deposit is a condition for a contract's formation or effectiveness, but the party required to pay the deposit fails to do so, and the main obligations of the contract have been fully performed and accepted by the other party, the court should consider the contract as formed or effective from the time the other party accepted the performance.[958] The failure to deliver the deposit would, under normal circumstances, mean that the contract does not take effect or is not formed. However, exceptions arise when the primary intent

955. Paragraph 1 of Art. 67 of the SPC Interpretation on the Contract Book (2023).
956. *Ibid.*
957. Paragraph 2 of Art. 67 of the SPC Interpretation on the Contract Book (2023).
958. Paragraph 3 of Art. 67 of the SPC Interpretation on the Contract Book (2023).

of the contract is fulfilled through the performance and acceptance of its main obligations. If the primary obligations under the contract have been performed by one party (e.g., delivery of goods, provision of services), this demonstrates a clear intent to perform the contract. The acceptance of performance by the other party reinforces mutual consent to the contractual terms, effectively overriding the initial failure to meet the deposit condition. It prioritises the substantive execution of the contract over the failure to meet a formal condition (the deposit).

1016. Courts scrutinise the proportionality of the deposit amount relative to the main contract and enforce the 20% cap. The 20% cap strikes a balance between securing the creditor's rights and protecting the debtor from undue financial strain, fostering equitable and sustainable business practices. If disputes arise regarding whether the deposit was actually delivered, the party claiming the deposit's validity bears the burden of proof. Since the deposit contract only becomes effective upon actual delivery, retaining evidence of payment is crucial for ensuring enforceability. By capping the deposit amount and linking its validity to the actual delivery, the law provides clarity and predictability, encouraging compliance and minimising disputes.

1017. When parties agree to both liquidated damages and a deposit, the non-breaching party may choose to invoke either the liquidated damages clause or the deposit clause in the event of a breach.[959] The ability to choose between liquidated damages and the deposit provides flexibility for the non-breaching party to pursue the remedy that best aligns with their interests.

1018. Unlike liquidated damages, the amount of a deposit penalty cannot be adjusted at the court's discretion. If the deposit is insufficient to cover the losses caused by the breach, the non-breaching party may also request compensation for the portion of the losses that exceed the amount of the deposit.[960] This rule ensures that the deposit does not cap the non-breaching party's recovery, preserving their right to full compensation for actual losses. The non-breaching party must provide evidence of the losses exceeding the deposit amount, aligning with principles of procedural fairness and evidentiary requirements.

1019. While the non-breaching party can claim additional compensation, this is subject to reasonable loss calculation. Courts will assess whether the claimed losses are reasonable and directly attributable to the breach. The non-breaching party cannot claim both liquidated damages and retain the deposit simultaneously, preventing double recovery.

959. Paragraph 1 of Art. 588 CC.
960. Paragraph 2 of Art. 588 CC.

§6. Creditor's Unjustified Refusal or Delay to Accept Performance

1020. If the debtor performs their obligation in accordance with the agreement and the creditor refuses to accept the performance without a valid reason, the debtor may request the creditor to compensate for the increased costs incurred.[961] During the period of the creditor's delay in accepting performance, the debtor is not required to pay interest.[962] The rule governing creditor's delay (受领迟延) and unjustified refusal to accept performance (拒绝受领) provides important protections for debtors, ensuring that creditors cannot unfairly hinder the fulfilment of contractual obligations. This framework addresses the imbalance that occurs when a creditor's refusal to cooperate imposes unnecessary costs or burdens on the debtor.

1021. If the debtor performs their obligations as agreed, but the creditor unjustifiably refuses to accept performance, the debtor can claim compensation for any additional costs incurred due to the delay. These costs might include storage fees, transportation expenses, or other direct financial losses caused by the creditor's failure to cooperate. During the period of the creditor's refusal or delay, the debtor is exempt from paying interest on any outstanding monetary obligations. This provision prevents the creditor from benefitting financially from their own wrongful delay in accepting performance.

1022. This rule applies broadly to reciprocal obligations, where performance by one party is contingent upon cooperation by the other. The debtor must have fulfilled their obligation in line with the terms of the contract, including time, place, and method of performance. The rule does not apply if the debtor's performance is defective or inconsistent with the agreement.

1023. The rule safeguards debtors from bearing the financial burden of the creditor's unjustified non-cooperation. It reinforces the principle of good faith (诚信原则) in contractual relationships, emphasising that creditors must not obstruct performance unreasonably. By exempting debtors from paying interest during the creditor's delay, the rule prevents creditors from profiting at the expense of the debtor. This ensures that creditors cannot use delay tactics to gain an unfair financial advantage.

1024. The United Nations Convention on Contracts for the International Sale of Goods (CISG) includes a related principle: a party cannot rely on the other party's non-performance if their own actions or omissions caused it.[963]

1025. Determining the 'increased costs' attributable to the creditor's delay can be complex, especially in high-value or time-sensitive contracts. Judicial interpretations could clarify what constitutes recoverable additional costs to reduce disputes

961. Paragraph 1 of Art. 589 CC.
962. Paragraph 2 of Art. 589 CC.
963. Article 80 of the United Nations Convention on Contracts for International Sale of Goods (CISG).

and ensure fair application. While interest suspension applies to monetary obligations, this may not address other forms of damages or penalties associated with delayed performance. Parties should explicitly outline the consequences of a creditor's delay in their contracts to avoid ambiguity and reliance solely on statutory provisions.

§7. Exceptio Non Adimpleti Contractus (The Defence of Non-performance by the Other Party)

1026. Articles 525, 526 and 527 of the Civil Code provide legal standards for simultaneous performance defences, prior performance defences, and anticipatory breach defences, establishing a framework for resolving disputes where parties invoke these defences to suspend their performance obligations. These three articles are set out below.

1027. Simultaneous performance defence is available when parties owe reciprocal obligations. One party may withhold its performance until the other has fulfilled its corresponding obligation.[964] This defence aims to ensure mutual security in performance, especially in contracts with interdependent obligations.

1028. Prior performance defence arises where one party's obligation is due first; the counterparty may withhold performance if the first party fails to fulfil its obligation.[965] This defence protects the counterparty from performing when there is no assurance of receiving the corresponding benefit.

1029. Anticipatory breach defence is invoked when a party suspends performance if there is clear evidence that the other party will fail to perform due to insolvency or other severe risks.[966] This defence is based on commercial reasonableness and the principle of good faith.

964. Article 525 CC provides that where both parties have obligations to one another, and there is no order of priority in respect of the performance of obligations, the parties shall perform the obligations simultaneously. Each party is entitled to reject the other party's demand for performance prior to the performance by the other party. If one party's performance of the obligations is not in conformity with the agreement, the other party is entitled to reject its demand for corresponding performance.

965. Article 526 CC provides that where both parties have obligations to each other, and there is an order of priority in respect of the performance, if the party who is to perform first fails to perform, the party who is to perform next in line is entitled to reject the other party's demand for performance. If the performance of the obligations of the party who is to perform first is not in conformity with the agreement, the party who is to perform next in line is entitled to reject the other party's demand for corresponding performance.

966. Article 527 CC provides that the party who is required to perform first may suspend its performance if it has conclusive evidence showing that the other party is under any of the following circumstances: (1) where its business operations have seriously deteriorated; (2) where it has engaged in the transfer of assets or withdrawal of funds for evading debts; (3) where it has lost its business creditworthiness;(4) where there is any other circumstance which causes or may cause it to lose its ability to perform. Where a party suspends performance without conclusive evidence, it shall be liable for breach of contract.

1030. Invoking a defence solely as a pretext to avoid performance is inconsistent with the principle of good faith under Article 7 of the Civil Code. Courts may deny the defence if the refusal to perform appears opportunistic or motivated by bad faith. In practice, disputes often arise when a debtor refuses to perform a primary obligation, citing the counterparty's failure to perform secondary or non-primary obligations, such as delivering documents or materials unrelated to the core subject matter of the contract. Contracts often do not clearly distinguish between primary and secondary obligations, leading to disputes about their relative importance. For instance, a seller might argue that failing to deliver minor technical documentation does not justify the buyer's refusal to pay for the main goods. A buyer might insist that incomplete documentation undermines their ability to use the goods as intended, thus justifying withholding payment. Using a minor non-performance (e.g., delayed delivery of non-critical documents) to refuse significant performance (e.g., full payment for delivered goods) may violate principles of fairness and good faith. Here, a proportionality test is employed.

1031. Courts usually assess whether the obligation cited is essential to the contract's purpose. Non-performance of secondary obligations typically does not justify withholding performance unless the breach significantly makes it impossible to achieve the purpose of the contract or the parties have otherwise agreed to prioritise the non-major obligation.[967] A debtor's refusal to perform must be proportionate to the counterparty's non-performance. This rule highlights the principle of proportionality and the importance of distinguishing between major and non-major obligations. Courts aim to prevent disproportionate withholding of major obligations for minor breaches, aligning with principles of good faith and contractual fairness. The exceptions ensure flexibility where non-major obligations are critical to achieving the contract's purpose, reflecting a pragmatic approach.[968] In common law, this aligns with doctrines like substantial performance, where minor breaches typically do not justify withholding performance unless they undermine the contract's fundamental purpose.[969]

1032. If a plaintiff sues for performance and the defendant successfully invokes the simultaneous performance defence without filing a counterclaim, the court will order both parties to perform simultaneously. The judgment will specify that enforcement actions against the defendant can proceed only after the plaintiff has

---

967. Paragraph 1 of Art.31 of the SPC Interpretation on the Contract Book (2023).
968. *Company A Ltd., Company B Ltd., Company C Ltd., and Company D Ltd. v. Guangzhou Company*, Supreme People's Court (2021) SPC Min Zhong No.1079; 某甲有限公司、某乙有限公司、某丙有限公司、某丁有限公司、广州公司股权转让纠纷民事二审民， 最高人民法院(2021)最高法民终1079号. In this case, the SPC held that 'the characteristics of ancillary obligations lie in the varying degree of cooperation required between the parties as the contractual relationship evolves. Therefore, whether a breach of ancillary obligations affects the achievement of the contract's purpose cannot be determined universally. Instead, it should be assessed comprehensively, taking into account the progress of contract performance and the specific circumstances involved.'
969. MP Furmston, Cheshire, Fifoot & Furmston's Law of Contract ch. 18(17th ed, OUP 2017) ; *Hoenig v. Isaacs* [1952] EWCA Civ 6.

fulfilled their obligations.[970] By tying the defendant's performance to the plaintiff's fulfilment of their obligation, the court maintains mutual security in contractual performance. The enforcement mechanism reduces the risk of either party being left without recourse, balancing the rights and obligations of both sides. Chinese law's explicit focus on enforcement mechanics provides greater procedural predictability.

1033. Where the defendant files a counterclaim in addition to invoking the simultaneous performance defence, the court will order both parties to perform their obligations simultaneously and specify that either party may apply for enforcement, but enforcement against the other party will only proceed after the applicant fulfils their obligation.[971] The simultaneous performance judgment ensures that all disputes between the parties are resolved in a single proceeding. The enforcement mechanism further emphasises reciprocity, reducing potential enforcement disputes.

1034. When the plaintiff sues for performance, and the defendant invokes the prior performance defence, if the defence is upheld, the court will dismiss the plaintiff's claim. However, this dismissal does not preclude the plaintiff from re-filing the lawsuit after fulfilling their obligation.[972] This provision reinforces the importance of fulfilling prior obligations in sequential performance relationships. The dismissal prevents premature lawsuits and incentivises the plaintiff to perform their obligations promptly. The option to re-file ensures access to justice while prioritising contractual order.

1035. Article 31 of the SPC Judicial Interpretation provides a detailed framework for addressing disputes involving simultaneous and sequential performance obligations. By distinguishing between major and non-major obligations, integrating defences and counterclaims, and specifying enforcement mechanics, it reflects principles of reciprocity, proportionality, and procedural fairness. There are five elements in Article 31.

First, the simultaneous performance defence requires that the two obligations between the parties must be corresponding and interdependent. A party can withhold performance only when the obligations are reciprocal and their fulfilment is conditional on the other party's corresponding performance.[973] This aligns with the principle of reciprocity (Gegenseitigkeitsprinzip) in civil law systems, where mutual obligations must be balanced to ensure fairness and security.

1036. Second, for cases involving the simultaneous performance defence, the court may issue a counter-performance judgment. This judgment conditions the defendant's obligation to perform on the plaintiff's fulfilment of their corresponding

970. Paragraph 2 of Art. 31 of the SPC Interpretation on the Contract Book (2023).
971. *Ibid.*
972. Paragraph 3 of Art. 31 of the SPC Interpretation on the Contract Book (2023).
973. *Chongqing Jintang Real Estate Development Co., Ltd. v. Chongqing Nengtou Real Estate Co., Ltd.* Supreme People's Court (2019) SPC Min Zhong No.454; 重庆金唐房地产开发有限公司、重庆能投置业有限公司合资、合作开发房地产合同纠纷二审民事判决书， 最高人民法院（2019）最高法民终454号.

obligation. The judgment explicitly orders both parties to perform simultaneously. This system is rooted in the principle of good faith (bona fides), ensuring that neither party is unfairly disadvantaged or placed in a position of uncertainty. By conditioning performance, the court enforces the contractual balance while protecting both parties' interests.

1037. Third, the rule distinguishes between the mere invocation of the simultaneous performance defence and situations where the defendant files a counterclaim. If a counterclaim is made, the court must address both parties' claims and issue a judgment requiring simultaneous performance by both sides. This distinction reflects the principle of procedural efficiency and ensures that courts address all related issues in a single proceeding. It also prevents the misuse of the defence to delay litigation or evade liability.

1038. Fourth, the law explicitly provides that counter-performance judgments serve as a basis for enforcement, and the court must specify this in the judgment. This ensures that the judgment can be executed without ambiguity. This reflects the principle of certainty in enforcement, a cornerstone of civil law systems. Linking the judgment directly to enforceability reduces post-judgment disputes and ensures that the defence is not used as a stalling tactic.

1039. Fifth, it also addresses prior performance defences, allowing the court to issue judgments requiring the party with the earlier performance obligation to fulfil their duty as a condition for the other party's subsequent performance. This is grounded in the sequential order of obligations (Leistungspflichten) and reflects the principle of fair risk allocation. It prevents unjust enrichment and ensures that parties fulfil their obligations in the agreed order.

1040. In view of the above rules, it is suggested that parties should clearly define primary and secondary obligations in contracts, specifying the consequences of non-performance for each. For example, a sales contract might state that delivery of goods is independent of ancillary documentation. The party invoking a defence should demonstrate how the counterparty's failure to fulfil a secondary obligation materially affects the overall contract.

§8. Liquidated Damages and Penalty Clauses

I. Concept

1041. Under Chinese law, there are three related yet different legal concepts, namely, liquidated damages, penalty clauses, and punitive damages. Both the notions of liquidated damages and punitive damages are provided in the Chinese Civil Code.[974] Liquidated damages refer to a pre-determined monetary amount

974. For example, the notion of punitive damages was provided in Art. 1095 CC: Where there is an intentional infringement of another's intellectual property rights, if the circumstances are serious,

agreed upon by contracting parties as compensation in the event of a breach of contract. These damages are typically set forth in the contract itself, allowing the parties to avoid lengthy litigation over the actual losses incurred from the breach.

1042. The punitive damages can be invoked where there is an infringement in areas such as product liability,[975] intellectual property rights,[976] and environmental protection.[977] Punitive damages are distinct from compensatory damages intended to make the plaintiff whole for the loss suffered. Punitive damages go beyond compensation and are aimed to punish the defendant and deter similar conduct. It is mainly applicable in the tort realm. Nonetheless, the penalty clauses, while they were widely discussed in the academic community[978] and legal practitioners, have not yet been specifically addressed in the Civil Code or the SPC Interpretation on the Contract Book.

1043. Penalty clauses refer to contractual provisions that impose a financial penalty on a breaching party in the event of non-performance or other specified breaches. The financial penalty amount exceeds the actual financial loss caused by the breach. These clauses are commonly used to ensure compliance with contractual obligations, provide certainty regarding potential compensation, and serve as a deterrent against non-performance. One can immediately notice that the notions of penalty clauses and liquidated damages share a great deal of commonalities.

1044. From a functional perspective, there are two major types of liquidated damages under Chinese law, namely, compensatory (or restorative) damages and penalty clauses. Penalty clauses primarily serve as a performance guarantee and economic sanction. By imposing an economic deterrent and psychological pressure on the debtor, penalty clauses encourage good faith and diligent performance of contractual obligations. In contrast, compensatory damages (liquidated damages) represent an estimate of the anticipated damages agreed upon by both parties at the contract's inception. The purpose is to lower potential litigation costs in the event of a breach by pre-setting a damages amount, thereby avoiding disputes over the precise extent and value of actual losses.

---

the victim of the tort shall be entitled to seek corresponding punitive damages. The notion of liquidated damages was provided in Arts 179 and 585 CC.

975. Article 1207 CC specifically addresses product liability, stating that if a product defect causes death or serious injury and the manufacturer or seller is found to have acted intentionally or with gross negligence, the injured party may claim punitive damages in addition to compensatory damages. This is particularly relevant in cases where the safety of consumers is severely compromised due to the actions of manufacturers or sellers.

976. Article 1185 CC: Where there is an intentional infringement of another's intellectual property rights, if the circumstances are serious, the victim of the tort shall be entitled to seek corresponding punitive damages.

977. For intentional environmental pollution and ecological destruction by a tortfeasor, punitive damages can be sought. (Art. 1232 CC) Additionally, an environmental public interest litigation system has been established to restore the ecological environment, along with a state compensation system for ecological damage.

978. Shiyuan Han, Contract Law 824-826 (4th edn, Law Press China 2018); Haiyan Xu, Interpretation and Reconstruction of the Exception-Based Reduction System for Punitive Liquidated Damages: A Balanced Perspective on Contractual Freedom and Contractual Justice, 44 Law Journal 85 (2023).

1045. Compensatory damages aid in overcoming the evidentiary and calculation challenges associated with property damage claims, reducing the creditor's burden of proof. By establishing an estimated amount of damages in advance, compensatory damages simplify the process of claiming losses and ensure that the outcome aligns with the intent of 'making the creditor whole' – as if the breach had not occurred.

II. Penalty Clause

1046. The distinction between penalty clauses and compensatory damages reflects a broader intent in contract law to balance enforcement with efficiency.[979] Penalty clauses not only deter breaches but reinforce the principles of trust and good faith, which are especially important in contexts where performance cannot be easily substituted or losses are difficult to quantify. By adding an element of economic consequence beyond mere compensation, punitive damages encourage parties to take contractual obligations seriously, potentially minimising the likelihood of a breach.

1047. Conversely, compensatory damages focus on minimising disputes over the amount owed after a breach. This approach recognises that proving actual losses can be complex, especially when damages are non-quantifiable or difficult to attribute directly to the breach. By agreeing to liquidated damages, parties essentially agree to a simplified, efficient method of addressing potential losses, promoting contractual certainty and reducing post-breach litigation.

1048. The pre-set target for compensatory damages aligns with the broader goal of contract law to 'put the injured party in the position they would have been in if the contract had been performed'. This restorative intent demonstrates the function of compensatory damages as a tool for efficient, fair resolution, ensuring that the contract can achieve its economic purpose without prolonged litigation or uncertainty.

1049. In summary, the choice between penalty clauses and compensatory damages reflects strategic decisions about enforcement, deterrence, and efficiency within contractual relationships. Courts generally respect this choice, adjusting only where damages appear unreasonable or disproportionate, thus supporting a balance between deterrence, fairness, and practical enforceability in contract law.

979. In English law, the key to distinguishing penalties and liquidated damages is the parties' intentions when they create the contract. In *Cavendish Square Holding BV (Appellant) v. Talal El Makdessi (Respondent)* [2015] UKSC 67, the test to identify whether the contract clause is a penalty clause or a liquidated damages clause requires two criteria: 1) whether there is a detriment on the contract-breaker 'out of all proportions', which means that whether the detriment was 'exorbitant or unconscionable' ; 2) Whether there was a legitimate interest in doing so. The court is 'looking for a very high degree of disproportionality before they will label the clause as a penalty'.

1050. Nonetheless, distinguishing between compensatory and punitive functions of liquidated damages can sometimes be complex, especially when contract terms are ambiguously worded or when both functions are arguably present. When it is challenging to differentiate the nature and function of the liquidated damages clearly, it should be presumed to be a penalty clause. By presuming liquidated damages to be punitive, courts prioritise deterrence and accountability for breaches. This presumption may also streamline judicial decisions by providing a default stance that favours enforcing contractual terms as a form of penalty unless compelling evidence indicates a solely compensatory intent.

1051. The legal rationale for the principle that punitive liquidated damages should not be subject to judicial reduction.[980] First, penalty clauses serve as a deterrent by imposing a financial consequence that exceeds mere compensation for actual losses. By upholding the full amount of penalty damages without reduction, the law reinforces the idea that breaching contractual obligations comes with significant repercussions. When parties willingly agree to a penalty in a contract, they exercise their freedom to structure remedies that align with their expectations and risk assessments. Respecting the agreed-upon punitive amount underscores the principle of autonomy, allowing parties to determine the level of deterrence appropriate for their relationship and to agree on the terms that best serve their interests.

1052. In addition, penalty clauses often serve to address non-tangible consequences of a breach, such as reputational harm, disruption of business relationships, or lost opportunities. These types of damages are difficult to quantify precisely but are nonetheless real and impactful. By not allowing reductions in penalty amounts, the law acknowledges these broader impacts and provides a remedy that considers both direct and indirect consequences of the breach, supporting the non-breaching party's broader interests.

1053. Furthermore, if penalty amounts were open to reduction based on the actual loss, it would frustrate the very purpose of the liquidated damages being a pre-estimate of loss, saving hassle for judicial calculation when a breach occurs. When Chinese courts readily reduce the agreed sum by the parties, they would be drawn into detailed evaluations of proportionality and fairness, potentially leading to inconsistent outcomes. This would invite arbitrary interventions and cause unpredictability, thus not creating a business-friendly legal environment.

1054. Finally, by imposing a penalty that cannot easily be reduced, the law incentivises parties to act in good faith, knowing that a breach will result in

---

980. This view has been taken by some Chinese courts, such as *Qingdao Wuchan Haohai International Trade Co., Ltd. v. Wen'an County Baoying International Trade Co., Ltd and Others*, Intermediate People's Court of Langfang Hebei (2020) Ji 10 Min Zhong No.3862; 青岛物产浩海国际贸易有限公司、文安县宝盈国际贸易有限公司、潘少峰买卖合同纠纷二审民事判决书， 河北省廊坊市中级人民法院（2020)冀10民终3862号案.

enforceable financial consequences. This legal certainty reinforces the integrity ofcontractual relationships, where parties can rely on the agreed penalties to safeguard against misconduct. Penalty serves a moral and social function by underscoring society's intolerance for breaches of contract. Contracts represent mutual trust and cooperation, and violating them undermines these principles. Upholding the penalty clauses reflects a public policy stance that values the sanctity of contracts and seeks to deter behaviour that would erode this foundational element of commerce and social interactions.

1055. In summary, the principle of non-reduction for punitive liquidated damages supports both the enforcement of contracts and broader social and economic objectives. By protecting the full scope of punitive damages, the law sends a clear message that contractual breaches are unacceptable and that penalties, when agreed upon, should be respected in full to ensure fairness, accountability, and the proper functioning of the legal system.

III. Adjusting Liquidated Damages

1056. Nonetheless, this does not mean that liquidated damages or penalties once agreed upon, are immune from challenge in court or arbitration proceedings. Courts should have the discretion to review these clauses, though with a degree of deference. If the penalty is found to be exorbitant or unconscionable, the courts should intervene by reducing it in proportion to the actual loss suffered by the non-breaching party. Non-reduction should be the general rule, with reduction as the exception.

1057. Nevertheless, as it stands, the judicial position on penalty clauses in China emphasises fairness and the principle of compensation. Courts have the authority and wide discretion to adjust agreed amounts to prevent unjust enrichment or punitive outcomes. The court or arbitration institution, upon the request of a party, can increase or decrease the penalty to a reasonable level based on the actual loss.[981] Parties are permitted to agree in advance on a set amount of liquidated damages payable in the event of a breach or to establish a formula for calculating the compensation owed for breach-related losses.[982] It also mandates that, even after paying liquidated damages for delayed performance, the breaching party must still fulfil their contractual obligations.

1058. Additionally, the SPC Judicial Interpretation defines excessive liquidated damages as those exceeding 30% of the actual losses incurred.[983] The liquidated

981. Paragraph 2 of Art. 585 CC.
982. Paragraph 1 of Art. 585 CC.
983. Paragraph 2 of Art. 65 of the SPC Interpretation on the Contract Book (2023).

damages are subject to the adjustment rules and emphasise the burden of proof on the breaching party.[984] If the non-breaching party claims that the agreed liquidated damages are reasonable, they must provide corresponding evidence to support their claim.[985]

1059. The court's discretionary power is alarmingly extensive. The request can be made by way of claim, counterclaim or defence.[986] In addition, even if the breaching party fails to appear in court, resulting in a default judgment, the court can still make appropriate adjustments if it finds that the agreed standard for liquidated damages is excessively high.[987]

1060. Furthermore, the court may still adjust liquidated damages even if the contract explicitly states that no adjustments are allowed.[988] The court will not uphold a claim based solely on such a contractual provision.

1061. Finally, procedure-wise, a party requests liquidated damages for breach of contract, and the opposing party raises defences like invalidity of the contract, lack of breach, or absence of losses but does not request an adjustment to the liquidated damages. It mandates that the court clarify (释明) whether the party seeks an adjustment of excessive liquidated damages if their defences fail.[989] If the first-instance court finds the defence to be valid and does not provide clarification, but the second-instance court determines that liquidated damages should be awarded, the second-instance court may directly provide clarification.[990] The appellate court allows a defendant who, due to objective reasons, failed to attend the first-instance proceedings but participates in the second-instance proceedings to request a reduction of liquidated damages. The appellate court, after considering evidence, cross-examination, and arguments from both parties, may lawfully adjust the liquidated damages if deemed appropriate.[991]

---

984. Paragraph 2 of Art. 64 of the SPC Interpretation on the Contract Book (2023).
985. *Ibid.*
986. Paragraph 1 of Art. 64 of the SPC Interpretation on the Contract Book (2023).
987. *Wang Yuanyuan v. Zhang Wei*, People's Court of Chaoyang District, Beijing (2016) Jing 0105 Min Chu No.33953; 王源源与张伟房屋买卖合同纠纷一审民事判决书, 北京市朝阳区人民法院(2016)京0105民初33953号; The Sixth Circuit Court of the SPC, Adjudication Rules of the Sixth Circuit Court of the SPC (People's Court Press 2022).
988. Paragraph 3 of Art. 64 of the SPC Interpretation on the Contract Book (2023).
989. Paragraph 1 of Art. 66 of the SPC Interpretation on the Contract Book (2023).
990. *Ibid. Chen v. Liu*, People's Court of Chaoyang District, Beijing (2016) Jing 0105 Min Chu No. 32945; 陈某与刘某, 北京市朝阳区人民法院（2016）京0105民初32945号民事判决; *Liu v. Chen*, No.3 Intermediate People's Court of Beijing (2016) Jing 03 Min Zhong No. 13939, 刘某与陈某合同纠纷二审民事判决书, 北京市第三中级人民法院 （2016）京03民终13939号. The courts would have addressed the legal issues presented, applying the relevant laws and considering the facts of the case.
991. Paragraph 2 of Art. 66 of the SPC Interpretation on the Contract Book (2023).

1062. By asking the breaching party if they wish to request an adjustment, the court ensures that no issue is overlooked due to procedural errors or lack of awareness on the part of the litigants. If the first-instance court did not provide clarification, the appellate court can address the issue directly, avoiding the need for remand. This promotes efficiency in resolving disputes while ensuring the parties' rights are preserved.

1063. However, appellate courts may face added responsibilities if the first-instance court does not clarify. Allowing significant adjustments in the second-instance proceedings may undermine the authority and finality of first-instance judgments, leading to a perception that such judgments are provisional.

1064. More to the point, by actively prompting parties to request an adjustment, the court risks overstepping its neutral role and interfering with party autonomy. There is a risk of diluting party autonomy by judicially steering the litigation process. After all, parties bear the primary responsibility for presenting their claims and defences. The breaching party, prompted by the court, may raise an adjustment claim even when the agreed damages were reasonable, leading to unnecessary delays and abuse of judicial resources. That said, introducing new arguments or evidence regarding liquidated damages in the second-instance proceedings can prolong the appellate process, increasing the workload for appellate courts and potentially delaying justice.

1065. Further, defendants might exploit the rule by deliberately skipping the first-instance proceedings, claiming objective reasons later, and raising critical defences in the appellate stage to delay judgment or gain leverage. Courts may differ in their assessment of what constitutes 'objective reasons' for absence, leading to inconsistent application and uncertainty for litigants.

1066. Finally, perhaps more concerning than anything else, if courts inconsistently apply the rule or fail to clarify the issue sufficiently, it may lead to appeals or claims of procedural unfairness.

IV. Factors Affecting the Adjustment of Liquidated Damages

1067. When deciding whether to reduce an agreed sum at the request of a party, the court must consider several key factors to ensure fairness and equity.[992] These factors include:

1. Actual losses caused by the breach: the court will assess the proven losses suffered by the non-breaching party, including direct losses and any consequential

992. Paragraph 1 of Art. 65 of the SPC Interpretation on the Contract Book (2023).

damages that can be substantiated. This serves as the baseline for determining whether the agreed sum is excessive.[993] Chinese courts typically base their assessment of liquidated damages on actual losses combined with anticipated profits. After considering the agreed-upon amount of liquidated damages, the courts then exercise discretion to determine whether a reduction is necessary and, if so, the specific amount of reduction. When the stipulated liquidated damages exceed 30% of the actual loss or 20% of the principal sum in disputes, the courts often consider this to be excessively high in relation to the losses incurred.[994]

2. Nature of the contracting parties: the court considers the characteristics and bargaining positions of the parties, such as whether they are consumers or commercial entities, and evaluates any potential power imbalances that may have influenced the agreement.[995]
3. Type of transaction: the nature of the transaction plays a role, with complex, high-value contracts often justifying higher liquidated damages, while routine agreements may not warrant excessive penalties.[996]
4. Performance of the contract: the degree to which the contract was performed is a relevant factor. For instance, partial or good faith performance by the breaching party might warrant a reduction of the agreed sum.[997] During contract performance, even in cases of breach, the court will take into account the breaching party's performance and efforts, as well as the impact of the breach on the non-breaching party, to make a reasonable adjustment to the liquidated damages.

---

993. *Guangdong Feigou Technology Co., Ltd. v. Shanghai Dianfan Intelligent Technology Co., Ltd.*, Supreme People's Court (2022) SPC Zhi Min Zhong No.108; 广东飞购科技有限公司、上海典泛智能科技有限公司 最高人民法院（2022）最高法知民终108号.
994. *Xinjiang Danlu Fashion Department Store Co., Ltd. V Xinjiang Guanghui Real Estate Development Co., Ltd.* Supreme People's Court (2020) SPC Min Shen No.6938; 新疆丹璐时尚百货有限公司、新疆广汇房地产开发有限公司房屋租赁合同纠纷再审审查与审判监督民事裁定书，最高人民法院（2020）最高法民申6938号民事裁定书.
995. *Haikou Telecom Urban Construction Investment Co., Ltd. v. Haikou Housing and Urban-Rural Development Burea, Supreme People's Court* (2016) SPC Min Zhong No.469; 海口电信城市建设投资有限公司与海口市人民政府、海口市住房和城乡建设局房屋租赁合同纠纷二审民事判决书，最高人民法院（2016）最高法民终469号; *Liu Lian v. Beijing Yigao Anjie Information Technology Co., Ltd.* No.1 Intermediate Court of Beijing (2016) Jing 01 Min Zhong No.6979; 刘恋诉北京益高安捷信息技术有限公司， 北京市第一中级人民法院（2016）京01民终6979号民事判决书.
996. *Li Chengjian v. Zhejiang Zhuojing Venture Capital Co., Ltd. Supreme People's Court* (2015) Min Shen Zi No.2593, 黎承健、浙江卓景创业投资有限公司与浙江卓景创业投资有限公司申请再审民事裁定书 最高人民法院 (2015)民申字第2593号.
997. *Wu Shanmeiand Li Yaosheng v. Liang Xinye and Song Hanzhi Supreme People's Court* (2016) SPC Min ZhongNo. 51, 吴善媚、李耀生与梁新业、宋汉之等股权转让纠纷二审民事判决书，最高人民法院（2016）最高法民终51号.

5. Degree of fault: the court evaluates the breaching party's level of fault, distinguishing between intentional, negligent, or minor breaches.[998] Intentional or bad-faith breaches will not result in a reduction in principle.[999]
6. The context of performance: external conditions, such as market fluctuations or unforeseen circumstances, may affect the reasonableness of the agreed sum and influence the court's decision.[1000]
7. Fairness and good faith: the court adheres to principles of fairness and good faith, seeking to balance the interests of both parties. It avoids allowing the non-breaching party to gain an unjustified advantage or excessive compensation.[1001] Courts carefully evaluate the evidence to determine the extent of each party's fault and adjust remedies accordingly. For example, the non-breaching party's failure to fulfil contractual duties, such as cooperation, can mitigate the breaching party's liability. By considering the contributory fault of both parties, courts ensure fairness in allocating liability and calculating damages.

1068. By carefully weighing these factors, the court determines whether the agreed sum aligns with the actual harm caused and the circumstances of the breach, ensuring that the outcome is just and proportionate.

1069. Consequently, the adjustment of liquidated damages is a common phenomenon in judicial practice, primarily manifesting as reductions rather than increases. In a study of 1,032 cases involving the adjustment of liquidated damages across three levels of courts in a certain municipality, the courts supported claims of excessive liquidated damages in 773 cases, accounting for a substantial 74.9% of the total.[1002] The fact that reductions are so commonly applied highlights a judicial preference for compensatory rather than punitive damages. By frequently intervening to lower damages, courts effectively signal that liquidated damages should not become a means of punishment disproportionate to the actual harm caused. This judicial practice reinforces the notion that, while parties have the autonomy to set liquidated damages, such autonomy is limited by overarching principles of fairness, ensuring that stipulated damages are reasonable and justifiable. However, the crux of the issue is to what extent the judicial reduction of the agreed sum by the party

---

998. *Datong Tianli Real Estate Development Co., Ltd. V Shanxi Tongzhiren Commercial Management Co., Ltd.* Supreme People's Court (2015) Min Yi Zhong Zi No.340; 大同市天力房地产开发有限责任公司诉山西同至人商业管理有限公司，最高人民法院（2015）民一终字第340号.
999. Paragraph 3 of Art. 65 of the SPC Interpretation on the Contract Book (2023); *Beijing Urban Construction Heavy Industry Co., Ltd. v. Beijing Longchang Weiye Trading Co., Ltd.,* No.2 Intermediate People's Court of Beijing(2017) Jing 02 Min Zhong No.8676 (SPC Guiding Case No.166); 北京城建重工有限公司与北京隆昌伟业贸易有限公司合同纠纷二审民事判决书， 北京市第二中级人民法院 (2017)京02民终8676号合同纠纷案 (最高院指导案例166号).
1000. Liming Wang and Hu Zhu, The Interpretation and Commentary of the SPC Interpretation concerning the General Principles of Contract Book of the Civil Code 620 (Renmin University Press 2024).
1001. *Shanghai Panda Interactive Entertainment Culture Co., Ltd. v. Li Cen and Kunshan Bo'aiyou Information Technology Co., Ltd.*, SPC Guiding Case No.189; 上海熊猫互娱文化有限公司诉李岑、昆山播爱游信息技术有限公司合同纠纷案，最高院指导案例189号.
1002. Songtao Liu, China's Liquidated Damages System Urgently Needs Reconstruction, 1 Chinese Case Law Review 17 (2016).

impacts the certainty and predictability. A related question is whether it is market-driven and proportional for the Chinese judges to rewrite contractual terms by reducing the penalty amounts in the name of fairness.

1070. As mentioned, the Civil Code does not distinguish between penalty clauses and compensatory liquidated damages. Regardless of the type of liquidated damages stipulated, the court is expected to use actual losses plus anticipated profit losses as the foundation for its assessment while also taking into account relevant factors outlined in the provision to decide on possible adjustments. The absence of a clear distinction between punitive and compensatory liquidated damages in this provision underscores a uniform approach to all forms of stipulated damages. By focusing on actual and anticipated losses, the courts prioritise the goal of fair compensation rather than strict enforcement of contractual penalties. The 30% threshold for considering damages 'excessively high' introduces a level of flexibility, enabling courts to tailor liquidated damages according to the circumstances. This threshold acts as a guideline rather than a strict cap, providing judicial discretion to assess the fairness of the penalty based on the contract's specific context. In cases of malicious or bad-faith breaches, the court's reluctance to reduce damages reflects an intent to uphold accountability and deter wrongful conduct, reinforcing the principle of good faith in contractual relationships.

1071. To summarise, the rules governing penalty clauses under the Civil Code ensure that these clauses are valid and enforceable while allowing for judicial discretion to adjust penalties to align with actual damages. This approach balances contractual certainty with the principle of fairness, helping to prevent disproportionate penalties that could result in unjust outcomes.

1072. However, a downside is that frequent judicial intervention in adjusting penalties may introduce uncertainty for parties relying on these clauses. The potential for courts to reduce stipulated penalties based on perceived excessiveness could undermine the deterrent effect intended by penalty clauses. This unpredictability may also complicate contract drafting, as parties may hesitate to rely on penalty clauses if there is a high likelihood of judicial modification. Additionally, the lack of a clear distinction between punitive and compensatory liquidated damages in the law can create ambiguities, making it difficult for parties and courts to interpret and enforce these clauses consistently. This uncertainty could reduce the effectiveness of penalty clauses as a tool for ensuring compliance and protecting contractual interests.

§9. Limitation of Actions

I. Nature and Function

1073. The statute of limitations in China, while embedded in substantive law, is fundamentally procedural, focusing on the right to seek judicial protection rather than the extinction of substantive rights. From a legislative perspective, provisions on the statute of limitations are embedded within substantive law, including the General Principles of Civil Law, the General Provisions of Civil Law, and the Civil Code, due to historical reasons.[1003]

1074. China's Civil Procedure Law, enacted in 1991,[1004] came five years after the General Principles of Civil Law, which had already introduced specialised rules on civil procedure. In the absence of a comprehensive procedural law, incorporating statute of limitations provisions into the General Principles of Civil Law (1986), a substantive law, addressed practical litigation needs and safeguarded litigation rights. This approach was retained in the 2017 General Provisions of Civil Law and fully integrated into the first part of the Civil Code in 2020.

1075. The statute of limitations refers to a legal system in which a right holder loses their ability to seek judicial protection of their civil rights if they fail to act within the prescribed legal period.[1005] It primarily governs the right to seek judicial protection, which is a procedural right. Expiry of the limitation period bars the right holder from pursuing a lawsuit while granting the obligor a time-bar defence. This aligns with the procedural concept of preserving judicial efficiency and ensuring timely resolution of disputes. Despite its procedural focus, the statute of limitations does not extinguish substantive rights. This means the underlying legal relationship (e.g., debt, contract, obligation) remains intact, allowing voluntary performance by the obligor even after the limitation period expires. The civil rights enjoyed by the right holder under the civil legal relationship continue to exist. When the obligor voluntarily fulfils their obligation after the statute of limitations expires, the right holder retains the right to accept the performance, and the statute of limitations does not restrict this. Additionally, if the obligor, having voluntarily fulfilled their obligation, cannot later attempt to retract their performance by citing the expiration of the statute of limitations.[1006]

1076. The statute of limitations for requesting the protection of civil rights (remedies against breach) in a court is three years unless otherwise provided by law.[1007] The limitation period begins when the right holder knows or should have known of the infringement of their rights and the identity of the obligor unless otherwise provided by law.[1008] However, when more than twenty years have passed since the infringement occurred, the court will not protect the right, except in special circumstances where the court may decide to extend the limitation period upon the right holder's application.[1009]

1003. In the civil law system, it is primarily included in the Civil Code. For example, in Germany, limitation periods (Verjährung) under the German Civil Code (BGB) are substantive.
1004. The Chinese Civil Procedure Law, enacted on 9 April, 1991, revised in 2007, 2012, 2017, 2021, and 2023 respectively.
1005. Article 188 CC describes the statute of limitations as used to request the protection of civil rights through the people's court is three years.
1006. Article 192 CC.
1007. Paragraph 1 of Art. 188 CC.
1008. Paragraph 2 of Art. 188 CC.
1009. *Ibid.*

1077. The general limitation period of three years encourages parties to promptly resolve disputes while ensuring that claims are brought forward when evidence and facts are still accessible. The three-year period strikes a balance between the right holder's opportunity to pursue a claim and the obligor's interest in not being subject to indefinite uncertainty.

1078. The limitation period begins when the right holder knows or should have known of the damage. The inclusion of 'should have known' prevents claimants from indefinitely delaying the start of the limitation period by claiming ignorance. This dual standard holds parties accountable for reasonable diligence in protecting their rights. In cases of fraud or hidden breaches, the limitation period might start much later than the date of the actual infringement, offering protection to the victim.

1079. The twenty-year maximum limitation period serves as a safeguard for legal certainty, ensuring that claims are not pursued excessively long after the event. This long-stop provision prevents the indefinite revival of claims. The allowance for extensions in 'special circumstances' demonstrates flexibility, particularly in cases involving significant impediments (e.g., natural disasters, fraud, or incapacity of the right holder).

1080. When the parties agree that the same debt will be performed in instalments, the statute of limitations begins from the date the final instalment becomes due. The rule reflects the nature of instalment obligations, where the debt is divided into multiple performance periods. This approach treats the debt as a whole, ensuring that the creditor's rights are not fragmented across multiple limitation periods for each instalment. It simplifies legal claims by allowing the creditor to address the entire debt in a single action after the final instalment becomes due. It prevents the debtor from exploiting earlier instalments' expiration to argue that parts of the debt are time-barred while other parts remain actionable.

II. Suspension of Limitation Period

1081. If any of the following obstacles prevent the exercise of a claim within the final six months of the limitation period, the statute of limitations is suspended:

1) Force majeure;
2) The right holder is a person without or with limited civil capacity and lacks a legal representative, or their legal representative dies, loses civil capacity, or loses their authority as a representative;
3) After inheritance proceedings begin, the heirs or estate administrator has not been determined;
4) The right holder is under control by the obligor or another person;

5) Other obstacles that prevent the right holder from exercising their claim.[1010]

1082. The statute of limitations resumes after the obstacle is removed, and the period shall expire six months from the date the reason for suspension ceases to exist. The suspension rule recognises that certain extraordinary circumstances can prevent a right holder from exercising their claim, even with diligence. To ensure fairness, the law allows the limitation period to be paused, protecting the right holder from losing their legal recourse due to obstacles beyond their control.

1083. Force Majeure, such as natural disasters, wars, or pandemics that make it impossible for the right holder to file a claim, suspend the limitation period. This reflects the principle of objective impossibility.

1084. When the right holder is a minor or lacks civil capacity and does not have a legal representative, the statute of limitations is paused until representation is re-established. The law also accounts for situations where the representative loses their authority, ensuring that vulnerable parties are not disadvantaged.

1085. In cases involving inheritance, where the heirs or estate administrator remain undetermined, the limitation period is suspended. This prevents the estate's rightful claimants from being penalised for delays in identifying legal successors.

1086. If the right holder is under the physical or psychological control of the obligor or a third party, their inability to exercise their rights is recognised as a valid reason for suspension. This provision protects against coercion or undue influence that may delay the initiation of legal proceedings.

1087. The law allows flexibility for unanticipated obstacles not explicitly listed, ensuring comprehensive protection of the right holder's rights. After the obstacle ceases, the right holder is granted an additional six months to file their claim, even if the original limitation period has expired. This ensures that the right holder has a fair chance to prepare and assert their claim.

III. Interruption of Limitation Period

1088. In any of the following circumstances, the statute of limitations is interrupted, and the limitation period is recalculated starting from the date of interruption or the conclusion of the relevant proceedings:

1) The right holder makes a demand for performance from the obligor;
2) The obligor agrees to perform their obligations;
3) The right holder files a lawsuit or applies for arbitration;

1010. Article 194 CC.

4) Other circumstances that have the same legal effect as filing a lawsuit or applying for arbitration.

1089. The rule on interruption ensures that the statute of limitations does not unjustly bar claims when the right holder takes significant steps to assert their rights. It strikes a balance between protecting claims where efforts are made to pursue them and encouraging the right holder to enforce their rights rather than remaining passive actively.

1090. First, a clear request from the right holder to the obligor to fulfil their obligations interrupts the limitation period. The SPC provides the following examples to illustrate what amounts to a clear request to fulfil the contractual obligation:

1. If one party delivers a document asserting their rights directly to the other party, and the other party signs, stamps, or affixes their fingerprint on the document, or if there is other evidence to prove that the document was received by the other party even without such acknowledgement.
2. If one party asserts their rights by sending a letter or electronic data message, and the letter or data message is delivered to or should reasonably be delivered to the other party.
3. If one party is a financial institution, it may assert its rights by deducting the owed principal and interest from the other party's account in accordance with legal provisions or their agreement.
4. If one party's whereabouts are unknown, the other party may publish a notice asserting their rights in a nationally influential media outlet or in a provincial-level media outlet where the missing party's domicile is located unless otherwise specifically provided by laws or judicial interpretations.

1091. For Item (1), if the other party is a legal person or organisation, the recipient can be its legal representative, the principal person in charge, the department responsible for handling correspondence, or an authorised person. If the other party is a natural person, the recipient can be the individual, a cohabiting relative with full civil capacity, or an authorised person.[1011] Even if a creditor calls the debtor's phone and the call is answered by someone other than the debtor, the act may still constitute an interruption of the statute of limitations.

1092. In the case, the content of the recorded phone call provided by the plaintiff (the creditor) proves that the creditor dialled the debtor's phone number and discussed the repayment of the loan. Although the call was not answered directly by the debtor, it is sufficient to establish the fact that the creditor was asserting their

1011. Article 8 of the SPC Provisions on the Application of the Statute of Limitations in the Trial of Civil Cases.

claim. Therefore, it was determined that the statute of limitations for the disputed loan was interrupted at that time, and the limitation period should restart from the following day.[1012]

1093. Second, if the obligor acknowledges its obligation and agrees to fulfil it, the limitation period restarts. This protects the right holder from having its claim time-barred while waiting for the obligor to act in good faith. Whether the statute of limitations interrupted when a debtor failed to fulfil obligations after the agreed deadline but issued an IOU without a specified repayment date? According to Article 195 of the Civil Code, this situation constitutes an interruption of the statute of limitations. If the supplier fails to assert their rights after the interruption, the limitation period should be recalculated starting from the date the supplier received the IOU issued by the buyer.[1013] This rule ensures that the issuance of an IOU without a repayment date restarts the statute of limitations, providing clarity and fairness for both parties.

1094. Third, filing a lawsuit or initiating arbitration is a formal assertion of rights that interrupts the limitation period. This ensures that legal proceedings are not precluded due to procedural delays or prolonged court or arbitration processes. Is the limitation period interrupted when a lawsuit was filed but subsequently withdrawn? If the lawsuit is withdrawn, resulting in the termination of the legal proceedings, the statute of limitations period will restart from the date the civil ruling approving the withdrawal is delivered and takes effect.[1014] The limitation period's restart is tied to the effective date of the court's ruling approving the withdrawal, providing a clear reference point for both parties. As long as a party files a lawsuit, the statute of limitations is interrupted, regardless of whether the lawsuit is later withdrawn.[1015] The statute of limitations is interrupted from the date the court receives the plaintiff's complaint, even if the case is later deemed automatically withdrawn due to the plaintiff's failure to pay court fees.[1016] This principle ensures that filing a lawsuit, regardless of its subsequent withdrawal, effectively interrupts the statute of limitations. It prioritises intent over outcome.

1012. *Weinan City Huazhou District Hongli Real Estate Development Co., Ltd. v. Tongguan County Xinlong Investment Co., Ltd.*, Supreme People's Court (2021) Min Shen No. 2434; 渭南市华州区鸿力房地产开发有限公司诉潼关县鑫龙投资有限责任公司， 最高人民法院（2021）最高法民申2434号.

1013. The SPC's Reply on the Issue of When the Statute of Limitations Begins to Run for an IOU Without a Repayment Date Issued by the Debtor After Failing to Fulfil Obligations Upon the Expiration of the Agreed Deadline (2020 Revision) (Fa Shi (2020] No. 17).

1014. Article 10 of the SPC Provisions on the Application of the Statute of Limitations in the Trial of Civil Cases.

1015. *Ningxiang Zhongyu Plastics Co., Ltd., Zhang Ailian, and Others v. Mao De'an,* Supreme People's Court (2019) SPC Min Shen No. 1151; 宁乡中宇塑业有限公司、张爱连民间借贷纠纷再审审查与审判监督民事裁定书，最高人民法院（2019）最高法民申1151号.

1016. *Shaoyang Daxiang District Shengchu Coal Trade Co., Ltd. v. Guodian Hunan Baoqing Coal and Electricity Co., Ltd.*, Supreme People's Court (2017) SPC Min Shen No. 3316; 邵阳市大祥区圣矗煤炭贸易有限公司、国电湖南宝庆煤电有限公司买卖合同纠纷再审审查与审判监督民事裁定书，最高人民法院（2017）最高法民申3316号.

1095. Fourth, courts recognise the following actions as having the same effect as filing litigation or arbitration in interrupting the statute of limitations: (1) applying for a payment order; (2) filing for bankruptcy or declaring bankruptcy claims; (3) applying for a declaration of the obligor as missing or deceased to assert rights; (4) applying for pre-litigation measures, such as property preservation or interim injunctions; (5) applying for enforcement; (6) applying to add parties or notify individuals to participate in litigation; (7) asserting a set-off during litigation; (8) other actions that have the same effect as filing a lawsuit in interrupting the statute of limitations.[1017]

1096. After the interruption, the limitation period starts anew from the date of interruption or the conclusion of related proceedings, giving the right holder additional time to pursue their claim. Right holders must retain evidence of actions taken to assert their rights, such as formal demands, written acknowledgements, or case filings.

1097. The duration, calculation method, and reasons for suspension or interruption of the statute of limitations are prescribed by law, and any agreement between the parties regarding these matters is invalid.[1018] A party's pre-emptive waiver of their statute of limitations rights is also invalid.[1019] For example, an agreement to shorten or extend the limitation period or to disregard events triggering suspension or interruption would be unenforceable. Limitation periods are not only a private matter but also serve a public interest by promoting the resolution of disputes within a reasonable time and reducing prolonged uncertainty. This protects weaker parties, such as consumers or employees, who might otherwise be pressured into unfavourable agreements that limit their ability to pursue claims. The rules governing the statute of limitations, including its duration and calculation, are standardised by law to ensure consistency and predictability in the application of time limits for legal claims.

1098. If the law provides specific rules for the arbitration limitation period, those rules shall apply. In the absence of such provisions, the rules governing the statute of limitations for litigation shall apply.[1020] A review of China's current legal provisions reveals no specific rules regarding the limitation period tailored for commercial arbitration. Therefore, the limitation period for commercial arbitration is governed by the relevant provisions of the statute of limitations for litigation.[1021] This omission means that arbitration proceedings rely on general limitation rules applicable to civil litigation.

1017. Article 11 of the SPC Provisions on the Application of the Statute of Limitations in the Trial of Civil Cases.
1018. Article 197 CC.
1019. *Ibid.*
1020. Article 198 CC.
1021. Article 74 of the Arbitration Law.

Part II. Specific Contracts

General Introduction

1099. The Civil Code provides rules for typical contracts in Part Two, Book III. It includes 18 kinds of typical contracts. Most of them originated from typical contracts in the repealed Contract Law.[1022] They are Chapter 9: Sale Contracts; Chapter 10: Contracts for the Supply and Use of Electricity, Water, Gas or Heat; Chapter 11: Gift Contracts; Chapter 12: Loan Contracts; Chapter 13: Guaranty Contracts; Chapter 14: Lease Contracts; Chapter 15: Financial Lease Contracts; Chapter 16: Factoring Contracts; Chapter 17: Contracts for work; Chapter 18: Construction Contracts; Chapter 19: Transport Contracts; Chapter 20: Technology Contracts; Chapter 22: Warehousing Contracts; Chapter 23: Mandate Contracts; Chapter 24: Property Service Contracts; Chapter 25: Contracts of Commission Agency; Chapter 26: Intermediary Contracts and Chapter 27: Partnership Contracts.[1023] Most of them originated from typical contracts in the repealed Contract Law. The new typical contracts that did not exist in the Contract Law are guaranty contract in Chapter 13, factoring contract in Chapter 16, property service contract in Chapter 24, and partnership contract in Chapter 27.

1100. There are different reasons for the new typical contracts in the Civil Code. First, the guaranty contract was regulated by the Guaranty Law before the Civil Code. After the Civil Code took effect in 2021, the Guaranty Law has been repealed. Therefore, the guaranty contract is regulated in the Civil Code. Second, the factoring business is developing fast in China, but there is no law on the factoring contract. There are more and more factoring contract disputes in Chinese judicial practice. Therefore, it is necessary to provide fundamental rules for factoring contracts in law. Third, with the acceleration of China's urbanisation process and people's living conditions, the number of disputes relating to property service contracts is increasing. Therefore, the Civil Code treats the property service contract as a typical contract and provides rules for outstanding issues such as the owners' right to terminate the contract, preliminary property service contracts and property

1022. The Contract Law has been replaced by the Book III of the Civil Code.
1023. Those chapter numbers are original chapter numbers in the Civil Code.

handovers. Last, the partnership includes both civil partnership and commercial partnership. The civil partnership is regulated by the General Principles of the Civil Law 1987 and the commercial partnership is regulated by the Partnership Enterprise Law. However, the General Principles of the Civil Law 1987 were repealed after the Civil Code took effect. Therefore, the Civil Code provides the rules for partnership contracts.[1024]

1101. Part II of the Civil Code does not cover all typical contracts in practice. When the contractual relations are regulated by specific laws, the specific laws may apply to the specific contracts. For example, the Consumer Protection Law 2013 Revision applies to contractual disputes between businesses and customers;[1025] the Tourism Law applies to contractual disputes between travel agents and tourists;[1026] the Insurance Law applies to insurance contract disputes between insurers and insured;[1027] the Maritime Law applies to marine insurance contract disputes between insurers and insured;[1028] the Commercial Banks Law 2003 applies to savings deposit contract disputes between banks and depositor;[1029] the Labour Contract Law applies to labour contract disputes between employers and employees.[1030] Of course, the general rules in Part I of the Civil Code still apply to those specific contracts, although they are not regulated by Part Two, Book III of the Civil Code. Some contracts cover a very wide range, and the content is extremely complex. It is difficult to abstract general rules from those contracts, such as service contracts and internet service contracts. Some contracts still have controversial issues in theory and practice, such as administrative contracts. Therefore, it is not appropriate to regulate those contracts as typical contracts in the Civil Code.[1031]

1024. Hong S, 'Significant Developments and Innovations in Contract Book' (2020) 4 China Legal Studies (Zhong Guo Fa Xue) 40, 48.
1025. *Zheng Chuanxin v. China Telecom Corporation Ltd Lianyungang Branch*, Gazette Case of the SPC, Issue 5, 2017; 郑传新诉中国电信股份有限公司连云港分公司电信服务合同纠纷案,《最高人民法院公报》案例，2017年05期.
1026. *Chen Ming, Xu Yanfang and Chen Jie v. Shanghai Ctrip International Travel Service Co., Ltd.*, Gazette Case of the SPC, Issue 4, 2015; 陈明、徐炎芳、陈洁诉上海携程国际旅行社有限公司旅游合同纠纷案，《最高人民法院公报》案例，2015年04期.
1027. *Zheng Shiqi v. Samsung Property & Casualty Insurance Company (China), Ltd*, Gazette Case of the SPC, Issue 5, 2022; 郑诗琦诉三星财产保险（中国）有限公司财产保险合同纠纷案,《最高人民法院公报》案例，2022年05期.
1028. *China Shipping Industry Co., Ltd. (Jiangsu) v. China Pacific Property Insurance Co., Ltd. Yangzhou Central Branch and China Pacific Property Insurance Co., Ltd.*, Gazette Case of the SPC, Issue 10, 2013; 中海工业（江苏）有限公司诉中国太平洋财产保险股份有限公司扬州中心支公司、中国太平洋财产保险股份有限公司海上保险合同纠纷案，《最高人民法院公报》案例，2013年10期.
1029. *Wang Yongsheng v. Bank of China Limited Nanjing Hexi Branch*, Gazette Case of the SPC, Issue 2, 2009; 王永胜诉中国银行股份有限公司南京河西支行储蓄存款合同纠纷案，《最高人民法院公报》案例，2009年02期.
1030. *Li Linxia v. Chongqing Manka Cultural Communication Co., Ltd.*, Gazette Case of the SPC, Issue 10, 2020; 李林霞诉重庆漫咖文化传播有限公司劳动合同纠纷案,《最高人民法院公报》案例，2020年10期.
1031. S Hong, Significant Developments and Innovations in Contract Book, 48-49.

Chapter 1. Sales Contracts

§1. Concept of Sale Contract

1102. A sale contract in the Civil Code refers to a contract whereby the seller transfers its ownership of the subject matter to the buyer and the buyer pays the price therefor.[1032] The subject matter for a valid sale must be a legal subject matter. In *Wu Hailan v. Shanghai Juren Biological Technology Co., Ltd.*,[1033] the subject matter of sale is stem cells. Stem cells originate from the human body. Based on their unique biological properties, they cannot be directly used as transaction targets in law. Stem cell technology, as a new type of biotherapeutic technology, shall be applied to clinical research and health needs. Therefore, the stem cell sale contract is invalid because it has harmed social and public interests. Similarly, a media account should not be the subject matter for sale. In *Cheng v. Zhao*,[1034] the subject matter for sale is a WeChat account. It was held that the sale of a WeChat account is not valid. It was pointed out that the essence of buying WeChat accounts is buying personal information of the holders of WeChat accounts. It violates the mandatory provisions of the law and shall be deemed invalid.

1103. Under the SPC Interpretation on Issues Concerning the Application of Law in the Trial of Disputes Over Sales Contracts (2012, 2020 revision) (the SPC Interpretation on the Sales Contracts (2020)),[1035] where there is no written contract between the parties and one party claims that a sales contract exists on the basis of delivery notes, goods received notes, settlement statements, and invoices, the Chinese court shall determine whether a sales contract has been formed by considering the transaction methods and customary business practices between the parties as well as other relevant evidence. The Chinese court may accept evidence for proving that a sales contract exists even if no name of a creditor is recorded in correspondence or certificates such as confirmation letters on account reconciliation or written confirmations of creditor's rights unless it can be invalidated by sufficient evidence to the contrary.[1036]

1104. The buyer's obligation to pay the price is based on the seller's real transfer of ownership of the subject matter in the sale contract. The existence of real

1032. Article 595 CC.

1033. *Wu Hailan v. Shanghai Juren Biological Technology Co., Ltd.*, Shanghai First Intermediate People's Court (2020) Hu 01 Min Zhong No. 4321; 吴海澜诉上海聚仁生物科技有限公司, 上海市第一中级人民法院（2020）沪01 民终4321 号. This case is included in the Gazette Case of the SPC, Issue 6, 2021; 《最高人民法院公报》案例，2021年06期. For comments on this case, *see* H Jian, Validity Determination and Application of Law in the First Stem Cell Sales Contract in China, 2 Journal of Law Application (Fa Lv Shi Yong) 127 (2022).

1034. *Cheng v. Zhao*, Jiangyin People's Court (2020) Su 0281 Min Chu No. 7297; 程某诉赵某, 江苏省江阴市人民法院（2020）苏0281民初7297号.

1035. The SPC Interpretation on Issues Concerning the Application of Law in the Trial of Disputes Over Sales Contracts (2012, 2020 revision).

1036. Article 1 of the SPC Interpretation on the Sales Contract (2020).

goods transactions is a prerequisite to support the seller's payment claim. In *A Company Fuzhou Branch v. Fuzhou B Company and Wu*,[1037] the seller and the buyer concluded a contract of sale of goods, and the third parties agreed to provide a guarantee for the payment of goods involved in the case. The seller claimed against the buyer and the third parties as the guarantors for the unpaid price of goods. The seller provided evidence of invoices, warehouse-out orders and goods receipt orders to support its claim. However, the guarantors believed that the evidence was not sufficient to prove that the goods involved in the case had been delivered and that the parties to the sale contract had a genuine sales contract. They argued that the contract involved in the case was a false contract and should be deemed invalid according to law, and the guaranty contract should also be invalid. The court found that the seller did not provide relevant evidence, such as the actual transportation and warehousing of the goods to support the authenticity of the transactions involved in the case. The seller's evidence was not sufficient to determine the true transactions of goods. Since there was no real transaction of goods, the claim for payment of goods was not supported, and the guarantors were not liable for payment under the guaranty.

1105. A sale contract generally includes terms as to the name, quantity, quality and price of the subject matter, the time, place and means of performance, packaging, the methods and standards of inspection, the means of payment settlement, and the terms used in the contract and their effects.[1038] The definition shows the nature of the sale contract, namely the transfer of ownership. If a sale contract is signed not for this purpose but for a loan between parties, the contract will not be recognised as a sale contract. In *Rizhao Port Co., Ltd. Coal Distribution Department v. Shanxi Coking Coal Group International Development Co., Ltd.*,[1039] one party sold a cargo to another party at a low price and then purchased the cargo back from that party at a high price. It was believed by the court that the sale contract was against the business purpose of profit and common sense of business. The real purpose of the sale contract is for inter-business lending between parties. Thus, this sale contract should be considered as a loan contract and the dispute should be a loan contract dispute.

1106. Since the purpose of the sale of goods is to transfer the ownership of the subject matter, the Contract Law provides rules for the transfer of ownership based on contract. It was provided that 'The ownership of a subject matter shall be transferred upon the delivery thereof unless otherwise prescribed by law or agreed upon

1037. *A Company Fuzhou Branch v. Fuzhou B Company and Wu*, Fujian High People's Court (2022) Min Min Zhong No. 162; 某公司福州分公司诉福州某公司及吴某某，福建省高级人民法院（2022）闽民终162号.

1038. Article 596 CC.

1039. *Rizhao Port Co., Ltd. Coal Distribution Department v. Shanxi Coking Coal Group International Development Co., Ltd.*, the SPC (2015) Min Ti Zi No. 74 (Gazette Case of the SPC, Issue 6, 2017); 日照港集团有限公司煤炭运销部诉山西焦煤集团国际发展股份有限公司，最高人民法院（2015）民提字第74号（《最高人民法院公报》案例，2017年06期）.

by the parties concerned.'[1040] However, it does not make a distinction between movables and immovable property, i.e., real estate, for the subject matter in sale contracts. In Chinese judicial practice, Chinese courts realised this problem and made such a distinction in judgments for disputes of transfer of property rights based on sale contracts.[1041] The Civil Code does not regulate the transfer of ownership under the sale contract in the chapter of sale contracts because ownership is regulated in relevant chapters of property rights of the Civil Code.[1042] In the Civil Code, the creation or transfer of movable property rights shall become effective upon delivery, unless otherwise provided by law.[1043] The transfer of immovable property rights shall become effective upon registration in accordance with law; it shall not become effective without registration unless otherwise provided by law.[1044] The registration is important for effective transfer of real estate, but it does not affect the legal effect of the sale contract for transfer of real estate.

1107. The relation between the legal effect of a sale contract of real estate and registration of transfer was explained in *Chengdu Xunjie Communication Chains Co., Ltd. v. Sichuan Shudu Industry Co., Ltd. and Sichuan Youli Investment Holding Co., Ltd.*[1045] In this case, the seller transferred the possession of a building under a sale contract but did not accordingly register the transfer of the building. The buyer applied to the Chinese courts requesting the seller to register the transfer of the building. The seller applied to Chinese courts requesting to terminate the sale contract. The first instance court held that the seller had no right to terminate the contract and should register the transfer of the real estate under the sale contract. In the appeal of the case, the second instance court took the view that the seller had the right to deal with the real estate, including termination of the sale contract before registration of transfer of the real estate under the sale contract. It held that the buyer should move out and return the building to the seller. However, the SPC overruled the judgement and affirmed the judgement of the first instance court. It pointed out that the second instance judgment was against the basic principle of contract law for protecting transaction security. In the view of the SPC, it was an error in application of property. The fact that the seller still had ownership of the building does not mean that it was entitled to terminate the sale contract without any legal or contractual basis. It was held that, when the sale contract was legally concluded, as the

---

1040. Article 133 of the Contract Law.

1041. *Dalian Haneda Steel Tube Co., Ltd. v. Hongfeng Steel Industry & Trade Co., Ltd. in Dalian Free Trade Zone, Haneda Steel Pipe Works Co., Ltd. and Dalian High-tech Industrial Park Longwangtang Subdistrict Office*, the SPC (2011) Min Ti Zi No. 29 (Gazette Case of the SPC, Issue 6, 2012); 大连羽田钢管有限公司与大连保税区弘丰钢铁工贸有限公司、株式会社羽田钢管制造所、大连高新技术产业园区龙王塘街道办事处物权确认纠纷案，最高人民法院（2011）民提字第29号（《最高人民法院公报》案例，2012年06期）.

1042. CC, Book II, Part One, Chapter 2.

1043. Article 224 CC.

1044. Paragraph 1 of Art. 209 CC.

1045. *Chengdu Xunjie Communication Chains Co., Ltd. v. Sichuan Shudu Industry Co., Ltd. and Sichuan Youli Investment Holding Co., Ltd.*, the SPC (2013) Min Ti Zi No. 90; 成都讯捷通讯连锁有限公司诉四川蜀都实业有限责任公司、四川友利投资控股股份有限公司，最高人民法院（2013）民提字第90号. This case is included in the Gazette Case of the SPC, Issue 1, 2015; 《最高人民法院公报》案例，2015年01期.

owner of the building, the seller should perform its obligation to register the transfer of the building under the sale contract.

§2. Consumer Sale Contract

1108. The concept of sale contract in the Civil Code does not make a distinction between businesses and individuals. It seems to infer that the sale contract rules should apply to all kinds of sale contracts. However, Chinese courts do not apply the sale contract rules in the Civil Code to the sale contract between businesses and individuals. In *Zhangli v. Beijing Heli Huatong Automobile Service Co., Ltd.*,[1046] the Chinese courts applied the Consumer Protection Law 2013 (Consumer Protection Law) to a dispute of a sale contract for the purchase of a car between a commercial seller and an individual buyer.[1047] In the sale contract, the seller promised that the car was a new car without any repairs. The buyer paid the price but found the car was repaired before delivery of the car. The buyer applied to the court requesting cancellation of the contract. The court held that the buyer was entitled to cancel the contract and return the car to the seller, and the seller must repay the payment to the buyer.[1048] The appellate court upheld the decision.[1049] The courts pointed out that the buyer purchased the car for personal use and not for business or non-living consumption, and therefore the Consumer Protection Law applied to such a sale contract.

1109. The SPC publishes this case as a Guiding Case and confirms that the Consumer Protection Law applies to fraud disputes in sale contracts of cars for household consumption.[1050] This Guiding Case clarifies the application of law to sale contracts between businesses and consumers, namely the Consumer Protection Law. However, it narrows this kind of sale contract dispute to fraud dispute, although the judgments themselves do not have such narrow application. In fact, disputes may occur for other reasons, e.g., the defect of a car without a fraud element. The narrow application may not be the real intention of the SPC in this Guiding Case. It is believed the Consumer Protection Law will apply to all kinds of disputes based on sale contracts of cars between businesses and consumers.

1046. *Zhang Li v. Beijing Heli Huatong Automobile Service Co., Ltd.*, SPC Guiding Case No. 17; 张莉诉北京合力华通汽车服务有限公司买卖合同纠纷案，最高人民法院，第17号指导性案例.

1047. *See also Deng Meihua v. Shanghai Yongda Pirui Auto Sales Service Co., Ltd.*, Gazette Case of the SPC, Issue 11, 2018; 邓美华与上海永达霹悦汽车销售服务有限公司买卖合同纠纷案，《最高人民法院公报》2018年第11期.

1048. Bejing Chaoyang District People's Court (2007) Chao Min Chu Zi No. 18230); 北京市朝阳区人民法院（2007）朝民初字第18230号.

1049. Beijing Second Intermediate People's Court (2008) Er Zhong Min Zhong Zi No. 00453; 北京市第二中级人民法院（2008）二中民终字第00453号.

1050. SPC Guiding Case No. 17, guiding note 1.

1110. Besides the Consumer Protection Law, the Chinese courts may apply specific laws to sell contract disputes between businesses and consumers. In *Sun Yinshan v. Nanjing Auchan Supermarket Co., Ltd. Jiangning Store*,[1051] the consumer purchased fourteen packs of sausage and found the best before the date expired. The consumer claimed damage against the supermarket as the seller based on the Consumer Protection Law. To determine whether the sausage complied with the food safety standard, the Chinese court applied the Food Safety Law[1052] and held that the supermarket as the seller should pay damages to the consumer under the Consumer Protection Law because the sausage failed to comply with the relevant standard. This case has also been published by the SPC as a Guiding Case.[1053]

§3. CISG

I. Application

1111. For sale of goods contracts, either the Civil Code or the United Nations Convention on Contracts for the International Sale of Goods in 1980 (CISG) may apply in different circumstances. On the one hand, the rules of the sale contract in the Civil Code apply to both domestic sale of goods contracts and international sale of goods contracts.[1054] On the other hand, the CISG applies to contracts of sale of goods between parties whose places of business are in different States (a) when the States are Contracting States; or (b) when the rules of private international law lead to the application of the law of a Contracting State.[1055] China ratified the CISG, which came into force in China in 1988. The CISG applies to international sales of goods unless the parties have excluded the application of the CISG in the contract.[1056] In judicial practice, Chinese courts refuse to apply the CISG to a contract

1051. *Sun Yinshan v. Nanjing Auchan Supermarket Co., Ltd. Jiangning Store*, Nanjing Jiangning District People's Court (2012) Jiang Ning Kai Min Chu Zi No. 646; 孙银山诉南京欧尚超市有限公司江宁店买卖合同纠纷案，江苏省南京市江宁区人民法院（2012）江宁开民初字第646号.

1052. It has been amended in 2021.

1053. SPC Guiding Case No. 23, 最高人民法院，第23号指导性案例.

1054. The Law on Foreign-related Economic Contracts 1985 has been repealed. For the development of Chinese contract law, *see* Chen L and DiMatteo LA, History of Chinese Contract Law, in Chinese Contract Law: Civil and Common Law Perspectives 3 (DiMatteo LA and Chen L eds., Cambridge University Press 2017).

1055. Article 1 of the CISG. *See Sino Chem International (Overseas) Pte Ltd v. Thyssen Krupp Metallurgical Products GmbH*, the SPC (2013) Min Si Zhong Zi No. 35; 中化国际（新加坡）有限公司诉蒂森克房伯冶金产品有限责任公司国际货物买卖合同纠纷案，最高人民法院（2013）民四终字第35号. This is also the Guiding Case No. 107 in which Chinese private international law led to the application of the CISG under the law of the New York State of the US as a Contracting State to the CISG.

1056. Article 6 of the CISG. *See The United States Joint Enterprises Ltd v. Shandong Foreign Trade Corporation Ltd Yantai Branch*, the SPC (1998) Jing Zhong Zi No. 358; 美国联合企业有限公司与中国山东省对外贸易总公司烟台公司购销合同纠纷案，最高人民法院（1998）经终字第358号.

for both sale and exhibition of goods because the exhibition of goods is not regulated by the CISG.[1057] It must be noted that there is no such condition in either the CISG or the Civil Code to exclude the application of the CISG. Therefore, this practice is inconsistent with the conditions for application of the CISG and should not be followed.

1112. Because both the Civil Code and the CISG apply to the international sale of goods contract, problems arise if the provisions are inconsistent between the Chinese Contract Law and the CISG regarding the same issues. The provisions of the CISG automatically apply to the international sale of goods between Chinese parties and the parties of other Contracting States of the CISG, except for other choice of law, and the disputes or lawsuits thereof shall be disposed of according to the CISG.[1058] In *Sino Chem International (Overseas) Pte Ltd .v Thyssen Krupp Metallurgical Products GmbH*,[1059] the SPC confirmed that the CISG has priority over the Chinese law in the application to international sale of goods. It clarified that, unless the parties have excluded the application of the CISG in the contract, the CISG should apply in priority to the contracts of international sale of goods between parties whose places of business are in different Contracting States. For the issues that are not regulated by the CISG, the agreed applicable law in the contract shall apply.[1060]

II. Formation of Contract

1113. In the CISG, a contract of sale does not need to be concluded in or evidenced by writing and is not subject to any other requirement as to form. It may be proved by any means, including witnesses.[1061] The word 'writing' in the CISG includes telegram and telex.[1062] Similarly, in the Civil Code, the parties may conclude a contract in written form, verbal form or any other form.[1063] 'Written form' shall refer to any form that serves to reflect the information contained therein in a tangible form, such as a written instrument, a letter, a telegram, a telex, a facsimile, etc. electronic messages in the forms of electronic data interchange, email, etc., which serve to reflect the information contained therein in a tangible form and can be obtained and used at any time shall be deemed as written form.[1064]

1057. *Shunde Westband Furniture Co., Ltd. v. Panda S.R.L.*, the SPC (2004) Min Si Ti Zi No. 4; 顺德市韦邦家具有限公司与熊猫有限公司，最高人民法院（1998）经终字第358号.
1058. Article 1 of the Notice on the Problems for Attention of the Ministry of Foreign Economic Cooperation and Trade on implementing the United Nations Convention on Contracts for the International Sale of Goods (1987).
1059. SPC Guiding Case No. 107. 最高人民法院，第107号指导性案例.
1060. SPC Guiding Case No. 107, guiding note 1.
1061. Article 11 of the CISG.
1062. Article 13 of the CISG.
1063. Paragraphs 1 of Art. 469 CC.
1064. Paragraphs 1 and 2 of Art. 469 CC.

1114. Under the CISG, an offer becomes effective when it reaches the offeree.[1065] An offer under the Civil Code becomes effective only when the counterparty becomes aware of the contents of the offer.[1066] The CISG provides that if, by virtue of the offer or as a result of practices that the parties have established between themselves or of usage, the offeree may indicate assent by performing an act, the acceptance is effective at the moment the act is performed.[1067] Similarly, an acceptance of the Civil Code may be made by conduct according to trade practices or as indicated in the offer.[1068] The CISG provides that silence or inactivity does not in itself amount to acceptance,[1069] but the Civil Code does not have such provisions. In both the CISG and the Civil Code, a reply to an offer that purports to be an acceptance but contains additions, limitations or other modifications is a rejection of the offer and constitutes a counteroffer. However, a reply to an offer that purports to be an acceptance but contains additional or different terms that do not materially alter the terms of the offer constitutes an acceptance. Additional or different terms relating, among other things, to the price, payment, quality and quantity of the goods, place and time of delivery, the extent of one party's liability to the other or the settlement of disputes are considered to alter the terms of the offer materially.[1070]

1115. Under both the Civil Code and the CISG, a contract is concluded when an acceptance of an offer becomes effective.[1071] The Civil Code provides more rules for the conclusion of contracts. Where the parties concerned conclude the contract in the form of a written contract, the contract shall be established at the time when the parties concerned affix their signatures, seals, or fingerprints to the contract. If one party concerned has performed main obligations before the affixation of signatures, seals, or fingerprints, such contract shall be established at the time of acceptance by the other party.[1072]

III. Seller's Obligations and Buyer's Remedies

1116. In both the CISG and the Civil Code, the seller must deliver the goods, hand over any documents relating to them and transfer the property in the goods.[1073] The seller must also deliver the goods that are of the quantity, quality and description required by the contract and which are contained or packaged in the manner required by the contract.[1074] In the Civil Code, if the seller breaches the contract, the buyer's remedies include repair, replacement, rework, return of the subject

1065. Article 15 (1) of the CISG; para. 1 of Art. 16 of the Contract Law.
1066. Article 474 and Art. 137 CC.
1067. Article 18 (3) of the CISG.
1068. Article 480 CC.
1069. Article 18 (1) of the CISG.
1070. Article 19 of the CISG; Arts 488 and 489 CC.
1071. Article 23 of the CISG; Art. 483 CC.
1072. Article 490 CC.
1073. Article 30 of the CISG; Arts 598 and 601 CC.
1074. Article 35 (1) of the CISG; Arts 615 and 619 CC.

matter, reduction in payment of prices or remunerations, etc.[1075] Similarly, in the CISG the buyer can claim damages for the seller's breach of contract.[1076] The CISG further provides that the buyer is not deprived of any right he may have to claim damages by exercising his right to other remedies.[1077] If the goods do not conform to the contract, the buyer's remedies include the substitute goods if the lack of conformity constitutes a fundamental breach of contract and the repair of conformity unless this is unreasonable having regard to all the circumstances.[1078] The Civil Code does not provide such remedies, but they are not forbidden by Chinese law.

1117. Furthermore, the CISG provides the buyer with the right to declare the contract avoided if the failure by the seller to perform any of his obligations amounts to a fundamental breach of contract, or the seller does not deliver the goods.[1079] In the CISG, a breach of contract committed by one of the parties is fundamental if it results in such detriment to the other party as substantially deprives him of what he is entitled to expect under the contract unless the party in breach did not foresee and a reasonable person of the same kind in the same circumstances would not have foreseen such a result.[1080] There is no concept of fundamental breach in the Civil Code. The Civil Code provides that a party to a contract may terminate a contract if the counterparty breaches the contract, making it impossible to achieve the purposes of the contract.[1081] In the sale of goods contract, the buyer can refuse to accept the goods or terminate the contract if the purposes of a contract cannot be fulfilled because the goods do not meet quality requirements.[1082] The substantial difference in the remedy between the Civil Code and the CISG is the consequence of the fundamental breach, e.g., the goods do not meet quality requirements so the purposes of a contract cannot be fulfilled. The remedy in the Civil Code is termination of contract, whereas the remedy in the CISG is avoidance of contract. Therefore, for a fundamental breach, a buyer may terminate but not avoid a contract if the Civil Code applies, whereas a buyer may avoid but not terminate a contract if the CISG applies.[1083]

IV. Buyer's Obligations and Seller's Remedies

1118. The buyer must pay the price for the goods and take delivery of them.[1084] The CISG provides a concept of anticipatory breach under which a party may suspend the performance of his obligations if it becomes apparent that the other party

1075. Article 582 CC.
1076. Articles 74 to 77 of the CISG.
1077. Article 45 (1) and (2) of the CISG.
1078. Article 46 (2) and (3) of the CISG.
1079. Article 49 (1) of the CISG.
1080. Article 25 of the CISG.
1081. Article 563 (4) CC.
1082. Article 610 CC.
1083. The difference also applies to the sale of goods contract for delivery of goods by instalments. *See* Art. 73 of the CISG and Art. 633 CC.
1084. Article 53 of the CISG; Art. 626 CC.

will not perform a substantial part of his obligations as a result of: (a) a serious deficiency in his ability to perform or in his creditworthiness; or (b) his conduct in preparing to perform or in performing the contract.[1085] This concept applies to both the seller and the buyer in the international sale of goods. In particular, the CISG provides that if the seller has already dispatched the goods before the buyer's anticipatory breach becomes evident, he may prevent the handing over of the goods to the buyer even though the buyer holds a document which entitles him to obtain them.[1086] By contrast, the Civil Code does not have the concept of anticipatory breach but provides that, where either party to a contract explicitly expresses or indicates by its acts its intention not to perform its obligations under the contract, the other party may, before the expiry of the period of performance, demand that the former bear the liability for breach of contract.[1087] It can be seen that the difference in the Civil Code is that, if one party's breach is anticipated, the counterparty cannot suspend its performance of the contract but is entitled to claim damages for breach of contract.

1119. In the CISG, the unpaid seller may prevent the handing over of the goods to the buyer even though the buyer holds a document which entitles him to obtain them. However, the seller may not be able to prevent the delivery of the goods to the buyer if the seller is not the shipper in the contract of carriage of goods by sea. Even if the seller is the shipper, the seller may not be able to prevent the delivery of goods if the buyer demands the delivery of goods from the carrier by presenting a shipping document, e.g., a bill of lading as a document of title. In either of the two circumstances, the carrier may deliver the goods to the buyer, and the seller, even if unpaid, may not be able to prevent such delivery, although the CISG provides such remedy. The CISG emphasises that the stoppage in transit remedy relates only to the rights of the goods between the buyer and the seller,[1088] but does not provide solutions for the unpaid seller to prevent the delivery of goods. By contrast, although the Civil Code does not provide the remedy of stoppage in transit for the unpaid seller in the sale of goods, it does provide a potential solution for the stoppage of goods in transit in Chapter 19 'Carriage Contract'. The Civil Code provides the shipper with the right, before the carrier delivers the goods to the consignee, to ask the carrier to stop the carriage, return the goods, change the place of destination or deliver the goods to another consignee, provided that the shipper shall compensate for the losses thus caused to the carrier.[1089]

1085. Article 71 (1) of the CISG.
1086. Article 71 (2) of the CISG. However, a party suspending performance, whether before or after dispatch of the goods, must immediately give notice of the suspension to the other party and must continue with performance if the other party provides adequate assurance of his performance. *See* Art. 71 (3) of the CISG.
1087. Article 578 CC.
1088. Article 71 (2) of the CISG.
1089. Article 829 CC.

V. Breach and Remedies

1120. In the CISG, damages for breach of contract by one party consist of a sum equal to the loss, including loss of profit, suffered by the other party as a consequence of the breach. Such damages may not exceed the loss which the party in breach foresaw or ought to have foreseen at the time of the conclusion of the contract, in the light of the facts and matters of which he then knew or ought to have known, as a possible consequence of the breach of contract.[1090] Similarly, in the Civil Code, if either party causes loss to the other party by breach of contract, the amount of compensation for loss shall include the profit obtainable after the contract is performed but shall not exceed the amount of the loss that may be caused by breach of contract and that has been or ought to be foreseen by the party in breach in concluding the contract.[1091]

1121. In the CISG, the innocent party may declare the contract avoided if the wrongful party has a fundamental breach of contract. Avoidance of the contract releases both parties from their obligations under it, subject to any damages which may be due.[1092] On the one hand, a party who has performed the contract either wholly or in part may claim restitution from the other party of whatever the first party has supplied or paid under the contract. If both parties are bound to make restitution, they must do so concurrently.[1093] On the other hand, if the contract is avoided and if, in a reasonable manner and within a reasonable time after avoidance, the buyer has bought goods in replacement or the seller has resold the goods, the party claiming damages may recover, in addition to the normal damage for breach of contract, the difference between the contract price and the price in the substitute transaction.[1094] If there is no such substitute transaction, the party claiming damages may recover the difference between the prices fixed by the contract and the current price at the time of avoidance as well as any further damages for breach of contract.[1095]

1122. By contrast, the innocent party in the Civil Code can terminate a contract if the wrongful party has a fundamental breach.[1096] When a contract is terminated, the rights and obligations under the contract shall be terminated.[1097] After termination, performance of the contract shall be ceased if it has not been performed. If the

1090. Article 74 of the CISG.
1091. Article 584 CC.
1092. Article 81 (1) of the CISG. Avoidance does not affect any provision of the contract for the settlement of disputes or any other provision of the contract governing the rights and obligations of the parties consequent upon the avoidance of the contract.
1093. Article 81 (2) of the CISG.
1094. Article 75 of the CISG.
1095. Article 76 (1) of the CISG. For this purpose, the current price is the price prevailing at the place where delivery of the goods should have been made or, if there is no current price at that place, the price at such other place as serves as a reasonable substitute, making due allowance for differences in the cost of transporting the goods. *See* Art. 76 (2) of the CISG.
1096. Article 563 (4) CC.
1097. Article 557 CC.

contract has already been performed, a party may, according to the situations of performance and the nature of the contract, demand restoration to the original status or other remedial measures to be taken and shall be entitled to claim damages.[1098] By comparing with the damages after avoidance of contract in the CISG, it can be seen that the legal consequence of avoidance of contract in the CISG is the same as that of termination of contract in the Civil Code.

§4. Ownership under Sale

1123. Under the Civil Code, it is assumed that the seller has the right to disposal of the subject matter in the contract. Where the ownership of the subject matter cannot be transferred for want of the right to dispose on the part of the seller, the buyer may terminate the contract and request the seller to bear liability for breach of contract. Where the transfer of the subject matter is prohibited or restricted by any law or administrative regulation, such law or regulation shall prevail.[1099] Meanwhile, the ownership under the sale contract shall not be affected by third parties. Under the Civil Code, the seller is obliged to warrant that no third party has any rights in the subject matter with regard to the subject matter delivered unless otherwise prescribed by law.[1100] This obligation of warranty is to avoid cloud on title in property transactions. For the judgment of cloud on title, the standard is a possibility rather than a reality. It does not require that a third party actually exercises its rights with respect to the subject matter or that the third party's exercise of rights has caused actual obstruction to the buyer. So long as a third party has the ability to exercise its rights with respect to the subject matter, and such possibility poses a potential obstacle or risk to the buyer's ability to obtain complete rights to the subject matter, it can be deemed to constitute a cloud on title.[1101] However, where the buyer knows or ought to know that a third party has rights in the subject matter of the sale when entering into the contract, the seller shall not bear such obligation of warranty.[1102] Furthermore, the buyer may suspend payment of the corresponding price if it proves the presence of a third party's rights in the subject matter, except that the seller has provided appropriate security.[1103]

1124. For the transfer of ownership of the subject matter in the sale contract, the seller shall perform the obligations of delivering to the buyer the subject matter or handing over the documents for taking delivery and transferring to the buyer the

1098. Article 566 CC.
1099. Article 597 CC.
1100. Article 612 CC.
1101. *Zhang Zhiwei and Yu Liping v. Jia Haiqing*, Shanghai Second Intermediate People's Court (2016) Hu 02 Min Zhong No. 9503; 张志伟、俞利平等与贾海庆房屋买卖合同纠纷案，上海市第二中级人民法院 （2016）沪02民终9503号.
1102. Article 613 CC.
1103. Article 614 CC.

ownership of the subject matter.[1104] Where the subject matter is an electronic information product that does not need to be delivered in a corporeal medium, the parties have not explicitly agreed upon the delivery mode, and the delivery mode also cannot be determined according to Article 510 of the Civil Code, delivery shall be deemed to be made when the buyer receives the agreed-upon electronic information product or a certification of rights.[1105] The seller shall also, in accordance with the contract or any trade practice, deliver to the buyer any relevant certificates or documents other than the documents for taking delivery of the subject matter.[1106] The certificates or documents mainly include insurance policies, warranties, ordinary invoices, special value added tax (VAT) invoices, product qualification certificates, quality guarantee certificates, quality appraisal certificates, quality inspection certificates, product entry-exit quarantine certificates, certificates of origin, users' manuals, and packing lists.[1107] In the sale of a subject matter to which an intellectual property right is attached, the intellectual property right in the subject matter shall not vest in the buyer, unless otherwise provided by law or agreed between the parties.[1108] Unless otherwise agreed by the parties, all fruits of the subject matter generated prior to delivery shall belong to the seller, and all fruits generated after delivery shall belong to the buyer.[1109]

1125. Parties to a sale contract may agree to reserve the ownership in some circumstances. In the Civil Code, the parties concerned may agree in a sale contract that the seller shall have ownership of the subject matter if the buyer fails to perform the obligation to pay the price or other obligations. Where the seller retains the ownership of the subject matter, such ownership, if not registered, cannot be alleged against a bona fide third party.[1110] This agreement on the retention of ownership does not apply to immovables.[1111] If the parties agree that the seller reserves the ownership of the subject matter of the contract and the buyer before the ownership to the subject matter is transferred, falls under any of the following circumstances, causing harm to the seller, the seller shall have the right to take back the subject matter unless otherwise agreed upon by the parties: (1) failing to pay the price as agreed and still failing to pay it within a reasonable period after the seller's demand for payment; (2) failing to perform specified obligations as agreed; or (3) selling, pledging or otherwise improperly disposing of the subject matter.[1112] However, where a third party has acquired ownership or any other real right of the subject matter in good faith in accordance with Article 311 of the Civil Code, if the seller claims reclamation of the subject matter, the Chinese court shall not support such claim.[1113]

1104. Article 598 CC.
1105. Article 2 of the SPC Interpretation on the Sales Contracts (2020).
1106. Article 599 CC.
1107. Article 3 of the SPC Interpretation on the Sales Contracts (2020).
1108. Article 600 CC.
1109. Article 630 CC.
1110. Article 641 CC.
1111. Article 25 of the SPC Interpretation on the Sales Contracts (2020).
1112. Paragraph 1 of Art. 642 CC.
1113. Paragraph 2 of Art. 26 of the SPC Interpretation on the Sales Contracts (2020).

1126. The seller may negotiate with the buyer to take back the subject matter; if the negotiation fails, the procedure for realisation of the security interest may apply as reference.[1114] In Chinese judicial practice, the seller shall comply with the following legal conditions when it disposes of the subject matter with reference to the procedure for realisation of the security interest. First, both parties to the sales contract should reach an agreement on the retention of ownership; second, the buyer has a breach of contract, which causes substantial damage to the seller's creditor's rights; third, the seller fails to exercise the right of retrieval to retrieve the subject matter; last, the subject matter exists, and ownership has not been transferred.[1115]

1127. Parties may also agree to the buyer's redemption of the subject matter within a certain period of time even if the seller takes back the subject matter. If, after the seller takes back a subject matter in the aforementioned circumstances, the buyer extinguishes the seller's cause for taking back the subject matter during the redemption period agreed upon by both parties or designated by the seller, the buyer may claim for the redemption of the subject matter. If the buyer does not redeem the subject matter during the redemption period, the seller may sell the subject matter to a third party at a reasonable price, and the surplus of proceeds from the sale of the subject matter after deduction of the amount not paid by the buyer and necessary expenses, if any, shall be returned to the buyer; any shortfall shall be made up for by the buyer.[1116] This is a balance of interests of parties between the seller's right to take back the subject matter and the buyer's right of redemption of the subject matter in the Civil Code.

§5. Delivery of the Subject Matter

1128. The seller shall deliver the subject matter by the agreed time. Where a period of time for delivery is agreed upon, the seller may deliver the subject matter at any time during the agreed period.[1117] Where the parties have not agreed upon the time for the delivery of the subject matter or where their agreement is equivocal, the general rules of the Civil Code shall apply.[1118] First, where, after the contract becomes effective, there is no agreement in the contract between the parties on such contents as quality, price or remuneration, or place of performance, etc., or such agreement is ambiguous, the parties may agree upon supplementary terms; if a supplementary agreement cannot be reached, such terms shall be determined in accordance with the relevant terms, nature, and purpose of the contract, or the trade practices.[1119] Second, if the time of performance is not clarified, the obligor may

1114. Paragraph 2 of Art. 642 CC. The procedure could be found in the Civil Procedure Law.
1115. *Liebherr (China) Co., Ltd. v. Ningxia Ruichen Aodisi Engineering Machinery Co., Ltd.*, Shanghai Pudong New Area People's Court (2021) Hu 0115 Min Chu No. 55963; 利勃海尔（中国）有限公司与宁夏瑞宸奥迪斯工程机械有限公司等买卖合同纠纷案，上海市浦东新区人民法院（2021）沪0115民初55963号.
1116. Article 643 CC.
1117. Article 601 CC.
1118. Article 602 CC.
1119. Article 510 CC.

perform, and the obligee may require performance at any time, provided that the other party shall be given adequate time required for preparation.[1120]

1129. The seller shall deliver the subject matter at the agreed place. Where the parties have not agreed on the place of delivery or their agreement is equivocal and could not be ascertained in accordance with the relevant terms, nature, and purpose of the contract, or the trade practices, the following rules shall apply: (1) where carriage is required, the seller shall deliver the subject matter to the first carrier for delivery to the buyer; (2) where carriage is not required, and both the seller and the buyer knew at the conclusion of the contract the location of the subject matter, the seller shall deliver the subject matter at that location. Where there is no knowledge of the location of the subject matter, delivery of the subject matter shall be effected at the location of the seller's place of business when the contract was concluded.[1121] Furthermore, the seller shall deliver the subject matter in accordance with the contractual requirements for packaging. Where the parties have not agreed on the requirements as to packaging or their agreement is equivocal, a usual manner of packaging shall be used. Where there is no usual manner of packaging, packaging shall be made in a manner sufficient to protect the subject matter.[1122]

1130. The seller should deliver the subject matter in the agreed quantity or amount. If the quantity of the subject matter being delivered by the seller exceeds the agreed quantity, the buyer may accept or reject the excessive portion of the subject matter. If the buyer accepts the excessive portion, it shall pay for the excessive portion at the agreed price. If the buyer rejects the excessive portion, it shall promptly notify the seller.[1123] The Civil Code does not clarify the consequence if the buyer does not give the seller a timely notice for rejecting the excessive portion. It is submitted that the notice is only a subsidiary obligation of the buyer. The buyer may be liable for loss or damage to the seller if it fails to give such notice. However, silence without notice should not be considered as acceptance of an excessive portion of the subject matter by the buyer. Where the buyer rejects the excess over the subject matter, the buyer may keep custody of the excess for the seller. Where the buyer claims that the seller should assume reasonable expenses during the custody period, the Chinese court shall support such claim. Where the buyer claims that the seller should assume any losses not caused by the intentional conduct or gross negligence of the buyer during the custody period, the Chinese court shall support such claim.[1124]

1131. Where the seller concludes several sales contracts for the same ordinary movables, and the buyers all demand actual performance of the contracts and all the sales contracts are valid, the Chinese court shall handle the matter differently according to the following circumstances: (1) where the buyer is the first to take

---

1120. Article 511 (4) CC.
1121. Article 603 CC.
1122. Article 619 CC.
1123. Article 629 CC.
1124. Article 3 of the SPC Interpretation on the Sales Contracts (2020).

delivery and requests confirmation of transfer of ownership, the court shall support such requests; (2) where no buyer takes delivery, and the buyer is the first to make payment and requests that the seller perform contractual obligations including the delivery of the subject matter, the court shall support such requests; or (3) where no buyer takes delivery of the subject matter or makes payment, but the buyer whose contract has been formed in accordance with law requests that the seller performs contractual obligations including delivery of the subject matter, the court shall support such requests.[1125]

1132. Where the seller concludes several sales contracts for the same special movables, such as a ship, aircraft or motor vehicle, and the buyers all demand the actual performance of the contracts and all the sales contracts are valid, the Chinese court shall handle the matter differently according to the following circumstances: (1) where the buyer first to take delivery requests that the seller perform contractual obligations including the handling of formalities for transferring and registering ownership, the court shall support such requests; (2) where no buyer takes delivery, and the buyer that has handled the formalities for transferring and registering ownership in advance requests that the seller perform contractual obligations including the delivery of the subject matter, the court shall support such requests; (3) where no buyer takes delivery of the subject matter or handles the formalities for transferring and registering ownership, if the buyer that has first formed the contract in accordance with law requests that the seller perform contractual obligations including the delivery of the subject matter and the handling of formalities for transferring and registering ownership, the court shall support such requests; or (4) where the seller delivers the subject matter to one of the buyers and handles the formalities for registering ownership for another buyer, if the buyer that has taken delivery of the subject matter requests registration of ownership of the subject matter under its name, the court shall support such requests.[1126]

§6. Risks and Transfer

1133. The risk of subject matter in a sale contract under the Civil Code is basically allocated upon delivery. Unless otherwise provided by law or agreed between the parties, the risk of damage to or loss of the subject matter shall be borne by the seller before delivery and shall pass to the buyer after delivery.[1127] If the buyer designates the place for delivery of subject matter to the carrier, after the seller carries the subject matter to the place designated by the buyer and delivers it to the carrier in accordance with the contract, the risk of damage to or loss of the subject matter shall be borne by the buyer,[1128] except as otherwise agreed upon by the parties.[1129]

1125. Article 6 of the SPC Interpretation on the Sales Contracts (2020).
1126. Article 7 of the SPC Interpretation on the Sales Contracts (2020).
1127. Article 604 CC.
1128. Paragraph 1 of Art. 607 CC. This is a new rule in the Civil Code which does not exist in the Contract Law.
1129. Article 9 of the SPC Interpretation on the Sales Contracts (2020).

If the parties have not agreed on the place of delivery or their agreement is equivocal, and carriage of the subject matter is required after the seller delivers the subject matter to the first carrier, the risk of damage or loss shall be borne by the buyer.[1130] In addition, if the subject matter being sold by the seller has been delivered to a carrier and is in transit, unless otherwise agreed upon by the parties concerned,[1131] the risk of damage or loss shall be borne by the buyer from the time of concluding the contract.[1132]

1134. Where the seller sells subject matter that has been delivered to a carrier for transport and it is in transit, and the seller knows or should have known that the subject matter has been damaged or lost at the time of the formation of the contract but fails to inform the buyer, if the buyer claims that the seller assumes risk of damage to or loss of the subject matter, the Chinese court shall support such claims.[1133] Where the parties do not agree upon the assumption of risk, the subject matter is a general product class, and the seller fails to clearly specify the subject matter of the sales contract by recognisable means such as shipping documents, affixing marks, and notification of the buyer if the buyer claims that it does not assume risk of damage to or loss of the subject matter, the Chinese court shall support such claims.[1134]

1135. The risk allocation is subject to the parties' breach of contract. On the one hand, if the subject matter is not delivered by the agreed time for reasons attributable to the buyer, the buyer shall bear the risk of damage to or loss of the subject matter from the time of the breach of contract.[1135] Moreover, if the seller has placed the subject matter at the place of delivery but the buyer fails to collect the subject matter in breach of the contract, the risk of damage to or loss of the subject matter shall be borne by the buyer from the time of the breach of contract.[1136] On the other hand, the passing of the risk of damage to or loss of the subject matter is not affected by the failure of the seller to deliver certificates or documents relating to the subject matter in accordance with the contract.[1137] Where the subject matter fails to conform to the requirements as to the quality so that the purpose of the contract cannot be fulfilled, the buyer may refuse to accept the subject matter or terminate the contract. Where the buyer refuses to accept the subject matter or terminates the contract, the risk of damage to or loss of the subject matter shall be borne by the seller.[1138] Where the risk of damage to or loss of the subject matter is borne by the buyer, the buyer's right to demand that the seller bear liability for breach of contract by reason of the seller's performance not conforming to the contract is not affected.[1139]

1130. Paragraph 2 of Art. 607 CC.
1131. This is common for international sale of goods contracts.
1132. Article 606 CC.
1133. Article 10 of the SPC Interpretation on the Sales Contracts (2020).
1134. Article 11 of the SPC Interpretation on the Sales Contracts (2020).
1135. Article 605 CC.
1136. Article 608 CC.
1137. Article 609 CC.
1138. Article 610 CC.
1139. Article 611 CC.

§7. Quality Requirements

1136. The seller shall deliver the subject matter pursuant to the contractual requirements as to quality. Where the seller has provided descriptions as to the quality of the subject matter, the delivered subject matter shall conform to such descriptions.[1140] The Civil Code provides detailed provisions on quality and other matters when certain contents agreed upon by the parties in the contract are ambiguous and cannot be determined by contract. Where the parties have not agreed upon the requirements as to the quality of the subject matter or their agreement is equivocal, and such requirements cannot be ascertained under Article 510 of the Civil Code, Article 511(1) of the Civil Code shall be applied.[1141] Article 510 of the Civil Code provides that, where, after the contract becomes effective, there is no agreement in the contract between the parties on quality or such agreement is ambiguous, the parties may agree upon supplementary terms; if a supplementary agreement cannot be reached, such terms shall be determined in accordance with the relevant terms, nature and purpose of the contract, or the trade practices.[1142] Article 511(1) provides that, if the quality requirement is not specified, performance shall be rendered in accordance with the mandatory state standard; where there is no mandatory state standard, the recommended state standard shall be adopted; where there is no recommended state standard, the industry standard shall be adopted; in the absence of any state or industry standard, performance shall be in accordance with the customary standard or any particular standard consistent with the purpose of the contract.[1143] Where the parties agree to reduce or exempt the seller's liability for any defect in the subject matter, and the seller deliberately or by gross negligence fails to inform the buyer of any defect in the subject matter, the seller is not entitled to assert the reduction or exemption of its liability.[1144]

1137. For the quality of subject matter, parties to a sale contract may specify the requirements for the quality in the contract. If there is no such agreed requirement, Chinese courts may refer to other standards or requirements for determining the quality of the subject matter. In *Japon Elektronik Teknoloji Ticaret Limited Sirketi v. Qingdao Hisense Import & Export Co., Ltd.*,[1145] parties agreed to import wireless communication equipment from Turkey to China, and the dispute is about the quality of the equipment.[1146] In normal international sales, parties may adopt quality standards of export or import state or international standards. In this case, the parties did not specify the requirement of equipment in the sale contract. Because of

1140. Article 615 CC.
1141. Article 616 CC.
1142. This article also applies to matters of price or remuneration, place of performance, etc.
1143. This article applies when certain contents agreed upon by the parties in the contract are ambiguous and cannot be determined in accordance with the provisions in Art. 510.
1144. Article 618 CC. This is a new article in the CC which does not exist in the Contract Law.
1145. *Japon Elektronik Teknoloji Ticaret Limited Sirketi v. Qingdao Hisense Import & Export Co., Ltd.*, Gazette Case of the SPC, Issue 11, 2013; 捷跑电子科技有限公司诉青岛海信进出口有限公司国际货物买卖合同纠纷案，《最高人民法院公报》案例，2013年11期.
1146. The Contract Law applied to the dispute. The relevant provisions are identical to the corresponding provisions in the Civil Code.

the defects, the buyer recalled the equipment from the market. Later the equipment was recalled by Turkish authorities. The buyer refused to accept the equipment, terminated the contract and claimed damages against the seller. The core issue in the dispute is whether the equipment failed to conform to the requirements as to the quality. Before the import of the equipment, the seller entrusted an independent third party to have a survey of the quality of the equipment. The buyer received the survey report and did not raise any objections. The Chinese court pointed out that the survey report itself did not prove that the quality requirements of the equipment were satisfied even if it was accepted by the buyer. The quality standards of export and import states should be referred to and considered for the purpose of the contract. Furthermore, although the equipment was recalled by authorities, it had no direct relation to the damage caused by defective quality. In the view of the Chinese court, the buyer did not pay necessary and careful attention to the quality of the equipment. The equipment was recalled after the buyer sold it in the market and consumers complained. Thus, the seller had no chance to be involved in risk assessment and recalling procedures. Therefore, the Chinese court held the seller and the buyer to bear 60% and 40% of the damage caused by the defective quality of the equipment. It is submitted that the ideal practice is to specify the requirements as to the quality of subject matter in the contract.

1138. Where there are no contractual requirements on the quality of subject matter, Chinese courts may refer to standard requirements from industries or authorities. In *Wuyuan Antai Real Estate Development Co., Ltd. v. Lin Xihai*,[1147] the issue in dispute is the quality standard of commodity apartments in a real estate sale contract. Although there were no contractual requirements of quality, the Chinese court held that the commodity apartments as special products shall comply with the requirements approved by building authorities. Only the approved building can be registered by housing authorities, and the property ownership certificate is issued only for the registered building. The purpose of the real estate sale contract can be fulfilled only when the buyer obtains the property ownership certificate. Therefore, the Chinese court applied the quality requirements from the building authorities, although there were no such requirements in the sale contract.

1139. Even if the standard requirements from industries or authorities are satisfied, the subject matter delivered by the seller may fail to satisfy the requirements as to quality for the contract purpose. In *Yang Jun v. Dongtai Dongsheng Real Estate Development Co., Ltd.*,[1148] the house delivered under the sale contract had cracks and leak problems, and the buyer claimed that the house did not satisfy the quality requirement. The reasons for the quality problems identified by a professional surveyor were the lack of an insulation layer and poor quality of wall

1147. *Wuyuan Antai Real Estate Development Co., Ltd. v. Lin Xihai*, Guide on Adjudication Supervisions (2018) Issue 1, People's Court Press (2019) pp. 52-68; 婺源县安泰房地产开发有限责任公司诉林细海，《审判监督指导》2018年第1辑，人民法院出版社，2019年版，第52-68页.

1148. *Yang Jun v. Dongtai Dongsheng Real Estate Development Co., Ltd.*, Gazette Case of the SPC, Issue 11, 2010; 杨珺诉东台市东盛房地产开发有限公司商品房销售合同纠纷案，《最高人民法院公报》案例，2010年11期.

masonry. The seller argued that the authorities had approved the design and completion of the house. It seemed to imply that the requirement was satisfied when the authorities approved the building of the house. However, this argument was not accepted by the Chinese courts. It was pointed out by courts that, although there were approvals from authorities, the house delivered under the contract had apparent quality defects and it could not be used by the buyer for contractual purpose. More importantly, the requirement from authorities did not include the requirement of an insulation layer. The approvals were only the recognition of the authorities for administration purpose; they were not evidence denying the fact that the house had quality defects. Therefore, the house delivered by the seller did not satisfy the quality requirement and the buyer was entitled to claim damages caused by the quality defects.

1140. For the damage caused by quality problems, the Civil Code provides that, where the subject matter delivered by the seller fails to satisfy the requirements as to quality, the buyer may claim for breach of contract in accordance with Articles 582–584 of the Civil Code.[1149] First, where performance fails to satisfy the agreement, the liability for breach of contract shall be borne as agreed upon by the parties. If there is no agreement in the contract on the liability for breach of contract or such agreement is not clarified, the adversely affected party may, in light of the nature of the subject matter and the degree of loss, reasonably choose to request the other party to bear the liability for breach of contract, such as repairing, redoing, replacing, returning the goods, reducing the price or remuneration.[1150] Second, even if the breaching party, e.g., the seller continues performance or takes remedial measures after breach of contract, he shall compensate the buyer if the buyer still suffers other losses.[1151] The Civil Code does not specify what other losses can be reimbursed. It is submitted that such other losses should be losses caused by the breach of contract. In any event, the amount of compensation for losses shall be equal to the losses caused by the breach of contract, including the benefits receivable after the performance of the contract, but shall not exceed the amount of the loss that may be caused by the breach of contract and that has been or ought to be foreseen by the breaching party in concluding the contract.[1152]

1141. Besides the basic rules for assessment of damage in the Civil Code, the damage is also assessed on a case-by-case basis in judicial practice. In *Li Mingbo v. Nanjing Jinling Property Development Co., Ltd.*,[1153] the house in the sale contract had the quality problem, and the actual damage was assessed based on the rent of the same kind of house for the same period. For the amount of rent, the references included the rent provided by the authority, the Price Certification Centre of the local Price Bureau, and the rent of other houses in the local area for the same

1149. Article 617 CC.
1150. Article 582 CC.
1151. Article 583 CC.
1152. Article 584 CC.
1153. *Li Mingbo v. Nanjing Jinling Property Development Co., Ltd.*, Gazette Case of the SPC, Issue 12, 2016; 李明柏诉南京金陵置业发展有限公司商品房预售合同纠纷案，《最高人民法院公报》案例，2016年12期.

period. The Chinese courts considered the references but did not adopt any of them for determining the amount of actual damage. On the one hand, the courts pointed out that the opinion of price provided by the local authorities should be considered according to the relevance between the opinion and the facts. If the opinion could not reflect the real facts of the case, it should not be accepted as evidence for determining the case. In this case, it was found that the price in the opinion was much lower than the real market rent of the similar house in the same period. Thus, it would be unfair to the innocent party if the damage were assessed based on the rent in the opinion from the local authorities. On the other hand, the buyer provided evidence of rent by referring to the rent of other similar houses in the local area for the same period. But the courts found that those similar houses were located in different places and had different internal decorations. Therefore, the courts pointed out the rent provided by the buyer was not representative for the average rent of the local houses. The Chinese courts held that the assessment of damage based on rent should be decided according to the real market price of the rent in the same period.[1154]

§8. INSPECTION

1142. Inspection is an important measure for the buyer to make sure the subject matter in a sale contract complies with the pre-agreed quantity or quality. Under the Civil Code, upon receipt of the subject matter, the buyer shall conduct inspection within the agreed inspection period. Where there is no agreed inspection period, inspection shall be carried out timely.[1155] The buyer has an obligation to notify the seller of any non-conformity to the contract after inspection. First, where the parties have agreed on a period for inspection, the buyer shall, within the inspection period, notify the seller of any non-conformity to the contract in respect of the quantity or quality of the subject matter. Where the buyer neglects to give such notification, the quantity or quality of the subject matter shall be deemed to conform to the contract.[1156] It must be noted that the seller should not only inspect the subject matter within the inspection period if it is agreed upon, but also give the notice within the inspection period. So, if the seller completes the inspection within the agreed period but gives a notice of non-conformity after the period, the notice may not be accepted unless the parties otherwise agreed. If the buyer claims product quality defects after the expiration of the agreed inspection period, the agreement on the inspection period shall not be disregarded unless there are statutory circumstances.[1157]

1143. Second, where the parties have not agreed on a period for inspection, the buyer shall notify the seller of any non-conformity to the contract in respect of the quantity or quality of the subject matter within a reasonable period after it discovers

1154. The Chinese courts have discretion for determining a reasonable price with reference to market price.
1155. Article 620 CC.
1156. Paragraph 1 of Art. 621 CC.
1157. *A Battery Co., Ltd. v. B Auto Co., Ltd.*, the SPC (2021) Zui Gao Fa Min Shen No. 2163; 某电池公司诉某汽车公司买卖合同纠纷案（2021）最高法民申2163号.

or ought to discover such non-conformity. Where the buyer fails to notify the seller within the reasonable period or two years from the date of receipt of the subject matter, the quantity or quality shall be deemed to conform to the contract. However, where there is a period of warranty as to the quality, the period of warranty shall apply in place of the provisions on the two-year limit.[1158] When determining the 'reasonable period', the Chinese court shall comprehensively take into account the transaction naturc, purpose, methods, and customary business practice between the parties, the category, quantity and nature of the subject matter, the circumstances regarding installation and use, the nature of any defects, the duty of reasonable care to be assumed by the buyer, the inspection methods and their degree of difficulty, the specific environment at the location of the buyer or inspector and their own skills as well as other reasonable factors, and make a judgment based on the principle of good faith.[1159]

1144. The period of 'two years' means the maximum reasonable period. This period is a non-variable period to which the provisions on the suspension, interruption or extension of extinctive prescription do not apply.[1160] In any event, where the seller knows or ought to know that the subject matter to be supplied fails to conform to the contract, the buyer is not subject to the restrictions as to the notification period in the aforementioned circumstances.[1161] After the inspection period, the reasonable period, and the two-year period have passed, where the buyer claims that the quantity or quality of the subject matter does not comply with the contractual agreement, the Chinese court shall not support such claim. If the seller reneges on a voluntary assumption of liability for breach of contract on the ground that the inspection periods have expired, the Chinese court shall not support such reneging.[1162]

1145. Inspection period may be subject to practices and law. Where the agreed inspection period is too short in light of the nature of the subject matter and trade practice, and the buyer cannot complete a full-scale inspection of the subject matter within the inspection period, such a period shall be deemed merely as the period for the buyer to raise an objection as to any external defect of the subject matter.[1163] Where the agreed period for inspection or the period of warranty as to the quality is shorter than that required by laws or administrative regulations, the period prescribed under such laws or administrative regulations shall prevail.[1164] If the parties have not agreed on a period for inspection, but the buyer has signed for a delivery note, confirmation slip or other document which states the quantity, model and specifications of the subject matter, it is presumed that the buyer has inspected the

1158. Paragraph 2 of Art. 621 CC.
1159. Article 12 of the SPC Interpretation on the Sales Contracts (2020).
1160. Article 13 of the SPC Interpretation on the Sales Contracts (2020).
1161. Paragraph 3 of Art. 621 CC.
1162. Article 14 of the SPC Interpretation on the Sales Contracts (2020).
1163. Paragraph 1 of Art. 622 CC.
1164. Paragraph 2 of Art. 622 CC.

quantity and any external defect of the subject matter, unless there is relevant evidence sufficient to rebut such a presumption.[1165] If the subject matter is required to be recovered after the expiry of the period of effective use in accordance with the provisions of laws or administrative regulations or the agreement between the parties, the seller shall have the obligation to recover or entrust a third party to recover the subject matter.[1166]

1146. If parties have agreed on the standard of inspection, they should follow the standard. There is a special rule on inspection standards among more than two parties in the Civil Code. It is provided that, where, as instructed by the buyer, the seller delivers the subject matter to a third party, and the inspection standard agreed by the seller and the buyer is inconsistent with the inspection standard agreed by the buyer and the third party, the inspection standard agreed by the seller and the buyer shall prevail.[1167] This special rule does not clarify what it is for when the inspection standard agreed upon by the seller and the buyer prevails. It is believed that the special rule is the application of the general contract law rule to the sale contract. In the Civil Code, it is provided that, where the parties agree that the obligor shall perform the obligations to a third party, and the obligor fails to perform its obligations to such a third party or its performance of the obligations is not in conformity with the agreement, the obligor shall be liable to the obligee for breach of contract.[1168] Applying this general rule to the special rule, it can be inferred that the inspection standard agreed by the seller and the buyer prevails when the seller is liable to the buyer for breach of contract. In other words, the seller cannot reply on the inspection standard agreed by the buyer and the third party as a defence to deny its liability for breach of contract. This is also the result of the application of the principle of privity of contract in the Civil Code.[1169]

1147. Where the buyer retains a portion of the price as a financial warranty of quality as agreed, and the seller fails to resolve the quality issue in a timely manner within the period for warranty of quality, which affects the value or utility of the subject matter, if the seller claims the payment of the portion of the price, the Chinese court shall not support such claim.[1170] Where the buyer raises an objection regarding quality within the inspection period, period for warranty of quality, or reasonable period, if the seller fails to repair the subject matter as demanded or, due to emergency, the buyer repairs the subject matter itself or through a third party, and the buyer claims that the seller should assume the reasonable expenses incurred thereby, the Chinese court shall support such claim.[1171]

1165. Article 623 CC.
1166. Article 625 CC.
1167. Article 624 CC.
1168. Paragraph 1 of Art. 522 CC.
1169. Paragraph 2 of Art. 465 CC provides that 'a lawfully formed contract will be legally binding only on the parties, except otherwise provided by law.'
1170. Article 15 of the SPC Interpretation on the Sales Contracts (2020).
1171. Article 16 of the SPC Interpretation on the Sales Contracts (2020).

§9. Payment Obligation

1148. Paying the price is an important obligation of the buyer. Under the Civil Code, the buyer shall pay the price in accordance with the agreed amount and method of payment. Where there is no agreement on the amount or method of payment or the agreement is equivocal, Articles 510, 511(2) and 511(5) of the Civil Code shall apply.[1172] Article 510 provides that the parties may agree upon supplementary terms on price; if a supplementary agreement cannot be reached, such terms shall be determined in accordance with the relevant terms, nature and purpose of the contract, or the trade practices. If the price cannot be determined in accordance with the provisions in Article 510, Article 511 will apply. The price can be determined in accordance with the prevailing market price at the place of performance at the time when the contract was concluded; where adoption of a price commissioned by the government or based on government-issued pricing guidelines is required by law, such requirement shall apply.[1173] If the method of payment is not clarified, performance shall be rendered in a manner conducive to realising the purpose of the contract.[1174] In addition, where the buyer has paid 75% or more of the total price of the subject matter, and the seller claims the reclamation of the subject matter, the Chinese court shall not support such claim.[1175]

1149. The SPC considered the payment obligation of the buyer in *Dongfang Turbine Co., Ltd. v. Dafeng Construction and Installation Co., Ltd. of Daqing High-tech Industrial Development Zone and Daqing Dafeng Energy Technology Service Co., Ltd.*.[1176] In this case, the seller and the buyer concluded a sale contract for the sale and purchase of wind turbine generator units. After inspection, the units were accepted by the buyer in October 2012. After acceptance, the quality warranty period started from November 2012 for five years. During the quality warranty period, the buyer did not raise any objections to the quality of the units. According to the sale contract, the buyer should pay the price by instalments from May 2016 to the end of 2017, but the buyer failed to pay the instalments. The seller claimed against the buyer for unpaid instalments. The buyer argued that the units had quality problem, and it was entitled to refuse to pay the instalments. The buyer also argued that the seller breached the contract because it did not deliver relevant technical documents to the buyer. The first instance court found that, although the buyer had concerns about the quality of the units, it agreed to pay the instalments without any condition of quality issue. The buyer also brought another lawsuit against the

1172. Article 626 CC.
1173. Article 511 (2) CC.
1174. Article 511 (5) CC.
1175. Article 26 of the SPC Interpretation on the Sales Contracts (2020).
1176. *Dongfang Turbine Co., Ltd. v. Dafeng Construction and Installation Co., Ltd. of Daqing High-tech Industrial Development Zone and Daqing Dafeng Energy Technology Service Co., Ltd.*, Gazette Case of the SPC, Issue 11, 2020; 东方电气集团东方汽轮机有限公司与大庆高新技术产业开发区大丰建筑安装有限公司、大庆大丰能源技术服务有限公司买卖合同纠纷案,《最高人民法院公报》案例，2020年11期.

seller for damage due to the quality problem. Therefore, it was held that the buyer should pay the unpaid instalments according to the sale contract.[1177]

1150. In the second instance of the case, the SPC upheld the decision of the first instant court. First, it was pointed out that the buyer was not entitled to raise the defence of first performance when it accepted and used the subject matter but did not challenge the quality within the quality warranty period.[1178] The buyer had brought another lawsuit for a quality issue. So, it could seek indemnity from that lawsuit. It should not affect the seller's claim against the buyer for the unpaid instalments. Second, delivery of documents is the seller's secondary obligation of delivery of the subject matter in the sale contract. The buyer may claim against the seller for breach of this obligation. However, if the seller breaches the secondary obligation but the undelivered documents do not affect the buyer's normal use of the subject matter or the purpose of the contract, the buyer cannot refuse to pay the price to the seller because of the breach of the secondary obligation.[1179] It was found that the buyer had never raised any objection to the technical documents during the use of the units, and there were no circumstances in which the units did not run due to lack of technical documents or the contract purpose could not be realised. Therefore, the SPC held that, even if the seller did not delivery relevant technical documents of the units, the buyer was not entitled to refuse to pay the price of the units.[1180] This SPC's judgment confirmed the overriding obligation of the buyer for payment of price under sale contract. However, this judgment is made based on special facts. If good quality of subject matter and delivery of technical documents are conditions of payment obligation, and the buyer can prove a quality problem or lack of technical documents, it might be entitled to refuse to pay the price according to the sale contract.

1151. Parties to a sale contract may agree on a place and time for payment. In the Civil Code, the buyer shall pay the price at the agreed place of payment. Where there is no agreement as to the place of payment or the agreement is equivocal, and the place cannot be ascertained under Article 510 of the Civil Code, the buyer shall pay at the seller's place of business. However, where it is agreed that payment is conditional on the delivery of the subject matter or of certificates for its collection, payment shall be made at the place of delivery of the subject matter or the certificates for its collection.[1181] The buyer shall pay the price at the agreed time. Where there is no agreement on the time for payment or the agreement is equivocal, and the time cannot be ascertained under Article 510 of the Civil Code, the buyer shall pay upon receipt of the subject matter or certificates for its collection.[1182]

1177. Heilongjiang High People's Court (2018) Hei Min Chu No. 34; 黑龙江省高级人民法院（2018）黑民初34号.
1178. Summary Note 1 of the Gazette Judgment.
1179. *Ibid*, Summary Note 2.
1180. The SPC (2019) Zui Gao Fa Min Zhong No. 185; 最高人民法院（2019）最高法民终185号.
1181. Article 627 CC.
1182. Article 628 CC.

§10. Termination of Contract

1152. Besides the general rules of termination of contract in the Civil Code,[1183] the chapter of sale contract provides four specific rules for termination of sale contract. The first rule is about the termination effect between the principal article in subject matter and the ancillary article in the subject matter. Where a contract is terminated due to the non-conformity of the principal article in the subject matter to the contract, the effect of the termination extends to any ancillary article. Where a contract is terminated due to the non-conformity of the ancillary article in the subject matter of the contract, the effect of the termination does not extend to the principal article.[1184] Second, where the subject matter comprises more than one article, and one of them does not conform to the contract, the buyer may terminate the contract in respect of that article. However, where the separation of such an article from other articles manifestly impairs the value of the subject matter, the contract may be terminated in respect of all of those articles.[1185]

1153. Third, if the seller delivers the subject matter in instalments, and the seller fails to deliver one of the instalments or the delivered instalment fails to conform with the contract, with the consequence that the purpose of the contract in respect of such an instalment cannot be fulfilled, the buyer may terminate the contract in respect of such an instalment.[1186] It means that the buyer cannot terminate the whole contract in this circumstance because other instalments are still valid. If the seller fails to deliver one of the instalments or the delivered instalment fails to conform to the contract, with the consequence that the purpose of the contract cannot be fulfilled by the delivery of subsequent instalments, the buyer may terminate the contract in respect of that and all subsequent instalments.[1187] It means that the buyer cannot terminate the whole contract because delivery of the previous instalments are valid. If the buyer terminates the contract in respect of one of the instalments of the subject matter, and that instalment is interdependent with every other instalment, the buyer may terminate the contract in respect of all delivered and undelivered instalments.[1188] In this circumstance, the buyer in fact terminates the whole contract.

1154. Last, where payments are to be made in instalments, if the unpaid instalments that are due amount to one-fifth of the total price and the buyer fails to pay the overdue price within a reasonable period after the seller's demand for payment, the seller may request the buyer to pay the total sum or terminate the contract.[1189] The phrase 'instalment payment' means that the buyer pays the total price payable to the seller at a minimum in three instalments within a certain period.[1190] If a sales contract permitting instalment payment contains a clause in violation of this rule of

1183. *See* the CC, Book III, Part One, Chapter 7 Termination of Contractual Rights and Obligations.
1184. Article 631 CC.
1185. Article 632 CC.
1186. Paragraph 1 of Art. 633 CC.
1187. Paragraph 2 of Art. 633 CC.
1188. Paragraph 3 of Art. 633 CC.
1189. Paragraph 1 of Art. 634 CC.
1190. Paragraph 1 of Art. 27 of the SPC Interpretation on the Sales Contracts (2020).

the Civil Code and injurious to the interest of the buyer, such a clause is void.[1191] Where the seller terminates the contract, it may require the buyer to pay the fee for the use of the subject matter.[1192] Where the seller, in an agreement on instalment payment in a sales contract, may retain payment already received when the contract is rescinded, if the amount retained by the seller exceeds fees for use of the subject matter and compensation for damages to the subject matter, the buyer is entitled to request the return of the excess amount.[1193] In addition, after a sales contract is rescinded due to breach of contract, where the non-breaching party claims that the liquidated damages clause should continue to apply, the Chinese court shall support such claim.[1194]

§11. Sale by Sample and Sale by Trial

1155. For the sale by sample, the Civil Code provides that 'the party shall seal the sample and may give descriptions of the quality of the sample'.[1195] But it does not mean that parties must seal the sample and give descriptions. It does not suggest that the sale by sample is not valid if parties do not seal the sample or fail to describe the sample. If the parties seal the sample and give a description, the subject matter delivered by the seller shall conform to the quality of the sample and its descriptions.[1196] However, where a sales contract contains any of the following contents, it is not a sale by trial: (1) when the subject matter satisfies certain requirements upon trial or inspection, the buyer shall purchase the subject matter; (2) when a third party approves the subject matter upon testing, the buyer shall purchase the subject matter; (3) when the buyer may request a replacement of the subject matter within a certain period; or (4) when the buyer may return the subject matter within a certain period.[1197]

1156. In a sale by sample, if the buyer is not aware of a latent defect in the sample, the quality of the subject matter delivered by the seller shall conform to the usual standards of the subject matter, notwithstanding that the delivered subject matter is identical to the sample.[1198] Where the quality of a sample as agreed upon in a contract is inconsistent with written descriptions and the parties fail to reach consensus when a dispute arises, if there are no changes to the external appearance and the internal qualities of the sample after being sealed, the sample shall be the standard used by the Chinese court. If there are changes to external appearance and

---

1191. Paragraph 2 of Art. 27of the SPC Interpretation on the Sales Contracts (2020).
1192. Article 634, para. 2 CC.
1193. Article 28, para. 1 of the SPC Interpretation on the Sales Contracts (2020).
1194. Article 20 of the SPC Interpretation on the Sales Contracts (2020).
1195. Article 635 CC.
1196. *Ibid.*
1197. Article 30 of the SPC Interpretation on the Sales Contracts (2020).
1198. Article 636 CC.

internal qualities, or the parties have disputes over whether there are changes but there is no way to ascertain any changes, the written descriptions shall be the standard used by the Chinese court.[1199]

1157. In a sale by trial, the parties may agree on a period of trial of the subject matter. Where the parties have not agreed on a period of trial or their agreement is equivocal, and the period cannot be ascertained under Article 510 of the Civil Code, the period shall be determined by the seller.[1200] Within the period of trial, the buyer may purchase or refuse to purchase the subject matter. Upon expiry of the period of trial, where the buyer does not indicate whether to purchase the subject matter, it shall be deemed to have purchased it. Where the buyer in a sale by trial has made partial payment of the price or has sold, leased or created a security interest over the subject matter during the period of trial, it shall be deemed to have agreed to the purchase.[1201] Where the parties in a sale by trial have not agreed on the fees for the use of the subject matter or their agreement is equivocal, the seller is not entitled to seek payment of such fees from the buyer.[1202] The risk of damage to or loss of the subject matter during the period of trial is borne by the seller.[1203] This risk allocation does not consider the circumstance in which the loss or damage resulted from an act or omission of the buyer done with intent to cause damage, or recklessly and with knowledge that damage would probably result. In this circumstance, it is not the seller's liability, and loss or damage should be borne by the buyer.

§12. OTHERS

1158. The chapter of the sale contract contains rules for some special sale contract. For the sale by tender, the rights and obligations of the parties and tendering procedures, etc., shall be governed by the relevant laws and administrative regulations.[1204] For the auction sale, the rights and obligations of the parties in an auction and the auction proceedings, etc., shall be governed by the relevant laws and administrative regulations.[1205] In Chinese judicial practice, both contract law rules and auction law rules will apply to auction sale disputes. The contract law rules will govern the legal relation between the seller and the buyer, and the auction law rules will govern the auction procedures.[1206] Where the parties have agreed on a barter

1199. Article 29 of the SPC Interpretation on the Sales Contracts (2020).
1200. Article 637 CC.
1201. Article 638 CC.
1202. Article 639 CC.
1203. Article 640 CC.
1204. Article 644 CC. The law is the Tendering and Bidding Law.
1205. Article 645 CC. The law is the Auction law.
1206. *Zeng Yilong v. Jiangxi Golden Horse Auction Co., Ltd., Bank of China Limited Shangrao Branch and Xu Shengju*, the SPC (2005) Min Yi Zhong Zi No. 43 (Gazette Case of the SPC, Issue 1, 2006); 曾意龙与江西金马拍卖有限公司、中国银行股份有限公司上饶市分行、徐声炬案，最高人民法院（2005）民一终字第43号（《最高人民法院公报》案例，2006年01期）.

transaction under which the ownership of the subject matter is transferred, the relevant provisions on sales contracts shall be referred to and applied.[1207] Where there are provisions in laws for other non-gratuitous contracts, such legal provisions shall prevail.[1208] Otherwise, the relevant provisions on sale contracts shall be referred to and applied.[1209]

§13. Sale of Commercial Real Estate

I. Commercial Real Estate Sale

1159. The Civil Code does not have special provisions for the sale of commercial real estate. The SPC promulgated the SPC Interpretation on Certain Issues Concerning the Application of Law in Trying Cases Involving Disputes over Contracts on Sale of Commercial Real Estate in 2003. It has been revised by the SPC according to the Civil Code in 2020 (the SPC Interpretation on the Sale of Commercial Real Estate (2020)).[1210] The 'Contracts on Sale of Commercial real estate' means the contracts by which the real estate enterprises, namely the sellers, sell houses that are not yet completed or that are already completed in the open market and transfer the ownership of the houses to the buyers who pay for the houses.[1211] From this concept, it can be seen that the SPC Interpretation on the Sale of Commercial Real Estate (2020) only applies to the dispute over commercial real estate sales with the real estate enterprises. In other words, the SPC Interpretation on the Sale of Commercial Real Estate (2020) does not apply to the sale of the commercial real estate between individuals. A sale contract shall be deemed as a sale contract of commercial real estate even if it is in the form of an agreement of subscription, order, or advance reservation for commercial real estate, provided that the agreement contains the main contents of the sale, and the seller has received the price of the sale in accordance with the agreement.[1212]

1207. Article 647 CC.
1208. For example, the Consumer Protection Law applies to the consumer contract, the Insurance Law applies to the insurance contract, the Tourism Law applies to the travel contract, the Maritime Law applies to marine insurance contract, and the Commercial Banks Law applies to the savings deposit contract.
1209. Article 646 CC. For example, the contracts for assignment of rights such as claims or equities, assignment of rights or any other onerous contract, *see* Art. 32 of the SPC Interpretation on the Sales Contracts (2020). *See also Wuxi Humei Thermal Power Engineering Co., Ltd. v. DBS Bank Ltd*, The SPC (2017) Zui Gao Fa Min Zhong No. 327 (Gazette Case of the SPC, Issue 11, 2018); 无锡湖美热能电力工程有限公司与新加坡星展银行信用证纠纷案， 最高人民法院（2017）最高法民终327号（《最高人民法院公报》案例，2018年11期）.
1210. The SPC Interpretation on the Sale of Commercial Real Estate (2020).
1211. Article 1 of the SPC Interpretation on the Sale of Commodity Houses (2020).
1212. Article 5 CC.

II. Offer and Validity of Contract

1160. There are special rules in the Interpretation on the formation and validity of sale contracts of commercial real estate. First, advertisements and promotional materials of commercial real estate in the Interpretation are invitations to offer. However, if the explanations and promises made by the seller concerning the real estate and related facilities within the scope of the real estate's development plan are clear and certain and have significant influence on the conclusion of the contract of sale of the real estate, they shall be deemed as an offer. Such explanations and promises shall be deemed as contents of the contract even if they are not included in the contract of sale of the commercial real estate. Any party in violation of such contents shall be liable for breach of the contract.[1213]

1161. Second, the seller must obtain the presale permit from authorities for the sale of commercial real estate in China. If a sale contract of commercial real estate is concluded before the seller obtains the permit, such a contract shall be deemed as void. However, if the seller obtains the permit before an action is instituted concerning the sale contract, the contract shall be deemed as valid.[1214] Furthermore, all contracts for presale of commercial real estate in China must be registered for record in accordance with the law and administrative regulation. Where a party files a request for invalidating a presale contract of commercial real estate because no formalities are completed for the registration of the contract, such request will not be upheld by Chinese courts. However, if the parties have agreed that the completion of registration formalities shall be a condition to the effectiveness of the presale contract, the condition shall be satisfied for the effectiveness unless one party concerned has already fulfilled its main obligations and the other party accepts the performance.[1215] Last, if a buyer cannot obtain the real estate as a result of malicious collusion between the seller and a third party in a separate sale contract of commercial real estate and the delivery of the real estate to such third party for use, the buyer can file a request to invalidate such a contract; the request shall be upheld by Chinese courts.[1216]

III. Risk and Quality Concerns

1162. In the SPC Interpretation on the Sale of Commercial Real Estate (2020), transfer of possession of real estate shall be deemed as delivery for use of the real estate, unless otherwise agreed by the parties. The risks of damage to, and destruction of, the real estate shall be borne by the seller before the real estate is delivered for use and by the buyer after they are delivered for use. If the buyer receives the seller's written notice of delivery of the real estate but refuses, without justified reasons, to take the delivery of the real estate, the risks of damage to, and destruction

1213. Article 3 CC.
1214. Article 2 CC.
1215. Article 6 CC.
1216. Article 7 CC.

of, the real estate shall be borne by the buyer from the date of delivery for use specified in the written notice, except as otherwise specified in the law or agreed upon by the parties.[1217]

1163. If the real estate fails to be delivered for use because of the unqualified main structure, or if the main structure is found to be unqualified upon testing and inspection after delivery for use, the buyer is entitled to terminate the contract and claim damages.[1218] If any quality problem of the real estate seriously affects the normal use for habitation, the buyer is entitled to terminate the contract and claim damages. In the event of quality problems occurring in the real estate that have been delivered for use during the warranty period, the seller shall bear the liability for repair; if the seller refuses to repair or delays doing so within a reasonable time limit, the buyer may repair it by itself or have it repaired by another person. The cost of the repair and other losses caused during the repair period shall be borne by the seller.[1219]

IV. Breach and Remedies

1164. The Civil Code provides that, if one party delays performance of its principal obligation and fails to perform within a reasonable period after the demand, the other party is entitled to terminate the contract.[1220] The SPC Interpretation on the Sale of Commercial Real Estate (2020) specifies the reasonable period for the sale contract of commercial real estate. It provides that if the seller delays the delivery of the real estate or the buyer delays the payment of the purchase price for the real estate and fails to do so within a reasonable time limit of three months after a reminder, the innocent party is entitled to terminate the contract, unless otherwise agreed upon by the parties. The Interpretation also provides a reasonable time limit for exercising the termination right. It provides that, in the absence of provisions in law or agreement between the parties concerned, the reasonable time limit for exercising the right of termination shall be three months after a reminder from the other party. In the absence of a reminder from the other party, the right of termination shall be exercised within one year from the date that the innocent party knows or should have known the event causing the termination. If the right is not exercised within the time limit, it shall be extinguished.[1221] The reasonable time limits for the entitlement of the termination right and the extinguishment of the termination right keep the balance of interests between parties and encourage parties to exercise rights in a timely manner.

1165. The Civil Code provides that the parties may agree on a certain sum of the liquidated damage in light of the circumstances when breach of contract occurs.

1217. Article 8 CC.
1218. Article 9 CC.
1219. Article 10 CC.
1220. Article 563(3) CC.
1221. Article11 of the SPC Interpretation on the Sale of Commodity Houses (2020).

Where the sum of the liquidated damage agreed upon is lower than the actual damage incurred, the Chinese courts or arbitration institutions may increase the amount upon the request of a party; where the sum of the liquidated damage agreed upon is excessively higher than the actual damage incurred, the Chinese courts or arbitration institutions may reduce the amount upon the request of party.[1222] The SPC Interpretation on the Sale of Commercial Real Estate (2020) specifies the standard of the amount of increase or decrease. It provides that, if a party requests a reduction of the amount of the liquidated damage that is extortionate, the amount of liquidated damages shall be appropriately reduced to 30% of the losses caused. If a party requests an increase of the amount of the liquidated damage that is less than the losses caused, the amount of the liquidated damage shall be determined by the amount of loss caused by the breach of contract.[1223]

1166. In the absence of a specific amount of liquidated damages or method for calculation of compensation for losses in a sale contract of commercial real estate, the amount of compensation for losses can be determined by referring to the following standards: (1) in the case of overdue payment, it shall be calculated by referring to the interest rate on outstanding loans set by the People's Bank of China for financial institutions on the basis of the amount of the total unpaid purchase price; (2) in the case of overdue delivery of the real estate for use, it shall be calculated according to the standard of the rent of the real estate of the same type in the same locality as published by the relevant competent authorities or as appraised by qualified real estate appraisal organisations for the period of the delay.[1224]

1167. The Civil Code provides that the creation, alteration, transfer or extinction of immovable property rights shall become effective upon registration in accordance with law; it shall not become effective without registration unless otherwise provided by law.[1225] Therefore, the registration of the real estate is very important for the buyer of the commercial real estate. Parties to the sale contract of commercial real estate may agree on a certain period of time for registration of the real estate. But the agreed period shall not be longer than the period required by law. Article 32 of the Regulations on Administration of Urban Real Estate Development and Management provides that the buyer of the commercial real estate shall register the real estate within ninety days from the date of delivery of the presale real estate or from the date of conclusion of the contract for completed real estate. It also provides that the real estate enterprises shall assist the buyer in the registration of the real estate and provide necessary documents. The SPC Interpretation on the Sale of Commercial Real Estate (2020) provides that if the buyer fails, due to reasons attributable to the seller, to register ownership of the real estate after one year from the

1222. Paragraphs 1 and 2 of Art. 585 CC.
1223. Article 12 of the SPC Interpretation on the Sale of Commodity Houses (2020).
1224. *Ibid.*; Art. 13.
1225. Article 209, para. 1 CC.

expiry of the time limit for registration specified in a contract or in Article 32 of the Regulations on Administration of Urban Real Estate Development and Management, the buyer is entitled to terminate the contract and claim damages thereby caused.[1226]

1226. Article 15 of the SPC Interpretation on the Sale of Commodity Houses (2020).

Chapter 2. Contracts for the Supply and Use of Electricity, Water, Gas or Heat

§1. Concept and Responsibility

1168. A contract for the supply and use of electricity in the Civil Code is a contract whereby the electricity supplier supplies electricity to the electricity user, and the user pays electricity charges therefore.[1227] The content of a contract for the supply and use of electricity generally includes terms as to the means, quality and time of the supply of electricity, the capacity, address and nature of the use of electricity, the means of calculating electricity quantity and settling electricity rate and charges, the responsibility for maintaining the facilities for the supply and use of electricity, etc.[1228] The Civil Code does not provide a concept of contract for the supply and use of water, gas and heat, but it provides that, for contracts for the supply and use of water, gas and heat, the relevant provisions of the contract for the supply and use of electricity shall be referred to and applied.[1229] The concept of the contract for the supply and use of electricity is not changed from the Contract Law, but the Civil Code adds that an electricity supplier who supplies electricity to the public shall not refuse a reasonable request made by the electricity user for entry into a contract.[1230] The electricity suppliers in China are large enterprises and have strong bargaining power in the market. This new provision is to balance the bargaining powers between the electricity suppliers and the electricity user. It also applies to contracts for the supply and use of water, gas and heat.

1169. The suppliers have not only the contractual obligations but also social responsibility. They may have a higher burden of proof to discharge their responsibilities and liabilities. In *Yancheng Tianmu Food Cot Ltd v. Yancheng Water Supply Co., Ltd.*,[1231] the water user found that the daily use of water increased substantially and unreasonably after the replacement of the water meter by the water supplier company. It claimed that the water supplier should refund the payment for the extra water charged according to the water meter in dispute. The water supplier argued that the water meter had no problem according to the survey report. It was agreed in the contract that the survey should be conducted jointly by parties, but the survey was actually done by the water supplier only. The courts refused to accept the report. The courts found that there was no change in daily use of water by the user, but the water use increased unreasonably. The courts pointed out that it is the water supplier's public service to install, replace and repair water meters under the water supply contract relationship. The water suppliers have dominance in water supply contracts in terms of information, technology and performance and they

1227. Article 648, para. 1 CC.
1228. Article 649 CC.
1229. Article 656 CC.
1230. Paragraph 2 of Art. 648 CC.
1231. *Yancheng Tianmu Food Co., Ltd. v. Yancheng Water Supply Co., Ltd.*, Gazette Case of the SPC, Issue 3, 2020; 盐城市天孜食品有限公司诉盐城市自来水有限公司供水合同纠纷案，《最高人民法院公报》案例，2020年03期.

should have a high level of public service and social responsibility. Since the water supplier could not prove that the water user actually used extra water, the courts held that the water supplier should return the extra payment.

1170. The suppliers have restricted freedom to terminate the supply contract if they supply water, gas and heat to a public community. In *Golf (Nanjing) Real Estate Development Co., Ltd. v. Wu Yongmei,*[1232] the Chinese courts rejected the heat supplier's claim for terminating the heat supplier contract with a heat supplier user and held that whether the contract could be terminated should be decided by the owners' general meeting. In this case, the commercial real estate seller sold houses to buyers and supplied heat to the buyers of the real estate. One of the buyers, as the heat supply user, applied for discontinuation of the heat supply. The commercial real estate seller, as the heat supplier, applied to the courts for termination of the heat supply contract. The courts held that the supplier has a mandatory obligation to enter into a contract. The courts found that the heat user just applied to discontinue the heat supply but did not apply for termination of the contract. The user was still paying the maintenance fee for the heat facilities and did not intend to terminate the contract. The courts also found that the heat was supplied to all the owners of the community and the heat facilities were public utilities. The courts pointed out that the termination would affect the interests of both the user in dispute and all other users of the community. Therefore, whether the heat contract could be terminated should be decided by the owners' general meeting, and the supplier's claim for termination was rejected.

§2. Performance of Contract

1171. Because of the special features of the contracts for the supply and use of electricity, water, gas and heat, the Civil Code provides special rules for the performance of contracts. First, the place of performance of a contract for the supply and use of electricity is determined by the parties' agreement. Where the parties have not agreed on the place or their agreement is equivocal, the place of performance shall be the place that defines the border of the property right to the facilities for the supply of electricity.[1233] Second, the electricity supplier shall supply electricity safely in accordance with the electricity quality of national standards and the contract. Where the electricity supplier fails to do so, thereby causing loss to the electricity user, the electricity supplier shall be liable for damages.[1234] Next, where the electricity supplier has to suspend the supply of electricity for reasons such as planned or ad hoc inspections or repairs of the facilities for the supply of electricity, lawful restrictions on the supply of electricity, or the user's unlawful use of electricity, the electricity supplier shall notify the user in advance in accordance with

1232. *Golf (Nanjing) Real Estate Development Co., Ltd. v. Wu Yongmei*, Gazette Case of the SPC, Issue 12, 2012; 高尔夫（南京）房地产有限公司诉吴咏梅供用热力合同纠纷案，《最高人民法院公报》案例，2012年12期.

1233. Article 650 CC.

1234. Article 651 CC.

the relevant regulations. Where the electricity supply is suspended without advance notification, thus causing loss to the electricity user, the electricity supplier shall be liable for damages.[1235] Where the electricity supply is suspended due to natural disasters or other similar reasons, the electricity supplier shall carry out timely repairs in accordance with the relevant regulations. Where timely repairs are not carried out, thereby causing loss to the electricity user, the electricity supplier shall be liable for damages.[1236]

1172. Furthermore, the electricity user shall pay electricity charges punctually in accordance with the relevant regulations and the contract between the parties. Where the electricity, water, gas or heat supply contract does not specify the charging standard, the two parties shall negotiate with each other to determine it. If the negotiation fails, it shall be determined according to transaction practices.[1237] Where the user fails to pay electricity charges by the due time, it shall pay agreed damages in accordance with the contract. Where the user fails to pay electricity charges and agreed damages within a reasonable period upon demand for payment, the electricity supplier may suspend the electricity supply in accordance with the procedures stipulated in regulations.[1238]

1173. Where the electricity supplier suspends the electricity supply in this circumstance, it shall notify the electricity user in advance.[1239] This notice requirement is a new rule in the Civil Code which does not exist in the Contract Law. It is to protect the interests of the users. However, it does not clarify what the liability the supplier may have or what damage the user may claim if the supplier fails to give the advance notice. Generally speaking, the supplier should be liable for the damages caused to the user if it fails to give the advance notice. Last, the electricity user shall, in accordance with the relevant regulations and the contract between the parties, use electricity in a safe, economical and planned manner. Where the user fails to use electricity safely in accordance with the relevant regulations and the contract between the parties, thereby causing loss to the electricity supplier, the user shall be liable for damages.[1240]

1235. Article 652 CC.
1236. Article 653 CC.
1237. *Dong Limin v. Hailin Changhai Heat Supply Co., Ltd.*, Heilongjiang High People's Court (2021) Hei Min Zai No. 707; 董立敏诉海林市长海供热有限公司，黑龙江省高级人民法院（2021）黑民再707号.
1238. Paragraph 1 of Art. 654 CC.
1239. Paragraph 2 of Art. 654 CC.
1240. Article 655 CC.

Chapter 3. Gift Contracts

§1. General Provisions

1174. A gift contract in the Civil Code is a contract whereby the donor transfers its property to the donee without consideration, and the donee accepts the gift.[1241] Where the gift property is lawfully required to be registered or to go through other formalities, such registration or formalities shall be satisfied.[1242] Gifts may be made subject to obligations. Where a gift is made subject to obligations, the donee shall perform such obligations as agreed.[1243] Gifts may also be made subject to conditions. Under the Civil Code, a civil juridical act may be subject to a condition. A civil juridical act subject to a suspensive condition becomes effective at the moment when the condition is fulfilled. A civil juridical act subject to a resolutive condition ceases to be effective at the moment when the condition is fulfilled.[1244] Where a gift, as a civil juridical act, is subject to a resolutive condition, it may cease to be effective at the moment when the condition is fulfilled. Disputes may occur in this circumstance. For example, if a large amount of property is donated based on a romantic relationship, and then the relationship ends without the parties entering into a marriage, the donor often goes to court to request the return of the donated property.

1175. For this kind of dispute, Chinese courts often regard the donation of a large amount of property based on a romantic relationship as a 'donation with conditions for resolution' and support the donor's request for property return when the condition (marriage in the future) for resolution is met (no marriage has been concluded). This judicial practice has been criticised. It is pointed out that the so-called condition of non-conclusion of marriage in the future in the gift contract is essentially a fabrication of the parties' intention. This fabrication is far-fetched and inconsistent with the reality of life and common social concepts.[1245] It is argued that, in the absence of clear agreement, assuming that the parties have the intention to set certain conditions is undoubtedly a violation of the parties' real intention. This arbitrary interpretation is contrary to the principle of autonomy of parties.[1246] It is submitted that the donor's request for property return when the implied marriage condition for resolution is met should not be supported.

1176. If a gift is made against public order and good morals, the Chinese courts may not recognise the legal effect of the gift contract. In *Zeng v. Ke and Wang*,[1247] Zeng and Wang married in 1995 and divorced in 2018. After the divorce, Zeng

1241. Article 657 CC.
1242. Article 659 CC.
1243. Article 661 CC.
1244. Article 158 CC.
1245. Z Wang, Unjustified Enrichment 105(2nd edn, Beijing University Press 2015).
1246. J Xia, Principles and Rules for Returning Donated Property Due to Lack of Cause, 1, SJTU Law Review (Jiao Da Fa Xue) 64, 69 (2024).
1247. *Zeng v. Ke and Wang*, 3 China Law Report 83-92 (People's Court Press 2021); 曾某诉柯某某和王某案,《人民法院案例选》2021年3辑, 人民法院出版社, 2021年版, 第83-92页.

found Wang gave rewards on a live-stream platform and transferred money to a network anchorwoman Ke before the divorce. She also found that they kept an indefinable relationship before divorce. Zeng applied to the courts requesting the refund of the rewards and the transferred money. The Chinese courts supported the request and held that Ke should return the rewards and the transferred money.[1248] On the one hand, the courts pointed out that, because the performance on a live-stream platform is independent and non-specific, and the rewards for the performance are completely voluntary without consideration, the relationship between the anchors and audiences established by rewards is actually a gift contractual relationship. The courts denied the validity of the gift contract in this case because Wang aimed to have an extramarital affair with Zeng as an extramarital third party by giving rewards and transferring money with unauthorised use of marital property. The gift contract was against the legal obligation of faithful requirement between husband and wife. It was against public order and good morals. In the Civil Code, a civil juridical act going against public order and good morals is void.[1249] Therefore, it was held that the gift contract was void and Ke should return the money under the contract.

§2. Performance of Contract

1177. There are special rules on the performance of the gift contracts. First, where the gift property is defective, the donor shall not be liable. Where the gift is made subject to obligations and the gift property is defective, the donor shall, to the extent of the annexed obligations, be liable in the same manner as a seller. Where the donor deliberately conceals the defects or warrants that the subject matter is free from defects, thereby causing loss to the donee, the donor shall be liable for damages.[1250] Second, the donor may rescind the gift before the transfer of the rights in the gifted property. But this does not apply to gift contracts that have been notarised or legally irrevocable gift contracts of a public interest or moral obligation nature involving disaster relief, poverty alleviation, disability aids, etc.[1251] For those kinds of gift contracts, the donee may seek delivery if the donor fails to deliver the property. If the property to be delivered under those kinds of gift contracts has been damaged, destroyed or lost due to the deliberate acts or gross negligence on the part of the donor, the donor shall be liable for damages.[1252]

1178. The gift contract in the Civil Code may be rescinded in some circumstances. The donor may rescind the gift contracts if the donee: (1) severely infringes

1248. Chongqing First Intermediate People's Court (2020) Yu 01 Min Zhong No. 3046; 重庆市第一中级人民法院（2020）渝01民终3046号.
1249. Paragraph 2 of Art. 153 CC. Civil juridical acts are acts carried out by civil subjects to create, alter, or discontinue civil legal relationships through manifestation of intent. *See* Art. 133 CC.
1250. Article 662 CC.
1251. Article 658 CC.
1252. Article 660 CC.

the lawful rights or interests of the donor or his/her close relatives;[1253] (2) is subject to an obligation to support the donor but fails to perform it; or (3) fails to perform the obligations under the gift contract. The right to rescind the contracts shall be exercised by the donor within one year from the date on which the donor knows or ought to have known the cause of rescission.[1254] Although failing to support the donor is one of the circumstances in which the donor is entitled to rescind the gift contract, the Chinese courts may not permit the donor to rescind the contract in some special circumstances.

1179. The special circumstances can be seen in *Hu X v. Hu Y*.[1255] In this case, the donor agreed to transfer 50% of ownership of a property to the donee under a gift contract. The donee applied to the Chinese courts to enforce the transfer of the property, and the court supported the donee's application. After that, the donor applied to the Chinese courts to rescind the gift contract. The donor argued that the donee did not support the donor, which was against his real intention of the gift contract. The donor's argument was rejected by the courts. The decision was made based on the following facts. First, the donor was rich and did not need economic support from the donee. Second, the donee was still studying abroad and had no financial ability to support the donor in life. The donor knew that the donee needed financial support when he made the gift but did not require any support. The purpose of the gift contract was to provide financial support to the donee and reduce the economic pressure on the donee. Third, the economic situations of the donor and the donee were not changed when the donor claimed to rescind the contract, and the donee was still studying abroad. In summary, the special circumstances are the donee's weak finances and the donor's strong finances. The donor's claim to rescind the gift contract was against the principle of good faith and the rescission will exacerbate financial difficulty, which might result in an unbalance of interests of the parties.

1180. Furthermore, if, as a result of illegal conduct on the part of the donee, the donor dies or loses his or her civil capacity, the heir or statutory agent of the donor may rescind the gift. The right to rescind of the heir or statutory agent of the donor shall be exercised within six months from the date on which he or she knows or ought to know the cause of rescission.[1256] Upon rescission of a gift by a person entitled to rescind, that person may seek recovery of the gift property from the donee.[1257] The donor may cease to perform the gift contract where its financial condition deteriorates so markedly that its business or family life has been severely affected.[1258]

1253. Close relatives in the Civil Code are the spouse, parents, children, siblings, paternal and maternal grandparents, paternal and maternal grandchildren. *See* para. 2 of Art. 1045 CC.
1254. Article 663 CC
1255. *Hu X v. Hu Y*, 胡某某v胡某案 (2018) 4 China Law Report, People's Court Press (2018), pp. 113-119; 《人民法院案例选》2018年4辑，人民法院出版社，2018年版，第113-119页.
1256. Article 664 CC.
1257. Article 665 CC.
1258. Article 666 CC.

Chapter 4. Loan Contracts

§1. CONCEPT

1181. A loan contract is a contract whereby the borrower obtains a loan from the lender and repays the loan with interest when the loan becomes due.[1259] A loan contract shall be made in writing, unless otherwise agreed by natural persons who are parties to the loan. The content of a loan contract generally includes terms as to the type of loan, currency, purpose, amount, interest rate, term of the loan, means of repayment, etc.[1260] If a loan contract is concluded between natural persons without a written form of contract, parties to the contract need to prove the contents of the contract in other ways. Chinese courts may refer to other evidence or use logical reasoning to examine such contracts.

1182. In *Zhao Jun v. Xiang Huimin and He Xueqin*,[1261] the lender claimed against the borrowers, a married couple for repayment of a loan under a loan contract. The husband, as one of the borrowers, admitted that the lender gave the alleged money in cash and there was no written contract but only an 'IOU' for the amount of money.[1262] The husband explained that the money under the loan was for repayment of a mortgage. The wife denied the existence of the loan contract. The court pointed out that evidence was needed for proving the existence of the contract, including the necessity of the loan, the purpose of the loan, the financial situation of the parties, source of the loan, delivery method of the loan, witness of transactions, etc. Based on evidence of bank transaction, the court found that the husband paid the mortgage with money in his bank account, not the alleged cash borrowed from the lender. The court also found the facts that the mortgage had discount, but the borrowed money had a high interest rate. The court required the lender to prove his financial situation in order to prove his ability to lend the money. But the lender failed to provide any evidence for this requirement. The court pointed out that only the IOU could not prove the existence of the loan contract and thus rejected the lender's claim.

1183. A loan contract may be concluded via a third party for the borrower and the lender. In this circumstance, it is necessary to clarify the rights and obligations of the third party in the loan contract. In *Guangzhou Youdai Micro-Lending Co., Ltd. v. Li*,[1263] a loan contract was concluded via a third party who managed the loan business for the borrower and the lender. The borrower found that he was charged more money than the agreed loan and interests. The borrower claimed against the

1259. Article 667 CC.
1260. Article 668 CC.
1261. *Zhao Jun v. Xiang Huimin and He Xueqin*, Gazette Case of the SPC, Issue 12, 2014; 赵俊诉项会敏、何雪琴民间借贷纠纷案，《最高人民法院公报》案例，2014年12期.
1262. An 'IOU', a phonetic acronym of the words 'I owe you', is a document that acknowledges the existence of a debt.
1263. *Guangzhou Youdai Micro-Lending Co., Ltd. v. Li*, Guangzhou Internet Court (2019) Yue 0192 Min Chu No. 45769; 广州优贷小额贷款有限公司诉李某、第三人深圳市前海吉顺信科技发展有限公司，广州互联网法院（2019）粤0192民初45769号.

lender and the third party for returning the extra payment. It was found that the third party was responsible for building up the loan platform, finding clients, verifying IDs, reviewing credits, concluding contracts, arranging monthly repayment, collecting repayment, and providing a guaranty for the loan. The lender did not pay any service fee to the third party. In fact, the third party charged a service fee to the borrower. This is the reason why the borrower repaid the extra money. The court held that the third party's responsibilities were for the benefits of the lender, and the lender should pay the service fee. There was no contractual basis for such a charge on the borrower, and it was unfair for the borrower to pay the service fee. It was held that the third party and the lender should refund the extra payment.[1264]

1184. The third party in the loan contract may act as an intermediary. It has responsibility as an intermediary under an intermediary contract. In *Tang Jun v. Li Yuling and Shanghai Paipaidai Finance Information Service Co., Ltd.*,[1265] the lender and the borrower concluded a loan contract via a P2P platform. The borrower failed to repay the loan. The lender claimed against the borrower for repayment of the loan and against the platform for joint and several liability. The central issue in this case is whether the P2P platform should be liable for payment of the loan. The court found that the main activities of the platform in this loan relationship are to provide a platform and review information, and its status should be that of an intermediary, not the borrower or guarantor. It was held that the borrower should be liable for the overdue repayment of the loan, and the platform did not have joint and several repayment responsibilities.

1185. In the course of making a loan contract, the borrower shall, in accordance with the requests made by the lender, provide true information as to its business activities in relation to the loan and its financial position.[1266] If the borrower deliberately conceals the true information of business activities and financial conditions, the lender may have remedies from the civil law. Under the Civil Code, where one party, by means of fraud, causes the other party to perform a civil juridical act against his true intentions, the latter shall be entitled to apply with the court or arbitration agency to rescind the act.[1267] A void or rescinded civil juridical act is not legally binding *ab initio*.[1268] Therefore, the lender may rescind the loan contract if the borrower deliberately conceals the relevant true information.

1264. (2021) 4 China Law Report, People's Court Press 157-162 (2021) .
1265. *Tang Jun v. Li Yuling and Shanghai Paipaidai Finance Information Service Co., Ltd.*, Shanghai Pudong New Area People's Court (2014) Pu Min Yi (Min) Chu Zi No. 14813; 唐骏诉李玉玲、上海拍拍贷金融信息服务有限公司，上海市浦东新区人民法院 （2014）浦民一（民）初字第14813号.
1266. Article 669 CC.
1267. Article 148 CC.
1268. Article 155 CC.

§2. Performance of Loan Contracts

1186. The performance of loan contracts is mainly subject to the contract itself. First, the lender may, in accordance with the contract, inspect and supervise the use of the loan. The borrower shall, in accordance with the contract, regularly provide the lender with the relevant financial and accounting statements and other information.[1269] Second, where the borrower fails to use the loan for the agreed purpose, the lender may withhold further releases of loans, recall the loan prior to its due date or terminate the contract.[1270]

1187. The Civil Code provides rules for damages and interests when the lender fails to provide, or the borrower fails to collect the agreed loan. On the one hand, if the lender fails to provide the loan in accordance with the agreed date or amount, thereby causing loss to the borrower, the lender shall be liable for damages. On the other hand, if the borrower fails to collect the loan in accordance with the agreed date or amount, it shall pay interest calculated on the basis of the agreed date and amount.[1271] Furthermore, the interest of a loan shall not be deducted from the principal in advance. Where interest has been deducted from the principal in advance, repayment shall be made, and interest calculated, on the basis of the actual amount borrowed.[1272]

1188. As an obligation, the borrower should repay the loan according to the loan contract. First, the borrower shall repay the loan by the agreed time. Where there is no agreement on the term of the loan or the agreement is equivocal, the borrower may repay the loan at any time. The lender may demand repayment to be made within a reasonable time by the borrower.[1273] Where the borrower repays the loan ahead of schedule, the interest accrued thereon shall be calculated according to the actual term of the loan unless otherwise agreed upon by the parties.[1274] The borrower may also apply to the lender for an extension of the loan term before the expiry of the time limit for repayment. The term of the loan may be extended if the lender agrees.[1275]

1189. The interest, compound interest and penalty interest stipulated in the financial loan contract should be supported if they are not legally invalid. However, the Chinese courts may adjust the agreed interests in the financial loan contract if they significantly deviate from the actual loss.[1276] This judicial practice is based on the general rule of contract law in the Civil Code. It is provided that, where the sum

1269. Article 672 CC.
1270. Article 673 CC.
1271. Article 671 CC.
1272. Article 670 CC.
1273. Article 675 CC.
1274. Article 677 CC.
1275. Article 678 CC.
1276. *Zhongyuan Bank Co., Ltd. v. Fujian Start Group Co., Ltd.*, Henan High People's Court (2021) Yu Min Zhong No. 949; 中原银行股份有限公司诉福建实达集团股份有限公司等金融借款合同纠纷案，河南省高级人民法院（2021）豫民终949号.

of damages agreed upon is excessively higher than the actual damages incurred, the court or an arbitration institution may reduce the amount upon the request of a party.[1277] Where there is no stipulation as to the payment of interest in the loan contract, it is deemed that there is no interest payable. Where the loan contract is equivocal about the payment of interest and the parties cannot reach a supplementary agreement, the interest rate is determined in accordance with the mode of trade and trade practice at the place of the loan or between the parties, market interest rate, etc.; where the loan is made between natural persons, it is deemed that there is no interest.[1278] However, if the borrower fails to repay the loan by the agreed time, it shall pay overdue interest in accordance with the contract or the relevant regulations.[1279]

1190. For the time of payment of interests, the Civil Code provides that, where there is no agreement on the time for the payment of interest or the agreement is equivocal, interest shall be paid at the time of full repayment of the loan where the term of the loan is under a year; interest shall be paid at each anniversary of the loan where the term of the loan is one year or longer but shall be paid at the time of the full repayment of the loan where the term remaining is less than one year.[1280] In any event, the Civil Code provides that lending money at usury shall be prohibited and the interest rate on lending shall not contravene any regulations.[1281]

§3. Private Loan Contracts

1191. The Civil Code does not provide definition of a private loan between natural persons. In the SPC Provisions on Certain Issues concerning Application of Law in Trial of Cases involving Private Lending (2020) (the SPC Provisions on Private Lending 2020),[1282] the private lending refers to the activities of financing between natural persons, legal persons and non-legal-person organisations.[1283] In other words, all non-financial lending are private lending if the loan is not from the financial institutions. Therefore, the SPC Provisions on Private Lending 2020 do not apply to the disputes arising out of loans and other relevant financial business from the financial institutions which are established upon approval by the financial regulatory authorities and engaging in loan business.[1284] If a financial institution engages in loan business without approval, its loans should be included in the category of

1277. Paragraph 2 of Art. 585 CC.
1278. Paragraphs 2 and 3 of Art. 680 CC.
1279. Article 676 CC.
1280. Article 674 CC.
1281. Paragraph 1 of Art. 680 CC.
1282. The SPC Provisions on Certain Issues concerning Application of Law in Trial of Cases involving Private Lending (2015, 2020 revision).
1283. Paragraph 1 of Art. 1 of the SPC Provisions on Private Lending (2020).
1284. Paragraph 2 of Art. 1 of the SPC Provisions on Private Lending (2020).

private lending. Chinese courts should apply the relevant provisions of the judicial Interpretation on private lending to handle such cases.[1285]

1192. The Civil Code provides a rule for the formation of a private loan contract between natural persons. It provides that a loan contract between natural persons shall be concluded when the lender disburses the loan.[1286] This provision is different from the old rule of the Contract Law in which it was provided that a loan contract between natural persons shall take effect when the lender disburses the loan.[1287] The substantial change is the result of the disbursement of the loan. The Contract Law recognises the legal effect of the loan contract when the loan is disbursed, whereas the Civil Code only recognises the conclusion of the contract in this circumstance. The legal effect is subject to law and contract itself. This special rule applies to the loan contract between natural persons only. There is no such rule for other loan contracts. A contract of private lending, other than a loan contract between natural persons, becomes effective as of the conclusion of the contract, unless otherwise agreed upon by the parties or otherwise provided for by laws and administrative regulations.[1288]

1193. The main purpose of the change in law for the loan contracts between natural persons is to crack down on usury. If a private loan with usury is concluded, the Civil Code only recognises the establishment of a contractual relationship between the natural persons. But such a loan contract is illegal because of usury. Therefore, the loan with usury does not take effect, although it is concluded, and the borrower shall not repay the interests based on an illegal high rate. If the loan money for usury is disbursed under the Contract Law, the loan contract takes effect. But the contract is void because the loan contract is for usury. This problem has been solved by the new rule of the Civil Code.

1194. The SPC Provisions on Private Lending 2020 provide detailed rules on the conclusion of a private loan contract between natural persons. It provides that a loan contract between natural persons that falls under any of the following circumstances may be deemed as concluded: (1) when the borrower receives the loan from the lender in the case of payment in cash; (2) when the fund enters the borrower's account in the case of payment through bank transfer, online electronic remittance or any other form; (3) when the borrower obtains the right to the bill in accordance with the law in the case of payment by bill; (4) when the borrower obtains the right to actually dispose of the specific capital account in the case that the lender grants

1285. *Sichuan Jinyu Financing & Guarantee Co., Ltd. v. Sichuan Jujuyuan Real Estate Co., Ltd.*, Cheng Du Qingyang District People's Court (2021) Chuan 0105 Min Chu No. 9112; 四川省金玉融资担保有限公司诉四川聚合源置业有限公司等借款合同纠纷案, 成都市青羊区人民法院（2021）川0105民初9112号.

1286. Article 679 CC.

1287. Article 210 of the Contract Law.

1288. Article 10 of the SPC Provisions on Private Lending (2020).

the right to dispose of the account to the borrower; and (5) when the lender provides the loan in any other method agreed upon with the borrower and completes the actual performance.[1289]

1195. The SPC Provisions on Private Lending 2020 also provide rules under which a private loan contract is void. It provides that a private loan contract is void under any of the following circumstances: (1) fraudulently obtaining the loan from a financial institution for relending; (2) relending the funds borrowed from another for-profit legal person, raised from its employees, taken in as deposit illegally from the public or through any other method; (3) offering lending by a lender without obtaining lending qualification in accordance with the law to unspecific targets in the society for profit-making purpose; (4) offering lending by a lender which knows or should know in advance that the borrower will use the borrowing for illegal or criminal activities; (5) violating the compulsory provisions under laws and administrative regulations; and (6) violating public order and good morals.[1290]

1196. The Civil Code provides that if there is no stipulation as to the payment of interest in the loan contract, it is deemed that there is no interest payable.[1291] The SPC Provisions on Private Lending 2020 detailed the rules on the agreement of interest. First, where the borrower and the lender fail to agree upon the interest, the Chinese court shall not uphold the lender's claims for payment of the interest. Second, where the interest on the loan between natural persons is not clearly agreed upon and the lender raises the claim for payment of interest, the Chinese court shall not uphold the claim. Third, except for the lending between natural persons, where the borrower and the lender fail to clearly agree upon the interest on the loan and the lender claims the interest, the Chinese court shall determine the interest in light of the content of the contract for private lending and according to the method of transaction adopted locally or by the parties concerned, usage of trade, market-quoted interest rate and other factors.[1292]

1197. Where the lender requests the borrower to pay interest according to the interest rate agreed upon in the contract, the Chinese court shall uphold the request unless the interest rate agreed upon by the parties exceeds four times the market-quoted interest rate for the one-year loan prevailing at the time of the establishment of the contract.[1293] There is no such provision of interest for financial loan contracts. Furthermore, where the borrower and the lender, after settlement of the principal and interest of the preliminary loan, include the interest in the principal of the latter loan and re-issue a voucher of the creditor's rights, if the preliminary interest rate does not exceed four times the market-quoted interest rate for the one-year loan

1289. Article 9 of the SPC Provisions on Private Lending (2020).
1290. Article 10 of the SPC Provisions on Private Lending (2020).
1291. Paea. 2 of Art. 680 CC.
1292. Article 24 of the SPC Provisions on Private Lending (2020).
1293. *Ibid.*; Art. 26, para. 1. The 'market-quoted interest rate for the one-year loan' shall refer to the market-quoted interest rate for the one-year loan published by the National Interbank Funding Center authorised by the People's Bank of China on a monthly basis starting from 20 August 2019.

prevailing at the time of the establishment of the contract, the amount stated in the reissued voucher of the creditor's right may be determined as the principal of the latter loan and the extra amount of the interest shall not be determined as the principal of the latter loan. Where the sum of the principal and interest payable by the borrower upon maturity of the loan term calculated according to the aforementioned method exceeds the sum of the principal of the preliminary loan and the interest for the entire term of the loan calculated with the principal of the preliminary loan as a base number and according to four times the market-quoted interest rate for the one-year loan prevailing at the time of the establishment of the contract, the Chinese court shall not uphold the sum.[1294]

1198. Where the borrower and the lender have agreed upon the interest rate applicable to late payment, such agreement shall be formed, provided that such interest rate shall not exceed four times the market-quoted interest rate for the one-year loan prevailing at the time of the establishment of the contract. Where the interest rate for late payment is not agreed upon or clearly agreed upon, the Chinese court may handle the case according to different situations: (1) where neither the interest rate for the loan term nor the interest rate for the late payment is agreed upon and the lender requests the borrower to bear the default liability for late payment from the date when the payment becomes due and payable, the court shall uphold the request; and (2) where the interest rate for the loan term is agreed upon but the interest rate for the late payment is not agreed upon and the lender requests the borrower to pay the interest for the period when the borrower occupies the fund calculated from the date when the payment becomes due and payable, the court shall uphold the request.[1295] Where the lender and the borrower have agreed upon both the interest rate for late payment and the liquidated damages or other fees, the lender may choose to claim the payment of the interest for late payment, the liquidated damages or other fees, or claim the payment of all of the preceding amounts. However, the Chinese court shall not uphold the claim for the part of the total amount that exceeds four times the market-quoted interest rate for the one-year loan prevailing at the time of the establishment of the contract.[1296]

1199. It can be seen that the interest rate rules are different for the financial loan and the private loan. The financial loan interest rate is decided by banks with reference to the Loan Prime Rate published on 20th of each month by the People's Bank of China.[1297] Therefore, it is important to identify the nature of a loan contract when there is a dispute about the interest rate that occurs relating to the loan contract. The difficulty in identifying the nature of a loan contract can be seen in *Shanghai Pudong Development Bank Co., Ltd. Shenzhen Branch v. Meizhou Dizhonghai*

1294. Article 28 of the SPC Provisions on Private Lending (2020).
1295. Article 29 of the SPC Provisions on Private Lending (2020).
1296. Article 30 of the SPC Provisions on Private Lending (2020).
1297. The Loan Prime Rate has been published since 2019.

Hotel Co., Ltd. and Others.[1298] In this case, there was an entrusted loan contract in dispute. The principal was a natural person who entrusted a bank to lend money to a hotel as the borrower. In the dispute over the interest of the loan, the court needed to identify the nature of the loan contract first because the interest rate rules were different under different loan contracts. In this case, the bank claimed against the borrower for repayment of the loan.

1200. The SPC pointed out that the entrusted loan contract looks like a financial contract, but it also has similarities with the private loan contract. First, in the entrusted loan contract, the financial institution is the lender, but it has a loan relationship as the trustee with the borrower. It does not decide matters of the loan. The main rights and obligations of the loan contract are the intentions of the principal. Second, it is the principal who is benefitted from the loan contract and takes the risks of non-repayment and overdue repayment of the loan. Third, the money in the entrusted loan contract is from the principal; it has no substantial difference from the private loan. In this case, the principal rather than the bank confirmed the interest rate of the loan and other main contract clauses and actually charged the interest. The loaned money was from the principal. The SPC held that the loan contract in dispute was a private loan contract, and therefore the rules of interest for private loan contracts should apply, even though the bank used its own name claiming against the borrower.[1299]

1298. *Shanghai Pudong Development Bank Co., Ltd. Shenzhen Branch v. Meizhou Dizhonghai Hotel Co., Ltd. and Others*, Gazette Case of the SPC, Issue 4, 2020; 上海浦东发展银行股份有限公司深圳分行与梅州地中海酒店有限公司等借款合同纠纷，《最高人民法院公报》案例，2020年04期.

1299. The SPC (2018) Zui Gao Fa Min Zai No. 54; 最高人民法院（2018）最高法民再54号.

Chapter 5. Guaranty Contracts

§1. General Provisions

1201. The provisions of the guaranty contract in the Civil Code are mainly from the provisions of the guaranty contract in the Guaranty Law 1995 and the SPC Interpretation on Certain Issues Concerning the Application of the Guaranty Law 2000 with necessary amendments for the purpose of the Civil Code. The current valid judicial interpretation is the SPC Interpretation on Several Issues Concerning the Application of the Security System in the Civil Code (2020) (the SPC Interpretation on Security System 2020).[1300] Therefore, the rules of the guaranty contract are mainly from the Civil Code and the SPC Interpretation on Security System 2020.

1202. A guaranty contract in the Civil Code is a contract whereby, to safeguard the performance of obligations, the guarantor and the creditor agree that the guarantor will perform obligations or bear liability where the debtor fails to perform its obligations when they fall due or where an event agreed upon by the parties occurs.[1301] The guarantor may raise against the creditor defences available to the debtor. Where the debtor waives its defences, the guarantor may nevertheless raise the defences against the creditor.[1302] Where the debtor is entitled to a set-off or rescission against the creditor, the guarantor may refuse to bear the guaranty liability to the corresponding extent.[1303] An independent guarantee is not such a guaranty contract. Therefore, the provisions of the guaranty contract in the Civil Code do not apply to the independent guarantee.[1304]

1203. The guarantor may request the debtor to provide a counter-guaranty.[1305] The Civil Code does not clarify whether the provisions of the guaranty contract apply to the counter-guaranty contract. The Guaranty Law applied to the counter-guaranty.[1306] Therefore, it is reasonably believed that the provisions of the guaranty contract in the Civil Code shall apply to the counter-guaranty contract if it satisfies the concept of the guaranty contract in the Civil Code. Where a guaranty contract

1300. The SPC Interpretation on Several Issues Concerning the Application of the Security System in the Civil Code (2020).
1301. Article 681 CC.
1302. Article 701 CC.
1303. Article 702 CC.
1304. The SPC Provisions on Several Issues concerning Trial of Disputes over Independent Guarantees (2016) apply to disputes arising from independent guarantees issued by financial institutions. *See also Anhui Foreign Economic Construction (Group) Co., Ltd. v. Inmobiliaria Palacio Oriental SA*, the SPC Guiding Case No. 109; 安徽省外经建设（集团）有限公司诉东方置业房地产有限公司保函欺诈纠纷案，最高人民法院，第109号指导性案例.
1305. Article 689 CC.
1306. Paragraph 2 of Art. 4 of the Guaranty Law.

is invalid, if the guarantor has been held liable for compensation under the guaranty, the counter-guarantor shall be liable to the guarantor for compensation in accordance with the counter-guaranty contract within the scope of the guarantor's liability for compensation.[1307]

1204. In the Civil Code, a governmental legal person shall not be a guarantor, except for those, with the approval of the State Council, making sub-loans out of loans from foreign governments or international economic organisations. The non-profit legal person for a public-welfare purpose or the unincorporated organisation shall not be a guarantor.[1308] Where a neighbourhood or villagers' committee provides a guaranty, the guaranty contract shall be invalid, except where the villagers' committee functioning as a village collective economic organisation in accordance with the law provides a guaranty to external parties according to the discussion and decision procedures stipulated in the Village Committees Organisation Law.[1309] Where non-profit schools, kindergartens, medical institutions, elderly care institutions, etc. for the purpose of public welfare provide guaranty, the guaranty contracts are invalid, except in any of the following circumstances: (1) when purchasing or renting under financial leases educational facilities, medical and health facilities, elderly service facilities and other public welfare facilities, the seller or lessor retains the ownership of the public welfare facilities in order to secure the realisation of the price or the rent; or (2) security interests are created on immovable property, movable property or property rights other than educational facilities, medical and health facilities, elderly service facilities and other public welfare facilities. Where schools, kindergartens, medical institutions, elderly care institutions, etc. registered as for-profit legal persons provide a guaranty, they cannot deny the validity of the guaranty contracts on the grounds that they are unqualified to provide guaranty.[1310]

1205. For the relation between the principal contract and the guaranty contract, the Civil Code provides that a guaranty contract is a collateral contract to the principal contract between the creditor and the debtor.[1311] It does not, however, mean that the guaranty contract must be included in the principal contract, although the former is collateral to the latter. In *Bank of Wenzhou Co., Ltd. Ningbo Branch v. Zhejiang Chuangling Electric Appliance Co., Ltd. and Others*,[1312] the lender had a loan contract as the principal contract with the borrower and a guaranty contract with the guarantor for securing the repayment of the loan under the principal contract. When the borrower failed to repay the loan, the lender claimed against the guarantor for the repayment of the loan. The guarantor argued that it was not liable

1307. Paragraph 1 of Art. 19 of the SPC Interpretation on Security System (2020).
1308. Article 683 CC.
1309. Paragraph 2 of Art. 5 of the SPC Interpretation on Security System (2020).
1310. Article 6 of the SPC Interpretation on Security System (2020).
1311. Paragraph 1 of Art. 682 CC.
1312. *Bank of Wenzhou Co., Ltd. Ningbo Branch v. Zhejiang Chuangling Electric Appliance Co., Ltd. and Others*, SPC Guiding Case No. 57; 温州银行股份有限公司宁波分行诉浙江创菱电器有限公司等金融借款合同纠纷案，最高人民法院，第57号指导性案例.

for the repayment because the guaranty contract was not included in the loan contract. It was so argued because there were two other guaranty contracts under the same loan contract that had been included in the loan contract. However, this argument was not accepted by the courts. It was held that the guarantor was liable for the repayment under the guaranty contract.[1313]

1206. As a guiding case, the SPC summarised the reasons for the decision. First, although the loan contract did not include the guaranty contract, it does not mean that the lender waives the right of claim under the guaranty contract. The lender did not expressly waive its right under the guaranty contract. Second, the lender's claim was within the duration of the guaranty. Third, the contractual relationship between the lender and the guaranty was governed by the guaranty contract, not the loan contract. Their contractual relation under the guaranty contract was not subject to the loan contract between the lender and the borrower. Last, the guarantor had partly repaid the loan under the guaranty contract. It indicates that the guarantor had a contractual obligation to perform the guaranty contract. The second and the last reasons are based on the facts of the case. However, the second and the third reasons are general rules clarifying the relations between the principal contract and the guaranty contract.

1207. Because of the collateral relationship, the guaranty contract may be affected if the principal contract is void. Unless otherwise provided by law, where the principal contract is void, the guaranty contract is void. Where a guaranty contract is void, the debtor, guarantor and creditor shall be liable to the extent of their respective degrees of fault.[1314] Where the parties agree in a guaranty contract that the effect of the guaranty contract is independent of the principal contract, or that the guaranty provider is liable for securing the legal consequences of the invalidity of the principal contract, the agreement on the independence of the guaranty shall be invalid. Where the principal contract is valid, the invalidity of the agreement on the independence of the guaranty does not affect the effect of the guaranty contract.[1315]

1208. In the context of commodity house sale, where a contract on the purchase and sale of commodity premises is determined to be invalid or is revoked or terminated, thereby resulting in the frustration of the purposes of a guaranty contract of secured loan for the commodity premises, the parties are allowed to terminate the guaranty contract of secured loan for the commodity premises.[1316] However, if a guaranty contract is void due to the fault of the debtor and guarantor, they shall be liable to the creditor to the extent of their respective degrees of fault. In *China Everbright Bank Co., Ltd. Shanghai Qingpu Branch v. Shanghai Donghe Real Estate*

1313. Zhejiang Ningbo Intermediate People's Court (2014) Zhe Yong Shang Zhong Zi No. 269; 浙江省宁波市中级人民法院（2014）浙甬商终字第369号.
1314. Paragraph 2 of Art. 682 CC.
1315. Article 2 of the SPC Interpretation on Security System (2020).
1316. Article 20 of the SPC Interpretation on the Sale of Commodity Houses (2020).

Development Co., Ltd. and Chen Siqi,[1317] the developer of the commodity premises colluded with the buyer in signing a fake presale commercial housing sale contract and the buyer obtained a loan from a bank with a guaranty from the developer. The fake contract was held invalid because of the fraud of the developer and the buyer. However, it was held that the developer was still liable jointly and severally with the buyer for the unpaid loan to the bank because of their fault.

1209. A guaranty contract may be made in writing separately or as guaranty terms incorporated in the principal contract between the creditor and the debtor. Where a third party makes a guaranty in writing in favour of the creditor, the guaranty contract is concluded once the creditor receives and does not object to the guaranty.[1318] An intention for providing a guaranty is required for a valid guaranty contract. Where a person affixes his signature or seal to the debit note, receipt for a loan, credit note or other vouchers of creditors' rights or the contract for private lending without indicating that he acts as the guarantor or assumes guarantee liability or without being presumed to be the guarantor by other facts, that person shall not bear guarantee liability.[1319]

1210. Where an arbitration clause is stipulated in the principal contract or the guaranty contract, the court shall have no jurisdiction over disputes between the parties to the contract which stipulates the arbitration clause. If the creditor sues the debtor and the guarantor together, the court with jurisdiction shall be determined in accordance with the principal contract. If the creditor can sue the guarantor alone and only sues the guarantor according to the law, the court with jurisdiction shall be determined in accordance with the guaranty contract.[1320] A guaranty contract generally includes terms as to the type and amount of the guaranteed principal obligation, the time for the debtor to perform its obligations, and the means, extent and period of the guaranty, etc.[1321]

§2. The Forms of Guaranty

1211. The forms of guaranty include general guaranties and guaranties with joint and several liability. Where the parties fail to agree or to explicitly agree to the form of guaranty in the guaranty contract, the guaranty liability shall be borne in the form of a general guaranty.[1322] This default guaranty form is different from the form in

1317. *China Everbright Bank Co., Ltd. Shanghai Qingpu Branch v. Shanghai Donghe Real Estate Development Co., Ltd. and Chen Siqi*, Gazette Case of the SPC, Issue 9, 2014; 中国光大银行股份有限公司上海青浦支行诉上海东鹤房地产有限公司、陈思绮保证合同纠纷案,《最高人民法院公报》案例, 2014年09期. The guaranty in dispute was a guaranty with joint and several liability.
1318. Article 685 CC.
1319. Article 20 of the SPC Provisions on Private Lending (2020).
1320. Article 21 of the SPC Interpretation on Security System (2020).
1321. Article 684 CC.
1322. Article 686 CC.

the Guaranty Law in which the guaranty liability shall be borne in the form of a joint and several liability.[1323] This change lessens the liability of the guarantor in the Civil Code.

1212. A general guaranty is an arrangement whereby the parties to a guaranty contract agree that the guarantor bears the guaranty liability when the debtor fails to perform its obligations.[1324] Where the parties agree in the guaranty contract that the guarantor will be liable under the guaranty only when the debtor fails to perform the debt or is unable to repay the obligation, it is an intention that the debtor shall assume liability first. Such a guaranty is a general guaranty.[1325] Where the guarantor under a general guaranty provides the creditor with true information about the executable property of the debtor after the principal obligation falls due, and the creditor waives or neglects to exercise its rights rendering such property not executable, the guarantor does not bear guaranty liability to the extent of the value of the executable property about which it has informed the creditor.[1326]

1213. The guarantor under a general guaranty may refuse to bear guarantee liability towards the creditor before a dispute over the principal contract is tried or arbitrated and the obligations cannot be fulfilled even after enforcement of the debtor's assets in accordance with the law, except for any of the following circumstances: (1) the whereabouts of the debtor are unknown and there is no property for enforcement; (2) a case filed for the bankruptcy of the debtor has been accepted by a court; (3) the creditor has evidence to show that the property of the debtor is insufficient for the full satisfaction of all obligations or that the debtor has lost the ability to perform its obligations; and (4) The guarantor waives in writing its rights provided in this paragraph.[1327]

1214. In *China CITIC Bank v. Beijing Jinggong Real Estate Development Co., Ltd.*,[1328] the guarantor agreed to provide a guaranty in the form of a general guaranty. Before the enforcement of the debtor's assets, it was found that the debtor's corporate business licence was revoked by the local authorities and its address was unknown after revocation. The investor of the debtor was also unknown. In this circumstance, the court pointed out that it was very difficult for the creditor to claim against the debtor to pay off the debt. Therefore, it was held that the guarantor bears the guaranty liability. This decision was made based on the Guaranty Law in which the circumstance was that the debtor's address was changed and the enforcement against the property of the debtor was seriously difficult.[1329] If this case were tried

1323. Article 16 of the Guaranty Law.
1324. Article 687, para. 1 CC.
1325. Paragraph 1 of Art. 25 the SPC Interpretation on Security System (2020).
1326. Article 698 CC.
1327. Paragraph 2 of Art. 687 CC.
1328. *China CITIC Bank v. Beijing Jinggong Real Estate Development Co., Ltd.*, Gazette Case of the SPC, Issue 6, 2002; 中信实业银行诉北京市京工房地产开发总公司保证合同纠纷案，《最高人民法院公报》案例，2002年06期.
1329. Article 17 (1) of the Guaranty Law.

under the Civil Code, the same decision could be made according to the circumstance in the Civil Code that the whereabouts of the debtor are unknown and there is no property for enforcement.[1330]

1215. A guaranty with joint and several liability is an arrangement whereby the parties to a guaranty contract agree that the guarantor and the debtor are jointly and severally liable for the obligations. Where the debtor under a guaranty with joint and several liability fails to perform its obligations when they fall due or where an event agreed upon by the parties occurs, the creditor may seek performance by the debtor of its obligations, or demand that the guarantor bear a guaranty liability to the extent of the guaranty.[1331] Where the parties agree in the guaranty contract that the guarantor will be liable under the guaranty when the debtor fails to perform the obligation or does not repay the obligation, or be liable for the guaranty unconditionally, it is not an intention that the debtor shall be liable first. Such a guaranty is a guaranty with joint and several liability.[1332]

1216. For the cases involving private lending, the SPC provides rules for the guarantor's liability in the different forms of guaranty. Where the guarantor provides the general guarantee for the borrower and the lender institutes a lawsuit against the guarantor only, the court shall add the borrower as the co-defendant; where the lender institutes a lawsuit against the borrower only, the court may not add the guarantor as the co-defendant. Where the guarantor provides the joint and several liability guarantee for the borrower and the lender institutes a lawsuit against the borrower only, the court may not add the guarantor as the co-defendant; where the lender institutes a lawsuit against the guarantor only, the court may add the borrower as the co-defendant.[1333]

1217. In financial transactions, the balance replenishment commitment is usually used as a credit enhancement measure for making up the difference in funds in commercial transactions, such as asset management plans, private equity funds, exchange-listed products, entrusted financial management, etc. It is to provide credit protection for financial products. For determining the nature of such a commitment to make up the balance, it needs to be based on the full text of the contract and restoring the original intention of the parties. If the nature of the balance replenishment commitment is unclear, it can be examined from the following aspects. First, it could be examined from the name description. It can be judged by the name of the document of the balance replenishment commitment, examining whether it contains guarantees, debt addition words, recovery agreements, etc. Second, it can be examined whether a commitment is independent. A supplementary and contingent commitment may be presumed to be guarantees, and an independent and deterministic commitment may be presumed to be debt addition. Third, it can be examined whether the right of recourse is agreed upon. If the right of recourse is agreed upon,

1330. Article 687 (1) CC.
1331. Article 688 CC.
1332. Paragraph 2 of Art. 25 of the SPC Interpretation on Security System (2020).
1333. Article 4 of the SPC Provisions on Private Lending (2020).

it is a guarantee. Fourth, it can be examined whether the guarantee period has been agreed upon. If it is so agreed, the commitment is a guaranty. Fifth, if the agreement is unclear and it is difficult to determine whether it is a guarantee or a debt addition, it is recognised as a guaranty. Sixth, if it neither conforms to the guaranty nor the nature of debt addition, it constitutes an independent contractual liability.[1334]

§3. Guaranty Liability

I. Duration of Guaranty

1218. The guarantor bears guaranty liability within the duration of a guaranty as the guaranty period. The duration of a guaranty shall not be suspended, interrupted or extended. The creditor and the guarantor may agree on the guaranty period. However, where the guaranty period elapses before or at the same time as the performance of the principal obligation falls due, it is deemed that no agreement has been reached. Where there is no agreement or the agreement is equivocal, the guaranty period shall be six months from the date when the performance of the principal obligation falls due. Where the creditor and the debtor fail to agree or to explicitly agree on the time for the performance of the principal obligation, the guaranty period shall commence from the date on which the grace period for the creditor to seek performance by the debtor of its obligation expires.[1335]

1219. The SPC Interpretation on Security System 2020 provides special rules for the duration period where there are two or more guarantors for the same debt. In this circumstance, if the creditor claims that it has exercised its rights against other guarantors during the guaranty period on the grounds that it has exercised its rights against some guarantors during the guarantee period, the court will not support such a claim. Where there are two or more guarantors with mutual recourse for the same debt and the creditor fails to exercise recourse against some guarantors during the guarantee period, causing other guarantors to lose the recourse after being liable for the guaranty, if other guarantors claim to be exempted from the guaranteed liability within the scope for which they cannot have recourse, the court will support such claim.[1336]

1220. The SPC Interpretation on Security System 2020 also provides special rules for the duration period under different forms of guaranty. Where the creditor of a general guaranty who files a lawsuit or applies for arbitration against the debtor during the guaranty period withdraws the lawsuit or arbitration application, and the

1334. *Chen Tongtong v. Beijing Gaohua Caixin Investment Consulting Co., Ltd. and Ma Chao*, Beijing Chaoyang District People's Court (2020) Jing 0105 Min Chu No. 36603; 陈彤彤诉北京高华财信投资顾问有限公司、马超保证合同纠纷案，北京市朝阳区人民法院（2020）京0105民初36603号.

1335. Article 692 CC.

1336. Article 29 of the SPC Interpretation on Security System (2020).

creditor does not file a lawsuit or apply for arbitration before the end of the guaranty period, if the guarantor claims no longer to undertake the guaranteed liability, the court will support such claim. Where the creditor of a guaranty with joint and several liability who files a lawsuit or applies for arbitration against the guarantor during the guaranty period withdraws the lawsuit or arbitration application, if a copy of the complaint or arbitration application has been served on the guarantor, the court will accept that the creditor has already exercised the right with the guarantor during the guaranty period.[1337]

1221. Where the creditor under a general guaranty fails to institute legal proceedings or apply for arbitration against the debtor within the guaranty period, the guarantor shall cease to bear any guaranty liability. Where the creditor under a guaranty with joint and several liability does not assert guaranty liability against the guarantor within the guaranty period, the guarantor shall cease to bear any guaranty liability.[1338] Where the creditor under a general guaranty institutes legal proceedings or applies for arbitration against the debtor before the expiry of the guaranty period, the limitation of action for the guaranteed obligation shall commence from the date on which the right of the guarantor to refuse to bear guaranty liability extinguishes. Where the creditor under a guaranty with joint and several liability claims that the guarantor bear guaranty liability before the expiry of the guaranty period, the limitation of action for the guaranteed obligation shall commence from the date on which the creditor makes the claim.[1339]

1222. The guarantor and the creditor may negotiate and conclude a contract of maximum amount guaranty, under which they agree that the guaranty is provided for obligations occurring continuously within a certain period of time to the extent of a maximum amount. The relevant provisions on the maximum amount charged in the Book on Property Rights shall, in addition to the provisions in this chapter, be referred to and applied in respect of contracts for maximum amount guaranty.[1340] Where the maximum guaranty contract has an agreement on the calculation and starting time of the guaranty period, the agreement shall prevail. Where the maximum guaranty contract has no or unclear agreement on the calculation and starting time of the guaranty period if the performance period of the secured claims has expired, the guaranty period shall begin to be calculated from the date of determination of the claims; if the performance period of the secured claims has not yet

1337. Article 31 CC.
1338. Article 693 CC.
1339. Article 694 CC.
1340. Article 690 CC. For maximum amount charge under mortgages, *see also Industrial and Commercial Bank of China Limited Xuancheng Longshou Branch v. Xuancheng Boguan Trading Co., Ltd. and Jiangsu Kaisheng Real Estate Co., Ltd.*, SPC Guiding Case No. 95; 中国工商银行股份有限公司宣城龙首支行诉宣城柏冠贸易有限公司、江苏凯盛置业有限公司等金融借款合同纠纷案，最高人民法院，第95号指导性案例; *China CITIC Bank Co., Ltd. Dongguan Branch v. Chen Zhihua and Others*, SPC Guiding Case No. 168; 中信银行股份有限公司东莞分行诉陈志华等金融借款合同纠纷案，最高人民法院，第168号指导性案例.

expired, the guaranty period shall begin to be calculated from the date on which the performance period of the last due claims expires.[1341]

II. Scope of Guaranty

1223. The scope of a guaranty includes the principal obligation and its interest, agreed damages, damages and expenses for the enforcement of the obligation. Where the parties agree otherwise, such agreement shall prevail.[1342] Where the parties agree on special liability for guaranty liability, or the scope of the agreed guaranty liability exceeds the scope of the debtor's liability, the guarantor is liable only within the scope of the debtor's liability. Where a guarantor bears liability exceeding the scope of the debtor's liability, the guarantor has a recourse right against the debtor and the debtor is liable only within the scope of its responsibilities.[1343]

1224. The maximum amount of claims in the maximum guaranty refers to all claims including the principal claims and interest thereon, liquidated damages, damages, costs for keeping the secured property, and costs for satisfying the claims or security interests, unless otherwise agreed by the parties.[1344] However, parties may agree on other damages and costs in addition to the maximum amount guaranty in contracts for maximum amount guaranty. Those agreed damages and costs are not subject to the maximum amount in the guaranty. In *China Great Wall Asset Management Co., Ltd. Shanxi Branch v. Huamei Aochongsheng Coal Industry Co., Ltd. of Pinglu District, Shuozhou, Shanxi and Others*,[1345] it was agreed that the maximum amount guaranty was RMB 500 million plus the relevant interest, penalty interest, liquidated damage, damages, all costs for enforcing debts, security rights, etc., and all other payable costs. The lower-level courts held that the guarantor should be liable to the creditor within RMB 500 million for all claims. The SPC overturned the decision. The SPC held that the guarantor should be liable for the secured principal debt within the maximum limit in the principal contract and other agreed interest, damage and costs beyond the maximum limit.

1225. Where the parties to a principal contract agree to refinance an existing loan with a new loan, if the creditor requests the security provider of the existing

---

1341. Paragraph 1 of Art. 30 of the SPC Interpretation on Security System (2020).
1342. Article 691 CC.
1343. Article 3 of the SPC Interpretation on Security System (2020). For special guaranty liabilities relating to company and insolvency, *see* the SPC Interpretation on Security System (2020), Arts 7-12 for company and Arts 22-24 for insolvency.
1344. Article 15, para. 1 of the SPC Interpretation on Security System 2020. If the registered maximum amount of claims is inconsistent with that agreed by the parties, the scope of creditors' priority to be paid shall be determined based on the registered maximum amount of claims: para. 2 of Art. 15 of the SPC Interpretation on Security System (2020).
1345. *China Great Wall Asset Management Co., Ltd. Shanxi Branch v. Huamei Aochongsheng Coal Industry Co., Ltd. of Pinglu District, Shuozhou, Shanxi and Others*, the SPC (2019) Zui Gao Fa Min Zhong No. 823 (Gazette Case of the SPC, Issue 5, 2020); 中国长城资产管理股份有限公司山西省分公司与山西朔州平鲁区华美奥崇升煤业有限公司等借款合同纠纷案，最高人民法院（2019）最高法民终823号（《最高人民法院公报》案例，2020年05期）.

loan to be liable for the security, the court shall not support such request. If the creditor requests the security provider of the new loan to be liable for the security, it shall be handled according to the following circumstances: (1) If the security provider of the new loan is the same as that of the existing loan, the court shall support such request; (2) If the security provider of the new loan is different from that of the existing loan, or if the existing loan is unsecured and the new loan is secured, the court shall not support such request, except where the creditor has evidence to prove that the security provider of the new loan knows or should know of the fact that an existing loan is being refinanced with a new loan when providing security.[1346]

1226. Where the principal contract is valid but the guaranty contract is invalid, the liabilities shall be determined in the following circumstances: (1) Where both the creditor and the guarantor are at fault, the guarantor shall be liable for compensation which shall not exceed half the value of the debtor's obligations that remain unfulfilled; (2) If the guarantor is at fault while the creditor is not at fault, the guarantor shall be liable for compensation to the value of the debtor's obligations that remain unfulfilled; (3) If the creditor is at fault but the guarantor is not at fault, the guarantor shall not be liable for compensation. Where the principal contract is invalid and the guaranty contract is thus invalid, the liabilities shall be determined in the following circumstances: (1) Where the guarantor is not at fault, he shall not be liable for compensation; (2) Where the guarantor is at fault, he shall be liable for no more than one third of the value of the debtor's obligations that remain unfulfilled.[1347] Those rules apply to the counter-guaranty.[1348]

III. Change of guaranty

1227. The guaranty may be affected by the change of the principal contract. Where, in the absence of written consent from the guarantor, the creditor and the debtor agree to change the content of the principal contract on the creditor's rights and obligations, the guarantor remains bearing guaranty liability for the changed obligation if the principal obligation is reduced; if the principal obligation is increased, the guarantor does not bear guaranty liability for the increased portion. Where, in the absence of written consent from the guarantor, the creditor and the debtor change the time for performance under the principal obligation contract, the guaranty period is unaffected by such change.[1349]

1228. The guaranty may also be affected by the assignment of the debt under the principal contract. Where the creditor assigns its claim in whole or in part to a third party, the guarantor bears corresponding guaranty liability to the assignee after the guarantor has been notified. Without notification, such assignment shall have no effect on the guarantor. Where the guarantor and the creditor agree that guaranty

1346. Article 16, para. 1 of the SPC Interpretation on Security System (2020).
1347. Article 17 CC.
1348. Paragraph 2 of Art. 19 CC.
1349. Article 695 CC.

liability is borne to specific creditors or that an assignment is prohibited, and the creditor, in the absence of written consent from the guarantor, assigns its claim in whole or in part, the guarantor ceases to bear guaranty liability to the assignee.[1350] Where, in the absence of written consent from the guarantor, the creditor consents to the transfer by the debtor of its obligation in whole or in part, unless otherwise agreed by the creditor and the guarantor, the guarantor ceases to bear guaranty liability in respect of any obligation transferred without its consent. The guaranty liability of the guarantor is unaffected by a third party joining as a debtor.[1351]

1229. A third party may join as a debtor, a guarantor or a new contract party. It is necessary to analyse the third party's liability in the guaranty relationship. The addition of debt does not discharge the original debtor from the debt relationship but adds a new debtor with the function of guaranteeing the realisation of the creditor's rights. In the absence of a clear debtor, to determine whether the third party's promise constitutes a guarantee, a debt addition, or a new contractual obligation, the party's true expression of intention should be examined on the party's autonomy in conjunction with the definition of the guaranty contract and on whether the third party's commitment is subordinate, conditional and recoverable. When the agreement is unclear, it should be deemed to be a guarantee.[1352]

1230. In *Guangdong Jiedong Rural Commercial Bank Co., Ltd. v. Wu Liebiao and Others*,[1353] the guarantor agreed to provide a guaranty for the borrower's repayment of a loan to the lender. After the guaranty agreement was concluded, a third party agreed to provide a joint guaranty for the borrower's repayment of the loan. The third party also agreed to 'repay on behalf of' the borrower for the unrepaid loan. The borrower failed to repay the loan, and the lender claimed against the borrower, the guarantor and the third party. The guarantor argued that the debt was transferred to the third party without the consent of the guarantor and the guarantor would no longer bear guaranty responsibility. The argument was not accepted by the court. It was pointed out that the term 'repay on behalf of' does not automatically mean that the debt has been transferred. In this case, the content of the original loan contract was changed, and the creditor did not exempt the borrower from its repayment obligation. Furthermore, the lender had clearly stated that it did not recognise that the debt had been transferred. Therefore, it was held that the third party joined the relationship as a debtor by agreeing to replay on behalf of the borrower. The liability guarantors jointly bear repayment obligations to creditors. The guaranty liability of the guarantor in this case was unaffected by a third party joining as a

1350. Article 696 CC.

1351. Article 697 CC.

1352. *Jia Min v. Fuhua Holdings Limited*, Beijing Chaoyang District People's Court (2019) Jing 0105 Min Chu No. 34308; 贾敏与复华控股有限公司保证合同纠纷案, 北京市朝阳区人民法院（2019）京0105民初34308号.

1353. *Guangdong Jiedong Rural Commercial Bank Co., Ltd. v. Wu Liebiao and Others*, Guangdong Jieyang Intermediate People's Court (2019) Yue 52 Min Zhong No. 421; 广东揭东农村商业银行股份有限公司诉吴列标等金融借款合同纠纷案, 广东省揭阳市中级人民法院（2019）粤52民终421号.

debtor. Therefore, it was held that the third party should bear repayment obligations to the lender jointly with the debtor and the jointly and severally liable guarantor.

IV. More Than One Guarantor

1231. Where, in respect of the same obligation, there are two or more guarantors, the guarantors shall bear guaranty liability in accordance with the guaranty shares as agreed in the guaranty contract. Where there is no agreement on the guaranty shares, the creditor may demand that any guarantor bear guaranty liability to the extent of its guaranty.[1354] After the guarantor has borne guaranty liability, unless otherwise agreed by the parties, the guarantor is entitled to seek compensation from the debtor to the extent of the guaranty liability it has borne, enjoying the creditor's rights against the debtor, provided that no prejudice is caused to the interests of the creditor.[1355]

1232. The SPC provides rules for special circumstances of guaranty with more than one guarantor. First, where two or more guarantors provide guaranty for the same debt and the guarantors agree on mutual recourse and respective shares, the guarantor who has been liable for the guaranty is entitled to request other guarantors to bear their respective liability as agreed; if the guarantors agree to undertake a joint and several joint guaranty, or agree on mutual recourse but fail to agree on respective shares, each guarantor shall share proportionately the part in relation to which it cannot have recourse against the debtor. Second, where two or more guarantors provide guaranty for the same debt and the guarantors agree on neither mutual recourse nor joint and several guaranty, but the guarantors have signed, sealed or fingerprinted the same contract, the guarantor who has been liable for the guaranty is entitled to request other guarantors to share proportionately the part in relation to which it cannot have recourse against the debtor. Except for these two specified circumstances, the guarantor who has been liable for the guaranty is not entitled to request other guarantors to share the part in relation to which it cannot have recourse against the debtor.[1356] Where two or more guarantors provide security for the same debt, if one of the guarantors accepts the claims, it means that the guarantor has borne the guaranty obligation. Where the guarantor which accepts the obligation as a creditor, it is not entitled to request other guarantors to be liable for the guaranty. However, such guarantor is entitled to request the share from other guarantors in the above two specified circumstances.[1357]

1354. Article 699 CC.
1355. Article 700 CC.
1356. Article 13 of the SPC Interpretation on Security System (2020).
1357. Article 14 CC.

Chapter 6. Lease Contracts

§1. General Provisions

1233. A lease contract in the Civil Code is a contract whereby the lessor delivers the leased item to the lessee for its use or benefit, for which the lessee pays the rent.[1358] The content of a lease contract generally includes terms as to the name, quantity and use of the leased item, term of lease, rent, time and means of payment of rent, and the maintenance and repair of the leased item, etc.[1359] Some lease contracts may need registration and record-filing. The Civil Code has special rules on the lease term of the lease contracts. The term of the lease shall not exceed twenty years. Where the lease exceeds twenty years, the excessive portion of the lease is void. Upon expiry of the lease, the parties may renew the lease provided that the renewed term shall not exceed twenty years from the date of the renewal.[1360] It means that the renewed lease contract is also subject to twenty years, and the excessive portion of the renewed lease is void.

1234. The lease term in the lease contract may be agreed upon in various ways, e.g., '×+×' upon renewal, the lease term should be determined upon judicial interpretation. In *Tianjin Baiyang Zhaojun Advertising Co., Ltd. v. Tianjin Aozhong Development Co., Ltd.*,[1361] the lease contract stated the lease term as '5+5 years', and then defined the sixth to tenth years as 'lease renewal'. For the sixth to tenth years, the rent limit was agreed upon, but the specific amount was not specified. The lease contract also provided the conditions for renewing the lease. First, the lessee should notify the lessor in writing six months before the expiration of the lease term, and then the consent of the lessor must be obtained for renewal. Both parties also needed to negotiate and sign a renewal contract. It was held that from the literal meaning of the contract terms, the lease term should be five years, and the term from the sixth year to the tenth year was only intention to renew the lease contract.

1235. Although contracts can be made in any form, e.g., in writing or in oral form, the Civil Code has special rules on the form upon the lease term. Where the term of the lease is not less than six months, the lease shall be made in writing. Where the lease is not in writing and the term of the lease cannot be ascertained, it shall be deemed that the lease is for an indefinite term.[1362] It is not clarified in the Civil Code whether the indefinite lease is subject to the twenty-year requirements for the validity of lease contracts. It is submitted that the indefinite lease should not be subject to the twenty-year requirement because the indefinite lease has no lease term, and the twenty-year requirement applies to lease contracts with definite lease terms. Where the parties have not agreed on the term of the lease or their agreement

1358. Article 703 CC. The definition has no change from that of the Contract Law.
1359. Article 704 CC.
1360. Article 705 CC.
1361. *Tianjin Baiyang Zhaojun Advertising Co., Ltd. v. Tianjin Aozhong Development Co., Ltd.*, Tianjin High People's Court (2019) Jin Min Zhong No. 194; 天津市佰扬兆俊广告有限公司诉天津澳中发展有限公司租赁合同纠纷案，天津市高级人民法院（2019）津民终194号.
1362. Article 707 CC.

is equivocal, and the term cannot be ascertained under Article 510 of this Code, it shall be deemed that the lease is for an indefinite term. The parties may terminate the contract at any time, provided that a notice has been served on the other party a reasonable time before the termination.[1363]

1236. The validity of the lease contract is unaffected by the fact that the parties fail to adhere to registration or filing formalities for lease contracts in accordance with the laws or administrative regulations.[1364] However, a lease contract may be void if the failure to adhere to registration or filing formalities is contrary to the public order and good morals and harms the public interest in civil law. In *Rao Guoli v. Jiangxi Provincial Prison Administration Material Supply Station*,[1365] the house under a lease contract was a dilapidated house, and it was found that the house under a lease contract had serious structural risks and might cause a major safety incident. The local authorities rated the house as a D-level dilapidated house and recommended the house be demolished as quickly as possible. According to the regulation from the Ministry of Housing and Urban-Rural Development, a house is not allowed to be leased if the house does not meet the construction standards for safety and disaster prevention purposes. The Chinese courts pointed out that the regulation is to protect the public safety and maintain public order and good morals. In this case, leasing this dilapidated house was obviously contrary to the public interests, public order and good morals. The Chinese courts should not uphold this lease contract. Therefore, the lease contract was held void according to the civil law and the contract law.[1366]

§2. Rights and Obligations of the Lessor

1237. The lessor shall, in accordance with the contract, deliver the leased item to the lessee and keep the leased item fit for the purpose of the contract during the term of the lease.[1367] If the purpose of the lease contract cannot be released, the lessee may apply for termination of the contract. In *Jiang Weimin v. Nanjing Hongyang Real Estate Brokerage Co., Ltd.*,[1368] the indoor air quality was in dispute under the lease contract. The lessee was ill after moving into the leased house. The lessor

1363. Article 730 CC.
1364. Article 706 CC.
1365. *Rao Guoli v. Jiangxi Provincial Prison Administration Material Supply Station*, the Supreme People's Court, (2019) SPC Min Zai No. 97; 饶国礼诉江西省监狱管理局物资供应站，最高人民法院（2019）最高法民再97号. SPC Guiding Case No. 170, 最高人民法院，第170号指导性案例.
1366. The decision is still valid under the current rules of the Civil Code. Article 8 of the Civil Code provides that civil subjects shall not carry out civil activities in violation of law, nor contrary to the public order and good morals. Art. 132 CC provides that civil subjects shall not abuse their rights in a way that harms the interest of the State, the public, or the lawful rights and interests of others.
1367. Article 708 CC.
1368. *Jiang Weimin v. Nanjing Hongyang Real Estate Brokerage Co., Ltd.*, Gazette Case of the SPC, Issue 11, 2022; 江卫民诉南京宏阳房产经纪有限公司房屋租赁合同纠纷案，《最高人民法院公报》案例，2022年11期.

refused to provide an air quality certificate, and the lessee invited a surveyor to conduct the air quality testing. The result showed that the formaldehyde value and total volatile organic compound value in indoor air exceeded the standard. The Chinese courts accepted the testing results and held that the lease contract was terminated because the contract purpose could not realise, and the lessor should return the paid rent to the lessee. In addition, the Civil Code provides that, where the leased item endangers the safety or health of the lessee, the lessee may terminate the contract at any time irrespective of its knowledge at the time of contract that the leased item fails to meet the quality requirements.[1369]

1238. Furthermore, the lessor shall perform its obligation to maintain and repair the leased item, unless otherwise agreed by the parties.[1370] Where the leased item is in need of maintenance or repair, the lessee may demand that the lessor maintain or repair it within a reasonable period. Where the lessor fails to perform its obligation to maintain and repair, the lessee may maintain and/or repair on its own initiative, at the lessor's cost. Where the maintenance or repair affects the use by the lessee, the rent shall be reduced, or the lease term shall be extended accordingly. Where the need for maintenance or repair of the leased item arises by virtue of the lessee's fault, the lessor does not bear those obligations.[1371]

1239. The lessor has the right to dispose of the ownership of the leased item during the lease term. However, any change in ownership of the leased item during the period in which the lessee possesses the item in accordance with the lease contract shall not affect the validity of the lease contract.[1372] Where the lessor sells property subject to a lease, the lessor shall notify the lessee within a reasonable period before the sale and the lessee has a right of first refusal under equal conditions, unless a co-owner by shares of the property exercises its right of first refusal or the lessor sells its property to a close relative.[1373] Where the lessor has performed its obligation to notify and the lessee fails to indicate its intention to purchase unequivocally within fifteen days, it is deemed that the lessee waives its right of first refusal.[1374]

1240. After the conclusion of the property sale contract between the lessee and the lessor, if another property sale contract between the lessor and a third party does not take effect or is invalid, there will be no conflict of rights between the lessee and the third party on the property, and the lessee can obtain ownership of the property through the performance of the contract between the lessee and the lessor. However, if the sale contract between the lessor and the third party still exists, there will be a dispute of dual sales under dual contracts between the lessor, the lessee and the third party. In this circumstance, whether the lessee can obtain ownership of the property in priority over the third party depends on the legal effect of the lessee's

1369. Article 731 CC.
1370. Article 712 CC.
1371. Article 713 CC.
1372. Article 725 CC.
1373. Close relatives in the Civil Code are the spouse, parents, children, siblings, paternal and maternal grandparents, paternal and maternal grandchildren. *See* para. 2 of Art. 1045 CC.
1374. Article 726 CC.

right of first refusal. It is believed that the lessee's right of first refusal has no adversarial effect against third parties. Therefore, if the lessor has transferred the property ownership to a third party, the lessee can only claim damages against the lessor.[1375] However, before the ownership of the house is transferred to a third party, if both the lessee and the third party request the lessor to transfer the ownership of the house, it is argued that the lessor shall fulfil its obligation to transfer the ownership of the property to the lessee.[1376]

1241. In the case where a rental house has a courtyard attached to it, the courtyard can be regarded as land attached to the rental house. According to the principle that 'the land follows the house' in real estate,[1377] the lessee has the right of first refusal to purchase the leased house and its courtyard.[1378] This right gives the lessee the right to be first in line to purchase the property when the landlord decides to sell. However, if the subject matter of the lease contract is only or mainly for land, the lessee does not have the right of first refusal to purchase the land.[1379] Furthermore, if the contract, in addition to the use and income of the house, also involves the use of the production and operation-related licences of the contracting party and the supervision and management of production safety, the contract is not a pure property rental contract, and the contractor does not have the right of first refusal as a lessee.[1380]

1242. In the case where the lessor sells the leased house together with other houses or ancillary facilities as a whole, the lessee may not have the right of first refusal on this part of the house. In a reply to a local court, the SPC took a view that, from the perspective of the use function of the house, if the part of the house rented by the lessee is separable from other parts of the house and the use function can be relatively independent, the lessee's right of first refusal should only extend to the part of the house rented. If the house is indivisible or the division will significantly reduce its overall value, the lessee cannot exercise the right of first refusal

1375. Mengyong Dai, Commentary on Article 726 of the Civil Code (Housing Lessee's Right of First Refusal), 4 Tsinghua University Law Journal (Qing Hua Fa Xue) 140, 156-157 (2023).
1376. The SPC First Civil Trial Division (ed), *Understanding and Application of the Judicial Interpretation of the Supreme People's Court on Hearing Cases Involving Disputes over Urban Housing Lease Contracts* (People's Court Press 2016) p. 292.
1377. Article 357 CC.
1378. *Wang Liya v. Lushi Hardware, Electricity and Chemical Products Co., Ltd., Yang Dongfen and Xue Maosheng*, (2006) 1 China Law Report 141-145 (People's Court Press 2006); 王利亚诉卢氏县五交化公司、杨冬粉、薛茂生承租房屋优先购买权案，《人民法院案例选》，2006 年第1 辑，人民法院出版社，2006 年版，第141-145 页.
1379. The SPC (2018) Zui Gao Fa Zhi Fu Zi No. 17; 最高人民法院（2018）最高法执复字第17 号 (names of the parties in the judgment were not released).
1380. *Ge Lanying v. Urban Agricultural Machinery Station*, (2003) 1 China Law Report, People's Court Press (2003), pp. 211-213; 葛兰英诉城镇农机站抵押借款后又将抵押物发包给其承包经营现抵押物被判决执行给债权人应按租赁关系由其行使优先购买权案，《人民法院案例选》2003 年第1 辑，人民法院出版社，2003 年版，第211-213 页.

on part of the leased house.[1381] However, this view has not been widely accepted in Chinese judicial practice. Some Chinese courts including the SPC take a different view that the lessee should not have the right of first refusal on this part of the house because the house sold as a whole is not the same subject as the part of the house rented by the lessee.[1382] It is argued that the latter view in judicial practice should be supported because the previous view was complicated and may cause uncertainty in the sale contract between the lessor and the third party.[1383]

1243. In the case where the lessee of a partial house claims to exercise the right of first refusal on a house sold as a whole, the SPC took a view from the same reply to the local court that if the part of the house rented by the lessee accounts for more than half of the whole house sold by the lessor, the lessee shall have the right of first refusal on the whole house sold by the lessor; if it is less than half of the whole house, it should not have the right of first refusal on all the house sold by the lessor.[1384] However, some Chinese courts take a different view that the lessee should not have the right of first refusal on the whole house because the partial house rented by the lessee and the house sold as a whole by the lessor are not of the same subject.[1385] Although the SPC's view in its reply has been widely applied in judicial practice,[1386] this view is also complicated and makes the lessee's right of first refusal uncertain when the part of the house rented by the lessee accounts for just half of the whole house sold by the lessor. It is submitted that the view that the lessee should not have the right of first refusal on the whole house should be supported.

1244. Where the lessor entrusts an auctioneer with placing a leased property into auction, the lessor shall notify the lessee five days prior to the auction. Where the lessee does not participate in the auction, it is deemed that the lessee waives its right

---

1381. Reply from the SPC on whether a lessee who rents part of a house has the right of first refusal when the lessor sells the house as a whole; The SPC [2004] Min Yi Ta Zi No. 29. 《最高人民法院关于承租部分房屋的承租人在出租人整体出卖房屋时是否享有优先购买权的复函》[2004] 民一他字第29 号.

1382. *Luo Zhiguang v. Guangdong Huaqiao Real Estate Agency Co., Ltd., Chen Liangyi and Huang Qujiao* (2009) China Law Report, China Legal Publishing House (2009), pp. 21-22; 罗志广诉广东省华侨房产建设公司、陈良义、黄取娇优先购买权纠纷案，《人民法院案例选》2009 年，中国法制出版社，2009 年版，第21-22 页.

1383. Mengyong Dai, Commentary on Article 726 of the Civil Code (Housing Lessee's Right of First Refusal), 149.

1384. Reply from the Supreme People's Court on whether a lessee who rents part of a house has the right of first refusal when the lessor sells the house as a whole; The SPC [2004] Min Yi Ta Zi No. 29. 《最高人民法院关于承租部分房屋的承租人在出租人整体出卖房屋时是否享有优先购买权的复函》[2004] 民一他字第29 号.

1385. *Chen Weiwen v. Lianping Hardware, Electricity and Chemical Products Co., Ltd.* (2007) 3 China Law Report, People's Court Press (2008), pp. 86-88; 陈伟文诉连平县五金交电化工公司确认优先购买权纠纷案，《人民法院案例选》，2007 年第3 辑，人民法院出版社，2008 年版，第86-88 页.

1386. *See* The SPC (2018) Zui Gao Fa Min Shen Zi No. 3900, 最高人民法院（2018）最高法民申字第3900 号; Beijing High People's Court (2020) Jing Min Shen Zi No. 278, 北京市高级人民法院（2020）京民申字第278 号; and Sichuan High People's Court (2019) Chuan Zhi Jian Zi No. 2, 四川省高级人民法院（2019）川执监字第2 号 (names of the parties in the judgment were not released).

of first refusal.[1387] Where the lessor does not notify the lessee or otherwise conducts itself so as to impair the lessee's exercise of its right of first refusal, the lessee may seek damages from the lessor. However, this does not affect the validity of the contract for the sale of the property between the lessor and the third party.[1388]

§3. Rights and Obligations of the Lessee

1245. The lessee has the right to use and have benefit from the use of the leased item. He also has an obligation to keep the leased item in good custody. On the one hand, benefits that accrue from the possession or use of the leased item during the lease are owned by the lessee, unless otherwise agreed by the parties. Where the lessee is unable to use or derive benefits from the leased item due to any claim by a third party, the lessee may seek reduction in or non-payment of the rent. The lessee shall notify the lessor in a timely fashion about any claims made by a third party.[1389] On the other hand, the lessee shall keep the leased item in good custody, and be liable for damages where its failure to do so causes the leased item to be damaged, destroyed or lost.[1390] With the consent of the lessor, the lessee may improve upon or affix other items to the leased item. Where the lessee improves upon or affixes other items to the leased item without the consent of the lessor, the lessor may demand that the lessee restore the leased item to its original state or pay damages.[1391]

1246. Furthermore, the lessee shall use the leased item in accordance with the agreed manner. Where there is no agreement on the manner of use or the agreement is equivocal, and the manner of use cannot be ascertained under Article 510 of the Civil Code, the leased item shall be used in a manner consistent with its nature.[1392] Where the lessee uses the leased item in the agreed manner or according to its nature, thereby causing wear and tear to the leased item, the lessee is not liable for damages.[1393] Where the lessee fails to use the leased item in the agreed manner or according to its nature, thereby causing damage to the leased item, the lessor may terminate the contract and claim damages.[1394] According to the Civil Code, the parties to a contract may terminate the contract as provided by law.[1395] The lessor's termination right is such a kind of right as provided by law. It is identical to the same right in the Contract Law. It means that the lessor's termination right is not changed from the Contract Law to the Civil Code. However, it is questioned whether it is appropriate to allow the lessor to terminate the lease contract if the lessee's

1387. Article 727 CC.
1388. Article 728 CC.
1389. Article 723 CC.
1390. Article 714 CC.
1391. Article 715 CC.
1392. Article 709 CC.
1393. Article 710 CC.
1394. Article 711 CC.
1395. Article 563 (5) CC.

improper use of the leased item causes minor damage only. It might not be reasonable to terminate the contract if the minor damage could be remedied without affecting the main purpose of the lease contract.

1247. The lessee shall pay the rent in accordance with the agreed time. Where there is no agreement on the time for the payment of the rent or the agreement is equivocal, and the time cannot be ascertained under Article 511 of this Code,[1396] the rent shall be paid when the term of the lease expires where the term of the lease is under one year,and where the term of the lease is one year or longer, the rent shall be paid at each anniversary of the lease, or if the remaining term is under one year, when the term of the lease expires.[1397] Where the lessee fails to pay or delays in paying the rent without justification, the lessor may seek payment by the lessee within a reasonable period. Where the lessee fails to pay within that period, the lessor may terminate the contract.[1398] This is not to impose an obligation on the lessor to seek payment after the lessee's breach of payment obligation but to provide the lessor a statutory right to terminate the lease contract if the breach cannot be remedied within a reasonable period. Where the lessee defaults in the payment of rent, the sub-lessee may pay the outstanding rent and agreed damages for the lessee, except where the sub-lease contract has no legal binding force on the lessor. The sub-lessee may offset the rent payable to the lessee by the rent and agreed damages paid for the lessee. Where the amount paid exceeds the rent payable, the sub-lessee may seek compensation from the lessee.[1399]

1248. The lessee may sub-lease the leased item to a third party. With the consent of the lessor, the lessee may sub-lease the leased item to a third party. Where there is a sub-lease, the lease contract between the lessor and the lessee remains valid. Where the third party causes damage to the leased item, the lessee shall be liable for damages. Where the lessee sub-leases without the consent of the lessor, the lessor may terminate the contract.[1400] Where the lessor knows or ought to know of the sub-lease by the lessee but raises no objection within six months, it is deemed that the lessor consents to the sub-lease.[1401] Where the lessee sub-leases the leased item to a third party with the consent of the lessor and the term of the sub-lease exceeds the remaining term of the lease, the excessive portion of the sub-lease contract has no legal binding force on the lessor, unless otherwise agreed by the lessor and the lessee.[1402]

1396. Article 510(4) CC provides that if the time of performance is not clarified, the obligor may perform, and the obligee may require performance, at any time, provided that the other party shall be given adequate time required for preparation.
1397. Article 721 CC.
1398. Article 722 CC.
1399. Article 719 CC.
1400. Article 716 CC.
1401. Article 718 CC.
1402. Article 717 CC. The lessee may be liable for damage to the sub-lessee caused by the exceeding period.

1249. The lessee may terminate the contract where the leased item cannot be used for reasons attributable to the lessor under any of the following circumstances: (1) The leased item is lawfully seized by judicial or executive authorities; (2) The ownership of the leased item is in dispute; (3) The leased item contravenes any mandatory provisions on the conditions for use under the laws or administrative regulations.[1403] Furthermore, where, for reasons not attributable to the lessor, the leased item is damaged, destroyed or lost in whole or in part, the lessee may seek a reduction in or non-payment of the rent. Where the purpose of the contract cannot be fulfilled due to damage to or loss of the leased item in whole or in part, the lessee may terminate the contract.[1404]

1250. Where the lessee dies during the term of the lease, its co-habitants or co-operators of the business may, in accordance with the original lease contract, lease the property.[1405] The lessee shall return the leased item upon expiry of the term of the lease. The returned leased item shall be in the same state as agreed in the contract or according to the nature of the leased item after being used.[1406] Where the lessee continues to use the leased item after the expiry of the term of the lease and the lessor raises no objection to it, the original lease contract remains effective, but the term of the lease will be indefinite. Upon expiry of the term of the lease, the lessee has a right of first refusal under equal conditions to renew the lease on the same terms.[1407]

§4. Lease Contracts on Urban Buildings

1251. The SPC provides special rules on contracts for the lease of urban buildings in the SPC Interpretation on Several Issues concerning the Application of Law in the Trial of Cases about Disputes Over Lease Contracts on Urban Buildings (2020) (the SPC Interpretation on Urban Buildings).[1408] The term 'urban buildings' in this interpretation refers to buildings located in the planned areas of cities and towns. Cases of disputes over lease contracts on buildings located in the planned areas of townships and villages may be governed by this interpretation by analogy, unless it is otherwise provided for by law.[1409]

1252. A lease contract on a building constructed without a building permit or in violation of the building permit shall be void. However, the lease contract is valid if a building permit or a construction approval from the competent department is

1403. Article 724 CC.
1404. Article 729 CC.
1405. Article 732 CC.
1406. Article 733 CC.
1407. Article 734 CC.
1408. The SPC Interpretation on Several Issues concerning the Application of Law in the Trial of Cases about Disputes Over Lease Contracts on Urban Buildings (2020).
1409. Article 1 of the SPC Interpretation on Urban Buildings (2020). This Interpretation shall not apply to cases of disputes over the lease of public housing, low-rent housing or low-income housing under the welfare policies of the state.

obtained before the close of court debate in the first instance.[1410] A lease contract on a temporary building constructed without approval or beyond the scope of approval shall be void. However, the lease contract is valid if a construction approval is obtained from the competent department before the close of court debate in the first instance. If the lease term exceeds the service life of a temporary building, the excessive part shall be void. However, the lease term within the extended service life of the temporary building is valid if an approval of the competent department on the extension of service life is obtained before the close of court debate in the first instance.[1411] However, where a property leasing contract is invalid, and a party claims payment of a fee for possession and use of the property according to the rent rate stipulated in the contract, the court shall generally support the claim.[1412]

1253. When a lessor concludes multiple lease contracts with respect to the same property, and if all contracts are valid, each lessee claims performance of the contract, the court shall determine the lessee performing the contract in the following order: (1) The lessee that has had legal possession of the leased property; (2) The lessee that has initiated the registration or filing procedures; (3) The lessee that is the first to form the contract. If a lessee that is unable to acquire the leased property claims rescission of the contract and compensation for loss, the relevant provisions of the Civil Code shall apply.[1413]

1254. Where a lease contract is nullified, if the lessee has decorated or remodelled the leasehold upon the lessor's consent, the lessor may, as it desires, own the detachable decorations and furnishings made by the lessee to the leasehold after paying a price; otherwise, the lessee may dismantle them. If the leasehold is damaged in the process of dismantling, the lessee shall restore it to the original state. The lessor may, as it desires, own the undetachable decorations or furnishings to the leasehold after paying a price; otherwise, the current value loss shall be shared by both parties in proportion to their respective faults leading to the nullification of the lease contract.[1414] Where the lease term expires or a lease contract is rescinded, if the lessee has decorated or remodelled the leasehold upon the lessor's consent, unless it is otherwise agreed upon between them, the detachable decorations or furnishings made by the lessee to the leasehold may be dismantled by the lessee. If the leasehold is damaged in the process of dismantling, the lessee shall restore it to the original state.[1415]

1255. Where a lease contract is rescinded, if the lessee has decorated or remodelled the leasehold upon the lessor's consent and both parties have not agreed upon the disposal of the undetachable decorations or furnishings made by the lessee to the leasehold, the court shall deal with it as follows: (1) If the contract is rescinded

1410. Article 2 CC.
1411. Article 3 CC.
1412. Paragraph 1 of Art. 4 CC.
1413. Article 5 CC.
1414. Article 7 CC.
1415. Article 8 CC.

due to the lessor's default, the lessee is entitled to claim against the lessor for compensation for the residue value loss of the decorations or furnishings for the rest of the lease term; (2) If the contract is rescinded due to the lessee's default, the lessee's request against the lessor for compensation for the residue value loss of the decorations or furnishings for the rest of the lease term shall be rejected, but if the lessor agrees to use them, it shall properly indemnify the lessee with the extent of the use value of them; (3) If the contract is rescinded due to both parties' defaults, the residue value loss of the decorations or furnishings for the rest of the lease term shall be assumed by both parties in proportion to their respective faults; and (4) If the contract is rescinded for a cause not attributable to either of the parties, the residue value loss of the decorations or furnishings for the rest of the lease term shall be assumed by both parties under the equity principle, unless it is otherwise provided for by law.[1416]

1256. Where the lease term expires, if the lessee has decorated or remodelled the leasehold upon the lessor's consent, the lessee is not entitled to claim against the lessor for compensation for the undetachable decorations or furnishings to the leasehold unless it is otherwise agreed upon by both parties.[1417] Where the lessee decorates, remodels or expands the leasehold without the lessor's consent, the costs arising therefrom shall be assumed by the lessee. The lessor is entitled to request the lessee to restore the leasehold to the original state or compensate the lessor for losses.[1418]

1257. Where a lease contract is nullified, the term of the lease contract expires or the contract is rescinded, the lessor is entitled to request the sub-lessee with the obligation of vacating the leasehold to pay a possession and use fee for its failure to vacate the leasehold.[1419] Where the ownership of a leased property changes during the period when the lessee is in possession in accordance with the lease contract, and the lessee claims continued performance of the original lease contract by the transferee of the property, the court shall support the claim, unless the leased property falls under any of the following circumstances, or the parties agree otherwise: (1) The leased property has been mortgaged before being leased, and the ownership of the leased property changes as a result of the realisation on the mortgage by the mortgagee; (2) The leased property has been placed under seal by the court before being leased.[1420] Where the lessor and the mortgagee agree to valuate or sell the leasehold for repayment of debts, the lessor shall notify the lessee within a reasonable period of time. If the lessee requests purchase of the leasehold on equal footing by exercising its pre-emptive right, the court shall uphold such a request.[1421]

1416. Article 9 CC.
1417. Article 10 CC.
1418. Article 11 CC.
1419. Article 13 CC.
1420. Article 14 CC.
1421. Article 15 CC.

1258. Where the lessee expands the leasehold upon the lessor's consent but both parties have not agreed upon the expansion costs, the court shall deal with it as follows: (1) If the construction formalities have been legally handled, the expansion costs shall be assumed by the lessor; (2) If the construction formalities have not been legally handled, the expansion costs shall be shared by both parties in proportion to their respective faults.[1422] When a lessee changes the body and load-bearing structure of or expands the property without authorisation, and refuses to restore the original condition within a reasonable period required by the lessor, if the lessor claims rescission of the contract and requires compensation for loss, Article 711 of the Civil Code shall apply to the claim.[1423] Where a property lease contract is invalid, the lessor is entitled to claim the payment of a fee for possession and use of the property according to the rent rate stipulated in the lease contract. If a party claims compensation for the loss arising from the invalidity of the contract, article 157 of the Civil Code shall apply to the claim.[1424]

1422. Article 12 CC.
1423. Article 6 CC.
1424. Article 4 CC.

Chapter 7. Financial Lease Contracts

§1. General Provisions

1259. A financial lease contract in the Civil Code is a contract whereby the lessor, in accordance with the lessee's choice as to the seller and leased item, purchases the leased item from the seller and provides it for the use of the lessee, for which the lessee pays the rent.[1425] Under the Civil Code, the lessor's ownership over the leased matter shall not, without being registered, be asserted against any bona fide third party.[1426] The content of a financial lease contract generally includes terms as to the name, quantity, specifications, technical performance of the leased item, means of inspection, term of lease, components of rent and time, means and currency of its payment, ownership of the leased item upon expiry of the lease, etc.[1427] It can be seen that the leased item is the basis of the financial lease contract. Therefore, if the parties enter into a financial lease contract by fabricating the leased item, the financial lease contract is void.[1428]

1260. Financial leasing transactions have the dual attributes of financing and property lease, and both are indispensable. Where a financial lease contract stipulates that if the lessee sells its own property to the lessor and then leases the leased property back from the lessor, only when the ownership of the subject matter is transferred to the lessor, the two parties will form a financial lease contract relationship. Otherwise, it is only named as a financial lease but actually is a loan contract. It should be handled in accordance with the actual legal relationship, that is, the loan contract relationship.[1429]

1261. According to the SPC Interpretation on Issues concerning the Application of Law in the Trial of Cases Involving Disputes over Financial Lease Contracts (2020) (the SPC Interpretation on Financial Lease Contracts 2020),[1430] where no legal relation of financial lease actually exists under a contract titled financial lease contract, the court shall handle the matter according to the actually formed legal relation.[1431] There is an atypical financial lease in business, e.g., shipping finance in which the lessee sells its own property to the lessor and then leases back the property from the lessor under a financial leasing contract. This practice, based on a sale-leaseback contract, does not need the handover of the property, and the lessee can

1425. Article 735 CC.
1426. Article 745 CC.
1427. Paragraph 1 of Art. 736 CC.
1428. Article 737 CC. This is a new rule in the CC which does not exist in the Contract Law.
1429. *China Financial Leasing Co., Ltd. v. Beijing Homyear Capital Holdings Co., Ltd. and Beijing Gaosheng Huafang Real Estate Development Co., Ltd.*, Tianjin High People's Court (2018) Jin Min Chu No. 150; 中国金融租赁有限公司诉北京华业资本控股股份有限公司、北京高盛华房地产开发有限公司借款合同纠纷案，天津市高级人民法院（2018）津民初150号.
1430. The SPC Interpretation on Issues concerning the Application of Law in the Trial of Cases Involving Disputes over Financial Lease Contracts (2020).
1431. Paragraph 2 of Art. 1 of the SPC Interpretation on Financial Lease Contracts (2020).

continually possess and use the leased property. This practice can satisfy the lessee's demands of cash flow and financing funding need. It can also provide the lessor a security on the leased property for payment of debt. The character of a sale-leaseback contract as a special type of financial lease contract is that the lessee and the seller are the same party, whereas they are different parties under the Civil Code. The Chinese court shall not determine that there is no legal relationship of financial leasing simply because the lessee and the seller are the same party.[1432]

1262. In Chinese judicial practice, some courts have recognised the sale-leaseback contract as a financial lease contract; some others have recognised it as a loan contract. In the former practice, the courts determine the authenticity of the leased property from three aspects: the authenticity of the leased property, the corresponding relationship between the value of the leased property and the transfer price, and the transfer of ownership of the leased property from the lessee to the lessor. When the requirement for 'financing the leased property' is met, a sale-leaseback contract will be recognised as a financial lease contract.[1433] In the latter practice, for legal relationships that lack the requirement of 'financing the leased property', the sale-leaseback contracts are not recognised as financial lease contracts.[1434] If the property does not really exist under a sale-leaseback contract, and there is no transfer of property but only transfer of money, the contract is a loan contract in essence.[1435]

1263. In the dispute of whether a sale-leaseback contract is a loan contract or a financial lease contract, the focus of the review is on the authenticity of the leased property. This should be considered from the following three aspects. First, the lessor shall bear the burden of proof regarding the requirement for 'financing the leased property' under the financial lease contract. Second, the lessor's true intention should be examined. This can be inferred through its review behaviour when signing the contract. If the lessor's true intention is to establish a financial lease contract, careful attention should be paid to the authenticity and ownership of the leased property. Third, the degree of deviation between the actual value of the leased property and the agreed value should be investigated. The overestimation of leased property is the same as that of fictitious leased property. They are both unable to guarantee the lessor's rights. A sale-leaseback contract is a loan contract if there is no financing property but only a transfer of funds.[1436]

1432. Article 2 CC.
1433. *See* the SPC (2019) Zui Gao Fa Min Zhong No. 222; (2019) 最高法民终222 号; the SPC (2016) Zui Gao Fa Min Zhong No. 480, (2016); 最高法民终480 号 (parties' names are not released).
1434. M Li, Analysis on the Legal Nature of Sale-leaseback Contracts in the Context of the Civil Code of the People's Republic of China, 4 Chinese Journal of Maritime Law (Zhong Guo Hai Shang Fa Yan Jiu) 14, 20 (2020).
1435. *Liulin Haobo Coking Coal Co., Ltd. v. Shanxi Liansheng Energy Investment Co., Ltd.*, the SPC (2016) Zui Gao Fa Min Zhong No. 286; 柳林县浩博煤焦有限责任公司、山西联盛能源投资有限公司融资租赁合同纠纷案，最高人民法院（2016）最高法民终286 号.
1436. *Nahe People's Hospital and Nahe City Investment Co., Ltd. v. Shanghai Electric Leasing Co., Ltd.*, Shanghai Financial Court (2021) Hu 74 Min Zhong No. 87; 讷河市人民医院、讷河市城市投资有限公司与上海电气融资租赁有限公司融资租赁合同纠纷案，上海金融法院（2021）沪74民终87号.

1264. When a dispute relating to a financial lease contract occurs, more than two parties may be involved in the dispute. Third parties who have legal interests in the dispute may join the action of the dispute. First, where a dispute arises between the seller and the buyer out of the sales contract or between the lessor and the lessee out of the financial lease contract, and a party institutes an action involving only one of the contractual relationships, the court may notify a party to the other contractual relationship to join the action as a third party if the court believes after examining the case that the party has a legal interest in the outcome of the case. Second, where the lessee and the party actually using the leasehold are different, and an action instituted by a party to the financial lease contract is not against the party actually using the leasehold, if the court believes after examining the case that the party actually using the leasehold has a legal interest in the outcome of the case, the court may notify such a party to join the action as a third party. Third, where the lessee claims a right under the sales contract, such as its right to take delivery of the leasehold or right to compensation directly against the seller based on the sales contract and the financial lease contract, a court shall notify the lessor to join the action as a third party.[1437]

1265. For the form of financial lease contract, the Civil Code requires that a financial lease contract shall be made in writing.[1438] It is not clarified what the legal effect of a financial lease contract is if it is not concluded in writing. It is understood that a financial lease contract in this circumstance shall not be valid and have legal effect if it is not concluded in writing.[1439] However, it must be noted that, according to the general contract law rules in the Civil Code, if one party has performed the principal obligation and the other party has accepted it, the contract is concluded even though the law requires it in written form, but the contract is not concluded in written from.[1440] Furthermore, where, in accordance with the law or administrative regulations, the lessee shall obtain administrative approval for the use and business operation of the leased item, the validity of the financial lease contract is unaffected by the failure of the lessor to obtain such administrative approval.[1441]

§2. Performance of the Financial Lease Contract

1266. For the financial lease purpose, the lessee may choose the leased item from a seller and the lessor concludes the sale contract with the seller. In this circumstance, the contents relating to the lessee in a sales contract concluded by the lessor in accordance with the lessee's choice as to the seller and leased matter shall

1437. Article 13 of the SPC Interpretation on Financial Lease Contracts (2020).
1438. Paragraph 2 of Art. 736 CC. For the meaning of 'in writing', *see* para. 2 of Art. 469 CC.
1439. The SPC Civil Code Implementation Leadership Group, *Understanding and Application of the Contract Section of the Civil Code of the People's Republic of China* (People's Court Press 2020) vol 4, pp. 694-695.
1440. Article 490, para. 2 CC.
1441. Article 738 CC.

not, without consent from the lessee, be varied by the lessor.[1442] The lessor shall be liable for damage if it modifies without authorisation the seller or the leased item that has been chosen by the lessee.[1443] Under a sales contract concluded by the lessor in accordance with the lessee's choice as to the seller and leased item, the seller shall deliver the leased item to the lessee in accordance with the contract, and the lessee enjoys the same rights as a buyer in respect of the taking delivery of the subject matter.[1444] When the lessee causes loss to the lessor by rejecting the leased item without timely notice to the lessor or without justification, the lessor is entitled to claim damages against the lessee.[1445] Where the seller breaches its obligation to deliver the leased item to the lessee, the lessee may refuse to take delivery of the leased item tendered to it by the seller if: (1) The leased item fails miserably to conform to the contract; (2) The seller fails to deliver the leased item in accordance with the contract and fails to do so within a reasonable period upon demand by the lessee or the lessor. Where the lessee refuses to take delivery of the leased item, it shall timely notify the lessor.[1446]

1267. Parties may agree who is entitled to claim damage to the leased item. The lessor, seller and lessee may agree that, where the seller fails to perform its obligations under the sales contract, the lessee may exercise the right to claim damages. Where the lessee exercises the right to claim damages, the lessor shall provide assistance.[1447] The lessee may demand that the lessor bear the corresponding liability where the lessor causes the failure of the lessee to claim damages against the seller by: (1) Failing to inform the lessee of any quality defects with knowledge of the defects; or (2) Failing to provide the necessary assistance in the course of the lessee exercising the right to claim damages. Where the lessor neglects to exercise any right to claim damages that only the lessor can exercise against the seller, thereby causing loss to the lessee, the lessee may claim damages against the lessor.[1448] However, the exercise by the lessee of the right to claim damages against the seller does not affect its obligation to pay the rent. However, where the lessee relies on the skills of the lessor in selecting the leased item or the lessor interferes in the selection of the leased item, the lessee may seek a reduction of the rent correspondingly.[1449]

1268. Since the leased item is sold by the seller, the lessor is not liable for any non-conformity of the leased item with the contract or the purpose of use, except where the lessee relies on the skills of the lessor in selecting the leased item or the lessor interferes in the selection of the leased item.[1450] Those exceptions apply when the lessor plays a decisive role in the choice of the leasehold when the lessee chooses the seller and the leased item, or the lessor requires the lessee to choose the

1442. Article 744 CC.
1443. Article 8 of the SPC Interpretation on Financial Lease Contracts (2020).
1444. Article 739 CC.
1445. Article 3 of the SPC Interpretation on Financial Lease Contracts (2020).
1446. Article 740 CC.
1447. Article 741 CC.
1448. Article 743 CC.
1449. Article 742 CC.
1450. Article 747 CC.

seller or the leased item according to the lessor's will. Where the lessee claims that it depends on the lessor's skills in determining the leased item or the lessor interferes with the choice of the leased item, the lessee shall have the burden of proving the above fact.[1451]

1269. During the contract period, the lessor has obligation for undertaking the lessee's possession and use of the leased item. The lessor shall provide a warranty as to the lessee's possession and use of the leased item. The lessee may claim damages against the lessor if the lessor: (1) recovers the leased item without justification; (2) obstructs or interferes with the lessee's possession or use of the leased item without justification; (3) causes a third party to assert rights over the leased item; or (4) otherwise improperly affects the lessee's possession or use of the leased item.[1452] The lessee may also terminate the financial lease contract if the lessee cannot possess or use the leased item because of the lessor.[1453]

1270. The lessor also has an obligation for proper and safe use of the leased item. The lessee shall keep the leased item in good custody and make proper use of it. The lessor shall perform its obligation to maintain and repair the leased item for the duration of its possession.[1454] In the course of the lessee's possession of the leased item, the lessor may seek continual payment of rent by the lessee notwithstanding the damage to or loss of the leased item, unless otherwise provided by law or agreed by the parties.[1455] Furthermore, the lessor is not liable for any personal injury or property damage caused to a third party by the leased item in the course of the lessee's possession of the leased item.[1456] It means that the lessee shall be liable for such injury or damage.

1271. The rent under a financial lease contract shall, unless otherwise agreed by the parties, be determined in accordance with the whole or majority of the cost of purchasing the leased item plus the lessor's reasonable profit.[1457] The lessee shall pay the rent in accordance with the contract. Where the lessee fails to pay the rent within a reasonable period upon demand, the lessor may seek payment of the rent in full or termination of the contract and recovery of the leased item.[1458] The SPC specifies the circumstances in which a lessor may terminate the financial lease contract: (1) The lessee fails to pay rent according to the period and amount specified in the contract, which satisfies the conditions for rescission as set out in the contract, and upon demand by the lessor, the lessee still fails to pay within a reasonable period; and (2) The contract does not clearly provide for the circumstances under which the contract may be rescinded due to rental arrears, but the lessee owes two

1451. Article 8 of the SPC Interpretation on Financial Lease Contracts (2020).
1452. Article 748 CC.
1453. Article 6 of the SPC Interpretation on Financial Lease Contracts (2020).
1454. Article 750 CC.
1455. Article 751 CC.
1456. Article 749 CC.
1457. Article 746 CC.
1458. Article 752 CC.

or more instalments of rent, or the amount owed is 50% or more of all the rent, and upon demand by the lessor, the lessee still fails to pay within a reasonable period.[1459]

§3. Termination of Contract

1272. Where the lessee, without consent from the lessor, transfers, creates a charge over, pledges, invests or otherwise disposes of the leased item, the lessor may terminate the financial lease contract.[1460] The lessor or lessee may terminate the financial lease contract if: (1) the sales contract between the lessor and the seller is terminated or declared void or rescinded, and no sales contract is concluded anew; (2) the leased item is damaged, destroyed or lost for reasons not attributable to the parties and cannot be repaired, with no substitute being identifiable; or (3) the purpose of the financial lease contract cannot be fulfilled for any reason attributable to the seller.[1461]

1273. Parties have different liabilities when the financial lease contract is terminated. First, where a financial lease contract is terminated by reason of the sales contract being terminated, declared void or rescinded, and the seller and the leased item are chosen by the lessee, the lessor may seek compensation against the lessee for the corresponding loss. However, where the lessor's loss is already compensated when the sales contract is terminated, declared void or rescinded, the lessee shall no longer be liable to compensate the corresponding loss.[1462] Second, where a financial lease contract is terminated by virtue of any reason not attributable to the parties, such as accidental damage to or loss of the leased item, after it is delivered to the lessee, the lessor may seek damages against the lessee according to its state of depreciation.[1463]

1274. It is important to clarify the ownership of the leased item after the completion of the financial lease contract. The lessor and lessee may agree on the ownership of the leased item upon expiry of the term of the lease. Where there is no agreement on the ownership of the leased matter or the agreement is equivocal, and the ownership cannot be ascertained under Article 510 of the Civil Code,[1464] the ownership of the leased item shall vest in the lessor.[1465] Where the parties agree that, upon expiry of the term of the lease, the lessee is required only to pay a nominal

1459. Article 5(1) and (2) of the SPC Interpretation on Financial Lease Contracts (2020).
1460. Article 753 CC.
1461. Article 754 CC.
1462. Article 755 CC.
1463. Article 756 CC.
1464. Article 510 CC provides that the parties may agree upon supplementary terms; if a supplementary agreement cannot be reached, such terms shall be determined in accordance with the relevant terms, nature and purpose of the contract, or the trade practices.
1465. Article 757 CC.

price to the lessor, it is deemed that the ownership of the leased item shall, upon full performance of the contractual obligations to pay rent, vest in the lessee.[1466]

1275. Where the parties agree that, upon expiry of the term of the lease, the leased item is to be owned by the lessee, and the lessee has paid the majority of the rent but is unable to pay the outstanding rent, and the lessor thereby terminates the contract and recovers the leased item, the lessee may seek partial restitution if the value of the recovered leased item is greater than the outstanding rent and other expenses payable by the lessee. Where the parties agree that, upon expiry of the term of the lease, the leased item is to be owned by the lessor, and the lessee cannot return the leased item due to its destruction, damage or loss, affixation or mixing with other items, the lessor may seek reasonable compensation from the lessee.[1467]

1276. Where a financial lease contract is void, and the parties have agreed on the ownership of the leased item, such an agreement shall prevail; where there is no agreement or the agreement is equivocal, the leased item shall be returned to the lessor. However, where the contract is void for reasons attributable to the lessee, and the lessor does not seek recovery or the efficacy of the leased item would manifestly diminish after recovery, the ownership of the leased item shall vest in the lessee, and the lessee shall pay reasonable compensation to the lessor.[1468]

1466. Article 759 CC.
1467. Article 758 CC.
1468. Article 760 CC.

Chapter 8. Factoring Contracts

1277. Factoring contract is a newly named contract in the Civil Code that did not exist in the Contract Law. Before the Civil Code, the factoring business was regulated by the regulations from authorities, e.g., the China Banking Regulatory Commission. The Chinese courts applied the SPC's judicial interpretations for disputes about factoring contracts. The Civil Code provides the rules of the factoring contract for the first time in Chinese law. The new rules in the Civil Code are simple but fundamental. Although the Civil Code provides important provisions for factoring contracts, it cannot provide all rules for it. The relevant provisions in Chapter Six of Book III: Contracts on the assignment of obligations shall apply to matters not provided for by this chapter.[1469] This means that the factoring contract has the character of assignment of obligations. It, however, has special characters more than the assignment of obligations. It can be seen from the definition of the factoring contract in the Civil Code.

1278. In the Civil Code, a factoring contract is a contract whereby a receivables creditor assigns its current or future receivables to a factor, and the factor provides services including financial accommodation, receivables management or collection, and arrangement for debtors' payment of and security over the receivables, etc.[1470] A factoring contract shall be made in writing. A factoring contract generally includes terms as to the nature of the business, scope and period of service, circumstances of the basal transactional contract, information about receivables, price of assignment, service fees and their means of payment, etc.[1471] The significance of this definition is that it recognises the factoring contract as a typical contract. It does not need to be considered as a loan, transfer of creditor's rights, guaranty or other types of contracts for evaluation. Instead, it should be evaluated in accordance with the provisions of the factoring contract in the Civil Code and the stipulations of the factoring contract for determining the relationship between the factor and the creditor of the accounts receivable.[1472]

1279. From the definition of the factoring contract, it is emphasised that: (1) the factoring contract only refers to the contract between the receivable creditor and the factor and does not include the debtor. The debtor is not the party to the factoring contract. Therefore, the stipulations in the factoring contract cannot apply to the debtor; (2) the factoring contract and the underlying transaction contract are two related contracts, but they are independent legal relationships, not principal contract and accessory contract; (3) the factor obtains the right to claim receivables based on the factoring contract; it does not mean that the factor has fully acquired the legal

1469. Article 769 CC.
1470. Article 761 CC.
1471. Article 762 CC.
1472. Zhigang Li, A three-dimensional perspective on the factoring contract in the Civil Code, 15 Journal of Law Application (Fa Lv Shi Yong) 39, 42 (2020).

status of the parties in the underlying transaction contract.[1473] This definition clarifies that the core element for determining the nature of a factoring contract is the transfer of receivables. If there is no transfer of receivables, it does not constitute factoring. If parties only agree on collection, it is a mandate contract; if parties only agree on financing, it is a loan contract; if parties only agree that receivables are to be used as a pledge of rights, it is a loan pledge guaranty.[1474]

1280. In Chinese judicial practice, it was controversial whether future receivables could be the object of factoring business because of restrictions from administrative regulations. In *Ping An Bank Co., Ltd. Wuhan Branch v. Datang Henan Clean Energy Co., Ltd.*,[1475] the factoring contract in dispute did not comply with relevant regulations. It was found that the factoring contract was concluded before the regulations took effect, and the contract did not violate compulsory provisions of law or regulations. The Chinese courts held that the factoring contract for future receivables was valid. Now, the Civil Code has clarified that receivables under a factoring contract include future receivables, and this controversial issue should not be an issue again in Chinese judicial practice. In judicial practice, for determining whether future receivables belong to the 'future receivables' under the Civil Code, the court may consider the predictability and certainty of the receivables based on factors such as the counterparty of the future receivables, the subject of the transaction, the nature of the contract, and historical transaction data.[1476]

1281. The factoring contract is based on the existence of receivables of the underlying contract. In business, there are three main situations of fictitious receivable. The first is that the factor colludes with the creditor, and the factor still provides financing to the creditor, even knowing that the creditor has no real receivables without an underlying transaction contract. In this case, the factor's financing risk increases significantly, but it can control the risk by increasing financing interest, providing additional guaranty by a third party, etc. The second situation is that the factor does not collude with the creditor, but it concludes the factoring contract only based on the confirmation of the false receivables submitted by the creditor and the debtor of the fictitious underlying transaction contract, but the debtor later defends on the grounds that the receivables are false. The third situation is that the factor has conducted the necessary review of the underlying transaction contract and related documents but has not found that the receivables are fictitious. The Chinese judicial practice protects the debtor in the first situation and the factor in the third situation. It was controversial what degree of review the factor should have for confirmation of receivables in judicial practice.[1477]

1473. Zhigang Li, A three-dimensional perspective on the factoring contract in the Civil Code, 43.
1474. *Ibid.*
1475. *Ping An Bank Co., Ltd. Wuhan Branch v. Datang Henan Clean Energy Co., Ltd.*, Hubei High People's Court (2017) E Min Zhong No. 3113; 平安银行股份有限公司武汉分行、大唐河南能源有限责任公司合同纠纷案，湖北省高级人民法院（2017）鄂民终3113号.
1476. Zhigang Li, A three-dimensional perspective on the factoring contract in the Civil Code, 45.
1477. *Ibid*, 46.

1282. For the answer to the second situation, the Civil Code provides that, where the receivables creditor fabricated with the receivables debtor the subject matter of the assignment and entered into a factoring contract with the factor, the debtor shall not raise against the factor a defence that the receivables do not exist, unless the factor knew that the receivables were fabricated.[1478] This provides a clear answer to the second situation. This answer only requires 'knew' rather than 'should know'. It shows that the standard of the requirement for the review obligation of the factor is relatively low. Accordingly, it is suggested that the standard for determining 'knew' should be based on the common sense of an ordinary person. The review of the underlying transaction contract or debt confirmation should be based on formal review rather than the review of the entire underlying transaction and all possible transaction documents.[1479]

1283. For the assignment of the receivables from the receivables creditor to the factor, the receivables debtor should be notified. Before the Civil Code, only the receivables creditor could give the notice of assignment to the receivables debtor according to the general contract law.[1480] It was uncertain in Chinese judicial practice whether the assignment is effective if the factor gives such notice.[1481] Under the Civil Code, the factor's notice of assignment is recognised. The factor shall, when issuing notice of the assignment of the receivables to the receivables debtor, indicate its capacity as a factor with necessary certification.[1482] The recognition of the factor's assignment notice provides flexibility to the factor business.

1284. Because the factor contract relates to the underlying contract, any change or termination of the underlying contract may affect the factor contract. In the Civil Code, upon receipt by the receivables debtor of the notice of assignment, where the receivables creditor and debtor agree to vary or terminate the underlying contract without justification, thereby adversely affecting the factor, such acts shall have no effect on the factor.[1483] This is to protect the interests of the factor in this circumstance. However, this protection is subject to two restrictions. First, there must be legitimate reasons for the subjective motivation, namely, the lack of justification for changing or terminating the underlying transaction contract and the negative effect on the factor. This protection with two restrictions has well balanced the interests of parties.[1484]

1478. Article 763 CC.
1479. Zhigang Li, A three-dimensional perspective on the factoring contract in the Civil Code, 48.
1480. Article 80 of the Contract Law.
1481. *Jiangyin Xinjiyang Petroleum Co., Ltd. v. China Construction Bank Jiangyin Lingang Xincheng Branch*, Wuxi Intermediate People's Court (2014) Xi Shang Zhong Zi No. 0306; 江阴市新暨阳石油有限公司与中国建设银行股份有限公司江阴临港新城支行债权转让纠纷案, 无锡市中级人民法院（2014）锡商终字第0306号. In this case, the Chinese courts held that the factor's notice of assignment was valid and effective.
1482. Article 764 CC.
1483. Article 765 CC.
1484. Zhigang Li, A three-dimensional perspective on the factoring contract in the Civil Code, 49.

1285. For enforcing the contractual right under the factoring contract, the factor may assert the receivables rights against the receivables debtor or the receivables creditor. The factor's rights are different depending on the types of factoring. Where the parties agree on a recourse factoring, the factor may claim restitution of the principal and interest of the funds it advanced or buy back the receivables rights from the receivables creditor or assert the receivables rights against the receivables debtor. Where the factor asserts the receivables rights against the receivables debtor, it shall return to the receivables creditor the balance of the receivables after deducting the principal and interest of the funds the factor advanced and relevant expenses.[1485]

1286. This rule of recourse factoring treats the transfer of receivables as security of a loan for financing the creditor of the receivables. In this case, the factor's reimbursement cannot exceed the principal and interest of the original financing, and any excess will be refunded. However, this is not the case in business. The reason why factors choose the factoring transaction model is not just to collect principal and interest from creditors of receivables, but also includes judgment of the time value of receivables and compensation risks, and also includes service prices for collection and management. Therefore, this rule of the Civil Code is not completely consistent with the actual factoring business. Parties may have a special agreement on the receivables rights in business that are different from the aforementioned rule of the Civil Code. A question arises as to whether the special agreement is valid when it is inconsistent with the rule of the Civil code.[1486] It is summarised that there are three types of rules in the Civil Code, namely arbitrary rules, advocacy rules and mandatory rules.[1487] It is understood that the transaction of a factoring contract only involves the factor and the receivables creditor and the aforementioned rule should be an arbitrary rule in the Civil Code. Therefore, parties should be allowed to have special agreements that are different from the aforementioned rule.[1488]

1287. Before the Civil Code, both the Chinese judicial practice and the regulations allowed the factor to assert the receivables rights against the receivables debtor first under the recourse factoring. Unless parties otherwise agreed, the factor can assert the receivables rights against the receivables creditor only for the portion that the receivables debtor cannot be paid off.[1489] This may not be reasonable for protecting the factor's interests. The Civil Code provides new rules for this circumstance. This new rule changed the Chinese judicial practice based on old contract law rules. In this circumstance, the receivables debtor and the receivables creditor actually have a joint and several liability under the recourse factoring. This is for

1485. Article 766 CC.
1486. Zhigang Li, A three-dimensional perspective on the factoring contract in the Civil Code, 50.
1487. Y Wang, Normative Types and Their Configuration Relationships in the Civil Code, 6 Tsinghua University Law Journal (Qing Hua Fa Xue) 58-61 (2014).
1488. Zhigang Li, A three-dimensional perspective on the factoring contract in the Civil Code, 51.
1489. *China Resource Bank of Zhuhai Co., Ltd. v. Jiangxi Fuel Co., Ltd.*, The SPC (2017) Zui Gao Fa Min Zai No. 164; 珠海华润银行股份有限公司与江西省电力燃料有限公司保理合同纠纷案，最高人民法院（2017）最高法民再164号.

the benefit of the factor who can assert rights against any of the receivables debtors and the receivables creditor or both of them for their joint liability.

1288. Where the parties agree on a no-recourse factoring, the factor shall assert the receivables rights against the receivables debtor and is not bound to return to the receivables creditor any excess portions of the receivables beyond the principal and interest of the funds the factor advanced and relevant expenses.[1490] This is also a new rule that has changed the current practice of no-recourse factoring. On the one hand, this new rule reflects the buyout nature of the no-recourse factoring. In this circumstance, the factor only has the right against the receivables debtor, not the receivables creditor. Therefore, the factor takes the risk of bad debts of the receivables debtor. On the other hand, the factor under no-recourse factoring may obtain extra benefit beyond the principal and interest of the funds. It was always agreed in a factor contract that the factor should return the extra benefit. This new rule allows the factor to keep the benefit as a statutory right. This will boost the motivation of the no-recourse factoring business in which the factors may obtain extra benefit.

1289. The Civil Code provides provisions for factoring with more than one factor for the same receivables. Where, in respect of the same receivables, the receivables creditor has entered into several factoring contracts so that multiple factors assert their claims, registered claims shall take precedence over unregistered claims in their satisfaction; where they are all registered, they shall be satisfied according to the chronological order of the respective registrations; where none of them is registered, the factor named in the first notice of assignment to arrive at the receivables debtor is entitled to have its claim satisfied; where none of them is registered or notified, they shall be satisfied in proportion to the receivables amount.[1491] This rule emphasises the importance of the registration of claims for priority in the enforcement of factoring rights.

1490. Article 767 CC.
1491. Article 768 CC.

Chapter 9. Contracts for Work

1290. The provisions of the contracts for work in the Civil Code are identical to those in the Chinese Contract Law. A contract for work is a contract whereby the contractor completes and delivers work in accordance with the requirements of the ordering party, and the ordering party pays remuneration. Work includes processing, custom-made work, repairs, reproduction, testing, inspections, et cetera.[1492] The content of a contract for work generally includes terms as to the subject matter, quantity, quality, remuneration and methods of work, supply of materials, time of performance, criteria and means of inspection, etc.[1493]

1291. Parties may conclude a contract for free work. The voluntary work under this kind of contract is different from the contract for work for remuneration. In *Zhang Minhua v. Wuxi Rongxin Metal Coating Technology Co., Ltd.*,[1494] the court summarised the differences between the contract for work and the relationship based on voluntary work. First, the subjects are different. Contracts for work generally occur between commercial entities such as enterprises, while voluntary work relationships usually occur between individuals such as neighbours, relatives, and friends. Second, things at work are different. The work under the contract for remuneration is generally for a highly professional work matter, while the voluntary work is usually for a less professional work matter. Third, the labour tools are different. Contractors generally earn their main source of income by providing work to ordering parties, so they usually bring their own tools or equipment when working; volunteer workers do not often provide work for ordering parties as their main source of income, and their work is based on friendship. Last, the remuneration is different. Remuneration is an important consideration in the contract of law, whereas the voluntary work is free.

1292. Where the parties do not agree on the remuneration for work in a contract, the ordering party may refuse to pay the remuneration and argue that the contract is for voluntary work. It might be difficult to determine whether there is remuneration for work, especially between acquaintances. In this circumstance, the distinction should be made based on factors such as the specific occupation, economic source, and trading habits of the parties. If the contractor has long been engaged in the job he was engaged in at the time of dispute as his occupation, and this job is his main source of income, and both parties have had similar transactions, it can be determined that the relationship between the two parties is a contract for work. Otherwise, it should be regarded as a voluntary service relationship.[1495]

1492. Article 770 CC.
1493. Article 771 CC.
1494. *Zhang Minhua v. Wuxi Rongxin Metal Coating Technology Co., Ltd.*, Jiangsu Wuxi Intermediate People's Court (2021) Su 02 Min Zhong No. 3616; 章敏华、无锡荣鑫金属涂装科技有限公司承揽合同纠纷案，江苏省无锡市中级人民法院（2021）苏02民终3616号.
1495. *Ibid.*

1293. Work delivered under a contract for work could be the subject matter of a sale contract. It is necessary to clarify the difference between the contract for work and the contract of sale, which is a contract whereby the seller transfers the ownership of a subject matter to the buyer, and the buyer pays the price.[1496] The SPC summarised the differences in *Fangchenggang Huayu High-tech Fiber Co., Ltd. v. Shaoyang Textile Machinery Co., Ltd.*.[1497] In this case, Huayu and Shaoyang Textile concluded contracts for the purchase of a production line. It was agreed that Huayu ordered a production line from Shaoyang Textile and Shaoyang Textile was responsible for engineering design and installation of it. Shaoyang Textile did not deliver the ordered production line and relevant materials. Huayu claimed against Shaoyang Textile for termination of the contracts and damage caused by the breach of contracts. One of the issues in this case is the nature of the contracts in dispute because liabilities and damages were different under different types of contracts. Huayu contended that the contracts in dispute were contracts for work. Shaoyang Textile argued that the contracts were a sale contract. The SPC pointed out that the contract for work and the contract of sale have certain similarities. However, they have different contents of rights and obligations.

1294. The SPC summarised the main differences in theory. First, the purposes of contracts are different. The purpose of a contract of sale is for the transfer of ownership of the subject matter, whereas the purpose of the contract for work is to obtain the specific results of the work. The second difference is the specificity of the subject matter of the contract. The subject matter of a sale contract generally is a kind of indefinite thing for common use and has national or industrial standards. The subject matter of the contract for work is specially made according to the special requests of the ordering party. It usually has a special purpose for satisfying special needs of the ordering party. It is usually for the use of the ordering party, not for sale in the market. Even if it could be sold in the market, it will lose its worthwhile value. Third, a contract for work focuses on the human nature of the contractor. In a contract for work, the ordering party is always concerned about the qualification, technical level, and equipment condition. There is no such concern in the sale contract. The buyer is concerned about the transfer of the ownership, not the maker of the subject matter, manufacturing conditions or process. Fourth, the ordering party has certain control over the production process in the contract for work. The contractor has an obligation to accept necessary supervision and inspections from the ordering party, whereas a sale contract usually has no such requirement. The buyer normally inspects whether the subject matter delivered satisfies the quality requirement but does not have the rights of supervision and inspections on the working process of the subject matter. Fifth, the contractor has an obligation to maintain confidentiality in contract for work, whereas sale contract usually does not have such obligation agreement. Last, the nature of price is different. The price in a sale

1496. Article 595 CC.
1497. *Fangchenggang Huayu High-tech Fiber Co., Ltd. v. Shaoyang Textile Machinery Co., Ltd.*, The SPC (2019) Zui Gao Fa Min Zai No. 383; 防城港华裕特纤科技有限公司、邵阳纺织机械有限责任公司买卖合同纠纷案，最高人民法院（2019）最高法民再383号.

contract is the value of the subject matter itself, whereas the price in a contract for work is the labour remuneration for the contractor's completion of a specific work product.

1295. The SPC applied those differences in theory to this case. On the one hand, Huayu contended that the contract should be a contract for work, but it admitted that it had no instructions to Shaoyang Textile or supervision obligation because Shaoyang Textile provided technical support. On the other hand, Shaoyang Textile argued that the techniques for Huayu's order of a production line were well developed. It had provided a similar production line to other ordering parties. For minimising the damage, it had used the part of ordered work for other orders. It was found that the projection line in dispute was not customisable and Huayu had no actual control or supervision right on the process of the production line. The SPC pointed out that Huayu's contractual right was different from the ordering party in a contract for work. It also pointed out that Shaoyang Textile's technical support is a supplementary obligation under the sale contract, not special work in accordance with the requirements of the ordering party in the contract for work. Therefore, the SPC held that the contracts in dispute were contracts of sale.

1296. The differences summarised by the SPC in this case should be followed by Chinese courts in judicial practice. Those differences can be reflected by the relevant rules in the Civil Code. First, the contractor shall, unless otherwise agreed by the parties, complete the principal work using its own equipment, skills and labour. Where the contractor assigns its principal work to a third party for completion, the contractor shall be liable to the ordering party for the work completed by the third party. The ordering party may terminate the contract where its consent to the assignment has not been obtained.[1498] Second, the contractor may assign its auxiliary work to a third party for completion. Where the contractor assigns its auxiliary work to a third party for completion, the contractor shall be liable to the ordering party for the work completed by the third party.[1499] Third, the contractor shall accept necessary supervision and inspections from the ordering party in the course of the work. The ordering party shall not obstruct the normal course of work of the contractor because of any supervision or inspection.[1500] The contractor shall, as required by the ordering party, maintain confidentiality and, without consent from the ordering party, shall not retain any replica or technical information.[1501]

1297. Parties to a contract for work are free to agree on who supplies the materials for the work. Where the contractor supplies the materials, it shall select the materials in accordance with the contract and make such materials available for inspection by the ordering party.[1502] Where the ordering party supplies the materials, it shall supply the materials in accordance with the contract. The contractor shall

1498. Article 772 CC.
1499. Article 773 CC.
1500. Article 779 CC.
1501. Article 785 CC.
1502. Article 774 CC.

timely inspect the materials supplied by the ordering party and timely notify the ordering party of any non-conformity with the contract for the ordering party to replace, supplement, or take other remedial measures. However, the contractor shall not unilaterally replace any material supplied by the ordering party or any components not in need of repair.[1503]

1298. The ordering party may change their request for the work. It may be liable for the damage caused by the change. Where the contractor discovers that the drawings or technical specifications provided by the ordering party are unreasonable, it shall notify the ordering party in a timely manner. The ordering party shall be liable for damages where it causes loss to the contractor due to its neglect in replying or other reasons.[1504] Where the ordering party, in the course of the work, changes its requirements for the work, thereby causing loss to the contractor, it shall be liable for damages.[1505] Furthermore, the contractor has an assistance obligation. Where the performance of the work requires assistance from the ordering party, the ordering party is obliged to provide such assistance. Where the work cannot be completed due to the ordering party's failure to assist, the contractor may demand that the ordering party perform its obligations within a reasonable period and may extend the time for performance. Where the ordering party fails to perform within the extended period, the contractor may terminate the contract.[1506]

1299. The Civil Code does not provide rules of compensation when the contractor terminates the contract if the ordering party fails to provide the required assistance within the extended period. It is recommended to apply the general rule of contract law for the compensation in this circumstance.[1507] It is provided in the Civil Code that where a party fails to perform its obligations under the contract or its performance fails to satisfy the agreement, thereby causing losses to the other party, the amount of compensation for losses shall be equal to the losses caused by the breach of contract, including the benefits receivable after the performance of the contract, provided that it does not exceed the probable losses caused by the breach that are foreseen or ought to be foreseen when the party in breach concludes the contract.[1508] By applying this general rule, it is suggested that when the ordering party refuses to perform necessary assistance obligations and the contractor has to terminate the contract, the contractor's right to claim remuneration for the work that has been completed should not be affected. For the work that has not been completed, the contractor should also have the right to claim remuneration according to the contract, but the benefits obtained by the contractor due to the termination of

1503. Article 775 CC.
1504. Article 776 CC.
1505. Article 777 CC.
1506. Article 778 CC.
1507. B Zhang, On the Right of the Contractor to Claim Damages when the Order Party Fails to Perform the Duty of Assistance, 2 Xiamen University Law Review (Xia Men Da Xue Fa Lv Ping Lun) 118, 134 (2022).
1508. Article 584 CC.

the contract shall be deducted.[1509] This suggestion is reasonable and fills the gap of law on compensation when the contractor legally terminates the contract if the ordering party breaches the obligation of assistance.

1300. Upon completion of the work, the contractor shall deliver the work to the ordering party and provide it with the necessary technical information and quality certificates. The ordering party shall inspect the work for acceptance.[1510] Where the work delivered by the contractor does not conform to the requirements as to quality, the ordering party may demand that the contractor bear liability for breach of contract in such forms as repair, redoing, a reduction of remuneration, damages, et cetera.[1511] On the other hand, the ordering party shall pay the remuneration by the agreed time. Where there is no agreement on the time for payment of the remuneration or the agreement is equivocal, and the time cannot be ascertained under Article 510 of the Civil Code, the ordering party shall pay upon delivery of the work by the contractor; where the work is delivered in part, the ordering party shall pay the corresponding remuneration.[1512]

1301. Where the ordering party fails to pay the contractor its remuneration or expenses in relation to the materials, et cetera, unless otherwise agreed by the parties, the contractor is entitled to a lien over, or to refuse to deliver, the work.[1513] The contractor shall keep in good custody the materials provided by the ordering party and the completed work and shall be liable for damages for damage or loss caused to them by a failure to do so.[1514] Furthermore, joint contractors shall be liable to the ordering party jointly and severally, unless otherwise agreed by the parties.[1515] Meanwhile, the ordering party may terminate the contract at any time before completion of the work and shall be liable for damages for any loss caused to the contractor.[1516]

1509. B Zhang, On the Right of the Contractor to Claim Damages when the Order Party Fails to Perform the Duty of Assistance, 133.
1510. Article 780 CC.
1511. Article 781 CC.
1512. Article 782 CC.
1513. Article 783 CC.
1514. Article 784 CC.
1515. Article 786 CC.
1516. Article 787 CC.

Chapter 10. Construction Contracts

§1. The Construction Contracts

1302. The Civil Code duplicates all provisions of construction contracts in the Contract Law and adds two new rules for the legal consequences where a construction contract is void but the construction is nevertheless inspected and accepted and where the contractor assigns or illegally subcontracts the construction. For the purposes of accurately trying cases regarding disputes over construction contracts for construction projects, the SPC issued the Interpretation on Issues concerning the Application of Law in the Trial of Cases Regarding Disputes over Construction Contracts for Construction Projects (I) (2020) (the SPC Interpretation on Construction Contracts (2020)).[1517]

1303. A construction contract in the Civil Code is a contract whereby the contractor undertakes construction, and the employer pays the price.[1518] Construction work is a kind of work under contract for work. Therefore, the relevant provisions on contracts for work shall be applied in respect of matters not provided for by the chapter of construction contracts.[1519] A construction contract shall be made in writing.[1520] Contracts for major state construction work shall be concluded in compliance with procedures stipulated by the state and documents approved by the state, including investment plans, feasibility reports, et cetera.[1521]

1304. Construction contracts include contracts for project survey, design and construction.[1522] The content of a contractor for survey or design generally includes terms as to the time for submitting documents, including basic information and summary budgets, quality requirements, fees, other conditions on cooperation, etc.[1523] The content of a construction contract generally includes terms as to the scope of the construction, term of the construction, commencement and completion times for intermittent handover constructions, quality and price of the construction, time of delivery for technical information, responsibilities for supplying materials and equipment, funding and account settlement, inspection of completed works, scope and period of quality warranties, mutual assistances, etc.[1524] Where the construction is subject to supervision, the employer shall enter into a mandate contract for supervision with the supervisor in writing. The rights, obligations and liabilities of the employer and the supervisor shall be governed by the chapter on mandate contracts and other laws and administrative regulations.[1525]

1517. The SPC Interpretation on Issues concerning the Application of Law in the Trial of Cases Regarding Disputes over Construction Contracts for Construction Projects (I) (2020) .
1518. Paragraph 1 of Art. 788 CC.
1519. Article 808 CC.
1520. Article 789 CC.
1521. Article 792 CC.
1522. Paragraph 2 of Art. 788 CC.
1523. Article 794 CC.
1524. Article 795 CC.
1525. Article 796 CC.

1305. In judicial practice, there are two relatively controversial issues regarding the scope of construction contracts. One is whether the supply and construction contract between the construction project equipment supplier and the construction employer or contractor is a construction contract. It is a question because the equipment supplier is responsible not only for the purchased equipment but also for the installation and maintenance of the equipment for the construction project. It is pointed out that whether such a contract belongs to the scope of the construction contract depends on whether the equipment is an integral part of the construction project and whether it is relatively independent from the project construction. If the installation of equipment itself is an integral part of the project construction, such as air conditioning, elevator, etc., which belongs to the scope of the construction project, the supply and construction contract should be a construction contract. If the equipment is not directly related to the project construction itself and is not part of the construction project and the supplier installs the equipment to fulfil the obligation stipulated in the supply and construction contract, rather than the obligations stipulated in the construction contract, such a contract does not belong to the construction contract defined in the Civil Code.[1526]

1306. The second question is whether the decoration project contract is considered a construction contract under the Civil Code. The SPC takes the view that the payment for decoration and decoration projects is within the scope of the exercise of the right to receive priority payment for construction project prices.[1527] It can be seen that the decoration and renovation projects are within the scope of construction projects. Therefore, the decoration project contract is a kind of construction contract. However, it is pointed out that, after the construction project is completed and put into use, the construction activities carried out by the users to decorate the building should not be included in the construction project because they do not involve the use function of the building. Such decoration contracts should be considered as contracts for work.[1528]

1307. In the case of any dispute between the parties over the commencement date of a construction project, the Chinese court shall determine the date respectively under the following circumstances: (1) the commencement date shall be that specified in the commencement notice sent by the employer or the supervisor; after the commencement notice is issued and the commencement conditions are not met, the commencement date shall be the time when the commencement conditions are met; and where the commencement time is delayed due to reasons attributable to the contractor, the time specified in the commencement notice shall be the commencement date; (2) where a contractor has actually entered the site for construction with consent of the employer, the actual date of entry shall be the commencement date; and (3) where an employer or a supervisor fails to issue a

---

1526. Y Wang, Research on Ten Major Issues in Construction Project Contracts from the Perspective of Civil Code, 1 Shandong Justice (Shan Dong Shen Pan) 61, 63-64 (2023).
1527. Reply from the SPC regarding whether the payment for renovation and decoration projects enjoys the priority right to compensation as stipulated in Article 286 of the Contract Law.
1528. Y Wang, Research on Ten Major Issues in Construction Project Contracts from the Perspective of Civil Code, 65.

commencement notice and there is no relevant evidence proving the actual commencement date, the commencement date shall be determined according to the time specified in the commencement report, contract, construction permit, completion acceptance report or completion acceptance registration form, in consideration of the fact whether the commencement conditions are met.[1529]

1308. In the case of any dispute between the parties over the date of substantial completion of a construction project, the Chinese court shall determine the date respectively under the following circumstances: (1) where a construction project has passed the completion acceptance, the date of completion acceptance shall be the completion date; (2) where a contractor has filed a completion acceptance report, and the employer delays the acceptance, the date on which the contractor files the acceptance report shall be the completion date; and (3) where an employer uses a construction project having not passed the completion acceptance without permission, the date of transfer or occupation of the construction project shall be the completion date.[1530]

1309. Where the parties have agreed on the pricing standard or method of construction project, the project price shall be settled as agreed. Where the quantity or quality standard of the construction project changes due to design changes, and the parties cannot agree on the price of this part of the project, the project price may be settled with reference to the pricing method or pricing standard issued by the local competent construction administrative department when the construction contract is signed.[1531]

§2. Construction Contract and Tendering

1310. A construction contract may require tendering. The tendering processes for construction shall be conducted in an open, fair and impartial manner in accordance with the law.[1532] Article 3 of the Tendering and Bidding Law provides that large-scale infrastructure, public utilities and other projects related to social public interests and public safety, projects using state-owned capital investment, state financing, and projects using loan assistance funds from international organisations or foreign governments, tendering must be conducted. For projects that are not subject to bidding as stipulated in Article 3 of the Tendering and Bidding Law, the construction contract signed by the parties before bidding shall generally be deemed valid.[1533] For commercial residential projects, there is no doubt that commercial housing projects invested with fiscal funds or state-owned assets fall within the scope of construction projects that require bidding as stipulated in Article 3 of the

---

1529. Article 8 of the SPC Interpretation on Construction Contracts (2020).
1530. Article 9 CC.
1531. Article 19 CC.
1532. Article 790 CC.
1533. *Haitian Construction Group Co., Ltd. v. Yunnan Fenggu Real Estate Co., Ltd.*, The SPC (2018) Zui Gao Fa Min Zhong No. 475; 海天建设集团有限公司、云南金丰谷置业有限公司建设工程施工合同纠纷案，最高人民法院（2018）最高法民终475.

Tendering and Bidding Law. However, for commercial housing projects invested with private investment rather than non-state-owned funds, it is not appropriate to determine that the construction project contract violates the provisions of the Tendering and Bidding Law and is thus void.[1534]

1311. An employer and a bid winner may conclude another construction contract after the awarded contract. In the event of any discrepancy between the construction contract for the construction project otherwise signed by and between an employer and a bid winner and the awarded contract in respect of the scope of project, construction period, project quality, project cost or any other substantive content, the rights and obligations of the parties shall be determined according to the awarded contract. Therefore, where an employer and a bid winner otherwise enter into a contract on the purchase of a constructed house at a price obviously higher than the market price, free construction of house-supporting facilities, surrender of profits, and donation of property to the construction entity, among others, for reducing the project cost in a disguised manner, the construction contract is invalid on the grounds of the contract's deviation from the substantive content of the awarded contract.[1535]

1312. In other words, the awarded contract shall prevail because the awarded contract is the basis of the construction project. Accordingly, where such discrepancy exists in respect of the scope of project, construction period, project quality and project cost, the bidding documents, bids, and bid winning notice shall prevail as the basis for settling project cost.[1536] This rule applies to a construction project that does not fall under the circumstance where bids must be invited unless the parties otherwise enter into a construction contract for the construction project due to unforeseeable changes arising from objective conditions at the time of bidding.[1537] This exception does not apply to the project where bids must be invited.

§3. SUBCONTRACTING

1313. The employer may enter into a construction contract with a main contractor or enter into contracts for survey, design and construction respectively with the surveyors, designers and constructor. However, if construction work ought to be completed by one contractor, the employer shall not divide construction work into parts and contract them out to several contractors.[1538] Meanwhile, the main contractor or contractors for survey, design or construction may, with the consent of the employer, engage a third party to complete a part of its work. The third party shall

1534. *Beihai Hengli Real Estate Development Co., Ltd. v. Guangxi Construction First Construction Engineering Group Co., Ltd.*, The SPC (2020) Zui Gao Fa Min Shen No. 2821; 北海恒立房地产开发有限公司、广西建工集团第一建筑工程有限责任公司建设工程施工合同纠纷案，最高人民法院（2020）最高法民申2821号.
1535. Article 2 of the SPC Interpretation on Construction Contracts (2020).
1536. Article 22 CC.
1537. Article 23 CC.
1538. Paragraph 1 of Art. 791 CC.

be liable to the employer jointly and severally with the main contractor or contractors for survey, design or construction in respect of the work completed by it.[1539]

1314. In the subcontracting situation, the construction contract could be referenced for the subcontract. In *Chaoyang Meili Construction Engineering Co., Ltd. v. Sanya Shuiyi Industrial Co., Ltd.*,[1540] the construction project contract stipulates that the final settlement will be based on the actual amount of work. The project involved has been actually completed by the actual constructor and handed over to the general contractor through the subcontractor. The general contractor paid the project price to the subcontractor, but the subcontractor refused to pay the actual constructor. It argued that there was no agreement on the project quantity with the actual constructor and there was no acceptance settlement. The SPC held that the project quantity under the subcontract could be determined according to the general contractor for the same project.

1315. However, there are some restrictions on the assignment of construction work based on subcontracts. First, the contractor shall not assign all of its construction work to a third party or divide all of its construction work into parts and assign them to third parties in the name of subcontracting.[1541] Next, the contractor is prohibited from subcontracting the construction work to units without the corresponding qualifications. The construction contracts shall be void if the construction work is subcontracted to any units without the corresponding qualifications.[1542] Furthermore, the subcontractor is prohibited from further subcontracting its construction work. Last, the work relating to the main structure of the construction must be completed by the contractor itself.[1543]

1316. Although subcontracting is restricted by law, it is still possible that construction work is done by a party without valid subcontracting. There are two types of invalid subcontracting. First, an unqualified entity or individual may enter into a construction contract for a construction project in the name of a qualified construction entity by borrowing qualification. In this circumstance, the employer may claim against the lender and borrower to bear the joint and several compensation liability for unacceptable construction project quality and other losses arising from lending of qualification.[1544]

1317. Second, because the main contractor or subcontractors may engage a third party to complete a part of its work, the third party may perform construction work under a construction contract with a subcontractor. However, the subcontracting

1539. Paragraph 2 of Art. 791 CC.
1540. *Chaoyang Meili Construction Engineering Co., Ltd. v. Sanya Shuiyi Industrial Co., Ltd.*, The SPC (2021) Zui Gao Fa Min Shen No. 6282; 朝阳美利建筑工程有限公司、三亚水亿实业有限公司等建设工程施工合同纠纷案，最高人民法院（2021）最高法民申6282号.
1541. Paragraph 1 of Art. 791 CC.
1542. X Feng, On the Principles for Judging the Legal Validity of Construction Contracts, in Reference and Guide to Civil Trial 111 (The SPC First Civil Trial Division ed., People's Court Press 2019).
1543. Paragraph 3 of Art. 791 CC.
1544. Article 7 of the SPC Interpretation on Construction Contracts (2020).

may not be valid for some reasons, e.g., the subcontracting was not permitted by the employer. In this circumstance, disputes may occur between those parties. In the SPC Interpretation on Construction Contracts 2020, this kind of third party is called the actual constructor. Because the actual constructor has a contract with the subcontractor, it can file a lawsuit against the subcontractor as the defendant if it suffers loss from the performance of construction work. Where an actual constructor makes claims against an employer as the defendant, the Chinese court shall add the subcontractor as a third party to the case. In this circumstance, the employer should assume liability to the actual constructor within the scope of the construction project cost owed by the employer after finding out the amount of the construction project cost owed by the employer to the subcontractor.[1545]

1318. Furthermore, if a subcontractor neglects to exercise its due creditor's right or the collateral rights related to such creditor's right against an employer, thereby affecting the realisation of an actual constructor's right that is due, the actual constructor may exercise its subrogation right according to Article 535 of the Civil Code.[1546] This subrogation right is to protect the interests of actual constructors who are vulnerable groups in the construction market in China, e.g., small private business, self-employed individuals or migrant workers.[1547] However, the actual constructor's subrogation right is not a replacement of the rights of suit of the subcontractor as the contractor in the construction contract. In *Xinxian Xincheng Construction Co., Ltd. v. Shandong Tianle Real Estate Co., Ltd.*,[1548] the contractor subcontracted the project to the actual constructor who actually completed the construction work. When the contractor claimed against the employer for the unpaid price of the construction, the local courts held that the contractor had no rights of suit against the employer because it did not actually complete the construction and had no real interest in the construction contract. The SPC overruled the decision and held the actual constructor's does not deny the contractor's rights of suit against the employer.

§4. Void Construction Contracts

1319. A construction contract for a construction project falling under any of the following circumstances shall be deemed invalid in accordance with the provisions

1545. Article 43 CC.
1546. Article 44 CC. Art. 535 CC provides that, where the obligor neglects to exercise its right or the collateral rights related to such creditor's right, thereby affecting the realisation of the obligee's creditor's right which is due, the obligee may apply for subrogation over the obligor in its own name, except where the rights exclusively belong to the obligor.
1547. Xie Y and Guo P, 'On the Civil Law Protection of Actual Construction Workers' (2021) 6 Journal of Law Application (Fa Lv Shi Yong) 69.
1548. *Xinxian Xincheng Construction Co., Ltd. v. Shandong Tianle Real Estate Co., Ltd.*, The SPC (2022) Zui Gao Fa Min Zai No. 96; 莘县莘城建设有限公司、山东天乐置业有限公司建设工程施工合同纠纷案，最高人民法院（2022）最高法民再96号.

of paragraph 1 of Article 153 of the Civil Code:[1549] (1) the contractor has not obtained the qualification for construction enterprise or has exceeded the qualification level; (2) the actual constructor without qualification borrows the name of a qualified construction enterprise; or (3) the bidding invitation must be conducted for a construction project, but it is not conducted, or the bid winning is invalid. Furthermore, a construction contract for a construction project signed by the contractor with another due to subcontracting or illegal subcontracting of the construction project shall be deemed void.[1550]

1320. The Chinese court will support either party's request for confirming the invalidity of a construction contract for a construction project on the ground of the failure of the employer to obtain the construction project planning permit and undergo other planning approval formalities unless the employer obtains the construction project planning permit and undergoes other planning approval formalities before a prosecution is initiated. However, the Chinese court will not support the request of any employer that can undergo the approval formalities but fails to undergo the formalities for confirming the invalidity of a construction contract for a construction project on the grounds of failure to undergo the approval formalities. Furthermore, where a contractor signs a construction contract for a construction project beyond the business scope corresponding to the qualification level and obtains the corresponding qualification level before the completion of the construction project, the Chinese court will not support either party's request for determining the contract to be void.[1551] Where a contractor signs a construction contract for a construction project beyond the business scope corresponding to the qualification level and obtains the corresponding qualification level before the completion of the construction project, the Chinese court will not support either party's request for determining the contract to be void.[1552]

1321. Where a construction contract for a construction project is invalidated, a party requesting the other party to compensate for the loss shall assume the burden of proof for the other party's default, amount of loss and causal relationship between the default and the loss. Where the amount of loss cannot be determined and a party requests determination of the amount of loss according to the quality standard, construction period, time for payment of the project cost, and other content, mutatis mutandis to the agreement of the contract, the Chinese court may render judgement, in consideration of the degree of the two parties' fault, the causal relationship between the fault and loss, and other factors.[1553]

1549. Paragraph 1 of Art. 153 CC provides that 'A civil juridical act violating any mandatory provision of law or administrative regulation is void, unless the mandatory provision in question does not lead to the voidness of the civil juridical act.'
1550. Article 1 of the SPC Interpretation on Construction Contracts 2020.
1551. *Ibid.*; Art. 3 CC.
1552. *Ibid.*; Art. 4 CC.
1553. *Ibid.*; Art. 6 CC.

1322. Where a construction contract is void but the construction is nevertheless inspected and accepted, the contractor may be compensated by reference to the contract provisions for the price of the construction. If a project construction contract is invalid and the project construction fails to pass acceptance inspection, the case shall be handled based on the following circumstances: (1) where the construction is inspected and accepted as up to standard after repairs are carried out, the employer may seek recovery of the expenses incurred for repairs against the contractor; (2) where the construction is substandard after inspection despite repairs being carried out, the contractor is not entitled to compensation by reference to the contract provisions for the price of the construction. Furthermore, where the employer is at fault in respect of the loss arising from the failure of the construction to meet the standard, it shall be liable correspondingly.[1554] Parties are free to reach a settlement agreement. Where such agreement is reached when the contract is concluded, the settlement agreement should be void if the contract is void.[1555] However, if such agreement is an independent agreement reached after the contract is determined void, the agreement shall be valid and shall bind the parties even though the contract is void.[1556] For construction projects that have not passed the completion acceptance inspection, if the parties cannot reach an agreement on the settlement of the project price, it is necessary to entrust judicial appraisal to settle the project price.[1557]

§5. Contractors' Rights and Obligations

1323. For construction work, all contractors, including the surveyor, designer and constructor, shall be responsible for the construction work. Where, for reasons attributable to the contractor, the construction causes personal injury or damage to property within a period of reasonable use, the contractor shall be liable for damages.[1558] Where the quality of the survey or design fails to conform to the requirements or the delay in submitting survey or design documents causes the term of construction to be extended, thereby causing loss to the employer, the surveyor or designer shall improve on the survey or design, reduce or waive the survey or design fees, and be liable for damages.[1559]

1324. Where the quality of the construction fails to conform to the contract for reasons attributable to the constructor, the employer is entitled to demand that the

---

1554. Article 793 CC.

1555. *Zhu Huayun v. hangchun Construction Engineering Xinjirun Construction Co., Ltd.*, The SPC (2020) Zui Gao Fa Min Shen No. 331; 朱华云、长春建工新吉润建设有限公司建设工程施工合同纠纷案，最高人民法院（2020）最高法民申331 号.

1556. *Changning Jiayuan Electric Power Development Co., Ltd. v. Baoshan Xinjie Construction Engineering Co., Ltd.*, The SPC (2020) Zui Gao Fa Min Shen No. 3395; 昌宁县珈源电力开发有限公司、保山市辛街建筑工程有限责任公司合同纠纷案，最高人民法院（2020）最高法民申3395 号.

1557. Wang Y, 'Research on Ten Major Issues in Construction Project Contracts from the Perspective of Civil Code', 78.

1558. Article 802 CC.

1559. *Ibid.*; Art. 800.

constructor repair, reconstruct or alter it free of charge within a reasonable period. Where late delivery is caused by such repair, reconstruction or alteration, the constructor shall bear liability for breach of contract.[1560] If the quality of a construction project does not meet the contractual requirements due to the contractor's reasons and the contractor refuses to repair, rework or rebuild the project, the employer has the right to request a reduction in the project price.[1561] The employer may claim against the constructor if the quality of construction fails to conform to the contract even if the inspection authority issues a certificate of inspection upon completion as evidence of quality. If the constructor fails or refuses to repair, reconstruct or alter the quality problem, the employer is entitled to contract with a third party to repair, reconstruct or alter it and claim against the constructor for the cost.[1562] If both the contractor and the constructor have defaults in the construction work, they may have joint and several liabilities for damage caused to the employer.[1563]

1325. Upon completion of the construction, the employer shall timely inspect for acceptance in accordance with the drawings, specifications, and the regulations on the inspection and quality standards of construction work. Where the construction is certified as in conformity, the employer shall pay the price in accordance with the contract and accept the construction. A construction may be delivered for use only after it has been inspected and accepted as up to standard and shall not be delivered for use where inspection has not been carried out or it is found on inspection to be substandard.[1564] The inspection upon completion is not only the employer's right but also its obligation. Without authority from the employer, the contractor has no right of inspection on behalf of the employer. In *Weihai Jingyuan Construction Co., Ltd. v. Weihai Welfare Enterprise Service Co., Ltd. and Weihai Shengfa Trade Co., Ltd.*,[1565] the contractor, without the consent of the employer, applied to a local quality inspection authority for the inspection upon completion and declaration of quality assessment grade. The SPC held that the contractor's application did not comply with the construction contract and the law.[1566] Therefore, the inspection upon completion report and the quality assessment grade had no legal effect.

1560. *Ibid.*; Art. 801.
1561. Article 12 of the SPC Interpretation on Construction Contracts 2020.
1562. *Jiangsu Nantong No. 2 Construction Engineering (Group) Co., Ltd. v. Wujiang Hengsen Real Estate Co., Ltd.*, Gazette Case of the SPC, Issue 8, 2014; 江苏南通二建集团有限公司与吴江恒森房地产开发有限公司建设工程施工合同纠纷案，《最高人民法院公报》案例，2014年08期.
1563. *Haiqing Heavy Industry Co., Ltd. v. Jiangsu Zhongxing Construction Co., Ltd. and China Construction Bank Taixing Branch*, The SPC (2012) Min Ti Zi No. 20; 海擎重工机械有限公司与江苏中兴建设有限公司、中国建设银行股份有限公司泰兴支行建设工程施工合同纠纷案，最高人民法院（2012）民提字第20号. This case is included in Gazette Case of the SPC, Issue 6, 2015; 《最高人民法院公报》案例，2015年06期.
1564. Article 799 CC.
1565. *Weihai Jingyuan Construction Co., Ltd. v. Weihai Welfare Enterprise Service Co., Ltd. and Weihai Shengfa Trade Co., Ltd.*, The SPC (2010) Min Ti Zi No. 210 (Gazette Case of the SPC, Issue 8, 2013); 威海市鲸园建筑有限公司与威海市福利企业服务公司、威海市盛发贸易有限公司拖欠建筑工程款纠纷案，最高人民法院（2010）民提字第210号（《最高人民法院公报》案例，2013年08期）.
1566. The law is article 279 of the Chinese Contract Law which is identical to article 799 CC.

1326. Parties may agree on the project quality guaranty deposit. Under one of the following circumstances, a contractor has the right to request a refund of the quality guaranty deposit from the employer: (1) the time limit for refund of the quality guaranty deposit agreed by the parties expires; (2) where the time limit for refund of the quality guaranty deposit is not agreed by the parties, two years have expired since the date when the construction project passes the completion acceptance and (3) where completion acceptance is not conducted for a construction project as scheduled due to reasons attributable to the employer, the time limit for refunding the agreed upon by the parties expires ninety days after the contractor's filing of the project completion acceptance report; and two years have expired ninety days after the contractor's filing of the project completion acceptance report where the time limit for refunding quality guaranty deposit is not agreed upon by the parties. However, the contractor's performance of the warranty obligations according to the contract or the law shall not be affected by the refund of the quality guaranty deposit from the employer.[1567]

§6. The Employer's Rights and Obligations

1327. Because a construction contract is a contract for work, the employer has the right to inspect the construction work. According to the Civil Code, the employer may, without interfering with the normal course of work of the contractor, inspect the progress of the construction and its quality at any time.[1568] For respect of concealed constructions, the contractor shall notify the employer that an inspection be conducted before concealment. Where the employer fails to inspect in time, the contractor may extend the period of construction and is entitled to claim damages for losses arising from the suspension of or delay in work, etc.[1569]

1328. The employer has obligations under both the construction contract and the Civil Code. The employer shall provide raw materials, equipment, site, funds or technical information in accordance with the agreed time or requirements. If the employer fails to do so, the contractor may extend the term of construction and is entitled to demand compensation for losses arising from the suspension of or delay in the work and so forth.[1570] The parties' agreement of the extension of the construction period shall be confirmed by the employer or supervisor by issuing certificates and other methods. Even though the contractor has not obtained the confirmation for postponement of the construction period, he is allowed to extend the construction period if he is able to prove that he has applied to the employer or supervisor for postponement of the construction period within the time limit agreed in the contract and the grounds for postponement comply with the contract.[1571]

1567. Article 17 of the SPC Interpretation on Construction Contracts (2020).
1568. Article 797 CC.
1569. Article 798 CC.
1570. Article 803 CC.
1571. Paragraph 1 of Art. 10 of the SPC Interpretation on Construction Contracts (2020).

Furthermore, where, before the completion of a construction project, the parties have a dispute over the project quality, and the project has been appraised and satisfied the quality requirement, the appraisal period shall be the extended construction period.[1572]

1329. The employer shall be liable for loss and expenses to the contractor, surveyor or designer caused by the fault of the employer. First, where, for reasons attributable to the employer, the construction was suspended or delayed in the course of construction, the employer shall take measures to remedy or reduce the damage and compensate the contractor for losses and actual expenses, including those arising from the suspension of or delay in the work, reshipment, relocation of machinery, overstocking of materials and components, et cetera.[1573] Second, where, due to the employer's change of plan, provision of inaccurate information, or failure to provide the necessary conditions for conducting a survey or design on time, the survey or design has to be reconducted, suspended or altered, the employer shall pay extra expenses for the additional actual workload assumed by the surveyor or designer.[1574]

1330. On the other hand, where the contractor assigns or illegally subcontracts the construction, the employer may terminate the contract. Where the main construction materials, components or equipment supplied by the employer do not conform to mandatory standards or the employer fails to perform its obligation to assist, thereby making it impossible for the contractor to construct, and the employer still fails to perform such obligations within a reasonable period of time upon demand, the contractor may terminate the contract. After the contract is terminated, the employer shall pay the corresponding price as agreed for the completed construction whose quality conforms to the standards. Where the quality of the completed construction does not conform to the standards, the matter shall be dealt with by reference to Article 793 of the Civil Code.[1575]

1331. Where the quality of a construction project is acceptable, the court shall support the contractor's request for priority of compensation for the price of the discount or auction of the part of the project undertaken by it.[1576] The contractor shall exercise the priority right of compensation for the construction project price within

1572. Article 11 CC.
1573. Article 804 CC.
1574. Article 805 CC.
1575. Article 806 CC.
1576. Article 38 of the SPC Interpretation on Construction Contracts 2020. The price of the discount includes the discount of part of the construction project. *See Haitian Construction Group Co., Ltd. v. Shanxi Yufeng Real Estate Development Co., Ltd.*, The SPC (2021) Zui Gao Fa Min Shen No. 6178; 海天建设集团有限公司、山西宇丰房地产开发有限公司建设工程施工合同纠纷案，最高人民法院（2021）最高法民申6178号.

a reasonable time. The period for exercising the priority right shall not exceed eighteen months commencing from the date when the employer shall pay the construction project price.[1577] This maximum period is pre-emption for exercising the priority right against the construction project. Once it expires, the substantive rights will be extinguished.[1578]

1332. In judicial practice, when a court executes against the employer's construction project upon the application of other creditors, the contractor may apply to the court for the execution of his priority right against the construction project. In this circumstance, it is assumed that the contractor has exercised his priority right within the pre-emption when he raises such application.[1579] The employer and contractor may agree on waiver or restriction of the priority right of compensation for the construction project price. However, this agreement shall be void if it prejudices the interests of construction workers.[1580] This is to protect interests of construction workers with the priority right against the construction project payment of price.

1333. An employer falling under any of the following circumstances and having caused defects in the construction project quality shall be liable for fault: (1) the provided design is defective; (2) the building materials, building components, and equipment provided or designated for purchase do not meet the mandatory standards; or (3) a subcontractor is directly appointed to subcontract a professional project. However, the contractor with fault shall also assume corresponding liability for the fault.[1581] Furthermore, an employer shall use the construction project after completion acceptance. If an employer uses a construction project before completion acceptance without permission, he is not allowed to claim on the grounds that the quality of the used part does not conform to the agreement. However, a contractor shall, within the reasonable service life of a construction project, assume responsibility for the quality of the ground foundation project and main structure.[1582]

1334. The employer has the obligation to pay the contract price. Where the employer fails to pay the price in accordance with the contract, the contractor may demand that the employer pay it within a reasonable period of time. Where the employer fails to pay within that time, except where the nature of the construction makes it unsuitable for valuation or auction, the contractor may negotiate with the employer to recoup the value of the construction or apply to a court for sale of the

---

1577. Article 41 of the SPC Interpretation on Construction Contracts (2020).
1578. *Chongqing Construction Engineering Group Co., Ltd. v. Chongqing Tongyao Transportation Equipment Co., Ltd.*, The SPC (2022) Zui Gao Fa Min Zai No. 114; 重庆建工工业有限公司、重庆通耀交通装备有限公司建设工程施工合同纠纷案， 最高人民法院 （2022）最高法民再114号.
1579. *Zhongtian Construction Group Co., Ltd. v. Henan Henghe Real Estate Co., Ltd.*, The SPC (2019) Zui Gao Fa Min Zhong No. 255 (SPC Guiding Case No. 171); 中天建设集团有限公司诉河南恒和置业有限公司建设工程施工合同纠纷案， 最高人民法院（2019）最高法民终255号（最高人民法院，第171号指导性案例）.
1580. Article 42 of the SPC Interpretation on Construction Contracts (2020).
1581. Article 13 CC.
1582. Article 14 CC.

construction by lawful auction. The price for the construction shall be paid in priority from the value or the proceeds of auction.[1583] This priority in payment not only applies to the contractor by law but also applies to the actual constructor or actual contractor in Chinese judicial practice.[1584] Furthermore, the contractor's right of priority to repay the construction project price is superior to mortgage rights and other debt claims.[1585]

1583. Article 807 CC.

1584. *Ningxia Yulong Engineering Co., Ltd. v. Anhui Sanjian Construction Engineering Co., Ltd. and Ningxia Lantian Real Estate Development Co., Ltd.*, The SPC (2019) Zui Gao Fa Min Shen No. 6085; 宁夏钰隆工程有限公司、安徽三建工程有限公司、宁夏蓝天房地产开发有限责任公司建设工程施工合同纠纷案最高人民法院（2019）最高法民申6085号.

1585. Article 36 of the SPC Interpretation on Construction Contracts (2020).

Chapter 11. Transport Contracts

§1. General Provisions

1335. A carriage contract in the Civil Code is a contract whereby the carrier carries passengers or goods from the place of departure to the agreed destination, and the passenger, consignor or consignee pays the fare or carriage fees.[1586] It includes a contract of carriage of passengers, carriage of goods and multimodal carriage. The carrier has a carriage obligation to the passenger, consignor or consignee. The passenger, consignor or consignee has a payment obligation to the carrier. The carrier shall, in accordance with the agreed or usual routes, safely carry the passengers or goods to the agreed destination within the agreed or a reasonable period of time.[1587] Meanwhile, the passenger, consignor or consignee shall pay the fare or carriage fees. Where the carrier fails to carry in accordance with the agreed or usual routes and thereby increases the fare or carriage fees, the passenger, consignor or consignee may refuse to pay the increased fare or carriage fees.[1588]

1336. The carrier includes public carriers and private carriers. A public carrier has social responsibility for public carriage. Therefore, a carrier who engages in public transport shall not refuse a usual and reasonable request for carriage made by the passenger or consignor.[1589] It was controversial whether liner shipping is a public carrier in Chinese judicial practice. Liner shipping carriage is the process of transporting goods from one destination to another by large ocean ships that move through regular routes on fixed schedules. In *Maersk (China) Shipping Co., Ltd. and Maersk (China) Shipping Co., Ltd. Xiamen Branche v. PRIME International (XIAMEN) Co., Ltd. and China Xiamen Ocean Shipping Agency Co., Ltd.*,[1590] Maersk China operated shipping carriage through regular routes from Xiamen but refused to continue business with Prime Xiamen for liner shipping carriage from Xiamen. Prime Xiamen claimed to Chinese courts requesting Maersk China to continue usual carriage business with Prime Xiamen. The SPC rejected Prime Xiamen's claim. It was pointed out by the SPC that the public carriage has features of public welfare and monopoly.[1591] However, international liner shipping carriage is commercial business for international trade. It is not for public service and has no features of

1586. Article 809 CC.
1587. Articles 811 and 812 CC.
1588. Article 813 CC.
1589. Article 810 CC.
1590. *Maersk (China) Shipping Co., Ltd. and Maersk (China) Shipping Co., Ltd. Xiamen Branche v. PRIME International (XIAMEN) Co., Ltd. and China Xiamen Ocean Shipping Agency Co., Ltd.*, The SPC (2010) Min Ti Zi No. 213 (Gazette Case of the SPC, Issue 10, 2011); 马士基（中国）航运有限公司及其厦门分公司与厦门瀛海实业发展有限公司、中国厦门外轮代理有限公司国际海上货运代理经营权损害赔偿纠纷案， 最高人民法院民事判决书（2010）民提字第213号（《最高人民法院公报》案例，2011年10期）.
1591. It was Art. 289 of the Contract Law that applied to the case. This article is identical to article 810 of the Civil Code.

public welfare or monopoly. Therefore, a liner shipping carrier is not a public carrier. It was held that Prime Xiamen had no right to enforce Maersk China to continue business without the consent of Maersk China.

§2. Carriage of Passengers Contracts

1337. For carriage of passengers, not only the Civil Code but also international conventions may apply the carriage contract for passengers.[1592] The international conventions may apply according to the carriage contract or the conflict of law rules.[1593] In the Civil Code, the ticket in passenger carriage plays an important role. First, a carriage contract of passengers is concluded upon delivery of the ticket by the carrier to the passenger, unless otherwise agreed by the parties or directed by the trade practice.[1594] Second, the passenger shall travel in accordance with the time, schedule and seat number specified in the ticket. Where the passenger travels without a ticket or exceeds the range or class of the ticket, or with invalid tickets, he or she shall pay the balance of the fare, and the carrier may charge an increased fare in accordance with regulations. Where the passenger fails to pay the fare, the carrier may refuse carriage. Where a passenger under a carriage contract bearing his/her genuine name loses his or her ticket, he or she may ask the carrier to record the loss of and re-issue the ticket, and the carrier shall not charge again for the ticket or levy other unreasonable fees.[1595] Where the passenger fails to travel at the time specified on the ticket for reasons attributable to the passenger him/herself, he or she shall obtain a refund or change the ticket by the agreed time. The carrier may refuse to refund and may be relieved from the obligation to carry if the passenger fails to do it within that time.[1596]

1338. Passengers have certain obligations in carriage under the Civil Code. First, passenger luggage shall conform to the agreed quantity limits and requirements as to its type. Where the passenger travels with luggage exceeding the quantity limits or does not conform to the requirements as to its type, such luggage shall be checked in to the carrier.[1597] Second, passengers shall not carry on themselves or in the luggage any inflammable, explosive, toxic, corrosive, radioactive articles or any dangerous or prohibited articles that may endanger the safety of persons or property on board. Where a passenger contravenes this requirement, the carrier may

1592. The conventions include the Warsaw Convention, the Guadalajara Convention, the Montreal Convention and their protocols.
1593. *Abdul Waheed v. China Eastern Airlines Co., Ltd.*, SPC Guiding Case No. 51; 阿卜杜勒・瓦希德诉中国东方航空股份有限公司航空旅客运输合同纠纷案，最高人民法院，第151号指导性案例. In this case, the amended Warsaw Convention and the Guadalajara Convention applied.
1594. Article 814 CC.
1595. Article 815 CC.
1596. Article 816 CC.
1597. Article 817 CC.

discharge, destroy or deliver the prohibited article to the relevant authorities. Where the passenger insists on carrying or conceals the prohibited article, the carrier shall refuse carriage.[1598]

1339. Carriers also have certain obligations under the Civil Code. First, the carrier shall strictly perform its obligations to provide safe transport and shall timely notify the passengers of matters concerning safe transport. Passengers shall assist and cooperate in the reasonable arrangements made by the carrier for the safe carriage.[1599] Second, the carrier shall, in the course of carriage, assist passengers suffering from sudden illness, giving birth to a child or at risk to the best of its ability.[1600] Furthermore, the carrier shall provide agreed carriage service. If the carrier unilaterally reduces the service standards, it shall, at the passengers' request, refund or reduce fares. Where the service standards have been raised, the carrier shall not charge additional fares.[1601]

1340. The carrier shall also refund or reduce fares even if it is the actual carrier that reduced the service standards. In *Zhou v. An Airlines Co., Ltd.*,[1602] the passenger in dispute received a reduced standard service from an endorsed flight of the actual carrier and claimed against the carrier for a refund due to the reduced service. The carrier argued that it had no fault because it was the actual carrier that reduced the service standard. The argument was not accepted by the court. It was pointed out that the nature of flight endorsement is that a third party other than the original contracting party of the air passenger contract will perform the contract on its behalf. It is not an assignment of a contract including the transfer of contractual rights and obligations from the carrier to the actual carrier. After the flight is endorsed, the contracting carrier should still be responsible for all transportation agreed upon in the contract. If the actual carrier failed to perform the contract with the passenger, the contracting carrier should bear liability for breach of contract to the passenger. The losses suffered by passengers due to flight endorsements should be subject to the principles of full compensation and loss compensation. If the actual carrier has paid the passengers a partial loss, the passengers can claim against the contracting carrier for the remaining loss. The compensation from the actual carrier does not exempt the carrier from its liability under the contract.

1341. The carrier shall carry the passengers in accordance with the time, schedule and seat numbers specified in their tickets. The carrier is obliged to notify and remind passengers of any delay in carriage. If the carriage is delayed, or there are other circumstances that make the normal transportation impossible, the carrier shall promptly notify and remind the passengers, take necessary arrangements, and, at passengers' requests, arrange other shifts or flights for the passengers or refund their

1598. Article 818 CC.
1599. Article 819 CC.
1600. Article 822 CC.
1601. Article 821 CC.
1602. *Zhou v. An Airlines Co., Ltd.*, Shanghai Pudong New Area People's Court (2019) Hu 0115 Min Chu No. 26237; 周某诉甲航空公司等航空旅客运输合同纠纷案，上海市浦东新区人民法院（2019）沪0115民初26237号.

tickets. Where losses are caused to the passenger, the carrier shall be liable for damages unless the reasons are not attributable to the carrier.[1603] This exemption to the liability, e.g., bad weather, applies only when the carrier has notified passengers of any delay or abnormal circumstances and taken necessary arrangements.[1604]

1342. In judicial practice, this liability for delay and abnormal circumstances applies to the liability if the passenger misses a carriage due to reasons that are attributable to the carrier. In *Yang Yanhui v. China Southern Airlines and Minhui Company*,[1605] the air ticket stated 'PVG' as the abbreviation of the airport and the passenger went to Shanghai Hongqiao International Airport but found the booked flight actually started from Shanghai Pudong International Airport. The passenger missed the flight and requested for a refund of the air ticket. The request was rejected by the air carrier. The Chinese court pointed out that not all passengers know PVG refers to Shanghai Pudong International Airport. Since Shanghai has two international airports, the air carrier shall state the airport in Chinese name, not just PVG. The air carrier argued that the air ticket was a standard ticket, and they had no fault for using PVG. The arguments were rejected by the Chinese court. It was pointed out that since the air ticket contained Chinese characters, there was no reason that the air carrier could not print the Chinese name of the airport. Therefore, it was the fault of the air carrier to cause the loss to the passenger. The court applied the liability rule for delay and held that the carrier should refund the ticket and indemnify the relevant cost the passenger had paid for the change of carriage.[1606]

1343. Furthermore, the carrier shall be liable for death or injury suffered by passengers in the course of carriage, except where the death or injury is caused by the health conditions of the passenger or where the carrier proves that the death or injury is caused by the deliberate acts of or gross negligence on the part of the passenger. This liability rule applies to passengers travelling without a ticket in accordance with the regulations, with concessionary tickets or without a ticket by permission from the carrier.[1607] Where, in the course of carriage, articles carried on the passenger are damaged, destroyed or lost and the carrier is at fault, it shall be liable for damages. Damage to or loss of luggage checked in by passengers is governed by the provisions on carriage of goods.[1608]

1344. The injured passenger may claim against the air carrier for liability based on contract or in tort. If the injured passenger claims against the air carrier for liability based on both contract and tort, Chinese courts will decide the cause of action

1603. Article 820 CC.
1604. *See* similar requirements in *Abdul Waheed v. China Eastern Airlines Co., Ltd.*, SPC Guiding Case No. 51; 阿卜杜勒•瓦希德诉中国东方航空股份有限公司航空旅客运输合同纠纷案，最高人民法院，第151号指导性案例.
1605. *Yang Yanhui v. China Southern Airlines and Minhui Company*, Gazette Case of the SPC, Issue 5, 2003; 杨艳辉诉南方航空公司、民惠公司客运合同纠纷案，《最高人民法院公报》案例，2003年05期.
1606. It is Art. 299 of the Contract Law that applied to the case. This article is identical to Art. 820 CC.
1607. Article 823 CC.
1608. Article 824 CC.

between contract and tort. In *Lu Hong v. United Airlines*,[1609] the claimant passenger was injured during the carriage and claimed against the air carrier for liability in contract and liability in tort for mental damage. The Chinese court pointed out that the liabilities were different under contract and tort. The choice of cause of action should be made for the benefit of the claimant passenger. The court found that the liability in contract was mainly for damage to property, whereas the liability in tort includes both damage to property and mental damage. Therefore, the court chose tort claim as the cause of action for the benefit of the claimant passenger.

§3. Carriage of Goods Contracts

1345. In carriage contract of goods, the consignor has obligation to provide information on goods to the carrier. The consignor shall pack the goods in the agreed manner. Where there is no agreement on the manner of packaging or the agreement is equivocal, article 619 of the Civil Code shall apply.[1610] Where the consignor contravenes the package requirement, the carrier may refuse carriage.[1611] Where the carriage of goods is subject to approval, inspection, et cetera, the consignor shall submit to the carrier the relevant documents showing the completion of such procedures.[1612] Furthermore, where the consignor consigns any dangerous articles including those that are inflammable, explosive, toxic, corrosive or radioactive, it shall properly pack the dangerous articles in accordance with the State regulations on the carriage of dangerous goods, mark and label the dangerous articles, and provide the carrier with written information about the name, nature and precautionary measures of the relevant dangerous articles. Where the consignor contravenes the requirement, the carrier may refuse carriage or take measures to prevent losses, the expenses of which are to be borne by the consignor.[1613]

1346. When the consignor arranges for the carriage of goods, it shall accurately indicate the necessary information for the carriage of goods, including the name of the consignee or the consignee by order, nature, weight and quantity of the goods, the destination, etc. Where the indications made by the consignor are untrue or omit substantial information, thereby causing loss to the carrier, the consignor shall be liable for damages.[1614] In *Hong Long Industry Co., Ltd. v. Shanghai Railway Sub-Bureau Hejiawan Station*,[1615] the consignor did not accurately declare to the carrier

1609. *Lu Hong v. United Airlines*, Gazette Case of the SPC, Issue 4, 2002; 陆红诉美国联合航空公司国际航空旅客运输损害赔偿纠纷案，《最高人民法院公报》案例，2002年04期.
1610. Under Art. 619 CC, a usual manner of packaging shall be used. Where there is no usual manner of packaging, packaging shall be made in a manner sufficient to protect the subject matter.
1611. Article 827 CC.
1612. Article 826 CC.
1613. Article 828 CC.
1614. Article 825 CC.
1615. *Hong Long Industry Co., Ltd. v. Shanghai Railway Sub-Bureau Hejiawan Station*, Gazette Case of the SPC, Issue 1, 2001; 宏隆实业有限公司与上海铁路分局何家湾站等铁路货物运输合同逾期货损索赔纠纷再审案，《最高人民法院公报》案例，2001年01期.

the true weight of the cargo carried by the railway carrier. The overloaded cargo damaged the carrying units. The consignor was held to be liable for the damage to the carrying units.

1347. Before the carrier delivers the goods to the consignee, the consignor may ask the carrier to suspend the carriage, return the goods, alter the destination or deliver to a different consignee, provided that the consignor compensates the losses thereby suffered by the carrier.[1616] This is the consigner's right to change the contract of carriage of goods before the delivery of the goods. It is, however, not an absolute right to the change contract. The change of contract is subject to the consent of the parties to the contract. If the consignor requests the change to the contract, the change takes effect only when the carrier agrees to such change. There must be evidence to prove the consent.[1617]

1348. In international sales of goods, if the seller is the consignor, the seller can exercise this right before the delivery of cargo. However, if the seller is not the consignor, he cannot exercise this right even if he delivers the cargo to the carrier. In *Chun Wing Intimate Factory Ltd v. CEVA Freight (Shenzhen) Ltd and Others*,[1618] the seller delivered the cargo to the agent of the buyer under a sale contract with an FOB term,[1619] and the agent delivered the cargo to the ocean carrier. Before delivery of the cargo, the seller ordered the carrier not to deliver the cargo to the buyer, but the carrier refused to follow the order.[1620] The Chinese courts held that the seller was not entitled to exercise this right because the agent of the buyer is the shipper/consignor of the cargo on behalf of the buyer. In fact, it is the buyer, not the seller, that can exercise the right as the consignor.

1349. In ocean carriage of goods, the consignor is called the shipper. In the Maritime Law, the shipper means: (a) the person by whom or in whose name or on whose behalf a contract of carriage of goods by sea has been concluded with a carrier; (b) the person by whom or in whose name or on whose behalf the goods have been delivered to the carrier involved in the contract of carriage of goods by sea.[1621] The SPC published the Provisions on Certain Issues concerning the Trial of Cases of Disputes over Marine Freight Forwarding (2020) (the SPC Provisions on

---

1616. Article 829 CC.
1617. *Qingdao A Company v. B Shipping Company and Shanghai C Company*, The SPC (2020) Zui Gao Fa Min Shen No. 6908; 青岛某公司诉某航运公司、上海某公司多式联运合同纠纷案, 最高人民法院（2020）最高法民申6908号.
1618. *Chun Wing Intimate Factory Ltd v. CEVA Freight (Shenzhen) Ltd and Others*, Gazette Case of the SPC, Issue 7, 2019; 骏荣内衣有限公司诉宏鹰国际货运（深圳）有限公司等海上货运代理合同纠纷案, 《最高人民法院公报》案例，2019年07期.
1619. FOB stands for 'Free on Board' in ICC Incoterms. It means that the buyer is responsible for carriage, and the seller discharges his delivery obligation when he delivers the cargo to the carrier.
1620. The seller relied on article 308 of the Contract Law for exercising the right. This article is identical to Art. 829 CC.
1621. Article 42 (3) of the Maritime Law.

Marine Freight Forwarding 2020).[1622] The two types of shippers are named the contractual shipper and the actual shipper in the SPC Provisions on Marine Freight Forwarding 2020.[1623] In China's export trade based on FOB contracts, the foreign FOB buyer is the contractual shipper, and the FOB seller is called the actual shipper. In this circumstance, the FOB seller as a shipper is an exception to privity of contract in the carriage of goods by sea in the Maritime Law. Based on this exception, the FOB shipper has a statutory relation with the carrier even though he has no contractual relation with the carrier. Although the Maritime Law provides the concept of shipper, which has recognised the FOB seller as the shipper, it does not provide that the FOB seller shall have the same rights of suit as the contractual shipper.[1624]

1350. Although the consignor may give instructions to the carrier to control the cargo before delivery, the carrier may not be able to follow instructions even though the consignor may compensate the loss thereby suffered by the carrier. In this circumstance, the carrier is entitled to refuse to follow the consignor's instructions. In the SPC guiding case No. 108, *Zhejiang Longda Stainless Steel Co., Ltd. v. AP Moller-Maersk A/S*,[1625] the shipper requested the carrier to return the cargo two days before the vessel arrived at the port of destination, and the carrier refused to follow the shipper's order because it was not operational. The cargo was sold by auction sale in the port of discharge. The shipper claimed against the carrier for the loss of the cargo because the carrier did not follow return instructions. The SPC pointed out that ocean carriage has special features, such as a large volume of cargo, prescheduled voyages, and regularly fixed routes. Therefore, the shipper's right to change delivery ports or return the cargo may not be easily operated and may interfere with the normal operation of the carrier or cause loss or damage to other shippers and consignees. In this circumstance, it is unfair to request the carrier to unconditionally follow the shipper's instructions. Thus, in the carriage of goods by sea contract, the shipper may not be unconditionally allowed to give instructions to change the delivery, and the carrier may not follow the shipper's instructions in any circumstance. In order to keep the balance of interests among all parties, when the shipper exercises the right to change delivery, the carrier shall have a right of defence. If the instructions for change of delivery are impossible to perform or the performance will seriously interfere with the carrier's normal operation, the carrier can refuse to follow instructions but shall promptly notify the shipper of the reason for refusal. In this case, the SPC found that the shipper's instructions could not be followed with the short notice. Therefore, the carrier was entitled to refuse to follow the shipper's instruction for return of the cargo.

1622. The Provisions on Certain Issues concerning the Trial of Cases of Disputes over Marine Freight Forwarding (2020).

1623. Paragraphs 2 and 3 Art. 8, of the SPC Provisions on Marine Freight Forwarding (2020).

1624. Liang Zhao, OB seller under Chinese law and privity of contract in carriage of goods by sea, 2 Asia Pacific Law Review 286, 294 (2019).

1625. *Zhejiang Longda Stainless Steel Co., Ltd. v. AP Moller-Maersk A/S*, The SPC (2017) Zui Gao Fa Min Zai No. 412 (SPC Guiding Case No. 108); 浙江隆达不锈钢有限公司诉A. P. 穆勒-马士基有限公司海上货物运输合同纠纷案，最高人民法院（2017）最高法民再412号（最高人民法院第108号指导性案例）.

1351. In addition, the SPC summarised in this guiding case that the shipper's right under the Contract Law is a rule applying to general transport contract, and this rule shall be subject to the compulsory rules in the Maritime Law when this rule applies to the carriage of goods by sea contract. The SPC does not specify the compulsory rules in the Maritime Law in the case summary. Since the shipper's right in this rule relates to the delivery of the goods, the relevant compulsory rules from the Maritime Law are the rules of delivery under the bill of lading. In the Maritime Law, a bill of lading is a document based on which the carrier undertakes to deliver the goods against surrendering the same.[1626] When the goods have been taken over by the carrier or have been loaded on board, the carrier shall, on demand of the shipper, issue to the shipper a bill of lading.[1627] Therefore, when the shipper transfers the bill of lading to a third party as a bill of lading holder, the carrier has an obligation to deliver the cargo to the bill of lading holder. In this circumstance, the carrier may refuse to follow the shipper's instruction not to deliver the goods because the carrier will breach the compulsory rules of the bill of lading in the Maritime Law if he does not deliver the goods to the bill of lading holder.

1352. Upon arrival of the goods, the carrier shall timely notify the consignee where it is known to the carrier, and the consignee shall collect the goods timely. Where the consignee collects the goods after the due time, it shall pay the carrier expenses for storage, etc.[1628] Where the consignee is unknown or refuses to take delivery of the goods without justification, the carrier may lawfully place the goods in escrow.[1629] If no one collects the goods and the goods are lost or damaged, the carrier is not liable for the loss or damage if the carrier does not breach an obligation to take care of the goods.[1630] Furthermore, the consignee shall, in accordance with the agreed time, inspect the goods when collecting them. Where there is no agreement on the time for inspection or the agreement is equivocal, and the time cannot be ascertained under article 510 of the Civil Code, inspection shall be carried out within a reasonable period of time. Where the consignee fails to raise any objection to issues including the quantity of or damage to or destruction of the goods within either the agreed time or the reasonable period of time, it shall be deemed prima facie evidence that the carrier has delivered the goods in accordance with the carriage certificates.[1631]

1353. The carrier is liable for any damage to or loss of the goods in the course of carriage, except where the carrier shows that the damage to or loss of the goods is caused by force majeure, the nature or reasonable wear and tear of the goods, or

---

1626. Article 71 of the Maritime Law.
1627. Paragraph 1 of Art. 72 CC.
1628. Article 830 CC.
1629. Article 837 CC.
1630. *Zhejiang Longda Stainless Steel Co., Ltd. v. AP Moller-Maersk A/S*, The SPC (2017) Zui Gao Fa Min Zai No. 412 (SPC Guiding Case No. 108); 浙江隆达不锈钢有限公司诉A. P. 穆勒-马士基有限公司海上货物运输合同纠纷案，最高人民法院（2017）最高法民再412号（最高人民法院第108号指导性案例).
1631. Article 831 CC.

fault on the part of the consignor or consignee.[1632] The burden of proof for the exemptions is on the carrier. In *China Pacific Property Insurance Co., Ltd. v. COSCO Shipping Holdings Co., Ltd.*,[1633] the cargo of cars was damaged due to a fire occurred during a coastal carriage. The carrier argued that the damage was caused by the spontaneous combustion of the cars shipped by the consignor. However, the carrier did not provide evidence for the reason for the fire and failed to prove that the fire was caused by the spontaneous combustion of the cars. Therefore, the SPC held that the carrier was liable for the damage to the cargo.

1354. The carrier is also liable for any damage to or loss of the goods in the course of carriage even if the damage or loss is caused by the actual carrier. In *Shanghai A Medicine Co., Ltd. v. Shanghai B Logistics Co., Ltd.*,[1634] the carrier had a carriage contract with the shipper and subcontracted with the actual carriage for the carriage of the cargo. It was declared by the shipper that the value of the cargo was RMB 2,000. The cargo was totally damaged during the carriage. The shipper claimed against the carrier for the loss of the cargo in the amount of RMB 510,188. The carrier argued that it was liable for RMB 2,000 as the value declared by the shipper. It was held that the carrier subcontracted the carriage without authorisation and caused damage or loss to the cargo; it constitutes gross negligence. Therefore, the carrier could not reply on the declared value clause, and the carrier should pay the shipper the actual value of the cargo. However, the shipper did not declare the real value of the cargo in good faith, and it affected the carrier's normal business judgment. Therefore, the carrier's liability can be reduced accordingly. It was held that the carrier should pay the shipper 60% of the real value of the cargo. This case emphasises the importance of subcontracting with authorisation from the shipper. However, it did not well explain why the declared value clause could not be relied on by the carrier. The clause itself does not set up any condition for application. The purpose of the clause is to limit the carrier's liability. The carrier may limit its liability even if it subcontracted the carriage and the actual carriage damaged the cargo. This case imposes a strict obligation and liability on the carrier. Furthermore, if the declared value clause could not be used, it is not reasonable to consider the clause for reducing the carrier's liability due to the shipper's breach of the clause.

1355. For the liability, where the parties have agreed on the amount of damages payable for damage to or loss of the goods, such agreement shall be followed. Where there is no agreement or the agreement is equivocal, and the amount cannot be ascertained under Article 510 of the Civil Code, damages shall be calculated in accordance with the market price at the destination of the goods at the time when

1632. Article 832 CC.

1633. *China Pacific Property Insurance Co., Ltd. v. COSCO Shipping Holdings Co., Ltd.*, The SPC (2011) Min Ti Zi No. 12 (Gazette Case of the SPC, Issue 8, 2012); 中国太平洋财产保险股份有限公司与中远航运股份有限公司、第三人海南分公司海南一汽海马汽车销售有限公司水路货物运输合同货损赔偿纠纷案，最高人民法院（2011）民提字第12号（《最高人民法院公报》案例，2012年08期）.

1634. *Shanghai A Medicine Co., Ltd. v. Shanghai B Logistics Co., Ltd.*, Shanghai Second Intermediate People's Court (2022) Hu 02 Min Zhong No. 3258; 上海某医疗公司诉上海某物流公司运输合同纠纷案，上海市第二中级人民法院（2022）沪02民终3258号.

the goods are or are contracted to be delivered. Where any laws or administrative regulations provide otherwise about the assessment and limits of damages, such provisions shall prevail.[1635] In addition, where two or more carriers jointly carry the goods by the same means of carriage, the carrier who contracts with the consignor shall be responsible for the whole carriage. Where the loss occurs at a certain carriage segment, the carrier who contracts with the consignor and the carrier for that segment shall bear joint and several liability.[1636]

1356. Parties may agree to pay the freight in advance or upon delivery of the goods. Where the goods are lost by reason of force majeure in the course of carriage, and where the carriage fees have not been collected, the carrier shall have no claim for the carriage fees; where carriage fees have been paid, the consignor may demand a refund.[1637] Where the consignor or the consignee fails to pay the freight, storage or other fees, the carrier is entitled to a lien over the corresponding goods, unless otherwise agreed by the parties.[1638]

§4. Multimodal Transport Contracts

1357. The Civil Code provides rules for multimodal transport contracts, but it does not provide a definition of this contract. In the Maritime Law, a multimodal transport contract means a contract under which the multimodal transport operator undertakes to transport the goods, against the payment of freight for the entire transport, from the place where the goods were received in his charge to the destination and to deliver them to the consignee by two or more different modes of transport, one of which being sea carriage.[1639] This definition may apply to the Civil Code rules omitting the phrase 'one of which being sea carriage'. The Maritime Law also provides a definition of the multimodal transport operator which means the person who has entered into a multimodal transport contract with the shipper either by himself or by another person acting on his behalf.[1640] This can also apply to the Civil Code rules for multimodal transport contracts. A multimodal transport operator is responsible for performing or organising the performance of the multimodal transport contract and shall, in respect of the entirety of the transport, enjoy rights and assume obligations as a carrier.[1641]

1358. A multimodal transport operator may agree on the respective responsibilities over each carriage segment with the carrier of each carriage segment. However, such agreements do not affect the obligations assumed by the multimodal transport operator over the entirety of the transport.[1642] Upon receipt of the goods delivered

1635. Article 833 CC.
1636. Article 834 CC.
1637. Article 835 CC.
1638. Article 836 CC.
1639. Paragraph 1 of Art. 102 of the Maritime Law.
1640. Paragraph 2 of Art. 102 CC.
1641. Article 838 CC.
1642. Article 839 CC.

by the consignor, the multimodal transport operator shall issue a multimodal transport document. Such a document may, at the consignor's request, be a negotiable or non-negotiable instrument.[1643] For liabilities, on the one hand, where losses to the multimodal transport operator are caused by reason of the consignor's fault in the course of the consignment of the goods, the consignor is liable for damages notwithstanding that the consignor has assigned the multimodal transport document.[1644] On the other hand, where damage to or loss of the goods occurs at a certain carriage segment, the liability and limits to the liability of the multimodal transport operator to pay damages are governed by the relevant provisions of law applicable to the mode of carriage in that segment. Where the carriage segment in which damage to or loss of the goods occurs cannot be ascertained, liability to pay damages shall be assumed in accordance with this chapter.[1645]

1643. Article 840 CC.
1644. Article 841 CC.
1645. Article 842 CC.

Chapter 12. Technology Contracts

§1. General Provisions

1359. A technology contract in the Civil Code is a contract whereby the parties define their rights and obligations as to the development, transfer, licensing, consultancy or service of technology.[1646] The principle of technology contracts shall be beneficial to the protection of intellectual property rights and the advancement of science and technology, and promotion of the research and development, transformation, application and dissemination of scientific and technological achievements.[1647] The legal issues of technology contracts are governed by both the Civil Code and the SPC Interpretation on Certain Issues Concerning the Application of Law in Trying Cases Involving Technology Contract Disputes (2020) (the SPC Interpretation on Technology Contract 2020).[1648]

1360. The content of a technology contract generally includes terms as to the name, content, scope and requirements of the project, the arrangement, place and means of performance, the confidentiality of technical intelligence and information, ownership of technological product and distribution of income, standards and means of inspection, Interpretation on technical terms, et cetera. Furthermore, the materials as to the technological background, feasibility reports and technological evaluation reports, task plan and proposal of the project, technical standards and specifications, original designs and process documents, and other technical documents relating to the performance of the contract may, as agreed by the parties, form part of the contract. Where the technology contract involves a patent, the name, applicant and owner of the patent, date of application, number of applications, number of patents, and the expiry date of the patent shall be specified.[1649]

1361. The technology product means the technological solutions involving products, processes, materials and the improvements, etc., thereof, which are made with the utilisation of scientific and technological knowledge, information and experiences, including patents, patent applications, technical secrets, computer software, integrated circuit layout designs, new varieties of plant, etc.[1650] The technology product includes occupational technology products and non-occupational technology products. An occupational technology product is a technical product made in fulfilment of work tasks assigned by a legal person or an organisation of other types, or mainly from the use of materials and technology of the legal person or organisation.[1651]

1646. Article 843 CC.
1647. Article 844 CC.
1648. The SPC Interpretation on Certain Issues Concerning the Application of Law in Trying Cases Involving Technology Contract Disputes (2020).
1649. Article 845 CC.
1650. Paragraph 1 of Art. 1 of the SPC Interpretation on Technology Contract (2020).
1651. Paragraph 2 of Art. 847 CC.

1362. For the occupational technology product, the 'fulfilment of work tasks assigned by a legal person or an organisation' shall include: (1) implementing his post duties of the legal person or other organisation or undertaking other technology development tasks consigned by the legal person or other organisation; (2) within one year after his leaving the post, continuing to engage in the technology development related to his post duties of the former legal person or other organisation, or related to the tasks consigned by it, unless otherwise prescribed in laws or administrative regulations. The legal person or other organisation and its employee may agree on the rights and interests of the technical product accomplished by such employee during his employment or after his leaving the post.[1652]

1363. The 'materials and technology of the legal person or organisation' shall include funds, equipment, apparatus, raw materials, unpublicised technical information, data, etc.,[1653] the 'use' of such materials and technology shall include the employee's utilising the whole or major part of funds, equipment, apparatus, raw materials or other material conditions of a legal person or other organisation in the process of research and development of the technological achievement, and such material conditions have essential effects on the forming of the said technical product; it shall also include the circumstances under which the essential contents of the technical product are completed on the basis of the technical product of either the whole process or a certain stage which has not been publicised by the legal person or other organisation, with the exceptions of the following circumstances: (1) with respect to the utilisation of the material and technical conditions provided by the legal person or other organisation, it is stipulated that the funds should be refunded or the royalties should be paid; and (2) after the technical product is accomplished, the technical plan is verified or tested with utilisation of the material and technical conditions of the legal person or other organisation.[1654]

1364. Where the right to use or transfer an occupational technology product belongs to a legal person or an organisation, the legal person or organisation may conclude a technology contract in respect of the product. Where the legal person or organisation concludes a technology contract for the transfer of the product, the person who made the product has the right of first refusal under equal conditions.[1655] The right to use or transfer non-occupational technology products shall belong to the individual who completed such products, who may conclude a technology contract in respect of the products.[1656] The 'person who made the product' of an occupational technology product and the 'individual who completed such products' of a non-occupational technology product shall include the persons who independently or jointly make creative contributions to the technology products, that is, the inventors or designers of the technology products. The person who proposes the composition of the essential technology and therefore achieves the technical plan shall be

1652. Article 2 of the SPC Interpretation on Technology Contract (2020).
1653. Article 3 CC.
1654. Article 4 CC.
1655. Paragraph 1 of Art. 847 CC.
1656. Article 848 CC.

the person who makes creative contributions. The persons who provide funds, equipment, materials and conditions for experiments; carry out organisational management; assist in making drawings; and clear up documents and translating literature shall not be the individuals who accomplish the technological achievement.[1657] The individual who completed a technology product is entitled to identify himself/herself on the relevant documents on the technology product and to receive certificates of honour and awards.[1658]

1365. The means of payment for the price, remuneration or licence fees under the technology contract are as agreed by the parties, which may be by lump-sum payment upon a one-off account settlement, instalments upon a one-off account settlement, or by royalty payments or royalty payments with an advanced entry fee. Where royalty payments are agreed upon, the royalty may be calculated at a certain proportion of the price of the product or appreciation in product value, profits or sales proceeds following the use of the patent or technological secrets, or by other means as agreed. The rate of the royalty may be fixed, increased annually or reduced annually. Where royalty payments are agreed upon, the parties may agree on the manner in which the relevant books of accounts are inspected.[1659]

1366. Technology contracts involving unlawful monopoly of technology or infringement of another's technology products are void.[1660] The following circumstances shall belong to 'unlawful monopoly of technology': (1) restricting one party from making new research and development on the basis of the contractual subject technology, or restricting this party from using the improved technology, or the conditions for both parties to exchange the improved technologies with each other being not reciprocal, including such circumstances as requiring one party to gratuitously provide the other party with the improved technology, to transfer the improved technology to the other party non-reciprocally, to gratuitously and solely occupy, or jointly own the intellectual property of the improved technology; (2) restricting one party from obtaining, from other origins, the technology similar to or competitive against that of the technology provider; (3) impeding one party's sufficient exploitation of the contractual subject technology in a reasonable way pursuant to the market demands, including unreasonably restricting the quantity, varieties, price, sales channel or export market of the contractual subject technology exploited by technology acceptor in an obvious way to produce products or to provide services; (4) requiring the technology acceptor to accept attached conditions dispensable for exploiting the technology, including purchasing dispensable technologies, raw materials, products, equipment, services or accepting dispensable persons, etc.;[1661] (5) unreasonably restricting the channels or origins for the technology acceptor to purchase raw materials, parts and components, products or

1657. Article 6 of the SPC Interpretation on Technology Contract (2020).
1658. Article 849 CC.
1659. Article 846 CC.
1660. Article 850 CC.
1661. Whether the attached conditions are dispensable is a matter of fact to be determined by evidence. *See Dayang Company v. Huanghe Company*, The SPC (2003) Min San Zhong Zi No. 8

equipment, etc.; and (6) prohibiting the technology acceptor from making objections to the effectiveness of the intellectual property of the contractual subject technology or attaching conditions to the objections made.[1662]

1367. If, after a technology contract is invalidated or revoked, the researcher and developer under the technology development contract, the transferor under the technology transfer contract, or the entrusted party under the technical consulting contract or technical service contract has implemented or partially implemented the stipulated obligations, and the fault of causing invalidity or revocation of the contract lies in the other party, the Chinese court may ascertain the research and development fees ought to be charged for the implemented obligations, the technology royalties, or the remuneration from provision of consulting services as the losses caused by the other party from invalidity or revocation of the contract. If, after a technology contract is invalidated or revoked, the parties are unable to re-determine through agreement the new technological achievement accomplished due to the implementation of the contract, or the belongingness of rights and sharing of benefits of the technological achievement based upon the follow-up improvements of the technological achievements accomplished by others, the Chinese court may rule that the technological achievement shall be owned by the accomplishing party.[1663]

1368. Furthermore, if a technology contract infringing upon another's technical secret is confirmed as invalid, the party who obtained the technical secret in good faith may, unless otherwise prescribed by laws or administrative regulations, continue using this technical secret within the same scope as that when he obtained it, provided that he shall pay the obligee reasonable royalties and bear confidential obligations. Where both parties maliciously collude with each other to conclude or implement a contract, or one party who knows or ought to know the other party's infringement concludes a contract with such other party or implements the contract, such conclusion or implementation of the contract shall be joint infringement, and the Chinese court shall rule that the tortfeasors shall bear joint indemnity liabilities or confidential obligations; therefore the party who has obtained the technical secret may not continue using this technical secret.[1664]

§2. Contracts for Technology Development

1369. A contract for technology development is a contract concluded by the parties for the research and development of novel technology, products, techniques, varieties, materials or their systems.[1665] The 'novel technology, products, techniques, varieties, materials or their systems' include products, processes, materials,

（Gazette Case of the SPC, Issue 9, 2004）；大洋公司诉黄河公司专利实施许可合同纠纷案，最高人民法院（2003）民三终字第8号（《最高人民法院公报》案例，2004年09期）.

1662. Article 10 of the SPC Interpretation on Technology Contract (2020).
1663. Article 11 CC.
1664. Article 12 CC.
1665. Paragraph 1 of Art. 851 CC.

systems and other technical solutions that the parties have not mastered when entering into the technology contract. However, modifications, process changes, material formula adjustments, and verification, testing and use of technical achievements of existing products that are not technically innovative are excluded.[1666] Contracts for technology development shall be made in writing. A contract for technology development includes contracts for commissioned development and contracts for cooperative development. For contracts concluded between the parties on the transformation of technology products of practical value, the relevant provisions on contracts for technology development shall be referred to and applied.[1667] The transfer and licence of other intellectual property rights, including exclusive rights in integrated circuit layout designs, rights to new plant species, copyrights of computer software, and so forth, shall be regulated by reference to the relevant provisions in this section.[1668] Where laws or administrative regulations provide otherwise for contracts for the import or export of technology, contracts of patents or contracts for applications for patents, such provisions shall prevail.[1669]

1370. Both the commissioning party and the researcher and developer under the contract for commissioned development have obligations under the Civil Code. On the one hand, the commissioning party under a contract for commissioned development shall, in accordance with the contract, supply funds for the research and development and pay remuneration, provide technical information and raw data, identify requirements for the research and development, provide assistance, and accept the product.[1670] On the other hand, the researcher and developer under a contract for commissioned development shall prepare and implement research and development plans in accordance with the contract, make reasonable use of research and development funds, complete research and development, deliver the products timely, and provide the relevant technical information and necessary technical guidance to keep the commissioning party abreast of the products of the research and development.[1671] Where any party to a contract for commissioned development breaches the contract, thereby causing the research and development project to be suspended, delayed or to fail, the party shall bear liability for the breach of contract.[1672]

1371. The parties to a contract for cooperative development shall invest in accordance with the contract, including investment in the form of technology, divided participation in the research and development, and cooperation in the

---

1666. Article 17 of the SPC Interpretation on Technology Contract (2020).
1667. Paragraphs 2–4 of Art. 851 CC. The contract for the transformation of technology products refers to a contract between the parties that agrees on subsequent testing, development and application of scientific and technological achievements that have practical value but have not yet been industrialised, including phased technical achievements, with the goal of realising the industrial application of the scientific and technological achievements. *See* Art. 18 of the SPC Interpretation on Technology Contract (2020).
1668. Article 876 CC.
1669. Article 877 CC.
1670. Article 852 CC.
1671. Article 853 CC.
1672. Article 854 CC.

research and development.[1673] The 'divided participation in the research and development' includes that the parties jointly or separately undertake design, technology, testing, trial production, etc. in accordance with the agreed plan and allocation of work. If one party to a technology development contract only provides funds, equipment, materials and other material conditions or undertakes auxiliary collaboration matters, and the other party carries out research and development work, it is a contract for commissioned development.[1674] Where any party to a contract for cooperative development breaches the contract, thereby causing the research and development project to be suspended, delayed or to fail, the party shall be liable for the breach of contract.[1675]

1372. Where, in the course of performance of the contract for technology development, the research and development fail in whole or in part owing to any insurmountable technological difficulties, such risk shall be allocated as agreed by the parties. Where there is no agreement or the agreement is equivocal, and the allocation of risk cannot be ascertained under Article 510 of the Civil Code, the risk shall be reasonably shared between the parties. Where either party is aware of any possibility that the research and development may fail in whole or in part as provided in the preceding paragraph, it shall timely notify the other party and take appropriate measures to mitigate the losses. Where the party fails timely to notify and take appropriate measures, thereby causing an aggravation of the losses, the party shall be liable for the aggravated losses.[1676] Where, due to the disclosure by another of the subject matter of the contract for technology development, the performance of the contract for technology development is rendered meaningless, a party may terminate the contract.[1677]

1373. According to the general rule in the Civil Code, after the termination of a contract, performance shall cease if the contract has not been performed; if the contract has been performed, a party may, in accordance with the circumstances of performance or the nature of the contract, request the other party to restore such party to its original state or adopt other remedial measures, and such party shall have the right to demand compensation for losses.[1678] When the contract is terminated, if the developer only performs part of the contract, the completed part usually involves value assessment, and it is not appropriate to treat the previous payment as performance. In *Xuzhou Batian Ecotypic Engineering Co., Ltd. v. Shenzhen Parameter Navigator Technology Co., Ltd. and Shenzhen Batian Ecotypic Engineering Co., Ltd.*,[1679] based on the actual utilisation of the system completed by the developer and the appraisal conclusion of the proportion of completed functions in all functions, the court determined that the commissioning party should pay around 60% of

1673. Article 855 CC.
1674. Article 19 of the SPC Interpretation on Technology Contract (2020).
1675. Article 856 CC.
1676. Article 858 CC.
1677. Article 857 CC.
1678. Paragraph 1 of Art. 566 CC.
1679. *Xuzhou Batian Ecotypic Engineering Co., Ltd. v. Shenzhen Parameter Navigator Technology Co., Ltd. and Shenzhen Batian Ecotypic Engineering Co., Ltd.*, Jiangsu High People's Court (2017) Su

the total contract price for the system involved in the case. If the performed part is of no value or the value of the performance is low in terms of the desired result, it is believed that the developer's previous performance can be regarded as non-performance, and the commissioning party does not need to compensate the debtor for its performance.[1680]

1374. The Civil Code has different rules for the right to apply for a patent under a commissioned development and a cooperative development. Unless otherwise provided by law or agreed by the parties, the right to apply for a patent over inventions completed under a commissioned development shall vest in the researcher and developer. Where the researcher and developer obtain the patent, the commissioning party may lawfully exploit the patent. Where the researcher and developer transfer the right to apply for a patent, the commissioning party has the right of first refusal under equal conditions.[1681] Unless otherwise agreed by the parties, the right to apply for a patent over inventions completed under a cooperative development shall vest jointly in the parties to the cooperative development. Where any one of the parties transfers its share in the joint right to apply for a patent, the other parties have the right of first refusal under equal conditions. Where any party to a cooperative development expressly waives its share in the joint right to apply for a patent, application may be unilaterally made by the other party or by the other parties jointly. Where the patent is granted, the party who waives the right to apply may exploit the patent free of charge. Where any of the parties to a cooperative development refuse to apply for a patent, the other party or parties shall not apply for a patent.[1682]

1375. Furthermore, the right to use and transfer, and the distribution of income from, the technological secrets completed under a commissioned or cooperative development shall follow the parties' agreement. Where there is no agreement or the agreement is equivocal, and the agreement cannot be ascertained under article 510 of the Civil Code, all parties enjoy the right to use and transfer before any identical technology is patented. However, the researcher and developer under a commissioned development shall not transfer the research and development product to a third party before it is delivered to the commissioning party.[1683] The phrase 'all parties enjoy the right to use and transfer' means that each party has the right to use the technical secrets themselves without the consent of the other party or to license others to use the technical secrets in the form of a general use licence and to monopolise the benefits derived therefrom. If one party transfers the right to transfer the technical secret products to another person or licenses another person to use the

Min Zhong No. 2151; 徐州市芭田生态有限公司与深圳市参数领航科技有限公司、深圳市芭田生态工程股份有限公司技术委托开发合同案，江苏省高级人民法院（2017）苏民终2151号.

1680. Yali Bai, A Preliminary Study on the Issue of Technical Contract Termination in the Context of the Civil Code, 12 Journal of Law Application (Fa Lv Shi Yong) 86, 91 (2022).

1681. Article 859 CC.

1682. Article 860 CC.

1683. Article 861 CC.

technical secret in the form of an exclusive or exclusive-use licence, the transfer or licensing act shall be deemed to be invalid without the consent or ratification of the other party.[1684]

§3. Contracts for Technology Transfer and Technology Licence

1376. A contract for technology transfer is a contract whereby the legal owner of the technology transfers the rights relating to an existing and specific patent, application for a patent, or technological secret to another.[1685] A contract for a technology licence is a contract whereby the legal owner of the technology licences another to exploit and use the rights relating to an existing and specific patent or technological secret.[1686] Contracts for technology transfer and contracts for technology licences shall be made in writing.[1687] Agreements on the provision of special equipment or raw materials for the exploitation of the technology, or the provision of relevant technology consultations and services under a contract for technology transfer or a contract for technology licences form part of the contract.[1688] Furthermore, if the parties enter into a joint venture contract in the form of technology shares, but the technology shareholders do not participate in the operation and management of the joint venture, and the joint venture or the joint venture partner agrees in the form of a minimum guarantee clause to pay the price or royalties for its technology, it shall be regarded as a technology transfer contract or a technology licence contract.[1689]

1377. A technology contract may have the contents of both the contract for technology development and the contract for technology transfer. In *Suzhou Siyuan Natural Products Research and Development Co., Ltd. v. Nanjing Hailing Chinese Medicine Pharmaceutical Process Technology Research Co., Ltd.*,[1690] the parties in dispute concluded a technology transfer contract. However, the subject matter of the contract involved and the specific content of the rights and obligations agreed upon by both parties include not only the transfer of all preclinical research data of a certain oral liquid, project-related patents, preparation process pilot technology, and other existing research results, but also include clinical research approval documents, large-scale production technology of preparation processes, clinical trial research, etc. that need further research and development at the time of signing the contract, and those belong to new technology and new process. The first part has the nature of a technology transfer contract, and the second part has the nature of a

1684. Article 20 of the SPC Interpretation on Technology Contract (2020).
1685. Paragraph 1 of Art. 862 CC.
1686. Paragraph 2 of Art. 862 CC.
1687. Paragraph 3 OF Art. 863 CC.
1688. Paragraph 3 of Art. 862 CC.
1689. Paragraph 3 of Art. 22 of the SPC Interpretation on Technology Contract (2020).
1690. *Suzhou Siyuan Natural Products Research and Development Co., Ltd. v. Nanjing Hailing Chinese Medicine Pharmaceutical Process Technology Research Co., Ltd.*, The SPC (2021) Zui Gao Fa Min Shen No. 7796; 苏州思源天然产物研发有限公司、南京海陵中药制药工艺技术研究有限公司技术合同纠纷，最高人民法院（2021）最高法民申7796号.

technology development contract. Therefore, the SPC held that the contract in dispute was a mix of the two types of contracts. For determining the nature of a technology contract, it cannot be simply based on the name of the contract signed by the parties but should be comprehensively determined based on the subject matter of the contract and the rights and obligations stipulated in the contract.

1378. Contracts for technology transfer and contracts for technology licences may provide for the scope of the exploitation of the patent or the use of the technology secret, provided that technological competition and development are not restricted.[1691] The 'scope of the exploitation of the patent or the use of the technology secret' includes the term, region, method of implementing the patent or using the technical secret, and the persons who have access to the technical secret, etc. If the parties have not agreed on the time limit for exploiting the patent or using the technical secrets or the agreement is unclear, the transferee or licensee shall not be subject to the time limit for exploiting the patent or using the technical secrets.[1692] The parties may, according to the principle of mutual benefit, stipulate in the contract the distribution of the improved technological product following the exploitation of the patent or use of the technological secrets. Where there is no agreement or the agreement is equivocal, and the agreement cannot be ascertained under article 510 of the Civil Code, the post-exploitation improvement to the technological product made by a party shall not be shared by other parties.[1693]

1379. Contracts for technology transfer include contracts for the transfer of patents, transfer of the right to apply for patents, and transfer of technological secrets, et cetera.[1694] Contracts for technology licences includes contracts for the licence to exploit patents or use technological secrets.[1695] The transferor under a contract for technology transfer shall warrant that it is the legal owner of the technology provided and that the technology provided is complete, free from error, effective, and can fulfil the agreed purpose.[1696] A contract for the licence to exploit a patent is valid only within the term of the patent. Where the patent expires or is declared invalid, the patentee shall not conclude a contract with another for the licence to exploit the patent.[1697] For performance of a contract for the licence to exploit a patent, the licensor shall, in accordance with the contract, allow the licensee to exploit the patent, deliver technical information in relation to the exploitation of the patent, and provide the necessary technical guidance.[1698] Meanwhile, the licensee shall exploit the patent in accordance with the contract, pay the licence fee as agreed, and shall not licence a third party outside the contract to exploit the patent.[1699]

1691. Article 864 CC.
1692. Article 28 of the SPC Interpretation on Technology Contract (2020).
1693. Article 875 CC.
1694. Paragraph 1 of Art. 863 CC.
1695. Paragraph 2 of Art. 863 CC.
1696. Article 870 CC.
1697. Article 865 CC.
1698. Article 866 CC.
1699. Article 867 CC.

1380. For technological secrets, the Civil Code assumes the duty of confidentiality. On the one hand, the transferor under a contract for the transfer of technological secrets or the licensor under a contract for the licence to use technological secrets shall, in accordance with the contract, provide technical information, technical guidance, warrant the practicality and reliability of the technology, and assume the duty of confidentiality. The duty of confidentiality provided in the preceding paragraph shall, unless otherwise agreed by the parties, not prevent the transferor or licensor from applying for a patent.[1700] On the other hand, the transferee under a contract for the transfer of technological secrets or the licensee under a contract for the licence to use technological secrets shall, in accordance with the contract, use the technology, pay the licence fees and assume the duty of confidentiality.[1701] The transferee under a contract for technology transfer shall assume the duty of confidentiality in respect of the undisclosed parts of the technology provided by the transferor and in accordance with the agreed scope and period.[1702]

1381. The Civil Code provides rules of liability for breach of contract. First, where the transferor fails to transfer the technology in accordance with the contract, it shall return the licence fees in whole or in part and be liable for breach of contract; where the transferor exploits the patent or the use of the technological secrets beyond the agreed scope or unilaterally licenses a third party to exploit the patent or use the technological secrets in breach of the contract, it shall cease the act of breach and bear liability for the breach of contract. Where the transferor breaches the duty of confidentiality, it shall be liable for the breach of contract. This rule applies where the licensor is liable for breach of contract.[1703] Second, where the transferee fails to pay the licence fees in accordance with the contract, it shall pay the unpaid licence fees and pay agreed damages pursuant to the contract; where the transferee fails to pay the licence fees or agreed damages in full, it shall cease the exploitation of the patent or use of the technological secrets, return the technical information, and be liable for breach of contract; where the transferee exploits the patent or the use of the technological secrets beyond the agreed scope or unilaterally licenses to a third party the exploitation of the patent or the use of the technological secrets in breach of the contract, it shall cease the act of breach and be liable for the breach of contract; where the transferee breaches the duty of confidentiality, it shall be liable for the breach of contract. This rule applies where the licensee is liable for breach of contract.[1704] In addition, where the transferee or licensee infringes the lawful rights and interests of another in the course of the exploitation of the patent or use of the technological secrets in accordance with the contract, the transferor or licensor shall be liable, unless otherwise agreed by the parties.[1705]

1700. Article 868 CC.
1701. Article 869 CC.
1702. Article 871 CC.
1703. Article 872 CC.
1704. Article 873 CC.
1705. Article 874.

§4. Contracts for Technology Consultancy and Technology Services

1382. A contract for technology consultancy is a contract whereby a party uses its skills and knowledge to provide the other party with feasibility studies, technological forecasts, investigations in specific technology, analytical and evaluative reports, and so forth concerning a specific technological project.[1706] The specific technological project includes soft science research projects relating to the coordinated development of science and technology and economy and society, professional technical projects that use scientific knowledge and technical means to investigate, analyse, demonstrate, evaluate, and predict, such as promoting scientific and technological progress and management modernisation, and improving economic and social benefits.[1707] A contract for technology services is a contract whereby a party uses its skills and knowledge to resolve specific technical issues for the other party and does not include a contract for work or a construction contract.[1708] Specific technical issues include technical problems that require the use of professional technical knowledge, experience and information to solve problems related to improving product structure, improving process flow, improving product quality, reducing product costs, saving resources and energy consumption, protecting resources and the environment, achieving safe operations, and improving economic and social benefits.[1709]

1383. In the course of performance of a contract for technology consultancy, the commissioning party under a contract for technology consultancy shall, in accordance with the contract, clearly state the issues to be consulted on, provide the technological background materials and the relevant technical information and data, accept the product of the work conducted by the commissioned party, and pay the remuneration.[1710] Meanwhile, the commissioned party under a contract for technology consultancy shall, in accordance with the contract, complete the consultancy report or answer the questions by the agreed time, and the consultancy report submitted shall conform to the agreed requirements.[1711] Where the commissioning party under a contract for technology consultancy fails to provide the necessary information and data in accordance with the contract, thereby affecting the progress and quality of the work, and it refuses to accept or delays in accepting the product of the work, it shall not seek recovery of paid remuneration and shall be liable to pay the balance of the remuneration. Where the commissioned party under a contract for technology consultancy fails to provide the consultancy report by the agreed time or the report provided does not conform to the contract, it shall be liable for breach of contract in the form of reducing or waiving the remuneration, and so forth. The losses sustained by the commissioning party resulting from its decision making in reliance on the consultancy report and opinion, provided in accordance

1706. Paragraph 1 of Art. 878 CC.
1707. Article 30 of the SPC Interpretation on Technology Contract (2020).
1708. Paragraph 2 of Art. 878 CC.
1709. Article 33 of the SPC Interpretation on Technology Contract (2020).
1710. Article 879 CC.
1711. Article 880 CC.

with the contract by the commissioned party, shall be borne by the commissioning party unless otherwise agreed by the parties.[1712]

1384. The commissioning party under a contract for technology services shall, in accordance with the contract, provide the working conditions and complete assistance to the commissioned party, accept the product of the work and pay the remuneration.[1713] Meanwhile, the commissioned party under a contract for technology services shall, in accordance with the contract, complete the service work, resolve technical issues, warrant the quality of the work, and communicate the knowledge acquired in resolving the technical issues.[1714] Where the commissioning party under a contract for technology services fails to perform its contractual obligations or performs the work at variance with the contract, thereby affecting the progress and quality of the work, and it refuses to accept or delays in accepting the product of the work, it shall not seek recovery of paid remuneration and shall be liable to pay the balance of the remuneration. Where the commissioned party fails to complete the service work in accordance with the contract, it shall be liable for breach of contract in the form of waiving the remuneration, etc.[1715]

1385. In the course of performance of a contract for technology consultancy or technology services, the novel technological product that the commissioned party completes by using the technical information and working conditions provided by the commissioning party shall be owned by the commissioned party. The novel technological product that the commissioning party completes by using the commissioned party's work shall be owned by the commissioning party. Where the parties agree otherwise, such agreement shall prevail.[1716] Where a contract for technology consultancy or technology services makes no provision for the bearing of expenses necessary for the commissioned party to complete the work, or where such provision is equivocal, the expenses shall be borne by the commissioned party.[1717]

1712. Article 881 CC.
1713. Article 882 CC.
1714. Article 883 CC.
1715. Article 884 CC.
1716. Article 885 CC.
1717. Article 886 CC.

Chapter 13. Safekeeping Contracts

1386. A safekeeping contract is a contract whereby the depository keeps the deposited item delivered by the depositor and returns it.[1718] This definition in the Civil Code is the same as that of the Contract Law. The Civil Code clarifies further that where the depositor places an item at a place designated for shopping, dining, accommodation, and so forth on the depository's premises, this is deemed safekeeping, unless otherwise agreed by the parties or directed by trade practice.[1719] This clarification solves the problem of whether there is a safekeeping contract when a person keeps the deposited item in the shopping place for shopping purposes. A safekeeping contract takes effect on delivery of the deposited item, unless otherwise agreed by the parties.[1720] Parties may agree to issue a certificate of deposit. Where the depositor delivers the deposited item to the depository, the depository shall provide a certificate of deposit, unless otherwise directed by trade practice.[1721] If no deposited item is delivered but the depository fraudulently provides a certificate of deposit, the depository shall be liable for damage to the innocent party caused by the issuance of the fraudulent certificate of deposit.[1722]

1387. Under a safekeeping contract, the depositor shall pay safekeeping fees to the depository in accordance with the contract. Under a non-gratuitous safekeeping contract, the depositor shall pay the safekeeping fees to the depository by the agreed time. Where the parties have not agreed on the time of payment or the agreement is equivocal, and the time cannot be ascertained under 510 of the Civil Code, the payment shall be made when the deposited item is being collected.[1723] Where the parties have not agreed on the safekeeping fees or the agreement is equivocal, and the fees cannot be ascertained under article 510 of the Civil Code, it is deemed gratuitous safekeeping.[1724] Where the depositor fails to pay safekeeping fees or other fees in accordance with the contract, the depository is entitled to have a lien over the deposited item, unless otherwise agreed by the parties.[1725]

1388. For safekeeping purpose, the depository shall keep the deposited item in good custody. The parties may agree on the place and means of safekeeping. Except in an emergency or for protection of the interests of the depositor, the place and means of safekeeping shall not be altered unilaterally.[1726] Where the deposited item delivered by the depositor is defective or in need of special safekeeping measures

1718. Paragraph 1 of Art. 888 CC.
1719. Paragraph 2 of Art. 888 CC.
1720. Article 890 CC.
1721. Article 891 CC.
1722. *Dalian Fengqi Investment Management Co., Ltd. v. Sinotrans Liaoning Storage and Freight Co., Ltd. and Others*, The SPC (2016) Zui Gao Fa Min Zhong No. 650 (Gazette Case of the SPC, Issue 7, 2017); 大连俸旗投资管理有限公司与中国外运辽宁储运公司等借款合同纠纷案，(2016) 最高法民终650号（《最高人民法院公报》案例，2017年07期）.
1723. Article 902 CC.
1724. Article 889 CC.
1725. Article 903 CC.
1726. Article 892 CC.

due to its nature, the depositor shall notify the depository of such circumstances. Where the deposited item is damaged due to the depositor's failure to notify, the depository is not liable for damages. Where the depository sustains losses therefrom, the depositor shall be liable for damages, except where the depository knows or ought to know the above circumstances and fails to take remedial measures.[1727] Where, in the course of the safekeeping, the depository fails to keep the deposited item in good custody, thereby causing damage to or loss of the deposited item, the depository shall be liable for damages. However, where the safekeeping is gratuitous and the depository proves that there was no deliberate act or gross negligence on its part, it is not liable for damages.[1728]

1389. The depositor may collect the deposited item at any time. Where the parties have not agreed on the term of safekeeping or the agreement is equivocal, the depository may request the depositor to collect the deposited item at any time; where the term of safekeeping is agreed upon, the depository may not, without special reasons, request the depositor to collect the deposited item in advance.[1729] Upon expiry of the term of safekeeping or where the depositor collects the deposited item in advance, the depository shall return the deposited item with its fruits to the depositor.[1730]

1390. There are two rules for the safekeeping of valuables. First, where the depositor deposits currencies, valuable securities, or other valuable goods, it shall make a declaration so that the depository may inspect and accept or seal the deposited item. Where the depositor fails to declare, damage to or loss of the deposited item may be compensated for by the depository by the standard of an ordinary item.[1731] Second, where the depository keeps currencies, it may return the same type and quantity of the currencies. Where other fungible items are deposited, the depository may return items of the same type, quality, and quantity in accordance with the contract.[1732]

1391. The Civil Code provides rules relating to third parties for the safekeeping contract. First, the depository shall not give the deposited item to a third party for safekeeping unless otherwise agreed by the parties. Where the depository contravenes the preceding paragraph and gives the deposited item to a third party for safekeeping, thereby causing damage to the deposited item, it shall be liable for damages.[1733] Second, the depository shall not use or permit a third party to use the deposited item unless otherwise agreed by the parties.[1734] Third, where a third party asserts rights in the deposited item, the depository shall perform its obligation to return the deposited item to the depositor, except where interim measures or

1727. Article 893 CC.
1728. Article 897 CC.
1729. Article 899 CC.
1730. Article 900 CC.
1731. Article 898 CC.
1732. Article 901 CC.
1733. Article 894 CC.
1734. Article 895 CC.

enforcement orders are lawfully being implemented against the deposited item. Where a third-party institutes court proceedings against the depository or applies for seizure of the deposited item, the depository shall timely notify the depositor.[1735]

1735. Article 896 CC.

Chapter 14. Warehousing Contracts

1392. A warehousing contract in the Civil Code means a contract whereby the depository stores the warehoused item delivered by the depositor and the depositor pays warehouse fees.[1736] The warehousing contract is a kind of safekeeping contract, and the deposited item is the warehoused item. Therefore, the relevant provisions on safekeeping contracts shall apply to matters not provided for by this Chapter.[1737] A warehousing contract may be named in other ways. In *PetroChina Co., Ltd. Jiangsu Lianyungang Sales Branch v. Lianyungang Zejia International Logistics Co., Ltd.*,[1738] a logistics company, a petroleum company, and others concluded a single-vessel agreement. The logistics company claimed against the petroleum company for wrongful delivery of the cargo. The petroleum company argued that there was no warehousing contract between them, and the single-vessel agreement was just a port operation contract. The courts pointed out that the petroleum company was the actual warehousing person of the cargo, and the logistics company was responsible for handling storage and delivery matters under the contract. Moreover, the single-vessel agreement stipulated that the logistics company should negotiate with the petroleum company on the cargo delivery method and quantity confirmation method. Therefore, there was a warehousing contract between the logistics company and the petroleum company.

1393. The Civil Code provides that a warehousing contract is concluded upon the meeting of the minds between the depository and the depositor.[1739] This rule is different from the rule in the Contract Law in which it was provided that a warehousing contract takes effect once it is concluded.[1740] The Civil Code emphasises how a warehousing contract is concluded, whereas the Contract Law focuses on the time when a warehousing contract takes effect. First, the general rules for conclusion of contracts in the Civil Code can apply to the warehousing contract, and the warehousing contract has no special characters requiring the emphasis of the meeting of the minds between the depository and the depositor. Second, normal contracts take effect once they are concluded, and the warehousing contract has no special characters requiring any further conditions after the contract is concluded. Therefore, those two rules are not necessary, although they are not harmful to other rules.

1394. The depository has certain obligations to the depositor for the warehoused item. First, the depository shall, in accordance with the contract, inspect and accept the warehoused item entering the warehouse. Where the depository discovers in the course of inspection and acceptance that the warehoused item entering the

1736. Article 904 CC.
1737. Article 918 CC.
1738. *PetroChina Co., Ltd. Jiangsu Lianyungang Sales Branch v. Lianyungang Zejia International Logistics Co., Ltd.*, The SPC (2021) Zui Gao Fa Min Shen No. 6612; 中国石油天然气股份有限公司江苏连云港销售分公司、连云港泽嘉国际物流有限公司港口货物保管合同纠纷案，最高人民法院（2021）最高法民申6612号.
1739. Article 905 CC.
1740. Article 382 of the Contract Law.

warehouse does not conform to the contract, it shall notify the depositor timely. Where the type, quantity or quality of the warehoused item is found not to conform to the contract after the depository has inspected and accepted it, the depository shall be liable for damages.[1741] Second, after the depositor delivers the warehoused item, the depository shall issue certificates including warehouse warrants, warehouse receipts, and so forth.[1742]

1395. The depository shall sign or stamp the warehouse warrant, which shall state: (1) the name or business name and address of the depositor; (2) the type, quantity, quality, packaging and its number and marking of the warehoused item; (3) wear and tear standards of the warehoused item; (4) place of storage; (5) term of storage; (6) warehouse fees; (7) where the warehoused item is insured, the amount and term insured, and the name of the insurer; and (8) the issuer and the place and date of issue.[1743] The warehouse warrant is an important commercial document. It is a certificate for the collection of the warehoused item. The depositor or a bearer of the delivery note may assign the right to collect the warehoused item by endorsing and having the depositor sign or stamp the warehouse warrant.[1744]

1396. The warehouse warrant represents a right of debt. So, it is a certificate of debt. When it is in conflict with the property right, the property right prevails over the debt right evidenced by the warehouse warrant. This has been proved in *China Railway Materials Harbin Co., Ltd. v. Sinochem International Corporation.*[1745] In this case, the third party and the defendant concluded a warehousing contract for storage of a cargo carried by sea. The defendant issued a warehouse warrant to the third party. The claimant held a bill of lading for the same cargo. The claimant surrendered the bill of lading and obtained a delivery order for the cargo. The claimant demanded the delivery of the cargo from the defendant but was rejected. The claimant claimed to the court requesting the delivery of the cargo. The defendant argued that it had a duty to deliver the cargo under the warehouse warrant. A judgement from a Chinese court confirmed that the claimant had obtained the property right on the cargo. It was held that the defendant should deliver the cargo to the claimant or pay the loss of the cargo to the claimant if it could not deliver the cargo. This decision was made based on the property law. It is provided that the owner has the right to possess, use, profit from, and dispose of its immovable or movable property in accordance with law.[1746]

1397. During the warehousing term, the depository has continuing obligations on the warehoused item. First, the depository shall, at the request of the depositor or bearer of the warehouse warrant, agree to the depositor's or bearer's inspection

1741. Article 907 CC.
1742. Article 908 CC.
1743. Article 909 CC.
1744. Article 910 CC.
1745. *China Railway Materials Harbin Co., Ltd. v. Sinochem International Corporation*, The SPC (2019) Zui Gao Fa Min Shen No. 3187; 中国铁路物资哈尔滨有限公司、中化国际（控股）股份有限公司港口货物保管合同纠纷案，最高人民法院（2019）最高法民申3187号.
1746. Article 240 CC. It is identical to Art. 39 of the Property Law which was applied in the case.

of the warehoused item or extraction of samples.[1747] Second, where the depository discovers that the warehoused item stored in the warehouse is deteriorating or is otherwise damaged, it shall timely notify the depositor or bearer of the warehouse warrant.[1748] Third, where the depository discovers that the warehoused item stored in the warehouse is deteriorating or is otherwise damaged so as to endanger the safety and normal storage of other warehoused items, it shall demand that the depositor or bearer of the delivery note make the necessary disposition. The depository may make the necessary disposition in a state of emergency but shall timely notify the depositor or bearer of the delivery note of such circumstances.[1749] In the course of the storage, if the depository fails to keep the warehoused item in good custody, thereby causing its damage or loss, it shall be liable for damages. However, if the warehoused item does not conform to the contract by reason of its nature or packaging or is beyond the valid term of the storage, thereby causing its deterioration or damage, the depository is not liable for the damages.[1750]

1398. The depositor or bearer of the warehouse warrant has both the right and obligation to collect the warehoused item. First, where the parties have not agreed on the term of storage or their agreement is equivocal, the depositor or bearer of the warehouse warrant may collect the warehoused item at any time, and the depository may also request the depositor or bearer of the warehouse warrant to collect the warehoused item at any time but shall allow for necessary preparatory time.[1751] Upon expiry of the term of storage, the depositor or bearer of the warehouse warrant shall collect the warehoused item by presenting the warehouse warrant, the warehouse receipt, and so forth. Where the depositor or bearer of the warehouse warrant collects the warehoused item after the due time, additional warehouse fees shall be charged. No warehouse fees shall be deducted for early collection.[1752] If the depositor or bearer of the warehouse warrant does not collect the warehoused item upon expiry of the term of storage, the depository may demand collection within a reasonable period. If the warehoused item is not collected within the period, the depository may place the warehoused item in escrow.[1753]

1399. The Civil Code provides special rules on dangerous warehoused items. Where the warehoused item is dangerous goods, including those that are inflammable, explosive, toxic, corrosive, radioactive, et cetera, or perishable goods, the depositor shall state the nature of such items and provide the relevant information. Where the depositor contravenes the preceding paragraph, the depository may, at the depositor's expense, refuse to accept the warehoused item or take corresponding

1747. Article 911 CC.
1748. Article 912 CC.
1749. Article 913 CC.
1750. Article 917 CC.
1751. Article 914 CC.
1752. Article 915 CC.
1753. Article 916 CC.

measures to avoid the incurrence of loss. A depository that stores dangerous goods, including those that are inflammable, explosive, toxic, corrosive, radioactive, etc., shall possess the corresponding conditions for storage.[1754]

1754. Article 906 CC.

Chapter 15. Mandate Contracts

§1. General Provisions

1400. A mandate contract is a contract whereby the mandator and mandatory agree that the mandatory will handle the affairs of the mandator.[1755] The mandator may mandate the mandatory specifically to administer one or several affairs or generally to handle all its affairs.[1756] Under the Civil Code, the mandatory should properly handle the mandated affairs and report on the affairs. First, the mandatory shall handle the mandated affairs in accordance with the instructions given by the mandator. Where the instructions given by the mandator are to be altered, consent from the mandator shall be obtained. Where it is difficult to contact the mandator in an emergency, the mandatory shall handle the mandated affairs properly and report the circumstances to the mandator in a timely manner afterwards.[1757] Second, the mandatory shall, at the mandator's request, report on the state of administration of the mandated affairs. Upon termination of the mandate contract, the mandatory shall report on the results of the mandated affairs.[1758] Furthermore, property obtained by the mandatory during the administration of the mandated affairs shall be delivered to the mandator.[1759]

1401. Upon completion by the mandatory of the administration of the mandated affairs, the mandator shall pay it the remuneration in accordance with the contract. Where the mandate contract is terminated or the administration of the mandated affairs cannot be completed for reasons not attributed to the mandatory, the mandator shall pay corresponding remuneration to the mandatory. Where the parties agree otherwise, such agreement shall prevail.[1760] For the payment of the expenses for the mandated affairs, the default rule in the Civil Code is that the mandator shall pay expenses for the administration of the mandated affairs in advance. Any necessary expenses for the administration of the mandated affairs advanced by the mandatory shall be repaid together with interest by the mandator.[1761] Of course, it does not mean that the parties cannot agree otherwise on the payment of expenses.

§2. Damages

1402. Under a remunerative mandate contract, where the mandator sustains losses by reason of fault on the part of the mandatory, the mandator may claim damages. Under a gratuitous mandate contract, where the mandator sustains losses by

1755. Article 919 CC.
1756. Article 920 CC.
1757. Article 922 CC.
1758. Article 924 CC.
1759. Article 927 CC.
1760. Article 928 CC.
1761. Article 921 CC.

reason of deliberate acts or gross negligence on the part of the mandatory, the mandator may claim damages.[1762] If the mandator's loss is caused by the reason of the fault of both the mandator and the mandatory under a remunerative mandate contract or by the reasons of the fault of the mandator and deliberate acts or gross negligence of the mandatory under a gratuitous mandate contract, the mandatory shall bear the liability in proportion according to its fault or deliberate acts or gross negligence compared with the mandator's fault.[1763]

1403. The mandatory shall be liable for losses caused by its ultra vires acts in relation to the mandator.[1764] Even if the mandatory acts are within its authorisation, it may be liable to the mandator for the damage caused by its fault. In *Zhou Weijun and Zhou Weida v. Wang Xuqiong*,[1765] the mandatory sold the mandator's property within its authorisation under a mandate contract. However, the price of the sale was much lower than the actual market price of the property. The mandatory sold the property for the benefit of the buyer of the property. The mandator claimed a loss against the mandatory for the difference between the market price and the sale price. The court held that, although the sale contract was a valid contract, the sale activity was against the benefit of the mandator. The court pointed out that the mandatory should deal with the mandator's affairs in good faith, and it should be liable for the mandator's loss if the mandatory's authorised activity is against the real intention of the mandator and interests. In this case, the mandatory knew the market price of the mandator's property but deliberately sold the property at a low price. This activity caused the loss of the mandator. Therefore, the mandatory should be liable for such a loss. Meanwhile, the court found that the mandator also had fault because it did not take the necessary precautions to avoid the loss. The court held that the mandatory should reduce its liability to the mandator accordingly.

1404. The mandator may be liable for the mandatory's loss. First, where, in the course of administration of the mandated affairs, the mandatory sustains losses for reasons not attributable to itself, the mandatory may seek damages against the mandator.[1766] Second, with consent from the mandatory, the mandator may mandate another third party to handle the mandated affairs in addition to the mandatory. Where this causes loss to the mandatory, the mandatory may claim damages against

---

1762. Paragraph 1 of Art. 929 CC.

1763. *Suzhou Yangguang Xindi Real Estate Co., Ltd. Xindi Central Hotel v. Suzhou Cultural International Travel Service Co., Ltd. Xinqu Tayuanlu Business Department and Suzhou Cultural International Travel Service Co., Ltd.*, Gazette Case of the SPC, Issue 8, 2012; 苏州阳光新地置业有限公司新地中心酒店诉苏州文化国际旅行社有限公司新区塔园路营业部、苏州文化国际旅行社有限公司委托合同纠纷案，《最高人民法院公报》案例，2012年08期. In this case, the mandatory's gross negligence under a gratuitous mandate contract was the minor cause to the mandator's loss. Thus, the mandatory was liable for 20% of the loss.

1764. Paragraph 2 of Art. 929 CC.

1765. *Zhou Weijun and Zhou Weida v. Wang Xuqiong*, Gazette Case of the SPC, Issue 3, 2018; 周伟均、周伟达诉王煦琼委托合同纠纷案，《最高人民法院公报》案例，2018年03期. In this case, the relevant law is Art. 406 of the Contract Law, which is identical to Art. 929 CC.

1766. Article 930 CC.

the mandator.[1767] Meanwhile, where two or more mandatories jointly handle the mandated affairs, they are liable to the mandator jointly and severally.[1768]

§3. Mandate Contracts with Third Parties

1405. The Civil Code provides rules for mandate contracts with third parties. The first rule regulates the performance of the mandated matters by third parties. In principle, the mandatory shall handle the mandated affairs personally. With the mandator's consent, the mandatory may delegate the mandate. Where the delegation is consented to or ratified by the mandator, the mandator may instruct the delegated third party directly, and the mandatory is liable only for the appointment of the third party and the instructions that it gives to the third party. Where the delegation is not consented to or ratified, the mandatory shall be liable for the conduct of the delegated third party, except where the delegation is necessary for the protection of the interests of the mandator in an emergency.[1769]

1406. The second rule regulates the relationship between the mandator and the third party when the mandatory, using its own name, enters into a contract with the third party. Where the mandatory enters into a contract in its own name with a third party within the scope of authorisation of the mandator, and the third party is aware of the agency relationship between the mandatory and mandator at the time of the contract, the contract binds the mandator and the third party directly, unless it is shown that the contract binds only the mandatory and the third party.[1770] This rule applies to the agency of an unnamed principal only and does not apply to the agency of a named principal.[1771]

1407. In *Beijing Changfu Investment Fund v. Wuhan Zhongsenhua Century Real Estate Development Co., Ltd. and Others*,[1772] the mandator, the mandatory (a bank), and the third parties entered into a mandate loan contract under which the mandator provided fund, and the mandatory handled the matter of the loan to the third party. The contract provided that the mandatory shall, under written demand of the mandator, claim with the mandator's name against the third party, its guarantor, and relevant persons if the third party fails to repay the fund and interests thereof. The third party failed to repay the loan, and the bank claimed against the third party. It was

1767. Article 931 CC.
1768. Article 932 CC.
1769. Article 923 CC.
1770. Article 925 CC.
1771. *Hubei Jinhua Industry Co., Ltd. v. Su Jinshui and Others*, The SPC (2012) Min Kang Zi Di No. 24 (Gazette Case of the SPC, Issue 1, 2014); 湖北金华实业有限公司与苏金水等商品房买卖合同纠纷案， 最高人民法院（2012）民抗字第24号（《最高人民法院公报》案例，2014年01期）.
1772. *Beijing Changfu Investment Fund v. Wuhan Zhongsenhua Century Real Estate Development Co., Ltd. and Others*, The SPC (2016) Zui Gao Fa Min Zhong No. 124 (Gazette Case of the SPC, Issue 11, 2016); 北京长富投资基金与武汉中森华世纪房地产开发有限公司等委托贷款合同纠纷案， 最高人民法院（2016）最高法民终124号（《最高人民法院公报》案例，2016年11期）.

found by the courts that the third party was aware of the agency relationship between the bank and the mandator when they entered into the contract among them. Therefore, the contract should bind the relationship between the mandator and the third party.

1408. The purpose of identifying the relationship is to determine the nature of the loan contract. If it is a contract between the bank and the third party, it is a financial loan contract. If it is a contract between the mandator and the third party, it is a private loan contract, and the rules for private loan contracts shall apply. Although the contract in this case was a private loan contract between the mandator and the third party, the bank raised the claim because the bank was entitled to do so according to the contract. This entitlement is also the bank's obligation under the mandate contract. It was held that it did not imply that the contract should bind the relationship between the bank and the third party.

1409. The relationships among the mandator, the mandatory, and the third party are complicated when the mandate contract is concluded for matters more than the agency relationship. Whether a contract between the mandatory and the third party binds the mandator in a mandate contract will be decided based on the facts of those contracts. This complex can be found in *Xiamen Aviation Development Co., Ltd. v. Beijing Nangang Jinyi Trading Co., Ltd. and Xiamen Dongfanglong Metallic Materials Co., Ltd.*.[1773] In this case, under a contract for mandate, sale, loan and guaranty matters, the mandatory agreed to handle the matter of the mandator for the purchase of a steel cargo from a third party. Within the scope of authorisation of the mandator, the mandatory entered into a sale contract with the third party. It was agreed in the sale contract that the cargo was to be delivered in the warehouse of the third party, and the ownership of the cargo belongs to the mandatory after payment. The third party was aware of the agency relationship between the mandatory and mandator at the time of the sale contract. In the mandate contract, it was agreed that the mandator should obtain the cargo after payment, and the ownership of the cargo belongs to the mandatory before the mandate takes delivery of the cargo. This agreement was known to the third party. The mandatory paid the price of the cargo to the third party. However, the third party delivered the cargo before the mandator paid the price of the cargo to the mandatory. The mandator did not pay the price of the cargo to the mandatory.

1410. In this case, the mandatory claimed against the third party and the mandator for payment of the price of the cargo. Since the third party knew the agency relationship between the mandatory and mandator at the time of the sale contract, it seems that the sale contract should bind the mandator and the third party directly, and the mandatory had no direct right of claim against the third party. However, the

1773. *Xiamen Aviation Development Co., Ltd. v. Beijing Nangang Jinyi Trading Co., Ltd. and Xiamen Dongfanglong Metallic Materials Co., Ltd.*, The SPC (2014) Min Shen Zi Di No. 2225 (Gazette Case of the SPC, Issue 1, 2017); 厦门航空开发股份有限公司与北京南钢金易贸易有限公司及第三人厦门市东方龙金属材料有限公司买卖合同纠纷案，最高人民法院（2014）民申字第2225号（《最高人民法院公报》案例，2017年01期）.

SPC did not accept this presumption of the binding effect between the mandator and the third party. There are two reasons for this decision. First, the mandate contract in dispute was not a contract for a pure agency relationship; it also covered matters of sale, loan and guaranty. The presumption of binding effect between the mandator and the third party shall apply to the pure agency relationship under a mandate contract, but not the mandate contract with other relationships. Second, the agreement of ownership in the sale contract and the fact that the mandatory paid the price as a loan to the mandator are evidence of the proviso to the presumption of the binding effect between the mandator and the third party. Therefore, if the mandatory who has paid the price was excluded from the sale contract that bound the mandator and the third party only, the mandatory's rights will be prejudiced. The SPC emphasised that it would be against the purpose of the law in this circumstance. Therefore, the sale contract should bind the mandatory and the third party only. It was found that the third party breached the sale contract by delivering the cargo, which belonged to the mandatory, and the mandator accepted the cargo without paying the price. It was held that the third party should pay the price of the cargo to the mandatory. After payment, the third party may raise recourse action against the mandator.

1411. The third rule regulates the exercise of rights against the wrongful party among the mandator, the mandatory, and the third party. On the one hand, the mandator has the right to intervene in the contract with the third party. Where a third party is not aware of the mandatory relationship between the mandatory and mandator at the time when the mandatory enters into a contract in its own name with the third party, and the mandatory fails to perform its obligations to the mandator for reasons attributable to the third party, the mandatory shall disclose the third party to the mandator, who may thus exercise the mandatory's rights against the third party, except where the third party would not have entered into the contract had it been aware of the mandator at the time of contract.[1774]

1412. In Chinese judicial practice, even if the third party is not aware of the mandatory relationship between the mandator and the mandatory when the contract is concluded, if the mandator and the third party know each other's identity after the conclusion of the contract, the mandator can claim directly against the third party without the mandatory disclosing the third party to the mandator if the third party fails to perform its contractual obligations.[1775] This implies that the mandator has the right to intervene the contract with the third party, no matter whether the third party is aware of the mandatory relationship or not at the time when the mandatory enters into a contract in its own name with the third party. This judicial practice does not strictly follow the rule of the Civil Code in this circumstance. However, it does not substantially change the application of the rule because the

1774. Paragraph 1 of Art. 926 CC.

1775. *Li Zunji v. Peng Chao and Others*, Beijing Third Intermediate People's Court (2023) Jing 03 Min Zai No. 57; 李遵基与彭超等民间借贷纠纷案，北京市第三中级人民法院（2023）京03民再57号.

awareness of the third party matters only to the exception of the rule, namely the third party would not have entered into the contract had it been aware of the mandator when the contract is concluded.

1413. If the mandator chooses to exercise the mandatory's rights against the third party, the contract shall bind the relationship between the mandator and the third party. If the mandator chooses not to exercise such right, the contract shall bind the relationship between the mandatory and the third party only according to the principle of privity of contract. In the latter circumstance, the mandatory can claim directly against the third party, and any dispute between the mandatory and the mandator shall be solved separately.[1776] Furthermore, where the mandator exercises the mandatory's rights against the third party, the third party may raise defences available against the mandatory. Where the third party elects the mandator as the opposite party, the mandator may raise defences available to itself against the mandatory and defences available to the mandatory against the third party.[1777]

1414. On the other hand, where the mandatory fails to perform its obligations to the third party for reasons attributable to the mandator, the mandatory shall disclose the mandator to the third party, who may thus elect to assert its rights against either the mandator or the mandatory but shall not change its election of the opposite party.[1778] The election of the opposite party is the third party's option, not a compulsory choice. In other words, the third party does not have to choose both the mandator and the mandatory as the opposite party. In *Fengning Changge Mining Cot Ltd v. China Railway Beijing Group Co., Ltd.*,[1779] after disclosing the agency relationship between the mandatory and mandator, the third party chose to claim against the mandatory for breach of a contract between them. The mandatory applied to the court of first instance for adding the mandator as the opposite party in the litigation. However, the third party refused to add the mandator as the opposite party in the claim. The mandatory argued that it was not a proper defendant in the dispute. This argument was rejected by the court of first instance. The mandatory appealed to the SPC, but the appeal was rejected. The SPC upheld the decision of the first instance and held that the mandatory was the proper defendant and should be liable for its breach of contract.

1776. *Shanghai Minlurun Tarde Co., Ltd. v. Shanghai Gangyi International Trade Co., Ltd.*, The SPC (2015) Min Shen Zi Di No. 956 (Gazette Case of the SPC, Issue 1, 2016); 上海闽路润贸易有限公司与上海钢翼贸易有限公司买卖合同纠纷案，最高人民法院（2015）民申字第956号（《最高人民法院公报》案例，2016年01期）. In this case, the relevant law is article 403, paragraph 1 of the Contract Law, which is identical to para. 1 of Art. 926 CC.

1777. Paragraph 3 of Art 926 CC.

1778. Paragraph 2 of Art. 926 CC.

1779. *Fengning Changge Mining Cot Ltd v. China Railway Beijing Group Co., Ltd.*, The SPC (2017) Zui Gao Fa Min Zhong No. 724 (Gazette Case of the SPC, Issue 9, 2019); 丰宁长阁矿业有限公司与北京铁路局物权保护纠纷案，最高人民法院（2017）最高法民终724 号（《最高人民法院公报》案例，2019年09期）. In this case, the relevant law is para. 2 of Art. 403 of the Contract Law, which is identical to para. 2 of Art. 926 CC.

§4. TERMINATION OF CONTRACT

1415. The mandator or mandatory may terminate the mandate contract at any time. Where termination leads to loss to the other party, unless for reasons not attributable to the terminating party, the terminating party under a gratuitous mandate contract shall be liable for direct losses caused by the inappropriately timed termination, and the terminating party under a remunerative mandate contract shall be liable for direct losses sustained and benefits to be obtained by the other party if the contract were performed.[1780] This is different from the old rule of loss after termination of contract in the Contract Law. It was provided by the Contract Law that the mandator or mandatory may terminate the mandate contract at any time. If the termination of the contract by either party causes losses to the other party, the former shall compensate for the losses except for reasons not attributable thereto.[1781] The Contract Law's rule of loss after termination of the mandate contract is not clear enough for the scope or contents of the loss.

1416. Under the Contract Law, for the loss if the contract is terminated, the Chinese courts interpreted them as actual loss, excluding potential benefits from performing the contract. In *Shanghai Hongzheng Law Firm v. Marine Design and Research Institute of China*,[1782] the mandator terminated a legal service contract with a law firm, the mandatory. The mandatory claimed against the mandator for the loss of the agreed attorney fee. The Chinese courts held that the mandatory has no legal basis to claim the agreed attorney fee, but the actual loss caused by the termination of the mandate contract. Furthermore, the loss caused by the termination of the mandate contract is limited to the actual loss and does not extend to the expected benefit if there is termination. In *Shanghai Panqi Trade Co., Ltd. v. Panqi Industry (Dalian) Co., Ltd.*,[1783] the mandatory agreed to develop the network for sales of the mandator under a mandate contract. The mandator terminated the contract, and the mandatory claimed against the mandator for the loss of the cost for performing the mandate contract and the expected profit from performing the contract. The court of first instance held that the mandatory was entitled to claim the loss of the cost but denied the claim for the loss of profit. It was pointed out that the civil liability for the termination of a contract is different from the liability for a breach of contract. The mandator has the right to terminate the contract, and the mandatory has the right to claim the actual loss excluding the expected benefit.[1784]

1780. Article 933 CC.
1781. Article 410 of the Contract Law.
1782. *Shanghai Hongzheng Law Firm v. Marine Design and Research Institute of China*, Gazette Case of the SPC, Issue 12, 2009; 上海市弘正律师事务所诉中国船舶及海洋工程设计研究院服务合同纠纷案，《最高人民法院公报》案例，2009年12期.
1783. *Shanghai Panqi Trade Co., Ltd. v. Panqi Industry (Dalian) Co., Ltd.*, The SPC (2005) Min Er Zhong Zi No. 143 (Gazette Case of the SPC, Issue 4, 200); 上海盘起贸易有限公司与盘起工业（大连）有限公司委托合同纠纷案， 最高人民法院 （2005） 民二终字第143号（《最高人民法院公报》案例，2006年04期）.
1784. Liaoning High People's Court (2003) Liao Min San He Chu Zi No. 34; 辽宁省高级人民法院（2003）辽民三合初字第34号.

The SPC upheld the decision and clarified that the loss due to the termination of the mandate contract should not be interpreted in a wider way.

1417. These cases were determined based on the Contract Law. They are meaningful for the Interpretation on loss if the mandate contract is terminated. They can still be considered under the Civil Code for assessment of the direct loss of one party if the mandate contract is terminated by the other party. These cases, however, cannot be considered for all loss because the benefit to be obtained can also be claimed as additional loss after the termination of the mandate contract. It is understood that the rule of loss for the mandate contract under the Civil Code is to clarify that the direct loss does not include the benefit to be obtained where the mandate contract is terminated.[1785] Furthermore, it is also pointed out that the agreement of parties regarding the calculation of damage or loss after termination of the mandate contract should be recognised as a valid agreement because of the complexity of the calculation of damage or loss.[1786] In other words, the agreement of a liquidated damage is allowed for assessment of loss after termination of a mandate contract. It is also pointed out that if the parties agree to waive the right to terminate the mandate contract, the agreement of waiver should be recognised as a valid agreement.[1787] In *Sichuan Nanbu Jinli Real Estate Development Co., Ltd. v. Chengdu Hexin Zhiyuan Real Estate Consulting Co., Ltd.*,[1788] the SPC recognised the validity of the waiver clause and held that the mandator who terminated the contract breached the waiver clause and should be liable for the breach.

1418. In fact, the loss after termination of the mandate contract can also be assessed by the general rule of loss in the Civil Code. It provides that, where a party fails to perform its obligations under the contract or its performance fails to satisfy the agreement, thereby causing loss to the other party, the amount of compensation for losses shall be equal to the loss caused by the breach of contract, including the benefit receivable after the performance of the contract, provided that it does not exceed the probable losses caused by the breach that are foreseen or ought to be foreseen when the party in breach concludes the contract.[1789] The termination of a mandate contract can be understood as a circumstance in which a party fails to perform its obligation under the contract. The loss in the general rule includes the direct loss or actual loss and the benefit to be obtained, like the special rule of loss in the chapter of the mandate contract. Although these rules can be interpreted in the same way for compensation of loss, the special rule shall apply to the loss after termination of the mandate contract.

1785. Jianghong Zhou, Direct loss under Arbitrary Termination of the Entrustment Contract, 3 Zhejiang Academic Journal (Zhe Jiang Xue Kan) 230, 238 (2023).
1786. Weiheng Zhong, Research on the Legal Application of the Right to Terminate Non-gratuitous Entrustment Contracts, 17 Journal of Law Application (Fa Lv Shi Yong) 22 (2022).
1787. *Ibid*, 25.
1788. *Sichuan Nanbu Jinli Real Estate Development Co., Ltd. v. Chengdu Hexin Zhiyuan Real Estate Consulting Co., Ltd.*, The SPC (2015) Min Yi Zhong Zi Di No. 226; 四川南部县金利房地产开发有限公司与成都和信致远地产顾问有限责任公司商品房销售代理合同纠纷案，最高人民法院（2015）民一终字第226号.
1789. Article 584 CC.

1419. A mandate contract terminates on the mandator's or mandatory's death or loss or termination of the civil capacity to act, unless otherwise agreed by the parties or where the mandated affairs are by their nature unsuitable for termination.[1790] Furthermore, where termination of the mandate contract by reason of the mandator's death or loss or termination of the civil capacity to act would adversely affect its interests, the mandatory shall continue to handle the mandated affairs until they are taken over by the heir, estate administrator, statutory agent or liquidator of the mandator.[1791] Last, where the mandate contract is terminated by reason of the mandatory's death or loss or termination of the civil capacity to act, the heir, estate administrator, statutory agent or liquidator of the mandatory shall inform the mandator timely. Where the termination of the mandate contract would adversely affect the interests of the mandator, the heir, estate administrator, statutory agent or liquidator of the mandatory shall take all necessary measures before the mandator handles the aftermath of the event.[1792]

1790. Article 934 CC.
1791. Article 935 CC.
1792. Article 936 CC.

Chapter 16. Property Service Contracts

§1. General Provisions

1420. The property service contract was not regulated by the Contract Law. It is regulated by the Civil Code for the first time. A property services contract is a contract whereby the property service provider, within the service area, provides property services to the owners, including repair and maintenance of the building and its ancillary facilities, maintenance and management of the environment, hygiene and the community order, and the owners pay service fees. Property service providers include property service enterprises and other property managers.[1793] The content of a property services contract generally includes terms as to the content and quality of the services, rates and means of payment of service fees, use of the maintenance funds, management and use of service premises, term of services, handover of services, and so forth. Service promises made publicly by the service provider, which are beneficial to the owners, shall form part of the contract for property services. Property services contracts shall be made in writing.[1794]

1421. A property service contract relationship could be established by activities. In *Zhongshan A Property Management Co., Ltd. v. Fang*,[1795] although the commercial building involved in the case was not within the scope of property service management stipulated in the property service contract, and the owner of the commercial building involved was not the counterparty to the property service contract, the property service provider had performed basic maintenance, management, cleaning, and safety guarantees for the commercial building, and the owner of the commercial building had not raised any objection for a long time. It was held that the two parties had formed a de facto property service contract relationship, and the owner of the commercial building should pay the service fee to the property service provider.

1422. A property service contract may be concluded between a service provider and the developer. A property service contract may also be concluded between a service provider and a representative on behalf of owners, e.g., the owners' committee. This is common for owners living in the properties in the same building or the same area and using the services from the same service provider. Under the Civil Code, a preliminary property service contract lawfully made between the developer and the service provider and a contract for property services made between the owners' committee and a service provider lawfully appointed by the owners' general meeting bind the owners.[1796] In addition, if the owners' committee cannot be elected due to objective reasons before the new owners' committee is formed, the residents'

1793. Article 937 CC.
1794. Article 938 CC.
1795. *Zhongshan A Property Management Co., Ltd. v. Fang*, Zhongshan Intermediate People's Court (2022) Yue 20 Min Zhong No. 849; 中山市某物业管理有限公司诉方某某物业服务合同纠纷案，广东省中山市中级人民法院（2022）粤20民终849号.
1796. Article 939 CC.

committee where the property is located can, under the guidance and supervision of the government, take over the responsibilities of the owners' committee and sign the property service contract on behalf of the owners in the community. Such property service contract has a binding effect on all the owners.[1797]

1423. This binding effect of the preliminary property service contract cannot be excluded by agreement in the property sale contract between the individual buyer/owner and the developer. If an individual owner and the developer agree in the sale contract to exclude the preliminary property service contract, it will have no effect on the property service provider, and the owner shall still be bound by the preliminary property service contract.[1798] On the other hand, compared with the property service contract signed by the owners committee and the property service provider selected by the owners meeting in accordance with the law, the preliminary property service contract has differences in terms of contract signing parties, competitiveness and openness of price negotiations, social public awareness, owner acceptance, contract termination, etc., and neither individual owners nor owner committees have the opportunity to participate in the early negotiation of property service contracts. In this circumstance, it is possible that the service price in the preliminary property service contract may lead to an imbalance of interests between the service provider and owners. If there is a dispute regarding the service price in the preliminary property service contract, the court may adjust it, and the calculation of it should be based on the standard price in the preliminary property contract and the actual situation of the disputes.[1799]

1424. Where, before the term of a preliminary contract for property services lawfully made between the developer and the service provider expires, a property services contract made by the owners' committee or owners with a new service provider takes effect, the preliminary contract for property services terminates.[1800] Where an owners' committee is responsible for the services to the properties of its owners, the owners' committee may conclude property service contracts with its owners. The owners' committee may conclude another property service contract with a service provider for the actual services to the owners. In this circumstance, the owners shall pay a service fee to the owner's committee under the property service contract between the owner's committee and the owners.[1801]

1797. *Kaiping A Property Management Co., Ltd. v. Chen B and Wu C*, Jiangmen Intermediate People's Court (2022) Yue 07 Min Zhong No. 3418; 开平某物业分公司诉陈某权、吴某桃物业服务合同纠纷案，江门市中级人民法院（2022）粤07民终3418号.

1798. A *Property Management Co., Ltd. v. B Bank Qingdao Branch and C Business Co., Ltd.*, The SPC (2022) Zui Gao Fa Min Zai No. 223; 某物业公司诉某银行青岛分行、某商业公司物业服务合同纠纷案，最高人民法院（2022）最高法民再223号.

1799. *Ibid.*

1800. Article 940 CC.

1801. *A Community Owners Committee v. Deng*, (2017) 2 China Law Report, People's Court Press (2017), pp. 63-64; 某小区业主委员会诉邓某某物业服务合同纠纷案，《人民法院案例选》2017年2辑，人民法院出版社，2017年版，第63-64页.

§2. PERFORMANCE OF CONTRACT

1425. The service provider shall, in accordance with the contract and the property's nature, properly repair, maintain, clean, landscape and manage the common parts of the service area, maintain basic order within the service area, and take reasonable measures to protect the personal and property safety of the owners. The service provider shall, in relation to acts within the service area that contravene the laws on security and the environment, take timely and reasonable measures to stop such acts and report to the relevant administrative authorities and provide assistance.[1802]

1426. If an owner requires assistance from a service provider, the service provider may provide assistance in service, provided that such assistance could balance the interests of the owner and other owners. In *Fan v. Chongqing Ganghua Property Management Co., Ltd.*,[1803] the claimant owner requested the property service provider to issue a certificate for proving the installation of a charging pile in a closed parking space, but the request was rejected by the service provider for the reason of public security. The owner applied to the Chinese court for requesting the property service provider to issue the certificate. The property service contract in the dispute provides that the matters not specified in the contract shall be decided according to law and regulations. The court found that both the regulations and local rules required the property service provider to provide assistance to its owners to install the charging piles. It was held that the property service provider should issue the certificate according to the regulations and local rules. After the owner installs the charging pile, if the property service company discovers that there is a safety hazard in the charging facility, it can promptly exercise its property management power to correct it or stop it. Relevant stakeholders should also cooperate with the supervision of the property service company.[1804] In *Chen v. Zhuhai A Property Management Co., Ltd.*,[1805] the court pointed out that the owners' rights based on the exclusive parts will inevitably have the practical need to use the common parts. This demand should be a reasonable extension of the owner's exercise of exclusive rights in order to better utilise the exclusive part. This extension should be deemed as fair use if it does not violate the provisions of laws, regulations, and management regulations or affect the common interests of other owners in the community.

1802. Article 942 CC.

1803. *Fan v. Chongqing Ganghua Property Management Co., Ltd.*, 2 China Law Report 113-121 (People's Court Press 2021); 范某某诉重庆港华物业管理有限公司物业服务合同纠纷案,《人民法院案例选》2021年2辑，人民法院出版社2021年版，第113-121页.

1804. *Nie Qin v. Country Garden Life Services Group Co., Ltd. Dongguan Branch and Others*, Dongguan Intermediate People's Court (2021) Yue 19 Min Zhong No. 12866; 聂琴、碧桂园生活服务集团股份有限公司东莞分公司等物业服务合同纠纷案，广东省东莞市中级人民法院（2021）粤19民终12866号.

1805. *Chen v. Zhuhai A Property Management Co., Ltd.*, Zhuhai Xiangzhou District People's Court (2022) Yue 0402 Min Chu No. 1029; 陈某某诉珠海某物业公司物业服务合同纠纷案，珠海市香洲区人民法院（2022）粤0402民初1029号.

1427. On the other hand, the property service providers can reject such requests if it is not feasible to install charging piles for owners. In *Lin v. Hangzhou Heyi Property Management Co., Ltd.*,[1806] the owner requested assistance from the property service provider for installing a charging pile. The Chinese court rejected the owner claim because the community for installing the charging pile was an old community, and its power supply system could not afford the power demand for the charging pile. Installing the charging pile would inevitably involve a change of the community's power system and reallocation of public resources of the community. The owner's request could not be supported without permission of the owners' general meeting.

1428. The service provider shall regularly and in a reasonable fashion make public to the owners and report to the owners' general meeting or committee information about the content of services, responsible personnel, quality requirements, charged items, standards for fees, state of performance, the use of maintenance funds, and the business and financial status of the common parts, et cetera.[1807] The service provider may mandate certain specific services within the service area to a professional service organisation or any other third party. In this circumstance, the service provider shall be responsible to the owners for such specific services. However, the service provider shall not delegate to a third party the entirety of the property services that it shall provide or delegate separately to third parties parts divided from the entirety of its property services.[1808]

1429. For the service, the owners shall pay the service fees to the service provider in accordance with the contract. Where the service provider has provided services in accordance with the contract and the relevant regulations, the owners shall not refuse to pay the service fees on the ground that they have not accepted or do not need such services. Where the owners fail to pay the service fees by the agreed time, the service provider may demand payment within a reasonable period of time, and where the owners fail to pay upon expiry of that period, the service provider may institute court proceedings or apply for arbitration. However, the property service provider shall not adopt the methods such as cutting off the supply of power, water, heat or gas to urge the payment of service fee.[1809] For major decoration or renovation to their property, the owners shall inform the service provider in advance, comply with reasonable cautionary matters advised by the service provider, and cooperate with it in necessary site inspection. Where the owners transfer or lease individually owned areas in the property, create a habitation right, or lawfully alter the use of the common parts, they shall timely inform the service provider of such.[1810]

1806. *Lin v. Hangzhou Heyi Property Management Co., Ltd.*, Hangzhou Intermediate People's Court (2019) Zhe 01 Min Zhong No. 877; 林某某与杭州和亿物业管理有限公司物业服务合同纠纷案，杭州市中级人民法院（2019）浙01民终877号.
1807. Article 943 CC.
1808. Article 941 CC.
1809. Article 944 CC.
1810. Article 945 CC.

§3. TERMINATION OF CONTRACT

1430. Where the owners, through statutory procedures, jointly resolve to dismiss the service provider, the contract for property services may be terminated. Where a resolution to dismiss is made, the service provider shall be notified in writing sixty days in advance, unless the period for notification has been otherwise provided for in the contract. For this termination, unless for reasons not attributable to the owners, the owners shall be liable for damages to the service provider.[1811] The Civil Code does not specify the legal consequence if the service provider is not notified in writing sixty days in advance. It is believed that the contract is not so terminated unless the period for notification has been otherwise provided for in the contract.

1431. Prior to the expiry of the term of property services, where the owners jointly and lawfully resolve to renew the appointment, they shall renew the contract for property services with the property provider before the original contract expires. Where, prior to the expiry of the term of property services, the service provider refuses to renew the appointment, it shall notify the owners or the owners' committee in writing ninety days before the expiry of the contract, unless the period for notification has been otherwise provided in the contract.[1812] It seems to imply that the service provider agrees to renew the appointment if it does not notify the owners or the owners' committee in writing ninety days before the expiry of the contract, unless the period for notification has been otherwise provided in the contract.

1432. Where, on the expiry of the term of property services, the owners do not resolve lawfully to renew the appointment or to appoint another service provider, and the service provider continues to provide property services, the original contract for property services remains effective for an indefinite term. A party may at any time terminate a contract for property services for an indefinite term, provided that a written notice is served on the other party sixty days in advance.[1813] It means that the indefinite term contract should remain effective at least sixty days from the date of a written notice of termination.

1433. Upon termination of the contract for property services, the original service provider shall withdraw from the service area by the agreed time or within a reasonable period of time, return the relevant materials required by the maintenance of the property service premises, ancillary facilities, and property services to the owners' committee, the owners who have resolved to manage by themselves or their specified persons, assist the new service provider in the handover, and truthfully inform the new service provider about the state of use and management of the property. Where the original service provider fails to perform those obligations, it shall not claim payment of service fees from the owners accruing after termination of the contract for property services and shall be liable for any loss caused to the owners

1811. Article 946 CC.
1812. Article 947 CC.
1813. Article 948 CC.

by breach of those obligations.[1814] However, after a contract for property services is terminated, and before the new service provider or owners who have resolved to manage by themselves take over, the original service provider shall continue to deal with property service matters and may demand the payment from the owners of service fees for that period.[1815]

1814. Article 949 CC.
1815. Article 950 CC.

Chapter 17. Contracts of Commission Agency

1434. A contract of commission agency is a contract whereby the commission agent conducts trading activities in its own name for the principal, and the principal pays remuneration.[1816] For example, an auction company may have a contract of commission agency with its client. The auction company conducts auction activities in its own name for its client, and the client pays remuneration. Where the commission agent enters into a contract with a third party, the commission agent directly enjoys rights and assumes obligations under the contract. Where the third party's non-performance of obligations causes losses to the principal, the commission agent shall be liable in damages, unless otherwise agreed by the commissioning party and the principal.[1817] Upon full or partial completion of the commissioned affairs by the commission agent, the principal shall pay the corresponding remuneration to the commission agent. Where the principal fails to pay the remuneration by the due time, the commission agent is entitled to a lien over the commissioned item, unless otherwise agreed by the parties.[1818]

1435. The commission agency contract is a special type of mandate contract. Therefore, for matters not provided for by this Chapter, the relevant provisions on mandate contracts shall be referred to and applied.[1819] There are three main differences between the contract of commission agency and the mandate contract. First, the commission agent conducts trading activities in its own name, whereas the mandatory may conclude contracts with other parties in its own name or the principal's name. Second, the contract of commission agency is remunerative, whereas the mandate contract may be remunerative or gratuitous. Third, the expenses incurred by the commission agent in the course of handling the commissioned affairs shall be borne by the commission agent, unless otherwise agreed by the parties,[1820] whereas the mandatory's cost will be borne by the mandator under the mandate contract. Because of those differences, the relevant provisions on mandate contracts shall be referred to and applied to the commission agency contract for matters not provided for by this chapter. This is different from the application rule under the Chinese Contract in which it was provided that the relevant provisions on mandate contracts shall be applied to the commission agency contract for matters not provided for by the chapter of the commission agency contract.[1821] The Contract Law did not recognise the differences between the commission agency contract and the mandate contract. The Civil Code has rectified this legislative error.

1436. Where the commission agent possesses the commissioned item, it shall keep the commissioned property in good custody.[1822] Furthermore, where the commissioned item is defective, susceptible to deterioration, or perishable at the time of

1816. Article 951 CC.
1817. Article 958 CC.
1818. Article 959 CC.
1819. Article 960 CC.
1820. Article 952 CC.
1821. Article 423 of the Contract Law.
1822. Article 953 CC.

delivery to the commission agent, the commission agent may, with consent from the principal, dispose of the item. Where a timely contact cannot be made with the principal, the commission agent may dispose of it reasonably.[1823] Where the commission agent sells at a price lower than the price specified by the principal or purchases at a price higher than the price specified by the principal, the consent of the principal shall be obtained. If the consent of the principal has not been obtained, but the commission agent compensates for the difference in price, the transaction is effective to the principal. Where the commission agent conducts a sale at a price higher than the price specified by the principal or purchases at a price lower than the price specified by the principal, the commission agent may, in accordance with the contract, increase its remuneration. Where there is no agreement or the agreement is equivocal, and it cannot be ascertained under Article 510 of the Civil Code, the benefits shall vest in the principal. Where the principal gave specific instructions on the price, the commission agent shall not sell or purchase in breach of such instructions.[1824]

1437. Where the commission agent sells or purchases commodities with a market price, unless otherwise indicated by the principal, the commission agent may itself act as the buyer or seller. In this circumstance, the commission agency is still entitled to remuneration.[1825] Where the commission agent purchases the commissioned item in accordance with the contract, the principal shall take timely delivery of it. Where the principal refuses to take delivery of it without justification upon demand by the commission agent, the commission agent may lawfully place the commissioned item in escrow. Where the commissioned item cannot be sold or the principal withdraws it from sale, and the principal fails to retrieve or dispose of the item upon demand by the commission agent, the commission agent may lawfully place the commissioned item in escrow.[1826]

1823. Article 954 CC.
1824. Article 955 CC.
1825. Article 956 CC.
1826. Article 957 CC.

Chapter 18. Intermediary Contracts

§1. General Provisions

1438. An intermediary contract is a contract whereby the intermediary informs the principal of the opportunity to conclude a contract or acts as an intermediary for the conclusion of a contract, and the principal pays remuneration.[1827] This is the same definition of the intermediary contract under the Contract Law.[1828] However, the Civil Code provides two new rules for intermediary contracts in terms of payment of remuneration and expenses and the application of the mandate contract rules to the intermediary contract.[1829]

1439. An intermediary contract may not be named with a different title, e.g., a service contract. It is the contents, not the title of a contract that decide the nature of the contract. In *EV Capital Private Limited and Others v. Joyou Group Building Materials Co., Ltd.*,[1830] parties in dispute concluded a financing agreement in which party B agreed to introduce investors to Party A. It was agreed that Party B provides comprehensive financing consulting services to Party A in accordance with the terms of the agreement. The scope of service includes: (a) assisting Party A in preparing business plans and financing summaries; (b) assisting Party A in packaging business, highlighting Party A's advantages; (c) assist Party A to standardise and improve relevant legal matters; (d) assist Party A to standardise and improve relevant financial matters, including historical financial records; (e) assist Party A to prepare for Financial and cash flow forecasts in 2009 and 2010; (f) assist Party A in preparing for legal and financial documents, coordinate and respond to investor due diligence; (g) introduce potential investors; (h) assist Party A in negotiating investment terms; and (i) assist Party A to maintain relationships with investors. One of the questions in dispute is the nature of the agreement, i.e., whether it is an intermediary contract or a service contract. The court pointed out that the nature of the agreement in dispute should be determined according to the real intention of the parties. In this case, it was found that the real intention of Party A is to have investors, and Party B is to find the investors for Party A. The scope of the service does not change the intention of the parties. In the view of the court, the intermediary contract is a kind of service contract. Since the intermediary contract is a typical contract in Chinese law, it is reasonable to decide the agreement in dispute as an intermediary contract.[1831]

1827. Article 961 CC.
1828. Article 424 of the Contract Law.
1829. Articles 964, 965 and 966 CC.
1830. *EV Capital Private Limited and Others v. Joyou Group Building Materials Co., Ltd.*, The SPC (2014) Min Si Zhong Zi No. 14; 万嘉融资咨询私人有限公司等诉中宇建材集团有限公司中介合同纠纷案，最高人民法院（2014）民四终字第14号.
1831. In this case, the definition of the intermediary contract under the Contract Law was applied. It is the same as the definition in the CC.

§2. Intermediary's Report Obligation

1440. Under the Civil Code, an intermediary shall truthfully inform the principal of matters relating to the conclusion of the contract. Where the intermediary deliberately conceals material facts relating to the conclusion of the contract or provides false information, thereby damaging the interests of the principal, it shall have no claim for remuneration and shall be liable in damages.[1832] Parties in an intermediary contract may agree that the intermediary takes no responsibility for the advice or work it provides to its principal. In this circumstance, the intermediary can provide the relevant suggestions based on their own subjective understanding. If there is no fraud or malicious collusion, the suggestions should not be regarded as the basis for the principal to make independent business judgments. The intermediary is not responsible for the suggestions. The agreement is consistent with the nature of an intermediary contract. Since the intermediary's obligation to report truthfully is its main obligation, the agreement that it is not responsible for the advice or work should be interpreted as not being responsible for the transaction results for which the intermediary service is provided based on the purpose of the intermediary contract, transaction practice, and the principle of good faith. However, it is inappropriate to conclude that the intermediary is not responsible for fulfilling the obligation to truthfully report.[1833]

1441. It is understood that this obligation is a negative obligation of the intermediary. It was believed that the intermediary has no positive obligation to search and investigate the counterparties or trading partners. Rather, the intermediary has only a negative obligation to truthfully inform the matters relating to the conclusion of the contract under the Civil Code.[1834] However, this understanding is inconsistent with the Chinese judicial practice. Chinese courts have applied the positive obligation to the intermediary in the performance of the contract. In *Li Yandong v. Shanghai Hanyu Real Estate Consulting Co., Ltd.*,[1835] the intermediary and the principal concluded an intermediary contract for the purchase of a property. It was found that the date of birth of the seller of the property on a forged notarial certificate was different from that of the seller's identity card. The court pointed out that this difference could be easily identified without professional knowledge. However, the intermediary did not take any action to verify the notarial certificate. The principal paid money but did not obtain the property because of the fraud. In the view of the court, the intermediary, as a professional in intermediary business, should exercise due diligence to protect the principal's interests by investigating the real situation of

1832. Article 962 CC.
1833. *A Company v. Shanxi B Company*, The SPC (2019) Zui Gao Fa Min Zhong No. 402; 某公司诉山西某公司中介合同纠纷案，最高人民法院（2019）最高法民终402号.
1834. Jianghong Zhou, Several Suggestions for Modifications to the Contract Part of the Civil Code (Draft) (Second Review Draft), 2 Research on Rule of Law (Fa Zhi Yan Jiu) 20 (2019).
1835. *Li Yandong v. Shanghai Hanyu Real Estate Consulting Co., Ltd.*, Gazette Case of the SPC, Issue 2, 2015; 李彦东诉上海汉宇房地产顾问有限公司居间合同纠纷案，《最高人民法院公报》案例，2015年02期.

the property and keeping the deposit according to the intermediary contract. Based on the facts, the court held that the intermediary should be liable for the loss suffered by the principal.[1836]

1442. In summary, it is pointed out that the intermediary shall undertake the duty of care that meets the requirements of professional entities. In the intermediary business for the purchase of properties, the intermediary shall pay attention to reviewing and verifying the authenticity of the identity of the subject, property ownership, entrustment of agency, credit and other supporting materials related to the transaction. If an intermediary fails to discover major flaws or defects in relevant materials provided by one party because it fails to exercise necessary care, thereby causing the principal to suffer losses due to fraud, it shall be liable for compensation within the corresponding scope based on the degree of its fault.[1837] It can be seen that the intermediary has a very positive obligation or duty under the intermediary contract. It is not enough to only truthfully inform the principal of matters relating to the conclusion of the contract.

1443. Although this positive obligation is not expressly stated in the Civil Code, it is reasonable to have the implied obligation to protect the interests of the principal. The positive obligation also applies to crowdfunding platforms that inform the investors of the opportunity to conclude an investment contract as an intermediary for the conclusion of an investment contract. In *Chen Liyun v. Beijing Yuanshihui Investment Management Co., Ltd. and Beijing Wangxin Zhongchou Network Technology Co., Ltd.*,[1838] the intermediary operated an equity-based crowdfunding platform and provided an equity financing project online. The claimant invested in the project via the platform. The project was fabricated, and the claimant suffered a loss of the investment. It was found that the intermediary did not have substantive review and risk control of the project before it provided the information of the project online. The investor claimed against the project financier, but the financier had no financial ability to pay the investor's loss. The investor claimed against the crowdfunding platform.[1839] The court held that the crowdfunding platform was liable for the loss of the investor because it failed to fulfil its positive obligation as a financial intermediary. The liability is limited to the actual loss of the investor.

1444. This positive obligation is from relevant financial regulations. According to regulations from financial authorities, the crowdfunding platform as a financial intermediary has a positive obligation for intermediary business. It includes the duty

1836. In this case, the intermediary was not liable for the whole loss of the principal because the principal also had contributary negligence in performance of the contract.

1837. Case Summary of *Li Yandong v. Shanghai Hanyu Real Estate Consulting Co., Ltd.*, Gazette Case of the SPC, Issue 2, 2015.

1838. *Chen Liyun v. Beijing Yuanshihui Investment Management Co., Ltd. and Beijing Wangxin Zhongchou Network Technology Co., Ltd.*, 4 China Law Report 132-143 (People's Court Press 2019); 陈立耘与北京原始会投资管理有限公司、北京网信众筹网络科技有限公司居间合同纠纷案，《人民法院案例选》2019年4辑，人民法院出版社，2019年版，第132-143页.

1839. This is the first case about the intermediary dispute between the investor and crowdfunding platform in Chinese judicial practice.

to review the legality of financiers and financing projects, conduct timely and comprehensive disclosure of financier information; review the qualifications of investors, and make investors understand the basic rules and risks of equity crowdfunding through risk warnings; establish information communication channels between the financier and investor, maintain the neutrality of the intermediary, prevent and resolve fraud risks caused by information asymmetry; record and save key information in the investment and financing process, and protect the security of investors' personal information; and provide support for fund transfer and conduct against money laundering, etc. It is believed that this obligation is a reasonable basis for both remuneration to the intermediary and protection of principals and the financial market. The intermediary should exercise due diligence to fulfil this obligation.[1840]

1445. The judicial practice of positive obligation under the Contract Law is not changed under the Civil Code. In the judicial practice under the Civil Code, the scope of the intermediary's obligation to report truthfully should include the important matters related to the transaction that are required to be reported by the duty of loyalty and the duty of diligence. Violations of the obligation include intentional concealment and provision of false information, as well as omissions that are known or should be known but fail to inform due diligence. In *Wang v. Shanghai A Real Estate Agency Co., Ltd.*,[1841] the intermediary failed to inform the buyer of the change in tax policies on housing transactions. It caused the buyer suffering tax loss due to change in tax policies. It was held that the intermediary violated its obligation to report truthfully and should bear corresponding liability for compensation. The amount of compensation should be determined after taking into account factors such as the actual loss of the buyer, the degree of fault of both parties, the degree of causation of the damage, the actual performance of the intermediary agreement, and the amount of commission charged by the intermediary.

§3. Remuneration and Expenses

1446. Where the intermediary contributes to the conclusion of the contract, the principal shall pay remuneration in accordance with the contract. The intermediary's contribution should be substantial and decisive for the conclusion of the contract for a remuneration purpose. If the intermediary's contribution is limited, the intermediary can only claim partial remuneration according to its real contribution.[1842] Where there is no agreement on the remuneration of the intermediary or the agreement is equivocal, and the remuneration cannot be ascertained under

1840. *Chen Liyun v. Beijing Yuanshihui Investment Management Co., Ltd. and Beijing Wangxin Zhongchou Network Technology Co., Ltd.*, (2019) 4 China Law Report, People's Court Press (2019), pp. 142-143.

1841. *Wang v. Shanghai A Real Estate Agency Co., Ltd.*, Shanghai Second Intermediate People's Court (2022) Hu 02 Min Zhong No. 5071; 王某某诉上海某房地产经纪有限公司中介合同纠纷案，上海市第二中级人民法院（2022）沪02民终5071号.

1842. *Jia v. Shanghai A Trading Co., Ltd.*, Shanghai Second Intermediate People's Court (2013) Hu Er Zhong Min Yi (Min) Zhong Zi No. 483; 贾某诉上海某商贸有限公司居间合同纠纷案，上海市第二中级人民法院（2013）沪二中民一（民）终字第483号.

Article 510 of the Civil Code, remuneration shall be determined by reference to the labour provided by the intermediary. Where the intermediary acts as an intermediary for the conclusion of the contract and contributes to the conclusion of the contract, its remuneration shall be equally shared by the parties to the contract. Where the intermediary contributes to the conclusion of the contract, the expenses incurred for intermediary activities shall be borne by the intermediary.[1843] However, the Civil Code does not clarify whether parties can agree that the expenses incurred for intermediary activities are to be borne by the principal. It is uncertain whether the Chinese court will enforce such an agreement, which is different from the default rule of payment of the expenses incurred for intermediary activities. It is submitted that such an agreement should be respected and enforced based on the principle of freedom of contract.

1447. Where the intermediary fails to contribute to the conclusion of the contract, it shall have no claim for remuneration. However, it may, in accordance with the contract, seek payment by the principal of necessary expenses incurred for intermediary activities.[1844] This rule of payment of necessary expenses where the intermediary fails to contribute to the conclusion of the contract is different from that of the Contract Law in which it was provided that the intermediary may request payment by the principal of necessary expenses incurred for intermediary activities.[1845] The Contract Law seemed to balance the interests of the intermediary and the principal by payment of necessary expenses if the intermediary cannot claim remuneration where the intermediary fails to contribute to the conclusion of the contract. Although the balance was limited to the necessary expenses only, it had no appropriate legal basis for the allocation of the necessary expenses. If the expenses incurred for intermediary activities shall be borne by the intermediary when the intermediary contributes to the conclusion of the contract, there is no reason that the expenses (even if it is necessary only) incurred for intermediary activities shall not be borne by the intermediary when the intermediary contributes to do so. The Civil Code solves the problem based on the principle of freedom of contract.

1448. Where the principal, upon accepting the services provided by the intermediary, utilises the business opportunity or intermediary services provided by the intermediary and concludes the contract by circumventing the intermediary, the principal shall pay remuneration to the intermediary.[1846] This rule is to prevent 'skipping' order from the intermediary. There are three main forms of this situation: (1) The principal directly signs a contract with the counterparty of the contract without going through an intermediary; (2) The principal signs a contract with the counterparty of the contract through other intermediaries with lower quotations; (3) The principal discloses relevant information to relatives or friends, and the contract is signed with the counterparty in the name of the relatives or friends. The prohibition

1843. Article 963 CC.
1844. Article 964 CC.
1845. Article 427 of the Contract Law.
1846. Article 965 CC.

of 'skipping' orders from the intermediary is to promote the core values of integrity and is conducive to maintaining the healthy development of the real estate transaction market in China.

1449. There is no such remuneration rule in the Contract Law. This is a new remuneration rule for the intermediary contract in the Civil Code. The new rule is from the first SCP Guiding Case. In *Shanghai Zhongyuan Property Consulting Co., Ltd. v. Tao Dehua,*[1847] the intermediary and its principal concluded an intermediary contract for the purchase of a real estate property. Clause 2.4 of the intermediary contract provided that the principal shall not conclude a purchase contract by circumventing the intermediary utilising the business opportunity or intermediary services provided by the intermediary. The principal concluded a purchase contract without the intermediary. The intermediary claimed against the principal for the loss of remuneration in accordance with the intermediary contract due to the principal's breach of the contract. In this case, the court examined clause 2.4 of the contract. It was pointed out that the clause aims to prevent buyers from using the housing information provided by the intermediary but 'skipping' the intermediary to purchase a house, so that the intermediary cannot get the remuneration it deserves. This clause does not exempt one party from liability, increase the liability of the other party, or exclude the other party's major rights. Therefore, it was held that the clause was valid to the parties.

1450. However, it does not mean that the buyer must pay the remuneration to the intermediary when it circumvents the intermediary. It depends on whether the buyer utilises the business opportunity or intermediary services provided by the intermediary and concludes the contract. If the buyer does not take advantage of the information, opportunities and other conditions provided by the intermediary but obtains the same house information through other legitimate channels that are accessible to the public, the buyer has the right to choose an intermediary with a low price and good service to conclude a house sales contract, and it does not constitute a breach of contract. In this case, the original property owner listed the same house for sale through more than one intermediary. The principal learnt about the same house information through a different intermediary and concluded a house sales contract through another intermediary. Therefore, the principal did not take advantage of the intermediary's information and opportunities, so it did not constitute a breach of contract. This Guiding Case is not only a basis of the new remuneration rule for intermediary contracts in the Civil Code, but also a good application of the rule in Chinese judicial practice, although it is a case before the Civil Code.

1451. In the intermediary service for the purchase of real estate property, parties may agree that the intermediary acts as the exclusive intermediary for the principal to contract a property purchase contract. In this circumstance, if the principal may

1847. *Shanghai Zhongyuan Property Consulting Co., Ltd. v. Tao Dehua*, SPC Guiding Case, No. 1; 上海中原物业顾问有限公司诉陶德华居间合同纠纷案，最高人民法院, 第1号指导性案例.

breach the intermediary contract if it purchases a property through other intermediaries.[1848] When there is no explicit provision in the intermediary contract that prohibits the principal from conducting transactions with other intermediary service providers and multiple intermediary service agencies provide intermediary services for the property, the property buyer, as the principal, can choose a good intermediary after comparing the services of multiple intermediaries. This behaviour of providing services by high-quality and low-cost intermediary service does not constitute skipping orders.[1849]

§4. Application of the Mandate Contract Rules

1452. The Civil Code provides that, for matters not provided for by the chapter of intermediary contract, the relevant provisions on mandate contract shall be referred to and applied.[1850] This application rule is also a new rule for intermediary contracts in the Civil Code. A mandate contract in the Civil Code is a contract whereby the mandator and mandatory agree that the mandatory will handle the affairs of the mandator.[1851] It seems that the intermediary contract and the mandate contract have some characters in common. However, they also have different characters. Therefore, not all rules of the mandate contract can apply to the intermediary contract for matters not provided for by the chapter of the intermediary contract. Even if the rule of the mandate contract can apply to the intermediary contract, they apply as reference only, other than direct application.

1453. There are some rules of the mandate contract that may apply to the intermediary contract. First, the mandatory shall handle the mandated affairs in accordance with the instructions given by the mandator.[1852] It is believed that this rule can apply to the intermediary contract. In theory, the intermediary should follow the principal's instruction for intermediary service, including informing the principal of the opportunity to conclude a contract or acting as an intermediary for the conclusion of a contract. Therefore, this rule may apply to the intermediary contract in principle.[1853] Second, the mandatory shall handle the mandated affairs personally. With the mandator's consent, the mandatory may delegate the mandate.[1854] It is suggested that, by applying this rule, the intermediary should personally handle intermediary affairs and shall not hand over intermediary affairs to others without

1848. *Shanghai Zhongyuan Property Consulting Co., Ltd. v. Zhou Yunfei*, Shanghai Second Intermediate People's Court (2021) Hu 02 Min Zhong No. 342; 上海中原物业顾问有限公司诉周云飞居间合同纠纷案，上海市第二中级人民法院（2021）沪02民终342号.

1849. *Qingdao Yaleju Real Estate Brokerage Co., Ltd. v. You Zhenglei*, Shandong Qingdao Intermediate People's Court (2022) Lu 02 Min Zhong No. 4730; 青岛青雅居房产经纪有限公司诉由政磊中介合同纠纷案，山东省青岛中级人民法院（2022）鲁02民终4730号.

1850. Article 966 CC.

1851. *Ibid.*; Art. 919 CC.

1852. *Ibid.*; Art. 922 CC.

1853. The SPC Civil Code Implementation Leadership Group, Understanding and Application of the Contract Section of the Civil Code of the People's Republic of China vol. 4, 2729 (People's Court Press 2020) .

1854. Article 923 CC.

authorisation.[1855] It is also suggested that the intermediary may delegate the intermediary affairs to others with the consent of the principal.[1856] Those suggestions are reasonable, and this rule should be applicable to the intermediary contract in principle.

1454. Third, the mandator or mandatory may terminate the mandate contract at any time. Where termination leads to loss to the other party, unless for reasons not attributable to the terminating party, the terminating party under a gratuitous mandate contract shall be liable in damages for direct losses caused by the inappropriately timed termination, and the terminating party under a remunerative mandate contract shall be liable in damages for direct losses sustained and benefits to be obtained by the other party.[1857] Because the chapter of intermediary contract has no similar rule, the termination right in the rule of the mandate contract may apply to the intermediary contract in principle.[1858]

1455. However, the damage rule may not apply to the termination of the intermediary contract. In most cases, the intermediary contract is a remunerative contract. So, the damage issue of a gratuitous intermediary contract is not discussed. Where the intermediary terminates the contract before the principal concludes a contract, the principal will not suffer damage unless they have paid the remuneration. And the principal can claim the refund of payment because the intermediary does not contribute to the conclusion of a contract.[1859] Where the principal terminates the intermediary contract before it concludes a contract, the intermediary may claim damages against the principal. But the intermediary may not suffer damage. Unless otherwise agreed, expenses incurred for intermediary activities shall be borne by the intermediary.[1860] Furthermore, where the intermediary does not contribute to the conclusion of the contract, it shall have no claim for remuneration.[1861] Therefore, the intermediary may not suffer any loss even if it has the right to claim damage when it terminates the intermediary contract, unless the principal utilises the business opportunity or intermediary services provided by the intermediary and concludes the contract by circumventing the intermediary.[1862]

1855. Wei Huang (ed), Commentaries of the Book on Contracts of the Chinese Civil Code 1415 (Law Press 2020) .
1856. Jianghong Zhou, Changes and understanding of intermediary contracts in the Civil Code, 2 Journal of Comparative Law (Bi Jiao Fa Yan Jiu) 60 (2021).
1857. Article 933 CC.
1858. Hu Zhu, Between Separation and merger: the Arbitrary right to terminate a contract in the Civil Code (2020) 4 Peking University Law Journal (Zhong Wai Fa Xue) 1018.
1859. Article 964 CC.
1860. Article 963 CC.
1861. Article 964 CC.
1862. Article 965 CC.

Chapter 19. Partnership Contracts

§1. Definition

1456. A partnership contract is a contract concluded by two or more partners whereby they share profits and bear risks jointly for a common business endeavour.[1863] It was not regulated as a typical contract in the Contract Law. The purpose of the partnership contract in the Civil Code is to fill the gap of law when the General Principles of the Civil Law were repealed, and the relevant provisions of partnership were abandoned. It also has general rules for the special rules in the Partnership Enterprise Law, which regulate the partnership in the form of an enterprise.[1864]

1457. In business, a contract named as a partnership contract may not be a contract for a real partnership. The most common issue in judicial practice is that a partnership contract is concluded for a loan purpose. In this circumstance, the partnership contract will be considered as a sale contract in nature.[1865] Similarly, a partnership contract could be concluded for an employment purpose,[1866] a lease purpose,[1867] or a mandatary purpose.[1868] Conversely, a contract in other names may be regarded as a partnership contract. For example, a partnership contract in the names of a cooperative mining contract,[1869] a technical cooperation development contract,[1870] a Sino-foreign cooperative enterprise contract,[1871] or a Sino-foreign joint venture contract.[1872] In judicial practice, a partnership contract can be distinguished from other types of contracts based on the three characteristics of the partnership

1863. Article 967 CC.
1864. The SPC Civil Code Implementation Leadership Group, Understanding and Application of the Contract Section of the Civil Code of the People's Republic of China vol. 4, 2732-2734 (People's Court Press 2020).
1865. *Ibid*, p. 2737.
1866. Beijing High People's Court (2019); 北京市高级人民法院（2019） 京民申4269号 (names of the parties in the judgment were not released).
1867. Tongren Intermediate People's Court (2021) Qian 06 Min Zhong No. 735; 贵州省铜仁市中级人民法院（2021） 黔06民终735号 (names of the parties in the judgment were not released).
1868. Qitaihe Intermediate People's Court (2021) Hei 09 Min Zhong No. 475; 黑龙江省七台河市中级人民法院（2021） 黑09民终475号 (names of the parties in the judgment were not released).
1869. The SPC (2012) Min Kang Zi Di No. 1; 最高人民法院（2012） 民抗字第1号 (names of the parties in the judgment were not released).
1870. Yichang Intermediate People's Court (2020) E 05 Zhi Min Chu No. 185; 湖北省宜昌市中级人民法院（2020） 鄂05知民初185号 (names of the parties in the judgment were not released).
1871. Guangxi High People's Court (2014) Gui Min Si Zhong Zi Di No. 8; 广西壮族自治区高级人民法院（2014） 桂民四终字第8号 (names of the parties in the judgment were not released).
1872. Jiangmen Intermediate People's Court (2014) Jiang Zhong Fa Min Yi Zhong Zi Di No. 456; 广东省江门市中级人民法院（2014） 江中法民一终字第456号 (names of the parties in the judgment were not released).

contract. i.e., sharing profits and bearing risks jointly for a common business endeavour. Other types of contracts normally do not have those characteristics of the partnership contract.[1873]

§2. Performance of Contract

1458. For establishing a partnership, partners shall perform their obligations to make capital contributions in accordance with the agreed means, amount, and time of contribution.[1874] Capital contributions advanced by the partners and income and other assets lawfully obtained by the partnership shall be partnership property. Partners shall not request the division of partnership property prior to the termination of the partnership contract.[1875]

1459. For partnership affairs, where partners make a decision on partnership affairs, unless otherwise provided in the partnership contract, the unanimous consent of all partners shall be obtained. In principle, partnership affairs shall be jointly handled by all partners. In accordance with the partnership contract or a resolution of all partners, one or more partners may be mandated to handle partnership affairs. Other partners will cease to handle partnership affairs but are entitled to supervise the administration. Where the partners handle partnership affairs separately, a partner who handles partnership affairs may raise objections to other partners' administration of affairs. Where objections have been raised, the other partners shall cease the administration of such affairs.[1876] The Civil Code does not provide solutions to the objections after the administration of affairs has ceased. This should be left to the parties to work out solutions according to the terms of their partnership contract.

1460. Because the partnership contract is for the parties to share profit, partners shall not seek remuneration for the administration of partnership affairs unless otherwise provided in the partnership contract.[1877] For profits and losses of the partnership, they shall be distributed in accordance with the partnership contract. Where there is no agreement in the partnership contract or the agreement is equivocal, distribution shall be resolved through negotiation by the partners. Where negotiation fails, distribution shall be made in accordance with the shares of the actual capital contributions of each partner. Where it is not possible to ascertain the shares of capital contributions, distribution shall be made evenly.[1878]

1461. For the external liabilities, on the one hand, partners shall bear joint and several liability for obligations owed by the partnership. Where a partner satisfies

---

1873. The SPC (2018) Zui Gao Fa Min Shen No. 2450; 最高人民法院（2018） 最高法民申2450号 (names of the parties in the judgment were not released).
1874. Article 968 CC
1875. Article 969 CC.
1876. Article 970 CC.
1877. Article 971 CC.
1878. Article 972 CC.

partnership obligations beyond its own share, it is entitled to compensation from other partners.[1879] On the other hand, the creditors of a partner shall not subrogate and exercise the rights that the partner enjoys according to this chapter or the partnership contract, except for the partner's right to seek profits distribution.[1880]

§3. External Transfer of Share

1462. Unless otherwise provided in the partnership contract, where a partner transfers the whole or part of its share in the properties to a person who is not a partner, unanimous consent by all other partners must be obtained.[1881] The share in the properties normally means the partner's property in the partnership. It also could be debts or liabilities of the partner's property.[1882] The unanimous consent required for the transfer of the partner's property is based on the nature of the share in the properties in partnership. If the transfer of the share is valid with unanimous consent by all other partners, the partners will be changed after the transfer. Where the whole share of a partner in the properties is transferred, the partner will withdraw from the partnership, and the transferee of the share will join the partnership as a new partner. Where part of a partner's share in the properties is transferred, the transferor is still a partner, but it has less share in properties because of the transfer. Meanwhile, the transferee becomes a new partner because of its acceptance of the transferred share.[1883]

1463. Partnership property shares have special characteristics compared with general property interests. On the one hand, partnership share is the consideration for the partners' investment in the partnership; the share of partnership property has the attribute of property. On the other hand, the share of partnership property is a prerequisite for maintaining partner status in a partnership. Therefore, the partnership property share involves both the property interests of the partners and their participation in the partnership. Accordingly, the transfer of partnership property shares not only involves the personal property interests of the partners but also affects the status and interests of partners in the partnership. It has an indirect impact on the basis of personal trust of the partnership by transferring a share of partnership property to an external party. Therefore, if the transferee is allowed to transfer the property without the unanimous consent of other partners, becoming a new partner by acquiring a share of partnership property may damage the trust relationship between partners within the partnership.[1884]

1879. Article 973 CC.
1880. Article 975 CC.
1881. Article 974 CC.
1882. Leshan Intermediate People's Court (2017) Chuan 11 Min Zhong No. 1657; 四川省乐山市中级人民法院（2017）川11民终1657号 (names of the parties in the judgment were not released).
1883. Xu Q, On the transfer of partnership property shares, 5 The Jurist (Fa Xue Jia) 118, 128 (2023).
1884. Guangdong High People's Court (2017) Yue Min Shen 9026; 广东省高级人民法院（2017）粤民申9026号 (names of the parties in the judgment were not released).

1464. If a partner transfers the whole or part of its share in the properties to a person who is not a partner without unanimous consent of all other partners, this transfer is not valid to other partners within the partnership. On the one hand, it does not have the legal effect of an external transfer of shares in properties. On the other hand, the transfer agreement between the partner who intends to transfer its share and the person who is not a partner may be valid between them. The partner as the transferor may be liable for the loss suffered by the person as the transferee because the transfer is not valid due to the lack of unanimous consent of all other partners. It is believed that the transferee will not have the whole or part of the transferor's share as acquired in good faith.[1885]

§4. End and Termination of Partnership Contracts

1465. The end of partnership contracts depends on the term of the contracts. The term of partnership contracts may be definite or indefinite. Where the partners have not agreed on the term of partnership or the agreement is equivocal, and the term cannot be ascertained under Article 510 of the Civil Code, it is deemed that the partnership is for an indefinite term. Where, upon the expiry of the term of partnership, one or more partners continue to handle partnership affairs and other partners do not raise any objection, the original partnership contract remains valid for an indefinite term. Partners may terminate a partnership contract for an indefinite term at any time, provided that they notify other partners a reasonable period of time prior to the termination.[1886]

1466. A partnership contract may be terminated on the death or loss or termination of civil capacity to act of partners, unless otherwise provided in the contract or where the partnership affairs are unsuitable for termination by their nature.[1887] Upon termination of a partnership contract, any remaining partnership properties after deducting expenses incurred for the termination and payments in satisfaction of partnership obligations shall be distributed in accordance with the way of distribution of profits and losses of the partnership.[1888]

1885. Xu Q, On the transfer of partnership property shares, 127.
1886. Article 976 CC.
1887. *Ibid.*; Art. 977 CC.
1888. *Ibid.*; Art. 978 CC. The way of distribution of profits and losses of the partnership is in Art. 972 CC.

Part III. Quasi-contracts

§1. Negotiorum Gestio (Unauthorised Management)

1467. Unauthorised management is a traditional concept in Chinese civil law. In the Civil Code, where a manager handles another person's affairs for the purpose of avoiding any loss suffered by such person without owing any prior duty to such person either by operation of law or by consent, the manager has the right to claim against the beneficiary for reimbursement of the necessary expenses incurred due to the management; the manager also has the right to claim against the beneficiary an appropriate sum of money in the case where the manager suffered any loss due to the management. However, the manager does not have such rights if the management goes against the genuine intent of the beneficiary, unless the interested party's genuine intent violates the law or goes against public order and good morals.[1889] Where an unauthorised management is ratified by the beneficiary after the management, the relevant provisions of mandate contracts shall apply retrospectively from the commencement of the management, unless the manager manifests his intention otherwise.[1890]

1468. There is a related rule about tort liability in the Civil Code. It is necessary to clarify the relationship between the tort liability and the unauthorised management when the latter is caused by the tortfeasor. In the Civil Code, Article 183 provides that, where one suffers damage due to his or her act of protecting another's civil rights or interests, the tortfeasor shall bear civil liability, and the beneficiary may pay an appropriate compensation to the victim. In the case of no tortfeasor, an absconding tortfeasor, or a tortfeasor unable to bear civil liabilities, the beneficiary shall pay appropriate compensation to the victim. It is understood that this article actually stipulates a principle that 'tort liability shall be given priority to unauthorised management' because it requires the tortfeasor to bear civil liability first, and the unauthorised management applies only when no tortfeasor is to take the liability. This may limit the free choice of the manager for remedy in this circumstance.[1891]

1889. Article 979 CC.
1890. *Ibid.*; Art. 984 CC.
1891. Li Y, Research on Scope of Regulation for Unauthorised Management in China's Civil Code, 6 China Legal Studies (Zhong Guo Fa Xue) 24, 37 (2020).

1469. One of the conditions for unauthorised management is the lack of any prior duty to such a person either by operation of law or by consent. In the Civil Code, there are many situations where managers assume the management of other people's affairs in accordance with legal obligations. For example, the property custodian's proper management of the missing person's property in accordance with Article 43. The person who finds the property has legal obligations to properly keep the lost property in accordance with Article 316, and the lien holder has legal obligations to properly keep the property under lien in accordance with Article 451. Emergency suppliers have repair obligations when power is cut off due to disasters and other reasons. The lessor has the obligation to repair the leased property in accordance with Article 712. The inheritance administrator has the obligation to keep and divide the inheritance in accordance with Article 1147. Hotels, shopping malls, banks and other business premises, operators and managers of public places, or organisers of mass activities have safety guarantee obligations in accordance with Article 1198. In those examples, the actor's performance of the above obligations does not constitute unauthorised management.[1892]

1470. A manager in unauthorised management may not handle another person's affairs directly for the purpose of avoiding any loss suffered by such a person, it does not, however, deprive the manager's right to claim for reimbursement of the necessary expenses incurred due to the management. This circumstance is discussed in *Shenyang Dadong District Urban Construction Bureau v. Shenyang Hengyu Real Estate Development Co., Ltd.*.[1893] In this case, the project involved in the case was constructed and developed by Hengyu Company. Hengyu Company discontinued the project. The Dadong District Urban Construction Bureau (the Bureau) advanced the construction funds and entrusted Dongqiang Company to carry out the subsequent construction of the project. The Bureau claimed against Hengyu Company for the subsequent construction costs. Hengyu Company argued that the Bureau advanced the funds to Dongqiang Company, not Hengyu Company, and there might be unauthorised management only between Dongqiang Company and Hengyu Company.

1471. In the retrial of the case, the SPC found that the Bureau advanced the construction funds and entrusted Dongqiang Company to carry out the follow-up construction of the project involved in the case, which objectively avoided or mitigated Hengyu Company's breach of contract liability to the construction party. In fact, it has the effect of preventing Hengyu Company from suffering losses. Hengyu Company admitted that it knew at that time that the project involved in the case was being taken over by the Bureau but did not express any objection. Dongqiang Company made it clear that it was entrusted by the Bureau to actually take over the construction of the project. The relevant funds were allocated by the Bureau, and the

---

1892. Wu X, Commentary on Article 979 of the Civil Code (Constitutive Requirements of Unauthorised Management and the Manager's Right to Claim), 6 The Jurist (Fa Xue Jia) 169, 190 (2022).

1893. *Shenyang Dadong District Urban Construction Bureau v. Shenyang Hengyu Real Estate Development Co., Ltd.*, the SPC (2019) Zui Gao Fa Min Shen No. 4796; 沈阳市大东区城市建设局诉沈阳恒宇房地产开发有限公司，最高人民法院（2019）最高法民申4796号.

Bureau should exercise relevant rights. Based on the above facts, the SPC dismissed Hengyu's retrial application and held that the legal relationship between the Bureau and Hengyu Company was based on unauthorised management. In the retrial judgement, the SPC did not analyse the agency relationship between the Bureau and Dongqiang Company. It can be seen that the agency relationship does not prevent the Bureau, as the principal, from claiming the compensation under unauthorised management.

1472. There could be unauthorised management even if the management is not to avoid any loss. Where unauthorised management does not fall within the circumstances in which any loss may be avoided, but the beneficiary does receive a benefit due to such management,[1894] the manager has the right to claim against the beneficiary for reimbursement of the necessary expenses incurred due to the management. The manager also has the right to claim against the beneficiary an appropriate sum of money in the case where the manager suffered any loss due to the management. However, the manager's rights are limited to the extent of the benefit that the beneficiary receives.[1895] This is a new rule of unauthorised management in the Civil Code. In previous civil law rules, the purpose of unauthorised management was limited to management for avoiding any loss and did not include the management for any benefit.[1896] This new rule has been implemented by the Chinese courts before the enactment of the Civil Code. So, this new rule is a recognition of judicial practice in the Civil Code.

1473. The Chinese judicial practice can be seen in *Bai Bing v. Guangdong Rongqi Sea Wheel Container Service Co., Ltd.*.[1897] In this case, Rongqi Company chartered vessels from Bai Bing, who chartered them from the shipowner Yuanheng Company. It was agreed between Rongqi Company and Bai Bing that all claims and debts between Bai Bing and the shipowner should be settled by Bai Bing and the shipowner themselves and had nothing to do with Rongqi Company. During business, Bai Bing failed to pay a debt to Yuanheng Company. For chartering the vessels, Rongqi Company paid the debt to Yuanheng Company. It was agreed in a settlement agreement between them that Bai Bing had no right to collect the freight involved in the case and Rongqi Company had the right to recover compensation from Bai Bing. Rongqi Company claimed against Bai Bing for the compensation of the debt. In the retrial, the SPC upheld the decisions of the lower-level courts and supported the claim for compensation under unauthorised management. The SPC

1894. In Chinese judicial practice, the benefit is not limited to the benefit of the beneficiary; it also includes the benefits of both the manager and the beneficiary. *See Ningbo Yinzhou Ruixing Clothing Co., Ltd. v. Zheng Minghua*, Zhejiang Ningbo Intermediate People's Court (2009) Zhe Yong Shang Zhong No. 1054; 宁波市鄞州润兴服饰有限责任公司诉郑明华，浙江宁波中级人民法院（2009）浙甬商终1054号.

1895. Article 980 CC.

1896. *See* Art. 93 of General Principles of the Civil Law and Art. 121 of the General Provisions of the Civil Law.

1897. *Bai Bing v. Guangdong Rongqi Sea Wheel Container Service Co., Ltd.*, the SPC (2020), Zui Gao Fa Min Shen No. 3032; 白冰诉广东容奇水陆集运有限公司，最高人民法院（2020）最高法民申3032号.

pointed out that there was no direct contractual relationship between Rongqi Company and Yuanheng Company, and Rongqi Company had no contractual or legal obligation to pay freight to Yuanheng Company. Rongqi Company's payment of the debt of freight on behalf of Bai Bing constituted unauthorised management, and Bai Bing should reimburse Rongqi Company for the debt in accordance with the law.[1898] The payment of the debt by Rongqi Company is not to avoid any loss of Bai Bing but to make a benefit to Bai Bing. This circumstance has been recognised as unauthorised management, although previous civil law did not clarify the point of benefit.

1474. For balancing the interests of parties under unauthorised management, the Civil Code set up a certain obligation of the manager. First, the manager shall manage the affairs for the benefit of the beneficiary. Where suspension of management is to put the beneficiary at a disadvantageous position, the manager shall not suspend management without just cause.[1899] Second, during the unauthorised management, the manager shall promptly notify the beneficiary if he is able to do so. Where the managed affairs do not need emergency management, the manager shall wait for the beneficiary's instruction.[1900] Last, when an unauthorised management comes to an end, the manager shall make a report on the management affairs to the beneficiary. All assets acquired due to the unauthorised management shall be transferred to the beneficiary in a timely manner.[1901]

§2. Unjustified Enrichment

1475. Unjustified enrichment is also a traditional concept in Chinese civil law. In the Civil Code, where a party is unjustifiably enriched without a legal basis at the expense of another, the aggrieved party has the right to claim for restitution of the enrichment acquired by the enrichee, except where (i) the performance was made to discharge a moral obligation; (ii) an obligation was discharged before the due date; or (iii) an obligation was discharged that the performer knew did not exist.[1902] Where the enrichee knows or ought to know of the lack of legal basis for the enrichment, the aggrieved party has the right to claim against the enrichee for restitution of enrichment, as well as to claim for compensation of loss in accordance with law.[1903] However, where the enrichee does not know of and ought not to know of the lack of legal basis for the enrichment and the enrichment no longer exists, the enrichee has no duty to make restitution to the extent that the enrichee is no longer enriched.[1904] Where the enrichee has gratuitously transferred the acquired enrichment to a third party, the aggrieved party has the right to claim against that third

1898. It is Art. 93 of General Principles of the Civil Law that applied in this case.
1899. Article 981 CC.
1900. *Ibid.*; Art. 982 CC.
1901. *Ibid.*; Art. 983 CC.
1902. *Ibid.*; Art. 985 CC.
1903. *Ibid.*; Art. 987 CC.
1904. *Ibid.*; Art. 986 CC.

party for restitution to the extent of that third party's enrichment.[1905] It must be noted that this right to claim against the third party is limited to a gratuitous transfer of the acquired enrichment. If the enrichee transfers the acquired enrichment to a third party for the exchange of value, e.g., payment under a contract, the aggrieved party should have no right to claim against that third party for restitution.

1476. The enrichment under unjustified enrichment may relate to other factors in a complicated transaction. Thus, the determination of unjustified enrichment could be complicated. The complex of determination is illustrated in *Tianjin Zhongjurui International Trade Co., Ltd. v. Jiangsu Suzhou Port Group Co., Ltd.*.[1906] In this case, Zhongjurui Company purchased nickel ore from Jiajiaxin Company. Huarong Company acted as the agent of Zhongjurui Company and Suzhou Port Company acted as the agent of Jiajiaxin Company for respectively importing the goods. When the goods arrived at the port of destination, Zhongjurui Company paid the port fees to Huarong Company and Huarong Company paid the same charge to the local port. However, Suzhou Port Company applied for arrest of the goods due to its dispute with Jiajiaxin Company. After the arrest, Huarong Company agreed to act as the agent of Suzhou Port Company for importing the goods, and both of them agreed that Zhongjurui Company should pay the port fees. Suzhou Port Company then paid the storage charge and dispatch payment to Huarong Company and paid the customs a late declaration fee to the local customs. Upon Suzhou Port Company's application, Huarong Company was ordered by a local court to deliver the goods to Suzhou Port Company. After delivery, Suzhou Port Company sold the goods to a third party. Zhongjurui Company claimed against Suzhou Port Company and requested Suzhou Port Company to refund the port fees to it.

1477. In the first instance of the case, the court of first instance held that the port fees paid by Zhongjurui Company were unjustified enrichment of Suzhou Port Company.[1907] The court pointed out that whether it was unjust enrichment of Suzhou Port Company depends on whether it has obtained benefits, whether it has a legal basis, and whether it has caused losses to others.[1908] In the view of the court, the value of the goods included the port fees, and Suzhou Port Company, as the actual disposer of the goods, obtained the benefits of the charges. Although Suzhou Port Company and Huarong Company agreed that all relevant Zhongjurui Company should pay the port fees, there was no evidence that Zhongjurui Company accepted the agreement. This agreement had no effect on Zhongjurui Company, and Suzhou Port Company had no legal basis for obtaining this benefit. Zhongjurui Company paid relevant port fees but did not receive the goods involved in the case. Suzhou Port Company obtained this benefit, causing Zhongjurui Company to suffer losses from the charges. Therefore, the charges constituted unjust enrichment of Suzhou Port Company.

1905. *Ibid.*; Art. 988 CC.
1906. *Tianjin Zhongjurui International Trade Co., Ltd. v. Jiangsu Suzhou Port Group Co., Ltd.*, the SPC (2023) Zui Gao Fa Min Zai No. 16; 天津中钜锐国际贸易有限公司诉江苏苏州港集团有限公司，最高人民法院（2023）最高法民再16号.
1907. Tianjin Maritime Court (2020) Jin 72 Min Chu 293; 天津海事法院（2020）津72民初293号.
1908. Article 122 of the General Provisions of the Civil Law.

1478. Suzhou Port Company appealed. The appellate court overruled the decision of the first instance court and held that the port fees paid by Zhongjurui Company were not unjust enrichment of Suzhou Port Company.[1909] The appellate court's reasoning focused on the analysis of the benefit. In the view of the appellate court, a benefit received by one party means that one party obtains certain property interests based on certain factual results. Property interests acquired include both positive and negative increases in property. The appellate court pointed out that there was no positive or negative benefit of Suzhou Port Company in this case. First, Zhongjurui Company paid port fees to Huarong Company, and Huarong Company paid port fees to a port company. The above charges were not actually obtained by Suzhou Port Company, and Suzhou Port Company could not have a positive increase in property interests. Second, the appellate court explained that the negative increase in property interest refers to a decrease in property that should have been made but was not, including expenses that should have been expended but were not expended, and debts that should have been borne but were not borne. In this case, the prerequisite for Suzhou Port Company to have unjust enrichment due to negative increase in property interests is that it had the obligation to bear the port fees. However, according to the ascertained facts, Suzhou Port Company was not responsible for the payment of port fees. Furthermore, the port fees had no relation with the value of the goods but were determined according to relevant contracts. Therefore, the port fees paid by Zhongjurui Company were not unjust enrichment of Suzhou Port Company. In addition, the loss suffered by Zhongjurui Company was caused by the dispute between it and Jiajiaxin Company and had no relation with the disposal of the goods by Suzhou Port Company. The loss suffered by Zhongjurui Company could be solved through other means.

1479. Zhongjurui Company applied for retrial of the case to the SPC. The SPC overruled the decision of the appellate court and held that the port fees paid by Zhongjurui Company constituted unjust enrichment of Suzhou Port Company. The SPC analysed as follows. First, Zhongjurui Company suffered the loss of the port fees. Zhongjurui Company paid port fees to Huarong Company but did not actually obtain the goods, which resulted in a decrease in the property interests. Second, Suzhou Port Company had benefits. After taking the delivery of the goods to Suzhou Port Company, the port fees paid by Zhongjurui Company constituted a negative increase in property interests of Suzhou Port Company. There was a legal causal relationship between the negative increase in property interests and the loss suffered by Zhongjurui Company. Third, there was no legal basis for Suzhou Port Company to obtain the benefits. Legal basis includes the contractual basis and the basis of law. In this case, the delivery court order did not involve the issue of port fees. It was not the basis of law for Suzhou Port Company to obtain the benefits of port fees. Zhongjurui Company was not a party to the agreement between Suzhou Port Company and Huarong Company. The agreement was not a contractual basis

1909. Tianjin High People's Court (2021) Jin Min Zhong No. 238; 天津市高级人民法院（2021）津民终238号.

for Suzhou Port Company to obtain the benefits. Therefore, the SPC held that Zhongjurui Company's payment of port fees constitutes unjust enrichment of Suzhou Port Company.

1480. The decisions of the Chinese courts in this case indicate not only the complexity of the facts but also the uncertainty in the application of law. Both the first instance court and the SPC recognised the port charges as unjustified enrichment of Suzhou Port Company based on two main facts: Zhongjurui Company paid the port fees, but Suzhou Port Company obtained the goods. The first instance court and the SPC believed that the port fees should be included in the value of the goods, and therefore Suzhou Port Company had Suzhou Port Company when they received and disposed of the goods. However, it should be noted, as the appellate court clarified, that Zhongjurui Company paid the port fees according to relevant contracts, and Suzhou Port Company received the goods according to the local court order. They have no direct or causative relationship with each other. Even if the port fees were included in the value of the goods (this was not clarified by the courts), the port fees and the disposal of the goods are independent legal issues and should be solved separately. The appellate court suggested that the loss suffered by Zhongjurui Company could be solved through other means. The means could be a claim for a breach of relevant contracts according to which Zhongjurui Company paid the port fees. It should not be a claim for unjust enrichment in this case.

Bibliography

Books

Bing Ling, *Contract Law in China* (Sweet & Maxwell 2002)

Birks P, *An Introduction to the Law of Restitution* (Clarendon Press 1985)

Calnan R, *Principles of Contractual Interpretation* (2nd edn, Oxford University Press 2017)

Chen L 'The Security Interests in Chinese Law: Some Nuances' in Jiang H and Sirena P (eds), *The Making of the Civil Code: Promises and Persistent Problems* (Cambridge University Press 2023)

Chen L and DiMatteo LA, 'History of Chinese Contract Law' in DiMatteo LA and Chen L (eds), *Chinese Contract Law: Civil and Common Law Perspectives* (Cambridge University Press 2017)

Chen L et al. (eds), *The Civil Code of the People's Republic of China: English Translation* (Nijhoff: Brill 2021)

Chen L, 'Availability of Specific Remedies in Chinese Contract Law' in Chen-Wishart M, Loke A and Ong Burton (eds), *Remedies for Breach of Contract* (Oxford University Press 2016)

Chen L, 'Contextualizing Legal Transplant: China and Hong Kong' In Monateri PG (ed.), *Methods of Comparative Law* (Elgar Edward 2012)

Chen L, 'Damages and Specific Performance in Chinese Contract Law', in DiMatteo LA and Chen L (eds), *Chinese Contract Law: Civil and Common Law Perspectives* (Cambridge University Press 2017)

Chen L, 'Relaxations of Contractual Privity and the Need for Third Party Rights in Chinese Contract Law' in Chen-Wishart M, Loke A, and Vogenauer S (eds), *Formation and Third Party Beneficiaries* (Oxford University Press 2018)

Cui J, *Commentaries of the Chinese Civil Code: Book on Property Rights* (Renmin University Press 2020) vol 1

Davies PS, 'Construing Commercial Contracts: No Need for Violence' in Freeman M and Smith F (eds), *Law and Language: Current Legal Issues* (Oxford University Press 2013) vol 15, ch 26

Ding C, 'Contract Formation Under Chinese Law' in Chen-Wishart M, Loke A, and Vogenauer S (eds), *Studies in the Contract Laws of Asia II: Formation and Third Party Beneficiaries* (Oxford University Press 2018) https://ssrn.com/abstract=3237320 accessed October 4 2024

Eisenberg MA, 'Incomplete Contracts' in *Foundational Principles of Contract Law* (Oxford University Press 2018) ch 36

Bibliography

Enforcement of Civil Code Group of the SPC (ed), *Understanding and Applying the Contract Book of the Chinese Civil Code (II)* (People's Court Press 2020)

Enforcement of Civil Code Group of the SPC (ed), *Understanding and Applying the Contract Book of the Chinese Civil Code (I)* (People's Court Press 2020)

Feng X, 'On the Principles for Judging the Legal Validity of Construction Contracts' in The SPC First Civil Trial Division (ed), *Reference and Guide to Civil Trial* (People's Court Press 2019)

Furmston MP, *Cheshire, Fifoot & Furmston's Law of Contract* (17th ed, OUP 2017) ch.18

Gray K and Gray SF, *Elements of Land Law* (5th edn, Oxford University Press 2009)

Han S, 'A Snapshot of Chinese Contract Law from an Historical and Comparative Perspective' in *Towards a Chinese Civil Code* (Brill Nijhoff 2012)

Han S, 'General Principles under the CCL' in Chen L and DiMatteo LA (eds), *Chinese Contract Law: Civil and Common Law Perspectives* (Cambridge University Press 2017)

Han S, *The General Principles of Contract Law* (4th edn, Law Press China 2018)

Hohfeld WN, *Fundamental Legal Conceptions as Applied in Judicial Reasoning* (Yale University Press, 1919)

Huang W (ed), *Commentaries of the Book on Contracts of the Chinese Civil Code* (Law Press 2020)

Kötz H, 'Comparative Contract Law' in Reimann M and Zimmermann R (eds), *The Oxford Handbook of Comparative Law* (Oxford University Press 2019) https://doi.org/10.1093/oxfordhb/9780198810230.013.29 accessed 12 April 2024

Leng J and Shen W, 'The Evolution of Contract Law in China: Convergence in Law but Divergence in Enforcement' in Chung, Shen, and Wang (eds), *Private Law in China and Taiwan – Legal and Economic Analyses* (Cambridge University Press 2016) ch 3

Liang H and Chen H, *Property Law* (Law Press China 2016)

Liang H, *General Introduction of Civil Law* (5th edition, Law Press China 2017)

Loke A, 'Pre-contractual Liability through the Looking Glass of the Common Law' in DiMatteo LA and Chen L (eds), *Chinese Contract Law: Civil and Common Law Perspectives* (Cambridge University Press 2017)

MacQueen HL, Illegality and Immorality in Contracts: Towards European Principles in Hartkamp AS et al. (eds), *Towards a European Civil Code* (4th end, Kluwer Law International–Ars Aequi Libri 2011)

Mak V, *Performance-Oriented Remedies in European Sale of Goods Law* (Hart Publishing 2009)

Markesinis B, Unberath H and Johnston A, *The German Law of Contract: A Comparative Treatise* (Bloomsbury Publishing 2006)

McKendrick E and Liu Q, 'Good Faith in Contract Performance in the Chinese and Common Laws' in Chen L and DiMatteo LA (eds), *Chinese Contract Law: Civil and Common Law Perspectives* (Cambridge University Press 2017)

McKendrick E, *Contract Law: Text, Cases, and Materials* (7th edn, OUP 2016)

McMeel G, *The Construction of Contracts: Interpretation, Implication and Rectification* (3rd edn, Oxford University Press 2017)

Michael J. Bonell, 'Interpretation of Convention' in Bianca CM and Bonell MJ (eds), *Commentary on the International Sales Law* (Guiffre: Milan 1987)

Shen W, 'The Doctrine of Mistake and the Rule on Gross Misunderstanding in Chinese Contract Law' in Chen-Wishart M, Hiroo Sono, and Vogenauer S (eds), *Invalidity* (Oxford 2022)

Siems M, *Comparative Law* (Cambridge University Press 2022)

Sun X and Zhu G (eds), *Commentaries of the Civil Code: Book on Property Rights* (China Legal Publishing House 2020) vol 1

Sun X, *General Principles of Real Rights Law of China* (2nd edn, Beijing: Law Press 2009)

Swadling W, 'Restitution and Bona Fide Purchase' in W. Swadling (ed), *The Limits of Restitutionary Claims: A Comparative Analysis* (London: UKNCCL 1997)

The Sixth Circuit Court of the SPC, *Adjudication Rules of the Sixth Circuit Court of the SPC* (People's Court Press 2022)

The SPC Civil Code Implementation Leadership Group, *Understanding and Application of the Contract Section of the Civil Code of the People's Republic of China* (People's Court Press 2020) vol 1

The SPC Civil Code Implementation Leadership Group, *Understanding and Application of the Contract Section of the Civil Code of the People's Republic of China* (People's Court Press 2020) vol 4

The SPC First Civil Trial Division (ed), *Understanding and Application of the Judicial Interpretation of the Supreme People's Court on Hearing Cases Involving Disputes over Urban Housing Lease Contracts* (People's Court Press 2016)

The SPC Second Civil Division (ed), *The Guidance on Commercial Adjudication* (The People's Court Press 2010)

The SPC Second Civil Division (ed), *Understanding and Application of the SPC Interpretation of the General Provisions of the Contract Section of the Civil Code* (People's Court Press 2023)

The SPC Second Civil Division (ed), *Understanding and Application of the Minutes of the National Conference on Civil and Commercial Trial Work of Courts Nationwide* (People's Court Press 2019)

Twigg-Flesner C, 'General Principles of Chinese Contract Law: An English Common Law Perspective' in Chen L and DiMatteo LA (eds), *Chinese Contract Law: Civil and Common Law Perspectives* (Cambridge University Press 2017)

Von Bar C et al. (eds), *Definitions and Model Rules of European Private Law: Draft Common Frame of Reference* (OUP Oxford 2010)

Wang L and Zhu H, *The Interpretation and Commentary of the SPC Interpretation concerning the General Principles of Contract Book of the Civil Code* (Renmin University of China Press 2024)

Wang L, *Contract Law Studies* (Renmin University Press 2015) vol 1

Wang L, *Studies on Contract Law* (Renmin University Press 2002) vol 1

Wang Y, 'Duress and Exploitation in Chinese Contract Law' in Chen-Wishart M, Sono H, and Vogenauer S (eds), *Invalidity* (Oxford 2022) https://doi.org/10.1093/oso/9780192859341.003.0003 accessed 1 Jan. 2025

Wang Y, *On the Transfer of Real Rights* (Renmin University Press 2001)

Wang Z, *Unjustified Enrichment* (2nd edn, Beijing University Press 2015)

Xiong B, 'The determination of neglect in exercising authority affecting the realisation of due claims' in Wang L and Zhu H (eds), *Interpretation and Commentary on the Judicial Interpretation of the General Provisions of the Contract Chapter in the Civil Code* (Renmin University Press 2024)

Yin T, *Comments and Thoughts on Property Law Theories* (Renmin University Press 2004)

Journal Articles

Adams J and Brownsword R, 'Contract, consideration and the critical path' (1990) 53 The Modern Law Review 536

Bai Y, 'A Preliminary Study on the Issue of Technical Contract Termination in the Context of the Civil Code' (2022) 12 Journal of Law Application (Fa Lv Shi Yong) 86

Berg A, 'Thrashing Through the Undergrowth' (2006) 122 Law Quarterly Review 354

Cerchia RE, 'A Comparative Viewpoint on Illegal Contracts: In Favor of Flexibility and Proportionality' (2021) 21.2 Global Jurist 447

Chen L and DiMatteo LA, 'Inefficiency of Specific Performance as a Contractual Remedy in Chinese Courts: An Empirical and Normative Analysis' (2009) 40 Nw. J. Int'l L. & Bus. 275

Chen L and Wang Q, 'Demystifying the Doctrine of Change of Circumstances under Chinese Law – A Comparative Perspective from Singapore and English Common Law' (2021) 6 Journal of Business Law 475

Chen L, 'Continuity and change: some reflections on the Chinese Civil Code' (2021) 29(2) Asia Pacific Law Review 287

Chen L, 'Private Property with Chinese Characteristics: A Critical Analysis of the Chinese Law on Property of 2007' (2010) 18(5) European Review of Private Law 983

Chen L, 'Specific Performance as a Contractual Remedy in Chinese Courts: An Empirical Study' (2019) 7 The Chinese Journal of Comparative Law 95

Chen L, 'The historical development of the Civil Law tradition in China: a private law perspective' (2010) 78(1-2) Tijdschrift voor Rechtsgeschiedenis/Revue d'histoire du droit/The Legal History Review 159

Cui J, 'On Contracts for the Benefit of a Third Party' (2022) 62 Jilin University Journal Social Science Edition 152

Cui J, 'On the Elements of the Creditor's Right of Revocation' (2020) 3 Tsinghua University Law Journal 133

Cui J, 'Positivist Analysis of the Concept of Juridical Act of Real Rights and Chinese Civil Law' (2004) 2 Journal of Comparative Law 60

Cui J, 'The Distinction between Civil Contracts and Commercial Contracts' (20221 Political and Legal Forum 56

Dai M, ''Debtor's Waiver of Matured Claims' and the Creditor's Right of Revocation' (2014) 5 Journal of CUPL 48

Dai M, 'Commentary on Article 726 of the Civil Code (Housing Lessee's Right of First Refusal)' (2023) 4 Tsinghua University Law Journal (Qing Hua Fa Xue) 140

DeRey S and Chen L, 'Non-monetary relief for breach of contract: a European perspective on Chinese contract law' (2021) 29 Asia Pacific Law Review 325

DeVries G, 'Right to Specific Performance: Is There a Divergence between Civil- and Common-Law Systems and, If So, How Has It Been Bridged in the DCFR?' (2009) 17 European Review of Private Law 581
DiMatteo LA, 'Rule of Law in China: The Confrontation of Formal Law with Cultural Norms' (2018) 391 Cornell Int'l LJ 51
Fuller L, 'Consideration and Form' (1941) 41 Columbia Law Review 799
Gamage D and Kedem A, 'Commodification and Contract Formation: Placing the Consideration Doctrine on Stronger Foundations' (2006) 73 U. Chi. L. Rev 1299
Gao S and Tao X, 'On the Legal Application of Third-Party Debt Repayment: An Analysis Based on Article 30 of Interpretations of the General Provisions of the Contract Section of the Civil Code' (2024) 1 Social Science Research 42
Ge Y, 'Study on the Theory of Real Juridical Act' (2004) 6 Peking University Law Journal 702
Han S, 'Application of CISG in International Commercial Arbitration in China' (2016) 5 China Law Science 218
Han S, 'On Contracts for Performance to a Third Party: An Interpretation of Article 64 of the Chinese Contract Law' (2004) 22 Science of Law (Journal of Northwest University of Political Science and Law) 100
He J, 'Commentary on Article 54 (1), Item 2 of the Contract Law (Unconscionability)' (2017) 1 The Jurist 155
Herbots JH, 'The Chinese new Civil Code and the law of contract' (2021) 7 China-EU Law Journal 39
Hong S, 'Significant Developments and Innovations in Contract Book' (2020) 4 China Legal Studies (Zhong Guo Fa Xue) 40
Janssen A and Wahnschaffe CJ, 'COVID-19 and international sale contracts: unprecedented grounds for exemption or business as usual?' (2020) 25(4) Uniform Law Review 466
Jhering R, 'Culpa in contrahendo' (1861) 4 JherJb 1
Jian H, 'Validity Determination and Application of Law in the First Stem Cell Sales Contract in China' (2022) 2 Journal of Law Application (Fa Lv Shi Yong) 127.
Kessler F and Fine E, 'Culpa in Contrahendo, Bargaining in Good Faith, and Freedom of Contract: A Comparative Study' (1964) 77 Harvard LR 401
Klass G, 'To Perform or Pay Damages' (2012) 98 Virginia Law Rev 143
Kornet N, 'Contracting in China: Comparative Observations on Freedom of Contract, Contract Formation, Battle of Forms and Standard Form Contracts' (2011) Maastricht European Private Law Institute Working Paper No. 2011/06
Kramer A, 'Common Sense Principles of Contract Interpretation (and how we've been using them all along)' (2003) 23(2) Oxford Journal of Legal Studies 173'
Leonhard C, 'A Legal Chameleon: An Examination of the Doctrine of Good Faith in Chinese and American Contract Law' (2010) 25 Connecticut Journal of International Law 305
Li M, 'Analysis on the Legal Nature of Sale-leaseback Contracts in the Context of the Civil Code of the People's Republic of China' (2020) 4 Chinese Journal of Maritime Law (Zhong Guo Hai Shang Fa Yan Jiu) 14
Li W, 'The Reference Application of Debt Assumption to Guarantee Contract Rules' (2022) 4 Journal of CUPL 110

Li X, 'The Application and Limits of the Legal Corrective Function of the Principle of Good Faith' (2021) 2 Law Science 241
Li Y, 'A Legislative Analysis of Factoring Contracts' (2019) 12 Law Science 45
Li Y, 'Research on Scope of Regulation for Unauthorised Management in China's Civil Code' (2020) 6 China Legal Studies (Zhong Guo Fa Xue) 24
Li Z, 'A three-dimensional perspective on the factoring contract in the Civil Code' (2020) 15 Journal of Law Application (Fa Lv Shi Yong) 39
Liang H, 'Is Juridical Act of Real Rights Recognised in Chinese Civil Law?' (1989) 6 Chinese Journal of Law 56
Liang H, 'The Principle of Good Faith and Supplementing Loopholes' (1994) 2 Legal Studies 27
Liang Y, 'Judicial identification and handling of informal/social arrangements' (2014) 2 Journal of Law Application (Fa Lv Shi Yong) 30
Liu G and Wu G, 'Thinking Methods in the Application of Contract Law Book in the Civil Code: Focusing on the Interpretation of the General Principles of Contract Book' (2024) 1 The Jurist 57
Liu G, 'Issues Regarding the Formation of Contracts' (2022) 4 Journal of Law Application (Fa Lv Shi Yong) 3
Liu N, 'Challenge to the right to terminate the agreement under the limitation of minor breaches' (2023) 4 Law Science 74
Liu Q and Ren X, 'CISG in Chinese Courts: The Issue of Applicability' (2017) 65(4) The American Journal of Comparative Law 873
Liu S, 'China's Liquidated Damages System Urgently Needs Reconstruction' (2016) 1 Chinese Case Law Review 17
Lorenz S, 'Die culpa in contrahendo im französischen Recht' (1994) ZEuP 218
Maskin E and Tirole J, 'Unforeseen Contingencies and Incomplete Contracts' (1999) 66(1) The Review of Economic Studies 83
Nicholls L, 'My Kingdom for a Horse: the Meaning of Words' (2005) 121 Law Quarterly Review 577
Novaretti S, 'General Clauses and Practice: The Use of the Principle of Good Faith in the Decisions of Chinese Courts' (2010) 5(18) European Review of Private Law 953
Pan Z, 'The Typological Application of the Principle of Good Faith in China's Civil Law' (2023) 9 Jurisprudence 125
Pattison P and Herron D, 'The Mountains are High and the Emperor Is Far Away: Sanctity of Contract in China' (2003) 40 American Business Law Journal 459
Peng Z, 'An Inquiry into the Legal Status of Judicial Interpretation Documents Issued by the Supreme People's Court' (2018) 26(3) Science of Law 14
Ran K, 'The System of Third-Party Payment from the Perspective of the Codification of the Civil Code' (2015) 2 FASHANG YANJIU (Journal of South Central Institute of Political Science and Law) 36
Sanga S, 'Incomplete Contracts: An Empirical Approach' (2018) 34(4) The Journal of Law, Economics, and Organization 650
Shavell S, 'Specific Performance versus Damages for Breach of Contract: An Economic Analysis' (2005) 84 Texas Law Rev 831
Spigelman J, 'From Text to Context: Contemporary Contractual Interpretation' (2007) 81 Australian Law Journal 322

Staughton C, 'How do the courts interpret commercial contracts?' (1999) 58 Cambridge Law Journal 303
Sun X, 'The Principle of Separation Between the Reason and the Result of the Alteration of Property Rights' (1999) 5 Chinese Journal of Law 28
Tian Y, 'On Third-Party Contracts', (2001) 1 Legal Studies 33
Wang H, 'Commentary on Article 538 of the Civil Code (Revocation of Gratuitous Acts by the Debtor)' (2021) 58 Journal of Nanjing University (Philosophy, Humanities and Social Sciences) 133
Wang J and DiMatteo LA, 'Chinese Reception and Transplantation of Western Contract Law' (2016) 34 Berkeley J. Int'l L. 44
Wang L and Pan C, 'On the Triple Protection of the Revocation Right Holder under the Interpretation of the Contract Section: Focusing on Article 46 of the Interpretation of the Contract Section' (2024) 1 Journal of Shanghai University of Political Science and Law 1
Wang L and Xu C, 'Fundamental Principles of China's Contract Law' (1999) 13 Colum. J. Asian L. 1
Wang L, 'A Study on Major Complex Issues in the General Provisions of the Contract Section of the Civil Code' (2020) 1 Social Science in Yunan (Yunnan She Hui Ke Xue) 77
Wang L, 'On Performance by a Third Party: Focusing on Article 524 of the Civil Code' (2021) 8 LAW 5
Wang L, 'On Several Issues Concerning Juridical Act of Real Right' (1997) 3 Chinese Legal Science 58
Wang L, 'On the distinction between the informal/social arrangements and Civil Legal Conduct' (2013) 6 Tsinghua Law Journal 157
Wang L, 'On the Right of Recourse of the Debt Assumer: Focusing on Article 51 of the SPC Interpretation of the General Provisions of the Contract Sections of the Civil Code' (2024) 41 Studies in Law and Business 3
Wang L, 'The Impact of Arbitration Agreements on the Exercise of Subrogation Rights: A Commentary on Article 36 of the Interpretation of the General Provisions of the Contract Code' (2024) 1 Guangdong Social Science (Guangdong She Hui Ke Xue) 221
Wang Y, 'Normative Types and Their Configuration Relationships in the Civil Code' (2014) 6 Tsinghua University Law Journal (Qing Hua Fa Xue) 56
Wang Y, 'Research on Ten Major Issues in Construction Project Contracts from the Perspective of Civil Code' (2023) 1 Shandong Justice (Shan Dong Shen Pan) 61
Wright L, 'Ought the Doctrine of Consideration to be Abolished from the Common Law?' (1936) 49 Harvard LR 1225
Wu X, 'Commentary on Article 979 of the Civil Code (Constitutive Requirements of Unauthorised Management and the Manager's Right to Claim)' (2022) 6 The Jurist (Fa Xue Jia) 169
Wu Z and Chen L, 'Revisiting property transfer theory: English law and Chinese law compared' (2023) 43(2) Legal Studies 259
Wu Z and Swadling W, 'Unjustified Enrichment in the Chinese Civil Code: Questions from the Common Law' (2021) 29(2) Asia Pacific Law Review 402
Xia H, 'The Distinction Between Debt Assumption and Guarantee: Analysis and Development Based on Judicial Divergences' (2019) 6 The Jurist 102

Bibliography

Xia J, 'Principles and Rules for Returning Donated Property Due to Lack of Cause' (2024) 1, SJTU Law Review (Jiao Da Fa Xue) 64

Xiao J, 'Types and Structures of Debt Assumption: Starting from Article 552 of the Civil Code' (2020) 6 Oriental Law 125

Xie H, 'On the Intention to Establish Legal Relationships: The Limits of Legal Intervention in Social Life' (2012) 3 Global Law Review 5

Xie Y and Guo P, 'On the Civil Law Protection of Actual Construction Workers' (2021) 6 Journal of Law Application (Fa Lv Shi Yong) 69

Xu D, 'A Teleological Explanation of the Abstraction Principle' (2005) 2 Chinese Legal Science 84

Xu D, 'The Responsible Assets of the Debtor: The Common Basis of the Creditor's Right of Revocation, Subrogation, and the Corporate Creditor Protection System' (2024) 1 Tsinghua University Law Journal 25

Xu H, 'Interpretation and Reconstruction of the Exception-Based Reduction System for Punitive Liquidated Damages: A Balanced Perspective on Contractual Freedom and Contractual Justice'. (2023) 44 Law Journal 85

Xu Q, 'On the transfer of partnership property shares' (2023) 5 The Jurist (Fa Xue Jia) 118

Yang D, 'The Principle of Interpretation of the Expression of Intent' (2020) 7 Law Science 41

Yu F, 'The Case-based Application of the Corrective Legal Function of the Principle of Good Faith – the Supreme People's Court's judgment in the Huacheng Case as the object of analysis' (2022) 22(2) Chinese Journal of Law 63

Yu X, 'A Study on Practical Legal Issues of Debt Assumption: Summary of the Supreme People's Court's Adjudication Rules' (2015) 18 People's Judicature 44

Zhang B, 'On the Right of the Contractor to Claim Damages when the Order Party Fails to Perform the Duty of Assistance' (2022) 2 Xiamen University Law Review (Xia Men Da Xue Fa Lv Ping Lun) 118

Zhang G, 'Commercial Law, the Hermit Crab: On the Independence and Characteristics of Commercial Law' (2005) 2 Tsinghua Rule of Law 1-51

Zhang J, 'Recent developments in the law of secured transactions of movables under the new Chinese Civil Code' (2021) 26 Uniform Law Review 191

Zhao L, 'FOB seller under Chinese law and privity of contract in carriage of goods by sea' (2019) 2 Asia Pacific Law Review 286

Zhao W, 'A Commentary on Article 94 of Contract Law (Termination)' (2019) 4 The Jurist 175

Zhong W, 'Research on the Legal Application of the Right to Terminate Non-gratuitous Entrustment Contracts' (2022) 17 Journal of Law Application (Fa Lv Shi Yong) 22

Zhou J, 'Changes and understanding of intermediary contracts in the Civil Code' (2021) 2 Journal of Comparative Law (Bi Jiao Fa Yan Jiu) 60

Zhou J, 'Direct loss under Arbitrary Termination of the Entrustment Contract' (2023) 3 Zhejiang Academic Journal (Zhe Jiang Xue Kan) 230

Zhou J, 'Several Suggestions for Modifications to the Contract Part of the Civil Code (Draft) (Second Review Draft)' (2019) 2 Research on Rule of Law (Fa Zhi Yan Jiu) 20

Zhu H, 'A Study on the Scope and Effectiveness of Prohibition of Assignment of Claims: Focusing on the Rules of the Civil Code'(2020) 5 Science of Law (Journal of Northwest University of Political Science and Law) 121

Zhu H, 'Between Separation and merger: the Arbitrary right to terminate a contract in the Civil Code' (2020) 4 Peking University Law Journal (Zhong Wai Fa Xue) 1018

Zhu Y, 'A Study on Contracts Benefiting Third Parties' (2005) 23 Science of Law (Journal of Northwest University of Political Science and Law) 55

Others

Maastricht European Private Law Institute Working Paper, No. 2011/06 https://ssrn.com/abstract=1756750 or http://dx.doi.org/10.2139/ssrn.1756750 accessed on 3 November 2024

People's Court Daily, 'Maintain Social Fairness with Strict and Impartial Justice' (2023) https://www.chinacourt.org/article/detail/2023/01/id/7112342.shtml accessed on 11 January 2024

People's Daily Online, 'What makes CPC-led multi-party cooperation a success' (2011) http://english.people.com.cn/90001/90780/91342/7421713.html

The CCP, 'Opinion of the CPC Central regarding Insisting on and Perfecting the System of Multiparty Co-operation and Political Consultation under the Leadership of the CCP' (1990) State Council Gazette No.2, 38

The National Bureau of Statistics of China, 'The Seventh National Population Census' (2021) https://www.stats.gov.cn/english/PressRelease/202105/t20210510_1817185.html

Table of Cases

Chinese Cases

A Battery Co., Ltd. v. B Auto Co., Ltd., the SPC (2021) Zui Gao Fa Min Shen No. 2163; 某电池公司诉某汽车公司买卖合同纠纷案（2021）最高法民申2163号

A Community Owners Committee v. Deng, (2017) 2 China Law Report, People's Court Press (2017), pp. 63-64; 某小区业主委员会诉邓某某物业服务合同纠纷案，《人民法院案例选》2017年2辑，人民法院出版社，2017年版，第63-64页

A Company Fuzhou Branch v. Fuzhou B Company and Wu, Fujian High People's Court (2022) Min Min Zhong No. 162; 某公司福州分公司诉福州某公司及吴某某，福建省高级人民法院（2022）闽民终162号

A Company v. Shanxi B Company, The SPC (2019) Zui Gao Fa Min Zhong No. 402; 某公司诉山西某公司中介合同纠纷案，最高人民法院（2019）最高法民终402号

A Property Management Co., Ltd. v. B Bank Qingdao Branch and C Business Co., Ltd., The SPC (2022) Zui Gao Fa Min Zai No. 223; 某物业公司诉某银行青岛分行、某商业公司物业服务合同纠纷案，最高人民法院（2022）最高法民再223号

Abdul Waheed v. China Eastern Airlines Co., Ltd., SPC Guiding Case No. 51; 阿卜杜勒・瓦希德诉中国东方航空股份有限公司航空旅客运输合同纠纷案，最高人民法院，第151号指导性案例

Anhui Foreign Economic Construction (Group) Co., Ltd. v. Inmobiliaria Palacio Oriental SA, the SPC Guiding Case No. 109; 安徽省外经建设（集团）有限公司诉东方置业房地产有限公司保函欺诈纠纷案，最高人民法院，第109号指导性案例

Bai Bing v. Guangdong Rongqi Sea Wheel Container Service Co., Ltd., the SPC (2020), Zui Gao Fa Min Shen No. 3032; 白冰诉广东容奇水陆集运有限公司，最高人民法院（2020）最高法民申3032号

Baiyin Nonferrous Group Co., Ltd. v. Kaifeng Tokyo Air Separation Group Co., Ltd. & Henan Sijian Co., Ltd, the Supreme People's Court, (2018) SPC Min Zhong No. 377; 白银有色集团股份有限公司诉开封东京空分集团有限公司、河南四建股份有限公司，最高人民法院（2018）最高法民终377号

Bank of Wenzhou Co., Ltd. Ningbo Branch v. Zhejiang Chuangling Electric Appliance Co., Ltd. and Others, SPC Guiding Case No. 57; 温州银行股份有限公司宁波分行诉浙江创菱电器有限公司等金融借款合同纠纷案，最高人民法院，第57号指导性案例

Beihai Hengli Real Estate Development Co., Ltd. v. Guangxi Construction First Construction Engineering Group Co., Ltd., The SPC (2020) Zui Gao Fa Min Shen No. 2821; 北海恒立房地产开发有限公司、广西建工集团第一建筑工程有限责任公司建设工程施工合同纠纷案，最高人民法院（2020）最高法民申2821 号

Beijing Changfu Investment Fund v. Wuhan Zhongsenhua Century Real Estate Development Co., Ltd. and Others, The SPC (2016) Zui Gao Fa Min Zhong No. 124; 北京长富投资基金与武汉中森华世纪房地产开发有限公司等委托贷款合同纠纷案, 最高人民法院（2016）最高法民终124号. Gazette Case of the SPC, Issue 11, 2016; 《最高人民法院公报》案例，2016年11期

Beijing Junfield Real Estate Development Ltd v. Cinda Investment Limited and others, the Supreme People's Court, (2020) SPC Min Zai No. 15; 北京庄胜房地产开发有限公司诉信达投资有限公司等，最高人民法院 （2020） 最高法民再15号

Beijing Shangshi Culture Communication Co., Ltd. v. Mokexing Pictures (Beijing) Co., Ltd., Beijing Chaoyang District People's Court, (2021) Jing 0105 Min Chu No. 85353; 北京上狮文化传播有限公司诉墨客行影业（北京）有限公司，北京市朝阳区人民法院（2021）京0105民初85353号.

Beijing Shiying Hezhong Digital Technology Co., Ltd. v. Union Software (Beijing) Co., Ltd., the Supreme People's Court, (2019) SPC Zhi Min Xia No. 477; 北京世盈合众数字技术有限公司诉系联软件（北京）有限公司， 最高人民法院（2019）最高法知民辖终477号

Beijing Urban Construction Heavy Industry Co., Ltd. v. Beijing Longchang Weiye Trading Co., Ltd. No.2 Intermediate People's Court of Beijing (2017) Jing 02 Min Zhong No.8676 (SPC Guiding Case No.166); 北京城建重工有限公司与北京隆昌伟业贸易有限公司合同纠纷二审民事判决书 北京市第二中级人民法院 （2017） 京02民终8676号合同纠纷案（最高院指导案例166号）

Beijing Yougaoya Decoration Engineering Co., Ltd. v. Beijing Henry Dai Art Furniture Co., Ltd. Beijing No. 2 Intermediate People's Court Er Zhong Min Zhong Zi No.01756; 北京优高雅装饰工程有限公司诉北京亨利戴艺术家具有限公司 北京二中院（2007）二中民终字第01756号

Beijing Zuotengfei Refrigeration Equipment Engineering Co., Ltd. v. Guodian Power Jiuquan Power Generation Co., Ltd. Supreme People's Court (2016) SPC Min Shen No. 2296; 北京佐腾飞制冷设备工程有限公司与国电电力酒泉发电有限公司债权转让合同纠纷申诉、申请民事裁定书 最高人民法院（2016）最高法民申2296号

BY.O v. Yushang Group Co., Ltd, Gazette Case of the SPC, Issue 11, 2021; BY.O诉豫商集团有限公司，《最高人民法院公报》案例，2021年11期

Cao Canru v. Shanghai Lines Real Estate Co., Ltd. No.2 Intermediate People's Court of Shanghai (2010) Hu Er Zhong Min Er (Civil) Zhong Zi No.609; 曹灿如与上海莱因思置业有限公司 上海二中院（2010）沪二中民二（民）终字第609

Cargill International S.A. v. Fujian Jinshi Oil Manufacturing Co., Ltd., SPC Guiding Case No. 33; 瑞士嘉吉国际公司诉福建金石制油有限公司等确认合同无效纠纷案，最高人民法院指导案例33号

Cen Mingguang v. Tengxian Tianping Agricultural Development Co., Ltd, Intermediate People's Court of Wuzhou City, Guangxi Zhuang Autonomous Region (2015) Wu Min Er Zhong Zi No.94; 岑明广与梁志宏、藤县天平农业发展有限公司与公司有关的纠纷二审民事判决书　广西壮族自治区梧州市中级人民法院（2015）梧民二终字第94号

Chai v. Management Company, Case No. 10 of The SPC Typical Cases Related to the SPC Interpretation on the General Provisions of the Contract Book, 2023; 某石材公司与某采石公司买卖合同纠纷案，《关于适用中华人民共和国民法典合同编通则若干问题的解释》相关典型案例，第10号案例

Changning Jiayuan Electric Power Development Co., Ltd. v. Baoshan Xinjie Construction Engineering Co., Ltd., The SPC (2020) Zui Gao Fa Min Shen No. 3395; 昌宁县珈源电力开发有限公司、保山市辛街建筑工程有限责任公司合同纠纷案，最高人民法院（2020）最高法民申3395 号

Chaoyang Meili Construction Engineering Co., Ltd. v. Sanya Shuiyi Industrial Co., Ltd., The SPC (2021) Zui Gao Fa Min Shen No. 6282; 朝阳美利建筑工程有限公司、三亚水亿实业有限公司等建设工程施工合同纠纷案，最高人民法院(2021) 最高法民申6282号

Chaoyang Qinghua Mining Co., Ltd. v. Chaoyang Jinchang Mining Co., Ltd., the Supreme People's Court, (2013) SPC Min Shen No. 2018; 朝阳青花矿业有限公司诉朝阳金昌矿业有限公司，最高人民法院 (2013) 民申字第2018号

Chen Guangyu v. Lin Mingqiang & Wang Ying, Intermediate People's Court of Haikou City, Hainan Province, (2018) Qiong 01 Min Zhong No. 1393; 陈光玉诉林明强、王颖，　海南省海口市中级人民法院（2018）琼01民终1393号

Chen Jing v. Wang Weibin, Shanghai No. 2 Intermediate People's Court, (2016) Hu 02 Min Zhong No. 5427; 陈婧诉王伟斌，　上海市第二中级人民法院（2016）沪02民终5427号; Shanghai No. 2 Intermediate People's Court ruled that the contract was invalid as there was a violation of a mandatory legal provision.

Chen Liyun v. Beijing Yuanshihui Investment Management Co., Ltd. and Beijing Wangxin Zhongchou Network Technology Co., Ltd., (2019) 4 China Law Report, People's Court Press (2019), pp. 132-143; 陈立耘与北京原始会投资管理有限公司、北京网信众筹网络科技有限公司居间合同纠纷案，《人民法院案例选》2019年4辑，人民法院出版社，2019年版，第132-143页

Chen Ming, Xu Yanfang and Chen Jie v. Shanghai Ctrip International Travel Service Co., Ltd., Gazette Case of the SPC, Issue 4, 2015; 陈明、徐炎芳、陈洁诉上海携程国际旅行社有限公司旅游合同纠纷案，《最高人民法院公报》案例，2015年04期

Chen Tongtong v. Beijing Gaohua Caixin Investment Consulting Co., Ltd. and Ma Chao, Beijing Chaoyang District People's Court (2020) Jing 0105 Min Chu No. 36603;　陈彤彤诉北京高华财信投资顾问有限公司、马超保证合同纠纷案，北京市朝阳区人民法院（2020）京0105民初36603号

Chen v. Liu, People's Court of Chaoyang District, Beijing (2016) Jing 0105 Min Chu No. 32945; 陈某与刘某，北京市朝阳区人民法院（2016）京0105民初32945号民事判决

Chen v. Zhuhai A Property Management Co., Ltd., Zhuhai Xiangzhou District People's Court (2022) Yue 0402 Min Chu No. 1029; 陈某某诉珠海某物业公司物业服务合同纠纷案， 珠海市香洲区人民法院（2022）粤0402民初1029号

Chen Weiwen v. Lianping Hardware, Electricity and Chemical Products Co., Ltd. (2007) 3 China Law Report, People's Court Press (2008), pp. 86-88; 陈伟文诉连平县五金交电化工公司确认优先购买权纠纷案， 《人民法院案例选》，2007 年第3 辑，人民法院出版社，2008 年版，第86-88 页

Cheng Meiju v. Jiangxi Huirong Real Estate Investment and Development Co., Ltd. Jiangxi High People's Court (2016) Gan Civil Zai No.46; 程美菊与江西惠荣房地产投资开发有限公司商品房预约合同纠纷案 江西省高级人民法院 （2016）赣民再46号; Chengdu Pengwei Industrial Co., Ltd. v. Jiangsu Province Yongxiu County Government & the Office of the Leading Group for Sand Mining Management of Poyang Lake in Yongxiu County, Gazette Case of the SPC, Issue 4, 2010; 成都鹏伟实业有限公司诉江西省永修县人民政府、永修县鄱阳湖采砂管理工作领导小组办公室,《最高人民法院公报》案例，2010年04期

Cheng v. Zhao, Jiangyin People's Court (2020) Su 0281 Min Chu No. 7297; 程某诉赵某，江苏省江阴市人民法院（2020）苏0281民初7297号

Chengdu Xunjie Communication Chains Co., Ltd. v. Sichuan Shudu Industry Co., Ltd. and Sichuan Youli Investment Holding Co., Ltd., the SPC (2013) Min Ti Zi No. 90; 成都讯捷通讯连锁有限公司诉四川蜀都实业有限责任公司、四川友利投资控股股份有限公司，最高人民法院（2013）民提字第90号. The Gazette Case of the SPC, Issue 1, 2015; 《最高人民法院公报》案例，2015年01期

China CITIC Bank Co., Ltd. Dongguan Branch v. Chen Zhihua and Others, SPC Guiding Case No. 168, 中信银行股份有限公司东莞分行诉陈志华等金融借款合同纠纷案，最高人民法院，第168号指导性案例

China CITIC Bank v. Beijing Jinggong Real Estate Development Co., Ltd., Gazette Case of the SPC, Issue 6, 2002; 中信实业银行诉北京市京工房地产开发总公司保证合同纠纷案，《最高人民法院公报》案例，2002年06期

China Development Bank v. Shenyang High-Voltage Switchgear Co., Ltd., New Northeast Electric (Shenyang) High-Voltage Switchgear Co., Ltd., New Northeast Electric (Shenyang) High-Voltage Disconnecting Switch Co., Ltd., and Shenyang Beifu Machinery Manufacturing Co., Ltd. Gazette Case of the SPC, Issue 12, 2008国家开发银行与沈阳高压开关有限责任公司、新东北电气(沈阳)高压开关有限公司、新东北电气(沈阳)高压隔离开关有限公司、沈阳北富机械制造有限公司等借款合同、撤销权纠纷案,《最高人民法院公报》2008年第12期

China Everbright Bank Co., Ltd. Shanghai Qingpu Branch v. Shanghai Donghe Real Estate Development Co., Ltd. and Chen Siqi, Gazette Case of the SPC, Issue 9, 2014; 中国光大银行股份有限公司上海青浦支行诉上海东鹤房地产有限公司、陈思绮保证合同纠纷案，《最高人民法院公报》案例，2014年09期

China Financial Leasing Co., Ltd. v. Beijing Homyear Capital Holdings Co., Ltd. and Beijing Gaosheng Huafang Real Estate Development Co., Ltd., Tianjin High People's Court (2018) Jin Min Chu No. 150; 中国金融租赁有限公

司诉北京华业资本控股股份有限公司、北京高盛华房地产开发有限公司借款合同纠纷案，天津市高级人民法院（2018）津民初150号
China Great Wall Asset Management Co., Ltd. Shanxi Branch v. Huamei Aochongsheng Coal Industry Co., Ltd. of Pinglu District, Shuozhou, Shanxi and Others, the SPC (2019) Zui Gao Fa Min Zhong No. 823; 中国长城资产管理股份有限公司山西省分公司与山西朔州平鲁区华美奥崇升煤业有限公司等借款合同纠纷案，最高人民法院（2019）最高法民终823号. The Gazette Case of the SPC, Issue 5, 2020; 《最高人民法院公报》案例，2020年05期
China International Water & Electric Corp v. Shanghai Fumin Reclamation and Dredging Co., Ltd, Longwan Port Group Shanghai Industrial Co., Ltd & Hainan Longwan Port Dredging Group Co., Ltd, The Supreme People's Court (2009) Min Er Ti Zi No.58; 中国水利电力对外公司诉上海福岷围垦疏浚有限公司、龙湾港集团上海实业有限责任公司、海南龙湾港疏浚集团有限公司最高人民法院（2009）民二提字第58号
China National Petroleum Corporation North China Sales Branch v. Beijing Tianlong Construction Engineering Co., Ltd., No.2 Intermediate People's Court of Beijing (2014) Er Zhong Zhi Zi No.542; 中国石油天然气股份有限公司华北销售分公司申请执行北京天龙建筑工程有限公司国内非涉外仲裁裁决纠纷强制执行裁定书，北京市第二中级人民法院(2014)二中执字第542号
China Pacific Property Insurance Co., Ltd. v. COSCO Shipping Holdings Co., Ltd., The SPC (2011) Min Ti Zi No. 12; 中国太平洋财产保险股份有限公司与中远航运股份有限公司、第三人海南分公司海南一汽海马汽车销售有限公司水路货物运输合同货损赔偿纠纷案，
最高人民法院（2011）民提字第12号. Gazette Case of the SPC, Issue 8, 2012, 《最高人民法院公报》案例，2012年08期
China Railway 15th Bureau Group Second Engineering Co., Ltd. v. China Railway 15th Bureau Group Second Engineering Co., Ltd. Kunming Branch and Lin Jihui, No.2 Intermediate People's Court of Shanghai, (2018) Hu 02 Min Xia Zhong No.617; 中铁十五局集团第二工程有限公司与中铁十五局集团第二工程有限公司昆明分公司、林际晖 债权人代位权纠纷二审民事裁定书 上海市第二中级人民法院（2018）沪02民辖终617号
China Railway Materials Harbin Co., Ltd. v. Sinochem International Corporation, The SPC (2019) Zui Gao Fa Min Shen No. 3187; 中国铁路物资哈尔滨有限公司、中化国际（控股）股份有限公司港口货物保管合同纠纷案， 最高人民法院（2019）最高法民申3187号
China Resource Bank of Zhuhai Co., Ltd. v. Jiangxi Fuel Co., Ltd., The SPC (2017) Zui Gao Fa Min Zai No. 164; 珠海华润银行股份有限公司与江西省电力燃料有限公司保理合同纠纷案，最高人民法院（2017）最高法民再164号
China Shipping Industry Co., Ltd. (Jiangsu) v. China Pacific Property Insurance Co., Ltd. Yangzhou Central Branch and China Pacific Property Insurance Co., Ltd., Gazette Case of the SPC, Issue 10, 2013; 中海工业（江苏）有限公司诉中国太平洋财产保险股份有限公司扬州中心支公司、中国太平洋财产保险股份有限公司海上保险合同纠纷案， 《最高人民法院公报》案例，2013年10期
China Water Resources and Electric Power Foreign Company v. Shanghai Fumin Reclamation and Dredging Co., Ltd., Longwan Port Group Shanghai Industrial

Co., Ltd., and Hainan Longwan Port Dredging Group Co., Ltd. Supreme People's Court (2009) Min Er Ti Zi No.58; 中国水利电力对外公司诉上海福岷围垦疏浚有限公司、龙湾港集团上海实业有限责任公司、海南龙湾港疏浚集团有限公司最高人民法院（2009）民二提字第58号

China Water Resources and Electric Power Foreign Company v. Shanghai Fumin Reclamation and Dredging Co., Ltd., Longwan Port Group Shanghai Industrial Co., Ltd., and Hainan Longwan Port Dredging Group Co., Ltd., the Supreme People's Court (2009) Min Er Ti Zi No.58; 中国水利电力对外公司诉上海福岷围垦疏浚有限公司、龙湾港集团上海实业有限责任公司、海南龙湾港疏浚集团有限公司最高人民法院（2009）民二提字第58号民事判决书

China Xiamen Construction Group Co., Ltd. v. China Construction Bank Corporation Shanghai Second Branch, the Supreme People's Court, (2019) SPC Min Shen 1518; 中国建设银行股份有限公司上海第二支行诉中厦建设集团有限公司 最高人民法院（2019）最高法民申1518号

Chongqing Boda Mining Co., Ltd. v. Aluminum Corporation of China Chongqing Branch & Aluminum Corporation of China Limited, the Supreme People's Court, (2019) SPC Min Zhong No. 511; 重庆博达矿业有限公司诉中国铝业股份有限公司重庆分公司、中国铝业股份有限公司， 最高人民法院 （2019）最高法民终511号

Chongqing Construction Engineering Group Co., Ltd. v. Chongqing Tongyao Transportation Equipment Co., Ltd., the SPC (2022) Zui Gao Fa Min Zai No. 114; 重庆建工工业有限公司、重庆通耀交通装备有限公司建设工程施工合同纠纷案，最高人民法院 （2022）最高法民再114号

Chongqing Jintang Real Estate Development Co., Ltd. v. Chongqing Nengtou Real Estate Co., Ltd., the Supreme People's Court (2019) SPC Min Zhong No.454; 重庆金唐房地产开发有限公司、重庆能投置业有限公司合资、合作开发房地产合同纠纷二审民事判决书 最高人民法院（2019）最高法民终454号

Chongqing Port Logistics Group Industrial Co., Ltd. v. Chongqing Metallurgical Rolling Mill, the Supreme People's Court (2016) SPC Min Shen No.3020; 重庆港务物流集团实业有限公司诉重庆冶金轧钢厂，最高人民法院（2016）最高法民申3020号

Chun Wing Intimate Factory Ltd v. CEVA Freight (Shenzhen) Ltd and Others, Gazette Case of the SPC, Issue 7, 2019; 骏荣内衣有限公司诉宏鹰国际货运（深圳）有限公司等海上货运代理合同纠纷案， 《最高人民法院公报》案例，2019年07期

Civil Affairs Bureau of Linwei District, Weinan City, Shaanxi Province v. Weinan Xiangshan Cemetery Operations Management Co., Ltd. and Others, Supreme People's Court (2021) SPC Min Shen No.4557; 陕西省渭南市临渭区民政局、渭南象山公墓运营管理有限公司等合同纠纷案，最高人民法院民事申请再审审查民事裁定书，（2021）最高法民申4557号

Coal Sales Department of Rizhao Port Group Co., Ltd. v. Shanxi Coking Coal Group International Development Co., Ltd., the Supreme People's Court, (2015) SPC Min Ti No. 74; 日照港集团有限公司煤炭运销部诉山西焦煤集团国际发展股份有限公司，最高人民法院（2015）民提字第74号

Company A Ltd., Company B Ltd., Company C Ltd., and Company D Ltd. v. Guangzhou Company, Supreme People's Court (2021) SPC Min Zhong No.1079;

某甲有限公司、某乙有限公司、某丙有限公司、某丁有限公司、广州公司股权转让纠纷民事二审民 最高人民法院（2021）最高法民终1079号

Cui Chengqi v. Shandong Baoan Real Estate Development Ltd., Shandong Province Weihai City Intermediate People's Court, (2023) Lu 10 Min Zhong No. 229; 崔承歧诉山东宝安房地产开发有限公司，山东省威海市中级人民法院（2023）鲁10民终229号

Dalian Fengqi Investment Management Co., Ltd. v. Sinotrans Liaoning Storage and Freight Co., Ltd. and Others, The SPC (2016) Zui Gao Fa Min Zhong No. 650; 大连俸旗投资管理有限公司与中国外运辽宁储运公司等借款合同纠纷案，（2016）最高法民终650号. Gazette Case of the SPC, Issue 7, 2017; 《最高人民法院公报》案例，2017年07期

Dalian Haneda Steel Tube Co., Ltd. v. Hongfeng Steel Industry & Trade Co., Ltd. in Dalian Free Trade Zone, Haneda Steel Pipe Works Co., Ltd. and Dalian High-tech Industrial Park Longwangtang Subdistrict Office, the SPC (2011) Min Ti Zi No. 29; 大连羽田钢管有限公司与大连保税区弘丰钢铁工贸有限公司、株式会社羽田钢管制造所、大连高新技术产业园区龙王塘街道办事处物权确认纠纷案，最高人民法院（2011）民提字第29号. The Gazette Case of the SPC, Issue 6, 2012; 《最高人民法院公报》案例，2012年06期

Datang Huxian No. 2 Thermal Power Plant v. Shandong Sanrong Environmental Protection Engineering Co., Ltd., the Supreme People's Court, (2017) SPC Min Xia Zhong No. 83; 山东三融环保工程有限公司诉大唐户县第二热电厂，最高人民法院（2017）最高法民辖终83号

Datong Tianli Real Estate Development Co., Ltd. v. Shanxi Tongzhiren Commercial Management Co., Ltd. Supreme People's Court (2015) Min Yi Zhong Zi No.340; 大同市天力房地产开发有限责任公司诉山西同至人商业管理有限公司 最高人民法院（2015）民一终字第340号

Dawa Tianruixiang Chemical Co., Ltd. v. Jin'ao Technology (Hubei) Chemical Co., Ltd., Hanjiang Intermediate People's Court, Hubei Province (2016) E 96 Min Zhong No. 245; 大洼天瑞祥化工有限公司诉金澳科技（湖北）化工有限公司，湖北省汉江中级人民法院（2016）鄂96民终245号

Dayang Company v. Huanghe Company, The SPC (2003) Min San Zhong Zi No. 8; 大洋公司诉黄河公司专利实施许可合同纠纷案， 最高人民法院（2003）民三终字第8号. The Gazette Case of the SPC, Issue 9, 2004; 《最高人民法院公报》案例，2004年09期

Deng Meihua v. Shanghai Yongda Pirui Auto Sales Service Co., Ltd., Gazette Case of the SPC, Issue 11, 2018; 邓美华与上海永达霹悦汽车销售服务有限公司买卖合同纠纷案，《最高人民法院公报》2018年第11期

Dong Limin v. Hailin Changhai Heat Supply Co., Ltd., Heilongjiang High People's Court (2021) Hei Min Zai No. 707; 董立敏诉海林市长海供热有限公司，黑龙江省高级人民法院（2021）黑民再707号

Dongfang Turbine Co., Ltd. v. Dafeng Construction and Installation Co., Ltd. of Daqing High-tech Industrial Development Zone and Daqing Dafeng Energy Technology Service Co., Ltd., Gazette Case of the SPC, Issue 11, 2020; 东方电气集团东方汽轮机有限公司与大庆高新技术产业开发区大丰建筑安装有限公司、大庆大丰能源技术服务有限公司买卖合同纠纷案，《最高人民法院公报》案例，2020年11期

Dongyang Shangjiang Ham Factory v. Zhejiang Xuefang Industry and Trade Co., Ltd., Supreme People's Court (2014) Min Shen Zi No. 1233; 东阳市上蒋火腿厂诉浙江雪舫工贸有限公司，最高人民法院（2014）民申字第1233号

Du Changhang v. Wang Xuewei, Liaoning Shenyang Intermediate People's Court (2021) Liao 01 Min Zhong No. 12917; 杜畅航诉王学伟，辽宁沈阳中院（2021）辽01民终12917号

Du Yang & Feng Xuan v. Yuan Hairong & Zhao Qiang, Beijing No. 3 Intermediate People's Court (2019) Jing 03 Min Zhong No. 6313; 杜洋、冯轩诉袁海荣、赵强，北京市第三中级人民法院（2019）京03民终6313号

EV Capital Private Limited and Others v. Joyou Group Building Materials Co., Ltd., The SPC (2014) Min Si Zhong Zi No. 14; 万嘉融资咨询私人有限公司等诉中宇建材集团有限公司中介合同纠纷案，最高人民法院（2014）民四终字第14号

Fan v. Chongqing Ganghua Property Management Co., Ltd., (2021) 2 China Law Report, People's Court Press (2021), pp. 113-121; 范某某诉重庆港华物业管理有限公司物业服务合同纠纷案，《人民法院案例选》2021年2辑，人民法院出版社202I年版，第113-121页

Fangchenggang Huayu High-tech Fiber Co., Ltd. v. Shaoyang Textile Machinery Co., Ltd., The SPC (2019) Zui Gao Fa Min Zai No. 383; 防城港华裕特纤科技有限公司、邵阳纺织机械有限责任公司买卖合同纠纷案，最高人民法院（2019）最高法民再383号

Fengning Changge Mining Cot Ltd v. China Railway Beijing Group Co., Ltd., The SPC (2017) Zui Gao Fa Min Zhong No. 724; 丰宁长阁矿业有限公司与北京铁路局物权保护纠纷案，最高人民法院（2017）最高法民终724 号. Gazette Case of the SPC, Issue 9, 2019; 《最高人民法院公报》案例，2019年09期

Foshan Sanshui Huatongsheng Textile Printing and Dyeing Co., Ltd. v. Wu Shuxin, Foshan Intermediate People's Court of Guangdong Province, (2018) Yue 06 Min Chu No. 141; 佛山市三水华通盛纺织印染有限公司诉吴树新，广东省佛山市中级人民法院（2018）粤06民初141号

Fu Jiaqun v. Hubei Rongxingda Trading Co., Ltd. Intermediate People's Court of Hubei (2017) E 01 Min Zhong No.1576; 付家群、湖北荣兴达贸易有限公司，湖北省武汉市中级人民法院（2017）鄂01民终1576号

Fuxin Shengjin Investment Management Co., Ltd. v. Shenyang Ke Laisite International Real Estate First Co., Ltd. and Shenyang Jiazhou Yangguang Garden Housing Development Co., Ltd. Supreme People's Court (2016) SPC Zhi Fu No.48; 阜新盛金投资管理有限公司与沈阳克莱斯特国际置业第一有限公司、沈阳加州阳光花园房屋开发有限公司，最高人民法院（2016）最高法执复48号

Ge Lanying v. Urban Agricultural Machinery Station, (2003) 1 China Law Report, People's Court Press (2003), pp. 211-213; 葛兰英诉城镇农机站抵押借款后又将抵押物发包给其承包经营现抵押物被判决执行给债权人应按租赁关系由其行使优先购买权案，《人民法院案例选》2003 年第1 辑，人民法院出版社，2003 年版，第211-213 页

Golf (Nanjing) Real Estate Development Co., Ltd. v. Wu Yongmei, Gazette Case of the SPC, Issue 12, 2012; 高尔夫（南京）房地产有限公司诉吴咏梅供用热力合同纠纷案，《最高人民法院公报》案例，2012年12期

Gu Ming & Wang Youheng & Jiangsu Ruihao Real Estate Co., Ltd. v. Yancheng Dafeng District People's Government & Yancheng Dafeng District Land and Resources Bureau, the Supreme People's Court, (2016) SPC Min Zhong No. 822; 顾明、汪有恒、江苏瑞豪置业有限公司诉盐城市大丰区人民政府、盐城市大丰区国土资源局，最高人民法院（2016）最高法民终822号

Guangdong Feigou Technology Co., Ltd. v. Shanghai Dianfan Intelligent Technology Co., Ltd. Supreme People's Court (2022) SPC Zhi Min Zhong No.108; 广东飞购科技有限公司、上海典泛智能科技有限公司 最高人民法院（2022）最高法知民终108号

Guangdong Jiedong Rural Commercial Bank Co., Ltd. v. Wu Liebiao and Others, Guangdong Jieyang Intermediate People's Court (2019) Yue 52 Min Zhong No. 421; 广东揭东农村商业银行股份有限公司诉吴列标等金融借款合同纠纷案，广东省揭阳市中级人民法院（2019）粤52民终421号

Guangzhou Youdai Micro-Lending Co., Ltd. v. Li, Guangzhou Internet Court (2019) Yue 0192 Min Chu No. 45769; 广州优贷小额贷款有限公司诉李某、第三人深圳市前海吉顺信科技发展有限公司，广州互联网法院（2019）粤0192民初45769号

Haikou Telecom Urban Construction Investment Co., Ltd. v. Haikou Housing and Urban-Rural Development Burea, Supreme People's Court (2016) SPC Min Zhong No.469海口电信城市建设投资有限公司与海口市人民政府、海口市住房和城乡建设局房屋租赁合同纠纷二审民事判决书，最高人民法院（2016）最高法民终469号

Haiqing Heavy Industry Co., Ltd. v. Jiangsu Zhongxing Construction Co., Ltd. and China Construction Bank Taixing Branch, The SPC (2012) Min Ti Zi No. 20; 海擎重工机械有限公司与江苏中兴建设有限公司、中国建设银行股份有限公司泰兴支行建设工程施工合同纠纷案，最高人民法院（2012）民提字第20号. Gazette Case of the SPC, Issue 6, 2015; 《最高人民法院公报》案例，2015年06期

Haitian Construction Group Co., Ltd. v. Shanxi Yufeng Real Estate Development Co., Ltd., The SPC (2021) Zui Gao Fa Min Shen No. 6178; 海天建设集团有限公司、山西宇丰房地产开发有限公司建设工程施工合同纠纷案，最高人民法院（2021）最高法民申6178号

Haitian Construction Group Co., Ltd. v. Yunnan Fenggu Real Estate Co., Ltd., The SPC (2018) Zui Gao Fa Min Zhong No. 475; 海天建设集团有限公司、云南金丰谷置业有限公司建设工程施工合同纠纷案，最高人民法院（2018）最高法民终475号

Hangzhou Yishang Investment Management Partnership (General Partnership) v. Zhongzhu Medical Holdings Co., Ltd., the Supreme People's Court, (2020) SPC Min Zhong No. 137; 杭州忆上投资管理合伙企业(普通合伙)诉中珠医疗控股股份有限公司，最高人民法院（2020）最高法民终137号

Hebi Broadhouse Real Estate Co., Ltd. v. Qixian Rural Credit Cooperatives, the Supreme People's Court, (2019) Min Shen No. 4756; 淇县农村信用合作联社诉鹤壁市广厦房产置业有限公司， 最高人民法院（2019）最高法民申4756号

Heilongjiang Kunfeng Agricultural Development Group Co., Ltd. v. Wengfu Group Agricultural Materials Co., Ltd. & Keshan Xinglong Agriculture Co., Ltd. Supreme People's Court (2019) SPC Min Zhong No.1451; 黑龙江昆丰农业

发展集团有限公司、瓮福集团农资有限责任公司企业借贷纠纷二审民事判决书 最高人民法院 (2019)最高法民终1451号
Hong Kong Rilong Investment Co., Ltd. v. Shenzhen Lexin Enma Electronics Co., Ltd. & Shenzhen Lexin Jingmi Industry Co., Ltd, the Supreme People's Court (2017) SPC Min Zai No. 370; 日隆投资有限公司诉深圳乐新恩玛电子有限公司、深圳乐新精密工业有限公司， 最高人民法院（2017）最高法民再370号
Hong Long Industry Co., Ltd. v. Shanghai Railway Sub-Bureau Hejiawan Station, Gazette Case of the SPC, Issue 1, 2001; 宏隆实业有限公司与上海铁路分局何家湾站等铁路货物运输合同逾期货损索赔纠纷再审案， 《最高人民法院公报》案例，2001年01期
Hu X v. Hu Y, 胡某某v胡某案 (2018) 4 China Law Report, People's Court Press (2018), pp. 113-119; 《人民法院案例选》2018年4辑， 人民法院出版社，2018年版，第113-119页
Huang Ruzhen v. Lin Ping, Fujian High People's Court (2016) Min Zhong No.927; 黄如震、林萍债权人撤销权纠纷二审民事判决书 福建省高级人民法院 (2016) 闽民终972号民事判决书
Huang Wengui v. Beijing Ningke Real Estate Co., Ltd. The SPC (2019) SPC Min Shen No.2868; 黄文贵、北京宁科置业有限责任公司房屋买卖合同纠纷案 最高人民法院（2019）最高法民申2826号
Hubei Jinhua Industry Co., Ltd. v. Su Jinshui and Others, The SPC (2012) Min Kang Zi Di No. 24 (Gazette Case of the SPC, Issue 1, 2014); 湖北金华实业有限公司与苏金水等商品房买卖合同纠纷案， 最高人民法院（2012）民抗字第24号（《最高人民法院公报》案例，2014年01期）
Hunan Hongji Industrial Development Co., Ltd. v. Hengyang Mulin Real Estate Development Co., Ltd., the Supreme People's Court, (2019) SPC Min Zhong No. 1464; 湖南宏基实业开发有限公司诉衡阳市沐林房地产开发有限公司，最高人民法院 (2019) 最高法民终1464号
Industrial and Commercial Bank of China Limited Xuancheng Longshou Branch v. Xuancheng Boguan Trading Co., Ltd. and Jiangsu Kaisheng Real Estate Co., Ltd., SPC Guiding Case No. 95; 中国工商银行股份有限公司宣城龙首支行诉宣城柏冠贸易有限公司、江苏凯盛置业有限公司等金融借款合同纠纷案，最高人民法院，第95号指导性案例
Japon Elektronik Teknoloji Ticaret Limited Sirketi v. Qingdao Hisense Import & Export Co., Ltd., Gazette Case of the SPC, Issue 11, 2013; 捷跑电子科技有限公司诉青岛海信进出口有限公司国际货物买卖合同纠纷案，
《最高人民法
院公报》案例，2013年11期
Jia Min v. Fuhua Holdings Limited, Beijing Chaoyang District People's Court (2019) Jing 0105 Min Chu No. 34308; 贾敏与复华控股有限公司保证合同纠纷案，北京市朝阳区人民法院（2019）京0105民初34308号
Jia v. Shanghai A Trading Co., Ltd., Shanghai Second Intermediate People's Court (2013) Hu Er Zhong Min Yi (Min) Zhong Zi No. 483; 贾某诉上海某商贸有限公司居间合同纠纷案， 上海市第二中级人民法院（2013）沪二中民一（民）终字第483号

Jianfuxin Software Development Co., Ltd. v. Zhuhai Jinshan Office Software Co., Ltd., the Supreme People's Court, (2020) SPC Zhi Min Zhong No. 1319; 福建福昕软件开发股份有限公司诉珠海金山办公软件有限公司，最高人民法院（2020）最高法知民终1319号
Jiang Weimin v. Nanjing Hongyang Real Estate Brokerage Co., Ltd., Gazette Case of the SPC, Issue 11, 2022; 江卫民诉南京宏阳房产经纪有限公司房屋租赁合同纠纷案，《最高人民法院公报》案例，2022年11期
Jiangsu Jintao Investment Holding Co., Ltd. v. Jiangxi Kete Investment Co., Ltd. Supreme People's Court (2020) SPC Min Zhong No.295; 江苏金涛投资控股有限公司、江西省科特投资有限公司借款合同纠纷二审民事判决书，最高人民法院（2020）最高法民终 295 号民事判决书司
Jiangsu Nantong No. 2 Construction Engineering (Group) Co., Ltd. v. Wujiang Hengsen Real Estate Co., Ltd., Gazette Case of the SPC, Issue 8, 2014; 江苏南通二建集团有限公司与吴江恒森房地产开发有限公司建设工程施工合同纠纷案，《最高人民法院公报》案例，2014年08期
Jiangyin Xinjiyang Petroleum Co., Ltd. v. China Construction Bank Jiangyin Lingang Xincheng Branch, Wuxi Intermediate People's Court (2014) Xi Shang Zhong Zi No. 0306; 江阴市新暨阳石油有限公司与中国建设银行股份有限公司江阴临港新城支行债权转让纠纷案，无锡市中级人民法院（2014）锡商终字第0306号
Jinsha County Lengshuihe Tourism Development Co., Ltd. v. Jinsha County People's Government, the Supreme People's Court, (2020) SPC Min Shen No. 6933; 金沙县冷水河旅游开发有限责任公司诉金沙县人民政府，最高人民法院（2020）最高法民申6933号
Jiuyi Global (Jiamusi) Mining Equipment Co., Ltd. v. Datong Longmei Coal Mining Machinery Sales Co., Ltd, the Supreme People's Court, (2016) SPC Min Xia Zhong No. 39; 久益环球（佳木斯）采矿设备有限公司诉大同市龙煤煤矿机械销售有限公司，最高人民法院，（2016）最高法民辖终39号
Kaiping A Property Management Co., Ltd. v. Chen B and Wu C, Jiangmen Intermediate People's Court (2022) Yue 07 Min Zhong No. 3418; 开平某物业分公司诉陈某权、吴某桃物业服务合同纠纷案， 江门市中级人民法院（2022）粤07民终3418号
Ke Guoqing v. Maoming Weiheng Real Estate Co., Ltd., Maoming Bohui Investment Co., Ltd., and Others, Supreme People's Court (2015) Min Ti Zi No.221; 柯国庆与茂名市伟恒地产有限公司、茂名市博汇投资有限公司、茂名市志同贸易有限公司与黄世就民间借贷纠纷，最高人民法院再审，（2015）民提字第211号
Legal Evening News Agency v. Beiqing Hangmei Technology and Media Communication Co., Ltd., No.4 Intermediate People's Court of Beijing (2021) Jing 04 Min Te No.164; 法制晚报社与北青航媒科技传播有限公司申请撤销仲裁裁决民事裁定书 北京市第四中级人民法院（2021）京04民特164号
Li Chengjian v. Zhejiang Zhuojing Venture Capital Co., Ltd. Supreme People's Court (2015) Min Shen Zi No.2593; 黎承健、浙江卓景创业投资有限公司与浙江卓景创业投资有限公司申请再审民事裁定书 最高人民法院（2015）民申字第2593号

Li Guohui v. Zhang Li, Guangdong Province Shaoguan City Intermediate People's Court, (2022) Yue 02 Min Zhong No. 2240; 李国辉诉张力，广东省韶关市中级人民法院（2022）粤02民终2240号
Li Li v. Hunan Caixin Trust Co., Ltd, Supreme People's Court (2021) SPC Min Shen No.1754; 李莉、湖南省财信信托有限责任公司债权人撤销权纠纷再审审查与审判监督民事裁定书
最高人民法院（2021）最高法民申1754号案例
Li Linxia v. Chongqing Manka Cultural Communication Co., Ltd., Gazette Case of the SPC, Issue 10, 2020; 李林霞诉重庆漫咖文化传播有限公司劳动合同纠纷案，《最高人民法院公报》案例，2020年10期
Li Mingbo v. Nanjing Jinling Property Development Co., Ltd., Gazette Case of the SPC, Issue 12, 2016; 李明柏诉南京金陵置业发展有限公司商品房预售合同纠纷案，《最高人民法院公报》案例，2016年12期
Li Wenyuan v. Hong Meiliang & Wu Jiafu, High People's Court of Zhejiang (2013) Zhe Min Zai Zi No. 21; 李文渊诉洪美良、吴加富 浙江省高级人民法（2013）浙民再字第21号
Li Yandong v. Shanghai Hanyu Real Estate Consulting Co., Ltd., Gazette Case of the SPC, Issue 2, 2015; 李彦东诉上海汉宇房地产顾问有限公司居间合同纠纷案，《最高人民法院公报》案例，2015年02期
Li Zunji v. Peng Chao and Others, Beijing Third Intermediate People's Court (2023) Jing 03 Min Zai No. 57; 李遵基与彭超等民间借贷纠纷案，北京市第三中级人民法院（2023）京03民再57号
Liangxi District Manze Road Trading Company v. Zhejiang S.F. Express Co., Ltd., the Supreme People's Court, (2023) SPC Min Xia No. 142; 梁溪区漫泽道商贸商行诉浙江顺丰速运有限公司，最高人民法院民（2023）最高法民辖142号
Liebherr (China) Co., Ltd. v. Ningxia Ruichen Aodisi Engineering Machinery Co., Ltd., Shanghai Pudong New Area People's Court (2021) Hu 0115 Min Chu No. 55963; 利勃海尔（中国）有限公司与宁夏瑞宸奥迪斯工程机械有限公司等买卖合同纠纷案，上海市浦东新区人民法院（2021）沪0115民初55963号
Lin v. Hangzhou Heyi Property Management Co., Ltd., Hangzhou Intermediate People's Court (2019) Zhe 01 Min Zhong No. 877; 林某某与杭州和亿物业管理有限公司物业服务合同纠纷案，杭州市中级人民法院（2019）浙01民终877号
Liu Lian v. Beijing Yigao Anjie Information Technology Co., Ltd. No.1 Intermediate Court of Beijing (2016) Jing 01 Min Zhong No.6979; 刘恋诉北京益高安捷信息技术有限公司，北京市第一中级人民法院（2016）京01民终6979号民事判决书
Liu v. Chen, No.3 Intermediate People's Court of Beijing (2016) Jing 03 Min Zhong No. 13939; 刘某诉陈某，北京市第三中级人民法院（2016）京03民终13939号
Liu Xiangqian v. Anbang Property Insurance Co., Ltd., (Gazette Case of the SPC, Issue 8, 2013); 刘向前诉安邦财产保险公司，《最高人民法院公报》案例，2013年第08期

Liulin Haobo Coking Coal Co., Ltd. v. Shanxi Liansheng Energy Investment Co., Ltd., the SPC (2016) Zui Gao Fa Min Zhong No. 286; 柳林县浩博煤焦有限责任公司、山西联盛能源投资有限公司融资租赁合同纠纷案， 最高人民法院（2016）最高法民终286 号

Lu Hong v. United Airlines, Gazette Case of the SPC, Issue 4, 2002; 陆红诉美国联合航空公司国际航空旅客运输损害赔偿纠纷案， 《最高人民法院公报》案例，2002年04期

Lu Suyan v. Wujiang Taihu Industrial Waste Disposal Co., Ltd. & Others People's Court of New District Shanghai (2022) Hu 0115 Min Chu No. 95925; 陆肃燕与吴江市太湖工业废弃物处理有限公司等其他与公司有关的纠纷一审民事判决书 上海市浦东新区人民法院（2022）沪0115民初95925号

Lu Yuxiang v. China Power Engineering Co., Ltd. No.1 Intermediate People's Court of Beijing, (2015), Yi Zhong Min (Comm) Zhong Zi No.543; 鲁于翔与中国电力工程有限公司买卖合同纠纷二审民事裁定书 北京市第一中级人民法院（2015）一中民（商）终字第543号

Luo Zhiguang v. Guangdong Huaqiao Real Estate Agency Co., Ltd., Chen Liangyi and Huang Qujiao (2009) China Law Report, China Legal Publishing House (2009), pp. 21-22; 罗志广诉广东省华侨房产建设公司、陈良义、黄取娇优先购买权纠纷案， 《人民法院案例选》2009 年， 中国法制出版社， 2009 年版， 第21-22 页

Maersk (China) Shipping Co., Ltd. and Maersk (China) Shipping Co., Ltd. Xiamen Branche v. PRIME International (XIAMEN) Co., Ltd. and China Xiamen Ocean Shipping Agency Co., Ltd., The SPC (2010) Min Ti Zi No. 213 (Gazette Case of the SPC, Issue 10, 2011); 马士基（中国）航运有限公司及其厦门分公司与厦门瀛海实业发展有限公司、中国厦门外轮代理有限公司国际海上货运代理经营权损害赔偿纠纷案， 最高人民法院民事判决书（2010）民提字第213号（《最高人民法院公报》案例，2011年10期）

Malai Gen and Others v. Nanjing Jiangning Urban Construction and Development Co., Ltd. Intermediate People's Court of Nanjing Jiangsu (2017) Su 01 Min Zhong No.9469; 马来根等诉南京江宁城镇建设开发有限责任公司房屋租赁合同纠纷案 江苏省南京市中级人民法院（2017）苏01民终9469号

Nahe People's Hospital and Nahe City Investment Co., Ltd. v. Shanghai Electric Leasing Co., Ltd., Shanghai Financial Court (2021) Hu 74 Min Zhong No. 87; 讷河市人民医院、讷河市城市投资有限公司与上海电气融资租赁有限公司融资租赁合同纠纷案，上海金融法院（2021）沪74民终87号

Nanjing Gaoke Xinjun Growth Phase I Equity Investment Partnership (Limited Partnership) v. Fang Yongsheng and Liang Xilin, Shanghai No. 2 Intermediate People's Court, (2020) Hu 02 Min Chu No. 234; 南京高科新浚成长一期股权投资合伙企业（有限合伙）诉房永生、梁锡林， 上海市第二中级人民法院（2020）沪02民初234号

Nanjing Gaoke Xinjun Growth Phase I Equity Investment Partnership (Limited Partnership) v. Fang Yongsheng and Liang Xilin, Shanghai High People's Court, (2020) Hu 02 Min Chu No. 234; 南京高科新浚成长一期股权投资合伙企业（有限合伙）诉房永生、梁锡林，上海市高级人民法院（2021）沪民终745号

Ni Xiuping v. Yang Xigen & Li Ruifen, Wuxi Intermediate People's Court, (2017) Su 02 Min Zhong No. 1560; 倪惠平诉杨锡根、李瑞芬，江苏省无锡市中级人民法院（2017）苏02民终1560号.

Nie Jiawei v. Xinjiang Balingjiuling Automobile Service Co., Ltd., the People's Court of Shuimogou District, Urumqi City, Xinjiang Uygur Autonomous Region (2022) Xin 0105 Min Chu No. 5620; 聂嘉伟诉新疆捌零玖零汽车服务有限公司， 新疆维吾尔自治区乌鲁木齐市水磨沟区人民法院（2022）新0105民初5620号

Nie Qin v. Country Garden Life Services Group Co., Ltd. Dongguan Branch and Others, Dongguan Intermediate People's Court (2021) Yue 19 Min Zhong No. 12866; 聂琴、碧桂园生活服务集团股份有限公司东莞分公司等物业服务合同纠纷案，广东省东莞市中级人民法院（2021）粤19民终12866号

Ningbo Yinzhou Ruixing Clothing Co., Ltd. v. Zheng Minghua, Zhejiang Ningbo Intermediate People's Court (2009) Zhe Yong Shang Zhong No. 1054; 宁波市鄞州润兴服饰有限责任公司诉郑明华，浙江宁波中级人民法院（ 2009）浙甬商终1054号

Ningxia Qianzongbao Diabetes Kidney Disease Institute v. Jiangsu Hongrui Pharmaceutical Co., Ltd., the Supreme People's Court, (2019) SPC Min Shen No. 1173; 宁夏千宗宝糖尿病肾病研究所诉江苏红瑞制药有限公司， 最高人民法院（2019）最高法民申1173号

Ningxia Yulong Engineering Co., Ltd. v. Anhui Sanjian Construction Engineering Co., Ltd. and Ningxia Lantian Real Estate Development Co., Ltd., The SPC (2019) Zui Gao Fa Min Shen No. 6085; 宁夏钰隆工程有限公司、安徽三建工程有限公司、宁夏蓝天房地产开发有限责任公司建设工程施工合同纠纷案最高人民法院（2019）最高法民申6085号

Ningxiang Zhongyu Plastics Co., Ltd., Zhang Ailian, and Others v. Mao De'an (2019) SPC Min Shen No. 1151; 宁乡中宇塑业有限公司、张爱连民间借贷纠纷再审审查与审判监督民事裁定书 最高人民法院（2019）最高法民申1151号

PetroChina Co., Ltd. Jiangsu Lianyungang Sales Branch v. Lianyungang Zejia International Logistics Co., Ltd., The SPC (2021) Zui Gao Fa Min Shen No. 6612; 中国石油天然气股份有限公司江苏连云港销售分公司、连云港泽嘉国际物流有限公司港口货物保管合同纠纷案， 最高人民法院（2021）最高法民申6612号

Ping An Bank Co., Ltd. Wuhan Branch v. Datang Henan Clean Energy Co., Ltd., Hubei High People's Court (2017) E Min Zhong No. 3113; 平安银行股份有限公司武汉分行、大唐河南能源有限责任公司合同纠纷案， 湖北省高级人民法院（2017）鄂民终3113号

Qingdao A Company v. B Shipping Company and Shanghai C Company, The SPC (2020) Zui Gao Fa Min Shen No. 6908; 青岛某公司诉某航运公司、上海某公司多式联运合同纠纷案，最高人民法院（2020）最高法民申6908号

Qingdao Wuchan Haohai International Trade Co., Ltd. v. Wen'an County Baoying International Trade Co., Ltd and Others, Intermediate People's Court of Langfang Hebei (2020) Ji 10 Min Zhong No.3862; 青岛物产浩海国际贸易有限公司、文安县宝盈国际贸易有限公司、潘少峰买卖合同纠纷二审民事判决书河北省廊坊市中级人民法院（2020）冀10民终3862号案

Qingdao Yaleju Real Estate Brokerage Co., Ltd. v. You Zhenglei, Shandong Qingdao Intermediate People's Court (2022) Lu 02 Min Zhong No. 4730; 青岛青雅居房产经纪有限公司诉由政磊中介合同纠纷案，山东省青岛中级人民法院（2022）鲁02民终4730号

Qinghai Salt Lake Industrial Co., Ltd. v. Qinghai Haolin Machinery Equipment Leasing Co., Ltd., Qinghai Salt Lake Energy Co., Ltd., and Wan Shiliang, Supreme People's Court (2016) SPC Min Zhong No.27; 青海盐湖工业股份有限公司与青海皓林机械设备租赁有限公司与青海盐湖能源有限公司与万世良债权转让合同纠纷二审民事判决书 最高人民法院（2016）最高法民终27号

Rao Guoli v. Jiangxi Provincial Prison Administration Material Supply Station, the Supreme People's Court, (2019) SPC Min Zai No. 97 (SPC Guiding Case No. 170); 饶国礼诉江西省监狱管理局物资供应站，最高人民法院（2019）最高法民再97号（最高人民法院第170号指导性案例）

Rizhao Port Co., Ltd. Coal Distribution Department v. Shanxi Coking Coal Group International Development Co., Ltd., the SPC (2015) Min Ti Zi No. 74 (The SPC, Issue 6, 2017); 日照港集团有限公司煤炭运销部诉山西焦煤集团国际发展股份有限公司，最高人民法院（2015）民提字第74号（《最高人民法院公报》案例，2017年06期）

Shanghai A Medicine Co., Ltd. v. Shanghai B Logistics Co., Ltd., Shanghai Second Intermediate People's Court (2022) Hu 02 Min Zhong No. 3258; 上海某医疗公司诉上海某物流公司运输合同纠纷案，上海市第二中级人民法院（2022）沪02民终3258号

Shanghai Honghua Cultural Entrepreneurship Investment Co., Ltd. v. Chen Hao-kang & Shenzhen Quance Management Consulting Co., Ltd. & Li Ye, Shanghai No. 1 Intermediate People's Court, (2019) Hu 01 Min Chu No. 46; 上海宏华文化创业投资有限责任公司诉陈灏康、深圳市权策管理咨询有限公司、李野，上海市第一中级人民法院（2019）沪01民初46号

Shanghai Honghua Cultural Entrepreneurship Investment Co., Ltd. v. Chen Hao-kang & Shenzhen Quance Management Consulting Co., Ltd. & Li Ye, Shanghai High People's Court, (2020) Hu Min Zhong No. 512; 上海宏华文化创业投资有限责任公司诉陈灏康、深圳市权策管理咨询有限公司、李野，上海市高级人民法院（2020）沪民终512号

Shanghai Hongzheng Law Firm v. Marine Design and Research Institute of China, Gazette Case of the SPC, Issue 12, 2009; 上海市弘正律师事务所诉中国船舶及海洋工程设计研究院服务合同纠纷案，《最高人民法院公报》案例，2009年12期

Shanghai Minlurun Tarde Co., Ltd. v. Shanghai Gangyi International Trade Co., Ltd., The SPC (2015) Min Shen Zi Di No. 956 (Gazette Case of the SPC, Issue 1, 2016); 上海闽路润贸易有限公司与上海钢翼贸易有限公司买卖合同纠纷案，最高人民法院（2015）民申字第956号（《最高人民法院公报》案例，2016年01期）

Shanghai Minsheng Investment Co., Ltd. v. Jilin Dongli Comprehensive Investment (Group) Co., Ltd., Supreme People's Court, (2006) Min Er Zhong Zi No. 145; 上海民生投资有限公司诉吉林省东力综合投资（集团）有限公司，最高人民法院（2006）民二终字第145号

Shanghai Oriental Cultural Development Center v. Shanghai Shennan Real Estate Co., Ltd. Intermediate People's Court of Shanghai (2014), Hu Yi Zhong Min Er (Civil) Zhong Zi No.1; 上海东方文化发展中心诉上海申南置业有限公司等房屋租赁合同纠纷案 上海第一中级人民法院（2014）沪一中民二（民）终字第1号

Shanghai Panda Interactive Entertainment Culture Co., Ltd. v. Li Cen and Kunshan Bo'aiyou Information Technology Co., Ltd., SPC Guiding Case No.189; 上海熊猫互娱文化有限公司诉李岑、昆山播爱游信息技术有限公司合同纠纷案，最高院指导案例189号

Shanghai Panqi Trade Co., Ltd. v. Panqi Industry (Dalian) Co., Ltd., The SPC (2005) Min Er Zhong Zi No. 143 (Gazette Case of the SPC, Issue 4, 2006); 上海盘起贸易有限公司与盘起工业（大连）有限公司委托合同纠纷案， 最高人民法院（2005）民二终字第143号（《最高人民法院公报》案例，2006年04期）

Shanghai Pudong Development Bank Co., Ltd. Shenzhen Branch v. Meizhou Dizhonghai Hotel Co., Ltd. and Others, Gazette Case of the SPC, Issue 4, 2020; 上海浦东发展银行股份有限公司深圳分行与梅州地中海酒店有限公司等借款合同纠纷，《最高人民法院公报》案例，2020年04期

Shanghai Qinju Co Ltd. v. Beijing Yuner Computing Technology Ltd., Beijing Dongcheng District People's Court, (2021) Jing 0101 Min Chu No. 6309; 上海勤鞠实业有限公司诉北京云尔计算科技有限公司， 北京市东城区人民法院（2021）京0101民初6309号

Shanghai Zhedong Aluminium Co., Ltd. v. Changzhou Shifang International Trade Co., Ltd., Supreme People's Court (2013) Min Er Zhong Zi No.76; 上海浙东铝业有限公司诉常州世方国际贸易有限公司，最高人民法院（2013）民二终字第76号

Shanghai Zhongxiang (Group) v. Shanghai Zhabei District Economic Commission, High People's Court of Shanghai, (2009) Hu Gao Min Yi Min Zi Zhong No.21; 上海中祥（集团）与上海市闸北区经济委员会等代位权纠纷案， 上海市高级人民法院，（2009）沪高民一民终字第21号

Shanghai Zhongyuan Property Consulting Co., Ltd. v. Tao Dehua, SPC Guiding Case, No. 1; 上海中原物业顾问有限公司诉陶德华居间合同纠纷案，最高人民法院，第1号指导性案例

Shanghai Zhongyuan Property Consulting Co., Ltd. v. Zhou Yunfei, Shanghai Second Intermediate People's Court (2021) Hu 02 Min Zhong No. 342; 上海中原物业顾问有限公司诉周云飞居间合同纠纷案， 上海市第二中级人民法院（2021）沪02民终342号

Shanxi Gonghe Chuangzhan Investment Co., Ltd. & Shanxi Puda Coal Industry Group Co., Ltd. & Zhao Ming v. Shanxi Shuozhou Shanyin Youyi Coal Industry Co., Ltd. Supreme People's Court (2019) SPC Min Zhong No.1104; 山西共合创展投资有限公司、山西普大煤业集团有限公司合同纠纷二审民事判决书 最高人民法院（2019）最高法民终1104号

Shanxi Shuyuan Huashi Chemical Energy Co., Ltd. v. Shanxi Sanwei Group Co., Ltd. Supreme People's Court (2012) Min Yi Zhong Zi No.67; 山西数源华石化工能源有限公司、山西三维集团股份有限公司租赁合同纠纷，最高人民法院二审（2012）民一终字第67号

Shanxi Shuyuan Huashi Chemical Energy Co., Ltd. v. Shanxi Sanwei Group Co., Ltd. Supreme People's Court (2012) Min Yi Zhong Zi No.67; 山西数源华石化工能源有限公司、山西三维集团股份有限公司租赁合同纠纷，最高人民法院二审，（2012）民一终字第67号

Shaoyang Daxiang District Shengchu Coal Trade Co., Ltd. v. Guodian Hunan Baoqing Coal and Electricity Co., Ltd. Supreme People's Court (2017) SPC Min Shen No. 3316; 邵阳市大祥区圣矗煤炭贸易有限公司、国电湖南宝庆煤电有限公司买卖合同纠纷再审审查与审判监督民事裁定书 最高人民法院（2017）最高法民申3316号

Shenyang Dadong District Urban Construction Bureau v. Shenyang Hengyu Real Estate Development Co., Ltd., the SPC (2019) Zui Gao Fa Min Shen No. 4796; 沈阳市大东区城市建设局诉沈阳恒宇房地产开发有限公司， 最高人民法院（2019）最高法民申4796号

Shenyang Huajin Real Estate Co., Ltd. v. Shenyang Sujiatun District People's Government & Shenyang Municipal Bureau of Natural Resources Sujiatun Branch, the Supreme People's Court, (2021) SPC Min Zai No. 351; 沈阳华锦置业有限公司诉沈阳市苏家屯区人民政府、沈阳市自然资源局苏家屯分局，最高人民法院（2021）最高法民再351号

Shenyang Narnia Biomedical Technology Co., Ltd. v. Shanghai Jingfeng Pharmaceutical Co., Ltd., the Supreme People's Court, (2022) SPC Zhi Min Zhong No. 781; 沈阳纳尼亚生物医药科技有限公诉上海景峰制药有限公司， 最高人民法院（2022）最高法知民终781号

Shenzhen Hengchang Disheng Technology Co., Ltd. v. Xiamen Yongtongchang Investment Co., Ltd., the Supreme People's Court (2018) SPC Min Shen No. 5290; 深圳市恒昌迪生科技有限公司诉厦门永同昌投资有限公司，最高人民法院（2018）最高法民申5290号

Shizong Hongxin Manganese Industry Co., Ltd. v. Li Yinghui and Wang Duxian Supreme People's Court (2020) SPC Min Shen No.4691; 师宗宏鑫锰业有限责任公司、王都贤租赁合同纠纷再审审查与审判监督民事裁定书（2020）最高人民法院 最高法民申4691号

Shunde Westband Furniture Co., Ltd. v. Panda S.R.L., the SPC (2004) Min Si Ti Zi No. 4; 顺德市韦邦家具有限公司与熊猫有限公司， 最高人民法院（1998）经终字第358号

Sichuan Jinyu Financing & Guarantee Co., Ltd. v. Sichuan Jujuyuan Real Estate Co., Ltd., Cheng Du Qingyang District People's Court (2021) Chuan 0105 Min Chu No. 9112; 四川省金玉融资担保有限公司诉四川聚合源置业有限公司等借款合同纠纷案，成都市青羊区人民法院（2021）川0105民初9112号

Sichuan Nanbu Jinli Real Estate Development Co., Ltd. v. Chengdu Hexin Zhiyuan Real Estate Consulting Co., Ltd., The SPC (2015) Min Yi Zhong Zi Di No. 226; 四川南部县金利房地产开发有限公司与成都和信致远地产顾问有限责任公司商品房销售代理合同纠纷案，最高人民法院（2015）民一终字第226号

Sino Chem International (Overseas) Pte Ltd v. Thyssen Krupp Metallurgical Products GmbH, the SPC (2013) Min Si Zhong Zi No. 35 (SPC Guiding Case No. 107); 中化国际（新加坡）有限公司诉蒂森克虏伯冶金产品有限责任公司国际货物买卖合同纠纷案，最高人民法院（2013）民四终字第35号（最高人民法院第107号指导性案例）

Stone company v. Quarry Company, Case No. 9 of The SPC Typical Cases Related to the SPC Interpretation on the General Provisions of the Contract Book, 2023; 某石材公司与某采石公司买卖合同纠纷案，《关于适用中华人民共和国民法典合同编通则若干问题的解释》相关典型案例，第9号案例

Su Yueniu & Zhu Zhiping v. Wang Zhengpeng & Wang Zhenyou Intermediate People's Court of Xuancheng Anhui (2020) Wan 18 Min Zhong No. 1328; 苏月牛、朱治平股权转让纠纷案 安徽省宣城市中级人民法院（2020）皖18民终1328号

Sugiura Tatsumi v. Gong Yin, Shanghai Financial Court, (2018) Hu 74 Min Chu No. 585; 杉浦立身诉龚茵，上海金融法院（2018）沪74民初585号

Suiyang Anjie Motor Carriage of Goods Ltd. v. Tu Zhengui, Guizhou Province Zunyi City Intermediate People's Court, (2021) Qian 03 Min Zhong No. 10651; 绥阳县安捷汽车货运有限责任公司诉涂珍贵，贵州省遵义市中级人民法院（2021）黔03民终10651号

Sun Jianfa v. Shenyang High-grade Highway Construction Corporation & Shenyang High-grade Highway Construction Corporation Materials and Equipment Company, the Supreme People's Court, (2017) SPC Min Shen No. 3108; 孙建发诉沈阳高等级公路建设总公司、沈阳高等级公路建设总公司材料设备公司，最高人民法院（2017）最高法民申3108号

Sun v. Real Estate Company, Case No. 7 of The Typical Cases Related to the SPC Interpretation on Several Issues Concerning the Application of the General Provisions of the Contract Book of the Civil Code; 孙某诉某房地产公司，最高人民法院《关于适用＜中华人民共和国民法典＞合同编通则若干问题的解释》相关典型案例，第7号案例

Sun Yinshan v. Nanjing Auchan Supermarket Co., Ltd. Jiangning Store, Nanjing Jiangning District People's Court (2012) Jiang Ning Kai Min Chu Zi No. 646 (SPC Guiding Case No. 23); 孙银山诉南京欧尚超市有限公司江宁店买卖合同纠纷案，江苏省南京市江宁区人民法院（2012）江宁开民初字第646号（最高人民法院第23号指导性案例）

Suzhou Siyuan Natural Products Research and Development Co., Ltd. v. Nanjing Hailing Chinese Medicine Pharmaceutical Process Technology Research Co., Ltd., The SPC (2021) Zui Gao Fa Min Shen No. 7796; 苏州思源天然产物研发有限公司、南京海陵中药制药工艺技术研究有限公司技术合同纠纷，最高人民法院（2021）最高法民申7796号

Suzhou Yangguang Xindi Real Estate Co., Ltd. Xindi Central Hotel v. Suzhou Cultural International Travel Service Co., Ltd. Xinqu Tayuanlu Business Department and Suzhou Cultural International Travel Service Co., Ltd., Gazette Case of the SPC, Issue 8, 2012; 苏州阳光新地置业有限公司新地中心酒店诉苏州文化国际旅行社有限公司新区塔园路营业部、苏州文化国际旅行社有限公司委托合同纠纷案，《最高人民法院公报》案例，2012年08期

Swiss Cargill International v. Fujian Jinshi Oil Manufacturing Co., Ltd and others, SPC Guiding Case No. 33; 瑞士嘉吉国际公司诉福建金石制油有限公司等，最高人民法院第33号指导性案例

Tan v. Chang & Chang, Liaocheng Intermediate People's Court of Shandong Province, (2023) Lu 15 Min Zhong No. 3926; 谭某祥诉常某龙、常某峰，山东省聊城市中级人民法院（2023）鲁15民终3926号

Tang Jun v. Li Yuling and Shanghai Paipaidai Finance Information Service Co., Ltd., Shanghai Pudong New Area People's Court (2014) Pu Min Yi (Min) Chu Zi No. 14813; 唐骏诉李玉玲、上海拍拍贷金融信息服务有限公司，上海市浦东新区人民法院 （2014）浦民一（民）初字第14813号

Tianjin Baiyang Zhaojun Advertising Co., Ltd. v. Tianjin Aozhong Development Co., Ltd., Tianjin High People's Court (2019) Jin Min Zhong No. 194; 天津市佰扬兆俊广告有限公司诉天津澳中发展有限公司租赁合同纠纷案，天津市高级人民法院（2019）津民终194号

Tianjin Metal Tools Company v. Peishi Investment Company, , Gazette Case of the SPC, Issue 4, 2003; 天津市金属工具公司诉沛时投资有限公司，《最高人民法院公报》案例，2003年04期

Tianjin Zhongjurui International Trade Co., Ltd. v. Jiangsu Suzhou Port Group Co., Ltd., the SPC (2023) Zui Gao Fa Min Zai No. 16; 天津中钜锐国际贸易有限公司诉江苏苏州港集团有限公司，最高人民法院 (2023) 最高法民再16号

Tibet Zhongtaihengyuan Industrial Co., Ltd. v. Lhasa Liuwu New District Urban Investment, Construction and Development Group Co., Ltd., the Supreme People's Court (2019) SPC Min Zhong No. 760; 西藏中太恒源实业有限公司诉拉萨市柳梧新区城市投资建设发展集团有限公司，最高人民法院 (2019) 最高法民终760号

Tokio Marine Nichido Fire Insurance (China) Co., Ltd. Shanghai Branch v. Xinjie Logistics Group Co., Ltd., Gazette Case of the SPC, Issue 12, 2019; 东京海上日动火灾保险(中国)有限公司上海分公司诉新杰物流集团股份有限公司，《最高人民法院公报》案例，2019年12期

Wang Jian v. Manzhouli China International Travel Service Industrial Co., Ltd., the Supreme People's Court, (2019) SPC Min Shen No. 568; 王健诉满洲里中国国际旅行社实业有限公司，最高人民法院 (2019) 最高法民申568号

Wang Liya v. Lushi Hardware, Electricity and Chemical Products Co., Ltd., Yang Dongfen and Xue Maosheng, (2006) 1 China Law Report, People's Court Press (2006), pp. 141-145; 王利亚诉卢氏县五交化公司、杨冬粉、薛茂生承租房屋优先购买权案，《人民法院案例选》，2006 年第1 辑，人民法院出版社，2006 年版，第141-145 页

Wang v. Shanghai A Real Estate Agency Co., Ltd., Shanghai Second Intermediate People's Court (2022) Hu 02 Min Zhong No. 5071; 王某某诉上海某房地产经纪有限公司中介合同纠纷案，上海市第二中级人民法院（2022）沪02民终5071号

Wang Weibin v. Chen Jing No.2 Intermediate People's Court of Shanghai (2016) Hu 02 Min Zhong No. 5427; 王伟斌与陈婧委托理财合同纠纷案 上海市第二中级人民法院（2016）沪02民终5427号

Wang Xiaoli v. Dong Xunhu & Dong Xunlong, Anhui High People's Court (2020) Wan Min Zhong No.229; 王小丽、董训龙债权人撤销权纠纷二审民事判决书，安徽省高级人民法院 (2020) 皖民终229

Wang Yongsheng v. Bank of China Limited Nanjing Hexi Branch, Gazette Case of the SPC, Issue 2, 2009; 王永胜诉中国银行股份有限公司南京河西支行储蓄存款合同纠纷案，《最高人民法院公报》案例，2009年02期

Wang Yuanyuan v. Zhang Wei, People's Court of Chaoyang District, Beijing (2016) Jing 0105 Min Chu No.33953; 王源源与张伟房屋买卖合同纠纷一审民事判决书，北京市朝阳区人民法院 (2016)京0105民初33953号

Weihai Jingyuan Construction Co., Ltd. v. Weihai Welfare Enterprise Service Co., Ltd. and Weihai Shengfa Trade Co., Ltd., The SPC (2010) Min Ti Zi No. 210 (Gazette Case of the SPC, Issue 8, 2013); 威海市鲸园建筑有限公司与威海市福利企业服务公司、威海市盛发贸易有限公司拖欠建筑工程款纠纷案，最高人民法院（2010）民提字第210
（《最高人民法院公报》案例，2013年08期）

Weinan City Huazhou District Hongli Real Estate Development Co., Ltd. v. Tongguan County Xinlong Investment Co., Ltd. Supreme People's Court (2021) Min Shen No. 2434; 渭南市华州区鸿力房地产开发有限公司诉潼关县鑫龙投资有限责任公司，最高人民法院（2021）最高法民申2434号

Wen Bin v. Yunnan Radio and Television Real Estate Development Co., Ltd., The SPC (2020) SPC Civil Zai No.194; 文斌、云南广电房地产开发有限公司缔约过失责任纠纷案，最高人民法院（2020）最高法民再194号

Wu Hailan v. Shanghai Juren Biological Technology Co., Ltd., Shanghai First Intermediate People's Court (2020) Hu 01 Min Zhong No. 4321; 吴海澜诉上海聚仁生物科技有限公司，上海市第一中级人民法院（2020）沪01 民终4321 号

Wu Shanmeiand Li Yaosheng v. Liang Xinye and Song Hanzhi Supreme People's Court (2016) SPC Min ZhongNo. 51; 吴善娟、李耀生与梁新业、宋汉之等股权转让纠纷二审民事判决书 最高人民法院（2016）最高法民终51号

Wuhan Gas Company v. Chongqing Detection Instrument Factory, Gazette Case of the SPC, Issue 2, 1996; 武汉市煤气公司诉重庆检测仪表厂，《最高人民法院公报》案例，1996年02期

Wuxi Humei Thermal Power Engineering Co., Ltd. v. DBS Bank Ltd, The SPC (2017) Zui Gao Fa Min Zhong No. 327 (The Gazette Case of the SPC, Issue 11, 2018); 无锡湖美热能电力工程有限公司与新加坡星展银行信用证纠纷案，最高人民法院（2017）最高法民终327号 （《最高人民法院公报》案例，2018年11期）

Wuyuan Antai Real Estate Development Co., Ltd. v. Lin Xihai, Guide on Adjudication Supervisions (2018) Issue 1, People's Court Press (2019) pp. 52-68; 婺源县安泰房地产开发有限责任公司诉林细海，
《审判监督指导》2018年第
1辑，人民法院出版社，2019年版，第52-68页

Xiamen Aviation Development Co., Ltd. v. Beijing Nangang Jinyi Trading Co., Ltd. and Xiamen Dongfanglong Metallic Materials Co., Ltd., The SPC (2014) Min Shen Zi Di No. 2225 (Gazette Case of the SPC, Issue 1, 2017); 厦门航空开发股份有限公司与北京南钢金易贸易有限公司及第三人厦门市东方龙金属材料有限公司买卖合同纠纷案，最高人民法院 （2014） 民申字第2225号（《最高人民法院公报》案例，2017年01期）

Xi'an Qinghe Real Estate Co., Ltd. v. Electronic Comprehensive Survey and Research Institute of the Ministry of Information Industry, the Supreme People's

Court, (2022) SPC Min Shen No. 725; 西安清河置业有限公司诉信息产业部电子综合勘察研究, 最高人民法院 (2022) 最高法民申725号
Xinjiang Danlu Fashion Department Store Co., Ltd. v. Xinjiang Guanghui Real Estate Development Co., Ltd. Supreme People's Court (2020) SPC Min Shen No.6938; 新疆丹璐时尚百货有限公司、新疆广汇房地产开发有限公司房屋租赁合同纠纷再审审查与审判监督民事裁定书 最高人民法院（2020）最高法民申6938号民事裁定书
Xinjiang Yakun Trading Co., Ltd. v. Xinjiang Jinghe County Kangrui Cotton Processing Co., Ltd. (Gazette Case of the SPC, Issue 11, 2006); 新疆亚坤商贸有限公司与新疆精河县康瑞棉花加工有限公司买卖合同纠纷案（最高人民法院公报2006年11期）
Xinxian Xincheng Construction Co., Ltd. v. Shandong Tianle Real Estate Co., Ltd., The SPC (2022) Zui Gao Fa Min Zai No. 96; 莘县莘城建设有限公司、山东天乐置业有限公司建设工程施工合同纠纷案, 最高人民法院（2022）最高法民再96号
Xinyu Company v. Feng Yumei, Gazette Case of the SPC, Issue 6, 2006; 新宇公司诉冯玉梅, 《最高人民法院公报》案例, 2006年06期
Xu Tingde v. Linyi Yishui Hongxin Mall Ltd, Shandong Province Linyi City Intermediate People's Court, (2021) Lu 13 Min Zhong No. 3740; 徐廷德诉临沂市沂水虹鑫商城有限公司, 山东省临沂市中级人民法院 (2021) 鲁13民终3740号
Xuzhou Batian Ecotypic Engineering Co., Ltd. v. Shenzhen Parameter Navigator Technology Co., Ltd. and Shenzhen Batian Ecotypic Engineering Co., Ltd., Jiangsu High People's Court (2017) Su Min Zhong No. 2151; 徐州市芭田生态有限公司与深圳市参数领航科技有限公司、深圳市芭田生态工程股份有限公司技术委托开发合同案, 江苏省高级人民法院 (2017) 苏民终2151 号
Yancheng Tianmu Food Co., Ltd. v. Yancheng Water Supply Co., Ltd., Gazette Case of the SPC, Issue 3, 2020; 盐城市天孜食品有限公司诉盐城市自来水有限公司供水合同纠纷案, 《最高人民法院公报》案例, 2020年03期
Yang Jinguo v. Lin Jinkun, the Supreme People's Court, (2017) SPC Min Shen No. 2454; 杨金国诉林金坤, 最高人民法院（2017）最高法民申2454号
Yang Jun v. Dongtai Dongsheng Real Estate Development Co., Ltd., Gazette Case of the SPC, Issue 11, 2010; 杨珺诉东台市东盛房地产开发有限公司商品房销售合同纠纷案, 《最高人民法院公报》案例, 2010年11期
Yang Meihua v. Yang Wanyong and Others, The People's Court of Wusu City, Xinjiang Uyghur Autonomous Region (2021) Xin 4202 Min Chu No.5407; 杨某花杨某勇等债权人代位权纠纷案, 新疆维吾尔自治区乌苏市人民法院（2021）新4202民初5407号判决书
Yang Yanhui v. China Southern Airlines and Minhui Company, Gazette Case of the SPC, Issue 5, 2003; 杨艳辉诉南方航空公司、民惠公司客运合同纠纷案, 《最高人民法院公报》案例, 2003年05期
Yuhe Building Materials Factory of Moyu County, Xinjiang Uygur Autonomous Region v. Agricultural Bank of China, Moyu County Branch, Supreme People's Court (2004) Min Er Zhong Zi No.228; 新疆维吾尔自治区墨玉县玉

河建材厂与中国农业银行墨玉县支行为借款合同纠纷新疆维吾尔自治区墨玉县玉河建材厂与中国农业银行墨玉县支行为借款合同纠纷，最高人民法院二审（2004）民二终字第228号

Yunyu Co., Ltd. v. Shenzhen Zhongyuancheng Commercial Investment Holding Co., Ltd., the Supreme People's Court, (2019) SPC Min Te No. 1; 运裕有限公司与深圳市中苑城商业投资控股有限公司，最高人民法院（2019）最高法民特1号

Zaozhuang Mining (Group) Co., Ltd. Chaili Coal Mine v. Huaxia Bank Co., Ltd. Qingdao Branch & Qingdao Free Trade Zone International Trade Co., Ltd, Gazette Case of the SPC, Issue 6, 2010; 枣庄矿业（集团）有限公司柴里煤矿诉华夏银行股份有限公司青岛分行、青岛保税区画的国际贸易有限公司，《最高人民法院公报》案例，2010年06期

Zeng v. Ke and Wang; 曾某诉柯某某和王某案（2021）3 China Law Report, People's Court Press (2021), pp. 83-92; 《人民法院案例选》2021年3辑，人民法院出版社，2021年版，第83-92页

Zeng Yilong v. Jiangxi Golden Horse Auction Co., Ltd., Bank of China Limited Shangrao Branch and Xu Shengju, the SPC (2005) Min Yi Zhong Zi No. 43 (The Gazette Case of the SPC, Issue 1, 2006); 曾意龙与江西金马拍卖有限公司、中国银行股份有限公司上饶市分行、徐声炬案，最高人民法院（2005）民一终字第43号（《最高人民法院公报》案例，2006年01期）

Zhang & Cao v. Dongfeng County Hengdaohecheng Honest Development and Construction Co., Ltd, the People's Court of Longshan District, Liaoyuan City, Jilin Province, (2021) Liao 0882 Min Chu No.4534; 张某、曹某廷诉东丰县横道河诚实开发建设有限公司、东丰县东风建设有限责任公司，吉林省辽源市龙山区人民法院（2021） 辽0882 民初4534号

Zhang Jie v. Shanghai Haitong Securities Asset Management Co., Ltd. The SPC (2018) SPC Civil Min Shen No. 1423; 张杰、上海海通证券资产管理有限公司委托理财合同纠纷案，中华人民共和国最高人民法院（2018）最高法民申1423号

Zhang Jun and Xi'an Daniel Real Estate Development Co., Ltd, Shaanxi Province Xi'an Intermediate People's Court (2009) Xi Min Er Zhong Zi No.1376; 张军与西安丹尼尔房地产开发有限公司买卖合同纠纷案 陕西省西安市中级人民法院（2009）西民二终字第1376号

Zhang Li v. Beijing Heli Huatong Automobile Service Co., Ltd., SPC Guiding Case No. 17; 张莉诉北京合力华通汽车服务有限公司买卖合同纠纷案， 最高人民法院，第17号指导性案例

Zhang Minhua v. Wuxi Rongxin Metal Coating Technology Co., Ltd., Jiangsu Wuxi Intermediate People's Court (2021) Su 02 Min Zhong No. 3616; 章敏华、无锡荣鑫金属涂装科技有限公司承揽合同纠纷案， 江苏省无锡市中级人民法院（2021）苏02民终3616号

Zhang Zhiwei and Yu Liping v. Jia Haiqing, Shanghai Second Intermediate People's Court (2016) Hu 02 Min Zhong No. 9503; 张志伟、俞利平等与贾海庆房屋买卖合同纠纷案，上海市第二中级人民法院 （2016）沪02民终9503号

Zhangjiakou Xin Million Catering Co., Ltd. v. Xuanhua Hotel Co., Ltd., Zhangjiakou Intermediate People's Court (2007) Zhang Shang Zhong Zi No. 74; 张家口市鑫百万餐饮有限公司诉宣化饭店有限责任公司，张家口市中级人民法院（2007）张商终字第74号

Zhao Jun v. Xiang Huimin and He Xueqin, Gazette Case of the SPC, Issue 12, 2014; 赵俊诉项会敏、何雪琴民间借贷纠纷案，《最高人民法院公报》案例，2014年12期

Zhejiang Longda Stainless Steel Co., Ltd. v. AP Moller-Maersk A/S, The SPC (2017) Zui Gao Fa Min Zai No. 412 (SPC Guiding Case No. 108); 浙江隆达不锈钢有限公司诉A. P. 穆勒-马士基有限公司海上货物运输合同纠纷案， 最高人民法院（2017）最高法民再412号 （最高人民法院第108号指导性案例）

Zheng Chuanxin v. China Telecom Corporation Ltd Lianyungang Branch, Gazette Case of the SPC, Issue 5, 2017; 郑传新诉中国电信股份有限公司连云港分公司电信服务合同纠纷案，《最高人民法院公报》案例，2017年05期

Zheng Shiqi v. Samsung Property & Casualty Insurance Company (China), Ltd, Gazette Case of the SPC, Issue 5, 2022; 郑诗琦诉三星财产保险（中国）有限公司财产保险合同纠纷案，《最高人民法院公报》案例，2022年05期

Zhongcang Palace (Beijing) Culture Media Co., Ltd. Shanghai Branch & Zhongcang Palace (Beijing) Culture Media Co., Ltd. v. Shanghai Huanyu Hui Commercial Management Co., Ltd. No.2 Intermediate People's Court of Shanghai (2020) Hu 02 Min Zhong 3179; 中藏宫(北京)文化传媒有限公司诉上海寰宇汇商业管理有限公司房屋租赁合同纠纷二审民事判决书， 上海市第二中级人民法院 (2020) 沪02民终3179.

Zhongshan A Property Management Co., Ltd. v. Fang, Zhongshan Intermediate People's Court (2022) Yue 20 Min Zhong No. 849; 中山市某物业管理有限公司诉方某某物业服务合同纠纷案， 广东省中山市中级人民法院（2022）粤20民终849号

Zhongtian Construction Group Co., Ltd. v. Henan Henghe Real Estate Co., Ltd., The SPC (2019) Zui Gao Fa Min Zhong No. 255 (SPC Guiding Case No. 171); 中天建设集团有限公司诉河南恒和置业有限公司建设工程施工合同纠纷案，最高人民法院（2019）最高法民终255号 （最高人民法院， 第171号指导性案例）

Zhongyuan Bank Co., Ltd. v. Fujian Start Group Co., Ltd., Henan High People's Court (2021) Yu Min Zhong No. 949; 中原银行股份有限公司诉福建实达集团股份有限公司等金融借款合同纠纷案， 河南省高级人民法院（2021）豫民终949号

Zhou Lihui v. Huang Huili, High People's Court of Henan (2020) Yu Min Zai No. 515; 周利辉诉黄惠丽，河南省高级人民法院（2020）豫民再515号

Zhou v. An Airlines Co., Ltd., Shanghai Pudong New Area People's Court (2019) Hu 0115 Min Chu No. 26237; 周某诉甲航空公司等航空旅客运输合同纠纷案，上海市浦东新区人民法院（2019）沪0115民初26237号

Zhou Weijun and Zhou Weida v. Wang Xuqiong, Gazette Case of the SPC, Issue 3, 2018; 周伟均、周伟达诉王煦琼委托合同纠纷案，《最高人民法院公报》案例，2018年03期

Zhu Huayun v. hangchun Construction Engineering Xinjirun Construction Co., Ltd., The SPC (2020) Zui Gao Fa Min Shen No. 331; 朱华云、长春建工新吉润建设有限公司建设工程施工合同纠纷案，最高人民法院（2020）最高法民申331 号

Zhu Junmin, Wang Yazhuang & Zheng Lu v. Shanghai Yuankai (Group) Co., Ltd. & Song Guizhong, the Supreme People's Court, (2020) SPC Min Shen No. 4426; 祝军民、王亚壮、郑路诉上海源恺（集团）有限公司、宋贵中， 最高人民法院（2020）最高法民申4426号

Zibo Zichuan Ganglian Material Ltd. v. Building & Installing Engineer Co. Ltd. of China Railway 12th Bureau Group Shandong Province Zibo City Intermediate People's Court, (2023) Lu 03 Min Zhong No. 1307; 淄博市淄川钢联物资有限公司诉中铁十二局集团建筑安装工程有限公司， 山东省淄博市中级人民法院（2023）鲁03民终1307号

UK Cases

Adams v. Lindsell (1818) 1 B & Ald 681

Arcos Ltd v. Ronaasen & Son [1933] AC 470

Barton v. Armstrong [1976] AC 104

Bradford Third Equitable Benefit Building Society v. Borders [1941] UKHL J0509-1

British Westinghouse Electric & Manufacturing Co Ltd v. Underground Electric Railways Co of London Ltd [1912] AC 673

Cavendish Square Holding BV v. Talal EI Makdessi [2015] UKSC 67

Co-operative Insurance Society Ltd v. Argyll Stores (Holdings) Ltd [1997] 3 All ER 297

Crabb v. Arun DC (1976) 1 Ch 179

Dearle v. Hall (1828) 38 ER 475

Derry v. Peek (1889) App Cas 337

DHL Project & Chartering Ltd v. Gemini Ocean Shipping Co Ltd [2022] EWCA 1555

Grant v. Dawkins [1973] 1 WLR 1406

Hadley v. Baxendale (1854) 9 Exch 341

Hoenig v. Isaacs [1952] EWCA Civ 6

Investors Compensation Scheme Ltd. v. West Bromwich Building Society [1997] UKHL 28

Lloyds Bank v. Bundy [1975] QB 326, Lord Denning at para [339]

Occidental Worldwide Investment Corp. v. Skibs A/S Avanti, Skibs A/S Glarona, Skibs A/S Navalis (The 'Siboen' and the 'Sibotre') [1976] 1 Lloyd's Rep 293

Parsons (Livestock) Ltd v. Uttley Ingham & Co Ltd [1978] QB 791

Patel v. Mirza [2016] UKSC 42

Photo Production Ltd v. Securicor Transport Ltd [1980] AC 827

R v. A-G for England and Wales [2003] UKPC 22, Lord Hoffman at para [21]

Robinson v. Mollett (1875) LR 7 HL 802

Royal Bank of Scotland plc v. Etridge (No. 2) [2001] UKHL 44, Lord Nicolls at para [18]

Smith v. Hughes (1871) LR 6 QB597

Strydom v. Vendside Ltd [2009] EWHC 2130 (QB) [2009] All ER (D) 135 (Aug) Justice Blair at para [36]
Taylor v. Caldwell (1863) 3 B & S 826
William Brandt's Sons & Co v. Dunlop Rubber Co Ltd [1905] AC 454

Other Jurisdictions

BCY v. BCZ [2017] 3 SLR 357
Bhasin v. Hrynew, 2014 SCC 71, (2014) 379 DLR (4th) 385
Renard Constructions (ME) Pty v. Minister for Public Works (1992) 44 NSWLR 349

Table of Legislation

China

Law

Arbitration Law of the People's Republic of China 1994
Bidding Law of the People's Republic of China 2017 Revision
Chinese Civil Procedure Law of the People's Republic of China 2023 Revision
Civil Code of the People's Republic of China 2020
Commercial Banks Law of the People's Republic of China 2003 Revision
Company Law of the People's Republic of China 2023 Revision
Constitution of the People's Republic of China 2018 Revision
Construction Law of the People's Republic of China 2019 Revision
Consumer Protection Law 2013 Revision
Contract Law of the People's Republic of China 1999 (Expired)
E-Commerce Law of the People's Republic of China 2018
Economic Contract Law of the People's Republic of China 1993 Revision (Expired)
Electronic Signature Law of the People's Republic of China 2019 Revision
Enterprise Bankruptcy Law of the People's Republic of China 2006
Foreign Economic Contract Law of the People's Republic of China 1985 (Expired)
Foreign Investment Law of the People's Republic of China 2019
General Principles of the Civil Law 1987 (Expired)
Insurance Law of the People's Republic of China 2018 Revision
Labor Contract Law of the People's Republic of China 2012 Revision
Labour Law of the People's Republic of China 2018
Maritime Law of the People's Republic of China 1992
Organic Law of the People's Courts of the People's Republic of China 2018 Revision
Partnership Enterprise Law of the People's Republic of China 2006 Revision
Regional Ethnic Autonomy Law of the People's Republic of China 2021 Revision
Rural Land Contract Law of the People's Republic of China 2018 Revision
Technology Contract Law of the People's Republic of China 1987 (Expired)
Tourism Law of the People's Republic of China 2018 Revision
Trust Law the People's Republic of China 2001
Urban Real Estate Administration Law 2019 Revision

Table of Legislation

Administrative Regulation

Foreign Exchange Control Regulations of the People's Republic of China 2008 Revision

Departmental Rule

The Administrative Measures for the Quality Inspection of Construction Projects 2022

Judicial Interpretation

The SPC Interpretation Concerning Some Issues on Application of the Arbitration Law of the People's Republic of China (2006, 2008 revision)

The SPC Interpretation of on the Application of the Civil Procedure Law (2015, 2021 revision).

The SPC Interpretation on Certain Issues Concerning the Application of Law in Trying Cases Involving Disputes over Contracts on Sale of Commercial Real Estate (2003, 2020 revision)

The SPC Interpretation on Certain Issues Concerning the Application of Law in Trying Cases Involving Technology Contract Disputes (2020)

The SPC Interpretation on Issues Concerning the Application of Law in the Trial of Disputes Over Sales Contracts (2012, 2020 revision)

The SPC Interpretation on Issues concerning the Application of Law in the Trial of Cases Regarding Disputes over Construction Contracts for Construction Projects (I) (2020)

The SPC Interpretation on Issues concerning the Application of Law in the Trial of Cases Involving Disputes over Financial Lease Contracts (2020)

The SPC Interpretation on Issues Concerning the Application of the Contract Law (I) (1999)

The SPC Interpretation on Issues Concerning the Application of the Contract Law (II) (2009)

The SPC Interpretation on Several Issues Concerning the Application of the General Provisions of the Contract Book of the Civil Code (2023)

The SPC Interpretation on Several Issues Concerning the Application of the Administrative Litigation Law (2018)

The SPC Interpretation on Several Issues Concerning the Application of the General Provisions of the Civil Code (2022).

the SPC Interpretation on Several Issues Concerning the Application of the Security System in the Civil Code (2020).

The SPC Interpretation on Several Issues Concerning the Application of the Property Rights Book of the Civil Code (2021)

The SPC Interpretation on Several Issues Concerning the Application of International Treaties and International Customs in Foreign-Related Civil and Commercial Cases (2023)

The SPC Interpretation on Several Issues Concerning the Application of Law in the Trial of Disputes over Mining Rights (2017)

The SPC Interpretation on Several Issues concerning the Application of Law in the Trial of Cases about Disputes Over Lease Contracts on Urban Buildings (2020)

The SPC Interpretation on Several Issues Concerning the Ascertainment of Compensation Liability for Emotional Damages in Civil Torts (2001, 2020 revision)
The SPC Interpretation on the Application of Law in the Trial of Construction Contract Disputes
The SPC Interpretation on the Application of Laws in the Adjudication of Disputes over Contracts concerning State-owned Land Use Rights (2005, 2020 revision)

Judicial Document

Notice by the SPC of Issuing the Forty-First Group of Guiding Cases (2024).
Notice of the SPC on Issuing Some Opinions of the SPC about Providing Judicial Protection for the Construction of Socialist Harmonious Society (2007)
Notice of the SPC on Issuing the First Set of Guiding Cases (2011).
Several Opinions of the SPC on Cultivating and Practicing the Socialism Core Values (2015)
The Beijing High People's Court's Reference Opinions on the Implementation of the Civil Procedure Law in Civil Trial Work (2012)
The Detailed Implementing Rules on the SPC Provisions Concerning Work on Case Guidance (2015)
The Guiding Opinions on Several Issues Concerning the Trial of Civil and Commercial Contract Disputes under Current Situations (2009)
The Minutes of the National Courts Symposium on Foreign-Related Commercial and Maritime Adjudication Work (2021)
The Opinions of the Civil Division II of the Guangdong High People's Court on Resolving Difficult Legal Issues in Civil and Commercial Trial Practice (2012)
The Provisions of the SPC on Several Issues Concerning the Application of Law in the Trial of Cases about travel service contracts disputes.
The SPC Guiding Opinions on Several Issues Concerning the Trial of Civil and Commercial Contract Dispute Cases under the Current Situation (2009)
The SPC Guiding Opinions on Unifying the Application of Laws to Strengthen the Retrieval of Similar Cases (for Trial Implementation) (2020).
The SPC Minutes of the National Conference on Civil and Commercial Trial Work of Courts Nationwide (2019)
The SPC Notice on Improving Online Filing Procedures (2020).
The SPC Opinion on Strengthening the Judicial Protection of Intellectual Property Rights (2020)
The SPC Opinions on Several Issues Concerning the Implementation of the GPCL (1988).
The SPC Opinions on Several Specific Issues in Current Commercial Trials (2015)
The SPC Provisions Concerning Work on Case Guidance (2010)
The SPC Provisions on Certain Issues concerning Application of Law in Trial of Cases involving Private Lending (2020)
The SPC Provisions on Certain Issues Concerning the Adjudication of Cases Involving Foreign-Invested Enterprises (I) (2010)
The SPC Provisions on Certain Issues concerning the Trial of Cases of Disputes over Marine Freight Forwarding (2020)
The SPC Provisions on Citing Laws, Regulations, and Other Normative Legal Documents in Judicial Decisions (2009)

Table of Legislation

The SPC Provisions on the Application of the Statute of Limitations in the Trial of Civil Cases (2008, 2020 revision)

Judicial Reply

The Answers of the Jilin High People's Court to Several Questions on the Application of the Contract Termination System in Commercial Cases (2014)
The Reply from the SPC on whether a lessee who rents part of a house has the right of first refusal when the lessor sells the house as a whole; The SPC [2004] Min Yi Ta Zi No. 29
The Reply from the SPC regarding whether the payment for renovation and decoration projects enjoys the priority right to compensation as stipulated in Article 286 of the Contract Law
The Reply of the SPC on the Issue of When the Statute of Limitations Begins to Run for an IOU Without a Repayment Date Issued by the Debtor After Failing to Fulfil Obligations Upon the Expiration of the Agreed Deadline (2020 Revision) (Fa Shi (2020] No. 17)
The Reply of the SPC to the Request for Instructions on the Case of Dispute over outstanding debts in sales contract between Xiamen Sakura Garment Co., Ltd. and Japan Xijiasi Co., Ltd., (2002) Min Si Ta Zi No. 33
The Reply on Issues concerning Whether State-owned Transferred Land Use Rights of Bankrupt Enterprises Should be Included in Bankruptcy Property

Other Jurisdictions

Consumer Rights Act 2015
German Civil Code 2022 Revision
Law of Property Act 1925
Misrepresentation Act 1967
Principles of European Contract Law 1998
Restatement (Second) of Contracts § 21 (Am. Law Inst. 1981)
Unfair Contract Terms Act 1977
Unfair Terms in Consumer Contracts Directive 93/13/EEC 1993
Uniform Commercial Code 1952

International Law

United Nations Convention on Contracts for International Sale of Goods 1980
The UNIDROIT Principles of International Commercial Contracts 2016 Revision

Index

The numbers here refer to paragraph numbers.

Actions, 1073–1098
Administration, 47, 177, 243, 247, 488, 795, 1139, 1167, 1236, 1400, 1401, 1404, 1459, 1460
Administrative contracts, 62–77
Agency
  basis, 720
Agent, 354–357, 359, 409, 444, 755, 756, 934, 1101, 1180, 1348, 1419, 1434–1437, 1476
Agreement, 189–260, 705–737, 879–890
Application, 1111–1112, 1452–1455Authority, 11, 13, 16, 29, 32, 33, 38, 44, 66, 69, 71, 108, 118, 158, 176–178, 276, 364, 616, 617, 678, 755, 756, 823, 841, 1057, 1063, 1081, 1084, 1141, 1324, 1325
Bank of China, 473, 982, 1101, 1158, 1166, 1197, 1199, 1222
Banks, 364, 439, 440, 473, 561, 709, 774, 982, 1101, 1158, 1166, 1182, 1189, 1194, 1197, 1199, 1200, 1205, 1208, 1214, 1222, 1230, 1280, 1283, 1287, 1324, 1407, 1408, 1423, 1469
Bill, 1119, 1194, 1351, 1396
Buildings, 291, 347, 348, 367, 417, 451, 455, 488, 571, 819, 845, 982, 1107, 1138, 1139, 1183, 1251–1258, 1306, 1333, 1420–1422, 1439
Buyer, 84, 95, 112, 118, 144, 187, 382, 388, 389, 394, 444, 641, 797, 828, 933, 944, 971, 986, 987, 989, 1030, 1093, 1102, 1104, 1107, 1108, 1116–1119, 1121, 1123–1127, 1129–1159, 1161–1164, 1167, 1170, 1208, 1264, 1266, 1293, 1294, 1348, 1349, 1403, 1423, 1437, 1445, 1449–1451
Cancellation, 626, 636, 1108
Capacity, 15, 80, 227, 248, 340, 341, 349, 350, 352–359, 433, 515, 531, 616, 618, 674, 675, 698, 811, 989, 1081, 1084, 1091, 1168, 1180, 1283, 1419, 1466
Capital contributions, 1458, 1460
Carriage
  bill of, 1119, 1351
  contracts, 750, 899, 1119, 1129, 1133, 1335–1339, 1341–1358
Carrier, 636, 758, 1119, 1129, 1133, 1134, 1335–1358
Certificates, 71, 367, 1103, 1124, 1135, 1138, 1151, 1237, 1300, 1324, 1328, 1352, 1364, 1386, 1394–1396, 1426, 1441
Certification, 1124, 1141, 1283
Charge, 726, 1091, 1168, 1172, 1183, 1222, 1272, 1324, 1337, 1339, 1357, 1374, 1476–1478, 1480
Chinese Law of contracts, 45–121, 148–188
CIETAC, 609
Circumstances, special, 795, 1006, 1076, 1079, 1132, 1150, 1178, 1179, 1232, 1388
Civil
  law, 23–28
  relationships, 45, 63, 64, 87, 101, 124, 132, 138, 152, 163, 235, 238, 260, 283, 284, 403, 412, 420, 427, 430, 530, 560, 582, 606, 607, 642, 685, 705, 713, 746, 748, 846, 892, 961, 976, 1014, 1070, 1075, 1174, 1176, 1193, 1261, 1262, 1278, 1279, 1286, 1412, 1468, 1473
  rights, 45, 122, 398, 895, 1075, 1076, 1468

Index

Communist party of China (CCP), 10, 14–16, 33, 47
Compensation, 329–338
Concept, 39, 54, 103, 106, 110, 116, 122–125, 132, 182, 224, 244–246, 260, 290, 299, 305, 377, 391, 416, 429, 431, 440, 443, 476, 485, 489, 547, 637, 642, 663, 760, 761, 791–803, 813, 928–932, 956, 970, 980, 990, 1004, 1041–1045, 1075, 1102–1108, 1117, 1118, 1159, 1168–1170, 1175, 1181–1185, 1203, 1349, 1467, 1475
Consent, 103, 152, 241, 242, 245, 248, 253, 257, 269, 355, 356, 359–461, 527, 606, 618, 619, 671, 714, 725, 738, 792, 879, 884, 1015, 1227, 1228, 1230, 1234, 1245, 1248, 1254–1256, 1258, 1266, 1272, 1296, 1307, 1313, 1325, 1336, 1347, 1375, 1400, 1404, 1405, 1436, 1453, 1459, 1462–1464, 1467, 1469
Consignee, 758, 1119, 1335, 1346, 1347, 1350, 1352, 1353, 1356, 1357
Consignor, 1335, 1336, 1345–1350, 1353, 1355, 1356, 1358
Construction, 56, 59, 78, 124, 134, 152, 153, 169, 261, 291, 331, 348, 360, 364, 366, 436, 543, 577, 597, 636, 678, 750–754, 764, 818, 821, 828, 872, 971, 995, 1067, 1099, 1149, 1202, 1236, 1252, 1258, 1283, 1302–1334, 1382, 1470, 1471
Contracts. *See also* Administrative contracts, Carriage contracts; Economic contracts; Technology contract formation, 189-338, 1113-1115
Contractor, 543, 597, 636, 751, 752, 754, 950, 1241, 1290–1292, 1294, 1296–1305, 1307, 1308, 1313–1315, 1317–1320, 1322–1334
Contractual,
allocation of risk, 82, 937, 1135
Countries, 1, 2, 6, 190, 203, 564
Courts, 841–878CPPCC, 14, 16
Creditor, 1020–1025
Damages, 904–907, 977–1007, 1041–1071, 1402–1404
Debtor, 83, 144, 364, 558, 568, 569, 636, 640, 646–649, 652, 655–667, 670–693, 695–697, 699–704, 710–713, 715, 716, 718, 719, 721, 723, 725–729, 731–742, 744–749, 760–778, 780–785, 788–790, 811, 813, 835–839, 859, 922, 961, 966, 974, 975, 1008, 1009, 1016, 1020–1023, 1030, 1031, 1044, 1080, 1091–1093, 1202, 1203, 1205, 1207–1210, 1212–1215, 1218, 1220, 1221, 1223, 1226–1232, 1278, 1279, 1281–1285, 1287–1289, 1373
Defects, 271, 360–461, 606, 631, 828, 933, 935, 971, 1042, 1109, 1136, 1137, 1139, 1142, 1143, 1145, 1156, 1177, 1267, 1333, 1442
Department, 12, 15, 347, 365, 466, 469, 494, 513, 1067, 1091, 1105, 1252, 1309, 1402
Deposit, 311, 366, 473, 626, 818, 1008–1019, 1101, 1158, 1195, 1326, 1386–1392, 1441
Design, 14, 47, 88, 297, 408, 423, 477, 487, 615, 633, 676, 679, 692, 693, 703, 888, 1139, 1293, 1304, 1309, 1313, 1323, 1329, 1333, 1360, 1361, 1369, 1371, 1416
Disputes, 33, 38, 39, 42, 49, 51, 68, 77, 82, 84, 86, 93, 98, 99, 131, 133, 134, 138, 142, 156, 158, 163, 166, 179, 182, 183, 186–188, 193, 210, 213, 217, 238, 239, 262, 265, 274, 278–280, 282, 284–286, 289, 299, 315, 329, 331, 345, 346, 364, 391, 433, 469, 471, 514, 519, 525, 543, 549, 556, 558, 591, 597, 608–615, 617, 624, 627, 629, 631, 632, 636, 669, 694–697, 718, 732, 736, 751, 752, 754, 797, 827, 833, 837, 874, 890, 896, 898, 946, 947, 953, 956, 958, 983, 985, 986, 995, 998–1000, 1002, 1008, 1012, 1016, 1025, 1026, 1030, 1033, 1035, 1038, 1044, 1047, 1062, 1067, 1075, 1077, 1097, 1100, 1101, 1103, 1105, 1106, 1108–1110, 1112, 1114, 1121, 1137, 1138, 1156, 1158, 1159, 1169, 1170, 1174, 1175, 1191, 1199, 1200, 1202, 1208, 1210, 1213, 1237, 1240, 1249, 1251, 1261, 1263, 1264, 1277, 1280, 1292, 1293, 1295, 1302, 1307, 1308, 1317, 1328, 1340, 1349, 1359, 1377, 1410, 1413, 1414, 1423, 1426, 1439, 1443, 1476, 1478
Documents, 43, 44, 148, 149, 158, 167, 171–177, 221, 264, 276, 280, 281, 311–313, 317, 496, 506, 524, 528, 560, 561, 593, 597, 610, 625, 626, 628, 702, 846, 947, 1030, 1090, 1116, 1118, 1119, 1124, 1134, 1135, 1145, 1149, 1150,

1167, 1182, 1217, 1281, 1282, 1303, 1304, 1312, 1323, 1345, 1351, 1358, 1360, 1364, 1377, 1395, 1439
Duties, 69, 72, 94, 244, 525, 527, 811, 899, 912, 913, 935, 1067, 1362
Economic contracts, 48, 49, 1111
Expenses, 1446–1451
Expiration, 682, 837, 1075, 1080, 1093, 1142, 1234
Exploration, 932
Failure, 26, 74, 100, 119, 244, 270, 291, 320, 326, 528, 609, 625, 640, 660, 664, 679, 683, 684, 691, 738, 805, 810, 815, 817, 818, 928, 934, 943, 945, 948, 965, 968, 989, 994, 1009–1012, 1014, 1015, 1021, 1030, 1040, 1067, 1094, 1117, 1135, 1236, 1245, 1257, 1265, 1267, 1298, 1301, 1320, 1322, 1329, 1388
Faith, 122–147
FOB contracts, 1349
General Principles of, 26, 116, 124, 207, 226, 286, 381, 522, 528, 560, 563, 660, 1067, 1073, 1074, 1100, 1456, 1472, 1473
Chinese civil legislation
  civil law, 23–28
  contracts, 62–88
German law of contracts, 299
Goods
  carriage of, 750, 899, 1119, 1133, 1335, 1343, 1345–1356
  domestic, 1111
Government, 7, 8, 12–14, 17, 18, 21, 24, 25, 28, 29, 31, 35, 47, 66, 72, 73, 134, 135, 155, 156, 171–173, 195, 347, 362, 366–368, 477, 496, 506–508, 513, 528, 779, 875, 895, 1148, 1204, 1310, 1422
Governmental, 11, 17, 158, 1204
GPCL, 26, 49, 151, 339, 341, 351, 361, 377, 381, 396, 431, 432, 445–447
Guardians, 354, 674, 675
Harm, 89, 91, 93–95, 302, 305, 350, 398, 415, 419, 421, 424, 425, 429, 444–448, 453, 456, 457, 461, 469, 470, 486, 640, 663, 664, 668, 673, 676, 745, 749, 762, 766, 767, 770, 771, 855, 912, 919, 920, 978, 994, 1052, 1068, 1069, 1102, 1125, 1236
House, 117, 333, 334, 1139, 1141, 1159, 1164, 1165, 1167, 1170, 1208, 1236, 1237, 1240–1243, 1311, 1449, 1450
Individuals, 16, 29, 33, 63, 80, 82, 85, 92, 106, 110, 111, 134, 145, 147, 169, 340, 342, 350, 352–356, 358, 379, 433, 466, 481, 497, 503, 518, 552, 583, 606, 618, 636, 720, 747, 801, 803, 892, 1091, 1095, 1108, 1159, 1291, 1316, 1318, 1364, 1423
Injunction, 687, 1095
Institutions, 12, 63, 382, 397, 400, 401, 422, 433, 466, 609, 610, 616, 633, 698, 709, 799, 801, 815, 824, 869, 1057, 1090, 1165, 1166, 1189, 1191, 1195, 1200, 1202, 1204
Insurance
  contract, 92, 97, 153, 401, 636, 640, 642, 680, 750, 757, 795, 1101, 1124, 1158
Intention, 224–240
Interests, 47, 48, 63, 64, 66, 69, 72, 80, 85, 89, 110–112, 123, 124, 134, 135, 143, 157, 189, 249, 254, 257, 266, 325, 327–329, 331–333, 335, 336, 338, 341, 343, 350, 352, 364, 373, 377, 382, 385, 388, 397–399, 405, 408, 419, 421, 423, 425, 429, 436, 437, 444–448, 453–457, 469, 471, 477, 479, 483–486, 488, 497, 503, 508, 513, 516, 517, 525, 527, 530, 531, 537, 553, 568, 569, 600, 636, 640, 647, 651, 653, 657, 662–665, 668, 670, 679, 682, 684, 687, 691, 693, 705, 720, 722, 725, 734, 737, 739, 745, 746, 748, 749, 757, 761, 765, 771, 772, 778, 790, 811, 827, 844, 858, 859, 863, 873, 892, 895, 896, 904, 909, 916, 917, 919, 960–962, 971, 996, 1017, 1020, 1021, 1023, 1025, 1036, 1042, 1046, 1051, 1052, 1067, 1072, 1077, 1090, 1097, 1102, 1126, 1127, 1154, 1157, 1164, 1166, 1170, 1173, 1177–1179, 1181–1183, 1187–1190, 1193, 1196–1200, 1204, 1223, 1224, 1231, 1236, 1264, 1281, 1284–1288, 1310, 1318, 1332, 1350, 1362, 1381, 1388, 1401, 1403, 1405, 1407, 1419, 1423, 1426, 1440, 1441, 1443, 1447, 1463, 1468, 1474, 1478, 1479
International Sale of
  goods, 1024, 1111, 1112, 1118, 1133
Land
  ownership, 348, 638
Land–use right, 71, 261, 346, 347, 348, 366, 450–452, 454, 457

Law of
private, 25, 27, 47, 51, 63, 64, 71, 74, 91, 111, 125, 132, 135, 215, 518, 573, 863, 959, 1097, 1111, 1191–1195, 1310, 1318, 1336, 1439
public, 63, 65, 66, 72, 85, 124, 134, 135, 161, 166, 180, 238, 242, 250, 253, 341, 349, 350, 449, 462, 469, 477, 483–487, 518, 531, 578, 584, 863, 923, 1042, 1054, 1097, 1102, 1168, 1176, 1195, 1204, 1236, 1251, 1310, 1336, 1423, 1426, 1467, 1469
Lease, 56, 59, 64, 78, 82, 112, 152, 162, 194, 280, 378, 488, 543, 636, 862, 945, 993–996, 998, 1003, 1010, 1099, 1204, 1233–1276, 1429, 1457
Leased
property, 194, 945, 1010, 1239, 1241, 1244, 1250, 1253, 1257, 1260–1263, 1270, 1469
Legal persons, 45, 63, 72, 339, 419, 1091, 1191, 1195, 1204, 1361–1364
Legislation, 29–31, 36, 37, 40, 43, 49, 70, 138, 149–153, 159, 267, 584, 587, 642
Lessee, 543, 862, 1010, 1233, 1234, 1237–1250, 1253–1262, 1264–1276
Lessor, 543, 1204, 1233, 1234, 1237–1250, 1253–1276, 1469
Loan, 56, 64, 152, 378, 473, 537, 709, 829, 1092, 1099, 1105, 1166, 1181–1200, 1204–1206, 1208, 1209, 1225, 1230, 1260, 1262, 1263, 1278, 1279, 1286, 1310, 1407–1410, 1457
contracts, 1181–1200
Main obligations of parties, 76, 806, 813, 828, 1008, 1015, 1115, 1161, 1440
Mandate, 73, 106, 125, 261, 306, 307, 382, 554, 564, 605, 1057, 1061, 1099, 1279, 1304, 1400–1419, 1428, 1435, 1438, 1452–1455, 1467
Money
stipulated sum of, 509
Mortgaged property, 112, 347, 348, 1257
NPC, 7, 11–13, 17–22, 26, 29, 30, 32, 150, 167
Object, 103, 143, 424, 425, 469, 504, 702, 815, 1209, 1280
Obligations
primary, 74, 551, 656, 720, 726, 959, 977, 1015, 1030, 1040
Obligor, 293, 498, 528, 643, 705, 815, 1075–1077, 1081, 1086, 1088, 1090, 1093, 1095, 1128, 1146, 1247, 1318
Operation
joint, 1376
Organic Law of People's Court, 34
Other Conditions of validity, 462–530
Overdue delivery, 1166
Ownership, 49, 110, 113, 115, 118, 348, 493, 509, 510, 516, 638, 648, 1102, 1104–1107, 1123–1127, 1131, 1132, 1138, 1158, 1159, 1167, 1179, 1204, 1239, 1240, 1249, 1257, 1259, 1260, 1262, 1263, 1274, 1276, 1293, 1294, 1360, 1409, 1410, 1442
Packaging
materials, 1439
Partners, 667, 855, 1376, 1441, 1456, 1458–1466
Partnership, 81, 498, 501, 748, 800, 1099, 1100, 1456–1466
Passengers, 1335–1344
Payment, 1148–1151
Penalty, 84, 796, 926, 1009–1014, 1018, 1041–1072, 1189, 1224
People's Bank of China, 1197, 1199
People's Court, 11, 18, 22, 32–34, 68, 72, 86, 93, 99, 120, 127, 128, 134, 141, 143, 158, 179, 181, 260, 284, 325, 358, 364–366, 428, 450, 455, 468, 469, 471, 498, 500, 501, 516, 537, 558, 599, 609, 611, 625, 648, 650, 653, 678, 685, 693, 711–713, 721, 742, 746, 747, 760, 762, 764–766, 772, 777, 798–800, 807, 810, 811, 816, 825, 832, 840, 845, 872, 873, 880, 882, 888, 889, 893, 895, 899, 945, 982, 983, 985, 995, 1031, 1035, 1051, 1059, 1061, 1067, 1075, 1092, 1094, 1102, 1104, 1108, 1110, 1123, 1126, 1138, 1149, 1172, 1176, 1179, 1183, 1184, 1189, 1191, 1205, 1217, 1229, 1230, 1234, 1236, 1240, 1241, 1243, 1260, 1265, 1280, 1283, 1291, 1315, 1340, 1354, 1373, 1416, 1421, 1422, 1424, 1426, 1427, 1443–1446, 1451, 1453, 1456, 1457, 1462, 1463, 1472, 1478
People's Republic of China, 1–1480
Person, 1–1480
Plans, 19, 21, 228, 233, 819, 849, 1160, 1217, 1303, 1329, 1360, 1363, 1364, 1370, 1371, 1439
Pledgee

Port, 365, 711, 760, 762, 766, 1105, 1350, 1392, 1476–1480
Power, 11, 15–17, 19–22, 30, 32, 33, 40, 69, 72, 82, 120, 147, 358, 378, 399, 404, 406, 428, 439, 493, 527, 604, 606, 611, 712, 721, 760, 762, 924, 1059, 1067, 1158, 1168, 1322, 1426, 1427, 1429, 1469
Price, 59, 144, 193, 195, 210, 217, 218, 275, 314, 315, 321, 323, 333–335, 359, 366, 375, 378, 380, 389, 433, 436, 451, 455, 456, 459, 498, 501, 511, 540, 543, 544, 589, 641, 763, 772, 774, 775, 779–781, 849, 854, 858, 867, 872, 873, 875, 915, 919, 971, 974, 975, 985, 988–993, 995, 1102, 1104, 1105, 1108, 1114, 1116, 1118, 1121, 1123, 1125, 1127, 1128, 1130, 1136, 1140, 1141, 1147–1151, 1154, 1157, 1159, 1164, 1166, 1204, 1254, 1262, 1274, 1278, 1286, 1293, 1294, 1303, 1304, 1306, 1309, 1311, 1314, 1318, 1322, 1324, 1325, 1330–1332, 1334, 1355, 1365, 1366, 1373, 1376, 1403, 1409, 1410, 1423, 1436, 1437, 1450
Privity, 83, 634–790, 1146, 1349, 1413
Profits, 81, 87, 325, 330, 337, 365, 436, 494, 511, 514, 517, 528, 544, 820, 854, 905, 906, 918, 980, 982, 983, 985–987, 999, 1000, 1002, 1004, 1007, 1067, 1070, 1105, 1120, 1195, 1204, 1271, 1311, 1365, 1396, 1416, 1456, 1457, 1460, 1461, 1466
Project, 66, 78, 135, 169, 331, 494, 597, 622, 631, 751, 752, 754, 819–821, 828, 833, 1302, 1304–1312, 1314, 1316–1322, 1324, 1326, 1328, 1331–1334, 1360, 1370, 1371, 1377, 1382, 1443, 1444, 1470, 1471
Property
  law, 25, 34, 71, 96, 98, 106, 110–117, 119–121, 138, 160, 163, 175, 247, 264, 331, 348, 362, 429, 433, 487, 537, 636, 638, 663, 733, 737, 748, 757, 763, 922, 1041, 1042, 1099–1101, 1106, 1107, 1116, 1123, 1124, 1167, 1175, 1176, 1179, 1204, 1213, 1214, 1240, 1241, 1261, 1262, 1270, 1359, 1369, 1396, 1403, 1420, 1423–1426, 1441, 1449, 1469, 1479
  transfer ownership of, 1106, 1262
Raw materials, 986, 1328, 1363, 1366, 1376
Registration
  chronological order of, 1289
Regulations, 154–157
Rent, 162, 194, 862, 919, 945, 993–998, 1141, 1166, 1204, 1233, 1234, 1237, 1238, 1242, 1243, 1245, 1247, 1249, 1251, 1252, 1258, 1259, 1267, 1270, 1271, 1274, 1275
Repairs, 194, 962, 974, 975, 1108, 1116, 1147, 1163, 1169, 1171, 1233, 1238, 1270, 1290, 1297, 1300, 1322, 1324, 1420, 1425, 1469
Rescission, 99, 331, 357, 377, 382, 384–386, 392, 398, 404, 408, 412, 414, 415, 417, 428–431, 434, 1178–1180, 1202, 1253, 1258, 1271
Restitution, 117, 331, 404, 638, 784, 899–903, 919, 1006, 1007, 1121, 1275, 1285, 1475
Return, 105, 247, 366, 389, 452, 455, 517, 529, 534, 536–542, 544–546, 626, 730, 737, 784, 851, 890, 902, 975, 1009, 1010, 1012, 1107, 1108, 1116, 1119, 1127, 1154, 1155, 1169, 1174–1176, 1237, 1250, 1275, 1276, 1285, 1288, 1347, 1350, 1381, 1386, 1389–1391, 1433
Revolution, cultural, 26, 47, 48
Risk, 1133–1135, 1162–1163
Safekeeping contracts, 1386–1391
Sales, 279–1167
Schedule, 1188, 1336, 1337, 1341
Seals, 630, 1115, 1155, 1209, 1257, 1390
Second Restatement of contracts, 971
Security, 1008–1019
Seller, 116–119
Set forth, 1041
Settlement, 401, 597, 625, 627, 628, 775, 873, 874, 881, 882, 907, 1103, 1105, 1114, 1121, 1197, 1304, 1314, 1322, 1365, 1473
Ship, 1132, 1336
Standards, 598–607
State, 10–22
State Administration
  highest organ of, 11, 17
  StateCouncil, 11, 12, 17, 19–21, 30, 31, 74, 150, 154, 155, 167, 466, 494, 508, 1204
  ownership,

plans, 19, 21
provisions, 150, 155, 466, 494, 1204
socialist, 10
Station, 488, 1236, 1241, 1346
Stipulations, 203, 204, 264, 267, 642, 691, 797, 1189, 1196, 1278, 1279
Storage, 934, 944, 1021, 1352, 1356, 1386, 1392, 1395–1399, 1476
Subject matter, 77, 118, 193, 210, 217, 285, 311, 314, 315, 323, 359, 378, 380, 381, 512, 537, 539, 757, 786, 787, 974, 989, 993, 1030, 1102, 1104–1106, 1116, 1123–1140, 1142–1148, 1150–1158, 1177, 1241, 1260, 1266, 1282, 1290, 1293, 1294, 1345, 1372, 1377
Supplier, 144, 607, 1093, 1168–1173, 1305, 1469
Taking Delivery of goods, 118
Technology
contract, 49, 264, 375, 432, 450, 493, 609, 650, 811, 1067, 1099, 1102, 1149, 1169, 1291, 1359–1362, 1364–1373, 1375–1385, 1443
Termination, 49, 56, 67, 72, 75, 84, 99, 128, 152, 528, 621, 652, 653, 689, 791–916, 931, 990–992, 994–996, 1094, 1107, 1117, 1122, 1152–1154, 1164, 1170, 1235, 1237, 1246, 1271–1276, 1284, 1293, 1299, 1373, 1400, 1415–1419, 1423, 1430–1433, 1454, 1455, 1458, 1465, 1466
Third party, 406–412, 637–670, 1405–1414
Time limit, 201, 208, 428, 430, 815, 891, 1097, 1163, 1164, 1167, 1188, 1326, 1328, 1378
Transfer, 1133–1135, 1376–1381, 1462–1464
Transferee, 366, 544, 625, 705, 1257, 1378, 1380, 1381, 1462–1464
Transferor, 113, 117, 120, 366, 636, 705, 1367, 1379–1381, 1462, 1464
Transport, 60, 636, 758, 936, 1099, 1134, 1335–1358
UCC, 124, 607, 734, 971
UK, 483, 607, 622
UN Convention, 1024, 1111
United States of America (USA), 734
Vehicles, 388, 389, 1132
Water, 760, 762, 766, 1099, 1168–1173, 1429
Weight, 40, 172, 183, 580, 1346

www.ingramcontent.com/pod-product-compliance
Ingram Content Group UK Ltd.
Pitfield, Milton Keynes, MK11 3LW, UK
UKHW020130290926
15471UKWH00003B/395

9 789403 536293